[FROM 1865]

Experience
HISTORY
INTERPRETING AMERICA'S PAST

Experience History Guarantees Better Course Performance

Better-prepared students

Imagine the dynamic class discussions you could have or lively lectures you could give if your students came to class prepared.

Enter **McGraw-Hill's LearnSmart™**, the online adaptive learning system that guarantees students come to class prepared. As part of **McGraw-Hill's *Connect*® History** program, LearnSmart assesses students' knowledge of the chapter content and identifies gaps in understanding. Students come to class with a better grasp of the course material, resulting in livelier discussions and the freedom to lecture on what you think is important.

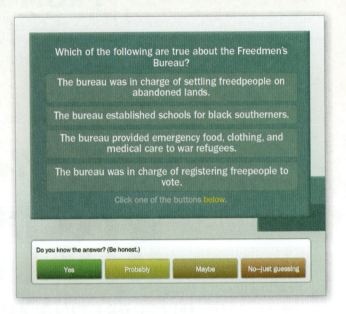

Which of the following are true about the Freedmen's Bureau?

The bureau was in charge of settling freedpeople on abandoned lands.

The bureau established schools for black southerners.

The bureau provided emergency food, clothing, and medical care to war refugees.

The bureau was in charge of registering freepeople to vote.

Click one of the buttons below.

Do you know the answer? (Be honest.)

Yes | Probably | Maybe | No—just guessing

STUDENTS TELL US:

- *"I just wanted to let you know that **I love this Connect thing**. The LearnSmart modules are great and really help me to learn the material. I even downloaded their app for my phone."*
—Colorado State University

AND THE INSTRUCTORS SAY:

- *"Five weeks into the semester, students in my three [course] sections have averages of 99.93, 99.97, and 100% respectively on the LearnSmart modules. **I would NEVER get that kind of learning and accuracy if I just assigned them to 'read the chapter and take notes'** or 'read the chapter and reflect'* or some other reading-based assignment."* —Florida State College at Jacksonville

- ***"LearnSmart has won my heart."*** —McLennan Community College

Better critical thinking skills

Experience History moves students beyond memorization of names and dates and promotes critical thinking:

- Now, map captions and "Daily Lives" feature more critical thinking prompts.

- Icons in the margins point to *Experience History*'s global, continental, and environmental coverage.

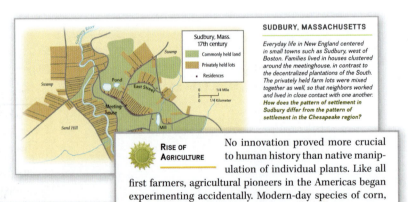

SUDBURY, MASSACHUSETTS

Everyday life in New England centered in small towns such as Sudbury, west of Boston. Families lived in houses clustered around the meetinghouse, in contrast to the decentralized plantations of the South. The privately held farm lots were mixed together as well, so that neighbors worked and lived in close contact with one another. ***How does the pattern of settlement in Sudbury differ from the pattern of settlement in the Chesapeake region?***

Sudbury, Mass. 17th century
- Commonly held land
- Privately held lots
- Residences

RISE OF AGRICULTURE No innovation proved more crucial to human history than native manipulation of individual plants. Like all first farmers, agricultural pioneers in the Americas began experimenting accidentally. Modern-day species of corn, for example, probably derive from a Mesoamerican grass known as teosinte. It seems that ancient peoples gathered teosinte to collect its small grains. By selecting the grains

WORLDWIDE SPREAD OF AMERICAN CROPS Indeed, ev... the grea... American... ples around the world. In addition to corn, the first Americans gave humanity scores of varieties of squash, potatoes, beans, and other basic foods. Today, plants domesticated by indigenous Americans account for three-fifths of the world's crops, including many that have revolutionized the global

Online activities in *Connect History* place students in an active environment where they develop analytical skills.

- *Connect History* builds advanced thinking and writing skills through "Critical Missions" projects that place students in a pivotal moment in time and ask them to develop a historical argument.

- Expanded and refined *Connect* resources, including new "Dueling Documents" and "Historian's Toolbox" activities, are now easier to assign and heighten the impact of text features.

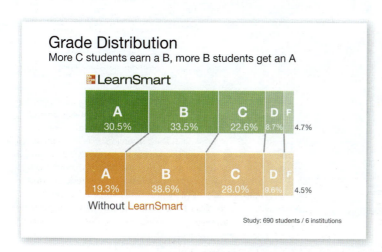

Grade Distribution
More C students earn a B, more B students get an A

LearnSmart

A	B	C	D	F
30.5%	33.5%	22.6%	8.7%	4.7%

A	B	C	D	F
19.3%	38.6%	28.0%	9.6%	4.5%

Without LearnSmart

Study: 690 students / 6 institutions

For a complete list of changes in the 8th edition of *Experience History*, go to **www.mhhe.com/eh8.**

Better grades

Research shows that students' grades improve using *Connect History* and LearnSmart. Imagine being able to document this type of grade improvement through easily-run reports.

Listen to instructors:

- *"My class that is using Connect scored higher than any other class in my 25 years of teaching."* —University of Colorado Denver

- *"The students really love Connect. They also got the best test scores on their first exam that I have ever seen in my teaching career."* —Georgia Southern University

Experience HISTORY

INTERPRETING AMERICA'S PAST

EIGHTH EDITION

James West Davidson

ooooo

Brian DeLay
UNIVERSITY OF CALIFORNIA, BERKELEY

ooooo

Christine Leigh Heyrman
UNIVERSITY OF DELAWARE

ooooo

Mark H. Lytle
BARD COLLEGE

ooooo

Michael B. Stoff
UNIVERSITY OF TEXAS, AUSTIN

Mc
Graw
Hill
Education

EXPERIENCE HISTORY: INTERPRETING AMERICA'S PAST, EIGHTH EDITION

1 2 3 4 5 6 7 8 9 0 DOW/DOW 1 0 9 8 7 6 5 4 3

ISBN   978-0-07-340701-2 (complete)
MHID   0-07-340701-1 (complete)
ISBN   978-0-07-750472-4 (volume I)
MHID   0-07-750472-0 (volume I)
ISBN   978-0-07-750473-1 (volume II)
MHID   0-07-750473-9 (volume II)

Senior Vice President, Products & Markets: *Kurt L. Strand*
Vice President, General Manager, Products & Markets: *Michael J. Ryan*
Vice President, Content Production & Technology Services: *Kimberly Meriwether David*
Managing Director: *Gina Boedeker*
Director: *Matt Busbridge*
Director of Development: *Rhona Robbin*
Managing Development Editor: *Nancy Crochiere*
Development Editor: *Sarah Remington*
Digital Development Editor: *Meghan Campbell*
Digital Product Analyst: *John Brady*

Brand Coordinator: *Kaelyn Schulz*
Executive Marketing Manager: *Stacy Best Ruel*
Director, Content Production: *Terri Schiesl*
Content Project Manager: *Angela Norris*
Senior Buyer: *Laura M. Fuller*
Design: *Trevor Goodman*
Senior Content Licensing Specialist: *Lori Hancock*
Media Project Manager: *Jennifer Barrick*
Typeface: *9/11 Kepler Std Regular*
Compositor: *Aptara®, Inc.*
Printer: *R. R. Donnelley*

The Library of Congress has cataloged the single-volume edition of this work as follows

Davidson, James West.
Experience history : interpreting America's past / James West Davidson, Brian DeLay, UNIVERSITY OF CALIFORNIA, BERKELEY, Christine Leigh Heyrman, UNIVERSITY OF DELAWARE, Mark H. Lytle, BARD COLLEGE, Michael B. Stoff, UNIVERSITY OF TEXAS, AUSTIN.—Eighth edition.
     pages cm
  Includes bibliographical references and index.
  ISBN-13: 978-0-07-340701-2 (complete text : acid-free paper)
  ISBN-10: 0-07-340701-1 (complete text : acid-free paper)
   1. United States—History.   2. United States—History—Study and teaching.   I. Title.
E178.1.E94 2014
973—dc23   2013010668

Brief Contents

Contents

After the Fact
Where Have All the Bison Gone? 496

Chapter 19
THE NEW INDUSTRIAL ORDER
1870–1914 500
∞∞∞ AN AMERICAN STORY ∞∞∞
"Waiting for Their Brains" 501

Chapter 20
THE RISE OF AN URBAN ORDER
1870–1914 530
∞∞∞ AN AMERICAN STORY ∞∞∞
"The Dogs of Hell" 531

Chapter 21

THE POLITICAL SYSTEM UNDER STRAIN AT HOME AND ABROAD 1877–1900 558

∞∞∞ AN AMERICAN STORY ∞∞∞

"The World United at Chicago" 559

After the Fact
En-Gendering the Spanish-American War 588

Chapter 22

THE PROGRESSIVE ERA 1890–1920 592

∞∞∞ AN AMERICAN STORY ∞∞∞

Burned Alive in the City 593

Chapter 25

THE GREAT DEPRESSION AND THE NEW DEAL 1929–1939 678

⚬⚬⚬⚬⚬ AN AMERICAN STORY ⚬⚬⚬⚬⚬

Letters from the Edge   679

Chapter 26

AMERICA'S RISE TO GLOBALISM 1927–1945 710

⚬⚬⚬⚬⚬ AN AMERICAN STORY ⚬⚬⚬⚬⚬

"Oh Boy"   711

After the Fact
Did the Atomic Bomb Save Lives?   **742**

Chapter 27
COLD WAR AMERICA
1945–1954   746

∞∞∞ AN AMERICAN STORY ∞∞∞
Glad to Be Home?   747

Chapter 32

THE UNITED STATES IN A GLOBAL COMMUNITY 1980–PRESENT   890

∞∞∞ AN AMERICAN STORY ∞∞∞

Of Grocery Chains and Migration Chains   891

LIST OF Maps and Charts

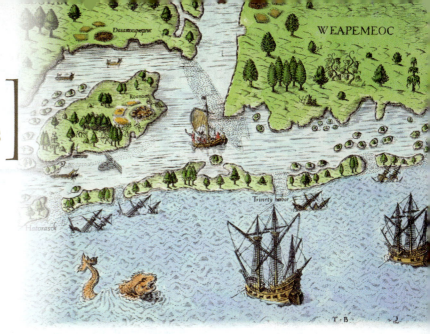

From the Authors

How do you make history?

There are two very different answers to the question, depending on whether you're living it or writing it. Yet both actions are more closely connected than appears at first glance. The American past is filled with people who have made history in ways they could not have anticipated when they were younger.

- Jean L'Archevêque, a 12-year-old French servant setting sail across the Atlantic in 1684 (see Chapter 5), could not have predicted that centuries later he would be remembered for his role as a decoy in an assassination plot, for the striking tattoos that were engraved on his face, and for his violent death along the Platte River, half a world away from his place of birth.

- Biology student Rachel Carson (Chapter 30) would have been astonished in 1928 to hear that 30 years later she would challenge the largest chemical companies in the United States, whose pesticides were damaging the environment.

- When a young Filipino soldier named Valentine Untalan (Chapter 26) was captured by the Japanese during World War II, the last thing on his mind, as he was herded into what was later called the Bataan death march, was whether one day his story might be told. He simply wanted to stay alive.

All these people made history—became a part of history—in large ways and small—as you yourself may someday, in a manner that is yet unknowable. However, there is another way to "make" history, and that is by thinking and writing about the past, as historians do.

THE EXPERIENCE OF "MAKING HISTORY"

The operative word is *make*. History is not the past; it is a reconstruction assembled from the past's raw materials. It is not a set of agreed-upon facts. Events happened and are relayed to us through a wide variety of surviving records, but—because we were not there—it is always through the gauze of someone's interpretation.

By nature textbook programs strive to be comprehensive, smooth, and seamless. They project an aura of omniscience; the narrative speaks with a single authoritative voice. But history does

not consist of one voice; it has multiple voices, like our diverse nation. It must take into account the dialogues, disagreements, and diverse actors that all have been a part of American history.

Of course, it is impossible to convey even a fraction of the debates that go into the "making" of history. However, in *Experience History,* we suggest a bit of the substance and flavor of the process by examining some of the debates and disagreements around a particular historical question. We place the reader in the role of historical detective. You are asked to examine historical evidence—whether a cartoon, an artifact, or two conflicting documents—and see what can be made of it. In short, you will learn what it means to make—to construct—history.

Experiencing the Stories of History

As historians, we use narrative as a way to give life to the past. The choice of narrative puts a great deal of emphasis on the individual and acknowledges that individuals can affect history in surprising ways. Personal decisions, sudden deaths, natural catastrophes, and chance all combine to make history unpredictable. And by telling these unpredictable stories we illustrate what historians refer to as "contingency"—the idea that history is not an inevitable series of events, but is changed and shaped by often-unanticipated events and actions of individuals.

Then, too, these stories fascinate us for the sheer wonder of watching individuals of all kinds grappling with how to shape the worlds around them.

- Take Wingina, chief of the Roanoke Indians, who in 1584 had to decide what to do about the savage, strangely behaved white men who had just landed on his shores;

- Or gaze in wonder at the quirky Henry Ford, who turned out identical Model T automobiles—because, as he put it, "Everybody wants to be somewhere he ain't"—and who also insisted that his factory workers wear identical expressions, which he referred to as "Fordization of the Face."

- Consider young Thurgood Marshall, crisscrossing the South in his own "little old beat-up '29 Ford," typing legal briefs in the backseat, trying to get black teachers to sue for equal pay, hoping to change African American lives for the better. Because (to quote Henry Ford) everybody wants to be somewhere he ain't.

Of course, narrative also allows us to comprehend broad trends—like the transportation revolution that proceeded from canals and steamboats to railroads and automobiles—but it does so without depriving us of history's irreducible details, like Wingina's dilemma or Marshall's dreams.

In *Experience History,* we hope we have combined a narrative whose stories engage you with a set of features that explore what historians do and how history is created. How you reflect upon the past, engage with it, and reconstruct it, will in no small measure determine your understanding and enjoyment of history, as well as your success in it.

Improve
Your
Course

Connect® History is a highly interactive learning environment designed to help students connect to the resources they will need to achieve success. Map activities, primary source exercises, image analysis, key term quizzes, and review questions provide a wealth of assignments to ensure that students are comprehending the reading and will succeed in the course. *ConnectPlus® History* offers all of the above with the addition of an integrated, interactive e-book. Optimized for the web, the e-book immerses students in a flexible, interactive environment.

ConnectPlus® History offers all of the above with the addition of an integrated, interactive e-book. Optimized for the web, the e-book immerses students in a flexible, interactive environment.

LearnSmart, McGraw-Hill's adaptive learning system, helps assess student knowledge of course content and maps out a personalized study plan for success. Accessible within *Connect History*, LearnSmart uses a series of adaptive questions to pinpoint the concepts students understand—and those they don't. The result is an online tool that helps students learn faster and study more efficiently and enables instructors to customize classroom lectures and activities to meet their students' needs.

 **SMARTBOOK™**

Fueled by LearnSmart—the most widely used and intelligent adaptive learning resource—SmartBook is the first and only adaptive reading experience available today.

Distinguishing what a student knows from what they don't, and honing in on concepts they are most likely to forget, SmartBook personalizes content for each student in a continuously adapting reading experience. Reading is no longer a passive and linear experience, but an engaging and dynamic one where students are more likely to master and retain important concepts, coming to class better prepared. Valuable reports provide instructors insight as to how students are progressing through textbook content, and are useful for shaping in-class time or assessment. As a result of the adaptive reading experience found in SmartBook, students are more likely to retain knowledge, stay in class and get better grades. This revolutionary technology is available only from McGraw-Hill Education and for hundreds of course areas as part of the LearnSmart Advantage series.

 **create™**

Design your ideal course materials with McGraw-Hill's **Create—www.mcgrawhillcreate.com!** Rearrange or omit chapters, combine material from other sources, and/or upload your syllabus or any other content you have written to make the perfect resources for your students. Search thousands of leading McGraw-Hill textbooks to find the best content for your students, then arrange it to fit your teaching style. You can even personalize your book's appearance by selecting the cover and adding your name, school, and course information. When you order a Create book, you receive a complimentary review copy. Get a printed copy in three to five business days or an electronic copy (eComp) via e-mail in about an hour. Register today at **www.mcgrawhillcreate. com** and craft your course resources to match the way you teach.

 **CourseSmart**

CourseSmart offers thousands of the most commonly adopted textbooks across hundreds of courses from a wide variety of higher education publishers. It is the only place for faculty to review and compare the full text of a textbook online, providing immediate access without the environmental impact of requesting a printed exam copy. At CourseSmart, students can save up to 50 percent off the cost of a printed book, reduce their impact on the environment, and gain access to powerful web tools for learning, including full text search, notes and highlighting, and e-mail tools for sharing notes among classmates. Learn more at **www.coursesmart.com**.

 **Campus**

McGraw-Hill Campus is the first-of-its-kind institutional service providing faculty with true single sign-on access to all of McGraw-Hill's course content, digital tools, and other high-quality learning resources from any learning management system (LMS). This innovative offering allows for secure and deep integration and seamless access to any of our course solutions such as McGraw-Hill *Connect*, McGraw-Hill Create, McGraw-Hill LearnSmart, or Tegrity. McGraw-Hill Campus includes access to our entire content library, including e-books, assessment tools, presentation slides, and multimedia content, among other resources, providing faculty open and unlimited access to prepare for class, create tests/quizzes, develop lecture material, integrate interactive content, and much more.

Online Learning Center for *Experience History*

The **Online Learning Center (OLC)** at **www.mhhe.com/eh8** contains a wealth of instructor resources, including an Instructor's Manual, Test Bank, and PowerPoint presentations for each chapter. All maps and most images from the print text are included.

A **Computerized Test Bank**, McGraw-Hill's EZ Test, allows you to quickly create a customized test using the publisher's supplied test banks or your own questions. You decide the number, type, and order of test questions with a few simple clicks. EZ Test runs on your computer without a connection to the Internet.

Primary Source Documents

The following primary source documents, carefully selected by the authors to coordinate with this program, are available on the Online Learning Center for *Experience History* at www.mhhe.com/eh8 and as assignable assessments on *Connect* at http://connect.mcgraw-hill.com. Documents include an explanatory headnote and are followed by discussion questions.

Choose from many of these documents—or hundreds of others—to customize your print text by visiting McGraw-Hill's Create at www.mcgrawhillcreate.com.

Acknowledgments

We are grateful to the many advisors and reviewers who generously offered comments and suggestions at various stages in our development of this manuscript. Our thanks go to:

Thomas Altherr,
Metropolitan State College of Denver

Melissa Anyiwo,
Curry College

Darren Bardell,
Ohlone College

Daniel Barr,
Robert Morris University

Melissa Biegert,
Temple College

Lisa Blank,
Tarrant County Community College

Margaret Brown,
Brevard College

Owen Chariton,
Metropolitan State College of Denver

Ann Short Chirhart,
Indiana State University

George Fain,
University South Carolina - Upstate

Jessica Feveryear,
Salt Lake Community College

Melody Flowers,
McLennan Community College

Amy Forss,
Metropolitan Community College

Rick Gianni,
Indiana University Northwest

Shawn Gladden,
Community College of Baltimore County

Mark Goldman,
Tallahassee Community College

Wendy Gunderson,
Collin College

David Haney,
Austin Community College

Ken Hansen,
Salt Lake Community College

Carmen Harris,
University of South Carolina - Upstate

Ely Janis,
Massachusetts College of Liberal Arts

Russell Jones,
Eastern Michigan University

Richard Kitchen,
New Mexico Military Institute

John Leland,
Salem International University

Charles Levine,
Mesa Community College

Manuel Medrano,
University of Texas, Brownsville

Mark Mengerink,
Lamar University

Don Mohr,
University of Alaska Anchorage

Kimberly Nichols,
Northeast Texas Community College

Michelle Anne Novak,
Houston Community College - Southeast

Shannon O'Bryan,
Greenville Technical College

Richard Owens,
West Liberty University

David Porter,
Northern Virginia Community College

Gretchen Reilly,
Temple College

John Selby,
Roanoke College

Richard Straw,
Radford University

Michael Thetford,
Lone Star College, Montgomery

Mark Van Ells,
Queensborough Community College

Melissa Weinbrenner,
Northeast Texas Community College

Scott Williams,
Weatherford College

Chad Wooley,
Tarrant County Community College

Digi-posium Attendees

Wayne Ackerson,
Technical College of Low Country

Ceci Barba,
El Paso Community College

Gene Barnett,
Calhoun Community College

Eric Duchess,
High Point University

Caroline Emmons,
Hampden-Sydney College

John Frongillo,
Florida Tech University

Mindy Green Reynolds,
Southern Union State Community College

Phyllis Jestice,
University of Southern Mississippi

Lloyd Johnson,
Campbell University

Haile Larebo,
Morehouse College

Jason Ramshur,
Pearl River Community College

Mark Roehrs,
Lincoln Land Community College

Robert A. Saunders,
Farmingdale State College

Keith Sisson,
University of Memphis

Matt Zembo,
Hudson Valley Community College

One acknowledgment we can never make too often is to the work of our co-author, colleague, and friend, William E. Gienapp. Bill traveled with us on this journey from the book's earliest conception up until his untimely passing in 2003. His insight, erudition, and good humor made him a pleasure to work with, and his contribution to the book will endure no matter how many new revisions appear.

JAMES WEST DAVIDSON, BRIAN DELAY,
CHRISTINE LEIGH HEYRMAN,
MARK H. LYTLE, MICHAEL B. STOFF

About the Authors

⊸⊸

JAMES WEST DAVIDSON

RECEIVED HIS PHD FROM YALE UNIVERSITY. A historian who has pursued a full-time writing career, he is the author of numerous books, among them *After the Fact: The Art of Historical Detection* (with Mark H. Lytle), *The Logic of Millennial Thought: Eighteenth-Century New England*, and *Great Heart: The History of a Labrador Adventure* (with John Rugge). He is co-editor with Michael Stoff of the *Oxford New Narratives in American History*, in which his own most recent book appears: *'They Say': Ida B. Wells and the Reconstruction of Race*.

BRIAN DELAY

RECEIVED HIS PHD FROM HARVARD University and is Associate Professor of History at the University of California, Berkeley. He is a frequent guest speaker at teacher workshops across the country and has won several prizes for his book *War of a Thousand Deserts: Indian Raids and the U.S.-Mexican War*. He is currently at work on the history of guns, business, and freedom in the Americas.

CHRISTINE LEIGH HEYRMAN

IS THE ROBERT W. AND SHIRLEY P. Grimble Professor of American History at the University of Delaware. She received a PhD in American Studies from Yale University and is the author of *Commerce and Culture: The Maritime Communities of Colonial Massachusetts, 1690–1750*. Her book *Southern Cross: The Beginnings of the Bible Belt* was awarded the Bancroft Prize in 1998.

MARK H. LYTLE

RECEIVED HIS PHD FROM YALE University and is Professor of History and Environmental Studies at Bard College. He served two years as Mary Ball Washington Professor of American History at University College, Dublin, in Ireland. His publications include *The Origins of the Iranian-American Alliance, 1941–1953*, *After the Fact: The Art of Historical Detection* (with James West Davidson), *America's Uncivil Wars: The Sixties Era from Elvis to the Fall of Richard Nixon*, and most recently, *The Gentle Subversive: Rachel Carson, Silent Spring, and the Rise of the Environmental Movement*. He is currently working on a book on the environmental impacts of consumerism in the post–World War II era.

MICHAEL B. STOFF

IS ASSOCIATE PROFESSOR OF HISTORY and Director of the Plan II Honors Program at the University of Texas at Austin. The recipient of a PhD from Yale University, he has been honored many times for his teaching, most recently with the University of Texas System Regents' Outstanding Teaching Award. He is the author of *Oil, War, and American Security: The Search for a National Policy on Foreign Oil, 1941–1947*, co-editor (with Jonathan Fanton and R. Hall Williams) of *The Manhattan Project: A Documentary Introduction to the Atomic Age*, and series co-editor (with James West Davidson) of the *Oxford New Narratives in American History*. He is currently working on a narrative of the bombing of Nagasaki.

[**FROM 1865**]

Experience
HISTORY
INTERPRETING AMERICA'S PAST

"There were swaying chimneys, tottering walls, streets impassable from piles of brick, stones, and rubbish," reported one journalist in Richmond at war's end. "Men stood speechless, haggard . . . gazing at the desolation." Many white southerners must have felt that way in defeat. But despite the ruins visible in this photograph, newly freed African Americans were understandably happy about their changed status.

CHAPTER 17

Reconstructing the Union

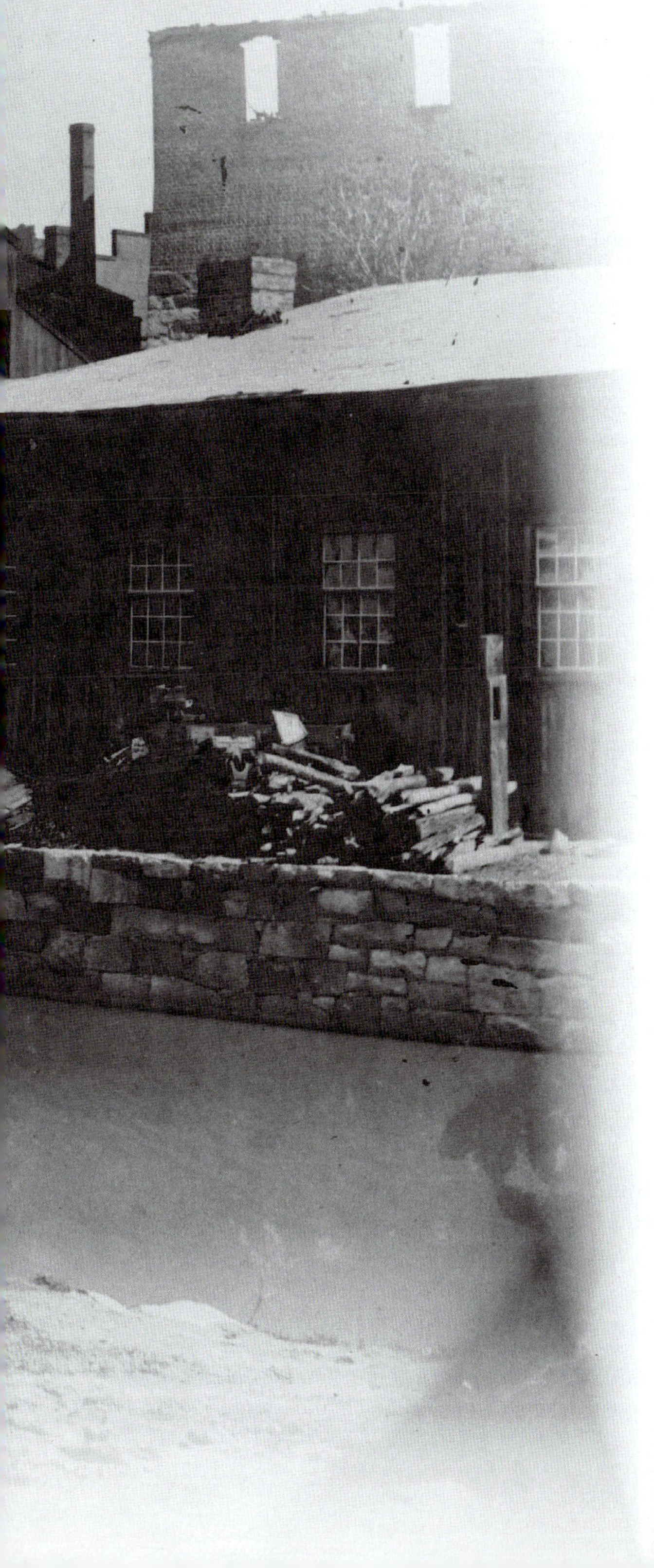

1865–1877

What's to Come

AN AMERICAN STORY

The Secret Sale at Davis Bend

Joseph Davis had had enough. Well on in years and financially ruined by the war, he decided to quit farming. In November 1866 he sold his Mississippi plantations Hurricane and Brierfield to Benjamin Montgomery and his sons. The sale of southern plantations was common enough after the war, but this transaction was bound to attract attention, since Joseph Davis was the elder brother of Jefferson Davis. Indeed, before the war the Confederate president had operated Brierfield as his own plantation, although his brother retained legal title to it. In truth, the sale was so unusual that the parties involved agreed to keep it secret, since the Montgomerys were black, and Mississippi law prohibited African Americans from owning land.

Though a slave, Montgomery had been the business manager of the two Davis plantations before the war. He had also operated a store on Hurricane Plantation for white as well as black customers with his own line of credit in New Orleans. In 1863 Montgomery fled to the North, but when the war was over, he returned to Davis Bend, where the federal government was leasing plots of the land on confiscated plantations, including Hurricane and Brierfield, to black farmers. Montgomery quickly emerged as the leader of the African American community at the Bend.

Then, in 1866, President Andrew Johnson pardoned Joseph Davis and restored his lands. By then Davis was over 80 years old and lacked the will and stamina to rebuild. Yet unlike many ex-slaveholders, he still felt bound by obligations to his former slaves. He was convinced that with proper encouragement African Americans could succeed economically in freedom. Only when the law prohibiting African Americans from owning land was overturned in 1867 did Davis publicly confirm the sale to his former slave.

| Benjamin Montgomery

For his part, Montgomery undertook to create a model society at Davis Bend based on mutual cooperation. He rented land to black farmers, hired others to work his own fields, sold supplies on credit, and ginned and marketed the crops. To the growing African American community, he preached the gospel of hard work, self-reliance, and education.

Various difficulties dogged these black farmers, including the destruction caused by the war, several disastrous floods, insects, droughts, and declining cotton prices. Yet before long, cotton production exceeded that of the prewar years, and in 1870 the black families at Davis Bend produced 2,500 bales. The Montgomerys eventually acquired another plantation and owned 5,500 acres, which made them reputedly the third-largest planters in the state. They won national and international awards for the quality of their cotton. Their success demonstrated what African Americans, given a fair chance, might accomplish.

The experiences of Benjamin Montgomery during the years after 1865 were not those of most black southerners, who did not own land or have a powerful white benefactor. Yet Montgomery's dream of economic independence was shared by all African Americans. As one black veteran noted, "Every colored man will be a slave, and feel himself a slave until he can raise him own bale of cotton and put him own mark upon it and say dis is mine!" Blacks could not gain effective freedom simply through a proclamation of emancipation. They needed economic power, including their own land that no one could unfairly take away.

For nearly two centuries the laws had prevented slaves from possessing such economic power. If those conditions were to be overturned, black Americans needed political power too. Thus the Republic would have to be reconstructed to give African Americans political power that they had been previously denied.

War, in its blunt way, had roughed out the contours of a solution, but only in broad terms. Clearly, African Americans would no longer be enslaved. The North, with its industrial might, would be the driving force in the nation's economy and retain the dominant political voice. But, beyond that, the outlines of a reconstructed Republic remained vague. Would African Americans receive effective power? How would the North and the South readjust their economic and political relations? These questions lay at the heart of the problem of Reconstruction. ∞∞∞

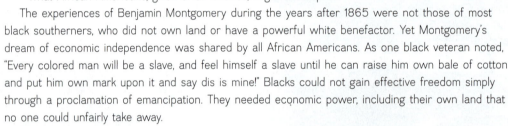

PRESIDENTIAL RECONSTRUCTION

THROUGHOUT THE WAR ABRAHAM LINCOLN had considered Reconstruction his responsibility. Elected with less than 40 percent of the popular vote in 1860, he was acutely aware that once the states of the Confederacy were restored to the Union, the Republicans would be weakened unless they ceased to be a sectional party. By a generous peace, Lincoln

hoped to attract former Whigs in the South, who supported many of the Republicans' economic policies, and build up a southern wing of the party.

Lincoln's 10 Percent Plan

Lincoln outlined his program in a Proclamation of **Amnesty** and Reconstruction issued in December 1863. When a

A Visit from the Old Mistress, by Winslow Homer, captures the conflicting, often awkward, emotions felt by both races after the war.

minimum of 10 percent of the qualified voters from 1860 took a **loyalty oath** to the Union, they could organize a state government. The new state constitution had to be republican in form, abolish slavery, and provide for black education, but Lincoln did not insist that high-ranking Confederate leaders be barred from public life.

Lincoln indicated that he would be generous in granting pardons and did not rule out compensation for slave property. Moreover, while he privately suggested permitting some black men to vote in the disloyal states, "as for instance, the very intelligent and especially those who have fought gallantly in our ranks," he did not demand social or political equality for black Americans, and he recognized pro-Union governments in Louisiana, Arkansas, and Tennessee that allowed only white men to vote.

RADICAL REPUBLICANS The Radical Republicans found Lincoln's approach much too lenient. Strongly anti-slavery, Radical members of Congress had led the struggle to make emancipation a war aim. Now they were in the forefront in advocating rights for the freed people. Lincoln argued that the executive branch should bear the responsibility for restoring proper relations with the former Confederate states. The Radicals, on the other hand, believed that it was the duty of Congress to set the terms under which states would regain their rights in the Union. Though the Radicals often disagreed on other matters, they were united in a determination to readmit southern states only after slavery had been ended, black rights protected, and the power of the planter class destroyed.

WADE-DAVIS BILL Under the direction of Senator Benjamin Wade of Ohio and Representative Henry Winter Davis of Maryland, Congress formulated a much stricter plan of Reconstruction. It proposed that Confederate states be ruled temporarily by a military governor, required half the white adult males to take an oath of allegiance before drafting a new state constitution, and restricted political power to the hard-core Unionists in each state. When the Wade-Davis bill passed on the final day of the 1864 congressional session, Lincoln exercised his right of a **pocket veto.** Still, his own program could not succeed without the assistance of Congress, which refused to seat Unionist representatives who had been elected from Louisiana or Arkansas. As the war drew to a close, Lincoln appeared ready to make concessions to the Radicals. At his final cabinet meeting, he approved placing the defeated South temporarily under military rule. But only a few days later Booth's bullet found its mark, and Lincoln's final approach to Reconstruction would never be known.

The Mood of the South

In the wake of defeat, the immediate reaction among white southerners was one of shock, despair, and hopelessness. Some former Confederates, of course, were openly antagonistic. A North Carolina innkeeper remarked bitterly that Yankees had stolen his slaves, burned his house, and killed all his sons, leaving him only one privilege: "To hate 'em. I git up at half-past four in the morning, and sit up till twelve at night, to hate 'em." Most Confederate

The mood of white southerners at the end of the war was mixed. Many, like the veteran caricatured here by northern cartoonist Thomas Nast, remained hostile. Others, like Texas captain Samuel Foster, came to believe that the institution of slavery "had been abused" and that men "who actually owned and held slaves up to this time,—have now changed in their opinions regarding slavery . . . to see that for a man to have property in man was wrong, and that the 'Declaration of Independence' meant more than they had ever been able to see before."

soldiers were less defiant, having had their fill of war. Even among hostile civilians the feeling was widespread that the South must accept northern terms.

This psychological moment was critical. To prevent a resurgence of resistance, the president needed to lay out clearly what white southerners had to do to regain their old status in the Union. Any wavering on the peace terms could only increase the likelihood of resistance. Perhaps even a clear and firm policy would not have been enough. But with Lincoln's death, the executive power came to rest in far less capable hands.

Johnson's Program of Reconstruction

JOHNSON'S CHARACTER AND VALUES
Andrew Johnson, the new president, had been born in North Carolina and eventually moved to Tennessee, where he worked as a tailor. Barely able to read and write when he married, he rose to political power by portraying himself as the champion of the people against the wealthy planter class. "Some day I will show the stuck-up aristocrats who is running the country," he vowed as he began his political career. He had not opposed slavery before the war—in fact, he hoped to disperse slave ownership more widely in southern society. Although he accepted emancipation as one consequence of the war, Johnson remained a confirmed racist. "Damn the negroes," he said during the war, "I am fighting these traitorous aristocrats, their masters."

Because Johnson disliked the planter class, Republican Radicals in Congress expected him to uphold their views on Reconstruction. In fact, the new president did speak of trying Confederate leaders and breaking up planters' estates. Unlike most Republicans, however, Johnson strongly supported states' rights. Furthermore, his prickly personality made conflict between the president and Congress

| Andrew Johnson

inevitable. Scarred by his humble origins, Johnson remained an outsider throughout his life. When challenged or criticized he became tactless and inflexible, alienating even those who sought to work with him.

JOHNSON'S PROGRAM
Johnson moved quickly to return the southern states to their place in the Union. He prescribed a loyalty oath that white southerners would have to take to regain their civil and political rights and to have their property, except for slaves, restored. Excluded were high Confederate officials and those with property worth over $20,000, who had to apply for individual pardons. Johnson announced that once a state had drafted a new constitution and elected state officers and members of Congress, he would revoke martial law and recognize the new state government. Suffrage was limited to white citizens who had taken the loyalty oath. This plan was similar to Lincoln's, though more lenient. Only informally did Johnson ask that the southern states renounce their ordinances of secession, repudiate the Confederate debt, and ratify the proposed Thirteenth Amendment abolishing slavery.

The Failure of Johnson's Program

SOUTHERN DEFIANCE
The southern delegates who met to construct new governments were in no frame of mind to follow Johnson's recommendations. Several states merely repealed instead of repudiating their ordinances of secession, rejected the Thirteenth Amendment, or refused to repudiate the Confederate debt.

BLACK CODES
Nor did the new governments allow African Americans any political rights or make any effective provisions for black education. In addition, each state passed a series of laws, often modeled on its old slave code, that applied only to African Americans. These **black codes** did grant African Americans some rights that had not been enjoyed by slaves. They legalized marriages performed under slavery and allowed black southerners to hold and sell property and to sue and be sued in state courts. Yet their primary purpose was to keep African Americans as propertyless agricultural laborers with inferior legal rights. The new freedmen, or freedpeople, could not serve on juries, testify against whites, or work as they pleased. South Carolina forbade blacks to engage in anything other than agricultural labor without a special license; Mississippi prohibited them from buying or renting farmland. Most states ominously provided that black people who were

vagrants could be arrested and hired out to land-owners. Many northerners were incensed by the restrictive black codes.

ELECTIONS IN THE SOUTH Southern voters under Johnson's plan also defiantly elected prominent Confederate military and political leaders to office, headed by Alexander Stephens, the vice president of the Confederacy, who was elected senator from Georgia. At this point, Johnson could have called for new elections or admitted that a different program of Reconstruction was needed. Instead, he caved in. For all his harsh rhetoric, he shrank from the prospect of social upheaval, and he found it enormously gratifying when upper-class planters praised his conduct and requested pardons. As the lines of ex-Confederates waiting to see him lengthened, he began issuing special pardons almost as fast as they could be printed. In the next two years he pardoned some 13,500 former rebels.

Thaddeus Stevens, Radical leader in the House

In private, Johnson warned southerners against a reckless course. Publicly he put on a bold face, announcing that Reconstruction had been successfully completed. But many members of Congress were deeply alarmed.

Johnson's Break with Congress

The new Congress was by no means of one mind. A small number of Democrats and a few conservative Republicans backed the president's program. At the other end of the spectrum, a larger group of Radical Republicans, led by Thaddeus Stevens, Charles Sumner, Benjamin Wade, and others, was bent on remaking southern society in the image of the North. Reconstruction must "revolutionize Southern institutions, habits, and manners," insisted Representative Stevens, "... or all our blood and treasure have been spent in vain." Unlike Johnson, Radicals championed civil and political rights for African Americans and believed that the only way to maintain loyal governments and develop a Republican Party in the South was to give black men the ballot.

As a minority, the Radicals could accomplish nothing without the aid of the moderate Republicans, the largest bloc in Congress. Led by William Pitt Fessenden and Lyman Trumbull, the moderates hoped to avoid a clash with the president, and they had no desire to foster social revolution or promote racial equality in the South. But they wanted to keep Confederate leaders from reassuming power, and they were convinced that the former slaves needed federal protection. Otherwise, Trumbull declared, the freedpeople would "be tyrannized over, abused, and virtually reenslaved."

Moderates agreed that the new southern governments were too harsh toward African Americans, but they feared that too great an emphasis on black civil rights would alienate northern voters.

In December 1865, when southern representatives to Congress appeared in Washington, a majority in Congress voted to exclude them. Congress also appointed a joint committee, chaired by Senator Fessenden, to look into how to implement Reconstruction. The split with the president became clearer when Congress passed a bill extending the life of the Freedmen's Bureau. Created in March 1865, the bureau provided emergency food, clothing, and medical care to war refugees (including white southerners) and took charge of settling freedpeople on abandoned lands. The new bill gave the bureau the added responsibilities of supervising special courts to resolve disputes involving freedpeople and establishing schools for black southerners. Although this bill passed with near unanimous Republican support, Johnson vetoed it. Congress failed to override his veto.

JOHNSON'S VETOES Johnson also vetoed a civil rights bill designed to overturn the most severe provisions of the black codes. The law made African Americans citizens of the United States and granted them the right to own property, make contracts, and have access to courts as parties and witnesses. For most Republicans Johnson's action was the last straw, and in April 1866 Congress overrode his veto, the first major legislation in American history to be enacted over a presidential veto. Congress then approved a slightly revised Freedmen's Bureau bill in July and promptly overrode the president's veto. Johnson's refusal to compromise drove the moderates into the arms of the Radicals.

The Fourteenth Amendment

To prevent unrepentant Confederates from taking over the reconstructed state governments and denying African Americans basic freedoms, the Joint Committee on Reconstruction proposed an amendment to the Constitution, which passed both houses of Congress with the necessary two-thirds vote in June 1866. The amendment, coupled with the Freedmen's Bureau and civil rights bills, represented the moderates' terms for Reconstruction.

PROVISIONS OF THE AMENDMENT The Fourteenth Amendment put a number of matters beyond the control of the president. The amendment guaranteed repayment of the national war debt and prohibited repayment of the Confederate debt. To counteract the president's wholesale pardons, it disqualified prominent Confederates from holding office and provided that only Congress by a two-thirds vote could remove this penalty. Because moderates, fearful of the reaction of white northerners, balked at giving the vote to African Americans, the amendment merely gave Congress the right to reduce the representation of any state

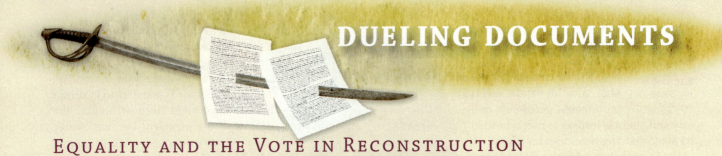

DUELING DOCUMENTS

EQUALITY AND THE VOTE IN RECONSTRUCTION

Debate swirled around not only the conditions southern states needed to fulfill to return to the Union but also the rights of citizenship granted to former slaves. At war's end, African Americans held a number of conventions to set forth their views (Document 1). Andrew Johnson privately conveyed to white southern leaders his idea of how they should act (Document 2). And Representative Thaddeus Stevens of Pennsylvania spoke for Radical Republicans (Document 3).

DOCUMENT 1 African Americans Seek the Vote

We, the delegates of the colored people of the State of Virginia . . . solemnly [declare] that we desire to live upon the most friendly and agreeable terms with all men; we feel no ill-will or prejudice towards our former oppressors . . . and that we believe that in this State we have still many warm and solid friends among the white people. . . .

We must, on the other hand, be allowed to aver and assert that we believe that we have among the white people of this State, many who are our most inveterate enemies . . .

who despise us simply because we are black, and more especially, because we have been made free by the power of the United States Government; and that they—the class last mentioned—will not, in our estimation, be willing to accord to us, as freemen, that protection which all freemen must contend for, if they would be worthy of freedom. . . .

We claim, then, as citizens of this State, the laws of the Commonwealth shall give to all men equal protection; that each and every man may appeal to the law for his equal

rights without regard to the color of his skin; and we believe this can only be done by extending to us the elective franchise, which we believe to be our inalienable right as freemen, and which the Declaration of Independence guarantees to all free citizens of this Government and which is the privilege of the nation.

Source: Proceedings of the Convention of the Colored People of Virginia . . . in Philip S. Foner and George E. Walker, eds., Proceedings of the Black State Conventions, 1840–1865 (Philadelphia, 1980), vol. 2, pp. 262–264.

DOCUMENT 2 President Johnson Advises Southern Leaders

I hope that without delay your convention will amend your State constitution . . . [to] adopt the amendment to the Constitution of the United States abolishing slavery. If you could extend the elective franchise to all persons of color who can read the Constitution of the United States in English and write their names, and to all persons of color who own real estate valued at not less

than two hundred and fifty dollars and pay taxes thereon, you would completely disarm the adversary and set an example the other States will follow. This you can do with perfect safety, and you would thus place Southern States in reference to the free persons of color upon the same basis with the free States. . . . And as a consequence the radicals, who are wild upon negro

franchise, will be completely foiled in their attempts to keep the Southern States from renewing their relations to the Union by not accepting their Senators and Representatives.

Source: Walter L. Fleming, ed., Documentary History of Reconstruction (Cleveland, 1906–1907), vol. 1, p. 177.

DOCUMENT 3 Representative Stevens on Equal Privileges

But this is not all that we ought to do before these inveterate rebels are invited to participate in our legislation. We have turned, or are about to turn, loose four million slaves without a hut to shelter them or a cent in their pockets. The infernal laws of slavery have prevented them from acquiring an education, understanding the commonest laws of contract, or of managing the ordinary business of life. This Congress is bound to provide for them until they can take care of themselves. If we do not furnish them with homesteads, and hedge them around with protective laws; if we leave them to the legislation of their late masters, we had better have left them in bondage . . . equal rights to all the privileges of the Government is innate to every immortal being, no matter what the

shape or color of the tabernacle which it inhabits. . . .

If equal privileges were granted to all, I should not expect to any but white men to be elected to office for long ages to come. . . . But it would still be beneficial to the weaker races. In a country where political divisions will always exist, their power, joined with just white men, would greatly modify, if it did not entirely prevent, the injustice of majorities. Without the right of suffrage in the late slave States, (I do not speak of the free States,) I believe the slaves had far better been left in bondage. . . .

[Men of influence] proclaim, "This is a white man's Government," and the whole coil of copperheads echo the same sentiment, and upstart, jealous Republicans join the cry. Is it any wonder ignorant foreigners and

illiterate natives should learn this doctrine, and be led to despise and maltreat a whole race of their fellow men?

Source: Congressional Globe, 39th Congress, 1st Session, 1865, pp. 72–73.

Thinking Critically

Each of the writers recommends that African Americans receive the vote in some way. Which document is the most radical? Which the least so? Who does President Johnson refer to as "the adversary"? How does he intend to "foil" the Radicals? And what does Thaddeus Steven not speak about? Why?

that did not have impartial male suffrage. The practical effect of this provision, which Radicals labeled a "swindle," was to allow northern states to restrict suffrage to whites if they wished, since unlike southern states they had few African Americans and thus would not be penalized.

The amendment's most important provision, Section 1, defined an American citizen as anyone born in the United States or naturalized, thereby automatically making African Americans citizens. Section 1 also prohibited states from abridging "the privileges or immunities" of citizens, depriving "any person of life, liberty, or property, without due process of law," or denying "any person . . . equal protection of the laws." The framers of the amendment probably intended to prohibit laws that applied to one race only, such as the black codes, or that made certain acts felonies when committed by black but not white people, or that decreed different penalties for the same crime when committed by white and black lawbreakers. The framers probably did not intend to prevent African Americans from being excluded from juries or to forbid segregation (the legal separation of the races) in schools and public places.

Nevertheless, Johnson denounced the proposed amendment and urged southern states not to ratify it. Ironically, of the seceded states only the president's own state ratified the amendment, and Congress readmitted Tennessee with no further restrictions. The telegram sent to Congress by a longtime foe of Johnson announcing Tennessee's approval ended, "Give my respects to the dead dog in the White House." The amendment was ratified in 1868.

The Elections of 1866

ANTIBLACK RIOTS

When Congress blocked his policies, Johnson undertook a speaking tour of the East and Midwest in the fall of 1866 to drum up popular support. But the president found it difficult to convince northern audiences that white southerners were fully repentant. News that summer of major race riots in Memphis and New Orleans heightened northern concern. Forty-six African Americans died when white mobs invaded the black section of Memphis, burning homes, churches, and schoolhouses. About the same number were killed in New Orleans when whites attacked both black and white delegates to a convention supporting black suffrage. "The negroes now know, to their sorrow, that it is best not to arouse the fury of the white man," boasted one Memphis newspaper. When the president encountered hostile audiences during his northern campaign, he made matters only worse by trading insults and ranting that the Radicals were traitors. Even supporters found his performance humiliating.

Not to be outdone, the Radicals vilified Johnson as a traitor aiming to turn the country over to rebels and Copperheads. Resorting to the tactic of "waving the **bloody shirt**," they appealed to voters by reviving bitter memories of the war. In a classic example of such rhetoric, Governor Oliver

This politician is literally "waving the bloody shirt"—using the bitter memories of the Civil War to rouse voters to side with Republicans.

Morton of Indiana proclaimed that "every bounty jumper, every deserter, every sneak who ran away from the draft calls himself a Democrat...Every 'Son of Liberty' who conspired to murder, burn, rob arsenals and release rebel prisoners calls himself a Democrat...In short, the Democratic Party may be described as a common sewer."

REPUDIATION OF JOHNSON Voters soundly repudiated Johnson, as the Republicans won more than a two-thirds majority in both houses of Congress, every northern gubernatorial contest, and control of every northern legislature. The Radicals had reached the height of their power.

✓ REVIEW

What were Lincoln's and Andrew Johnson's approaches to Reconstruction, and why did Congress reject Johnson's approach?

CONGRESSIONAL RECONSTRUCTION

WITH A CLEAR MANDATE IN hand, congressional Republicans passed their own program of Reconstruction, beginning with the first Reconstruction Act in March 1867. Like all later pieces of Reconstruction legislation, it was repassed over Johnson's veto.

Placing the 10 unreconstructed states under military commanders, the act directed officials to include black adult males as voters but not former Confederates barred from holding office under the Fourteenth Amendment. State conventions would frame constitutions that provided for black suffrage and that disqualified prominent ex-Confederates from office. The first state legislatures to meet under the new constitution were required to ratify the

Fourteenth Amendment. Once these steps were completed and Congress approved the new state constitution, a state could send representatives to Congress.

RESISTANCE OF SOUTHERN WHITES — White southerners found these requirements so insulting that officials took no steps to register voters. Congress then enacted a second Reconstruction Act, also in March, ordering the local military commanders to put the machinery of Reconstruction into motion. Johnson's efforts to limit the power of military commanders produced a third act, passed in July, that upheld their superiority in all matters. When elections were held to ratify the new state constitutions, white southerners boycotted them in large numbers. Undaunted, Congress passed the fourth Reconstruction Act (March 1868), which required ratification of the constitution by only a majority of those voting rather than those who were registered.

By June 1868 Congress had readmitted the representatives of seven states. Georgia's state legislature expelled its black members once it had been readmitted, granting seats to those barred by Congress from holding office. Congress ordered the military commander to reverse these actions, and Georgia was then admitted a second time in July 1870. Texas, Virginia, and Mississippi did not complete the process until 1869.

Post-Emancipation Societies in the Americas

With the exception of Haiti's revolution (1791–1804), the United States was the only society in the Americas in which the destruction of slavery was accomplished by violence. But the United States, uniquely among these societies, enfranchised former slaves almost immediately after the emancipation. Thus in the United States former masters and slaves battled for control of the state in ways that did not occur in other post-emancipation societies. In most of the Caribbean, property requirements for voting left the planters in political control. Jamaica, for example, with a population of 500,000 in the 1860s, had only 3,000 voters.

Moreover, in reaction to political efforts to mobilize disenfranchised black peasants, Jamaican planters dissolved the assembly and reverted to being a Crown colony governed from London. Of the sugar islands, all but Barbados adopted the same policy, thereby blocking the potential for any future black peasant democracy. Nor did any of these societies have the counterparts of the Radical Republicans, a group of outsiders with political power that promoted the fundamental transformation of the post-emancipation South. These comparisons highlight the radicalism of Reconstruction in the United States, which alone saw an effort to forge an interracial democracy.

The Land Issue

BLACKS' DESIRE FOR LAND — While the political process of Reconstruction proceeded, Congress confronted the question of whether land should be given to former slaves to foster economic independence. At a meeting with Secretary of War Edwin Stanton near the end of the war, African American leaders declared, "The way we can best take care of ourselves is to have land, and till it by our own labor." During the war, the Second Confiscation Act of 1862 had authorized the government to seize and sell the property, including land, of supporters of the rebellion. In June 1866, however, President Johnson ruled that confiscation laws applied only to wartime.

Congress debated land confiscation off and on from December 1865 until early 1867. Thaddeus Stevens, a leading Radical in the House, advocated confiscating 394 million acres of land from about 70,000 of what he termed the "chief rebels" in the South, who made up less than 5 percent of the South's white families. He proposed to give 40 acres to every adult male freedperson and then sell the remaining land, which would amount to nine-tenths of the total, to pay off the public debt, compensate loyal southerners for losses they suffered during the war, and fund Union veterans'

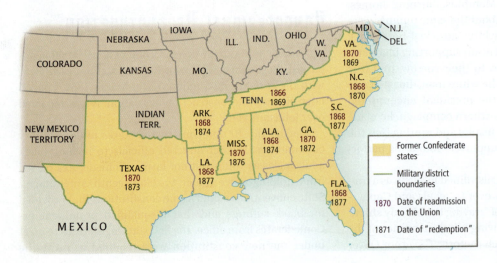

THE SOUTHERN STATES DURING RECONSTRUCTION

- Former Confederate states
- Military district boundaries
- 1870 Date of readmission to the Union
- 1871 Date of "redemption"

pensions. Land, he insisted, would be far more valuable to African Americans than the right to vote.

FAILURE OF LAND REDISTRIBUTION

But in the end Congress rejected all proposals. Given Americans' strong belief in self-reliance, little sympathy existed for the idea that government should support any group. In addition, land redistribution represented an attack on property rights, another cherished American value. By 1867 land reform was dead.

Few freedpeople acquired land after the war, a development that severely limited African Americans' economic independence and left them vulnerable to white coercion. It is doubtful, however, that this decision was the basic cause of the failure of Reconstruction. In the face of white hostility and institutionalized racism, African Americans probably would have been no more successful in protecting their property than they were in maintaining the right to vote.

Impeachment

TENURE OF OFFICE ACT

Throughout 1867 Congress routinely overrode Johnson's vetoes. Still, the president had other ways of undercutting congressional Reconstruction. He interpreted the new laws as narrowly as possible and removed military commanders who vigorously enforced them. Congress responded by restricting Johnson's power to issue orders to military commanders in the South. It also passed the Tenure of Office Act, which forbade Johnson to remove any member of the cabinet without the Senate's consent. The intention of this law was to prevent him from firing Secretary of War Edwin Stanton, the only Radical in the cabinet.

JOHNSON ACQUITTED

When Johnson tried to dismiss Stanton in February 1868, the determined secretary of war barricaded himself in his office (where he remained night and day for about two months). Angrily, the House of Representatives approved articles of impeachment. The articles focused on the violation of the Tenure of Office Act, but the charge with the most substance was that Johnson had conspired to systematically obstruct Reconstruction legislation. In the trial before the Senate, his lawyers argued that a president could be impeached only for an indictable crime, which Johnson clearly had not committed. The Radicals countered that impeachment applied to political offenses, not merely criminal acts. In May 1868 the Senate voted 36 to 19 to convict, one vote short of the two-thirds majority needed. The seven Republicans who joined the Democrats in voting for acquittal were uneasy about using impeachment as a political weapon.

REVIEW

What was Congress's approach to Reconstruction, and why did it not include a provision for giving land to former slaves?

RECONSTRUCTION IN THE SOUTH

THE REFUSAL OF CONGRESS TO convict Johnson sent a clear signal: the power of the Radicals in Congress was waning. Increasingly the success or failure of Reconstruction hinged on developments not in Congress but in the southern states themselves. Power there rested with the new Republican parties, representing a coalition of black and white southerners and transplanted northerners.

Black Officeholding

Almost from the beginning of Reconstruction, African Americans had lobbied for the right to vote. After they received the **franchise,** black men constituted as much as 80 percent of the Republican voters in the South. They steadfastly opposed the Democratic Party with its appeal to white supremacy.

Throughout Reconstruction, African Americans never held office in proportion to their voting strength. No African American was ever elected governor, and only in South Carolina, where more than 60 percent of the population was black, did they control even one house of the legislature. During Reconstruction between 15 and 20 percent of the state officers and 6 percent of members of Congress (2 senators and 15 representatives) were black. Only in South Carolina did black officeholders approach their proportion of the population.

BACKGROUND OF BLACK POLITICAL LEADERS

Blacks who held office generally came from the top levels of African American society. Among state and federal officeholders, perhaps four-fifths were literate, and more than a quarter had been free before the war, both marks of distinction in the black community. Their occupations also set them apart: two-fifths were professionals (mostly clergy), and of the third who were farmers, nearly all owned land. Among black members of Congress, all but three had a secondary school education, and four had gone to

| Hiram Revels, a minister and educator, became the first African American to serve in the U.S. Senate, representing Mississippi. Later he served as president of Alcorn University.

college. In their political and social values, African American leaders were more conservative than the rural black population was, and they showed little interest in land reform.

White Republicans in the South

Black citizens were a majority of the voters only in South Carolina, Mississippi, and Louisiana. Thus in most of the South the Republican Party had to secure white votes to stay in power. Opponents scornfully labeled white southerners who allied with the Republican Party **scalawags,** yet an estimated quarter of white southerners at one time voted Republican. Although the party appealed to some wealthy planters, they were outnumbered by Unionists from the upland counties and hill areas who were largely yeoman farmers. Such voters were attracted by Republican promises to rebuild the South, restore prosperity, create public schools, and open isolated areas to the market with railroads.

The other group of white Republicans in the South was known as **carpetbaggers.** Originally from the North, they allegedly had arrived with all their worldly possessions stuffed in a carpetbag, ready to plunder the defeated South. Some did, but northerners moved south for a variety of reasons. Those in political office were especially well educated. Though carpetbaggers made up only a small percentage of

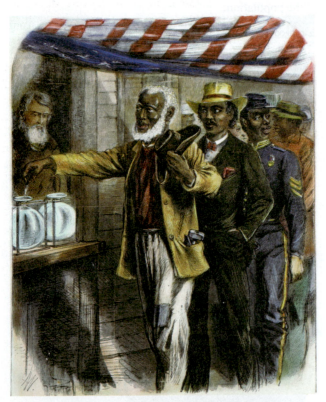

| Harper's Illustrated Weekly *celebrated African Americans who voted for the first time in 1867. First in line is a skilled craftworker, his tools in his pocket; then an urban resident of some sophistication, followed by a veteran. Why would the artist choose these men as examples?*

Republican voters, they controlled almost a third of the offices in the South. More than half of all southern Republican governors and nearly half of Republican members of Congress were originally northerners.

DIVISIONS AMONG SOUTHERN REPUBLICANS

The Republican Party in the South had difficulty maintaining unity. Scalawags were especially susceptible to the race issue and social pressure. "Even my own kinspeople have turned the cold shoulder to me because I hold office under a Republican administration," testified a Mississippi white Republican. As black southerners pressed for greater recognition and a greater share of the offices, white southerners increasingly defected to the Democrats. Carpetbaggers were less sensitive to race, although most felt that their black allies should be content with minor offices. The friction between scalawags and carpetbaggers, which grew out of their rivalry for party honors, was particularly intense.

The New State Governments

NEW STATE CONSTITUTIONS

The new southern state constitutions enacted several reforms. They put in place fairer systems of legislative representation, allowed voters to elect many officials who before had been appointed, and abolished property requirements for office-holding. In South Carolina, for the first time, voters were allowed to vote for the president, governor, and other state officers. (Previously, presidential electors as well as the governor had been chosen by the South Carolina legislature.) The Radical state governments also assumed some responsibility for social welfare and established the first statewide systems of public schools in the South.

RACE AND SOCIAL EQUALITY

All the new constitutions proclaimed the principle of equality and granted black adult males the right to vote. On social relations they were much more cautious. No state outlawed segregation, and South Carolina and Louisiana were the only states that required integration in public schools (a mandate that was almost universally ignored).

Economic Issues and Corruption

The war left the southern economy in ruins, and problems of economic reconstruction were as difficult as those of politics. The new Republican governments encouraged industrial development by providing subsidies, loans, and even temporary exemptions from taxes. These governments also largely rebuilt the southern railroad system, often offering lavish aid to railroad corporations. The investments in the South helped double its manufacturing establishments in the two decades after 1860. Yet the harsh reality was that the South steadily slipped further behind the booming industrial economy of the North. Between 1854 and 1879, 7,000 miles of railroad track were laid in the South, but in the same period 45,000 miles were constructed in the rest of the nation.

CORRUPTION The expansion of government services offered temptations for corruption. In many southern states, officials regularly received bribes and kickbacks for their award of railroad charters, franchises, and other contracts. By 1872 the debts of the 11 states of the Confederacy had increased by $132 million, largely because of railroad grants and new social services such as schools. The tax rate grew as expenditures went up; by the 1870s it was four times the rate of 1860.

Corruption, however, was not only a problem in the South: the decline in morality affected the entire nation. During these years in New York City alone, the Democratic Tweed Ring stole more money than all the Radical Republican governments in the South combined. Moreover, corruption in the South was hardly limited to Republicans. Many Democrats and white business leaders participated in the looting. "Everybody is demoralizing down here. Corruption is the fashion," reported Louisiana governor Henry Warmoth.

Corruption in Radical governments existed, but southern whites exaggerated its extent for partisan purposes. Conservatives just as bitterly opposed honest Radical regimes as they did corrupt ones. In the eyes of most white southerners the real crime of the Radical governments was that they allowed black citizens to hold some offices and tried to protect the civil rights of African Americans. Race was the conservatives' greatest weapon. And it would prove the most effective means to undermine Republican power in the South.

> ✓ **REVIEW**
>
> What roles did African Americans, southern whites, and northern whites play in the Reconstruction governments of the South?

BLACK ASPIRATIONS

EMANCIPATION CAME TO SLAVES IN different ways and at different times. For some it arrived during the war when Union soldiers entered an area; for others it came some time after the Confederacy's collapse, when Union troops or officials announced that they were free. Whatever the timing, freedom meant a host of precious blessings to people who had been in bondage all their lives.

Experiencing Freedom

The first impulse was to think of freedom as a contrast to slavery. Emancipation immediately released slaves from the most oppressive aspects of bondage—the whippings, the breakup of families, the sexual exploitation. Freedom also meant movement, the right to travel without a pass or white permission. Above all, freedom meant that African Americans' labor would be for their own benefit. One Arkansas freedman, who earned his first dollar working on a railroad, recalled that when he was paid, "I felt like the richest man in the world."

CHANGING EMPLOYMENT Freedom included finding a new place to work. Changing jobs was one concrete way to break the psychological ties of slavery. Even planters with reputations for kindness sometimes saw their former hands depart. The cook who left a South Carolina family even though they offered her higher wages than her new job explained, "I must go. If I stays here I'll never know I'm free."

IMPORTANCE OF NAMES Symbolically, freedom meant having a full name, and African Americans now adopted last names. More than a few took the last name of some prominent individual; more common was to take the name of the first master in the family's oral history as far back as it could be recalled. Most, however, retained their first name, especially if the name had been given to them by their parents (as most often had been the case among slaves). It had been their form of identity in bondage, and for those separated from their family it was the only link with their parents. Whatever name they took, it was important to black Americans that they make the decision themselves without white interference.

The Black Family

UPHOLDING THE FAMILY African Americans also sought to strengthen the family in freedom. Because slave marriages had not been recognized as legal, thousands of former slaves insisted on being married again by proper authorities, even though a ceremony was not required by law. Blacks who had been forcibly separated in slavery and later remarried confronted the dilemma of which spouse to take. Laura Spicer, whose husband had been sold away in slavery, received a series of wrenching letters from him after the war. He had thought her dead, had remarried, and had a new family. "You know it never was our wishes to be separated from each other, and it never was our fault. I had rather anything to had happened to me most than ever have been parted from you and the children," he wrote. "As I am, I do not know which I love best, you or Anna." Declining to return, he closed, "Laura, truly, I have got another wife, and I am very sorry. . . ."

SAML. DOVE wishes to know of the whereabouts of his mother, Areno, his sisters Maria, Neziah, and Peggy, and his brother Edmond, who were owned by Geo. Dove, of Rockingham county, Shenandoah Valley, Va. Sold in Richmond, after which Saml. and Edmond were taken to Nashville, Tenn., by Joe Mick; Areno was left at the Eagle Tavern, Richmond
Respectfully yours,
SAML. DOVE.
Utica, New York, Aug. 5, 1865–3m

| *A Tennessee newspaper advertisement seeking a family, 1865*

Like white husbands, black husbands deemed themselves the head of the family and acted legally for their wives. They often insisted that their wives would not work in the fields as they had in slavery, a decision that had major economic repercussions for agricultural labor. In negotiating contracts, a father also demanded the right to control his children and their labor. All these changes were designed to insulate the black family from white control.

The Schoolhouse and the Church

BLACK EDUCATION In freedom, the schoolhouse and the black church became essential institutions in the black community. Next to ownership of land, African Americans saw education as the best hope for advancement. At first, northern churches and missionaries, working with the Freedmen's Bureau, set up black schools in the South. Tuition represented 10 percent or more of a laborer's monthly wages. Yet these schools were full. Many parents sent their children by day and attended classes themselves at night. Eventually, the Bureau schools were replaced by the new public school systems, which by 1876 enrolled 40 percent of African American children.

Black adults had good reasons for seeking literacy. They wanted to be able to read the Bible, to defend their newly gained civil and political rights, and to protect themselves from being cheated. One elderly Louisiana freedman explained that giving children an education was better than giving them a fortune, "because if you left them even $500, some man having more education than they had would come along and cheat them out of it all."

TEACHERS IN BLACK SCHOOLS Teachers in the Freedmen's Bureau schools were primarily northern middle-class white women sent south by northern missionary societies. "I feel that it is a precious privilege," Esther Douglass wrote, "to be allowed to do something for these poor people." Many saw themselves as peacetime soldiers, struggling to make emancipation a reality. Indeed, on more than one occasion, hostile white southerners destroyed black schools and threatened and even murdered white teachers. Then there were the everyday challenges: low pay, dilapidated buildings, lack of sufficient books, classes of 100 or more children, and irregular attendance. Meanwhile, the Freedmen's Bureau undertook to train black teachers, and by 1869 most of the 3,000 teachers in freedmen's schools were black.

INDEPENDENT BLACK CHURCHES Before the war, most slaves had attended white churches or services supervised by whites. Once free, African Americans quickly established their own congregations led by black preachers. In the first year of freedom, the Methodist Church South lost fully half of its black members. By 1870 the Negro Baptist Church had increased its membership threefold when compared to the membership in 1850, and the African Methodist Episcopal Church expanded at an even greater rate.

Black churches were so important because they were the only major organizations in the African American community controlled by blacks. Black ministers were respected leaders, and many of the black men elected to political office during Reconstruction were preachers. As it had in slavery, religion offered African Americans a place of refuge in a hostile white world and provided them with hope, comfort, and a means of self-identification.

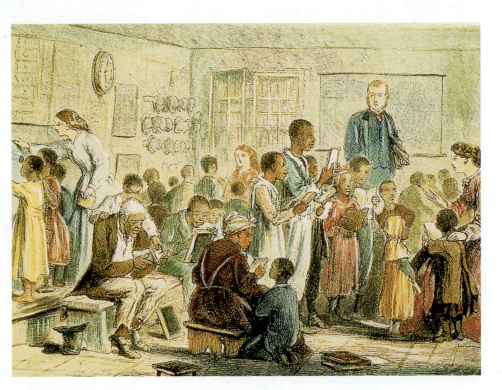

| After living for years in a society where teaching slaves to read and write was usually illegal, freedpeople viewed literacy as a key to securing their newfound freedom. African Americans were not merely "anxious to learn," a school official in Virginia reported, they were "crazy to learn."

New Working Conditions

As a largely propertyless class, blacks in the postwar South had no choice but to work for white landowners. Except for paying wages, whites wanted to retain the old system of labor, including close supervision, gang labor, and physical punishment. Determined to remove all emblems of servitude, African Americans refused to work under these conditions, and they demanded time off to devote to their own interests. Convinced that working at one's own pace was part of freedom, they simply would not work as long or as hard as they had in slavery. Because of shorter hours and the withdrawal of children and women from the fields, work output declined by an estimated 35 percent in freedom. Blacks also refused to live in the old slave quarters located near the master's house. Instead, they erected cabins on distant parts of the plantation. Wages at first were $5 or $6 a month plus provisions and a cabin; by 1867, they had risen to an average of $10 a month.

SHARECROPPING These changes eventually led to the rise of sharecropping. Under this arrangement, African American families farmed discrete plots of land and then at the end of the year split the crop with the white landowner. Sharecropping had higher status and offered greater personal freedom than being a wage laborer. "I am not working for wages," one black farmer declared in defending his right to leave the plantation at will, "but am part owner of the crop and as [such,] I have all the rights that you or any other man has." Although black per-capita agricultural income increased 40 percent in freedom, sharecropping was a harshly exploitative system in which black families often sank into perpetual debt.

The Freedmen's Bureau

The task of supervising the transition from slavery to freedom on southern plantations fell to the Freedmen's Bureau, a unique experiment in social policy supported by the federal government. Assigned the task of protecting freedpeople's economic rights, approximately 550 local agents supervised and regulated working conditions in southern agriculture after the war. The racial attitudes of Bureau agents varied widely, as did their commitment and competence. Then, too, they had to depend on the army to enforce their decisions.

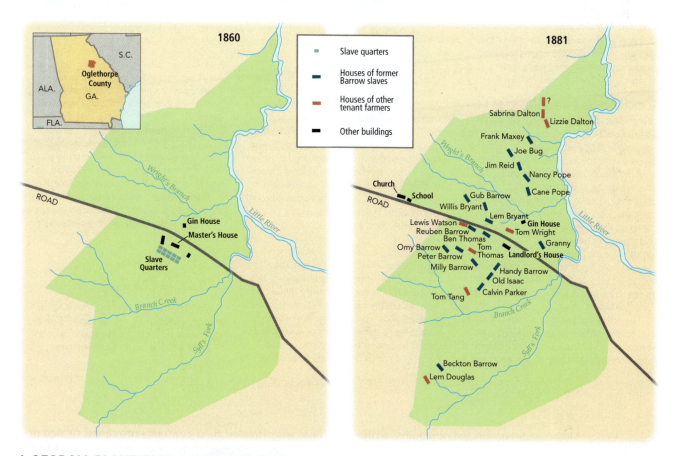

A GEORGIA PLANTATION AFTER THE WAR

After emancipation, sharecropping became the dominant form of agricultural labor in the South. Black families no longer lived in the old slave quarters but dispersed to separate plots of land that they farmed themselves. At the end of the year, each sharecropper turned over part of the crop to the white landowner. **How does the discussion of sharecroppers' cabins in Daily Lives (page 452) explain the difference of household locations on these two maps?**

THE BLACK SHARECROPPER'S CABIN

On the plantations of the Old South slaves had lived in cabins along a central path in the shadow of the white master's "big house." These quarters were the center of their community, where marriages and other festivals were celebrated and family life went on. But with the coming of emancipation, freedpeople looked to leave the old quarters, which stood as a symbol of bondage and of close white supervision. African Americans either built new housing or dismantled their old cabins and hauled them to the plots of land they rented as tenants or sharecroppers. Moving enabled them to live on the land they farmed, just as white farmers and tenants did.

Like slave cabins, most sharecroppers' dwellings were one story high, about 16 feet square, and usually built of logs chinked with mud. The few windows had shutters to protect against the weather; glass was rare. Though the inside walls normally lacked plaster or sheeting, they were given a coat of whitewash annually to brighten the dark interior.

The main room served as kitchen and dining room, parlor, bathing area, and the parents' bedroom. To one side might be a homemade drop-leaf table (essential because of cramped space), which served as a kitchen work counter and a dining table. The other side of the room had a few plain beds, their slats or rope bottoms supporting corn shuck or straw mattresses. The social center of the room was the fireplace, the only source of heat and the main source of light after dark. Pots and pans were hung on the wall near the fireplace, and the mother and daughters did the cooking stooped over an open fire. In the summer, cooking was done outdoors.

The cabin's chimney was made of small logs notched together and covered with several layers of clay to protect it from the heat. Sometimes its height was extended by empty flour barrels. A taller chimney drew better, which kept smoke from blowing back down into the house and kept sparks away from the roof. After the evening meal the family gathered around the fireplace, the children to play with homemade dolls and toys, the mother to sew, and the father perhaps to play the fiddle. At bedtime a trapdoor in the ceiling offered access up a ladder to the loft beneath the gabled roof, where older children slept, usually on pallets on the floor, as had been the case in slavery.

Gradually, as black sharecroppers scraped together some savings, they improved their homes. By the end of the century, frame dwellings were more common, and many older log cabins had been covered with wood siding. The newer homes were generally larger, with wood floors, and often had attached rooms such as a porch or kitchen. In addition, windows had glass panes, roofs were covered with shingles instead of planking, and stone and brick chimneys were less unusual.

Without question, the cabins of black sharecroppers provided more space than the slave quarters had, and certainly more freedom and privacy. Still, they lacked many of the comforts that most white Americans took for granted. Such housing reflected the continuing status of black sharecroppers as poverty-stricken laborers in a caste system based on race.

Chimneys on sharecroppers' cabins were often titled deliberately so that they could be pushed away from the house quickly if they caught fire.

Thinking Critically

How did housing serve to demonstrate independence for freedpeople? What other aspects of life in Reconstruction served to demonstrate independence?

BUREAU'S MIXED RECORD Most agents encouraged or required written contracts between white planters and black laborers, specifying not only wages but also the conditions of employment. Although agents sometimes intervened to protect freedpeople from unfair treatment, they also provided important help to planters. They insisted that black laborers not desert at harvest time; they arrested those who violated their contracts or refused to sign new ones at the beginning of the year; and they preached the gospel of work and the need to be orderly and respectful. Given such attitudes, freedpeople increasingly complained that Bureau agents were mere tools of the planter class. "They are, in fact, the planters' guards, and nothing else," claimed the *New Orleans Tribune*, a black newspaper.

END OF THE BUREAU

The primary means of enforcing working conditions were the Freedmen's Courts, which Congress created in 1866 to avoid the discrimination African Americans received in state courts. These new courts functioned as military tribunals, and often the agent was the entire court. The sympathy black laborers received varied from state to state.

But in 1869, with the Bureau's work scarcely under way, Congress decided to shut it down, and by 1872 it had gone out of business. Despite its mixed record, it was the most effective agency in protecting blacks' civil and political rights. Its disbanding signaled the beginning of the northern retreat from Reconstruction.

Planters and a New Way of Life

PLANTERS' NEW VALUES

Planters and other white southerners faced emancipation with dread. "All the traditions and habits of both races had been suddenly overthrown," a Tennessee planter recalled, "and neither knew just what to do, or how to accommodate themselves to the new situation."

The old ideal of a paternalistic planter, which required a facade of black subservience and affection, gave way to an emphasis on strictly economic relationships. Mary Jones, a Georgia slaveholder before the war who did more for her workers than the law required, lost all patience when two workers accused her of trickery and hauled her before a Freedmen's Bureau agent, with whom she won her case. Upon returning home, she announced to the assembled freedpeople that "I have considered them friends and treated them as such but now they were only laborers under contract, and only the law would rule between us." Only with time did planters develop new norms and standards to judge black behavior. What in 1865 had seemed insolence was viewed by the 1870s as the normal attitude of freedom.

Slavery had been a complex institution that welded black and white southerners together in intimate relationships. After the war, however, planters increasingly embraced the ideology of segregation. Because emancipation significantly reduced the social distance between the races, white southerners sought psychological separation and kept dealings with African Americans to a minimum. By the time Reconstruction ended, white planters had developed a new way of life based on the institutions of sharecropping and segregation and undergirded by a militant white supremacy.

Although most planters kept their land, they did not regain the economic prosperity of the prewar years. Rice plantations, unsuitable to tenant farming, largely disappeared after the war. In addition, southern cotton growers faced increased

Lucy Stone, a major figure in the women's rights movement

competition from new areas such as India, Egypt, and Brazil. Cotton prices began a long decline, and by 1880 the value of southern farms had slid 33 percent below the level of 1860.

> ✓ **REVIEW**
>
> Why were the church and the school central to African American hopes after the Civil War? To what degree did working conditions for African Americans change?

THE ABANDONMENT OF RECONSTRUCTION

ON CHRISTMAS DAY 1875, A white acquaintance approached Charles Caldwell on the streets of Clinton, Mississippi, and invited him into Chilton's store to have a drink to celebrate the holiday. A former slave, Caldwell was a state senator and the leader of the Republican Party in Hinds County, Mississippi. But the black leader's fearlessness made him a marked man. Only two months earlier, he had been forced to flee the county to escape a white mob angry about a Republican barbecue he and his fellow Republicans had organized. For four days the mob hunted down and killed nearly 40 Republican leaders for presuming to hold a political meeting. Despite that hostility, Caldwell had returned to vote in the November state election. Even more boldly, he had led a black militia company through the streets to help quell the disturbances. Now, as Caldwell and his "friend" raised their glasses in a holiday toast, a gunshot exploded through the window. Caldwell collapsed, mortally wounded from a bullet to the back of his head. He was taken outside, where his assassins riddled his body with bullets.

Charles Caldwell shared the fate of more than a few southern black Republicans. Southern whites used violence, terror, and political assassination to challenge the federal government's commitment to Reconstruction. If northerners had boldly countered such terrorism, Reconstruction might have ended differently. But in the years following President Johnson's impeachment trial in 1868, the influence of Radical Republicans steadily waned. The Republican Party was being drained of the crusading idealism that had stamped its early years.

The Election of Grant

Immensely popular after the war, Ulysses S. Grant was the natural choice of Republicans to run for president in 1868. Although Grant was elected, Republicans were shocked that despite his great military stature, his popular margin was only 300,000 votes. An estimated 450,000 black Republican votes had been cast in the South, which meant

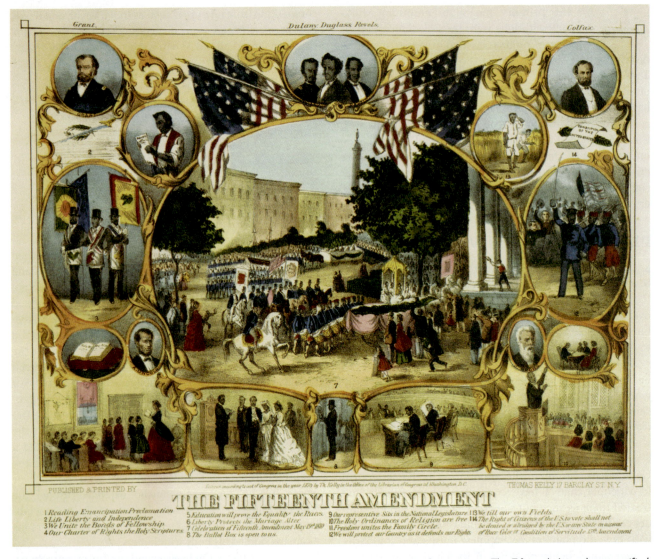

PUBLISHED & PRINTED BY   Entered according to act of Congress in the year 1870 by Th. Kelly in the Office of the Librarian of Congress at Washington. D.C.   THOMAS KELLY 17 BARCLAY ST. N.Y.

THE FIFTEENTH AMENDMENT

1 Reading Emancipation Proclamation
2 Life Liberty and Independence
3 We Unite the Bonds of Fellowship
4 Our Charter of Rights the Holy Scriptures

5 Education will prove the Equality the Races
6 Liberty Protects the Mariage Alter
7 Celebration of Fifteenth Amendment May 19th 1870
8 The Ballot Box is open to us.

9 Our representive Sits in the National Legislature
10 The Holy Ordinances of Religion are free
11 Freedom unites the Family Circle
12 We will protect our Country as it defends our Rights.

13 We till our own Fields.
14 The Right of Citizens of the U.S. to vote shall not be denied or abridged by the U.S. or any State on account of Race Color or Condition of Servitude. 15th Amendment

| From the beginning of Reconstruction, African Americans demanded the right to vote as free citizens. The Fifteenth Amendment, ratified in 1870, secured that right for black males. In New York, black citizens paraded in support of Ulysses S. Grant for president. Parades played a central role in campaigning: this parade exhibits the usual banners, flags, costumes, and a band. Blacks in both the North and the South voted solidly for the Republican Party as the party of Lincoln and emancipation, although white violence in the South increasingly reduced black turnout.

that a majority of whites casting ballots had voted Democratic. The 1868 election helped convince Republican leaders that an amendment securing black suffrage throughout the nation was necessary.

FIFTEENTH AMENDMENT   In February 1869 Congress sent the Fifteenth Amendment to the states for ratification. It forbade any state to deny the right to vote on grounds of race, color, or previous condition of servitude. Some Radicals had hoped to forbid literacy or property requirements to protect blacks further. Others wanted a simple declaration that all adult male citizens had the right to vote. But the moderates in the party were aware that many northerners were increasingly worried about the number of immigrants who were again entering the country and wanted to be able to restrict their voting. As a result, the final amendment left loopholes that eventually allowed

southern states to **disenfranchise** African Americans. The amendment was ratified in March 1870, aided by the votes of the four southern states that had not completed the process of Reconstruction and thus were also required to endorse this amendment before being readmitted to Congress.

WOMEN'S SUFFRAGE REJECTED   Proponents of women's suffrage were gravely disappointed when Congress refused to prohibit voting discrimination on the basis of sex as well as race. The Women's Loyal League, led by Elizabeth Cady Stanton and Susan B. Anthony, had pressed for first the Fourteenth and then the Fifteenth Amendment to recognize women's public role. But even most Radicals, contending that black rights had to be ensured first, were unwilling to back women's suffrage. The Fifteenth Amendment ruptured the feminist movement. Although disappointed that women were not included in its provisions, Lucy Stone and the American Woman Suffrage Association urged ratification. Stanton and Anthony, however, broke with their former allies among the Radicals, denounced the amendment, and organized the National Woman Suffrage Association to work for passage of a new amendment giving women the ballot. The division hampered the women's rights movement for decades to come.

The Grant Administration

Ulysses Grant was ill at ease with the political process. His simple, quiet manner, while superb for commanding armies, did not serve him as well in public life, and his well-known resolution withered when he was uncertain of his goal. Also, he lacked the moral commitment to make Reconstruction succeed.

CORRUPTION UNDER GRANT   A series of scandals wracked Grant's presidency. Although Grant did not profit personally, he remained loyal to his friends and displayed little zeal to root out wrongdoing. His relatives were implicated in a scheme to corner the gold market, and his private secretary escaped conviction for stealing federal whiskey revenues only because Grant interceded on his behalf. His secretary of war resigned to avoid impeachment.

Nor was Congress immune from the lowered tone of public life. In such a climate ruthless state machines, led by men who favored the status quo, came to dominate the party. Office and power became ends in themselves, and party leaders worked in close cooperation with northern industrial interests. The few Radicals still active in public life increasingly repudiated Grant and the Republican governments in the South. Congress in 1872 passed an amnesty act, removing the restrictions of the Fourteenth Amendment on officeholding except for about 200 to 300 ex-Confederate leaders.

As corruption in both the North and the South worsened, reformers became more interested in cleaning up government than in protecting blacks' rights. These liberal Republicans opposed the continued presence of the army in the South, denounced the corruption of southern governments as well as the national government, and advocated free trade and civil service reform. In 1872 they broke with the Republican Party and nominated for president Horace Greeley, the editor of the *New York Tribune*. A onetime Radical, Greeley had become disillusioned with Reconstruction and urged a restoration of home rule in the South as well as adoption of civil service reform. Democrats decided to back the Liberal Republican ticket. The Republicans renominated Grant, who, despite the defection of a number of prominent Radicals, won an easy victory with 56 percent of the popular vote.

Growing Northern Disillusionment

CIVIL RIGHTS ACT OF 1875   During Grant's second term, Congress passed the Civil Rights Act of 1875, the last major piece of Reconstruction legislation. This law prohibited racial discrimination in all public

Grant swings from a trapeze while supporting a number of associates accused of corruption. Among those holding on are Secretary of the Navy George M. Robeson (top center), who was accused of accepting bribes for awarding navy contracts; Secretary of War William W. Belknap (top right), who was forced to resign for selling Indian post traderships; and the president's private secretary, Orville Babcock (bottom right), who was implicated in the Whiskey Ring scandal. Although not personally involved in the scandals during his administration, Grant was reluctant to dismiss supporters accused of wrongdoing from office.

accommodations, transportation, places of amusement, and juries. At the same time, Congress rejected a ban on segregation in public schools, which was almost universally practiced in the North as well as the South. Although some railroads, streetcars, and public accommodations in both sections were desegregated after the bill passed, the federal government made little attempt to enforce the law, and it was ignored throughout most of the South. In 1883 the Supreme Court struck down its provisions except the one relating to juries.

Despite passage of the Civil Rights Act, many northerners were growing disillusioned with Reconstruction. They were repelled by the corruption of the southern governments, they were tired of the violence and disorder in the

South, and they had little faith in black Americans. "We have tried this long enough," remarked one influential northern Republican of Reconstruction. "Now let the South alone."

DEPRESSION AND DEMOCRATIC RESURGENCE As the agony of the war became more distant, the Panic of 1873 diverted public attention from Reconstruction to economic issues. In the severe depression that followed over the next four years, some 3 million people found themselves out of work. Congress became caught up in the question of whether printing greenbacks would help the economy prosper. Battered by the panic and the corruption issue, the Republicans lost a shocking 77 seats in Congress in the 1874 elections and, along with them, control of the House of Representatives for the first time since 1861. "The truth is our people are tired out with the worn out cry of 'Southern outrages'!!" one Republican concluded. "Hard times and heavy taxes make them wish the 'ever lasting nigger' were in hell or Africa." Republicans spoke more and more about cutting loose the unpopular southern governments.

The Triumph of White Supremacy

As northern commitment to Reconstruction waned, southern Democrats set out to overthrow the remaining Radical governments. White Republicans already in the South felt heavy pressure to desert their party. In Mississippi one party member justified his decision to leave on the grounds that otherwise he would have "to live a life of social oblivion" and his children would have no future.

RACISM To poor white southerners who lacked social standing, the Democratic appeal to racial solidarity offered great comfort. As one explained, "I may be poor and my manners may be crude, but . . . because I am a white man, I have a right to be treated with respect by Negroes. . . . That I am poor is not as important as that I am a white man; and no Negro is ever going to forget that he is not a white man." The large landowners and other wealthy groups that led southern Democrats objected less to black southerners voting. These well-to-do leaders did not face social and economic competition from African Americans, and in any case, they were confident that if outside influences were removed, they could control the black vote.

Democrats also resorted to economic pressure to undermine Republican power. In heavily black counties, white observers at the polls took down the names of black

| This campaign badge from 1868 made the sentiments of white Democrats clear.

residents who cast Republican ballots and published them in local newspapers. Planters were urged to discharge black tenants who persisted in voting Republican. But terror and violence provided the most effective means to overthrow the Radical regimes. A number of paramilitary organizations broke up Republican meetings, terrorized white and black Republicans, assassinated Republican leaders, and prevented black citizens from voting. The most famous was the Ku Klux Klan, founded in 1866 in Tennessee. It and similar groups functioned as unofficial arms of the Democratic Party.

CONTESTING THE NIGHT In the war for supremacy, contesting control of the night was of paramount concern to both southern whites and blacks. Before emancipation, masters attempted to control the nighttime hours, with a system of passes and patrols that chased slaves who went hunting or tried to sneak a visit to a family member at a neighboring plantation. For slaves the night provided precious hours not devoted to work: time to read, to meet for worship, school, or dancing. During Reconstruction, African Americans actively took back the night for a host of activities, including a custom that white Americans had enjoyed since the beginning of the republic: torchlight political parades. In Holly Springs, Mississippi, hundreds, even thousands of black citizens filled the streets during campaigns, holding aloft torches and "transparencies"—pictures painted on thin cloth, 10 to 12 feet long—the entire scene lit in an eerie, flickering glow.

Part of the Klan's mission was to recoup this contested ground and to limit the ability of African Americans to use the night as they pleased. Sometimes the Klan's threat of violence was indirect: one or two riders galloping through black neighborhoods rattling fences with lances. Other times several "dens" of the KKK might gather to ride from plantation to plantation over the course of a night, stopping in every black home they could reach and demanding all firearms. Other times the violence was direct: beatings and executions—again, heightened by the dark of night.

Congress finally moved to break the power of the Klan with the Force Act of 1870 and the Ku Klux Klan Act of 1871. These laws made it a felony to interfere with the right to vote; they also authorized use of the army and suspension of the writ of habeas corpus. The Grant administration eventually suspended the writ of habeas corpus in nine South Carolina counties and arrested hundreds of suspected Klan members throughout the South. Although these actions weakened the Klan, terrorist organizations continued to operate underground.

DRESSED TO KILL

Klan members drawn for Harper's Weekly magazine, 1868

Advertisement for a minstrel show, 1864

Why wear a hooded mask? Does the advertisement suggest more than one reason?

The costumes of Ku Klux Klan night riders—pointed hoods and white sheets—have become a staple of history books. But why use such outlandish disguises? To hide the identity of members, according to some accounts, or to terrorize freedpeople into thinking they were being menaced by Confederate ghosts. Historian Elaine F. Parsons has suggested that KKK performances took their cues from American popular culture: the costumes of Mardi Gras and similar carnivals, as well as minstrel shows. In behaving like carnival revelers, KKK members may have hoped to lull northern authorities into viewing the night rides as humorous pranks, not a threat to Radical rule. For southern white Democrats the theatrical night rides helped overturn the social order of Reconstruction, just as carousers at carnivals disrupted the night. The ritual garb provided seemingly innocent cover for what was truly a campaign of terror and intimidation that often turned deadly.

Thinking Critically

In what ways does the advertisement speak of experiences both frightening and humorous? In terms of popular culture, do modern horror films sometimes combine both terror and humor? Assess how this dynamic of horror and jest might have worked in terms of the different groups perceiving the Klan's activities: white northerners, white southerners, and African Americans. If this theory of why the Klan dressed as they did is true, does it make them more effective or less so as a terrorist organization?

MISSISSIPPI PLAN

Then in 1875 Democrats inaugurated what became known as the Mississippi Plan, the decision to use as much violence as necessary to carry the state election. Several local papers trumpeted, "Carry the election peaceably if we can, forcibly if we must." When Republican governor Adelbert Ames requested federal troops to stop the violence, Grant's advisers warned that sending troops to Mississippi would cost the party the Ohio election. In the end the administration told Ames to depend on his own forces. Bolstered by terrorism, the Democrats swept the election in Mississippi. Violence and intimidation prevented as many as 60,000 black and white Republicans from voting, converting the normal Republican majority into a Democratic majority of 30,000. Mississippi had been "redeemed."

The Disputed Election of 1876

With Republicans on the defensive across the nation, the 1876 presidential election was crucial to the final overthrow of Reconstruction. The Republicans nominated Ohio governor Rutherford B. Hayes to oppose Samuel Tilden, Governor of New York. Once again, violence prevented many Republican votes, this time an estimated quarter of a million, from being cast in the South. Tilden had a clear majority of 250,000 in the popular vote, but the outcome in the Electoral College was in doubt because both parties claimed South Carolina, Florida, and Louisiana, the only reconstructed states still in Republican hands. Hayes needed all three states to be elected, for even without them, Tilden had amassed 184 electoral votes, one short of a majority. Republican canvassing boards in power disqualified enough Democratic votes to give each state to Hayes.

To arbitrate the disputed returns, Congress established a 15-member electoral commission: 5 members each from the Senate, the House, and the Supreme Court. By a straight party vote of 8 to 7, the commission awarded the disputed electoral votes—and the presidency—to Hayes.

COMPROMISE OF **1877**

When angry Democrats threatened a filibuster to prevent the electoral votes from being counted, key Republicans met with southern Democrats on February 26 at the Wormley Hotel in Washington. There they reached an informal understanding, later known as the Compromise of 1877. Hayes's supporters agreed to withdraw federal troops from the South and not oppose the new Democratic state governments. For their part, southern Democrats dropped their opposition to Hayes's election and pledged to respect the rights of African Americans.

REDEEMERS TAKE CONTROL

Without federal support, the Republican governments in South Carolina and Louisiana promptly collapsed, and Democrats took control of the remaining states of the Confederacy. By 1877, the entire South was in the hands of the **Redeemers,** as they called themselves. Reconstruction and Republican rule had come to an end.

The Failure of Reconstruction

Reconstruction failed for a multitude of reasons. The reforming impulse that had created the Republican Party in the 1850s had been battered and worn down by the war. The new materialism of industrial America inspired in many Americans a jaded cynicism about the corruption of the age and a desire to forget uncomfortable issues. In the South, African American voters and leaders inevitably lacked a certain amount of education and experience; elsewhere, Republicans were divided over policies and options.

Yet beyond these obstacles, the sad fact remains that the ideals of Reconstruction were most clearly defeated by the deep-seated racism that permeated American life. Racism was why the white South so unrelentingly resisted Reconstruction. Racism was why most white northerners had little interest in black rights except as a means to preserve the Union or to safeguard the Republic. Racism was why northerners were willing to write off Reconstruction and with it the welfare of African Americans. While Congress might pass a constitutional amendment abolishing slavery, it could not overturn at a stroke the social habits of two centuries.

Certainly the political equations of power, in the long term, had been changed. The North had fought fiercely during the war to preserve the Union. In doing so, it had secured the power to dominate the economic and political destiny of the nation. With the overthrow of Reconstruction, the white South had won back some of the power it had lost in 1865. But even with white supremacy triumphant, African Americans did not return to the social position they had occupied before the war. They were no longer slaves, and black southerners who walked dusty roads in search of family members, sent their children to school, or worshiped in churches they controlled knew what a momentous change emancipation was. Even under the exploitative sharecropping system, black income rose significantly in freedom. Then, too, the Fourteenth

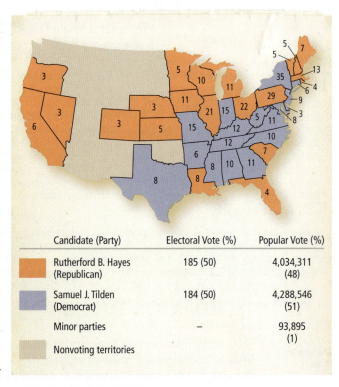

Candidate (Party)	Electoral Vote (%)	Popular Vote (%)
■ Rutherford B. Hayes (Republican)	185 (50)	4,034,311 (48)
■ Samuel J. Tilden (Democrat)	184 (50)	4,288,546 (51)
Minor parties	–	93,895 (1)
Nonvoting territories		

ELECTION OF 1876

Amendment principles of "equal protection" and "due process of law" had been written into the Constitution. These guarantees would be available for later generations to use in championing once again the Radicals' goal of racial equality.

END OF THE DAVIS BEND EXPERIMENT   But this was a struggle left to future reformers. For the time being, the clear trend was away from change or hope—especially for former slaves like Benjamin Montgomery and his sons, the owners of the old Davis plantations in Mississippi. In the 1870s bad crops, lower cotton prices, and falling land values undermined the Montgomerys' financial position, and in 1875 Jefferson Davis sued to have the sale of Brierfield invalidated. A lower court ruled against him, since he had never received legal title to the plantation. Davis appealed to the state supreme court, which, following the overthrow of Mississippi's Radical government, had a white conservative majority. In a politically motivated decision, the court awarded Brierfield to Davis in 1878, and the Montgomerys lost Hurricane as well. Reconstruction was over and done, along with the hopes that came with it.

 REVIEW

What factors in the North and the South led the federal government to abandon Reconstruction in the South?

CONCLUSION

THE WORLD AT LARGE

The waning days of Reconstruction were filled with such ironies: of governments "redeemed" by violence and Supreme Court decisions using Fourteenth Amendment rights to protect giant corporations rather than individual African Americans. Increasingly, the industrial North focused on the economic task of integrating the South and the West into the Union. Northern factories sought southern and western raw materials (cotton, timber, cattle, and minerals) to produce goods to sell in national and international markets.

This trend was global in scope. During the coming decades European nations also scrambled to acquire natural resources and markets. In the onrushing age of imperialism, Western nations would seek to dominate newly acquired colonies in Africa and Asia. There would be gold rushes in South Africa as well as in the United States, vast cattle ranches in Argentina and Canada as well as across the American Great Plains. Farmers would open up lands in New Zealand and Australia as well as in Oklahoma and Wyoming. And just as racism replaced slavery as the central justification for white supremacy in the South, it promoted the campaigns against Indians and Hispanics in the West and in a belief in "inferior races" to be swept aside by imperialists all across the world. The ideal of a truly diverse and democratic society remained largely unsought and unfulfilled. ∞∞∞

CHAPTER SUMMARY

PRESIDENTS ABRAHAM LINCOLN AND ANDREW Johnson and the Republican-dominated Congress each developed a program of Reconstruction to restore the Confederate states to the Union.

■ Lincoln's 10 percent plan required that 10 percent of qualified voters from 1860 swear an oath of loyalty to begin organizing state government.

■ Following Lincoln's assassination, Andrew Johnson changed Lincoln's terms and lessened Reconstruction's requirements.

■ The more-radical Congress repudiated Johnson's state governments and enacted its own program of Reconstruction, which included the principle of black suffrage.

• Congress passed the Fourteenth and Fifteenth Amendments and also extended the life of the Freedmen's Bureau, a unique experiment in social welfare.

• Congress rejected land reform, however, which would have provided the freedpeople with a greater economic stake.

• The effort to remove Johnson from office through impeachment failed.

■ The Radical governments in the South, led by black and white southerners and transplanted northerners, compiled a mixed record on matters such as racial equality, education, economic issues, and corruption.

■ Reconstruction was a time of both joy and frustration for former slaves.

• Former slaves took steps to reunite their families and establish black-controlled churches.

• They evidenced a widespread desire for land and education.

- Black resistance to the old system of labor led to the adoption of sharecropping.
- The Freedmen's Bureau fostered these new working arrangements and also the beginnings of black education in the South.

■ Northern public opinion became disillusioned with Reconstruction during the presidency of Ulysses S. Grant.

■ Southern whites used violence, economic coercion, and racism to overthrow the Republican state governments.

■ In 1877 Republican leaders agreed to end Reconstruction in exchange for Rutherford B. Hayes's election as president.

■ Racism played a key role in the eventual failure of Reconstruction.

ADDITIONAL READING

HISTORIANS' VIEWS OF RECONSTRUCTION HAVE dramatically changed over the past half century. Modern studies offer a more sympathetic assessment of Reconstruction and the experience of African Americans. Indicative of this trend is Eric Foner, *Reconstruction* (1988), and his briefer treatment (with photographic essays by Joshua Brown) *Forever Free: The Story of Emancipation and Reconstruction* (2005). Michael Les Benedict treats the clash between Andrew Johnson and Congress in *The Impeachment and Trial of Andrew Johnson* (1973). Political affairs in the South during Reconstruction are examined in Dan T. Carter, *When the War Was Over* (1985), and Thomas Holt, *Black over White* (1977), an imaginative study of black political leadership in South Carolina. Hans Trefousse, *Thaddeus Stevens: Nineteenth-Century Egalitarian* (1997), provides a sympathetic reassessment of the influential Radical Republican. Mark W. Summers, *A Dangerous Stir* (2009), deftly examines the ways in which fear and paranoia shaped Reconstruction.

Leon Litwack's Pulitzer Prize–winning *Been in the Storm So Long* (1979) sensitively analyzes the transition of enslaved African Americans to freedom. Heather Andrea Williams, *Self-Taught: African American Education in Slavery and Freedom* (2005), illustrates the black drive for literacy and education. The dialectic of black-white relations is charted from the antebellum years through Reconstruction and beyond in Steven Hahn, *A Nation under Our Feet: Black Political Struggles in the Rural South from Slavery to the Great Migration* (2003). Excellent studies of changing labor relations in southern agriculture include Amy Dru Stanley's *From Bondage to Contract* (1998), Julie Saville's *The Work of Reconstruction* (1995), and John C. Rodrigue's *Reconstruction in the Cane Fields* (2001). For contrasting views of the Freedman's Bureau, see George R. Bentley, *A History of the Freedman's Bureau* (1955)—favorable—and Donald Nieman, *To Set the Law in Motion* (1979)—critical. Heather Cox Richardson explores the postwar context in the North in *The Death of Reconstruction* (2004) and considers Reconstruction in the West in *West from Appomattox* (2008).

For a fuller list of readings, see the Bibliography at www.mhhe.com/eh8e.

SIGNIFICANT EVENTS

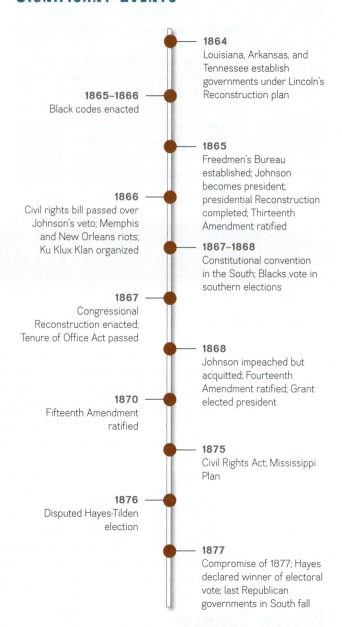

1864
Louisiana, Arkansas, and Tennessee establish governments under Lincoln's Reconstruction plan

1865–1866
Black codes enacted

1865
Freedmen's Bureau established; Johnson becomes president; presidential Reconstruction completed; Thirteenth Amendment ratified

1866
Civil rights bill passed over Johnson's veto; Memphis and New Orleans riots; Ku Klux Klan organized

1867–1868
Constitutional convention in the South; Blacks vote in southern elections

1867
Congressional Reconstruction enacted; Tenure of Office Act passed

1868
Johnson impeached but acquitted; Fourteenth Amendment ratified; Grant elected president

1870
Fifteenth Amendment ratified

1875
Civil Rights Act; Mississippi Plan

1876
Disputed Hayes-Tilden election

1877
Compromise of 1877; Hayes declared winner of electoral vote; last Republican governments in South fall

Radical Republicans	Advocated rights for freedpeople; believed Congress should set terms of Reconstruction
Moderate Republicans	Looked to bar Confederates from regaining power and to give slaves federal protection, but did not favor racial equality
African American officials	15–20 percent of state officeholders, 6 percent of members of Congress; generally more conservative than rural southern blacks
Scalawags	White southern Republicans; mostly yeoman farmers from upland counties; looked to restore prosperity, build railroads and schools
Carpetbaggers	White northerners in the South; made up a small percentage of Republican voters but held disproportionate number of political offices
Teachers, Freedmen's Bureau Schools	At first, northern middle-class white women sent by missionary societies; by 1869 black teachers made up a majority
Ministers, African American churches	Community leaders; black churches spread widely in the South after the war
White planters	Most did not regain prewar prosperity; developed a new way of life based on sharecropping and segregation
Redeemers	White Democrats who ousted Reconstruction governments; KKK and other paramilitary organizations used force to achieve their goals

RELIGIOUS SERVICES IN THE NORTH WING OF

African American migrants, known as Exodusters, hold a religious service in 1879 at Floral Hall on the Topeka, Kansas, fairgrounds. The Exodusters' journey was uncertain, as they often traveled with few resources; maintaining their faith gave them strength in their search for a better place to live in the West.

CHAPTER 18

The New South and the Trans-Mississippi West

RAL HALL.

1870–1914

What's to Come

∞∞∞ AN AMERICAN STORY ∞∞∞

"COME WEST"

The news spread across the South during the late 1870s. Perhaps a man came around with a handbill telling of cheap land, or a letter might arrive from friends or relatives and be read aloud at church. The news spread in different ways, but in the end, it always spelled Kansas.

Few black farmers had been that far west themselves. More than a few knew that the abolitionist Old John Brown had made his home in Kansas before coming east to raid Harpers Ferry and set off a chain of events that led to the

Civil War. After the war, it seemed that black folks might live more freely in Kansas. "You can buy land at from a dollar and a half to two dollars an acre," wrote one black settler to a friend in Louisiana. There was another advantage, he added: "They do not kill Negroes here for voting."

In 1878 such prospects excited hundreds of black families already stretched to their limits by hardship, even bloodshed. With Rutherford Hayes president, Reconstruction was at an end. Conservative whites had "redeemed" southern state governments from black and white Republicans. The future seemed uncertain.

"COME WEST," concluded *The Colored Citizen,* a newspaper in Topeka. "COME TO KANSAS."

St. Louis learned of these rumblings in the first raw days of March 1879, as steamers from downriver began unloading freedpeople in large numbers. Some came with belongings and money; others, with only the clothes on their backs. By the end of 1879 more than 20,000 had arrived. With the weather still cold, they sought shelter beneath tarpaulins along the river levee, built fires, and got out frying pans to cook meals.

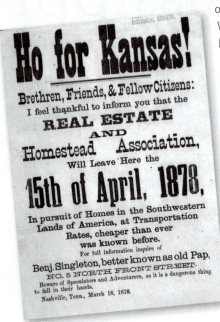

When the crowds overwhelmed the wharves and temporary shelters, the city's black churches banded together to house the "refugees," feed them and help them on to Kansas. Rumors that rail passage would not be free failed to shake their hopes. "We's like de chilun ob Israel when dey was led from out o' bondage by Moses," one explained, referring to the Bible's tale of the exodus of Jews from Egypt. So the "Exodusters," as they became known, pressed westward. In the end, black emigrants settled in growing towns such as Topeka and Kansas City. Men worked as hired hands; women took in laundry. With luck, couples made $350 a year, saved a bit for a home, and put down roots.

The host of Exodusters who poured into Kansas was part of a human flood westward. It had many sources—played-out farms of New England and the South, crowded cities, virtually all of Europe. In 1879, as African Americans traveled up the Mississippi to St. Louis, 1,000 white emigrants also arrived in Kansas every week. Special trains brought settlers to the plains, all eager to start anew. During the 1880s the number of Kansans jumped by 50 percent—from a million to a million and a half. Other western states experienced similar booms.

The optimism of boomers black and white could not mask the strains in the South and the Trans-Mississippi West. Largely agricultural, they struggled to find their place in the new age of industry. In the South, despite a strong push to industrialize, the continuing dominance of white supremacy helped to undercut economic growth, encouraging the scourge of sharecropping and farm tenancy and spawning a system of racial violence and caste to replace slavery. For their part, citizens of the booming West began to realize at least some of the dreams of antebellum reformers: free homesteads in Kansas and beyond, a railroad that spanned the continent, land-grant colleges to educate its people. Despite those differences, the West also built a society based on racial violence and hierarchy.

Much as the national markets emerging after the War of 1812 drew the lands beyond the Appalachian Mountains into their spheres, the industrial economy emerging after the Civil War incorporated the South and the Trans-Mississippi West in their domains. By the end of the nineteenth century, the South and the West had assumed their places as suppliers of raw materials, providers of foodstuffs, and consumers of finished goods. A nation of "regional nations" was thus knit together in the last third of the nineteenth century. Not all southerners and westerners were happy with the result. As we shall see in Chapter 21, their frustrations mounted as the Northeast enriched itself at their expense and the powers in Washington ignored their plight. ∞∞∞

THE SOUTHERN BURDEN

INEQUITIES BETWEEN THE AGRICULTURAL SOUTH and the industrial North infuriated Henry Grady, the editor of the *Atlanta Constitution.* Grady often told the story of the poor cotton farmer buried in a pine coffin in the piney woods of Georgia. Except the coffin hadn't been made in Georgia but in Cincinnati. The coffin nails had been forged in Pittsburgh, though an iron mine lay nearby. Even the farmer's cotton coat was made in New York and his trousers in Chicago. The "South didn't furnish a thing on earth for that funeral but the corpse and the hole in the ground!" fumed Grady.

The irony of the story was the tragedy of the South. The region had human and natural resources aplenty but few factories to manufacture the goods it needed and none of the profits more of them would surely bring.

THE GOSPEL OF A "NEW SOUTH" In the 1880s Grady campaigned to bring about a frothy "New South" of bustling industry, cities, and commerce. According to his gospel, the business class would displace the old planter class as southerners raced "to out-Yankee the Yankee." Grady and other publicists recognized the South's potential. Extending from Delaware south to Florida and west to Texas, the region took in a third of the nation's total area. It held a third of its arable farmlands, vast tracts of lumber, and rich deposits of coal, iron, oil, and fertilizers.

To overcome the destruction of the Civil War and the loss of slaveholding wealth, apostles of the New South campaigned to catch up with the industrial North. Yet well into the twentieth century, Grady's New South remained the poorest section of the country. Worse still, the South suffered the burden of an unwieldy labor system that was often unskilled, usually underpaid, and always divided by race.

Agriculture in the New South

A COTTON-DOMINATED ECONOMY For all the talk of industry, the economy of the postwar South remained agricultural, tied to cash crops like tobacco, rice, sugar, and especially cotton. By using fertilizers, planters were able to introduce cotton into areas once considered marginal. The number of acres planted with cotton more than doubled between 1870 and 1900. Some southern farmers sought prosperity in crops other than cotton. George Washington Carver, of Alabama's Tuskegee Institute (see page 573), persuaded many poor black farmers to plant peanuts. But most southern soils were too acidic and the spring rains too heavy for other legumes and grains to flourish. Parasites and diseases plagued cattle herds. Work animals like mules were raised more cheaply in other regions. Try as southerners might to diversify, cotton still dominated their economy.

From 1880 to 1900 world demand for cotton grew slowly, and prices fell. As farms in other parts of the country became larger and more efficient and tended by fewer workers per acre, southern farms decreased in size, the result of old plantations splintering and new births mushrooming. Across the country, the number of children born per mother was dropping, but in the South, large families remained common because more children meant more farmhands. Each year, fewer acres of land were available for each person to cultivate. Even though the southern economy kept pace with national growth, **per capita income** fell behind.

Tenancy and Sharecropping

The end of slavery brought hopes of economic independence to newly freed slaves across the South. John Solomon Lewis

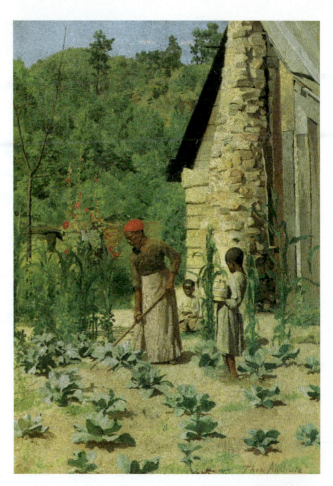

After the Civil War, African Americans marked their freedom by ending field labor for most women and children. The women instead played a vital role in the domestic economy. Home garden plots supplemented the family food supply.

rented land to grow cotton in Tensas Parish, Louisiana, after the Civil War. A depression in the 1870s dashed his dreams. "I was in debt," Lewis explained, "and the man I rented land from said every year I must rent again to pay the other year, and so I rents and rents and each year I gets deeper and deeper in debt."

AGRICULTURAL LADDER The dream of economic independence rested on a theory of landholding called the "agricultural ladder." According to this theory, any poor man willing to work hard and pinch pennies could eventually become a landowner, moving rung by rung up an imaginary ladder, first as a paid hand, then as a sharecropper reimbursed with a portion of the crop, then as a tenant who rented the land he worked, and finally emerging as an independent, landowning farmer.

In practice, harsh realities overwhelmed theory, as John Solomon Lewis and other poor farmers—black and white—learned. The South's best land remained in the hands of large plantation owners. Few freedpeople or poor whites ever had enough money to acquire property. The problem lay in a ruinous system of credit. The harvest, whether produced by croppers or tenants or even small, independent

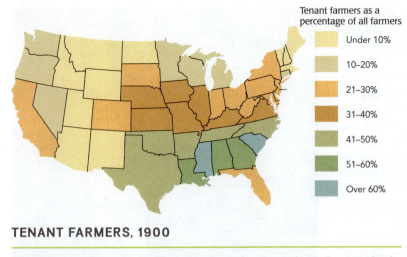

Tenant farmers as a
percentage of all farmers

	Under 10%
	10–20%
	21–30%
	31–40%
	41–50%
	51–60%
	Over 60%

TENANT FARMERS, 1900

Tenant farming dominated southern agriculture after the Civil War. But note that by 1900 it also accounted for much of the farm labor in the Trans-Mississippi West, where low crop prices, high costs, and severe environmental conditions forced independent farmers into tenancy. **Where are the heaviest concentrations of tenants? Why?**

farmers, was rarely enough for the worker to make ends meet, let alone to pay off debts and move up the agricultural ladder. Most farmers borrowed money in the spring just to buy seeds, tools, or necessities such as food and clothing. Usually the only source of supplies and credit was the country store.

When John Solomon Lewis and other tenants entered the store, they saw two prices: one for cash and one for credit. The credit price might be as much as 60 percent higher. Creditors justified the difference on the grounds that high interest rates protected them against unpaid loans. As security for the loan, independent farmers mortgaged their land and soon slipped into tenancy as debts mounted and creditors foreclosed on their farms. The only asset tenants had was the crop they owned or the share they received. So they put up a mortgage, or **lien,** on the crop. The lien gave the shopkeeper first claim on the crop until the debt was paid.

Across the South, sharecropping and crop liens reduced many farmers to virtual slavery by shackling them to perpetual debt. Year after year, they rented or worked the land and borrowed against their future returns until they found themselves so deeply in debt that they could never escape. This economic dependence, known as **debt peonage,** turned the agricultural ladder into an agricultural slide, robbing small farmers of their land and sending them to the bottom rungs of tenancy, sharecropping, and migrant-farm work. By the 1880s three of every four African American farmers in the Black Belt states of Mississippi, Alabama, and Georgia were croppers. Twenty years later a majority of southern white farmers had fallen into sharecropping. Few moved up. The landlord or shopkeeper (often the same person) could insist that tenants grow only cash crops such as cotton rather than things they could eat. Most landlords also required that cotton be ginned, baled,

and marketed through their mills—at rates they controlled.

 **DEBT PEONAGE IN INDIA, EGYPT, AND BRAZIL** The slide of sharecroppers and tenants into debt peonage occurred elsewhere in the cotton-growing world. In India, Egypt, and Brazil agricultural laborers gave up **subsistence farming** to raise cotton as a cash crop during the American Civil War, when the North prevented southern cotton from being exported. New railroad and telegraph lines built in these growing regions helped make the export of cotton more efficient and profitable. But when prices fell, growers borrowed to make ends meet, as in the American South. In India, moneylenders charged interest as high as 24 percent annually on such debts; in Egypt, sometimes 60 percent. In the mid-1870s, the pressures on cotton growers led them to revolt in India and Brazil, attacking moneylenders, destroying land records, and refusing to pay taxes. As we shall see in Chapter 21, in the 1890s, American farmers rose up too.

Southern Industry

The crusade for a New South did bring change. One of the most important adjustments began on May 30, 1886. The wider gauge or track width of southern railroads had presented endless difficulties for moving freight and passengers between North and South. In a single day 8,000 workers narrowed the gauge on 2,000 miles of the Lackawanna & Northern Railroad's southern line. Within three days thousands more workers converted the space between tracks across the South to the smaller standard of the North. For the first time trains moved easily from one region to another. Coupled with a railroad building boom starting in 1879, the South began knitting itself into a national transportation network and an industrialized economy. From 1869 to 1909, industrial production in the South grew faster than the national rate. So did productivity for southern workers.

BOOM IN TEXTILES Among the booming industries of the South, cotton remained king. With cotton fiber and cheap labor close at hand, 400 cotton mills were humming by 1900. They employed almost 100,000 workers. Most new textile workers were poor white southerners escaping competition from black farm laborers or fleeing the hardscrabble life of the mountains. Entire families worked in the mills. Older men had the most trouble adjusting. They lacked the experience, temperament, and dexterity to tend spindles and looms in cramped mills. Only over time, as farm folk adapted to the tedious rhythm of factories, did southerners become competitive with workers from other regions of the United States and western Europe.

This girl had been working in a cotton mill in Whitnel, North Carolina, for about a year, sometimes on the night shift. She made 48 cents a day. When asked how old she was, she hesitated, then said, "I don't remember." But then she added, confidentially, "I'm not old enough to work, but do just the same."

TOBACCO AND CIGARETTES The tobacco industry also thrived in the New South. Before the Civil War, American tastes had run to cigars, snuff, and chewing tobacco. In 1876 James Bonsack, an 18-year-old Virginian, invented a machine to roll cigarettes. That was just the device Washington Duke and his son James needed to boost the fortunes of their growing tobacco business. Cigarettes suited the new urban market in the North, "clean, quick, and potent" according to one observer.

Between 1860 and 1900 the annual rate of tobacco consumption nearly quadrupled. Americans spent more money on tobacco than on clothes or shoes. The sudden interest in smoking offered southerners a rare opportunity to control a national market. But its factories were so hot, the stench of tobacco so strong, and the work so exhausting that native-born white southerners generally refused the jobs. Duke solved the labor problem by hiring Jewish immigrants, experts in making cigars, to train black southerners in the techniques of tobacco work. He promoted cigarettes in a national advertising campaign, using gimmicks, such as collectible picture cards. By the 1890s his American Tobacco Company led the industry.

Timber and Steel

The realities of southern economic life were more accurately reflected in lumber and steel than in tobacco and textiles. After the Civil War, the South possessed more than 60 percent of the nation's timber resources. With growing demand from towns and cities across the nation, lumber and turpentine became the South's chief industries and employers.

If anything, however, aggressive lumbering left the South poorer. Corruption of state officials and a relaxed federal

Tobacco and sex became entwined in the nineteenth century, as this label for B. H. Watson's "Gentlemen's Delight" tobacco reveals. A bare-shouldered woman, her dark hair tumbling behind her, beckons buyers to purchase the product that promises nothing but the delight on the label's title.

timber policy allowed northerners and foreigners to acquire huge forest tracts at artificially low prices. The timber was then sold as raw lumber rather than as more profitable finished products such as cedar shingles or the coffins Henry Grady liked to mention. Overcutting added little to local economies. Logging camps were isolated and temporary. Visitors described the lumberjacks as "single, homeless, and possessionless." Once loggers leveled the forests around their camps, they moved on to other sites. Most sawmills operated for only a few years before the owners followed the loggers to a new area.

 ENVIRONMENTAL COSTS   The environmental costs were high. In the South, as elsewhere, overcutting and other logging practices stripped hillsides bare. As spring rains eroded soil and unleashed floods, forests lost their capacity for self-renewal. By 1901 a Georgian complained that "from most of the visible land the timber is entirely gone." With it went the golden eagles, the peregrine falcons, and other native species.

Turpentine mills, logging, and lumber milling provided young black southerners with their greatest source of employment. Occasionally an African American rose to be a supervisor, though most supervisors were white. Southerners often blamed these workers, not the operators or the dreadful working conditions and low pay, for the industry's high turnover rates and low morale among workers. As one critic complained, "The sawmill negro is rather shiftless and is not inclined to stay in any one location." In fact, most black workers left the mills in search of higher wages or to sharecrop in order to marry and support families.

BIRMINGHAM STEEL   The iron and steel industry most disappointed promoters of the New South. The availability of coke as a fuel made Chattanooga, Tennessee, and Birmingham, Alabama, major centers for foundries. By the 1890s the Tennessee Coal, Iron, and Railway Company (TCI) of Birmingham was turning out iron pipe for gas, water, and sewer lines vital to cities.

Unfortunately Birmingham's iron deposits were ill-suited for the kinds of steel in demand. In 1907 the financially strapped TCI was sold to the giant U.S. Steel Corporation, controlled by northern interests.

The pattern of lost opportunity was repeated in other southern industries—mining, chemical fertilizers, cottonseed oil, and railroads. Under the campaign for a New South, all grew dramatically in employment and value, but not enough to end poverty or industrialize the region.

The Sources of Southern Poverty

Why did poverty persist in the New South? Surely, as many southerners claimed, the South became a colonial economy controlled by northern business interests. Raw materials such as minerals, timber, and cotton were shipped to other regions, which earned larger profits by turning them into finished goods.

LATE START IN INDUSTRIALIZING   Three other factors also contributed to the region's poverty. First, the South began to industrialize later than the Northeast. Northern workers produced more not because they were more energetic or disciplined but because they were more experienced.

Second, the South commanded only a small technological community to guide its industrial development. Northern engineers and mechanics seldom followed northern capital into the region. Few people were available to adapt modern technology to southern conditions or to teach southerners how to do it themselves.

UNDEREDUCATED LABOR   Education might have overcome the problem by upgrading the region's workforce. But no region in the nation spent less on schooling than did the South. Southern leaders, drawn from the ranks of the upper class, cared little about educating ordinary white residents and openly resisted educating black southerners. And the region's low wages encouraged

| The booming timber industry often left the South poorer due to the harsh methods of extracting lumber. This crew in West Virginia is skidding logs downhill to market. The disturbed and newly bare terrain, however, eroded during rains. Soil washed off hillsides, polluting streams; farther downstream, tanneries, pulp mills and sawmills emptied waste and sewage into the water, making many streams into little more than open sewers.

educated workers to leave the South for higher pay. Few southern states invested much in technical colleges and engineering schools. As a result, none could match those of the North.

THE ISOLATED SOUTHERN LABOR MARKET Lack of education aggravated a third source of southern poverty: the isolation of its labor force. In 1900 agriculture still dominated the southern economy. It required unskilled, low-paid sharecroppers and wage laborers. Southerners feared that outsiders, with their new ways, might spread discontent among workers. So southern states discouraged social services and opportunities that might have attracted human and financial resources. The South remained poor because it received too little, not too much, outside investment.

REVIEW

What factors explain the failure of the campaign for a "New South" and which, in your view, is the most important?

LIFE IN THE NEW SOUTH

LIFE IN THE NEW SOUTH was a constant struggle to balance love of hell-raising with the equally powerful pull of Christian piety. Divided in its soul, the South was also divided by race. Even after the Civil War ended slavery, 90 percent of African Americans continued to live in the rural South. Without slavery, however, southerners lost the system of social control that had defined race relations. Over time they substituted a new system of **segregation,** or racial separation, that eased but never eliminated white fear that African Americans might overturn the racial hierarchy.

Rural Life

Pleasure, piety, race—all divided southern life, in town and country alike. Life separated along lines of gender as well, especially in the rural areas where most southerners lived.

HUNTING Southern males found one source of pleasure in hunting. Hunting offered men welcome relief from heavy farmwork. For rural people a successful hunt could also add meat and fish to a scanty diet. And through hunting many boys found a path to manhood. Seeing his father and brothers return with wild turkeys, young Edward McIlhenny longed for "the time when I would be old enough to hunt this bird."

The thrill of illicit pleasure also drew many southern men to events of violence and chance, including cockfighting. They valued combative birds and were convinced that their champions fought more boldly than did northern bantams. Gambling doubtless heightened the thrills. Such sport offended churchgoing southerners by its cruelty and wantonness. They condemned as sinful "the beer garden, the base ball, the low theater, the dog fight and cock fight and the ring for the pugilist and brute."

FARM ENTERTAINMENTS Many southern customs involved no such disorderly behavior. Work-sharing festivals such as house raisings, log rollings, quiltings, and roadwork gave isolated farm folk the chance to break their daily routine, to socialize, and to work for a common good. These events, too, generally segregated along gender lines. Men did the heavy chores and competed in contests of physical prowess. Women shared domestic tasks such as cooking, quilting, and sewing. Community gatherings also offered young southerners a relaxed place for courtship. In one courting game, the young man who found a rare red ear of corn could have the rare treat of kissing "the lady of his choice."

TOWN For rural folk a trip to town brought special excitement, along with a bit of danger. Saturdays, court days, and holidays drew throngs of people. Court week, when a district judge arrived to mete out justice, drew the biggest crowds. As ever, there were male and female domains. For men the saloon, the blacksmith shop, or the storefront was a place to do business and to let off steam. Few men went to town without participating in social drinking in the local saloon, but when men who had had one too many took to the streets, the threat of brawling and violence drove most women away.

The Church

At the center of southern life stood (and beyond its leadership very much the domain of women) the church as a great stabilizer and custodian of social order. "When one joined the Methodist church," a southern woman remembered, "he was expected to give up all such things as cards, dancing, theatres, in fact all so called worldly amusements." Many devout southerners pursued these ideals, although such restraint asked more of people than many could muster, except perhaps on Sunday.

RURAL RELIGION Congregations were often so small and isolated that they could attract a preacher only once or twice a month. The pious counted on the Sunday sermon to steer them from sin. In town, a sermon might last 30 to 45 minutes, but in the slower-paced countryside, a preacher could go on for two hours or more, whipping up worshipers until "even the little children wept."

By 1870 southern churches were segregated by race. Indeed, the black church was the only institution controlled by African Americans after slavery and thus a principal source of leadership and identity as well as comfort (see page 450). Within churches both black and white congregations were segregated by gender, too. As a boy entered manhood, he moved from the female to the male section. Yet churches were, at base, female domains. Considered guardians of virtue, more women than men were members, attended services, and ran church activities.

Church was a place to socialize as well as worship. Many of the young went simply to meet those of the opposite sex. Church picnics and all-day sings brought as many as 30 or 40 young people together for hours of eating, talk, services,

For Baptists in the South, both white and black, the ceremony of adult baptism included total immersion, often in a nearby river. The ritual symbolized the waters of newfound faith washing away sins that had been forgiven by God's free grace. Here, a black congregation looks on, some holding umbrellas to protect against the sun.

and hymn singing. Still, these occasions could not match the fervor of a weeklong camp meeting. In the late summer or early fall, town and countryside emptied as folks set up tents in shady groves and listened to two or three ministers preach day and night in the largest event of the year. The camp meeting refired faith while celebrating traditional values of home and family.

Segregation

Nothing challenged tradition in the South more than race. With the abolition of slavery and the end of Reconstruction, white northerners and southerners achieved sectional harmony by sacrificing the rights of black citizens. During the 1880s Redeemer governments moved to formalize a system of segregation or racial separation. Redeemers were Democratic politicians who came to power in southern states to end the Republican rule established during Reconstruction. They were eager to reap the benefits of economic expansion and to attract the business classes—bankers, railroad promoters, industrial operators. As their part of the bargain, the Redeemers assured anxious northerners that Redeemer rule would not mean political disenfranchisement of the freedpeople. That part of the bargain they would not keep.

Pressure to reach a new racial accommodation in the South increased as more African Americans moved into southern towns and cities, competing for jobs with poor whites and sharing public space,

especially on railroads and other public conveyances. One way to preserve the social and economic superiority of white southerners, poor as well as rich, was to separate blacks as an inferior caste. The first step came even before the end of Reconstruction. Starting in 1870, Tennessee—where whites outnumbered blacks by a ratio of nearly 3 to 1—outlawed racial intermarriage. Soon every southern state enacted similar laws. Over the next 20 years the white South began to construct a legal wall separating the races almost everywhere.

Federal laws designed to enforce the Civil Rights Act of 1866 and the Fourteenth Amendment, which promised

equal protection for all under law, stood in the way. In effect, these laws established social equality for all races in public places such as hotels, theaters, and railroads. But in 1883 the Supreme Court ruled (in the *Civil Rights Cases*) that hotels and railroads were not "public" institutions, because private individuals owned them. The Fourteenth Amendment was thus limited to protecting citizens from violations of their civil rights by states, not by private individuals. The national policy of **laissez faire** in race relations could not have been made any clearer.

JIM CROW LAWS Within 20 years every southern state had enacted segregation as law. The earliest laws legalized segregation in trains and other such public conveyances where blacks and whites were likely to mingle. Soon a complex web of "Jim Crow" statutes drew an indelible color line in prisons, parks, hotels, restaurants, hospitals, and virtually all public gathering places except streets and stores. (The term *Jim Crow,* used to denote a policy of segregation, originated in a song of the same name sung in minstrel shows of the day.)

In 1892 Homer Adolph Plessy, an African American, agreed to test a Louisiana law requiring segregated railroad facilities by sitting in the all-white section of a local train. He was promptly arrested. Slowly the case of *Plessy v. Ferguson* worked its way up to the Supreme Court. In 1896 the Court ruled that segregation did not constitute discrimination as long as accommodations for both races were "separate but equal." Justice John Marshall Harlan (ironically from a former slaveholding family) issued the lone dissent: separate, whether equal or not, was always a "badge of servitude" and a violation of the "color-blind" Constitution. The doctrine of **separate but equal** nonetheless became part of the fabric of American law and governed race relations for more than half a century to come. When coupled with a growing campaign in the 1890s to disenfranchise black voters across the South (see pages 571–572), segregation provided a formidable barrier to African American progress.

By the turn of the century segregation was firmly in place, stifling economic competition between the races and reducing African Americans to second-class citizenship. Many kinds of employment, such as work in the textile mills, went largely to whites. Skilled and professional black workers generally served black clients. African Americans were barred from juries and usually received far stiffer penalties than whites for the same crimes.

As Jim Crow laws became entrenched, so did stifling social custom. Black southerners always addressed white southerners as "Mister," "Miss," and "Ma'am"—even those of lower status. But white southerners called black southerners by their first names or more simply "Sister" or "Boy," no matter their age or profession. Any African American who crossed the color line risked violence. Some were tarred and feathered, others whipped and beaten, and many lynched. Of the 187 lynchings averaged each year of the 1890s, some 80 percent occurred in the South. The victims were almost always African Americans.

COST OF The cost of Jim Crow to southerners black
JIM CROW and white was incalculable. The race question trumped all other issues and produced a one-party region, where fear of black political participation hamstrung any opposition to all-white Redeemer Democrats. Since Democratic Party regulars controlled nominations and thus elections, politics sparked little public interest and fell into the hands of professionals who helped few ordinary southerners. Supporting a two-tiered system of public services drained money from southern treasuries no matter how inferior black institutions were. All suffered under the rule of racial separation, whether they realized it or not.

A long line of African American voters waits to cast ballots in Caddo Parish, Louisiana, in 1897. Clearly, interest in voting remained high among black citizens. Less clear from this photograph are the reasons for the interest of these particular voters. Were they clinging to the right to vote in a heroic line of resistance to the growing trend toward disenfranchisement, or were they being forced to vote in support of politicians who held power over them? Whatever the answer, there is no question about the trend playing out across the South. Two years after this picture was snapped, Louisiana followed the lead of other southern states in disenfranchising most of its black voters (as well as many poor whites).

Whites and the Western Environment: Competing Visions

WILLIAM GILPIN, A WESTERN BOOSTER

As discoveries of gold and silver lured whites into Indian territory, many whites adopted the decidedly un-Indian outlook of Missouri politician William Gilpin. Only a lack of vision prevented the opening of the West for exploitation, Gilpin told a Missouri audience in 1849. What was most needed were cheap lands and a railroad linking the two coasts "like ears on a human head." Distance, climate, topography, and the Indians were mere obstacles.

By 1868 a generous Congress had granted western settlers their two greatest wishes: free land under the Homestead Act of 1862 and a transcontinental railroad. As the new governor of Colorado, Gilpin crowed about the region's limitless resources. One day, he believed, the West would support more than a billion people. Scarce rainfall and water did not daunt him, for in his eyes the West was no

NATURAL ENVIRONMENT OF THE WEST

With the exception of Oregon and Washington in the Pacific Northwest, few areas west of the 20-inch rainfall line receive enough annual precipitation to support agriculture without irrigation. Consequently, water has been the key to growth and development in the area west of the 98th meridian, which encompasses more than half the land area of the continental United States. The dominance of short grasses and coniferous (evergreen) trees reflects the rainfall patterns.

"Great American Desert" but an Eden-like garden, awaiting only the plow and the rain that would follow it.

Gilpin subscribed to the popular notion that "rain follows the plow." The idea was as simple as it was widely held—and wrong. Settling dry lands and plowing fields would release moisture into the air, the theory maintained, thereby increasing cloud cover and rain. Early climatologist Cyrus Thomas and amateur scientist Charles Dana Wilbur helped popularize the notion. Whites settling the West and speculators profiting from developing it justified their actions as transforming "desert into a farm or garden." An unusually wet cycle from 1878 to 1886 helped to sustain the myth. The fact that such human activity did increase precipitation locally by drawing rain from nearby areas only undermined the few skeptics who rightly argued that the plow produced no change in climate over large regions.

JOHN WESLEY POWELL

Unlike the visionary Gilpin, John Wesley Powell knew something about water and farming. After losing an arm in the Civil War, geologist Powell went west. In 1869 and 1871 he led scientific expeditions down the Green and Colorado Rivers through the Grand Canyon. He returned to warn Congress that developing the West required more scientific planning. Much of the region had yet to be mapped or its resources identified.

WATER AS A KEY RESOURCE

In 1880 Powell became director of the recently formed U.S. Geological Survey. He, too, had a vision of the West, but one based on the limits of its environment. Water, not land, was the key. In the water-rich East, whoever owned the banks of a river or stream controlled as much water as they might take, regardless of the consequences for those downstream. The same practice in the water-starved West, Powell recognized, would enrich the small number with access while spelling ruin for the rest.

The alternative was to treat water as community property. The practice would benefit many rather than a privileged few. Powell suggested that the federal government establish political boundaries defined by watersheds and regulate the distribution of the scarce resource. Such scientific realism could not overcome the popular vision of the West as an American Eden. Powerful interests ensured that development occurred with the same helter-skelter, laissez-faire credo that was shaping the East.

 **REVIEW**

How did Indian conceptions of the environment compare and contrast with white conceptions?

THE WAR FOR THE WEST

SO MARGINAL DID FEDERAL OFFICIALS consider the Great Plains that they left the lands to the Indians. By the end of the Civil War some two-thirds of all Indian peoples lived on the Great Plains. Even before the war a series of gold and silver discoveries beginning in 1848 signaled the first serious interest by white settlers in the arid and semiarid lands beyond the Mississippi. White prospectors, settlers, merchants, and developers soon flooded the Trans-Mississippi West. The first to feel the effects of this unrestrained expansion were the Indians and Latinos of the region.

Those effects ripped the Navajo people from their land like a tornado. In January 1864, to solve the "Navajo problem," the army started rounding up thousands of the tribe. Over the next several months—in the dead of winter and the blazing heat of summer—armed guards marched them along seven trails from present-day Arizona and western New Mexico to an encampment called *Bosque Redondo* near Fort Sumner. Some walked as many as 450 miles. More than 200 died, among them stragglers shot for failing to keep up on the "Long Walk." Those who survived soon found themselves packed into a 40-square-mile stretch of short prairie grass and scorched desert that straddled the Pecos River. The encampment was originally designed to hold 5,000 people. By the spring of 1865, over 9,000 squeezed into ramshackle dwellings made of twigs and grimy canvas.

POLICY OF CONCENTRATION

The Long Walk was part of an experiment. To open more land to whites and to provide Indians a safe haven, federal officials had introduced a policy of "concentration" in 1851. They pressed tribes to sign treaties limiting the boundaries of their hunting grounds to "reservations"—the Sioux to the Dakotas, the Cheyenne to the foothills of Colorado. Some tribes like the Navajo were moved at rifle point. And for them, the experiment ended tragically. Conditions at *Bosco Redondo* were so horrid that nearly one in three Navajo died. In 1868, the government finally closed down the camp. The Navajo returned to their territory in one of the earliest instances of forced relocation home.

Despite treaty claims that their provisions would last "as long as waters run," land-hungry pioneers broke the promises of their government time after time by squatting on Indian territory and demanding federal protection. The government, in turn, forced more restrictive agreements on the western tribes. This cycle of promises made and broken continued, until a full-scale war for the West raged between whites and Indians.

Contact and Conflict

The policy of concentration began in the Pacific Northwest and produced some of the earliest clashes between whites and Indians. In an oft-repeated pattern Indian resistance led to war and war to Indian defeat. In the 1850s, as territorial governor Isaac Stevens was browbeating local tribes into giving up millions of acres in Washington Territory, a gold strike flooded the Indian homelands with miners. The tribes fought them off, only to be crushed and forced onto reservations.

In similar fashion, by 1862 the lands of the Santee Sioux had been whittled down to a strip 10 miles wide and

150 miles long along the Minnesota River. Lashing out in frustration, the tribe attacked several undefended white settlements on the Minnesota frontier. In response, General John Pope arrived in St. Paul declaring his intention to wipe out the Sioux. "They are to be treated as maniacs or wild beasts and by no means as people," he instructed his officers. When Pope's forces captured 1,800 Sioux, white Minnesotans were outraged that President Lincoln ordered only 38 hanged.

CHIVINGTON MASSACRE

The campaign under General Pope was the opening of a guerrilla war that continued on and off for 30 years. The conflict gained momentum in 1864, when Governor John Evans of Colorado sought to end all land treaties with Indian peoples in eastern Colorado. In November a force of 700 Colorado volunteers under Colonel John Chivington fell on a band of friendly Cheyenne gathered at Sand Creek under army protection. Chief Black Kettle raised an American flag to signal friendship, but Chivington would have none of it. "Kill and scalp all, big and little," he told his men. The troops massacred at least 150, including children holding white flags of truce and mothers with babies in their arms. A joint congressional investigation later condemned Chivington. A year later, in 1865, virtually all Plains Indians joined in the First Sioux War to drive whites from their lands.

BUFFALO SOLDIERS

Among the soldiers who fought the Plains Indians were African American veterans of the Civil War. In 1866 two regiments of black soldiers formed the Ninth and Tenth Cavalry under the command of white officers. Their Indian foes dubbed them "buffalo soldiers," reflecting the similarity they saw between African American hair and buffalo hair. It was also a sign of hard-won respect. The buffalo soldiers fought Indians across the West for more than 20 years. They also served as agents of white settlement, subduing bandits, cattle thieves, and gunmen for the safety of local businesses; locating water, wood, and grasslands for eager homesteaders; and laying the foundations for posts such as Fort Sill in Oklahoma.

White settlement undermined tribal cultures. Diseases introduced by settlers, including smallpox, measles, and cholera, killed more Indians than combat. Liquor furnished by white traders entrapped many a brave in a deadly cycle of alcoholism. Trading posts altered traditional ways of life with metal pots and pans, traps, coffee, and sugar but furnished no employment and thus few ways for their Indian customers to pay for these goods. Mines, crops, grazing herds, and fences disturbed native hunting and farming lands across the West.

On the Great Plains white incursions wreaked havoc with Indian life. The railroad disrupted the migratory patterns of the buffalo and thus the hunt on which Plains Indians depended for survival. Demand for buffalo products nearly destroyed the herds. When buffalo robes became popular in the East in the 1870s and hides a source of

leather for industrial belts, commercial companies hired professional hunters, who could kill as many as 100 bison an hour. Even Indians were caught up in the whirl of commercial trading, killing bison for profit rather than provisions. By 1883 the great herds had nearly disappeared from the Plains (see Historians Reconstruct the Past, "Where Have All the Bison Gone?" on pages 496–499). With them went a way of life that left Plains Indians more vulnerable to white expansion.

Custer's "Last Stand" —and the Indians'

In 1868 the Treaty of Fort Laramie capped four bloody years of fighting between whites and Indians, including the Santee and Lakota Sioux. The treaty established two large Indian reservations, one in Oklahoma and the other in the Dakota Badlands. Only six years later, Colonel George Armstrong Custer broke the treaty by leading an expedition into *Paha Sapa,* the sacred Black Hills of the Sioux. Custer, a Civil War veteran, already had a reputation for cruelty as a "squaw killer" from his days fighting Indians in western Kansas. To open the Black Hills to whites, his expedition spread rumors of gold "from the grass roots down." Prospectors poured into Indian country. When negotiations for a new treaty failed, President Grant ordered all "hostiles" in the area driven onto the reservations.

BATTLE OF LITTLE BIG HORN

In the summer of 1876 several army columns, among them Custer's Seventh Cavalry of over 600 troops, marched against the Sioux. Eager for glory, Custer arrived at the Little Big Horn River a day earlier than the other columns. Hearing of a native village nearby, he attacked, only to discover that he had stumbled onto an encampment of more than 7,000 Sioux and Cheyenne allied for the first time. From a deep ravine Sioux leader Crazy Horse charged Custer, killing him and 267 soldiers.

As he led the attack Crazy Horse yelled "It is a good day to die!"—the traditional war cry. He spoke more truth than he knew. Although Custer had been killed, railroads stood ready to extend their lines, prospectors to make fortunes, settlers to lay down roots, and soldiers to protect them all. By late summer the Sioux were forced to split into small bands to evade the army. Sioux holy man Sitting Bull barely escaped to Canada; Crazy Horse and 800 other Cheyennes and Sioux surrendered in 1876 after a winter of suffering and starvation.

These battles did not end the war between whites and Indians, but never again would it reach such proportions nor would Indians win many victories like that of the Little Big Horn. Even the peaceful Nez Percé of Idaho found no security once whites looked to their lands. The Nez Percé had become breeders of livestock, rich in horses and cattle that they grazed in the meadows west of the Snake River canyon. Their livestock business did not prevent the

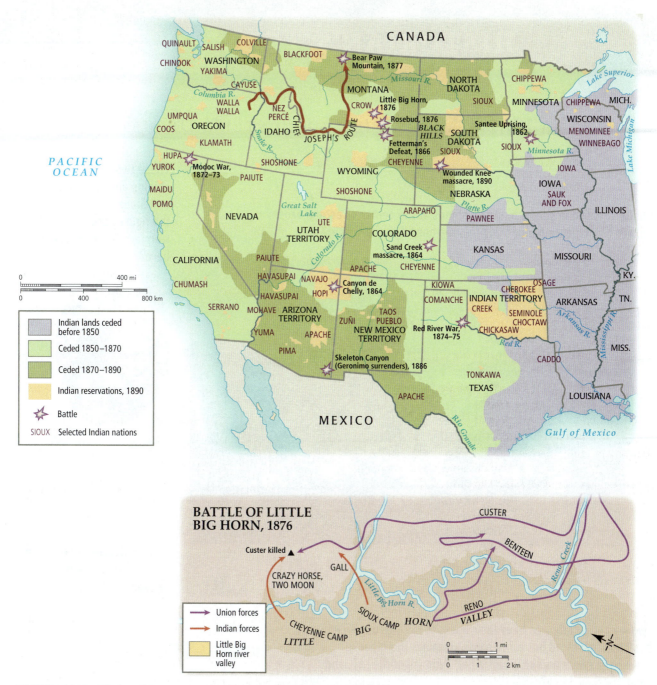

THE INDIAN FRONTIER

As conflict erupted between Indian and white cultures in the West, the government sought increasingly to concentrate tribes on reservations. Resistance to the reservation concept helped unite the Sioux and Cheyenne, traditionally enemies, in the Dakotas during the 1870s. In the Battle of Little Big Horn (known among Indians as "the Battle of the Greasy Grass"), the impetuous Custer underestimated the strength of his Indian opponents and attacked before supporting troops were in a position to help.

government from trying to force them onto a small reservation in 1877.

Rather than see his people humiliated, Chief Joseph led almost 600 Nez Percé toward Canada with the U.S. Army in hot pursuit. In just 75 days they traveled more than 1,300 miles. Every time the army closed to attack, Chief Joseph and his warriors drove them off. But before the Nez Percé

could reach the border, they were forced to surrender. Chief Joseph's words still ring with eloquence: "Hear me, my chiefs, I am tired; my heart is sick and sad. From where the sun now stands I will fight no more forever." The government then shipped the defeated tribe to the bleak Indian country of Oklahoma. There, disease and starvation finished what the army began.

A WHITE MAN'S VIEW OF CUSTER'S DEFEAT

Custer dressed in yellow buckskin stands at the center of action, saber raised. What message does this figure transmit to the viewer?

These two warriors carry shields and spears unlike any Sioux Indian's. In fact, the figures are African Zulu warriors. Why include them here?

CUSTER'S LAST FIGHT.
The Original Painting has been Presented to the Seventh Regiment U.S. Cavalry
ANHEUSER BUSCH BREWING ASSOCIATION.

These figures seem out of place. No one else is naked.

Two mysterious figures have their backs to us. The one kneeling has an Indian braid but white man's clothing. The other is dressed in buckskin and wears a hat. Who might they be, and what are they doing?

"When the legend becomes fact, print the legend," commented one cynical editor in the western *The Man Who Shot Liberty Valance*. Historians recognize that the evidence they examine often deals in legend. By the end of the nineteenth century the Battle of Little Big Horn had already slipped into the realm of myth, as can be seen in Otto Becker's chromolithograph *Custer's Last Fight*, based loosely on an earlier painting created by Casilly Adams in the 1880s. In 1896 the Anheuser Busch Brewing Association turned it into this advertising poster and plastered it in saloons across the country. But Becker was not content to copy Adams's painting. He added a number of his own details, borrowed from other art works of the day. The naked figures twisting in torment (lower right) imitate an illustration of hell by Gustave Doré. Even more interesting, the two shield-bearing African Zulu warriors (see the detail) seem to refer to another battle against native peoples. In 1879, three years after Custer's defeat, the Zulu slaughtered British forces at the Battle of Isandhlwana in present-day South Africa. Becker's additions are apparently based on engravings of that battle from *The Illustrated London News*.

Thinking Critically

Historian Frederick Jackson Turner in 1890 called the conquest of Indian peoples by whites the triumph of "civilization" over "savagery." Does Becker's lithograph make that point graphically? Or the opposite?

Killing with Kindness

Over these same years Indians saw their legal sovereignty being whittled away, sometimes even with the best intentions. Originally, federal authorities regarded various tribes as autonomous nations within the United States, with whom treaties could be made. That tribal status began shrinking in 1831, when the Supreme Court declared Indians "domestic dependent nations." Although the United States continued to negotiate treaties with the tribes, government officials began treating Indians as wards of the state who should be treated like inept children and raised with Christian values and white styles of living. Finally, in 1871, Congress abandoned the treaty system altogether and with it the legal core of Indian autonomy.

LA FLESCHE AND JACKSON

Some whites and Indians spoke out against the tragedy taking place on the Great Plains. In the 1870s Susan La Flesche, daughter of an Omaha chief and the first Indian woman in the United States to become a physician, lectured eastern audiences about the mistreatment of Indian peoples and inspired reformers to action. Similarly moved, the poet Helen Hunt Jackson lobbied for Indian rights and against government policy. In 1881 she published *A Century of Dishonor*, a best-selling exposé that detailed government fraud and corruption in Indian affairs, as well as the many treaties broken by the United States.

Reformers began pressing for assimilation of Indians into white society, ironically as the only means of preserving Indians in a society that seemed bent on destroying them. The Women's National Indian Association, created in 1874, and the later Indian Rights Association, joined by Helen Hunt Jackson, sought to end the Indian way of life by suppressing communal activities, reeducating Indian children, and establishing individual homesteads.

DAWES ACT

Reformers also recognized that the policy of concentrating Indians on reservations had failed. Deprived of their traditional lands and culture, reservation tribes became dependent on government aid. In any case, whites who coveted Indian lands were quick to violate treaty terms. With a mix of good intentions and unbridled greed, Congress adopted the Dawes Severalty Act in 1887. It ended reservation policy by permitting the president to distribute land to Indians

Le Sabre Indian School, Montana

After the end of the Indian wars of the late nineteenth century, government authorities and private philanthropists tried in many ways to encourage Indians to assimilate into mainstream white American society. One of the most ambitious, and controversial, was a series of boarding schools for Indian children, where white teachers worked to teach them the ways of the English-speaking world. Most such schools were for boys, but some—such as this school in Montana, run by Catholic nuns—were created for girls.

who had severed their attachments to their tribes. The goals of the policy were simple: to draw Indians into white society as farmers and small property owners and (less high-mindedly) to bring Indian lands legally into the marketplace.

In practice, the Dawes Act was more destructive than any blow struck by the army. It undermined the communal structure of tribal culture. Lands held by tribes were parceled out to individuals: 160 acres to the head of a family and 80 acres to a single adult or an orphan. Those who took the land and "adopted the habits of civilized life" received American citizenship. But as John Wesley Powell had warned, small homestead farms in the West could not support a family—white or Indian—unless the farms were irrigated. Most Indians, moreover, had no experience with farming, managing money, or other white ways. Perhaps worst of all, reservation lands not allocated to Indians were opened to non-Indian homesteaders. In 1881 Indians held more than 155 million acres of land. By 1900 the figure had dropped to just under 78 million.

WOUNDED KNEE Against such a dismal future some Indians assimilated, cutting their hair, abandoning the old ways and adopting the ways of the white man. Others, like the women of the Southern Utes, had more complex responses. They assimilated when it served their interests, resisted when it did not, in one instance openly opposing schools for their children outside of the reservation.

Still other tribes turned to cults and movements to revive Indian culture. In 1890 a religious revival swept the Indian nations when word came from the Nevada desert that a humble Paiute named Wovoka had received revelations from the Great Spirit. Wovoka preached that if his followers adopted his mystical rituals and lived together in love and harmony, the Indian dead would come back to life, whites would be driven from the land, and game would be plentiful again. As the rituals spread, alarmed settlers referred to their ritualized shuffling and chanting as the "Ghost Dance." The army moved to stamp out the Ghost Dance for fear of another uprising. At Wounded Knee in South Dakota the cavalry fell on a band of followers. As the soldiers were disarming the Indians, a shot rang out, setting off a blaze of army machine-gun fire. When the smoke cleared, some 300 Sioux men, women, and children and 25 soldiers lay dead.

Wounded Knee was a final act of violence against an independent Indian way of life. After 1890 the battle was over assimilation, not extinction. The system of markets, rail networks, and extractive industries was linking the Far West with the rest of the nation. Free-roaming bison were being replaced by herded cattle and sheep, nomadic tribes by prairie sodbusters, and sacred hunting grounds by gold fields. Reformers relied on education, citizenship, and allotments to move Indians into white society. Many Indians were equally determined to preserve their tribal ways and separateness as a people.

Borderlands

The coming of the railroad in the 1880s and 1890s brought wrenching changes to the Southwest as well, especially to the states and territories along the old border with Mexico. But here there was a twist. As new markets and industries sprang up, new settlers poured in not only from the east but also from the south, across the Mexican border. Indians such as the Navajo and the Apache thus faced the hostility of newcomers—Anglos and Mexicans alike—as well as of Hispanos, those settlers of Spanish descent long in the region. Before the Mexican War of 1846, the Spanish governors of northern Mexico had offered bounties for Indian scalps.

JUAN JOSÉ HERRERA AND THE WHITE CAPS Like Indians, Hispanos discovered that they had either to accommodate or to resist the flood of new Anglos. The elite, or Ricos, often aligned themselves with Anglos against their countryfolk to protect their status and property. Others, like Juan José Herrera, resisted the newcomers. When Anglo cattle ranchers began forcing Hispanos off their lands near Las Vegas, New Mexico, Herrera assembled a band of masked night riders known as *Las Gorras Blancas* (The White Caps). In 1889 and 1890 as many as 700 White Caps burned Anglo fences, haystacks, and occasionally barns and houses. In one fiery turn, Herrera's followers set thousands of railroad ties ablaze when the Atchison, Topeka and Santa Fe Railroad refused to raise the low wages of its Hispano workers.

New Anglos frequently fought Hispanos. But it was western lawyers and politicians, using legal tactics, who deprived Hispanos of most of their property. Thomas Catron, an ambitious New Mexico lawyer, squeezed out many Hispanos by contesting land titles so aggressively that his holdings grew to 3 million acres. Still, in those areas of New Mexico and California where they remained a majority, Hispanos continued to play a role in public life. During the early 1890s Herrera and his allies formed a "People's Party," swept local elections, and managed to defeat a bid by Catron to represent the territory in Congress.

MEXICAN IMMIGRANTS With the railroads came more white settlers as well as Mexican laborers. Just as the southern economy depended on African American labor, the economy of the Southwest rested on the backs of Mexicans. Mexican immigrants served mostly as contract and seasonal workers for railroads and large farms. Many of them settled in the growing cities along the rail lines: El Paso, Albuquerque, Tucson, Phoenix, and Los Angeles. They lived in segregated barrios, Spanish towns where their cultural traditions persisted. What little power they had lay in the hands of political bosses (see page 538), some Latino, some Anglo.

FORMATION OF REGIONAL COMMUNITIES To focus on cities alone would distort the experience of most southwesterners of Spanish descent, especially those who lived in the small villages of northern New Mexico

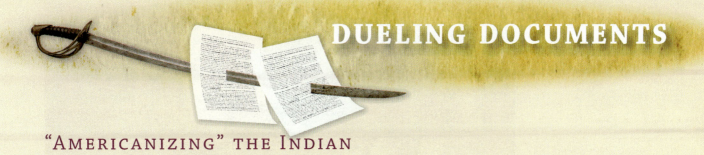

DUELING DOCUMENTS

"AMERICANIZING" THE INDIAN

The federal government began a program to "Americanize" Indians in 1887, by force if necessary. Children were separated from parents and sent to boarding schools such as the one at the Carlisle Barracks in Pennsylvania. Its founder, Captain Richard Pratt, explains the rationale for the schools in the first document below. In the second document, Zitkala-Sa (later known as Gertrude Simmons Bonnin) describes the experience from an Indian point of view.

DOCUMENT 1   Advantages of "Americanizing" Indians

A great general has said that the only good Indian is a dead one, and that high sanction of his destruction has been an enormous factor in promoting Indian massacres. In a sense, I agree with the sentiment, but only in this: that all the Indian there is in the race should be dead. Kill the Indian in him, and save the man. . . .

It is a sad day for the Indians when they fall under the assaults of our troops, as in the Piegan massacre, the massacre of Old Black Kettle and his Cheyennes at what is termed "the battle of the Washita," and hundreds of other like places in the history of our dealings with them; but a far sadder day is it for them when they fall under the baneful influences of a treaty agreement with the United States whereby they are to receive large annuities, and to be protected on reservations, and held apart from all association with the best of our civilization. The destruction is not so speedy, but it is far more general. . . .

The Indians under our care remained savage, because forced back upon themselves and away from association with

English-speaking and civilized people, and because of our savage example and treatment of them. . . .

We make our greatest mistake in feeding our civilization to the Indians instead of feeding the Indians to our civilization. America has different customs and civilizations from Germany. What would be the result of an attempt to plant American customs and civilization among the Germans in Germany, demanding that they shall become thoroughly American before we admit them to the country? Now, what we have all along attempted to do for and with the Indians is just exactly that, and nothing else. We invite the Germans to come into our country and communities, and share our customs, our civilization, to be of it; and the result is immediate success. Why not try it on the Indians? Why not invite them into experiences in our communities? Why always invite and compel them to remain a people unto themselves? . . .

The school at Carlisle is an attempt on the part of the government to do this. Carlisle has always planted treason to the

tribe and loyalty to the nation at large. It has preached against colonizing Indians, and in favor of individualizing them. It has demanded for them the same multiplicity of chances which all others in the country enjoy. Carlisle fills young Indians with the spirit of loyalty to the stars and stripes, and then moves them out into our communities to show by their conduct and ability that the Indian is no different from the white or the colored, that he has the inalienable right to liberty and opportunity that the white and the negro have. Carlisle does not dictate to him what line of life he should fill, so it is an honest one. It says to him that, if he gets his living by the sweat of his brow, and demonstrates to the nation that he is a man, he does more good for his race than hundreds of his fellows who cling to their tribal communistic surroundings. . . .

Source: Official Report of the Nineteenth Annual Conference of Charities and Correction (1892), pp. 46–59. Reprinted in Richard H. Pratt, "The Advantages of Mingling Indians with Whites," *Americanizing the American Indians: Writings by the "Friends of the Indian" 1880–1900* (Cambridge, Mass., 1973), pp. 260–271.

DOCUMENT 2   An Indian Girl's Experience

Late in the morning, my friend Judewin gave me a terrible warning. . . . She heard the paleface woman talk about cutting our long, heavy hair. Our mothers had taught us that only unskilled warriors who were captured had their hair shingled by the enemy. Among our people, short hair was worn by mourners, and shingled hair by cowards! We discussed our fate some moments, and when Judewin said, "We have to submit, because they are strong," I rebelled.

"No, I will not submit! I will struggle first!" I answered. . . .

I watched for my chance, and when no one noticed I disappeared, I crept up the stairs as quietly as I could in my squeaking shoes—my moccasins had been exchanged for shoes. . . . On my hands and knees

I crawled under [a] bed, and cuddled myself in the dark corner. . . .

What caused them to stoop and look under the bed I do not know. I remember being dragged out, though I resisted by kicking and scratching wildly. In spite of myself, I was carried downstairs and tied fast in a chair.

I cried aloud, shaking my head all the while until I felt the cold blades on the scissors, against my neck, and heard them gnaw off one of my thick braids. Then I lost my spirit. Since the day I was taken from my mother I had suffered extreme indignities. People had stared at me. I had been tossed about in the air like a wooden puppet. And now my long hair was shingled like a coward's! In my anguish I moaned for my mother, but no one came to comfort me. Not a soul reasoned quietly with me, as my own

mother used to do; for now I was only one of many little animals driven by a herder.

Source: Zitkala-Sa (Gertrude Simmons Bonnin), "The School Days of an Indian Girl," *Atlantic Monthly,* Vol. 89 (January–March 1900), pp. 45–47, 190, 192–194.

Thinking Critically

What does Captain Richard Pratt mean by "kill the Indian . . . and save the man"? How does he justify the Americanization program at Carlisle, and why might some whites at the time consider his reasoning to be "enlightened"? What effect do efforts at Americanization, in particular haircutting, have on Zitkala-Sa? In your view, who is more "civilized," Pratt or Zitkala-Sa?

Western cities attracted ethnically diverse populations. This chili stand in San Antonio served the city's large Latino population.

and southern Colorado. There a pattern of adaptation and resistance to Anglo penetration emerged. As the market economy advanced, Hispanic villagers turned to migratory labor to adapt. Women continued to work in the old villages; men traveled from wage job to wage job in mining, in farming, and on the railroads. A new culture developed rooted in the web of villages and migrant workers that furnished a base from which Hispanics could seek employment and a safe haven to which they could return. The resulting "regional community" served a dual purpose: preservation of the communal life of the old Hispanic village and transition into the new world of market capitalism that was transforming the West.

Ethno-Racial Identity in the New West

The New West met the Old South in the diamond-shaped Blackland Prairie of central Texas. Before the Civil War, King Cotton thrived in its rich soil. Afterward, Texas became the leading cotton-producing state in the country. Having embraced the slave system of the Old South, Texas also adopted the New South's system of race management, with its racial separation, restrictions on black voting, and biracial labor force of African Americans and poor whites. Yet Texas was part of the borderlands of the American West, where the Anglo culture of European Americans also confronted the Latino culture of Mexicans and Mexican Americans.

A NEW RACIAL TRIAD   Between 1890 and 1910 the Spanish-speaking population of the Southwest nearly doubled. In central Texas the presence of this large and growing force of Mexicano laborers complicated racial matters. The black-and-white poles of European and African Americans that had defined identity in the Old South were now replaced by a new racial triad of black,

white, and brown that negotiated identity and status among themselves.

Like African Americans, Mexican Americans and Mexican immigrants in Texas were separated from Anglos by a color line. Most whites considered them inferior and justified their prejudice on the grounds that Mexicans were shiftless, ignorant, and weak-minded, like all "darker races." But unlike African Americans, Texans of Mexican descent sometimes found themselves part of a three-cornered racial dynamic that left them swinging between the white world of privilege and the black world of disadvantage. In 1914, for example, Mexicans gained status by joining Anglos in the Land League, a radical organization of Texas

In the Far West, ethno-racial identity added other categories to the mix, including Chinese. These workers stop for refreshments at a stand with signs in English.

renters dedicated to land reform. Its white secretary, frustrated over the reluctance of other whites to sign on, extolled the courage and steadfastness of Mexican members, claiming that they would "starve before they will submit to a higher rent than the League and the law says is just."

In this fluid dynamic, whites could lose status, as had the many Texans who sank into landlessness and poverty on the eve of World War I. White landowners disdained them as "white trash" and a "white scourge," found them to be more expensive tenants, and thus were more likely to rent to what they now regarded as "hardworking" Mexican Americans and Mexican immigrants. As small white operators lost their farms and ranches to large corporations, they saw the social distance shrink between themselves and black and brown laborers, sharecroppers, and tenants. By the 1920s a multiracial labor force of landless wage earners worked on giant ranches and farms across the Southwest. In Texas the labor force was triracial, but in California it also included Asian Americans and, elsewhere, American Indians.

✓ REVIEW

Through what means did American Indians lose their independence and land?

BOOM AND BUST IN THE WEST

OPPORTUNITY IN THE NEW WEST lay in land and resources, but wealth also accumulated in towns and cities. Each time speculative fever struck, new communities sprouted to serve those who rushed in to grab riches. The western boom began in mining with the California gold rush of 1849 and the rise of San Francisco (see pages 364–365). In the decades that followed, new hordes threw up towns in Park City, Utah, Tombstone, Arizona, and other promising sites. All too often, busts followed booms and boom towns became ghost towns.

Mining Sets a Pattern

The gold and silver strikes of the 1840s and 1850s set a pattern followed by other booms. Stories of easy riches attracted single prospectors with their shovels and wash pans. Muddy mining camps sprang up in which a prospector could register a claim, get provisions, bathe, and buy a drink or a companion. Almost all the prospectors were male, and nearly half were born abroad. In local saloons English, Irish brogues, German, French, Spanish, Chinese, Italian, Hawaiian, and various Indian dialects collided noisily

PROSTITUTION — Prostitution flourished openly in mining towns (as it did in cattle towns). Such makeshift communities provided ideal conditions: large numbers of rootless men, few women, and money to purchase any favor. In the booming towns of Gold Hill and Virginia City near the Comstock Lode of Nevada, men outnumbered women 2 to 1 in 1875. Almost 1 woman in 12 was a prostitute. Usually prostitutes were young, in their teens and 20s. They walked the streets and plied their trade in one-room shacks called "cribs." If young and in demand, they worked in dance halls, saloons, and brothels. Pay varied by race, with Anglos at the top, followed by African Americans, Mexicans, and Indians. A far more profitable source of revenue came from outfitting these boom societies with the equipment they needed. Sales siphoned riches into the pockets of store owners and other suppliers, all with a stake in the town's survival. Once the quick profits were gone, a period of consolidation brought more order to towns destined to remain. Police departments replaced vigilantes. Brothels, saloons, and gambling dens were limited to "red-light" districts. Larger scale came to regional businesses.

ENVIRONMENTAL COSTS OF MINING — In the mine fields, that meant corporations with the capital for hydraulic water jets to blast ore loose and for the heavy equipment needed to crush rock and extract silver and gold from deeper veins. Their quest for profit often led to environmental disaster. With each snow melt and rain the gravel from hydraulic mining worked its way down into river systems. The resulting floods, mudslides, and dirty streams threatened the livelihood of farmers in the valleys below. Outside Sacramento 39,000 acres of farmland lay under the debris by the 1890s, and another 14,000 acres were nearly ruined. In Butte, Montana, smoke from sulfur-belching smelters turned the air so black that by the 1880s townsfolk had trouble seeing even in daylight.

In a common cycle, the rowdy mining frontier of small-scale prospectors was integrated into the industrial system of wage labor, large-scale resource extraction, and high-finance capital. Large corporations managed operations from afar. Paid laborers replaced the independent prospectors of earlier days. As these miners sought better wages and working conditions, shorter hours, and the right to unionize, management fought back. In Coeur d'Alene, Idaho, troops crushed a strike in 1892, killing seven miners. The miners then created the Western Federation of Miners, a union in which, in the decade after 1893, attracted some 50,000 members and gained a reputation for militancy.

The Transcontinental Railroad

As William Gilpin predicted in 1849, the development of the West awaited the railroads. Before the Central and Union Pacific railroads were joined to span the continent in 1869, travel was slow and dusty. Daunting distances and sparse population gave entrepreneurs little chance to follow the eastern practice of building local railroads from city to city.

Blasting away with pressurized water jets, miners loosen gold-bearing gravel. Such techniques damaged the environment in the rush to exploit western resources. The artist, Mrs. Jonas Brown, lived in Idaho City during the height of its gold rush.

RAILROAD LAND GRANTS

In 1862 Congress granted the Central Pacific Railroad the right to build the western link of the transcontinental railroad eastward from Sacramento. To the Union Pacific Corporation fell responsibility for the section from Omaha westward. Generous loans and gifts of federal and state lands made the venture wildly profitable. For every mile of track completed, the rail companies received between 200 and 400 square miles of land, eventually totaling some 45 million acres. Fraudulent stock practices, corrupt accounting, and wholesale bribery (involving a vice president of the United States and at least two members of Congress) swelled profits even more. "Our method of doing business is founded upon lying, cheating and stealing—all bad things," one railroad baron observed. Over 75 western railroads eventually benefited from such government generosity.

Millions of ordinary Americans eventually benefited, too, as did the national economy, but at the time the railroads were the chief beneficiaries. With legislators in their pockets and investors clamoring for a piece of the action, the companies ran seven lines across hundreds of miles of arid, empty grasslands containing few people or businesses to justify the often-inflated price tag. Then they enticed farmers with splashy handbills and posters to places along

their lines in western Nebraska and Kansas, where sparse rainfall doomed them to failure. Ruthless profiteering spawned incompetence, inefficiency, and waste. Even railroad boosters had to admit that, as one of them put it, "empty railroad trains ran across deserted prairies to vacant towns."

General Grenville Dodge, an army engineer on leave to the Union Pacific, recruited his immense labor force from Civil War veterans as well as Irish and other European immigrants. He drove them with army discipline, completing as much as 10 miles of track in a single day. Charles Crocker of the Central Pacific had no similar source of cheap labor in California to cut through the massive Sierra Nevada. When his partner Leland Stanford suggested importing workers from China, Crocker laughed, until he ran the numbers. Soon, 10,000 Chinese were inching eastward. They built trestles and chipped away at the Sierras' looming granite walls with picks, shovels, and deadly kegs of dynamite.

Once Chinese crews broke into the flat country of the desert basin, the two railroads raced to claim as much federal land as possible. On May 10, 1869, at Promontory Summit, Utah, with Chinese laborers banished from the scene, a silver hammer pounded a gold spike into the last tie. East and West were finally linked by rail. Travel time across the continent was slashed from months to barely a week.

Cattle Kingdom

Westerners realized that railroads were crucial components of the cattle industry. Cow towns such as Abilene, Denver, and Cheyenne flourished in the growing cattle kingdom. By 1860 some 5 million longhorn cattle were wandering the grassy plains of Texas. Ranchers allowed their herds to roam the unbroken or "open" range freely, identified only by a distinctive brand on their hides.

Cattle ranching in the United States already had a long history in Texas and California, developed largely by Tejanos and Californios of Spanish descent. Anglo-Americans who came to Texas readily adopted the equipment of Tejanos: the tough mustangs and broncos (horses suited to managing mean-spirited longhorns), the branding iron for marking the herds, the corral for holding cattle, and the riata, or lariat, for roping. The cowboys also wore Mexican chaps, spurs, and broad-brimmed sombreros, or "hats that provide shade." In Texas at least a third of all cowboys were Mexicans and black freedmen after the Civil War, the rest largely Confederate veterans. Rivalries sometimes developed among them. One Mexican *corrido*, or ballad, boasted of a herd of 500 steers that could not be corralled by 30 Anglo cowboys, when suddenly five Mexican *vaqueros* arrived: *"Esos cinco mexicanos al momento los echaron / y los trienta americanos se quedaron azorados."* ("Those five Mexicans in

THE MINING AND CATTLE FRONTIERS

In the vast spaces of the West, railroads, cattle trails, and mining for gold, silver, and other precious metals and minerals usually preceded the arrival of enough settlers to establish towns and cities. The railroads forged a crucial link between the region's natural resources and urban markets in the East and in Europe, but by transecting the plains they also disrupted the migratory patterns of the buffalo herds, undermining Plains Indian cultures while opening the land to cattle grazing and farming. **They also lured settlers to sometimes barely habitable areas of the country. What reasons might railroad barons have had for choosing the routes their lines took?**

a moment put in the steers / and the thirty Americans were left astonished.")

In 1866, as rail lines swept west, Texas ranchers began driving their herds north to railheads for shipment to market. These "long drives" lasted two to three months and sometimes covered more than 1,000 miles. When early routes to Sedalia, Missouri, proved unfriendly, ranchers scouted alternative paths. The Chisholm Trail led from San Antonio to Abilene and Ellsworth in Kansas. More westerly routes soon ran to Dodge City and even Denver and Cheyenne.

Home on the Range

Because cattle grazed on the open range, early ranches were primitive. Most had a house for the family, a bunkhouse for the hired hands, and about 30 to 40 acres of grazing land per animal. Women were scarce in the masculine world of the cattle kingdom. Most were ranchers' wives, strong and resourceful women who cooked, nursed the sick, and helped run the ranch. A few stalwart women ranched themselves. When Helen Wiser Stewart of Nevada learned in July 1884 that her husband had been murdered, she took over the ranch, buying and selling cattle, managing the hands, and tending to family and crops.

Farmers looking for their own homesteads soon became rivals to the cattle ranchers. The "nesters," as ranchers disdainfully called them, fenced off their lands, thus shrinking the open range. Vast grants to the railroads also limited the area of free land, and ranchers intent on breeding heavier cattle with more tender beef began to fence in their stock to prevent them from mixing with inferior strays. Before long, farmers and ranchers found themselves locked in deadly "range wars" over grazing and water rights. Farmers usually won.

Conflicts also arose between cattle ranchers and herders of another animal introduced by the Mexicans—sheep. Cattle ranchers had nothing but contempt for sheep raisers and their "woolies." Sheep cropped grasses so short that cattle could not graze. To protect the range they saw as their own from the "hooved locust," cattle ranchers attacked shepherds and their flocks. The feuds often burst into range wars, some more violent than those between farmers and ranchers.

A Boom-and-Bust Cycle

The cattle boom that began with the first long drive of 1866 reached its peak from 1880 to 1885. Ranchers came to expect profits of 25 to 40 percent a year. Millions of dollars

Clara Williamson painted this herd on the long drive north from Texas. Cowboys normally worked in pairs, opposite each other, as shown here; the chuck wagon can be seen at the rear of the train. So strenuous was the work that each cowboy brought with him about eight horses so that fresh mounts would be always available.

poured into the West from eastern and foreign interests eager to cash in on rocketing cattle prices.

INCREASING EROSION As in most booms, a bust often followed. High profits soon swelled the size of the herds and led to overproduction. Increased competition from cattle producers in Canada and Argentina caused beef prices to fall. And nature imposed its own limits. On the plains, nutritious buffalo and gamma grasses were eaten to the nub, only to be replaced by unpalatable species. When overgrazing combined with drought, as in New Mexico in the 1880s and 1890s, the results could be disastrous. In all these regions, as vegetation changed, erosion increased, further weakening the ecosystem. In 1870, 5 acres of plains land could feed a steer. By the mid-1880s, it took 50 acres.

By the 1890s the open range and the long drives had largely vanished. What prevailed were the larger cattle corporations such as the King Ranch of Texas. Only the large corporations had enough capital to acquire and fence vast grazing lands, hire foremen to manage herds, and pay for feed during winter months. Most cowboys became wage laborers employed by the ranching corporations. Like mining, cattle ranching was turning into a corporate industrial enterprise, succumbing to the eastern pattern of economic concentration and labor specialization.

✓ **REVIEW**

How were mining and cattle-ranching changed into large-scale operations in the decades after the Civil War?

THE FINAL FRONTIER

IN THE 1860S THEY HAD come in a trickle; in the 1870s they came in a torrent—farmers from the East and Midwest, black freedpeople from the rural South, and peasant-born immigrants from Europe. What bound them together was a craving for land. They had read railroad and steamship advertisements and heard stories from friends about millions of free acres west of the 98th meridian. Hardier strands of wheat like the "Turkey Red" from Russia, improved machinery, and new farming methods made it possible to raise crops in what once had been the "Great American Desert." The number of farms in the United States jumped from some 2 million on the eve of the Civil War to almost 6 million in 1900.

A Rush for Land

BOOMERS AND SOONERS The desire for land was so intense that in the spring of 1889 nearly 100,000 people made their way by wagon, horseback, carriage, mule, even on bicycles and on foot to a line near present-day Oklahoma City, in the center of land once

reserved for the Indians. These were "Boomers," gathered for the last great land rush in the Trans-Mississippi West. At noon on April 22, 1889, the Boomers raced across the line to claim some 2 million acres of Indian territory just opened for settlement. Beyond the line lay the "Sooners"—those who had jumped the gun and hidden in gullies and thickets, ready to leap out an instant after noon to claim their stake in prosperity.

Even as the hopefuls lined up in Oklahoma, thousands of other settlers were abandoning their farms to escape mounting debts. The dream of the West as a garden paradise was already being shaken by harsh weather, overproduction, and competition from abroad. Wheat sold for $1.60 a bushel during the Civil War. It fell to 49 cents in the 1890s.

Farming on the Plains

HOMESTEAD ACT Farmers looking to plow the plains faced a daunting task. Under the Homestead Act (1862), government land could be bought for $1.25 an acre or claimed free if a homesteader worked it for 5 years. But the best parcels—near a railroad line, with

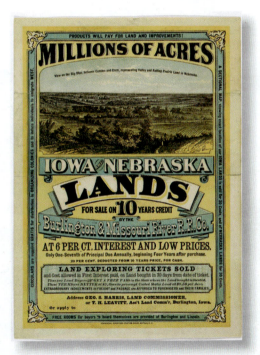

Land advertisements like this one were distributed widely in the East. Sellers promised credit at low interest rates as well as the inducement of "free rooms" for those interested in seeing what they might buy. The land in this ad is being offered by the Burlington and Missouri River Railroad Company. Railroads stood to profit not only from the sale of the land but also from the commodities that homesteaders might raise when they were ready to ship them to market.

access to eastern markets—were owned by the railroads or speculators and sold for much more, around $25 an acre.

Once land was acquired, expenses mounted. Sturdy steel-tipped plows and spring-toothed harrows, which turned over sunbaked prairie soil and left a blanket of dust to reduce evaporation, were needed for **dry farming** in parched climates. Newly developed threshers, combines, and harvesters brought in the crop, and powerful steam tractors pulled the heavy equipment. For such machinery, along with horses, seed, and other farm tools, the average farmer spent $1,200, a small fortune in 1880. (Bigger operators invested 10 or 20 times that total.) If their land abutted a ranch, farmers also had to erect fences to keep cattle from trampling fields. Lacking wood, they found the answer in barbed wire, first marketed by Illinois farmer Joseph Glidden in 1874. Crop yields of wheat increased tenfold as a result of these innovations.

BONANZA FARMS   Tracts of 160 acres granted under the Homestead Act might be enough for eastern farms, but in the drier West more land was needed to produce the same harvest. Farms of more than 1,000 acres, known as "bonanza farms," were most common in the wheat lands of the northern plains. A steam tractor working a bonanza farm could plow, harrow, and seed up to 50 acres a day—20 times more than a single person could do without machinery. Against such competition, small-scale farmers could scarcely survive. Like the southerners, many westerners became tenants on land owned by someone else, often in return for room, board, and 50 cents a day in wages.

A Plains Existence

For poor farm families, life on the plains meant sod houses or dugouts carved from hillsides for protection against the wind. Tough, root-bound sod was cut into bricks a foot wide and three feet long and laid edgewise to create walls. The average house was seldom more than 18 by 24 feet. In severe weather it had to accommodate animals as well as people. The thick walls kept the house warm in winter and cool in summer, but a heavy, soaking rain or snow could bring the roof down or drip mud and water into the living area. Armies of flies, gnats, mosquitoes, and fleas attacked inhabitants as soon as they moved in. Heavy burdens fell to women. With stores and supplies scarce, they spent countless hours over hot tubs preparing tallow wax for candles or soaking ashes and boiling lye with grease and pork rinds to make soap. In

Even out on the plains in sod huts, farmers cherished the culture they could bring from distant places. Here, family members proudly display the pump organ they imported from the East.

The Frontier Kitchen of the Plains

Food. Finding it was a problem for almost everyone in the Trans-Mississippi West. Out on the treeless plains the Indians had adjusted to scarcity by adopting a nomadic way of life. Their small kinship groups moved each season to wherever nature supplied sustenance. Such mobility discouraged families from acquiring many possessions. Tools and housing had to be light and portable. Even tribes that raised crops often moved with the seasons.

Unlike the Indians, farmers, ranchers, and townspeople rooted themselves in a single place. What the surrounding countryside could not supply had to be brought from afar, generally at great effort and expense. For those on the isolated prairie, keeping food on the table was nearly impossible in some seasons. Something as simple as finding water suitable for drinking or cooking became a problem in the West, where the choice might be between "the strong alkaline water of the Rio Grande or the purchase of melted manufactured ice (shipped by rail) at its great cost."

Gardening, generally a woman's responsibility, brought variety to the diet and color to the yard. The legume family of peas and beans, in particular, provided needed protein. Flowers were much prized but seldom survived the wind, heat, and droughts. To prepare for the lean winter months, women stocked their cellars and made wild fruits into leathery cakes eaten to ward off the scurvy that resulted from vitamin deficiency.

Until rail lines made the shipment of goods cheaper and until Sears, Roebuck "wishbooks" brought mail order to the frontier, a woman's kitchen was modest. One miner's wife in Montana during the 1870s considered her kitchen "well-furnished" with two kettles, a cast-iron skillet, and a coffee-pot. A kitchen cupboard might be little more than a box nailed to a log.

Without doctors, women learned how to take care of themselves. Whiskey and patent medicines were often more dangerous than the disease, but they were used to treat a range of ills from frostbite to snakebite and from sore throats to burns and rheumatism. Cobwebs could bandage small wounds; turpentine served as a disinfectant. Mosquitoes were repelled with a paste of vinegar and salt. Most parents thought the laxative castor oil could cure almost any childhood malady. Some women adapted remedies used on their farm animals. Sarah Olds, a Nevada homesteader whose family was plagued by fleas and lice, recalled that "we all took baths with plenty of sheep dip in the water. . . . I had no disinfectant . . . so I boiled all our clothing in sheep dip and kerosene."

Gradually, as the market system penetrated the West, families improvised less in diet and medicine. Through catalogs they could order spices as rare as white pepper and appliances such as grinders for real coffee. If a local stagecoach passed by the house, a woman might send her eggs and butter to town to be exchanged for store-bought goods such as thread and needles.

Like southern women, women in the West played an essential role in the family economy, not least by raising livestock with which to supply their "frontier kitchens." There was time for fun, too: this woman has found a rather remarkable way to feed her cat from the same source as she fed her family.

Thinking Critically

How did the environment of the West shape the experiences of women living there?

the early years of settlement, wool was in such short supply that resourceful women used hair from wolves and other wild animals to make cloth. Buttons had to be fashioned from old wooden spoons.

Nature added its hardships. In summer, searing winds blasted the plains for weeks. Grasses grew so dry that a single spark could ignite wildfires that engulfed thousands of acres. From Missouri to Oregon nothing spelled disaster like locusts. They descended without warning in swarms 100 miles long. Beating against houses like hailstones, they stripped all vegetation, including the bark of trees. Winter held special horrors. Blizzards swept the plains, piling snow to the rooftops and halting all travel. Settlers might awaken to find their food frozen and snow

on their beds. Weeks would pass before farm families saw an outsider.

THE COMFORT OF RELIGION
In the face of such hardships many westerners found comfort in religion. Indians turned to traditional spiritualism and Hispanics to the Catholic Church to cope with nature and hardship. Though Catholics and Jews came west, evangelical Protestants dominated the Anglo frontier in the mining towns and in other western communities. Worship offered an emotional outlet and intellectual stimulation as well as a means of preserving old values and sustaining hope. In the West, as in the rural South, circuit riders compensated for the shortage of preachers, while large-scale camp meetings offered the chance to socialize. Both

brought contact with a world beyond the prairie. In many communities it was the churches that first instilled order on public life, addressing problems such as the need for schools or charity for the poor.

The Urban Frontier

Not all westerners lived in isolation. By 1890 the percentage of those in cities of 10,000 or more was greater than in any other section of the country except the Northeast. Unruly, chaotic, and unplanned, western cities were usually the products of history, geography, technology, and commerce.

Some western cities—San Antonio, El Paso, and Los Angeles—were old Spanish towns whose growth had been sparked by Anglo migrants, Mexican immigrants, and the spread of railroad lines. Other cities profited from their location near commercial routes, such as Portland near the Columbia River in western Oregon. Still others, such as Wichita, Kansas, arose to serve the cattle and mining booms. As technology freed people from the need to produce their own food and clothing, westerners turned to the business of supplying goods and services, enterprises that required the labor of more-densely populated cities.

Most newer cities had wide streets and large blocks. Whereas the streets of eastern cities measured 30 to 60 feet across, street widths of 80 feet or more were common in the West, where thoroughfares had to be broad enough to allow ox-drawn wagons to turn. The dimensions also reflected the big plans of promoters for the future. "Every town in the West," marveled one European, "is laid out on a plan as vast as though it were destined, at no distant future, to contain a million of inhabitants."

DENVER   Denver, Colorado, was typical. Founded in 1859, Denver flourished with the discovery of gold at the mouth of Cherry Creek. The town catered largely to miners with a mix of supply stores, saloons, gambling parlors, and brothels. As it grew, so did its reputation for violence. "A man's life is of no more worth than a dog's," complained one disgusted visitor. Until the early 1860s, when the city hired its first police force, vigilante committees kept the peace with "the rope and the revolver."

In the 1870s Denver embarked on a new phase of growth. The completion of the Denver Pacific and Kansas Pacific Railroads made it the leading city on the eastern slope of the Rocky Mountains. Its economy diversified, and its population soared from about 5,000 in 1870 to more than 100,000 by 1890, when its population ranked behind only Los Angeles and Omaha among western cities.

Development was so rapid that Denver struggled to keep up with itself. By 1900 the city contained over 130,000 residents and 800 miles of streets, but only 24 miles of them were paved. A British observer marveled at "how [Denver's] future vast proportions seem to exist already in the minds of its projectors." So, too, with the rest of the urban West, where human imagination began to transform the natural landscape into man-made metropolises.

 ## The West and the World Economy

The ceaseless search for resources led all manner of people—and their money—west, including foreign investors. As raw materials flowed out of the region, capital flowed in, mostly from the East and from Europe.

Foreign investments varied from industry to industry but generally came in two forms: direct stock purchases and loans to western corporations and individuals. The great open-range cattle boom of the 1870s and 1880s brought an estimated $45 million into the western livestock industry from Great Britain alone. The Scottish-owned Prairie Cattle Company snapped up nearly 8,000 square miles of western cattle land in three huge tracts. By 1887 Congress had become so alarmed at foreign ownership that it enacted the Alien Land Law, which prohibited the purchase of any land in western territories by foreign corporations or by individuals who did not intend to become citizens. Capital-hungry westerners ignored it.

Like southerners, westerners rarely consumed what they took from the ground. In most instances, they located the resources, extracted them, and sent them outside the region to be turned into finished products. Only when manufactured goods returned to the West did westerners finally consume them, not simply as westerners but as part of a worldwide network of production and trade. Between 1865 and 1915, world population increased by more than 50 percent, and demand mushroomed. Better and cheaper transportation allowed westerners to supply raw materials and agricultural goods to places they knew only as exotic names on a map.

Global reach came at a cost. Decisions made elsewhere—in London and Paris, in Tokyo and Buenos Aires—now determined what westerners charged and how much they made. A bumper crop in Europe could drive down grain prices so sharply that debt-ridden farmers lost their land. And the effect in Europe was just as devastating, squeezing peasant farmers out and sending many of them to the Great Plains, where they increased the rivalry for land and profits.

No one linked the West to the wider world and shaped perceptions of the region more than William F. ("Buffalo Bill") Cody. Already a well-known scout for the frontier army and a buffalo hunter for hungry railroad crews, Cody garnered added fame when Edward Judson, writing under the pen name "Ned Buntline," published a series of novels in the 1870s based loosely on Cody's life. In them the dashing Buffalo Bill fought desperadoes and Indians, saved distressed damsels, and brought order to the wild frontier. He became an icon of a mythic West: where opportunity was

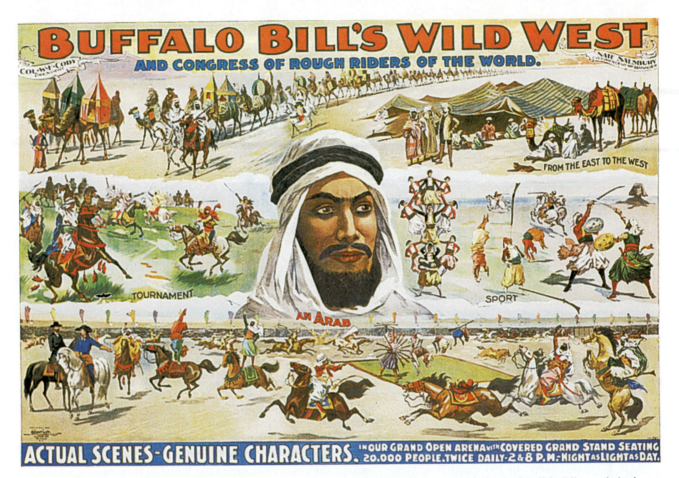

By the 1880s, when Cody created the show, Americans were already longing for the "vanishing frontier." Buffalo Bill provided it for them, complete with mythical stereotypes that reinforced the image of a savage land in need of taming but also as an Eden of boundless opportunity and adventure. The reach of such fantasies was truly global, and cultural exchange flowed in both directions, as the poster for the grand opening of the Wild West's new amphitheater suggests. Note the Arabs and cowboys on horseback and exotic camels. Note, too, the use of new technology—electric spotlighting—which allowed for a second, evening show by making "night as light as day."

there for the taking, where good always triumphed over evil, where all Indians hunted bison and lived in tepees, and where romance and adventure obscured the realities of Anglo conquest, unchecked exploitation, and growing corporate control.

BUFFALO BILL CODY'S WILD WEST SHOW

Trading on his fame and a flair for showmanship, Cody packaged the West in 1883, when he created the "Wild West, Rocky Mountain, and Prairie Exhibition" and took it on tour. Rope-twirling, gun-slinging cowboys, savage-looking Indians, and Annie Oakley, as celebrated for her beauty as for her pinpoint aim, entertained audiences as large as 40,000 or more in giant, open-air theaters. They re-enacted famous frontier events, including Custer's Last Stand, and performed daring feats of marksmanship, horseback riding, and calf-roping. Cody even hired Sitting Bull, the most famous Indian in America, to stare glumly at gawking ticket holders.

Marginalized as a people, Indians were now typecast and commercialized as a commodity and packaged along with other stereotypes of the American West, including the sturdy, brave cowboy of legend. Yet the show also broke stereotypes that spoke to Cody's own reformist impulses—for women's rights in the graceful, gun-toting Annie Oakley and for the preservation of Indian life in its remnant representatives whooping and galloping across the arena.

The popularity of Buffalo Bill's Wild West show soon extended overseas. Cody's troupe, animals and all, circled the globe by steamship, train, and wagon. The photograph on page 492 shows them embarking for London from New York in 1887, but they played to audiences as far away as Outer Mongolia. Queen Victoria saw them twice. For many Europeans the "Wild West" of Buffalo Bill Cody was America.

The South and the West in Sum

Examining the periodic population count taken in 1890, the superintendent of the census noted that landed settlements stretched so far that "there can hardly be said to be a frontier line." He might have added that in the process, the territories that had composed it were vanishing. One

This photograph of Buffalo Bill Cody (standing in front with his hand resting on a rope) and the cast of his Wild West was taken on a cross-Atlantic voyage to England in 1887. The troupe played to audiences as far away as Outer Mongolia.

after another, they were becoming states: Nebraska in 1867; Colorado in 1876; North Dakota, South Dakota, Montana, and Washington in 1889; Wyoming in 1890; Utah in 1896; Oklahoma in 1907; and New Mexico and Arizona in 1912. A new West was emerging as a mosaic of ethnicities, races, cultures, and climates, but with the shared identity of a single region.

That sense of a regional identity was heightened for both westerners and southerners because so many of them felt isolated from the mainstream of industrial America. Ironically, it was not their isolation from northern industry but their links to it that marginalized them. The campaign for a New South to out-Yankee the industrial Yankee could not overcome the low wages and high fertility rates of an older South. The promoters of the West had greater success in adapting large-scale industry and investment to mining, cattle ranching, and farming. Still, they, too, confronted the limits of their region, whose resources were not endless and whose rainfall did not follow the plow. Like easterners, westerners found that large corporations with near-monopoly control over markets and transportation bred inequality, corrupt politics, and resentment.

✓ **REVIEW**

What problems did the environment of the West present for farmers and ranchers?

CONCLUSION

THE WORLD AT LARGE

In the end, it was not simply the disappearance of the American "frontier" within the United States that was at work. Across the globe boundaries between peoples were being breached as the industrialized world scrambled for colonies rich in natural resources and potential for markets. Miners combed the hills of California for gold in 1849, as they did two years later in Victoria, Australia. In South Africa the rush was for diamonds discovered along the Vaal and Orange Rivers and gold near present-day Johannesburg.

In Canada, Argentina, Australia, and New Zealand, farmers and cattle ranchers moved steadily toward establishing the larger commercial farms seen in the American West.

In cities and on farms, deep in mineshafts, and atop towering forests, southerners and westerners were thus being linked to the world economy. Cotton picked by sharecroppers in the Mississippi delta might end up in the petticoats of royalty. Longhorn cattle that grazed on the prairies of Texas fed the cities of Europe. Timber from the piney woods of Georgia or the redwood forests of the Pacific Northwest could find its way into the coffins of Mexico City's dead or the hulls of British schooners.

Racialism—the era's widely accepted practice of categorizing people according to race—justified exploitation elsewhere in the world just as it was used to thwart southern black sharecroppers or Indians driven from their land by prospectors, cowhands, and sodbusters. Coolie laborers died by the thousands in India clearing jungles for tea plantations owned by British firms, while black miners labored in South Africa for Dutch diamond companies and Chinese workers in Australia for European investors, only to be excluded from mainstream society wherever they worked.

The small cotton growers in India, Egypt, and Brazil who faced plummeting prices were just as baffled by market economics as cotton farmers in the American South who found themselves deep in debt to merchants. One British official, traveling into a remote corner of India, reported that cotton growers there found "some difficulty in realizing . . . that, by means of the Electric Telegraph, the throbbings of the pulse of the Home markets communicate themselves instantly to Hingunghat and other trade centres throughout the country." Throughout the world, he might have added. Indeed, it was the "pulse of Home markets" worldwide that controlled the fortunes of those in the cotton fields of both India and the United States. A global industrial system increasingly determined interest rates, prices, and wages in ways that affected ordinary folk everywhere. ∞∞∞∞

CHAPTER SUMMARY

IN THE YEARS AFTER THE Civil War, both the South and the West became more closely linked to the industrial Northeast.

■ Despite differences in geography and history, the South and the West shared many features.

  • Both became sources of agricultural goods and raw materials that fed urban and industrial growth.

  • Both were racially divided societies in which whites often used violence to assert their dominance.

  • Both looked beyond their regions for the human and financial resources needed to boost their economies.

  • Southerners embraced the philosophy of the "New South" that industrialization would bring prosperity.

■ The South nonetheless remained wedded to agriculture, especially cotton, and to a system of labor that exploited poor whites and blacks.

  • Important in the South were the *crop-lien system,* which shackled poor southerners to the land through debt, and *Jim Crow segregation,* which kept blacks and whites apart.

■ White westerners, too, exploited people of other races and ethnicities through settlement, conquest, and capture.

  • By 1890 the emergence of the Ghost Dance and the closing of the frontier signaled that Indians must adapt to life within the boundaries set by white culture despite their efforts at resistance.

  • Latinos were increasingly subjected to similar exploitation but resisted and adapted more effectively to the intrusions of white culture and market economy.

  • In a pattern that became typical for western mining, ranching, and agriculture, small operators first grabbed quick profits and then were followed by large corporations that increased both the scale and the wealth of these industries.

ADDITIONAL READING

THE THEMES OF CHANGE AND continuity have characterized interpretations of southern history after Reconstruction. C. Vann Woodward's classic *The Origins of the New South* (1951) dominated thinking about the region. Edward Ayers, *The Promise of the New South* (1992), offers a comprehensive synthesis that sees both change and continuity. Ted Ownby, *Subduing Satan* (1990), provides a valuable discussion of southern social life, especially the role of religion. On race relations see Joel Williamson, *The Crucible of Race: Black-White Relations in the South since Emancipation* (1984) and on black migrations west, Nell Irvin Painter, *Exodusters: Black Migration to Kansas after Reconstruction* (1976).

The contours of western history were first mapped by Frederick Jackson Turner in his famous address "The Significance of the Frontier in American History" (1893) but have been substantially reshaped by Richard White, *"It's Your Own Misfortune and None of My Own": A New History of the American West* (1992); Patricia Limerick, *A Legacy of Conquest: The Unbroken Past of the*

American West (1987); and Gregory Nobles, *American Frontier: Cultural Encounter and Continental Conquest* (1997). Each describes the history of the West less as a saga of triumphs than as an analysis of how the region and its resources have been exploited by various peoples and cultures. White adds to his critique of western development in *Railroaded: The Transcontinentals and the Making of Modern* America (2011). For a well-written and superbly researched study of the Great Plains as a contested zone among environment, animals, and people, see Elliott West's *The Contested Plains: Indians, Goldseekers, and the Rush to Colorado* (1998). Studies of the environment are growing. Among the best are Shepherd Krech III, *The Ecological Indian: Myth and History* (1999); Karl Jacoby, *Crimes against Nature: Squatters, Poachers, Thieves and the Hidden History of American Conservation* (2001); and Dan T. Flores, *The Natural West: Environmental History in the Great Plains and Rocky Mountains* (2001). Donald Worster, *A River Running West: The Life of John Wesley Powell* (2002), chronicles that naturalist's feats. Sarah Deutsch, *No Separate Refuge: Culture, Class, and Gender on an Anglo-Hispanic Frontier in the American Southwest, 1880–1940* (1987), develops the concept of regional community in New Mexico and Colorado. Robert M. Utley expertly surveys *The Indian Frontier of the American West, 1846–1890* (1984). For the West's ethno-racial identities, see Neil Foley, *White Scourge: Mexicans, Blacks, and Poor Whites in Texas Cotton Culture* (1997); and for the African American experience, see Quintard Taylor, *In Search of the Racial Frontier: African Americans in the American West, 1528–1990* (1998).

For a fuller list of readings, see the Bibliography at www.mhhe.com/eh8e.

SIGNIFICANT EVENTS

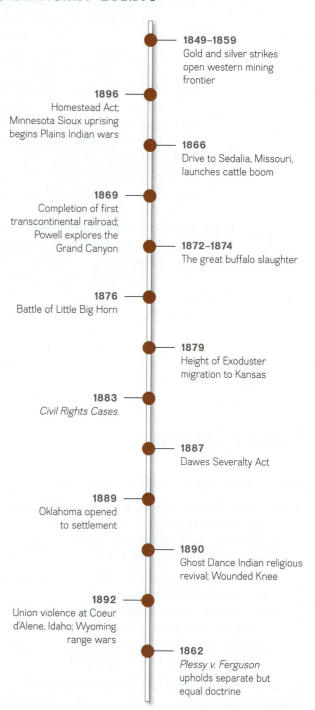

1849–1859
Gold and silver strikes open western mining frontier

1896
Homestead Act; Minnesota Sioux uprising begins Plains Indian wars

1866
Drive to Sedalia, Missouri, launches cattle boom

1869
Completion of first transcontinental railroad; Powell explores the Grand Canyon

1872–1874
The great buffalo slaughter

1876
Battle of Little Big Horn

1879
Height of Exoduster migration to Kansas

1883
Civil Rights Cases

1887
Dawes Severalty Act

1889
Oklahoma opened to settlement

1890
Ghost Dance Indian religious revival; Wounded Knee

1892
Union violence at Coeur d'Alene, Idaho; Wyoming range wars

1862
Plessy v. Ferguson upholds separate but equal doctrine

WAR/BATTLE	DATE	DESCRIPTION
Sioux Wars	1854–1890	Under Crazy Horse and Sitting Bull, Sioux resist whites streaming into their hunting grounds in Minnesota, South Dakota, and Wyoming.
Apache Attacks	1861	Led by Geronimo and Cochise, bands of Apaches escape reservations and begin to attack white outposts in New Mexico, Arizona, and Texas.
Santee Uprising	1862	Clashes between whites and Santee Sioux in southwestern Minnesota; 38 Indians are hanged in the largest-scale execution in U.S. history.
Battle of Canyon de Chelly	1864	Final battle between the Navajo and U.S. forces under Kit Carson. Survivors forced on "Long Walk" 400 miles from Arizona to Fort Sumner, New Mexico.
Sand Creek	1864	At Sand Creek, Colorado, white militia slaughter some 160 Cheyenne Indians.
Fort Kearny	1866	Near Fort Kearny, Wyoming, Cheyenne and Sioux kill Captain William J. Fetterman and his 80 men.
Modoc War	1872–1873	In the only Indian war in California, Captain Jack and 60 Modoc followers flee reservation to Tule Lake, where they fight until 1873.
Red River Wars	1874–1875	In northwestern Texas, General William T. Sherman leads an army force against the Arapaho, Cheyenne, Comanche, and Kiowa; final defeat of Plains Indians.
Battle of Little Big Horn	1876	Under Sitting Bull and Crazy Horse, Cheyenne and Sioux crush Custer's Seventh Cavalry.
Nez Percé War	1877	In Oregon, Chief Joseph and the Nez Percé resist white encroachment and then flee into Montana, surrendering 40 miles short of the Canadian border.
Battle of Skeleton Canyon	1886	Geronimo surrenders in southeastern Arizona, ending Apache Wars.
Wounded Knee	1890	At Wounded Knee, South Dakota, cavalry killed some 300 Lakota Sioux in what is regarded as the last engagement of U.S. soldiers and American Indians.

Southern Mail Route" east some 850 miles to Washington. Things had gone badly from the start. About 50 miles outside of town, a broken river bridge forced him to take a ferry, then a mule-drawn truck before learning that the rail line did not resume for another 40 miles. Disheartened, he returned to Memphis to try again.

The train to Memphis arrived six hours late, dawdled its way home, and then, barely three miles from the city, derailed in the middle of the night. When a few passengers decided to hike the remaining distance into town, Ferguson tagged along. It was then that he fell between the tracks onto a flimsy river bridge. Before he finally reached Washington, the Scot faced six more days of difficult travel. One line ended, and passengers and freight would be forced onto another because rail gauges—the width of the track—differed from line to line. Or a bridge was out, or there was no bridge at all. Trains had no meals "on board" or any sleeping cars. "It was certainly what the Americans would call 'hard travelling,'" Ferguson huffed.

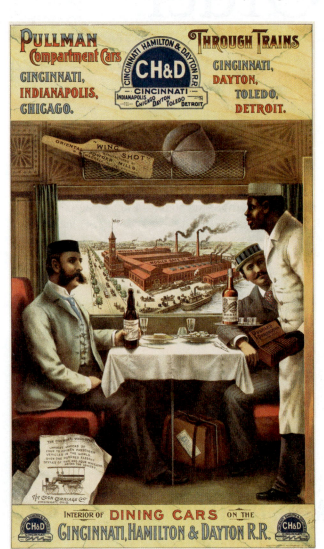

The Pullman "Palace" fantasy

Cross-country travel proved so rough that it inspired fantasy. In 1859, the *Southern Literary Messenger* carried the first of several installments of a futuristic "science romance" describing Miss Jane Delaware Peyton's trip to Washington, D.C., from Rasselas, Oregon, in 2029. Elegant trains whisked her across the country in only eight days at the "immense velocity" of 60 miles an hour. Like all train riders, Miss Peyton had to guard against "Tourbilliere," a common mental disorder of the future. After 10 hours on a speeding train, passengers found perception accelerating but memory lapsing. "The mind loses an idea almost as soon as it has been formed," Miss Peyton reported. The only cure was to stop and let the mind catch up to its changing surroundings. So every few days Miss Peyton and her fellow travelers sat quietly at a train station until their symptoms subsided. Such persons were said to be "waiting for their brains."

By the 1880s some of our writer's fantasies had come true, as British tourist T. S. Hudson discovered in 1882 when he launched a self-proclaimed "Scamper through America." Hudson did not cross the continent in quite 8 days, but it took him just 60 to go from England to San Francisco and back. He rode in Pullman "Palace" cars with luxury sleeping quarters and a full breakfast. Newly installed air brakes made trains safer and their stops smoother. Bridges appeared where none had been before, including a "magnificent" span over the Mississippi at St. Louis. Hudson also found himself in the midst of a communications revolution. Traveling across the plains he was struck by the number of telephone poles along the route.

What made America in the 1880s so different from just a few decades earlier was not the speed and comfort of travel or the wonders of new technologies. The true marvel was the emerging industrial order that underlay those technologies. Because this order was essentially in place by the beginning of the twentieth century, we tend to take its existence for granted. Yet its growth was at first slow and haphazard and required innovations in many different areas of society. The transformation brought pain along with progress. The demand for natural resources led to virgin forests being cut down and open-pit mines spewing hazardous runoffs. Factory-lined rivers of the Northeast were left toxic with industrial wastes. In 1882, the year Hudson scampered by rail across America, an average of 675 people were killed on the job every week. Like most people, workers scrambled—sometimes literally—to adjust. Few Americans anywhere had time to "wait for their brains" to catch up to the dizzying pace of change. ∞∞∞

The Development of Industrial Systems

THE PROCESS OF INDUSTRIALIZATION BEGAN in the United States at least three decades before the Civil War, with small factories producing light consumer goods such as clothing, shoes, and furniture. Much of the economy remained local. Only after the 1850s did the industrial economy develop a set of interlocking systems that allowed larger factories, using more and bigger machines, to produce goods with greater efficiency and market them on a national and international scale in a new industrial order of unprecedented scope.

The new order can best be understood as a web of complex industrial systems woven together in the second half of the nineteenth century. By "industrial system," historians mean a set of arrangements or processes—whether of extraction, production, transportation, distribution, or finance—organized to make the whole industrial order function smoothly. Look, for example, at the industrial systems required to build the bridge across the Mississippi that T. S. Hudson so admired. When James B. Eads constructed its soaring arches in 1874, he needed steel, probably from iron ore mined in northern Michigan. Giant steam shovels scooped up the ore and loaded whole freight cars in a few strokes. A transportation system—railroads, boats, and other carriers—moved the ore to Pittsburgh, where factories furnish the labor and machinery to finish the steel. The capital to create such factories came from a system of finance that linked investment banks and stock markets to entrepreneurs in need of money. Only with a national network of industrial systems could the Eads bridge be built and a new age of industry dawn.

Natural Resources and Industrial Technology

The earliest European settlers marveled at the "merchantable commodities" of America, from the glittering silver mines of the Spanish Empire to the continent's hardwood forests. What set the new industrial economy apart from that older America was the scale and efficiency of using such natural resources. New technologies made it possible to exploit them in ways undreamed of only decades earlier.

BESSEMER PROCESS — Steel, for example, had been made from iron and carbon alloyed with other metals and forged into swords as far back as the Middle Ages. In the 1850s inventors in England and America discovered a cheaper way—called the Bessemer process after its British developer—to convert large quantities of iron into stronger, more durable steel. By the late 1870s the price of steel had dropped by more than half. Steel tracks soon carried most rail traffic; steel girders replaced old cast-iron building frames; steel cables supported new suspension bridges.

PETROLEUM INDUSTRY — Industrial technology made some natural resources more valuable. New distilling methods transformed a thick, smelly liquid called petroleum into kerosene for lighting lamps, oil for lubricating machinery, and paraffin for making candles. Beginning in 1859, new drilling techniques began to tap vast pools of petroleum belowground. About the same time, Frenchman Etienne Lenoir constructed the first practical internal combustion engine. After 1900 new vehicles, such as the gasoline-powered carriage, turned the oil business into a major industry.

 **ENVIRONMENTAL CONSEQUENCES** — The scale of these operations used vast amounts of resources and produced huge quantities of waste. Coal mining, logging, and the industrial toxins of factories led to

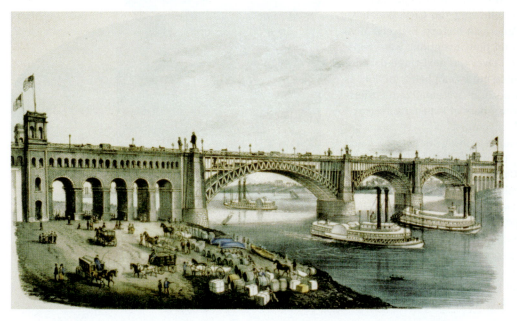

The magnificent steel arches of the Eads Bridge, the engineering marvel that awed T. S. Hudson, spanning the Mississippi River at St. Louis. At 6,442 feet, it was the longest bridge in the world and the first to cross the Mississippi and to carry railroad tracks. Its elegant steel arches also supported a roadway and two foot paths. The whole structure is supported by limestone piers sunk deeply into the bedrock of the river. The bridge took more than 7 years to build, cost over $10 million, and opened amid great fanfare on July 4, 1874. The steel came from the mills of Andrew Carnegie.

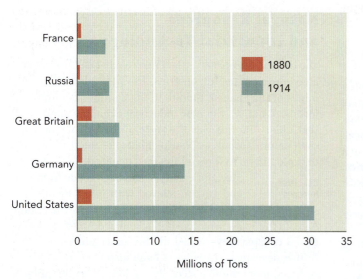

Steel Production, 1880 and 1914

While steel production jumped in Western industrial nations from 1880 to 1914, it skyrocketed in the United States because of rich resources, cheap labor, and aggressive management.

the most obvious forms of environmental degradation—scarred land, vanishing forests, contaminated waters. As giant water cannons blasted away hillsides in search of gold in California, rock and gravel washed into rivers, raising their beds and threatening populations downstream with floods. Some industrialists limited pollution, often to turn a profit as much as to protect the environment. Chicago meat packers used every conceivable part of the animals that came into their plants. Straight-length bones were turned into cutlery, hoofs and feet into glue and oil, fat into oleomargarine.

Systematic Invention

Industrial technology rested on invention. For sheer inventiveness, the 40 years following the Civil War have rarely been matched in American history. Between 1790 and 1860, 36,000 **patents** on new inventions were registered with the government. Over the next three decades the U.S. Patent Office granted more than half a million, as the process of invention became systematized. Orderly "invention factories"—forerunners of expensive research labs—replaced small-scale inventors.

EDISON'S CONTRIBUTIONS No one did more to bring system, order, and profitability to invention than Thomas Alva Edison. In 1868, at the age of 21, Edison went to work for a New York brokerage house and promptly improved the design of the company's stock tickers. A $40,000 bonus (worth perhaps $400,000 in current dollars) allowed him to become an independent inventor. For the next five years, Edison patented a new invention almost every five months.

Edison was determined to bring system and order to the process of invention. Only then could breakthroughs come in a steady and profitable stream. He moved 15 of his workers to Menlo Park, New Jersey, where in 1876 he created perhaps his greatest invention—an "invention factory." Like a manufacturer, Edison subdivided the work among gifted inventors, engineers, toolmakers, and others.

THE SPREAD OF AN ELECTRICAL POWER SYSTEM This orderly bureaucracy soon evolved into the Edison Electric Light Company. Its ambitious owner aimed at more than perfecting his new electric lightbulb. Edison wanted to create a unified electrical power system—central stations to generate electric current, wired to users, all powering millions of small bulbs in homes and businesses. To launch his enterprise, Edison won the backing of several large banking houses by lighting up the Wall Street district in 1882. It was like "writing by daylight," recorded one reporter. Soon Edison power plants sprang up in major cities across the country.

Electricity was more flexible than earlier sources of energy. Factories no longer had to be built near rivers and falls to make use of water power. Before the end of the century, electricity was running automatic looms, trolley cars, subways, and factory machinery. Electricity not only revolutionized industry; it also worked in

| *Thomas Edison, unkempt and wrinkled, in his research lab*

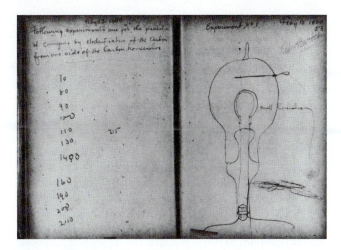

Edison's Notebook

This page from one of Thomas Edison's notebooks shows sketches of and notes on some of his early experiments with an incandescent lamp—what we know as an electric lightbulb. Edison was not only the most celebrated inventor of his day but by the early twentieth century also one of the greatest popular heroes in American life in a time when scientific and technological progress was considered the defining feature of the age.

the homes of ordinary citizens. The electric motor, developed commercially by George Westinghouse and Nikola Tesla in 1886, powered everything from sewing machines to Edison's "gramophone," later known as the record player.

George Eastman revolutionized photography by making the consumer a part of his inventive system. In the process, he democratized picture taking, once the province of the skilled professional, by inventing a camera that anyone could use at a price ($25) many could afford. In 1888 Eastman marketed the "Kodak" camera. The small black box weighed just over 2 pounds and contained a strip of celluloid film that replaced hundreds of pounds of photography equipment. After 100 snaps of the shutter, the owner simply sent the camera back to Eastman's Rochester factory, along with a $10 fee, then waited for the developed photos and a reloaded camera to return by mail. "You press the button—we do the rest" was Eastman Kodak's apt slogan. So successful was Eastman that competitors launched legal wars for control of his patents. In a pattern that has held ever since, other inventors faced similar court battles.

Transportation and Communication

THE PROBLEM OF SCALE
Abundant resources and new inventions remained worthless to industry until they could be moved to processing plants, factories, and offices. But distance was daunting. Where 100 miles of railroad track would do for shipping goods in Germany and England, 1,000 miles was necessary in America.

Nonetheless, by 1870 an efficient transportation system created an integrated national market and tied the United States into an emerging international economy. By the 1870s railroads crisscrossed the country, and steam-powered ships (introduced before the Civil War) were pushing barges down rivers and carrying passengers and freight across the oceans. The time of transatlantic travel was cut in half, to about 10 days. Eventually the rail and water transportation systems fused. By 1900 railroad companies owned nearly all the country's domestic steamship lines.

TELEGRAPH
A thriving industrial nation also required effective communication. Information was a precious commodity, as essential to industry as were resources or technology. In the early 1840s, it took newspapers as many as 10 days to reach Indiana from New York and 3 months to arrive by ship in San Francisco. In 1844 Samuel Morse succeeded in sending the first message over an electrical wire between cities. By 1861 the Western Union Company had strung 76,000 miles of telegraph lines across the country. If a bank collapsed in Chicago, bankers in Dallas knew of it that day. Railroads could keep traffic unsnarled through the dots and dashes of Morse's code. By the turn of the century a million miles of telegraph wire handled 63 million messages annually, not to mention those flashing across underwater cables to China, Japan, Africa, and South America.

TELEPHONE
A second innovation in communication, the telephone, vastly improved on the telegraph. Alexander Graham Bell, a Scottish immigrant, was teaching the deaf when he began experimenting with ways to transmit speech electrically. In 1876 he transmitted his famous first words to a young assistant: "Mr. Watson, come here! I want you." No longer did messages require a telegraph office, the unwieldy Morse code, and couriers to deliver them.

President Rutherford B. Hayes installed the first telephone in the White House in 1878, when the instrument was still a curiosity. The same year, the city of New Haven, Connecticut, opened the first telephone exchange in America. By 1900 there were 1.5 million of Bell's machines in America. The telephone patent proved to be the most valuable ever granted. In the scramble for profits, the Bell Telephone Company battled challenges from competitors and suits from rivals who claimed that their contributions were worth a share of the rights.

Along with other innovations in communication (see Daily Lives, "The Rise of Information Systems" on page 507), telephones modernized offices and eased business transactions. In 1915 the American Telephone and Telegraph Company opened the first transcontinental line. When commercial rates dropped after the turn of the century, the telephone became part of a social revolution. Like the railroad and the telegraph, it compressed distances and reduced differences across the country, tying the nation together through another network of communication.

A young Alexander Graham Bell with an early version of his "speaking telegraph."

Telegraph key

Finance Capital

As industry grew so did the demand for investment capital—the money spent on land, buildings, and machinery. The scale of industry required more funds than ever. Between 1870 and 1900 the number of workers in an average iron and steel firm grew from 100 to 400, and the capital invested jumped to nearly $1 million, about seven times what it had been in 1870.

SOURCES OF CAPITAL   Where did the money come from? For the first three-quarters of the nineteenth century, investment capital came mostly from the savings of firms. In the second half of the century, "capital deepening"—a process essential for industrialization—took place. Simply put, as national wealth increased, people began to save and invest more of their money, which meant that more funds could be loaned out.

Savings and investment grew more attractive with the development of a complex network of financial institutions. Commercial and savings banks, investment houses, and insurance companies gave savers new opportunities to channel money to industry. The New York Stock Exchange, in existence since 1792, linked eager investors with money-hungry firms. By the end of the nineteenth century, the stock market had established itself as the basic means of making capital available to industry.

The Corporation

For those business leaders with the skill to knit the industrial pieces together, large profits awaited. This was the era of the "robber barons," entrepreneurs who bullied their way to success at the expense of competitors and employees. To be sure, sheer ruthlessness went a long way in the fortune-building game. "Law? Who cares about law!" railroad magnate Cornelius Vanderbilt once boasted. "Hain't I got the power?"

To survive in the long term, business leaders could not depend on ruthlessness alone. They also needed ingenuity, an eye for detail, and the gift of foresight. The growing scale of enterprise and capital led them to adapt an old device, the corporation, to the new industrial order. Corporations had existed since colonial times, when governments granted charters of incorporation to organizations that ran facilities for public use such as turnpikes, canals, and banks. After the Civil War the modern corporation came into use for raising money and protecting business holdings.

ADVANTAGES OF THE CORPORATION   Colonial governments limited grants of incorporation only to those companies operating in the public interest, such as banks and canal companies, because of the many advantages corporations enjoyed over traditional forms of ownership: the single owner and the partnership. A corporation could raise large sums quickly by selling "stock certificates," or shares in its business. It could also outlive its owners or stockholders, requiring no legal reorganization if one of them died. It limited liability by relieving owners of personal responsibility for business debts. And it separated owners from day-to-day management of the company. A growing corps of highly skilled professional managers could now operate complex businesses. So clear were these advantages that before the turn of the century, corporations were making two-thirds of all manufactured products in the United States.

An International Pool of Labor

Last, but hardly least important for the new industrial order, was a pool of labor. In the United States the demand for workers far outstripped what native-born citizens could supply. In 1860 it took about 4.3 million workers to run all the factories, mills, and shops in the United States. By 1900 there were approximately 20 million workers in industrial and associated enterprises.

 GLOBAL LABOR NETWORK   In part, the United States relied on a vast global network to fill its need for workers. From the edges of the industrialized world in southern and eastern Europe as well as Latin America, Asia, Africa, and the Middle East, seasonal migrations provided a rich source of workers for many nations, including the United States. Beginning in the 1870s, for example, rural laborers and tenant farmers from the Mezzogiorno in Italy traveled throughout Europe seeking wage work in construction during the building season from

DAILY LIVES

THE RISE OF INFORMATION SYSTEMS

In 1877, a year after its invention, advertisements were already touting Alexander Graham Bell's "speaking telegraph": "Conversation can easily be carried on after slight practice and occasional repetition of a word or sentence. . . . [A]fter a few trials the ear becomes accustomed to the peculiar sound."

It was not so for everyone. Some people reported terrifying "stage fright" that left them speechless. Others had no idea how to greet callers. Bell answered with a chipper "Ahoy!" Operators at the first public telephone exchange used the old-fashioned "What is wanted?" But it was Thomas Edison's melodious "Hello" (derived from "Halloo," the traditional call to bring hounds to the chase) that won out by 1880.

At first Bell's electrical toys could be rented only in pairs by individuals who wanted to connect two places. In 1877 the advantages of such direct communication led to the first intercity hookup, between New York City and Boston. Before the turn of the century the Bell-organized American Telephone and Telegraph Company had combined more than 100 local telephone companies to furnish business and government with long-distance service. When rates dropped after 1900, telephones found their way into ordinary American homes.

The telephone revolutionized communications, cutting time and obliterating distances. It also liberated social relations by freeing people from the nineteenth-century convention of addressing only those to whom they had been properly introduced. And it acted as a great social leveler. Almost overnight, telephone operators (called "hello girls") began connecting people of different locales and classes who might never have spoken to each other at all, let alone as peers.

During the first half of the nineteenth century, information had traveled mostly through the mails. In 1844 Samuel F. B. Morse sent the first intercity message across electrical wires, thereby achieving instantaneous communication. But the telegraph had drawbacks. Instantaneous communication was hardly direct. Messages had to be taken to a telegraph office, where trained clerks could translate them into Morse code, an unwieldy system of dots and dashes. Only then could they be transmitted by electrical impulse. When they arrived at the receiving station, messages were recast into understandable language, then carried by hand to their precise destination.

The need for speed and efficiency in the office led to other breakthroughs. One device that increased business efficiency was the typewriter. C. Latham Sholes, a Milwaukee printer and editor, had been tinkering with an automatic numbering machine when a friend suggested he develop a mechanical letter-writing device. In 1868 he patented the "Type-Writer." By the early twentieth century the typewriter had taken its modern shape—a keyboard with upper- and lowercase letters and a carriage that allowed typists to see the output.

In 1890 Alfred Dick invented the mimeograph to reproduce many copies of a single document cheaply, a communications boon not only to businesses but also to churches, reform organizations, and political groups.

Systems of finance and communications intersected at Wall Street, New York City, where the nation's most important investment banks and markets were located. The Great Blizzard of 1888 buried the district with snow and also shadowed in white the crisscrossing "blizzard" of wires needed for the communications networks.

Thinking Critically

How did new systems of information pioneered in the late nineteenth century foreshadow the information revolution of the late twentieth century?

spring through early fall. Mechanization, poverty, oppression, and ambition pushed many of these rural laborers from farms into industrial cities and soon to other continents once steamships cut cross-Atlantic travel to under a week in the 1880s.

To draw these workers to the United States, industrialists advertised in newspapers, distributed pamphlets, and sent agents fanning out across the globe. Between 1870 and 1890, more than 8 million immigrants arrived in the United States, another 14 million by 1914. Some came from Asia and Latin America, but most came from Europe and settled in industrial cities. Like migratory laborers elsewhere, they hoped to find work, fatten their purses, and go home. According to one estimate, between 25 and 60 percent of all immigrants returned to their homelands from the United States during these years.

In the United States as in other countries, immigrants relied on well-defined migration chains of family and friends to get jobs. A brother might find work with other Slavs in the mines of Pennsylvania; or the daughter of Greek parents, in a New England textile mill filled with relatives. Labor contractors also served as a funnel to industry. Tough and savvy immigrants themselves, they met newcomers at the docks and train stations with contracts to work in local factories, mines, and other industries. For their trouble they took a fee or a slice of the new workers' wages. Among Italians they were known as *padrones;* among Mexicans, as *enganchistas.* By the end of the nineteenth century such contractors controlled two-thirds of the labor in New York City.

Mexicans, too, formed part of this transnational labor pool, streaming across the border especially after the Mexican Revolution in 1910. Even earlier, seasonal migration of Mexican laborers to plant and pick crops from Texas to California was common enough to spawn cross-border family networks. "Come! Come! Come over," a Mexican migrant remembered being told by family friends north of the Rio Grande. Mexican laborers also helped build the transcontinental railroad and, after the turn of the century, moved farther north to tanneries, meatpacking plants, foundries, and rail yards in Chicago, St. Louis, and other centers of industry.

Rural Americans—some 11 million between 1865 and 1920—provided a homegrown source of labor, similar to immigrants in the roots and patterns of their movements. Driven from the farm by machines and bad times or the desire for a new life, most lacked the skills for high-paying jobs. But unlike their foreign counterparts, they spoke English. Many could read and write, and few thought of returning home. In iron and steel cities as well as in coal-mining towns, the better industrial jobs and supervisory positions often went to them. Other rural migrants found work in retail stores or offices and slowly entered the new urban middle class of white-collar workers.

Most African Americans continued to work the fields of the South. About 300,000 moved to northern cities between 1870 and 1910, perhaps more to southern cities. Between 1880 and 1910 the black urban population across the South jumped, more than doubling in industrial cities such as Birmingham. In some instances black migrants were escaping domineering fathers; in

Chicago laborer

others, seeking the excitement of the city; and in still others, following a husband or fleeing the prejudices of the Old South. These migrants, too, relied on family migration chains in their journey, sometimes traveling in groups, sometimes alone. On occasion they brought siblings or spouses and children, often one by one, after they had found work.

Like immigrants and other migrants, African Americans came in search of opportunity, and all faced the burden of continued discrimination when they arrived. Newer industries such as textile manufacturing and railroad shop work refused to hire African Americans, but some businesses, such as Andrew Carnegie's steel mills in Pittsburgh, employed blacks as janitors and wage laborers. Women found jobs as domestic servants and laundresses. Still, by1890 less than 10 percent of black laborers worked in industry.

✓ REVIEW

What factors led to the development of industrial systems?

RAILROADS: AMERICA'S FIRST BIG BUSINESS

THE SYSTEM WAS A MESS: any good railroad executive knew as much. Along the tracks that spanned the country, each town—sometimes each rail station—set its clocks separately by the sun. In 1882, the year T. S. Hudson scampered across America, New York City and Boston were 11 minutes 45 seconds apart. Stations often had several clocks showing the time on different rail lines, along with one displaying "local mean time." In 1883, without consulting anyone, the railroad companies solved the problem by dividing the country into four zones, each an hour apart. Congress did not make the division official until 1918.

At the center of the new industrial systems lay the railroads, moving people and freight, spreading communications, reinventing time, ultimately binding the nation together. Railroads also stimulated economic growth, simply because building them required so many resources—coal, wood, glass, rubber, brass, and by the 1880s 75 percent of all U.S. steel. By lowering transportation costs, railroads allowed manufacturers to reduce prices, attract more buyers, and increase business. Perhaps most important, as America's first truly big business—spanning the country; employing hundreds of thousands; serving millions—railroads created modern management, soon adopted by other industries.

A Managerial Revolution

To the men who ran them, railroads provided a challenge in organization and finance. In the 1850s the Pepperell textile mills of Maine, one of the largest industrial enterprises in America, employed about 800 workers. By the early 1880s

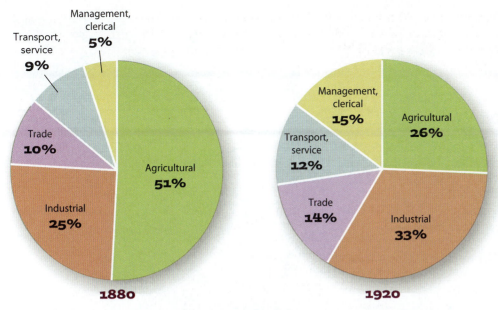

Between 1880 and 1920, management and industrial work—employing white- and blue-collar workers—grew at the expense of farmwork.

1880

Management, clerical **5%**

Transport, service **9%**

Trade **10%**

Industrial **25%**

Agricultural **51%**

1920

Management, clerical **15%**

Transport, service **12%**

Trade **14%**

Industrial **33%**

Agricultural **26%**

the Pennsylvania Railroad had nearly 50,000 people on its payroll. From setting schedules and rates to determining costs and profits, such size required a level of coordination unknown in earlier businesses.

PIONEERING TRUNK LINES The so-called trunk lines pioneered new systems of management. Scores of early companies serviced local networks of cities and communities, often with less than 50 miles of track. During the 1850s longer trunk lines emerged east of the Mississippi to connect the shorter branches, or "feeder" lines. By the outbreak of the Civil War, four great trunk lines linked the Eastern Seaboard with the Great Lakes and western rivers. After the war, trunk lines grew in the South and West.

THE NEW MANAGERS The operations of large lines gave rise to a new managerial elite, beneath owners but with complete authority over daily operations. Cautious by nature they preferred to negotiate and administer rather than compete. In the 1850s Daniel McCallum, superintendent of the New York and Erie Railroad, laid the foundation for this system by drawing up the first table of organization for an American company. A tree trunk with roots represented the president and board of directors; five branches constituted the main operating divisions; leaves stood for the local agents, train crews, and other workers. Information moved up and down the trunk so that managers could get daily reports to and from the separate parts.

By the turn of the century these managerial techniques had spread to other industries. Local superintendents were responsible for daily activities. Central offices served as corporate nerve centers, housing divisions for purchases, production, transportation, sales, and accounting. As a new class of middle managers imposed new order on business operations, executives, managers, and workers operated in increasingly precise and coordinated ways.

Competition and Consolidation

Although managers made operations more systematic, the struggle among railroad companies to dominate the industry was anything but precise and rational. In the 1870s and 1880s the pain of railroad expansion began to tell.

In addition to large start-up costs, railroads were saddled with enormous fixed costs—payrolls, equipment, debts. These remained constant regardless of the volume of traffic. Beginning in the 1860s railroads constructed more lines in hopes of increasing traffic and thereby revenues. Soon the railroads had overbuilt. With so much extra capacity, railroad owners schemed to win new accounts. They gave free passes to favored shippers, promised them free sidings at their plants, offered free land to lure businesses to their territory.

The most savage and costly competition came over the rates charged for shipping goods. Managers lowered rates for freight that was shipped in bulk, on long hauls, or on return routes (since the cars were empty anyway). They used "rebates"—secret discounts to preferred customers—to drop prices below the posted rates of competitors (and then recouped the losses by overcharging small shippers like farmers). When the economy plunged or a weak line sought to improve its position, rate wars broke out. By 1880, 65 lines had declared bankruptcy.

POOLING Cooperation worked better than competition. During the 1870s railroad managers created regional federations to combine traffic, set prices, and divide profits among members. Pooling—informal agreements among competing companies to act together—was designed to remove the competition that led to rate wars. Without the force of law, however, pools failed. Members broke ranks by cutting prices for quick gain. In the end, rate wars died down only when weaker lines failed or stronger ones bought up competitors.

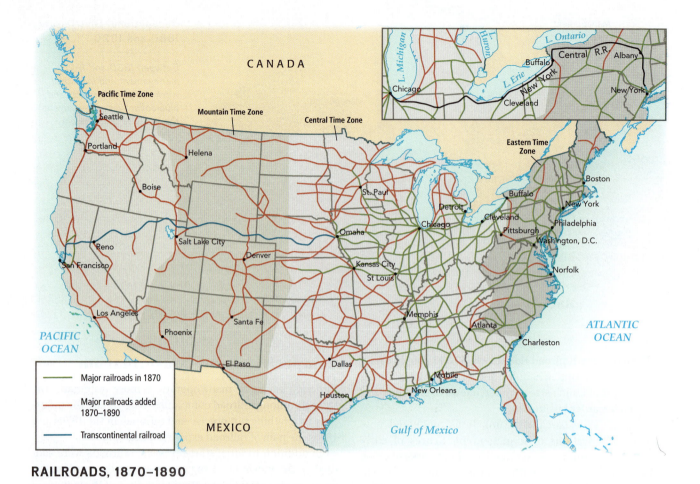

RAILROADS, 1870–1890

Legend:
- Major railroads in 1870
- Major railroads added 1870–1890
- Transcontinental railroad

By 1890 the railroad network stretched from one end of the country to the other, with more miles of track than in all of Europe. New York City and Chicago, linked by the New York Central trunk line, became the new commercial axes. **Beyond the Mississippi River a less dense network of trunk lines snaked their way to the West Coast. Note the cities they serviced along their lines. What role did railroads play in the settlement of the West?**

The Challenge of Finance

Earlier in the nineteenth century many railroads relied on state governments for financial backing. They also looked to counties, cities, and towns for bonds and other forms of aid. People living near the ends of rail lines, who stood to gain from construction, were persuaded to take railroad stock in exchange for land or labor. In the 1850s and 1860s western promoters went to Washington for help and returned with $65 million in loans to six western railroads and some 131 million acres of land.

NEW WAYS OF RAISING MONEY Federal aid helped to build only part of the nation's railroads. Most of the money came from private investors. The New York **Stock Exchange** expanded rapidly as railroad corporations began to trade their stocks and bonds. Large investment banks developed financial networks to track down money at home and abroad. By 1898 a third of the assets of American life insurance companies had gone into railroads, while Europeans owned nearly a third of all American railroad stocks.

Because investment bankers played such large roles in funding railroads, they found themselves advising companies about their business affairs. If a company fell into bankruptcy, bankers sometimes served as the "receivers" who oversaw the property until financial health returned. By absorbing smaller lines into larger ones, eliminating rebates, and stabilizing rates, the bankers helped reduce competition and impose order and centralization. In the process, they often came to control the companies they counseled.

By 1900 the new industrial systems had transformed American railroads. Nearly 200,000 miles of track were in operation, 80 percent of it owned by only six groups of railroads. Time zones coordinated schedules; standardized track made cross-country freighting easier. Soon passengers were traveling 16 billion miles a year. To that traffic could be added farm goods, raw materials, and factory-finished products. Everything moved with a new regularity that allowed businesses to plan and prosper.

✓ **REVIEW**

How did the railroads contribute to the rise of big business?

THE GROWTH OF BIG BUSINESS

IN 1865, 26-YEAR-OLD John D. Rockefeller sat stone-faced in the office of his Cleveland oil refinery, about to conclude the biggest deal of his life. Rockefeller's business was flourishing, but not his partnership with Maurice Clark. The two had fallen out over how quickly to expand. Rockefeller was eager to grow fast; the cautious Clark was not. They dissolved their partnership and agreed to bid for the company. Bidding opened at $500, rocketed to $72,500, and abruptly stopped. "The business is yours," said Clark. The men shook hands and a thin smile crept across Rockefeller's face.

Twenty years later Rockefeller's Standard Oil Company controlled 90 percent of the nation's refining capacity and an oil empire that stretched well beyond Cleveland. Around the clock, trains sped Standard executives to New York, Philadelphia, and other eastern cities. The railroads were a fitting form of transportation for Rockefeller's company; in many ways they were the key to his oil empire. They carried his oil products and discounted his rates, giving him the edge to squeeze out rivals. And they pioneered the business systems on which Rockefeller was building. As we shall see with other American firms, Standard Oil was improving on the practices of the railroads to do bigger and bigger business.

Strategies of Growth

First a great riddle had to be solved: how to grow and avoid the ravages of competition? In Michigan in the 1860s salt producers found themselves fighting for their existence. The presence of too many salt makers had begun an endless round of price-cutting that was driving them all out of business. In 1869, seeing salvation in combination, they drew together in the nation's first pool called the Michigan Salt Association. Pools voluntarily divided production, assigned markets, and set prices—in Michigan, at double the previous rate.

HORIZONTAL GROWTH Competition often plagued salt processing and other manufacturers of **consumer goods** because their start-up costs were low. **Horizontal combination**—joining loosely together with rivals that produced the same goods or services—had saved Michigan salt producers. The railroads were among the first big businesses to employ pools. By the 1880s there was a whiskey pool, a cordage pool, and countless others. Such informal arrangements ultimately proved unenforceable and therefore unsatisfactory. (After 1890 they were also considered illegal restraints on trade.) But other forms of horizontal growth, such as formal mergers, spread in the wake of an economic panic in the 1890s.

VERTICAL INTEGRATION Some makers of consumer products worried less about direct competition and concentrated on boosting efficiency and sales. They adopted a growth strategy called **vertical integration,** in which one company gained control of two or more stages of

a business operation. A fully integrated manufacturing company, for example, possessed its own raw materials, transportation facilities, factories, and marketing outlets.

Gustavus Swift, a New England butcher, saw the advantages of such integration when he arrived in Chicago in the mid-1870s. Aware of the demand for fresh beef in the East, he acquired new refrigerated railcars to ship meat from western slaughterhouses and a network of ice-cooled warehouses in eastern cities to store it. By 1885 he had created the first national meatpacking enterprise, Swift and Company. Swift moved upward, closer to consumers, by putting together a fleet of wagons to distribute his beef to retailers. He moved down toward raw materials, extending and coordinating the purchase of cattle at the Chicago stockyards. By the 1890s Swift and Company was a fully integrated, vertically organized corporation operating on a nationwide scale. Soon Swift, Armour and Company, and three other integrated giants—together called the "Big Five"—controlled 90 percent of the beef shipped across state lines.

Vertical growth generally brought producers of consumer goods closer to the marketplace. For them, profit came from high-volume sales. The Singer Sewing Machine Company and the McCormick Harvester Company created their own retail sales arms. Manufacturers began furnishing ordinary consumers with technical information, credit, and repair services in an effort to expand sales. Advertising expenditures grew to some $90 million by 1900, identifying markets, shaping buying habits, and drumming up business.

Carnegie Integrates Steel

Industrialization encouraged vertical integration in heavy industry but more often downward, toward reliable sources of raw materials. These firms made machinery and materials—called **producer goods**—for big users such as railroads and factory builders. Their markets changed little. For them, profits lay in securing limited raw materials and holding down costs.

Andrew Carnegie led the way in steel. A Scottish immigrant, he worked his way up from bobbin boy in a textile factory to expert telegrapher to superintendent of the western division of the Pennsylvania Railroad at the age of 24. A string of wise investments paid off handsomely. He owned a share of the first sleeping car, the first iron railroad bridge, a locomotive factory, and finally an iron factory that became the nucleus of his steel empire.

BESSEMER PROCESS In 1872, on a trip to England, Carnegie chanced to see the new Bessemer process for making steel. Awestruck by its fiery display, he rushed home to build the biggest steel mill in the world. The J. Edgar Thomson Steel Works (shrewdly named in honor of the president of the Pennsylvania Railroad) opened in 1875, in the midst of a severe depression. Over the next 25 years, Carnegie added mills at Homestead and elsewhere in Pennsylvania and moved from railroad

Carnegie steel furnaces, Braddock, Pennsylvania, on the banks of the Monongahela River, were opened in 1875 as part of the J. Edgar Thomson Steel Works. Its giant Bessemer converters were capable of producing as much as 225 tons of steel rails a day, many of which went into the construction of the Pennsylvania Railroad line.

building to city building. He supplied steel for the Brooklyn Bridge, New York City's elevated railway, and the Washington Monument.

KEYS TO CARNEGIE'S SUCCESS Carnegie succeeded, in part, by taking advantage of the boom-and-bust business cycle. He jumped in during hard times, building and buying when equipment and businesses were cheap. He also found skilled managers who employed the administrative techniques of the railroads. And Carnegie knew how to compete. He scrapped machinery, workers, even a new mill to undersell competitors.

The final key to Carnegie's success was expansion. His empire spread horizontally by purchasing rival steel mills and constructing new ones. It spread vertically, buying up sources of supply, transportation, and eventually sales. Controlling such an integrated system, Carnegie could ensure a steady flow of materials from mine to mill and market as well as a steady stream of profits. In 1900 his company turned out more steel than Great Britain and netted him $40 million.

Integration of the kind Carnegie employed expressed the logic of the new industrial age. More and more, the industrial activities of society were being linked in one giant, interconnected process.

Rockefeller and the Great Standard Oil Trust

John D. Rockefeller accomplished in oil what Carnegie achieved in steel. And he went further, developing an innovative business structure—the trust—that promised greater control than even Carnegie's integrated system. At first Rockefeller, who specialized in refining petroleum, grew horizontally by buying out or joining competing oil refiners. To cut costs, he expanded vertically, with oil pipelines, warehouses, and barrel factories. By 1870, when he and five partners formed the Standard Oil Company of Ohio, his high-caliber, low-cost products could compete with any other.

ROCKEFELLER'S METHODS OF EXPANSION Because the oil-refining business was a jungle of competitive firms, Rockefeller proceeded to twist arms. He bribed rivals, spied on them, created phony companies, and slashed prices. His decisive edge came from the railroads. Desperate for business, they granted Standard Oil not only rebates on shipping rates but also "drawbacks," fees that railroaders paid Standard for petroleum products shipped by a rival. Within a decade Standard dominated the oil business with a vertically integrated empire that stretched from drilling to selling.

Throughout the 1870s Rockefeller kept his empire stitched together through informal pools and other business combinations. But they were weak and afforded him too little control. He could try to expand further, except that corporations were restricted by state law. In Rockefeller's home state of Ohio, for example, corporations could not own plants in other states or own stock in out-of-state companies.

THE TRUST In 1879 Samuel C. T. Dodd, chief counsel of Standard Oil, came up with a solution, the "trust." Under the trust, the stockholders of corporations surrendered their shares "in trust" to a central board of

directors with the power to control all property. In exchange, stockholders received certificates of trust that paid hefty dividends. Because it did not literally own other companies, the trust violated no state law.

In 1882 the Standard Oil Company of Ohio formed the country's first great trust. It brought Rockefeller what he sought so fiercely—centralized management of the oil industry. Other businesses soon created trusts of their own—in meatpacking, wiremaking, and farm machinery, for example. Just as quickly, trusts became notorious for crushing rivals, fixing prices, and dominating markets.

The Mergers of J. Pierpont Morgan

The trust was only a stepping-stone to an even more effective means of avoiding competition, managing people, and controlling business: the corporate merger. The idea of two corporations merging—one buying out or pooling with another—remained impossible until 1889, when New Jersey began to permit corporations to own other corporations.

THE HOLDING COMPANY In 1890 the need to find a substitute for the trust grew urgent. Congress outlawed trusts under the Sherman Antitrust Act (page 515), which specifically banned business from "restraining trade" by setting prices, dividing markets, or engaging in other unfair practices. The ever-inventive Samuel Dodd came up with a new idea, the "holding company," a corporation of corporations that had the power to hold shares of other companies. Many industries converted their trusts into holding companies, including Standard Oil, which moved to New Jersey in 1899.

Two years later came the biggest corporate merger of the era, created by financial wizard J. Pierpont Morgan. His orderly mind detested the chaotic competition that threatened his profits. "I like a little competition," Morgan used to say, "but I like combination more." After the Civil War he had taken over his father's powerful investment bank. For the next 50 years the House of Morgan played a part in consolidating almost every major industry in the country.

Morgan's greatest triumph came in steel, where for years Carnegie had refused to combine with rivals. In January 1901, with the threat of a colossal steel war looming, Morgan convinced Carnegie to put a price tag on his company. When a messenger brought back the scrawled reply—more than $400 million—Morgan merely nodded and said, "I accept this price." He then bought Carnegie's eight largest competitors and announced the formation of the United States Steel Corporation.

U.S. Steel gobbled up more than 200 manufacturing and transportation companies, 1,000 miles of railways, and the whole Mesabi iron range of Minnesota. The mammoth holding company produced nearly two-thirds of all American steel. Its value of $1.4 billion exceeded the national debt and made it the country's first billion-dollar corporation, in 1901.

THE MERGER MOVEMENT What Morgan helped to create in steel was rapidly coming to pass in other industries. A wave of mergers swept through American business after the depression of 1893. As the economy plunged, cutthroat competition bled businesses until they were eager to sell out. Giants sprouted almost overnight. By 1904 in each of 50 industries one firm came to account for 60 percent or more of the total output.

Short- and Long-Term Costs of Doing Business

The heated debates between the critics and defenders of industrial capitalism made clear that the changes in American society were two-edged. Big businesses helped to order or rationalize production, increase national wealth, and tie the country together. Yet they also concentrated power, corrupted politics, and made the gap between rich and poor more apparent than ever. In 1890 the richest 9 percent of Americans held nearly three-quarters of all wealth in the United States. Meanwhile, by 1900 one American in eight (nearly 10 million people) lived below the poverty line.

THE BOOM-AND-BUST CYCLE The practices of big business subjected the economy to enormous disruptions. The banking system could not always keep pace with the demand for capital, and businesses failed to distribute enough profits to sustain the purchasing power of workers. The supply of goods periodically outstripped the appetite for them, and then the wrenching cycle of boom and bust set in. Three severe depressions—1873–1879, 1882–1885, and 1893–1897—rocked the economy in the last third of the nineteenth century. With hard times came fierce competition as managers searched frantically for ways to cut costs, and the industrial barons earned their reputations for ruthlessness.

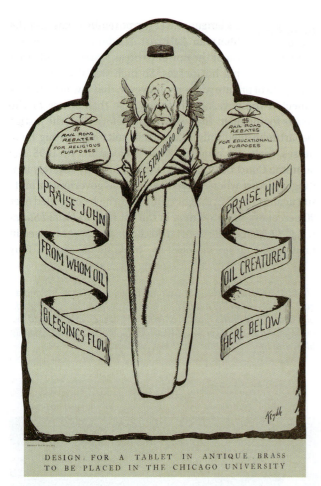

This drawing is from a 1905 edition of Collier's magazine, famous for exposing corporate abuses. Here it mocks John D. Rockefeller, head of the Standard Oil Company, as the new god of the industrial age by parodying the Protestant doxology of thanks: "Praise God from whom all blessings flow, Praise him all creatures here below!"

outside the authority of the Sherman Act. The ruling thus excluded most firms other than transportation companies that carried goods across state lines. Not until after the turn of the century would the law be used to bust a trust.

THE STUDY OF GLOBAL WARMING: FIRST STIRRINGS Some of the costs were unclear at the time. Although anyone could see the environmental impact of mining, logging, and smokestack industries on scarred hillsides, fouled rivers, and soot-filled air, the long-term effects were less apparent. In the nineteenth century most people, scientists included, assumed that Nature would maintain its own balance, largely unaffected by human action. And for the handful of observers interested in such things as climate change only the most basic calculations were possible. Still, step by small step, scientists

Boom-and-Bust Business Cycle, 1865–1900

Between 1865 and 1900 industrialization produced great economic growth but also wild swings of prosperity and depression. During booms productivity soared and near-full employment existed. But the rising number of industrial workers meant high unemployment during deep busts.

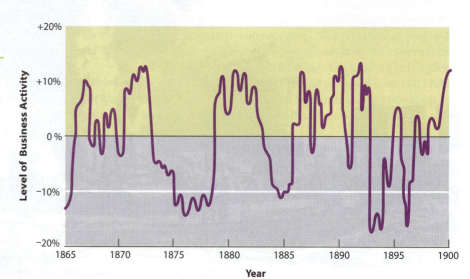

around the globe began to address a question that would obsess future generations: What controlled the temperature of the planet?

For eons, temperatures had ebbed and flowed in cycles stretching across vast intervals of time. Early in the nineteenth century, French scientist Joseph Fourier wondered why the Earth did not burn to a cinder given the power of solar energy. His answer: the Earth was venting heat into space. When he tallied the figures, he discovered an anomaly. On average the earth should be colder, not warmer, than he assumed. He concluded that the atmosphere must be trapping heat and radiating it back to the surface.

A Brit and a Swede, both consumed with discovering the cause of the prehistoric Ice Age, worked out the climatic ramifications. In 1859 British scientist John Tyndall posed the question of causality backward: Precisely what in the atmosphere *prevented* the Earth from freezing? By testing the gas emitted by burning coal from a jet in his laboratory, he found that methane and carbon dioxide thereby released captured heat. Historically such gases had come from volcanic eruptions and other natural occurrences, but growing amounts were now being thrown aloft by industry. In Sweden, Svante Arrhenius carried the idea one step further in 1896. If heat-trapping gases raised global temperatures even slightly, warmer air would absorb more of the biggest heat trapper of all—water vapor—raising temperatures still higher. With the age of industry in its infancy, few paid attention to the implications for what would later be called "global warming."

 REVIEW

What strategies and structures did businesses use to grow and at what costs?

THE WORKERS' WORLD

AT SEVEN IN THE MORNING Sadie Frowne sat at her sewing machine in a Brooklyn garment factory. The boss, a man she barely knew, dropped a pile of unfinished skirts next to her. She pushed one under the needle and began to rock her foot quickly on the pedal that powered her machine. Sometimes Sadie pushed the fabric too hastily, and the needle pierced her finger. "The machines go like mad all day because the faster you work the more money you get," Sadie explained of the world of industrial work in 1902.

The cramped sweatshops, the vast steel mills, the dank tunnels of the coalfields—all demanded workers and required them to work in new ways. Farmers or peasants who had once timed themselves by the movement of the sun now lived by the clock and labored in the twilight of gaslit factories. Instead of being self-employed, they were under the thumb of a supervisor and were paid by the piece or hour. Not the seasons but the relentless cycle of machines set their pace.

Industrial Work

In 1881 the Pittsburgh Bessemer Steel Company opened its new mill in Homestead, Pennsylvania. Nearly 400 men and boys went to work in its 60 acres of sheds. They kept the mill going around the clock by working in two shifts: 12 hours a day the first week, 12 hours a night the next. In the furnace room, some men fainted from the heat, while the vibration and screeching of machinery deafened others. There were no breaks, even for lunch.

PATTERN OF INDUSTRIAL WORK — Few industrial workers labored under conditions quite so harsh, but the Homestead mill reflected the common characteristics of industrial work: the use of machines for mass production; the division of labor into intricately organized, menial tasks; and the dictatorship of the clock. At the turn of the century two-thirds of all industrial work came from large-scale mills.

Under such conditions labor paid dearly for industrial progress. By 1900 most of those earning wages in industry worked 6 days a week, 10 hours a day. They held jobs that required more machines and fewer skills. Repetition of small chores replaced fine craftwork. In the 1880s, for example, almost all the 40 different steps that had gone into making a pair of shoes by hand could be performed by a novice, or "green hand," with a few days of instruction at a simple machine.

INDUSTRIAL ACCIDENTS — With machines also came danger. Tending furnaces in a steel mill or plucking tobacco from cigarette-rolling machines was tedious. If a worker became bored or tired, disaster could strike. From 1880 to 1900 industrial mishaps killed an average of 35,000 workers a year and injured over 536,000. Workers could expect no payment from employers or the government for death or injury. The law operated under the presumption that such accidents were the worker's fault.

TAYLORISM — Higher productivity and profits were the chief aims of business, and for Frederick W. Taylor, efficiency was the way to achieve them. During the 1870s and 1880s Taylor undertook careful time-and-motion studies of workers' movements in the steel industry. He set up standard procedures and offered pay incentives for beating his production quotas. On one occasion he designed 15 ore shovels, each for a separate task. One hundred forty men were soon doing the work of 600. By the early twentieth century "Taylorism" was a full-blown philosophy, complete with its own professional society.

For all the high ideals of Taylorism, ordinary laborers refused to perform as cogs in a vast industrial machine. In a variety of ways, they worked to maintain control. Many European immigrants continued to observe the numerous saints' days and other religious holidays of their homelands, regardless of factory rules. When the pressure of six-day weeks became too stifling, workers took an unauthorized

West Lynn Machine Shop

This machine tool shop in West Lynn, Massachusetts, photographed in the mid-1890s, suggests something of the growing scale of factory enterprise in the late nineteenth century—and also of the extraordinary dangers workers in these early manufacturing shops faced.

"blue Monday" off. Or they slowed down to reduce the grueling pace. Or they simply walked off the job. Come spring and warm weather, factories reported turnover rates of 100 percent or more.

WORKER CITIZENS For some laborers, seizing control of work was more than a matter of survival or self-respect. Many workers regarded themselves as citizens of a democratic republic. They expected to earn a "competence"—enough money to support and educate their families and enough time to stay abreast of current affairs. Few but highly skilled workers could realize such democratic dreams. More and more, labor was being managed as another part of an integrated system of industry.

Children, Women, and African Americans

The needs of industry for workers were so great that groups traditionally left out of the industrial ambit—children; women; African Americans—found themselves drawn into it. In the mines of Pennsylvania nimble-fingered eight- and nine-year-olds snatched bits of slate from amid the chunks of coal. In Illinois glass factories quick-footed "dog boys" dashed with trays of red-hot bottles to the cooling ovens. By 1900 the industrial labor force included some 1.7 million children, more than double the number 30 years earlier. Parents

| Workers fortunate enough to bring food used a "lunch pail" like this one.

often had no choice. As one union leader observed, "Absolute necessity compels the father . . . to take the child into the mine to assist him in winning bread for the family." On average, children worked 60 hours a week and carried home paychecks a third the size of those of adult males.

Women had always labored on family farms, but by 1870 one in four nonagricultural workers was female. In general they earned one-half of what men did. Nearly all were single and young, anywhere from their mid-teens to their mid-20s. Most lived in boardinghouses or at home with their parents. Usually they contributed their wages to the family kitty. Once married they took on a life of full-time housework and child rearing.

Only 5 percent of married women held jobs outside the home in 1900. Married black women (in need of income because of the low wages paid to their husbands) were four times more likely than married whites to work away from home. Domestic service was by far the most common occupation for these women. But industrialization inevitably pushed women into new jobs. Mainly they worked in industries considered extensions of housework: food processing, textiles and clothing, and cigar making. Many women actually preferred factory labor, with its long hours and dirty conditions, to being a live-in servant, where they were at work seven days a week and on call 24 hours a day.

New methods of management and marketing opened positions for

HISTORIAN'S TOOLBOX

DIGITAL DETECTING

Eastport, Maine: what adjectives would you use to describe the scene?

At first the view looks somewhat rural, but at least three elements in the photograph suggest otherwise. What are they?

What strikes you about this digitally enlarged portion of the photo?

Photographs can be both revealing and deceptive, but technology can help historians detect what the camera lens actually captured. This print (upper left) of a photo by Lewis Hine, a turn-of-the-century photographer, shows 8-year-old Phoebe Thomas returning to her house in Eastport, Maine. The scene seems to be nothing more than a little girl making her way home up a set of stairs. Hine tells us that the young Syrian worked all day in a cannery, shearing the heads off sardines with a butcher's knife. When the Library of Congress scanned the image nearly a century later, a portion of the photo could be digitally enlarged to reveal much more than meets the unaided eye. What appears to be an ordinary homecoming is, in fact, something much worse, as Hine's notes reveal. Phoebe was "running home from the factory all alone, her hand and arm bathed with blood, crying at the top of her voice. She had cut the end of her thumb nearly off, cutting sardines in the factory, and was sent home alone, her mother being busy."

Credit: Library of Congress Digital Photo ID: nclc 00966.

Thinking Critically

How does the close-up of Phoebe Thomas change the nature of the photograph? What would we make of the photograph without Hine's explanatory notes? Google "Lewis Hine" to learn what he photographed and why.

THE WORKERS' WORLD | 519

A sweatshop boss bellows at a seamstress.

Most unskilled and semiskilled workers in factories continued to receive low pay. In 1890 an unskilled laborer could expect about $1.50 for a 10-hour day; a skilled one, perhaps twice that amount. It took about $600 to make ends meet, but most manufacturing workers made under $500 a year. Native-born white Americans tended to earn more than immigrants, those who spoke English more than those who did not, men more than women, and all others more than African Americans, Latinos, and Asians.

SOCIAL MOBILITY
Few workers repeated the rags-to-riches rise of Andrew Carnegie. But some did rise despite periodic unemployment and ruthless wage cuts. About one-quarter of the manual laborers in one study entered the lower middle class in their own lifetimes. More often such unskilled workers climbed in financial status within their own class. Most workers, seeing some improvement, believed in the American dream of success, even if they did not fully share in it.

HORATIO ALGER
Anyone with doubts could turn to Horatio Alger to learn how to make the dream real. The son of a minister, Alger wrote over 100 books for boys between 1864 and 1899. His young heroes bore different names—Ragged Dick, Julius the Street Boy, Tony the Tramp—but their story was always the same. A chance encounter presents a poor young boy with an opportunity. In one book it's a runaway carriage with the daughter of a wealthy industrialist inside, in another a rich man's lost wallet. Through courage, honesty, hard work, and thrift, the boy makes the most of chance and lives a life of fame and fortune. With titles such as *Luck and Pluck, Strong and Steady, Slow and Sure,* and *Strive and Succeed,* Alger touted his simple keys for rising from what he called "rags to respectability." By the time he died at the turn of the century, his books had sold over a million copies and taught a generation how to succeed in business and life. Whether Alger's widely held virtues produced the same results in the real world was another matter.

✓ REVIEW
How did industrialization change the lives of workers?

white-collar women as "typewriters," "telephone girls," bookkeepers, and secretaries. On rare occasions women entered the professions, though law and medical schools still regarded them as unwelcome invaders. Such discrimination drove ambitious, educated women into nursing, teaching, and library work, all considered forms of feminine nurturance. Their growing presence soon "feminized" these professions, pushing men upward into managerial slots or out entirely.

Even more than women, African American men faced discrimination in the workplace. They were paid less than whites and given menial jobs. Their greatest opportunities in industry often came as strikebreakers to replace white workers. Once a strike ended, however, black workers were replaced and hated by the white regulars whose jobs they had taken. The service trades furnished the largest single source of jobs. Waiting on whites in restaurants or on railroads lay within the boundaries set by prevailing prejudice. Craftworkers and a sprinkling of black professionals could usually be found in cities. After the turn of the century, black-owned businesses thrived in the growing black neighborhoods of the North and the South.

The American Dream of Success

RISING REAL WAGES
Whatever their separate experiences, working-class Americans did improve their overall lot. Though the gap between the very rich and the poor widened, most wage earners made some gains. Between 1860 and 1890 real daily wages—pay in terms of buying power—climbed some 50 percent, more the result of gradually falling prices than of increases in pay. And after 1890, the number of hours on the job began a slow decline.

THE SYSTEMS OF LABOR

PUTTING IN MORE HOURS TO save a few pennies, walking out in exhaustion or disgust, slowing down on the job—in these ways individual workers coped with industrial America. Sporadic and unorganized, such actions stood little chance of bringing the new industrial order under the control of labor. For ordinary workers to begin to shape industrialization they had to combine, as businesses did. They needed to combine horizontally—organizing not just locally but on a national scale. They needed to integrate vertically by coordinating action across a wide range of jobs

Clerks' jobs, traditionally held by men, came to be filled by women as growing industrial networks created more managerial jobs for men. Here a factory floor full of neatly dressed female clerks bang away at their "Type-Writers," patented first in 1868.

and skills, as Andrew Carnegie coordinated the production of steel. Unions were the workers' systematic response to industrialization.

Early Unions

In the United States, **unions** began forming before the Civil War. Skilled craftworkers—carpenters, iron molders, cigar makers—joined together to protect themselves against the growing power of management. Railroad "brotherhoods" also furnished insurance for those hurt or killed on the accident-plagued lines. Largely local and exclusively male, these early craft unions remained weak and unconnected to each other as well as to the growing mass of unskilled workers.

NATIONAL LABOR UNION

After the Civil War a group of craft unions, brotherhoods, and reformers united skilled and unskilled workers in a nationwide organization. The National Labor Union (NLU) hailed the virtues of a simpler America, when workers controlled their workday, earned a decent living, and had time to be good citizens. NLU leaders attacked the wage system as unfair and enslaving and urged workers to manage their own factories. By the early 1870s NLU ranks had swelled to more than 600,000.

The NLU pressed energetically for the eight-hour workday, the most popular labor demand of the era. Workers saw it as a way not merely of limiting their time on the job but of limiting the power of employers over their lives. "Eight hours for work; eight hours for rest; eight hours for what we will!" proclaimed a banner at one labor rally. Despite the popularity of the issue, the NLU wilted during the depression of 1873.

The Knights of Labor

More successful was a national union born in secrecy. In 1869 Uriah Stephens and nine Philadelphia garment cutters founded the Noble and Holy Order of the Knights of Labor. They draped themselves in ritual and regalia to deepen their sense of solidarity and met in secret to evade hostile owners. Their strongly Protestant tone repelled Catholics, who made up almost half the workforce in many industries.

In this painting by Robert Koehler, titled The Strike (1886), labor confronts management in a strike that may soon turn bloody. One worker reaches for a stone as an anxious mother and her children look on.

TERENCE POWDERLY In 1879 the Knights elected Terence V. Powderly as their Grand Master Workman. Handsome, dynamic, Irish, and Catholic, Powderly threw off the Knights' secrecy, dropped their rituals, and opened their ranks. He called for "one big union" to embrace the "toiling millions"—skilled and unskilled, men and women, natives and immigrants, all religions, all races. By 1886 membership had leaped to over 700,000, including nearly 30,000 African Americans and 3,000 women.

Like the NLU, the radical Knights of Labor looked to abolish the wage system. In its place they wanted to construct a cooperative economy of worker-owned mines, factories, and railroads. The Knights set up more than 140 "cooperative workshops," where workers shared decisions and profits, and sponsored some 200 political candidates. To tame the new industrial order, they supported the eight-hour workday and the regulation of trusts. Underlying this program was a moral vision of society. If people only renounced greed, laziness, and dishonesty, Powderly argued, corruption and class division would disappear, and democracy would flourish. To reform citizens, the Knights promoted the prohibition of child and convict labor and the abolition of liquor.

It was one thing to proclaim a national union, quite another to coordinate the activities of so many members. Powderly soon found locals resorting to strikes and violence, actions he condemned. In the mid-1880s such stoppages wrung concessions from the western railroads, but the organization soon became associated with unsuccessful strikes and violent extremists. Even its impressive gains against railroads were wiped out when the Texas and Pacific Railroad broke a strike by local Knights. By 1890 the Knights of Labor, symbol of organized labor's resistance to industrial capitalism, teetered near extinction.

The American Federation of Labor

SAMUEL GOMPERS The American Federation of Labor (AFL) soon took up the Knights' position as the premier union in the nation. The AFL reflected the practicality of its leader, Samuel Gompers. Born in a London tenement, the son of a Jewish cigar maker, Gompers had immigrated in 1863 with his family to New York's Lower East Side. Unlike the visionary Powderly, Gompers preached accommodation, not resistance. He urged his followers to accept capitalism and the wage system. What he wanted was "pure and simple unionism"—a worker organization that accepted the idea of a fixed, wage-earning class and bargained for higher pay, fewer hours, improved safety, more benefits.

Gompers chose to organize highly skilled craftworkers, because they were difficult to replace. He bargained with employers and used strikes and boycotts only as last resorts. With the Cigar Makers' Union as his base, Gompers helped create the first national federation of craft unions in 1881. In 1886, it became the American Federation of Labor. Twenty-five labor groups joined, representing nearly 150,000 skilled workers. Stressing gradual, concrete gains, he made the AFL the most powerful union in the country.

By 1901 it had more than a million members, almost a third of all skilled workers in America.

FAILURE OF ORGANIZED LABOR Despite the success of the AFL the laboring classes did not organize themselves as systematically as did the barons of industry. For one thing, Gompers and the AFL were less interested in vertical integration that combined skilled and unskilled workers or included women and African Americans. For another, workers themselves were separated by language and culture, divided along lines of race and gender, and fearful of retaliation by management. A strong strain of individualism made many workers regard any collective action as un-American. In 1900 union membership made up less than 10 percent of industrial workers.

The Limits of Industrial Systems

As managers increased their control over the workplace, workers often found themselves at the mercy of the new industrial order. Even in boom times, one in three workers was out of a job at least three or four months a year. The word *unemployment* dates from the late nineteenth century.

SPONTANEOUS PROTESTS In hard times, when a worker's pay dropped and frustration mounted, when a mother worked all night and fell asleep during the day while caring for her children, when food prices suddenly jumped—anger might boil over into protest. "A mob of 1,000 people, with women in the lead, marched through the Jewish quarter of Williamsburg last evening and wrecked half a dozen butcher shops," reported the *New York Times* in 1902.

In the late nineteenth century a wave of labor activism swept the nation. More often than mobs, it was strikes and boycotts that challenged the authority of employers and gave evidence of working-class identity and discontent. Most strikes broke out spontaneously, organized by informal leaders in a factory. Thousands of rallies and organized strikes were staged as well, often on behalf of the eight-hour workday, in good times and bad, by union and nonunion workers alike.

MOLLY MAGUIRES Some workers resorted to terrorism to resist the new industrial order. In the coalfields of Pennsylvania, Irish miners organized a secret society called the Molly Maguires, named for an earlier group of protesters in Ireland who had disguised themselves as women and roamed the Irish countryside beating and sometimes killing tyrannical landlords. The American Mollys founded their society in 1866. For the next decade the small but dedicated band resorted to intimidation, arson, and murder to combat the horrid working conditions of coal miners. They saw it as "retributive justice" imported from Ireland and employed against a new set of oppressors. In 1876, 20 Mollys were brought to trial and a year later executed

for 16 murders. For most Americans justice was served, despite the questionable legality of the trial. In its wake the secret society vanished.

GREAT RAILROAD STRIKE In 1877, in the midst of a deep depression, the country's first nationwide strike opened an era of confrontation between labor and management. When the Baltimore and Ohio Railroad cut wages by 20 percent, a crew in Martinsburg, West Virginia, seized the local depot and blocked the line. President Hayes sent federal troops to enforce a court order ending the strike, but instead two-thirds of the nation's tracks shut down in sympathy. The novel tactic suggested a growing sense of solidarity among workers. The country ground to a halt.

When owners brought in strikebreakers, workers torched rail yards, smashed engines and cars, and tore up track. Local police, state militia, and federal troops finally quashed the strike after 12 bloody days. The "Great Railroad Strike" of 1877 left 100 people dead and more than $10 million worth of railroad property in rubble. It signaled the rising power and unity of labor and sparked fears, as one newspaper warned, that "this may be the beginning of a great civil war in this country, between labor and capital."

LAUNDRESSES STRIKE The Civil War between North and South was still fresh in the minds of Atlantans when 3,000 laundresses struck for higher wages in 1881. Over 98 percent of the city's domestic workers were black women, just a decade and a half out of slavery. Pitiful wages already had led many of them to employ informal strategies to protest. They took unauthorized breaks, pretended to be sick, or "pantoted" (stole) leftovers from the

Molly Maguires warning note: ". . . if you don't leave this place right away, you will be a dead man."

DUELING DOCUMENTS

Two Sides of Haymarket

The Haymarket Square Affair on May 4, 1886, led to the arrest and conviction of eight people for the murder of police officer Mathias J. Degan. Degan died as a result of the explosion of a pipe bomb at a labor rally organized by anarchists in the Haymarket Square in Chicago. In the first document one of the convicted defendants—an anarchist named August Spies—explains how he became a radical and what he did at Haymarket. The second document is part of Judge Joseph E. Gary's address to the convicted men.

DOCUMENT 1   A Radical Explains His Beliefs

The factory: the ignominious regulations, the surveillance, the spy system, the servility and lack of manhood among the workers and the arrogant arbitrary behavior of the boss and mamelukes—all this made an impression upon me that I have never been able to divest myself of. At first I could not understand why the workers, among them many old men with bent backs, silently and without a sign of protest bore every insult the caprice of the foreman or boss would heap upon them. I was not then aware of the fact that the opportunity to work was a privilege, a favor, and that it was in the power of those who were in the possession of the factories and instruments of labor to deny or grant this privilege. I did not then understand how difficult it was to find a

purchaser for one's labor, I did not know then that there were thousands and thousands of idle human bodies in the market, ready to hire out upon most any conditions, actually begging for employment. I became conscious of this, very soon, however, and I knew then why these people were so servile, whey [sic] suffered the humiliating dictates and capricious whims of their employers. . . .

My connection with the meeting on the Haymarket on May 4th 86 did not go beyond that of an invited speaker. I had been invited to address the meeting in German, but no German speakers being present I spoke in English. The meeting had been called by the representatives of a number of Trades Union. Those present were

workingmen of all beliefs and views; they were not Anarchists. Nor were the speeches anarchistic, they treated on the Eight Hour question. Anarchism was not even referred to by anyone. . . . But Anarchism was good enough to serve as a scapegoat for Bonfield. This fiend, in order to justify his murderous attack upon that meeting, said "They were Anarchists".— "Anarchists! Oh, Horror!" The stupid mass imagined that "Anarchists" must be something very bad and they joined in the chorus with their enemies and fleecers: "Crucify, Crucify!"

Source: August Spies, *Autobiography*, 1886, pp. 18–20, 31–33, Chicago Historical Society, Haymarket Affair Digital Collection, www.chicagohistory.org/hadc/manuscripts/M06/M06.htm, accessed 2.27.13.

DOCUMENT 2   The Judge Speaks of Murder and Free Speech

. . . the law is common sense. It holds each man responsible for the natural and probable consequences of his own acts. It holds that whoever advises murder, is himself guilty of the murder that is committed in pursuance of his advice, and that if men band together for a forcible resistance to the execution of the law, and advise murder, as a means to make such resistance effectual, whether such advice is to one man to murder another, or to a numerous class to murder men of another class, all who are so banded together, are guilty of any murder that may be committed in pursuance of such advice.

The People of this country love their institutions, love their homes, love their property. They will never consent that by violence and murder, those institutions shall be broken down, their houses despoiled, and their property destroyed.

And the People are strong enough to protect and sustain their institutions, and to

punish all offenders against their laws. And those who threaten danger to civil society, if the law is enforced, are leading to destruction whoever shall attempt to execute such threats.

The existing order of society can be changed only by the will of the majority.

Each man has a full right to entertain and advocate, by speech and print, such opinions as suit himself, and the great body of the People will usually care little what he says, but if he proposes murder as a means of enforcing his opinions, he puts his own life at stake. And no clamor about free speech, or evils to be cured, or wrongs to be redressed, will shield him from the consequences of his crime.

His liberty is not a license to destroy. The toleration that he enjoys, he must extend to others, and not arrogantly assume that the great majority are wrong, and may rightfully be coerced by terror, or removed by dynamite.

Source: Address by Judge Joseph E. Gary, 8 October 1886, Cook County (Ill.) Criminal Court, Chicago Historical Society, Haymarket Digital Collection, www.chicagohistory.org/hadc/manuscripts/m05/M05.htm, accessed 2.27.13.

Thinking Critically

What about "the factory" so disturbed August Spies and led to his becoming a radical? On what grounds does Judge Gary explain the conviction and the sentence? (At the time, those who advocated violence were legally responsible for violent consequences.) How, if at all, does knowing that Illinois Governor John Peter Altgeld pardoned the three surviving defendants as innocent only a few years later change your view of these two documents?

kitchens of their white employers. Washerwomen were among the most privileged domestics, because they neither worked nor lived with their employers. Instead, they labored together in common spaces in their neighborhoods, where they built social and political networks. In 1881 they formed the Washing Society and threatened to leave much of the city without clean clothes unless their demands for higher wages were met. Though little resulted from the strike, it nonetheless showed the appeal of organized protest against economic inequality and laid the groundwork for later civil rights protests.

HAYMARKET SQUARE RIOT In 1886 tension between labor and capital exploded in the "Great Upheaval"—a series of strikes, boycotts, and rallies. One of the most violent episodes occurred at Haymarket Square in Chicago. A group of anarchists was protesting the recent killing of workers by police at the McCormick Harvester Company. As rain drenched the small crowd, police armed with billy clubs and pistols ordered everyone out of the square. Suddenly a bomb was thrown into the procession of police. One officer was killed; 5 others were mortally wounded. The police opened fire, and the crowd fired back. Before the melee ended, nearly 70 policemen were injured, and at least 4 civilians died.

Conservatives charged that radicals were responsible for the "Haymarket Massacre." Though the bomb thrower was never identified, a jury found seven of eight anarchists guilty of conspiracy to commit murder and sentenced them to death. The eighth defendant received a 15-year prison sentence. Four were hanged, one killed himself, and three remained in jail until they were pardoned by Governor John Peter Altgeld in 1893. He considered their conviction a miscarriage of justice, but ordinary citizens who once had supported labor grew frightened of what newspapers called its "Samson-like power." Haymarket became a turning point in labor history. It ignited the nation's first "red scare", touching off years of official attacks on radicals for fear they were fomenting violence and revolution. (Red was the color often associated with radicals and revolutionaries.) Cities enlarged their police forces, and states built more National Guard armories on the borders of working-class neighborhoods to contain future violence. A succession of legal decisions hamstrung the union movement for decades, which in any case turned in more conservative directions.

Management Strikes Back

The strikes, rallies, and boycotts of 1886 were followed by a second surge of labor activism in 1892. In the remote silver mines of Coeur d'Alene, Idaho, at the Carnegie steel mill in Homestead, Pennsylvania, in the coal mines near Tracy City, Tennessee, strikes flared, only to be crushed by management. Often state and federal troops joined company guards and private detectives from the Pinkerton agency to fight workers.

PULLMAN STRIKE The broadest confrontation between labor and management took place two years later. A terrible depression had shaken the economy for almost a year when George Pullman, owner of the Palace Car factory and inventor of the plush railroad car, laid off workers and cut wages but kept rents high on company-owned

"GIVING THE BUTT"—THE WAY THE "REGULAR" INFANTRY TACKLES A MOB

Government troops were often called in to help management quell strikes. In the Pullman Strike of 1894, U.S. Regulars "give the butt" to angry laborers in this drawing by Frederick Remington.

housing. He refused to discuss any grievances. In 1894 workers struck and managed to convince the new American Railway Union to support them by boycotting all trains that used Pullman cars. Quickly the strike spread to 27 states and territories.

Anxious railroad owners appealed to President Grover Cleveland for federal help. On the slim pretext that the strike obstructed mail delivery (strikers had actually been willing to handle mail trains without Pullman cars), Cleveland secured a court order halting the strike. He then called several thousand special deputies into Chicago to enforce it. In the rioting that followed, 12 people died and scores were arrested. But the strike was crushed.

MANAGEMENT WEAPONS In all labor disputes the central issue was the power to shape the new industrial systems. Employers always enjoyed the advantage. They hired and fired workers, set the terms of employment, and ruled the workplace. They fought unions with "yellow dog" contracts that forced workers to refuse to join. Blacklists circulated the names of labor agitators. Lockouts kept protesting workers from plants, and company spies infiltrated their organizations. With a growing pool of labor, employers could replace strikers and break strikes.

Management could also count on local, state, and federal authorities for troops to break strikes. In addition, businesses used a powerful new legal weapon, the **injunction.** These court orders prohibited certain actions, including strikes, by barring workers from interfering with their employer's business.

It was just such an order that had brought federal deputies into the Pullman strike and put Eugene Debs, head of the American Railway Union, behind bars. The Indiana-born Debs, a former locomotive fireman and early labor organizer, received a six-month jail sentence for violating the court injunction. After his release, he abandoned the Democratic Party to become the foremost Socialist leader in America.

✔ **REVIEW**

How did workers respond to industrialization?

CONCLUSION

THE WORLD AT LARGE

In a matter of only 30 or 40 years, the new industrial order transformed the landscape of America and left its mark on the world at large. British railroad tracks covered some 20,000 miles by the 1870s, while Germany and France built even larger systems and Japan began constructing its own network with the help of hundreds of engineers from the United States and Great Britain. South Africa, Mexico, Argentina, and Egypt, all rich in raw materials and agricultural commodities, followed. None outstripped the United States. By 1915 its rail network was longer than the next seven largest systems combined.

With remarkable speed, networks of communication and transportation spread across the globe. Underwater telegraph cables were laid from the United States to Europe in 1866, to Australia in 1871 and 1872, to Latin America in 1872 and 1873, and to West Africa by 1886. The completion of the Suez Canal in 1869 (the same year a golden spike connected the last link in the U.S. transcontinental railroad) hastened the switch from sail-powered to steam-driven ships by slicing thousands of miles from the journey between Europe and Asia. Wheat from the United States and India, wool from Australia, and beef from Argentina poured into Europe, while Europe sent textiles, railroad equipment, coal, and machinery to Asia and the Americas.

As these networks tied together national economies, swings in the business cycle produced global consequences. When an Austrian bank failed in 1873, depression soon reached the United States. In the mid-1880s and again in the mid-1890s, recessions drove prices down and unemployment up across the industrialized world. Industrial workers bore the brunt of the burden, but in Europe they had greater success in unionizing, especially after anticombination laws forbidding strikes were abolished in the decades following 1850. By 1900 British unions had signed up 2 million workers, twice the number of members in either the United States or Germany. As strikes became more common and labor unions more powerful, industrializing nations passed social legislation that included the first social security systems and health insurance. Despite such laws, in the new industrial order material progress walked hand in hand with social pain and upheaval. ∞∞∞

Chapter Summary

IN THE LAST THIRD OF the nineteenth century a new industrial order reshaped the United States.

- New systems—of resource development, technology, invention, transportation, communications, finance, corporate management, and labor—boosted industrial growth and productivity.

- Businesses grew big, expanding vertically and horizontally to curb costs and competition and to increase control and efficiency.

- Industrialization came at a price.
  - Workers found their power, job satisfaction, and free time reduced as their numbers in factories mushroomed.
  - The environment was degraded.
  - A vicious cycle of boom and bust afflicted the economy.

- Workers both resisted and accommodated the new industrial order.
  - Some resisted through informal mechanisms such as slowdowns, absenteeism, and quitting and through spontaneous and more formal ones, including radical unions like the Knights of Labor.
  - Other workers were more accommodating, accepting low-paying jobs and layoffs and creating "pure and simple" unions, such as the American Federation of Labor, that accepted the prevailing system of private ownership and wage labor while bargaining for better wages and working conditions.

- The benefits of industrialization were equally undeniable.
  - Life improved materially for many Americans.
  - The real wages of even industrial workers climbed.

- The United States rocketed from fourth place among industrial nations in 1860 to first by 1890.

Additional Reading

FOR A USEFUL INTRODUCTION TO the period, see Edward C. Kirkland, *Industry Comes of Age: Business, Labor, and Public Policy, 1860–1897* (1967). Mechanization and its impact are the focus of Siegfried Giedion's classic *Mechanization Takes Command* (1948). The best overview of American labor is

American Social History Project, *Who Built America? Working People and the Nation's Economy, Politics, Culture, & Society,* Volume Two: *From the Gilded Age to the Present* (1992). Herbert Gutman, *Work, Culture, and Society in Industrializing America: Essays in American Working-Class History* (1976), explores the development of working-class communities in the nineteenth century, especially the role of ethnicity in creating a working-class culture. On wage earners, see Joshua L. Rosenbloom, *Looking for Work, Searching for Workers: American Labor Markets during Industrialization* (2002). David Montgomery offers a broad look at the impact of industrialization on American labor in *The Fall of the House of Labor: The Workplace, the State, and American Labor Activism, 1865–1925* (1987), and Leon Fink, *Workingmen's Democracy: The Knights of Labor and American Politics* (1983), examines early efforts of the Knights of Labor to challenge corporate capitalism by organizing workers and socializing them into a labor culture. Alice Kessler-Harris, *Out to Work: A History of Wage-Earning Women in the United States* (1982), surveys female wage earners and their effect on American culture, family life, and values. Paul Avrich's rich *The Haymarket Tragedy* (1984) sees the whole affair as a tragic miscarriage of justice. After looking at the actual trial transcript and a host of other original materials, Timothy Messer-Kruse concludes the trial followed common legal procedure and fairly convicted the eight anarchists, however tragic their deaths, in *The Trial of the Haymarket Anarchists: Terrorism and Justice in the Gilded Age* (2011).

No book did more to set the idea of big business as ruthless robber barons than Matthew Josephson, *The Robber Barons: The Great American Capitalists, 1861–1901* (1934). T. J. Stiles's *Tycoon: The Epic Life of Cornelius Vanderbilt* (2009) offers a detailed account of the public and personal life of the first great railroad baron. Ron Chernow's *Titan: The Life of John D. Rockefeller, Sr.* (1998) helps to debunk the image of business leaders as "robber barons," without minimizing their ruthlessness. Legal, social, and communal effects of the rise of railroads are addressed in Barbara Young Welke, *Recasting American Liberty: Gender, Race, Law, and the Railroad Revolution* (2001). Business historian Alfred D. Chandler Jr.'s *Strategy and Structure: Chapters in the History of American Industrial Enterprise* (1962) and *The Visible Hand: The Managerial Revolution in American Business* (1977) are seminal accounts of business organization and management that stress the adaptations of business structures and the emergence of a new class of managers. For a comparative view of the rise of big business in the United States, Great Britain, and Germany, see his *Scale and Scope* (1988). On the problem of climate change, see Spencer R. Weart, *The Discovery of Global Warming* (2003).

For a fuller list of readings, see the Bibliography at www.mhhe.com/eh8e.

SIGNIFICANT EVENTS

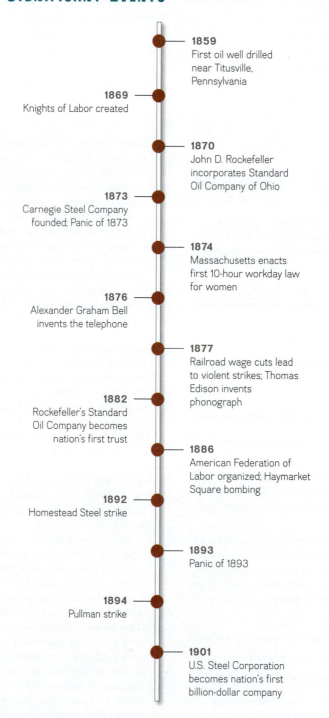

1859
First oil well drilled near Titusville, Pennsylvania

1869
Knights of Labor created

1870
John D. Rockefeller incorporates Standard Oil Company of Ohio

1873
Carnegie Steel Company founded; Panic of 1873

1874
Massachusetts enacts first 10-hour workday law for women

1876
Alexander Graham Bell invents the telephone

1877
Railroad wage cuts lead to violent strikes; Thomas Edison invents phonograph

1882
Rockefeller's Standard Oil Company becomes nation's first trust

1886
American Federation of Labor organized; Haymarket Square bombing

1892
Homestead Steel strike

1893
Panic of 1893

1894
Pullman strike

1901
U.S. Steel Corporation becomes nation's first billion-dollar company

The Structures and Strategies of Big Business

STRUCTURE	DESCRIPTION	ADVANTAGES
Corporation	Company owned by stockholders	Separation of ownership and management; limited liability of owners; expert managers; access to capital
Pool	Informal horizontal combination	Stifling competition
Trust	Shares of business held "in trust" by board of directors	Consolidation and control of several businesses; domination of markets
Holding Company	Company that only owns shares in other companies	Controlling management and operations of many companies

STRATEGY	DESCRIPTION	ADVANTAGES
Horizontal Combination	Combining with competitors	Stifling competition
Vertical Integration	Acquiring stages of business operation	Control of costs
Merger	Uniting two or more companies through purchase or mutual consent	Administrative centralization

every day; so crowded (according to Mark Twain), you "had to hang on by your eyelashes and toenails."

Civic leaders came to understand that the modern city could not survive, much less grow, without improved transportation. San Francisco installed trolley cars pulled by steam-driven cables. It worked so well in San Francisco that Chicago, Seattle, and other hilly cities installed cable systems in the 1880s. Some cities experimented with elevated trestles to carry steam locomotives; others, with cable lines high above crowded streets. But none of the breakthroughs quite did the trick. Cables remained slow and unreliable; the elevated railways, or "els," were dirty, ugly, and noisy.

ROLE OF ELECTRICITY
Electricity rescued city travelers. In 1888 Frank Julian Sprague, a naval engineer who had once worked for Thomas Edison, installed the first electric trolley line in Richmond, Virginia. Electrified streetcars were soon speeding along at 12 miles an hour, twice as fast as horses. By 1902 electricity drove nearly all city railways. Sprague's innovations also meant that "subways" could be built without having to worry about tunnels filled with a steam engine's smoke and soot. Between 1895 and 1897 Boston built the first underground electric line. New York followed in 1904 with a subway that ran from city hall on the southern tip of Manhattan north to Harlem. Once considered too far afield, Harlem soon became dotted with new apartments and tenements. When the white middle class refused to move so far uptown, Philip A. Peyton convinced landlords to allow his Afro-American Realty Company to handle the properties. Within a decade Harlem became the black capital of America.

The rich had long been able to keep homes outside city limits, traveling to and fro in private carriages. New systems of mass transit freed the middle class and even the poor to live miles from work. For a nickel or two, anyone could ride from central shopping and business districts to the suburban fringes and back. A network of moving vehicles held the segmented and sprawling city together and widened its reach out to "streetcar suburbs."

Bridges and Skyscrapers

Because cities often grew along rivers and harbors, their separate parts sometimes had to be joined over water. The principles of building large river bridges had already been worked out by the railroads. It remained for a German immigrant and his son, John and Washington Roebling, to make the bridge a symbol of urban growth.

The Brooklyn Bridge, linking Manhattan with Brooklyn, took 13 years to complete. It cost $15 million and 20 lives, including that of designer John Roebling. When it opened in 1883 it stretched more than a mile across the East River, with passage broad enough for a footpath, two double carriage lanes, and two railroad lines. Its arches were cut like giant cathedral windows, and its supporting cables hung, said an awestruck observer, "like divine messages from above." Soon other suspension bridges were spanning the railroad yards in St. Louis and the bay at Galveston, Texas.

Even as late as 1880 church steeples dominated the urban landscape. They towered over squat factories and office buildings. But growing congestion and the increasing value of land pushed architects to search for ways to make buildings taller. In place of thick walls of brick that restricted factory floor space, builders used cast-iron columns. The new "cloudscrapers" were strong, durable, and fire-resistant. Their open floors were ideal for warehouses and also for office buildings and department stores.

Steel, with greater flexibility and strength than iron, turned cloudscrapers into skyscrapers. William LeBaron Jenney first used steel in his 10-story Home Insurance

| Flatiron Building, New York City

Building (1885) in Chicago. By the end of the century steel frames and girders raised buildings to 30 stories or more. New York City's triangular Flatiron building (at left), named for its shape, used the new technology to project an angular yet remarkably delicate elegance. In Chicago, Daniel Burnham's Reliance Building (1890) relied so heavily on new plate glass windows that contemporaries called it "a glass tower fifteen stories high."

It was no accident that many of the new skyscrapers arose in Chicago. The Great Fire of 1871 engulfed more than 3 square miles of downtown and turned it into an architect's playground. John Root, aware that the decorative trim of buildings had fueled the blaze, designed new office towers that were sleek, simple, and immense. The young maverick Louis H. Sullivan promised a new urban profile in which the skyscraper would be "every inch a proud and soaring thing." In the Wainwright Building (1890) in St. Louis and the Carson, Pirie, and Scott department store (1889–1904) in Chicago, Sullivan produced sky-high structures that symbolized the modern industrial city and gave rise to what people were soon calling the "Chicago School of Architecture."

Architects did not create the towering landscapes of modern industrial cities without help. Reinforced concrete that could tolerate the weight and height of new buildings and plate glass that permitted people to see outside made the structures strong and supple. But soaring skyscrapers were of little value without an efficient, safe means of transporting people aloft. In 1861 Elisha Graves Otis developed a trustworthy, fast elevator. By the 1890s new electric elevators driven by hydraulic pumps were whisking people to the tops of skyscrapers in seconds. The elevator extended the city upward, just as the streetcar extended it outward, and in the process both knitted the physical and social fabric of urban America more tightly together.

The Urban Environment: Slum and Tenement

Far below the skyscrapers lay the slums and tenements of the inner city. In cramped rooms and sunless hallways, along narrow alleys and in flooded basements, lived the city's poor. They often worked there, too, in "sweaters' shops" where as many as 18 people labored and slept in foul two-room flats.

PERILS OF THE SLUM NEIGHBORHOOD
In New York City, whose slums were the nation's worst, crime thrived in places called "Bandit's Roost" and "Hell's Kitchen." Bands of young toughs with such names as the "Sewer Rats" and the "Rock Gang" stalked the streets in search of thrills and easy money. Gambling, prostitution, and alcoholism all claimed their victims most readily in the slums. The poor usually turned to such crime in despair. A 20-year-old prostitute supporting a sickly mother and four brothers and sisters made no apologies: "Let God Almighty judge who's to blame most, I that was driven, or them that drove me to the pass I'm in."

The poor diets of slum dwellers left them vulnerable to disease, but it was their close quarters and often filthy surroundings that raised their rates of infection to epidemic levels. Cholera, typhoid, and an outbreak of yellow fever in Memphis in the 1870s killed tens of thousands. Tuberculosis was deadlier still. As late as 1900, among infectious diseases it ranked behind only influenza and pneumonia *combined* as a killer. Slum children—all city children—were most vulnerable. Almost a quarter of children born in American cities in 1890 never lived to see their first birthday.

The installation of new sewage and water purification systems helped. The modern flush toilet came into use only after the turn of the century. Until then people relied on water closets and communal privies, some of the latter catering to as many as 800. All too often cities dumped waste into old private vaults or rivers used for drinking water. In 1881 an exasperated mayor of Cleveland called the Cuyahoga River "an open sewer through the center of the city."

Slum housing was often more dangerous than the water. The tubercle bacillus flourished in musty, windowless tenements. In 1879 New York enacted a new housing law requiring a window in all bedrooms of new **tenements.** Architect James E. Ware won a competition with a design that contained an indentation on both sides of the building. When two tenements abutted each other, the indentations formed a narrow shaft for air and light. From above, the buildings looked like giant dumbbells. Up to 16 families lived on a floor, with only two toilets in the hall.

Originally hailed as an innovation, Ware's dumbbell tenement spread over such cities as Cleveland, Cincinnati, and Boston "like a scab," said an unhappy reformer. Ordinary blocks contained 10 such tenements and housed as many as 4,000 people. The airshafts became giant silos for trash. They blocked what little light had entered and, worse still, carried fires from one story to the next. When

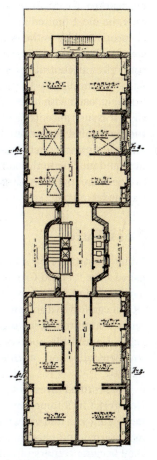

"Dumbbell" tenements were designed to use every inch of available space in the standard 25-by-200-foot city lot while providing ventilation and reducing the spread of disease.

the New York housing commission met in 1900, it concluded that conditions were worse than when reformers had started 33 years earlier.

 **REVIEW**

How did industrial cities grow and at what costs?

Running and Reforming the City

EVERY NEW ARRIVAL TO THE city brought dreams and altogether too many needs. Schools and houses had to be built, streets paved, garbage collected, sewers dug, fires fought, utility lines laid. Running the city became a full-time job, and a new breed of professional politician rose to the task. So, too, did a new breed of reformer, determined to help the needy cope with the ravages of urban life.

WEAKNESSES OF CITY GOVERNMENTS The need for change was clear. Many city charters dating from the eighteenth century included a paralyzing system of checks and balances. Mayors vetoed city councils; councils ignored mayors. Jealous state legislatures allowed cities only the most limited and unpopular taxes, such as those on property. But to the cities more than the states fell responsibility for providing services. Municipal governments were often decentralized—fragmented, scattered, at odds with one another. By 1890 Chicago had 11 branches of government, each with its own regulations and taxing authority. Just as such decentralization paralyzed city governments, the traditional sources of political leadership evaporated. The middle and upper classes were being drawn into business and moving to the suburbs. With cities mushrooming in size and population, the structures of urban government strained to adapt.

Boss Rule

"Why must there be a boss," journalist Lincoln Steffens asked Boss Richard Croker of New York, "when we've got a mayor—and a city council?" "That's why," Croker broke in. "It's because we've got a mayor and a council and judges—and—a hundred other men to deal with." The boss was right. He and his political system furnished cities with the centralization, authority, and services they sorely needed.

Bosses ruled through the **political machine.** Often, like New York City's Tammany Hall, machines dated back to the late eighteenth and early nineteenth centuries. They began as fraternal and charitable organizations. Over the years they became centers of political power. In New York City the machine was Democratic; in Philadelphia, Republican. Some were less centralized, as in Chicago; some less ethnically mixed, such as Detroit's. Machines could be found even in rural areas. In Duval County, Texas, for instance, the Spanish-speaking Anglo boss Archie Parr molded a powerful alliance with Mexican American landowners.

In an age of enterprise, the boss operated his political machine like a business corporation. His office might be a saloon, a funeral home, or, like New York's George Washington Plunkitt's, a shoe-shine stand. His managers were party activists, connected in a corporate-style chain of command. Local committeemen reported to district captains, captains to district leaders, district leaders to the boss or bosses who directed the machine.

A CRUDE WELFARE SYSTEM The goods and services of the machine were basic: a Christmas turkey, coal for the winter, jobs for the unemployed, English language classes for newcomers, flowers for the ill and deceased. Bosses sponsored fun, too—sports teams, glee clubs, balls and barbecues with bands playing and drink flowing. This system, rough and uneven as it was, served as a form of public welfare at a time when private charity could not cope with the crush of demand. To the unskilled, the boss doled out jobs in public construction. For bright, ambitious young men, he had places in city offices or in the party. These positions represented the first steps into the middle class, a concrete (if limited) example of social mobility for the masses.

In return, citizens were expected to show their gratitude at the ballot box. Sometimes the votes of grateful constituents were not enough, so bosses turned elsewhere. "Little Bob" Davies of Jersey City mobilized the "graveyard vote." He drew names from tombstones to pad lists of registered voters and hired "repeaters" to vote under the phony names. When reformers introduced the Australian (secret) ballot in the 1880s to prevent fraud, bosses pulled the "Tasmanian dodge" by pre-marking election tickets. Failing that, they dumped whole ballot boxes into the river or drove unpersuaded voters from the polls with hired thugs.

Rewards, Costs, and Accomplishments

Why did bosses go to such lengths? Some simply loved politics. More often bosses loved money. Their ability to get it was limited only by their ingenuity or the occasional success of reform. The record for sheer brass probably goes to Boss William Tweed. During his reign in the 1860s and 1870s Tweed swindled the city of New York out of a fortune. His masterpiece was a chunky three-story courthouse in lower Manhattan originally budgeted at $250,000. When Boss Tweed was through, the city had spent more than $13 million, over 60 percent of which ended up in the pockets of Tweed and his cronies. Tweed died in prison, but with such profits to be made, it was small wonder that bosses rivaled the pharaohs of Egypt as builders.

In their fashion, bosses played a vital role in the industrial city. Rising from the bottom ranks, they guided immigrants into American life and helped some of the underprivileged up from poverty. They changed the urban landscape with massive construction programs and modernized city government by uniting it and making it more effective. Choosing the aldermen, municipal judges, mayors,

MACHINE-AGE VOTING

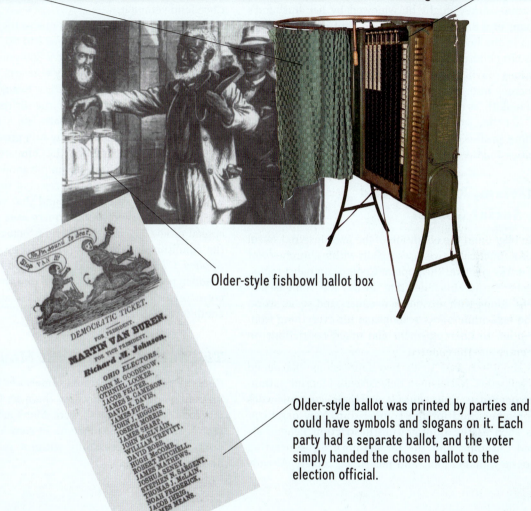

What is the purpose of the curtain?

Levers for mechanically marking ballots

Older-style fishbowl ballot box

Older-style ballot was printed by parties and could have symbols and slogans on it. Each party had a separate ballot, and the voter simply handed the chosen ballot to the election official.

In the late nineteenth century, political corruption often began with voting. Pre-marking ballots, stuffing ballot boxes, paying "repeaters" to vote more than once were all ways to fix the outcome of elections. Reformers fought back. The "Australian," or secret, ballot (first used in Victoria, Australia, in 1858 and in the United States in 1888) employed standardized paper ballots, distributed one to a voter at poll places and marked in a booth in secret. Each ballot had the names of candidates printed on it at government expense, as opposed to earlier ballots, which political parties printed and handed out, often with pictures or symbols

on them. Transparent "fishbowl" ballot boxes made it difficult to stuff the boxes beforehand. Taking the process one step further, Jacob A. Myers tested his new "gear-and-lever" voting machine in Lockport, New York, in 1892. He devised the machine, he said, to "protect mechanically the voter from rascaldom, and make the process of casting the ballot perfectly plain, simple and secret." Some called it "the inventive triumph of its age." The voter simply pulled a lever that closed a curtain around him for privacy. Other levers allowed him to vote for individual candidates or straight-party tickets. The machine recorded and tallied the votes.

Thinking Critically

What advantages did the voting machine offer over the Australian paper ballot? Over the older-style ballots provided by parties? What were the disadvantages of voting machines? Which system was better if voters could not read? What potential for voting fraud exists with today's electronic or optical-scan voting machines?

and administrative officials, bosses exerted new control to provide the contracts and franchises to run cities. Such accomplishments fostered the notion that government could be called on to help the needy. The welfare state, still decades away, had some of its roots here.

The toll was often outrageous. Inflated taxes, extorted revenue, and unpunished vice and crime were only the obvious costs. A woman whose family enjoyed a boss's Christmas turkey might be widowed by her husband's accident in a dangerous sweatshop kept open by timely bribes to the boss's political club. Filthy buildings might claim her children, as corrupt inspectors ignored serious violations. Buying votes and selling favors, bosses turned democracy into a petty business—as much a "business," said Plunkitt, "as the grocery or dry-goods or the drug business." Yet they were the forerunners of the new breed of full-time, professional politicians who would soon govern the cities and the nation as well.

Nativism, Revivals, and the Social Gospel

Urban blight and the condition of the poor inspired social as well as political activism, especially within churches. Not all of it was positive. The popular Congregationalist minister Josiah Strong concluded that the city was "a menace to society." Along with anxious economists and social workers, he held immigrants responsible for everything from corruption to unemployment and urged restrictions on their entry into the country.

In the 1880s and 1890s two depressions sharpened such anxieties. Nativism, a defensive and fearful nationalism, peaked as Americans blamed their economic woes on foreigners and foreign competition. New organizations such as the Immigration Restriction League attacked Catholics and the foreign-born for subverting democracy, taking jobs, and polarizing society. Already

the victims of racial prejudice, the Chinese were an easy target. In 1882 Congress enacted the Chinese Exclusion Act. It banned the entry of Chinese laborers, stranding a mostly male Chinese population in the States. It was the first time race was employed to exclude people and represented an important step in the drive to restrict immigration. In 1897 the first bill requiring literacy tests for immigrants passed Congress, but President Grover Cleveland vetoed it.

Some clergy took their missions to the slums to bridge the gap between the middle class and the poor. Beginning in 1870 Dwight Lyman Moody, a 300-pound former shoe salesman, won armies of lowly converts with revivals in Boston, Chicago, and other cities. Evangelists helped to found American branches of the British Young Men's Christian Association and the Salvation Army. By the end of the century the Salvation Army had grown to 700 corps staffed by some 3,000 officers. They ministered to the needy with food, music, shelter, and simple good fellowship.

A small group of ministers rejected the old ethos that weak character explained sin and that society would be perfected only as individual sinners were converted. They spread a new "Social Gospel" that focused on improving the conditions of society in order to save individuals. In *Applied Christianity* (1886), the influential Washington Gladden preached that the church must be responsible for correcting social injustices, including dangerous working conditions and unfair labor practices.

The Social Settlement Movement

Church-sponsored programs sometimes repelled the immigrant poor when they saw them as thinly disguised missionary efforts. Not all were. Many urban church programs, such as A. B. Simpson's in New York City, served body and soul successfully without relying on heavy-handed evangelizing.

| By the 1890s a flood of southern and eastern European immigrants were streaming into the new receiving center of Ellis Island in New York harbor, while the relatively fewer Asian immigrants who arrived (most were barred from entry by the Chinese Exclusion Act of 1882) came through Angel Island in San Francisco Bay. The rapid rise in immigration ignited nativist fears that immigrants were taking over the country. In the 1870s cartoon pictured here, Irish and Chinese immigrants in their native dress literally gobble up Uncle Sam.

THE GREAT FEAR OF THE PERIOD
THAT UNCLE SAM MAY BE SWALLOWED BY FOREIGNERS.

THE SETTLEMENT HOUSE Immigrants and other slum dwellers were more receptive to a bold experiment called the **settlement house.** Often situated in the worst slums, these early community centers were run by middle-class women and men to help the poor and foreign-born. At the turn of the century there were more than 100 of them, the most famous being Jane Addams's Hull House in Chicago. When Hull House opened in 1889 it occupied a crumbling mansion on South Halstead Street. Slowly it grew to a dozen buildings over more than a city block. In 1898 the Catholic Church sponsored its first settlement house in New York City, and in 1900 Bronson House opened its doors to the Latino community in Los Angeles.

High purposes inspired settlement workers. They left comfortable middle-class homes to live in settlement houses and dedicated themselves (like the "early Christians," said one) to service and sacrifice. Teaching immigrants American ways and creating a community spirit would foster "right living through social relations." But immigrants were also urged to preserve their heritages through festivals, parades, and museums. Like political bosses settlement reformers furnished help, from day nurseries to English language and cooking classes to playgrounds and libraries. Armed with statistics and personal experiences, they also lobbied for social legislation to improve housing, women's working conditions, and public schools.

 REVIEW

In what ways did boss rule represent "reform" of city government, and at whose expense did such reform come?

City Life

URBAN SOCIAL STRATIFICATION EVERY CITY HAD ITS GRIMY tenements and slums but also its fashionable avenues for the rich, who constituted barely 1 percent of the population but owned a fourth of all wealth. In between tenement and mansion lived the broad middle of urban society—educated professionals, white-collar clerks and salespeople, shopkeepers, corporate managers and executives, public employees, and their families. They composed nearly a third of the population and owned about half the nation's wealth. With more money and more leisure time, their power and influence were growing.

City life reflected the stratified nature of American society in the late nineteenth century. Class distinctions continued to be based not on lineage as in Europe but on wealth and income. No longer were dress and manners enough to distinguish one class from another in the United States. What told such differences were more often where people lived, what they bought, which organizations they joined, and how they spent their time.

The Immigrant in the City

When the ship put into port, the first thing an immigrant was likely to see was a city. Perhaps it was Boston or New York City or Galveston, Texas, where an overflow of Jewish immigrants was directed after the turn of the century. Enough of the newcomers traveled inland so that by 1900 three-quarters of the residents of Minnesota and Wisconsin and nearly two-thirds in Utah had at least one foreign-born parent.* But some 70 percent of all immigrants, exhausted physically and financially, settled in cities.

ETHNIC NEIGHBORHOODS Cities developed well-defined mosaics of ethnic communities, because immigrants usually clustered on the basis of Old World families, villages, or provinces. These neighborhoods were constantly changing. As many as half the residents moved out every 10 years, often because of better-paying jobs or more family members who worked. Though one nationality usually dominated a neighborhood, there were always others.

ADAPTING TO AMERICA Ethnic communities served as havens from an unfamiliar culture and as springboards to a new life. From the moment they stepped off the boat newcomers felt pressed to learn English, don American clothes, and drop their "greenhorn" ways. Yet in their neighborhoods they also found comrades who spoke their language, theaters that performed their plays and music, restaurants that served their food. Houses of worship were always at the center of neighborhood life, often reflecting the practices of individual towns or provinces. Foreign-language newspapers reported events from both the Old World and the New in a native tongue first-generation immigrants could understand. Meanwhile, immigrant aid societies furnished assistance with housing and jobs and sponsored insurance programs, English classes, and even baseball teams.

Sometimes immigrants combined the old and new in creative adaptations. Italians developed a pidgin dialect called "Italglish." The Fourth of July became "Il Forte Gelato" (literally "The Great Freeze"), a play on the sound of the words. The phrases permitted them to communicate quickly with Americans and to absorb American customs. Other immigrant groups invented similar idioms, like Chuco, a dialect that developed among border Mexicans in El Paso.

Where they came from often influenced the jobs immigrants took. Because Chinese men did not scorn washing or ironing, more than 7,500 of them could be found in San Francisco laundries by 1880. Sewing ladies' garments seemed unmanly to many native-born Americans but not to Russian and Italian tailors. Slavs tended to be physically robust and valued steady income over education. They often worked in the mines for better pay than in factories and pulled their children from school to earn a living.

*Mormons serving as missionaries in Europe and Great Britain especially swelled Utah's population with converts.

SIGNIFICANT EVENTS

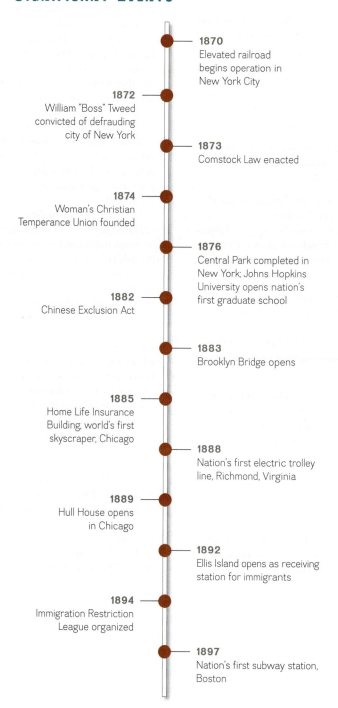

1870
Elevated railroad begins operation in New York City

1872
William "Boss" Tweed convicted of defrauding city of New York

1873
Comstock Law enacted

1874
Woman's Christian Temperance Union founded

1876
Central Park completed in New York; Johns Hopkins University opens nation's first graduate school

1882
Chinese Exclusion Act

1883
Brooklyn Bridge opens

1885
Home Life Insurance Building, world's first skyscraper, Chicago

1888
Nation's first electric trolley line, Richmond, Virginia

1889
Hull House opens in Chicago

1892
Ellis Island opens as receiving station for immigrants

1894
Immigration Restriction League organized

1897
Nation's first subway station, Boston

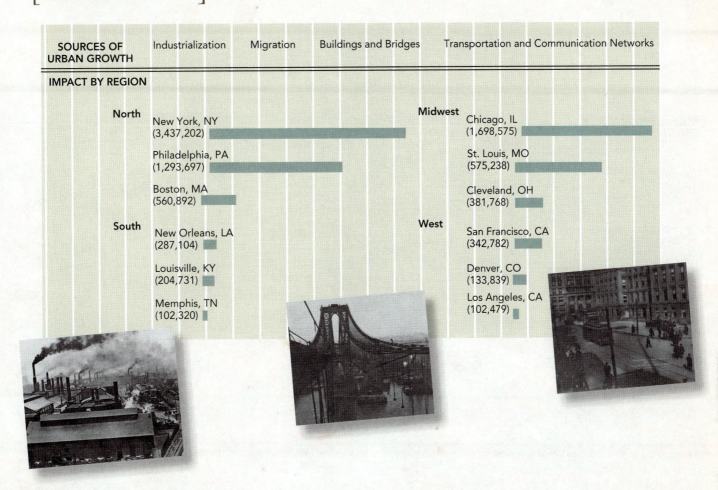

SOURCES OF URBAN GROWTH	Industrialization	Migration	Buildings and Bridges	Transportation and Communication Networks

IMPACT BY REGION

North

New York, NY
(3,437,202)

Philadelphia, PA
(1,293,697)

Boston, MA
(560,892)

South

New Orleans, LA
(287,104)

Louisville, KY
(204,731)

Memphis, TN
(102,320)

Midwest

Chicago, IL
(1,698,575)

St. Louis, MO
(575,238)

Cleveland, OH
(381,768)

West

San Francisco, CA
(342,782)

Denver, CO
(133,839)

Los Angeles, CA
(102,479)

The Statue of the Republic, by sculptor Daniel Chester French, stood 65 feet tall and dominated the Court of Honor at the World's Columbian Exposition in 1893. The fair's exotic buildings, with their domes, minarets, and flags from all nations, showed how conscious Americans were becoming of the wider world.

CHAPTER 21

The Political System under Strain at Home and Abroad

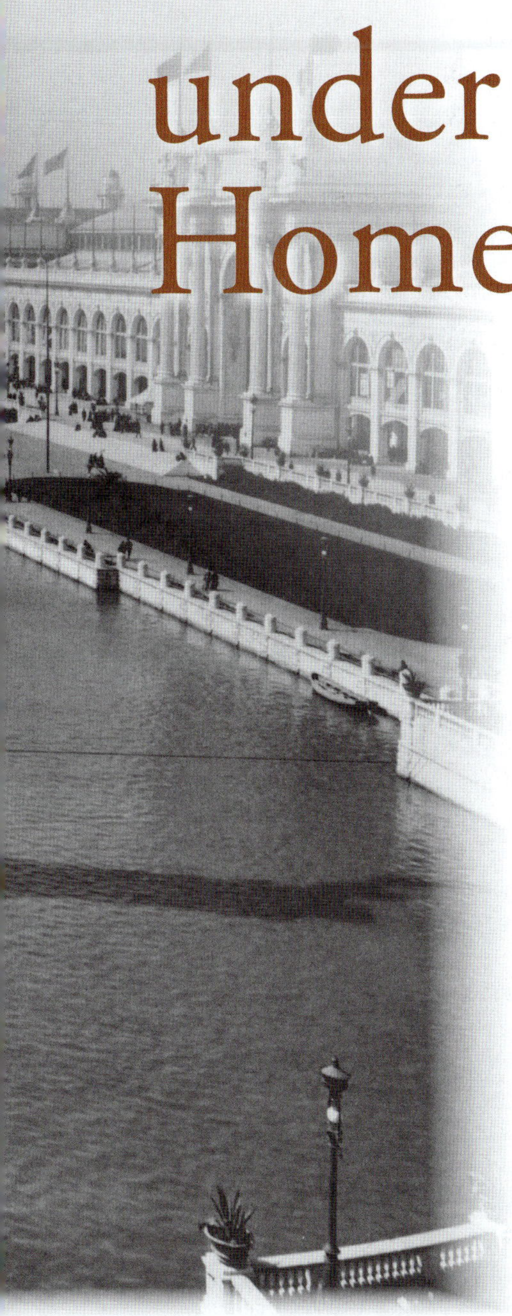

1877–1900

Whats to Come

AN AMERICAN STORY

"The World United at Chicago"

On May 1, 1893, nearly half a million people jostled into a dramatic plaza fronted on either side by gleaming white buildings overlooking a sparkling lagoon. Named the Court of Honor, the plaza was the center of a strange ornamental city that was at once awesome and entirely imaginary. At one end stood a building whose magnificent white dome exceeded even the height of the Capitol in Washington, D.C. Unlike the marble-built Capitol, however, this building was all surface: a stucco shell plastered onto a steel frame and then sprayed with white oil paint to make it glisten. Beyond the Court of Honor stretched thoroughfares encompassing over 200 colonnaded buildings, piers, islands, and watercourses. Located five miles south of Chicago's central business district, this city of the imagination proclaimed itself the "World's Columbian Exposition" in honor of the 400th anniversary of Columbus's voyage to America.

President Grover Cleveland opened the world's fair in a way that symbolized the nation's industrial transformation. He pressed a telegrapher's key. Instantly, electric current set 7,000 feet of shafting into motion, unfurling flags, setting fountains pumping, and lighting 10,000 electric bulbs. The lights played over an array of exhibition buildings soon known as the "White City."

One English visitor dismissed the displays within as little more than "the contents of a great dry goods store mixed up with the contents of museums." In a sense he was right. Visitors paraded by an unending collection of typewriters, pins, watches, agricultural machinery, cedar canoes, and refrigerators, to say nothing of a map of the United States made entirely of pickles. But this riot of

mechanical marvels, gewgaws, and bric-a-brac was symbolic too of the nation's industrial transformation. The fair resembled nothing so much as a tangible version of the new mail-order catalogs whose pages were introducing the goods of the city to the hinterlands.

The connections made by the fair were international as well. This event was the *World's* Columbian Exposition, with exhibits from 36 nations. Germany's famous arms manufacturer, Krupp, had its own separate building. It housed a 120-ton rifled gun. Easily within the range of its gunsights was a replica of the U.S. battleship *Illinois*, whose own bristling turrets stood just offshore of the exposition on Lake Michigan. At the fair's amusement park visitors encountered exotic cultures—not just temples, huts, and totems, but exhibits in the flesh. The Arabian village featured Saharan camels, veiled ladies, and elders in turbans. Nearby, Irish peasants boiled potatoes over turf fires while Samoan men threw axes.

Like all such fairs, the Columbian Exposition created a fantasy. Beyond its boundaries the real world was showing signs of strain. Early in 1893 the Philadelphia and Reading Railroad had gone bankrupt, setting off a financial panic. By the end of the year, nearly 500 banks and 15,000 businesses had failed.

The fair was opened by President Grover Cleveland, lower right.

Although millions of tourists continued to marvel at the fair's wonders, crowds of worried and unemployed workers also gathered elsewhere in Chicago. On Labor Day, Governor John Altgeld of Illinois told a crowd that the government was powerless to soften the "suffering and distress" brought by this latest economic downturn.

In truth, the political system was ill-equipped to cope with the economic and social revolutions reshaping America. The executive branch remained weak, while members of Congress and the courts found themselves easily swayed by the financial interests of the industrial class. The crises of the 1890s strained the political order and forced it to confront such inequities.

The political system also had to take into account developments abroad. Industrialization had sent American businesses scurrying around the world in search of raw materials and markets. As that search intensified, many influential Americans argued that the United States needed to compete with European nations in acquiring territory overseas. By the end of the century the nation's political system had taken its first steps toward modernization, including a major political realignment at home and a growing empire abroad. The changes launched the United States into the twentieth century and an era of prosperity and global power. ∞∞∞∞

THE POLITICS OF PARALYSIS

DURING THE 1880S AND 1890S, as the American political system came under strain, Moisei Ostrogorski was traveling across the United States. Part of a flood of foreign observers, the Russian political scientist had come to see the new democratic experiment in action. His verdict was as blunt as it was widely shared: "the constituted authorities are unequal to their duty." It seemed that the glorious experiment had fallen victim to greed, indifference, and political mediocrity.

In fact, there were deeper problems: a great gulf between rich and poor; a wrenching cycle of boom and bust; the unmet needs of African Americans, Indians, women and other "others." Politics was the traditional medium of resolution, but it was grinding into a dangerous stalemate.

Political Stalemate

From 1877 to 1897 American politics rested on a delicate balance of power that left neither Republicans nor Democrats in control. Republicans inhabited the White House for 12 years; Democrats, for 8. Margins of victory in presidential elections were paper thin. No president could count on having a majority of his party in both houses of Congress for his entire term. Usually Republicans controlled the Senate and Democrats the House of Representatives.

With elections tight, both parties worked hard to turn out voters. Brass bands, parades, cheering crowds of flag-wavers were "the order of the day and night from end to end of the country," reported a British visitor. When Election Day arrived, stores and businesses shut down. At political clubs and corner saloons men lined up for voting orders (along with free drinks) from ward bosses. Fields went untended as farmers took their families to town, cast their ballots, and bet on the outcome.

VOTER TURNOUT An average of nearly 80 percent of eligible voters turned out for presidential elections between 1860 and 1900, a figure higher than at any time since. New party discipline and organization helped to account for the turnout, but it is also true that the electorate made up a smaller percentage of the population. About one American in five actually voted in presidential elections from 1876 to 1892. Most voters were white males. Women could vote in national elections only in a few western states, and beginning in the 1880s, the South erected barriers that eventually disenfranchised many African Americans.

Party loyalty rarely wavered. In every election 16 states could be counted on to vote Republican and 14 Democratic (the latter mainly in the South). In only six states—the most important being New York and Ohio—were the results in doubt.

The Parties

What inspired such loyalty? While Republicans and Democrats shared broad values, they also had major differences. Both parties supported business and condemned radicalism; neither offered embattled workers or farmers much help. Democrats believed in states' rights and limited government, while Republicans favored federal activism to foster economic growth. The stronghold of Democrats lay in the South, where they reminded voters that they had led the states of the Old Confederacy, "redeemed" them from Republican Reconstruction, and championed white supremacy. Republicans dominated the North with strong support from industry and business. They, too, invoked memories of the Civil War to secure votes, black as well as white. "Not every Democrat was a rebel," they chanted, "but every rebel was a Democrat."

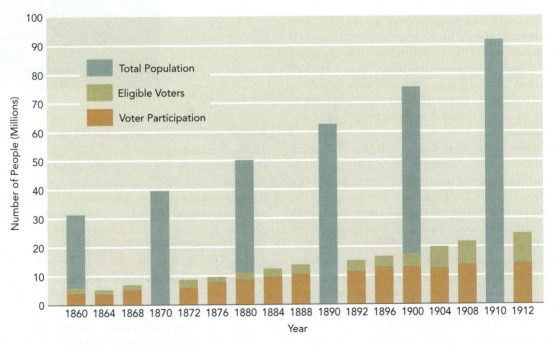

The Voting Public, 1860–1912

Between 1860 and 1910 the population and the number of eligible voters increased nearly threefold. As reforms of the early twentieth century reduced the power of political machines and parties, the percentage of voter participation actually declined.

Ethnicity and religion cemented voter loyalty. Republicans relied on old-stock Protestants, who feared new immigrants and put their faith in promoting pious behavior throughout society. In the Republican Party they found support for immigration restriction, prohibition, and English-only schools. In the North the Democratic Party attracted urban political machines, their immigrant voters, and the working poor. Often Catholic, these voters saw salvation in following their own religious rituals, not in dictating the conduct of others.

Outside the two-party system, reformers often fashioned political organizations of their own. Some groups aligned themselves behind issues rather than parties. Opponents of alcohol created the Woman's Christian Temperance Union (1874) and the Anti-Saloon League (1893). Champions of women's rights joined the National Woman Suffrage Association (1890), a reunion of two branches of the women's suffrage movement that had split in 1869.

Like these political organizations, third political parties also crystallized around an issue or a group. Advocates of temperance rallied to the Prohibition party (1869). Those who sought inflation of the currency formed the Greenback Party (1874). Angry farmers in the West and the South created the Populist, or People's, Party (1892). All drew supporters from both conventional parties, but as largely single-interest groups they mobilized minorities, not majorities.

The Issues

In Congress attention focused on well-worn issues: veterans' benefits, appointments, tariffs, and money. The presidency had been weakened by the impeachment of Andrew Johnson, the scandals of Ulysses S. Grant, and the contested victory of Rutherford B. Hayes in 1876. So Congress enjoyed the initiative in making policy. Time after time legislators squandered it amid electioneering and party infighting or simply were swamped by the ever-increasing flood of proposed legislation.

Some divisive issues were the bitter legacy of the Civil War. Republicans and Democrats waved the symbolic "bloody shirt," each tarring the other with responsibility for the war. The politics of the Civil War also surfaced in the lobbying efforts of veterans. The Grand Army of the Republic, an organization of more than 400,000 Union soldiers, petitioned Congress for pensions to make up for poor wartime pay and to support the widows and orphans of fallen comrades. By the turn of the century Union army veterans and their families were receiving $157 million annually. It was one of the largest public assistance programs in American history. It was also one of the first government programs to offer benefits to African Americans and laid the foundations of the modern welfare state.

More important than veterans' benefits was the campaign for a new method of staffing federal offices. From barely 53,000 employees at the end of the Civil War, the

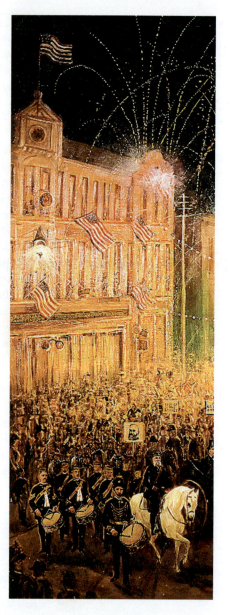

"For three months processions, usually with brass bands, flags, badges, crowds of cheering spectators, are the order of the day and night from end to end of the country," commented a British observer. Here, Denver Republicans lead a nighttime parade to celebrate the election of Benjamin Harrison in the presidential contest of 1888.

federal government had grown to 166,000 by the early 1890s. Far more of these new jobs required special skills. Dismantling the reigning **spoils system** proved difficult for politicians who had rewarded faithful supporters with government jobs regardless of their qualifications. American politics rested on such patronage. Without it, politicians—from presidents to lowly ward captains—feared they could attract neither workers nor money.

PENDLETON ACT   It took the assassination of President James Garfield by a frustrated office seeker in 1881 to break the log jam. In 1883 the Civil Service Act, or Pendleton Act, created a bipartisan civil service commission to administer competitive examinations for some federal jobs. By 1896 almost half of all federal workers came under civil service jurisdiction based on examination and merit.

The protective tariff also aroused Congress. As promoters of economic growth, Republicans usually championed this tax on imported goods. Democrats, with their strength in the agrarian South, generally sought to reduce tariffs in order to encourage foreign trade, lower prices on manufactured goods, and cut the growing federal surplus. In 1890, when Republicans controlled the House of Representatives, Congress enacted the McKinley Tariff. It raised tariff rates to new highs and contained a novel twist called "reciprocity." To promote freer trade, the president could lower rates if other countries did the same.

GOLD, SILVER, AND GREENBACKS

Just as divisive was the issue of currency. For most of the nineteenth century, currency was redeemable in both gold and silver. The need for more money during the Civil War had led Congress to issue "greenbacks"—currency printed on paper with a green back and not convertible to gold or silver. For the next decade and a half, Americans argued over whether to print more such paper money or take it out of circulation. Farmers and other debtors favored printing greenbacks as a way of inflating prices and thus reducing their debts. For the opposite reasons, bankers and creditors stood for "sound money" backed by gold. Fear of **inflation** led Congress first to reduce the number of greenbacks and then in 1879 to make all remaining paper money convertible into gold.

CRIME OF '73

A more heated battle was developing over silver-backed money. By the early 1870s so little silver was being used that Congress officially stopped coining it in 1873, touching off a steep economic slide as the supply of money contracted. With it came charges that a conspiracy of bankers had been responsible for "demonetizing" silver and wrecking the economy in what was widely referred to as the "Crime of '73."

BLAND-ALLISON ACT

In truth the money supply was inadequate to meet demand for the swelling number of manufactured goods. Interest rates—the charge for borrowing money—rose as consumers demanded more cash. Prices fell as too little money chased too many goods. All added to economic instability and increased calls for enlarging the supply of money. In 1878 the Bland-Allison Act inaugurated a limited form of silver coinage. But pressure for unlimited coinage of silver—coining all silver presented at U.S. mints—mounted as silver production quadrupled between 1870 and 1890. In 1890 the Sherman Silver Purchase Act obligated the government to buy 4.5 million ounces of silver every month. Paper tender called "treasury notes," redeemable in gold or silver, paid for the purchases. The compromise satisfied both sides only temporarily. The price of silver fell, pushing less money into the economy than silver enthusiasts wanted but more than the advocates of gold liked.

The White House from Hayes to Harrison

From the 1870s through the 1890s a string of nearly anonymous presidents presided over the country. Not all were mere caretakers. Some tried to energize the office, but Congress continued to dominate Washington.

Republican Rutherford B. Hayes was the first of the "Ohio dynasty," which included three presidents from 1876 to 1900. He moved quickly to end Reconstruction, but his pursuit of civil service reform ended only in splitting his party. Hayes left office after a single term, happy to be "out of a scrape." In 1880 Republican James Garfield, another Ohioan, spent his first hundred days in the White House besieged by office hunters. After Garfield's assassination only six months into his term, Chester A. Arthur, the "spoilsman's spoilsman," became president. To everyone's surprise, the dapper Arthur turned out to be an honest president. He broke with machine politicians, worked to lower the tariff, warmly endorsed the new Civil Service Act, and reduced the federal surplus by beginning construction

This cartoon, "The Tariff Tots," portrays various trusts as ill-tempered children playing roughly with dolls representing the public, consumers and small producers. Whenever reformers tried to reduce tariffs, political support for protection made the task nearly impossible. In 1882 Congress created a commission to consider lowering tariffs, but it was quickly captured by the interests who stood to gain most from high tariffs. Complained one senator: "There was a representative of the wool growers on the commission; . . . of the iron interest . . . of the sugar interest. . . . And those interests were very carefully looked out for."

of a modern navy. Such evenhandedness left him little chance for renomination from divided party leaders.

THE DIRTY ELECTION OF 1884

The election of 1884 was one of the dirtiest ever recorded. Senator James G. Blaine fought off charges of corrupt dealings with the railroads, while Democrat Grover Cleveland, the former governor of New York, admitted to fathering an illegitimate child. In the last week of the race a New York minister labeled the Democrats the party of "Rum, Romanism, and Rebellion" (alcohol, Catholicism, and the Civil War). In reaction the Irish Catholic vote swung strongly to Cleveland and with it New York and the election.

Cleveland was the first Democrat elected to the White House since James Buchanan in 1856 and was more active than many of his predecessors. He pleased reformers by expanding the civil service. His devotion to gold-backed currency, economy, and efficiency earned him praise from business. He supported the growth of federal power by endorsing a new federal regulatory agency created by the Interstate Commerce Act (1887), new agricultural research, and federal arbitration of labor disputes.

Cleveland's presidential activism nonetheless remained limited. He vetoed two of every three bills brought to him, more than twice the number of all his predecessors. Toward the end of his term, embarrassed by the large federal surplus, Cleveland finally reasserted himself by attacking the tariff, but to no avail. The Republican-controlled Senate blocked his attempt to lower it.

In 1888 Republicans nominated a sturdy defender of tariffs, Benjamin Harrison, the grandson of President William Henry Harrison. President Cleveland won a **plurality** of the popular vote but lost in the Electoral College. The "human iceberg" (as Harrison's colleagues called him) worked hard, rarely delegated management, and turned the White House into a well-regulated office. He helped to shape the Sherman Silver Purchase Act (1890), kept up with the McKinley Tariff (1890), and accepted the Sherman Antitrust Act (1890) to limit the power and size of big businesses. At the end of Harrison's term in 1893, Congress completed its most productive session of the era and enacted the nation's first billion-dollar peacetime budget.

A Chinese laborer, holding his queue of long hair in hand, proudly displays patches in support of the 1888 Democratic presidential candidate, Grover Cleveland, and his running mate, Allen B. Thurman. Cleveland and Thurman lost to Benjamin Harrison and Levi P. Morton, a wealthy New York banker. After his victory Harrison, a pious Presbyterian, grabbed the hand of Senator Matthew Quay and crowed, "Providence has given us the victory." "Providence hadn't a damn thing to do with it," Quay said later, irked that Harrison seemed to have no idea how many Republicans "were compelled to approach the gates of the penitentiary to make him President."

Ferment in the States and Cities

Despite its growing expenditures and more legislation, most people expected little from the federal government. Few newspapers even bothered to send correspondents to Washington. Public pressure to curb the excesses of the new industrial order mounted closer to home, in state and city governments. Experimental and often effective, state programs began to grapple with the problems of corporate power, discriminatory shipping rates, political corruption, and urban decay.

STATE COMMISSIONS

Starting in 1869 with Massachusetts, states established commissions to investigate and regulate industry, especially railroads, America's first big business. By the turn of the century almost two-thirds of the states had them. These weak commissions gathered and publicized information on shipping rates and business practices and furnished advice about public policy. On the West Coast and in the Midwest, state legislatures empowered commissions to end rebates and monitor freight rates. Illinois in 1870 became the first of several states to define railroads as public highways subject to regulation, including setting maximum rates.

NATIONAL MUNICIPAL LEAGUE

Concern over political corruption and urban blight led reformers to hold state municipal conventions to address urban problems. Iowa convened the first one in 1877. Philadelphia sponsored a national conference on good city government in 1894. A year later reformers founded the National

Mary Shelley's novel of a man-made monster who turns against its creator strikes the theme for this 1874 cartoon titled "The American Frankenstein." Here, the railroad is a monstrous creation that crushes the common people in its path. It carries the symbols of wealth and might—a cloak of ermine and a club of capital. "Agriculture, commerce, and manufacture are all in my power," the monster bellows in the caption. Figures of authority, like the policeman at the lower right, can only snap to attention and salute.

Municipal League. It soon had more than 200 branches. Its model city charter advanced such farsighted reforms as separate city and state elections, limited contracts for utilities, and more authority for mayors. Meanwhile, cities and states in the Midwest enacted laws closing stores on Sundays, prohibiting the sale of alcohol, and making English the language of public schools—all in an effort to standardize social behavior and control the habits of new immigrants.

 **REVIEW**

What factors led to the paralysis in the late nineteenth century?

THE REVOLT OF THE FARMERS

IN 1890 THE POLITICS OF stalemate cracked as the patience of farmers across the South and the western plains reached an end. Beginning in the 1880s a sharp depression drove down agricultural prices and forced thousands from their land. But farmers suffered from a great deal more, including heavy mortgages, widespread poverty, and railroad rates that sometimes discriminated against them. In 1890 their resentment boiled over. An agrarian revolt—called **Populism**—swept across the political landscape and helped break the political stalemate of the previous 20 years.

The Harvest of Discontent

TARGETS OF FARM ANGER The revolt of the farmers stirred first on the southern frontier, spreading eastward from Texas through the rest of the Old Confederacy, then west across the plains. Farmers blamed their troubles on obvious inequalities: manufacturers protected by the tariff, railroads with sky-high shipping rates, wealthy bankers who held their mounting debts, expensive intermediaries who stored and processed their commodities. All seemed to profit at the expense of farmers.

The true picture was more complex. The tariff protected industrial goods but also supported some farm commodities such as wool and sugar. Railroad rates, however high, actually fell from 1865 to 1890. Although mortgages were heavy, most were short, no more than four years. Farmers often refinanced them and used the money to buy more land and machinery, thus increasing their debts. Millers and operators of grain elevators or storage silos earned handsome profits, yet every year more of them came under state regulation.

In hard times, when debts mounted and children went hungry, complexity mattered little. And in the South many poor farmers seemed condemned forever to hard times. Credit lay at the root of their problem, because most southern farmers had to borrow money to plant and harvest their crops. The inequities of sharecropping and the crop-lien system (page 466) forced them into debt. When the prices for their crops fell they borrowed still more, stretching the financial resources of the South beyond their meager limits. Within a few years after the Civil War, Massachusetts's banks had five times as much money as all the banks of the Old Confederacy.

Beginning in the 1870s nearly 100,000 debt-ridden farmers a year picked up stakes across the Deep South and fled to Texas to escape this ruinous system of credit, only to find it waiting for them. Others stood and fought, as one pamphlet exhorted in 1889, "not with glittering musket, flaming sword and deadly cannon, but with the silent, potent and all-powerful ballot."

The Origins of the Farmers' Alliance

PATRONS OF HUSBANDRY Before farmers could vote together, they had to get together. Life on the farm was harsh, drab, and isolated. Such conditions shocked Oliver Hudson Kelley as he traveled across the South after the Civil War. In 1867 the young government clerk founded the Patrons of Husbandry to brighten the lives of farmers and broaden their horizons. Local chapters, called "granges," brought a dozen or so farmers and their families together to pray, sing, and learn new farming techniques. The Grangers sponsored fairs, picnics, dances, lectures—anything to break the bleakness of farm life. By 1875 there were 800,000 members in 20,000 locals, most in the Midwest, South, and Southwest.

At first Grangers swore off politics. But in a pattern often repeated, socializing led to economic and then political action. Pooling their money to buy supplies and equipment to store and market their crops, Grangers could avoid the high charges of intermediaries. By the early 1870s they also were lobbying midwestern legislatures to adopt "Granger laws" regulating rates charged by railroads, grain elevator operators, and other intermediaries.

GRANGER CASES Eight "Granger cases" came before the Supreme Court in the 1870s to test the new regulatory measures. *Munn v. Illinois* (1877) upheld the right of Illinois to regulate private property (in this case, the giant elevators for storing grain) as long as it was "devoted to a public use." Later decisions allowed state regulation of railroads, but only within state lines. Congress responded in 1887 by creating the Interstate Commerce Commission, a federal agency that could regulate commerce across state boundaries. In practice it had little power, but it was a key step toward establishing the public right to oversee private companies.

SOUTHERN ALLIANCE Slumping prices in the 1870s and 1880s bred new farm organizations. Slowly they blended into what the press called the "Alliance movement." The Southern Alliance, formed in Texas in 1875, spread rapidly after Dr. Charles W. Macune took command in 1886. A doctor and lawyer as well as a farmer, Macune planned to expand the state's network of local chapters, or suballiances, into a national network of state Alliance Exchanges. Like the Grangers the exchanges pooled their resources in cooperatively owned enterprises for buying and selling, milling and storing, banking and manufacturing.

For a brief period, between 1886 and 1892, the Alliance cooperatives grew to more than a million members throughout the South and challenged accepted ways of doing business. Macune claimed that his new Texas Exchange saved members 40 percent on plows and 30 percent on wagons. But most Alliance cooperatives were managed by farmers without the time or experience to succeed. Usually opposed by irate local merchants, the ventures eventually failed.

COLORED FARMERS' ALLIANCE Although the Southern Alliance admitted no African Americans, it encouraged them to organize. A small group of black and white Texans founded the Colored Farmers' National Alliance and Cooperative Union in 1886. By 1891 a quarter of a million farmers had joined. Its operations were largely secret, because public action often brought swift retaliation from white supremacists. When the Colored Farmers' Alliance organized a strike of black cotton pickers near Memphis in 1891, white mobs hunted down and lynched 15 strikers. The murders went unpunished, and the Colored Alliance began to founder.

The political and social turbulence of the era is reflected in this cartoon of a businessman being tossed and buffeted by agrarian Populists and "Silverites" as well as Republicans and Democrats.

The Alliance Peaks

The key to Alliance success was not organization but leadership, both at the top and in the middle. Alliance lecturers fanned out across the South and the Great Plains, organizing suballiances and teaching new members about finance and cooperative businesses. At least one-quarter of Alliance members were women. The Alliance movement continued the old Grange practice of sponsoring family-oriented activities, such as songfests, parades, picnics, and even burial services. Although the Alliance remained sharply divided over woman suffrage, more than a few women became speakers and organizers. "Wimmin is everywhere," noted one observer. The comment seemed to apply literally to Alliance member Mary Elizabeth Lease, who in the summer of 1890 alone gave 160 speeches.

OCALA DEMANDS In 1890 members of the Alliance met in Ocala, Florida, and issued the "Ocala Demands." The manifesto reflected their deep distrust of "the money power"—large corporations and banks whose financial power gave them the ability to manipulate the "free" market. The Ocala Demands called on government to correct such abuses by reducing tariffs, abolishing national banks, regulating railroads, and coining silver money freely. The platform also demanded a federal income tax and the popular election of senators to make government more responsive to the public.

The most innovative feature of the platform came from Charles Macune. His "subtreasury system" would have required the federal government to furnish warehouses for harvested crops and low-interest loans to tide farmers over until prices rose. Under such a system farmers would no longer have had to sell in a glutted market, as they did under the crop-lien system. And they could have exerted control over the money supply, expanding it simply by borrowing at harvest time.

In the elections of 1890 the old parties faced hostile farmers across the nation. In the South the Alliance continued to work within the Democratic Party and elected 4 governors, won 8 legislatures, and sent 44 members of Congress and 3 senators to Washington. In the Great Plains, Alliance candidates drew farmers from the Republican Party. Newly created farmer parties elected 5 representatives and 2 senators in Kansas and South Dakota and took over both houses of the Nebraska legislature.

In the West especially, Alliance organizers began to dream of a national third party that would be free from the corporate influence, sectionalism, and racial tensions that split Republicans and Democrats. In their minds it would be a party not just of farmers but also of the downtrodden and the "toilers," including industrial workers.

THE PEOPLE'S PARTY

In February 1892, as the presidential election year opened, a convention of 900 labor, feminist, farm, and other reform delegates (100 of them black) met in St. Louis. They founded the People's, or Populist, Party and called for another convention to nominate a presidential ticket. Initially southern Populists held back, clinging to their strategy of working within the Democratic Party. But when newly elected Democrats failed to support Alliance programs, southern leaders such as Tom Watson of Georgia abandoned the Democrats and began recruiting black and white farmers for the Populists. Although he was a wealthy farmer, Watson sympathized with the poor of both races.

The national convention of Populists met in Omaha, Nebraska, on Independence Day, 1892. Their impassioned platform promised to return government "to the hands of 'the plain people.'" More conservative southern Populists succeeded in blocking a plank for woman suffrage, though western Populists joined the campaign that would win women the right to vote in Colorado in 1893. Planks advocated the subtreasury plan, unlimited coinage of silver and expansion of the money supply, direct election of senators, an income tax, and government ownership of railroads, telegraph, and telephone. To attract wage earners the party endorsed the eight-hour workday, restriction of immigration, and a ban on the use of Pinkerton detectives in labor disputes—for the Pinkertons had engaged in a savage gun battle with strikers that year at Andrew Carnegie's Homestead steel plant. Delegates rallied behind the old greenbacker and Union general James B. Weaver, carefully balancing their presidential nomination with a one-legged Confederate veteran as his running mate.

The Election of 1892

The Populists enlivened the otherwise dull campaign of 1892, as Democrat Grover Cleveland and Republican incumbent Benjamin Harrison refought the election of 1888. This time Cleveland won, and for the first session since the Civil War, Democrats gained control of both houses of Congress. The Populists, too, enjoyed success. Weaver polled over a million votes, the first third-party candidate to do so. Populists elected 3 governors, 5 senators, 10 representatives, and nearly 1,500 members of state legislatures.

LONG-TERM WEAKNESSES OF THE POPULISTS

Despite these victories the election revealed dangerous weaknesses in the People's Party. Across the nation thousands of voters did change political affiliations, but most often from the Republicans to the Democrats, not to the Populists. No doubt a Democratic Party campaign of intimidation and repression hurt the People's Party in the South, where white conservatives had been appalled by Tom Watson's open courtship of black southerners. ("You are kept apart that you may be separately fleeced of your earnings," Watson had told his racially mixed audiences.) In the North, Populists failed to win over labor and most city dwellers. Both parties were more concerned with family budgets than with the problems of farmers and the downtrodden.

The darker side of Populism also put off many Americans. Its rhetoric was often violent; it spoke ominously of conspiracies and stridently in favor of immigration restriction. In fact, in 1892 the Alliance lost members, an omen of defeats to come. But for the present the People's Party had demonstrated two conflicting truths: it showed how far from the needs of many ordinary Americans the two parties had drifted and how difficult it would be to break their power.

✔ REVIEW

How did the Farmers' Alliance and the People's Party attempt to resolve the problems faced by farmers?

THE NEW REALIGNMENT

ON MAY 5, 1893, ONLY four days after President Grover Cleveland opened the World's Columbian Exposition in Chicago, a wave of bankruptcies swamped the economy. Overexpansion once again set in motion the boom-and-bust business cycle, ruining major firms and driving stock prices to all-time lows. By the time the exposition's gleaming White City shut its doors in October, nearly 200,000 workers had lost their jobs in Chicago alone. Millions more across the nation shared that fate, in what became the worst depression the Republic had yet experienced.

DUELING DOCUMENTS

WHAT SHOULD THE GOVERNMENT DO?

In 1887 President Grover Cleveland vetoed the "Texas Seed Bill," legislation designed to aid drought-stricken Texas farmers through the natural disaster (Document 1). Four years later, Nebraska farmer W. M. Taylor made a desperate plea for help in the face of natural and man-made disasters (Document 2).

DOCUMENT 1   Government Should Not Help Individuals: President Grover Cleveland

It is represented that a long-continued and extensive drought has existed in certain portions of the State of Texas, resulting in a failure of crops and consequent distress and destitution. Though there has been some difference in statements concerning the extent of the people's needs in the localities thus affected, there seems to be no doubt that there has existed a condition calling for relief; and I am willing to believe that, notwithstanding the aid already furnished, a donation of seed grain to the farmers located in this region, to enable them to put in new crops, would serve to avert a continuance or return of an unfortunate blight.

And yet I feel obliged to withhold my approval of the plan as proposed by this bill, to indulge a benevolent and charitable sentiment through the appropriation of public funds for that purpose.

I can find no warrant for such an appropriation in the Constitution, and I do not believe that the power and duty of the general government ought to be extended to the relief of individual suffering which is in no manner properly related to the public service or benefit. A prevalent tendency to disregard the limited mission of this power and duty should, I think, be steadfastly resisted,

to the end that the lesson should be constantly enforced that, though the people support the government, the government should not support the people.

The friendliness and charity of our countrymen can always be relied upon to relieve their fellow citizens in misfortune. This has been repeatedly and quite lately demonstrated. Federal aid in such cases encourages the expectation of paternal care on the part of the government and weakens the sturdiness of our national character, while it prevents the indulgence among our people of that kindly sentiment and conduct which strengthens the bonds of a common brotherhood.

It is within my personal knowledge that individual aid has, to some extent, already been extended to the sufferers mentioned in this bill. The failure of the proposed appropriation of $10,000 additional, to meet their remaining wants, will not necessarily result in continued distress if the emergency is fully made known to the people of the country.

It is here suggested that the Commissioner of Agriculture is annually directed to expend a large sum of money for the purchase, propagation, and distribution

of seeds and other things of this description, two-thirds of which are, upon the request of senators, representatives, and delegates in Congress, supplied to them for distribution among their constituents.

The appropriation of the current year for this purpose is $100,000, and it will probably be no less in the appropriation for the ensuing year. I understand that a large quantity of grain is furnished for such distribution, and it is supposed that this free apportionment among their neighbors is a privilege which may be waived by our senators and representatives.

If sufficient of them should request the Commissioner of Agriculture to send their shares of the grain thus allowed them, to the suffering farmers of Texas, they might be enabled to sow their crops; the constituents, for whom in theory this grain is intended, could well bear the temporary deprivation, and the donors would experience the satisfaction attending deeds of charity.

Source: President Grover Cleveland Vetoes Disaster Relief Legislation, February 16, 1887, reprinted in J. F. Watts and Fred Israel, eds., *Presidential Documents: The Speeches, Proclamations, and Policies That Have Shaped the Nation from Washington to Clinton* (New York: Routledge, 2000), pp. 164–165.

DOCUMENT 2   Farmers' Problems Are Beyond Their Control: W. M. Taylor

This season is without a parallel in this part of the country. The hot winds burned up the entire crop, leaving thousands of families wholly destitute, many of whom might have been able to run through this crisis had it not been for the galling yoke put on them by the money loaners and sharks—not by charging 7 per cent per annum, which is the lawful rate of interest of even 10 per cent, but the unlawful and inhuman country destroying rate of 3 per cent a month, some going still farther and charging 50 per cent per annum. We are cursed, many of us financially, beyond redemption, not by the hot winds so much as by the swindling game of the bankers and money loaners, who have taken the money and now are after the property, leaving the farmer moneyless and homeless. . . . I have borrowed

for example $1,000. I pay $25 besides to the commission man. I give my note and second mortgage of 3 per cent of the $1,000, which is $30 more. Then I pay 7 per cent on the $1,000 to the actual loaner. Then besides all this I pay for appraising the land, abstract, recording, etc., so when I have secured my loan I am out the first year $150. Yet I am told by the agent who loans me the money, he can't stand to loan at such low rates. This is on the farm, but now come the chattel loan. I must have $50 to save myself. I get the money; my note is made payable in thirty or sixty days for $35, secured by chattel of two horses, harness and wagon, about five times the value of the note. The time comes to pay, I ask for a few days. No I can't wait; must have the money. If I can't get the money, I have the

extreme pleasure of seeing my property taken and sold by this iron handed money loaner while my family and I suffer.

Source: W. M. Taylor to editor, *Farmer's Alliance* (Lincoln), January 10, 1891, Nebraska Historical Society, reprinted in Robert D. Marcus and David Burner, eds., *America Firsthand*, Vol. II (New York: St. Martin's Press, 1992), p. 90.

Thinking Critically

How does President Cleveland justify his veto of the "Texas Seed Bill"? What, in his view, is the role of the federal government in times of disaster? What problems does the farmer face? How would President Cleveland have responded to the farmer's letter?

Charles Dana Gibson, the Massachusetts-born illustrator famous for his portraits of well-bred young women in the 1890s, tackles a different subject in this ink drawing, a bread line of mixed classes during the depression of 1893.

The sharp contrast between the White City and the nation's economic misery demonstrated the inability of the political system to smooth out the economy's cycle of boom and bust. The new industrial order that had linked Americans economically had brought prosperity in the 1880s. But in 1893 the price of interdependence became obvious, as a downturn in one sector of the economy quickly affected others. With no way to control the swings in the business cycle, depression came on a scale as large as that of the booming prosperity. Out of it emerged a new political realignment that left the Republican Party in control of national politics for decades to come.

The Depression of 1893

Railroad baron and descendant of two presidents Charles Francis Adams Jr. called the depression a "convulsion," but the country experienced it as crushing idleness. In August 1893 unemployment stood at 1 million; by the middle of 1894 it was 3 million. At the end of the year nearly one worker in five was out of a job.

Working- and middle-class families took in boarders, laundry, and sewing to make ends meet. With so many fathers and husbands unemployed, more wives and children left home to work. In the 1890s the number of laboring women increased, from 4 million to 5.3 million, but mainly in the exploitative fields of domestic and clerical work. In the South, where half the nation's working children were employed, child labor rose by 160 percent in textile mills during the decade. Concern for the young became so acute that middle-class women created the League for the Protection of the Family in 1896. Among other things it advocated compulsory education to keep children out of factories and mines.

The federal government had no program to combat the effects of the depression. "While the people should

patriotically and cheerfully support their Government," President Cleveland had said at his inauguration, "its functions do not include the support of the people." The states offered little more. Relief, like poverty, was considered a private matter. The burden fell on local charities, benevolent societies, churches, labor unions, and ward bosses. In city after city citizens organized relief committees to distribute bread and clothing until their meager resources gave out.

Others were less charitable. As the popular preacher Henry Ward Beecher told his congregation, "No man in this land suffers from poverty unless it be more than his fault—unless it be his sin." But the scale of hardship was so great, its targets so random, that anyone could be thrown out of work—an industrious neighbor, a factory foreman with 20 years on the job, a bank president. Older attitudes about personal guilt and responsibility for poverty began to give way to new ideas about its social origins and the obligation of public agencies to help.

The Rumblings of Unrest

Even before the depression, rumblings of unrest had begun to roll across the country. The Great Railroad Strike of 1877 ignited nearly two decades of labor strife (pages 523–526). After 1893 discontent mounted as employers cut wages, laid off employees, and closed factories. During the first year of the depression 1,400 strikes sent more than half a million workers from their jobs.

COXEY'S ARMY Uneasy business executives and politicians saw radicalism and the possibility of revolution in every strike. But the depression of 1893 had unleashed a more elemental force: simple discontent. In the spring of 1894, it focused on government inaction. On Easter Sunday, "General" Jacob Coxey, a 39-year-old Populist and factory owner, launched the "Tramps' March on Washington" from Massillon, Ohio. His "Commonweal Army of Christ"—some 500 men, women, and children—descended on Washington to offer "a petition with boots on" for a federal program of public works. On May 1, Coxey's troops, armed with "clubs of peace," massed at the foot of the Capitol. When Coxey entered the Capitol grounds, 100 mounted police routed the demonstrators and arrested the general for trespassing on the grass. Nothing came of the protest, other than to signal a growing demand for federal action.

Federal help was not to be found. President Cleveland had barely moved into the White House when the depression struck. The country blamed him; he blamed silver. In his view the Sherman Silver Purchase Act (1890) had shaken business confidence by forcing the government to use its shrinking reserves of gold to purchase (though not to coin) silver. Repeal of the act, Cleveland believed, was the way to build gold reserves and restore confidence. After bitter debates Congress complied. The economic tinkering only strengthened the resolve of "silverites" in the Democratic Party to overwhelm Cleveland's conservative "gold" wing.

Worse for the president, repeal of silver purchases brought no economic revival. In the short run, abandoning silver hurt the economy by shrinking the money supply just when expansion might have stimulated it by providing needed credit. As panic and unemployment spread Cleveland's popularity wilted. Democrats were buried in the congressional elections of 1894. Dropping moralistic reforms and stressing national activism, Republicans won control of both the House and the Senate. With the Democrats now confined to the South, the politics of stalemate was over. All that remained for the Republican Party was to capture the White House in 1896.

The Battle of the Standards

The campaign of 1896 quickly became known as the "battle of the standards"—a reference to the burning question of whether gold alone or gold and silver should be the monetary standard. Most Republicans saw gold as the stable base for building business confidence and economic prosperity. They adopted a platform calling for "sound money" supported by gold alone. Their candidate, Governor William McKinley of Ohio, cautiously supported the gold plank and firmly believed in high tariffs to protect American industry.

FREE SILVER   Silverites campaigned for "free and independent" coinage of silver, in which the Treasury freely minted all the silver presented to it, independent of other nations. The supply of money would increase, prices would rise, and the economy would revive—or so the silverites' theory held. But the free silver movement was more than a monetary theory. It was a symbolic protest of region and class—of the agricultural South and West against the commercial Northeast, of debt-ridden farm folk against industrialists and financiers.

"CROSS OF GOLD" SPEECH   Silverites controlled the Democratic National Convention from the start. They paraded with silver banners, wore silver buttons, and wrote a plank into the platform calling for free and unlimited coinage of the metal. The high point came when William Jennings Bryan of Nebraska stepped to the lectern, threw back his head, and offered himself to "a cause as holy as the cause of liberty—the cause of humanity." The crowd was in a near frenzy as he reached the dramatic climax and spread his arms in mock crucifixion: "You shall not crucify mankind upon a cross of gold." The next day the convention nominated him for the presidency.

Populists were in a quandary. They expected the Democrats to stick with Cleveland and gold, sending unhappy silverites headlong into their camp. Instead, the Democrats stole their thunder. "If we fuse [with the Democrats] we are sunk," complained one Populist. "If we don't fuse, all the silver men we have will leave us for the more powerful Democrats." At a bitter convention, fusionists nominated Bryan for president. The best antifusionists could do was drop the Democrats' vice presidential candidate in favor of the fiery agrarian rebel from Georgia, Tom Watson.

Bryan knew he faced an uphill battle. Adopting a more active style that would be imitated in future campaigns, he traveled 18,000 miles by train, gave as many as 30 speeches a day, and reached perhaps 3 million people in 27 states. The nomination of the People's Party actually did more harm than good by labeling Bryan a Populist (which he was not) and a radical (which he definitely was not). Devoted to the "plain people," the Great Commoner spoke for rural America and Jeffersonian values: small farmers, small towns, small government.

McKinley knew he could not compete with Bryan's barnstorming, so he contented himself with sedate speeches from his front porch in Canton, Ohio. There thousands of his supporters flocked regularly to hear him promise a "full dinner pail" for everyone. The folksy appearance of the campaign belied its reality. From the beginning it had been engineered by Marcus Alonzo Hanna, a talented Ohio industrialist. Hanna relied on modern techniques of organization and marketing. He advertised McKinley, said Theodore Roosevelt, "as if he were patent medicine." Hanna also saturated the country with millions of leaflets, along with 1,400 speakers attacking free trade and free silver. McKinley won in a walk, the first president since Ulysses Grant to win a majority of the popular vote.

REPUBLICAN COALITION   The election proved to be one of the most critical in the Republic's history.* Over the previous three decades political life had been characterized by vibrant campaigns, slim party margins, high voter turnout, and low-profile presidents. The election of 1896 signaled a new era of dwindling party loyalties, stronger presidents, and Republican rule. McKinley's victory broke the political stalemate and forged a powerful coalition that dominated politics for the next 30 years. It rested on the industrial cities of the Northeast and Midwest and combined old support from business, farmers, and Union army veterans with broader backing from industrial wage earners. The Democrats controlled little but the South. And the Populists vanished, but not before leaving a compound legacy: as a catalyst for political realignment, a cry for federal action from the South and the West, and a prelude to a new age of reform.

The Rise of Jim Crow Politics

In 1892, despite the stumping of such Populists as Tom Watson, African Americans cast their ballots for Republicans, when they were permitted to vote freely. But increasingly, their voting rights were being curtailed across the South.

As the nineteenth century drew to a close, a long-standing racialism—categorizing people on the basis of

---

*Five elections, in addition to the contest of 1896, are often cited as critical shifts in voter allegiance and party alignments: the Federalist defeat of 1800, Andrew Jackson's rise in 1828, Lincoln's Republican triumph of 1860, Al Smith's Democratic loss in 1928, and—perhaps—Ronald Reagan's conservative tide of 1980.

PINNING THE WINNING TICKET

A lunch box (or "dinner bucket") used by workmen

What are the advantages of this transparent plastic (celluloid) button?

McKinley and Roosevelt

Metal pin easily affixed to clothing

EMPLOYMENT FOR LABOR

A FULL DINNER BUCKET

PROSPERITY

SOUND MONEY-GOOD MARKETS

Credit: Hervey Priddy Collection, Birdwell Library, Southern Methodist University.

Sometimes even the smallest objects yield a wealth of information to historians. This campaign button from the presidential election of 1900 offers a full assortment of campaign slogans as well as an unmistakable sign (even to those who could not read) of who is running and whom the wearer supports. Celluloid buttons first appeared in the presidential election of 1896. Cheap and easy to produce, they quickly turned into electioneering staples and signaled a shift from big political rallies and emotional appeals to promotional campaigns based on education and advertising. The Ohio industrialist Mark Hanna pioneered many of these practices, including the use of short newsreels of the candidate, when he managed McKinley's run for the White House in 1896. In 1900 McKinley's running mate Theodore Roosevelt at first deplored the unvarnished marketing of candidates (see page 570). Still, the techniques worked. Celluloid buttons became the fastest-growing article in the history of American political campaigns.

Thinking Critically

What slogans does the button contain? To which voting groups might these slogans have appealed? What do they tell us about turn-of-the-century politics? What visual cues reinforce the slogans? Why did political campaigns turn to advertising techniques, and what were the long-term effects of the shift?

race—deepened. The arrival of "new" immigrants from eastern and southern Europe and the acquisition of new overseas colonies highlighted differences among races and helped encourage prejudices that stridently justified segregation and other forms of racial control (see pages 470–472). In the South racialism was enlisted into a political purpose: preventing an alliance of poor blacks and whites that might topple white conservative Democrats. The white supremacy campaign, on the face of it directed at African Americans, also had a broader target in the world of politics: rebellion from below, whether black or white.

DISENFRANCHISEMENT Mississippi, whose Democrats had led the move to "redeem" their state from Republican Reconstruction, in 1890 took the lead in disenfranchising African Americans. A new state constitution required voters to pay a poll tax and pass a literacy test, requirements that eliminated the great majority of black voters. Conservative Democrats favored the plan because it also reduced voting among poor whites, who were most likely to join opposition parties. Before the new constitution went into effect, Mississippi contained more than 250,000 eligible voters, black and white. By 1892, after its adoption, there were fewer than 77,000.

Soon an all-white combination of conservatives and "reformers"—those disgusted by frequent election-stealing with blocs of black votes—passed disenfranchisement laws across the South. In 1898 the Supreme Court upheld these laws in *Williams v. Mississippi,* ruling that they were valid because they did not discriminate solely against African Americans. The decision dealt a mortal blow to the Republican Party in the South for generations because much of its support in the region came from African Americans. By 1908 campaigns to limit voting had won in every southern state.

The disenfranchisement campaign succeeded in achieving its broad aim of splitting rebellious whites from blacks, as the tragic fate of Tom Watson demonstrated. Only a dozen years after his biracial campaign of 1892, Watson was promoting black disenfranchisement and white supremacy in Georgia. Like other southern Populists, Watson returned to the Democratic Party still hoping to help poor whites. But under the increased atmosphere of intolerance, only by playing a powerful race card could he hope to win election. "What does civilization owe the negro?" he asked bitterly. "Nothing! Nothing!! NOTHING!!!"

To mount a successful campaign for disenfranchisement, white conservatives inflamed racial passions. They staged "White Supremacy Jubilees" and peppered newspaper editorials with complaints of "bumptious" and "impudent"

African Americans. The lynchings of blacks peaked during the 1890s, averaging over a hundred a year for the decade. Most took place in the South.

The African American Response

IDA B. WELLS African Americans worked out their own responses to the climate of intolerance. Ida B. Wells, a black woman born into slavery, turned her talents into a nationwide campaign against lynching when a friend, Thomas Moss, and two of his partners in the People's Grocery were brutally murdered in Memphis after a fight with a white competitor in 1892. Wells meticulously documented the murders of African Americans across the South, demonstrating an astounding 200 percent increase between 1882 and 1892. Wells turned antilynching into a personal crusade. She spent much of her time educating Americans about the use of lynching and other forms of mob violence as devices for terrorizing African Americans in the absence of slavery. Black men like Thomas Moss, who might want to start black-owned businesses or alter race relations in the South, were particular targets because they threatened the prevailing racial and economic hierarchy in the South. Though her lobbying failed to produce a federal antilynching law, Wells did help organize black women, eventually into the National Association of Colored Women in 1896. It supported wide-ranging reforms, including in education, housing, and health care, and, of course, antilynching.

Wells's campaign focused on mob violence, but another former slave, Booker T. Washington, stressed instead the need for accepting the framework for race relations and

In keeping with Booker T. Washington's emphasis on vocational training, the Tuskegee Institute, opened in Alabama in 1881, was training 1,400 students in 30 trades by 1900. Academic subjects received attention, too, as evidenced by this photograph of a history class (segregated by gender) learning about Captain John Smith and Pocahontas.

working within it. "I love the South," Washington reassured an audience of white and black southerners in Atlanta in 1895. He conceded that white prejudice against blacks existed throughout the region but nonetheless counseled African Americans to accept what was offered them and work for their economic betterment through manual labor. Every laborer who learned a trade, every farmer who tilled the land could increase his or her savings. And those earnings amounted to "a little green ballot" that "no one will throw out or refuse to count." Toward that end Washington organized the Tuskegee Institute in 1881 and created a curriculum stressing vocational skills for farming, manual trades, and industrial work.

ATLANTA COMPROMISE Many white Americans hailed what one black critic called the "Atlanta Compromise" because it struck the note of patient humility they were eager to hear. For African Americans it made the best of a bad situation. Washington, an astute politician, discovered that philanthropists across the nation hoped to make Tuskegee an example of their generosity. He was the honored guest of Andrew Carnegie at his imposing Skibo Castle. California railroad magnate Collis Huntington became his friend, as did other business executives eager to discuss "public and social questions."

Washington always preached accommodation to the racial caste system. He accepted segregation (as long as separate facilities were equal) and qualifications on voting (if they applied to white citizens as well). Above all, Washington sought economic self-improvement for common black folk in fields and factories. In 1900 he organized the National Negro Business League to help establish African Americans in business as the leaders of their people. The rapid growth of local chapters (320 by 1907) extended his influence across the country.

In the "Solid South" (as well as an openly racist North), it was Washington's restrained approach that set the agenda for most African Americans. The ferment of the early 1890s, among black Populists and white, was replaced by a lily-white Democratic Party that dominated the region but remained in the minority on the national level.

McKinley in the White House

In William McKinley, Republicans found a skillful chief with a national agenda and personal charm. He cultivated news reporters, openly walked the streets of Washington, and courted the public with handshakes and flowers from his own lapel. Firmly but delicately, he curbed the power of old-time state bosses. When necessary, he prodded Congress to action. In all these ways he foreshadowed "modern" presidents, who would act as party leaders rather than as executive caretakers.

Fortune at first smiled on McKinley. When he entered the White House, the economy had already begun its recovery. Factory orders were slowly increasing, and unemployment dropped. Farm prices climbed. New discoveries of gold in Alaska and South Africa expanded the supply of

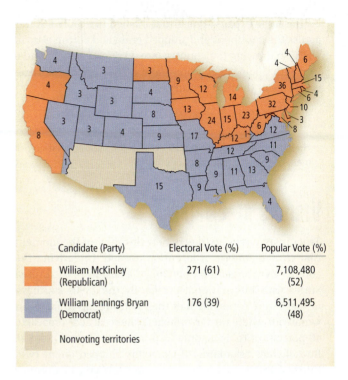

Candidate (Party)	Electoral Vote (%)	Popular Vote (%)
William McKinley (Republican)	271 (61)	7,108,480 (52)
William Jennings Bryan (Democrat)	176 (39)	6,511,495 (48)
Nonvoting territories		

ELECTION OF 1896

money without causing "gold bugs" to panic that currency was being destabilized by silver.

Freed from the burdens of the economic crisis, McKinley called a special session of Congress to revise the tariff. In 1897 the Dingley Tariff raised protective rates still higher but allowed tariffs to come down if other nations lowered theirs. McKinley also sought a solution for resolving railroad strikes, like the earlier Pullman conflict, before they turned violent. The Erdman Act of 1898 set up machinery for government mediation. McKinley even began laying plans for stronger regulation of trusts.

An 1896 Republican campaign poster features presidential hopeful William McKinley atop a giant gold coin engraved with the words "sound money" and supported by workers and businessmen alike. The poster promises domestic prosperity and respect overseas. The links between prosperity and empire as well as commerce and civilization were made not only in McKinley's campaign but also by later presidents.

The same expansiveness that pushed the United States across the continent and shipped grain and cotton abroad was also drawing the country into a race for empire and a war with Spain. Regulation—and a true age of reform—would await the next century.

✔ REVIEW

How did the election of 1896 resolve the politics of stalemate of the late nineteenth century?

VISIONS OF EMPIRE

THE CRISIS WITH SPAIN WAS only the affair of the moment that turned American attention abroad. Underlying the conflict were larger forces linking the destiny of the United States with international events. By the 1890s southern farmers were exporting half their cotton crop to factories worldwide, while western wheat farmers earned some 30 to 40 percent of their income from markets abroad. John D. Rockefeller's Standard Oil Company shipped about two-thirds of its refined products overseas, and Cyrus McCormick supplied Russian farmers with the reaper.

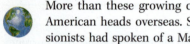 More than these growing commercial ties turned American heads overseas. Since the 1840s, expansionists had spoken of a Manifest Destiny to overspread the North American continent from the Atlantic to the Pacific. Between 1880 and 1914 they watched enviously as Western nations gobbled up large chunks of the rest of the world. In 1878 less than 10 percent of Africa lay under European rule. By 1900 nearly the entire continent was controlled by Europeans. In Asia, British influence radiated outward from its stronghold in India, while France ruled Indochina (present-day Vietnam, Cambodia, and Laos). Armed with new, rapid-firing machine guns and the drug quinine to control deadly malaria, Western soldiers, merchants, and missionaries established a new age of imperialism, sometimes through outright conquest and occupation, as in India and Indochina, sometimes by forging strong ties of trade and commerce, as in Latin America.

The results of European technological superiority could be devastating for native populations. In 1898, at the Battle of Omdurman, a small Anglo-Egyptian contingent under the command of British general Horatio Kitchener faced 40,000 Sudanese. The Anglo-Egyptian force was armed with machine guns and artillery, the Sudanese with little more than muskets and spears. When the smoke cleared hours later, 11,000 Sudanese had been shredded to pieces, whereas only 48 British had lost their lives.

Imperialism—European versus American Style

The scramble for empire was well under way by the time the Americans, Germans, and Japanese entered the race in the late nineteenth century. Spain and Portugal still clung to the remnants of their colonial empires, dating from the fifteenth and sixteenth centuries. In the early nineteenth century England, France, and Russia accelerated their drive to control foreign peoples and lands. But the late nineteenth century became the new age of **imperialism,** because the technology of arms and the networks of communication, transportation, and commerce brought the prospect of effective, truly global empires within much closer reach.

The speed and efficiency with which Europeans expanded prompted many Americans to argue for this European-style imperialism of conquest and possession. But other Americans preferred a more indirect imperialism: one that exported products, ideas, and influence. To them, this American imperialism seemed somehow purer, for without naked conquest Americans could be portrayed as bearers of long-cherished values: democracy, free-enterprise capitalism, and Protestant Christianity.

While Americans tried to justify imperial control in the name of such values, social, economic, and political forces were drawing them rapidly into the imperial race. The growth of industrial networks linked them to international markets as never before, whether they were Arkansas sharecroppers dependent on world cotton prices or Pittsburgh steelworkers whose jobs were made possible by orders for Singer sewing machines for Europe, China, and the Hawaiian Islands.

The Shapers of American Imperialism

Although the climate for expansion and imperialism was present at the end of the nineteenth century, the small farmer or steelworker was little concerned with how the United States advanced its goals abroad. An elite group—Christian missionaries, intellectuals, business leaders, and commercial farmers—joined navy careerists to shape a more active American imperialism.

Without a strong navy, imperialism of any sort was out of the question. By 1880 the once-proud Civil War fleet of more than 600 warships was rotting from neglect. The U.S. Navy ranked twelfth in the world, behind Denmark and Chile. The United States had a coastal fleet but no functional fleet to protect its interests overseas. Discontented navy officers now combined with trade-hungry business leaders to lobby Congress for a modern navy.

MAHAN CALLS FOR A STRONG NAVY

Alfred Thayer Mahan, a U.S. Navy captain and later admiral, formulated their ideas into a widely accepted theory of **navalism.** In *The Influence of Sea Power upon History* (1890), Mahan argued that great nations were seafaring powers that relied on foreign trade for wealth and might. In times of overproduction and depression, as had occurred repeatedly in the United States after the Civil War, overseas markets assumed even greater importance. The only way to

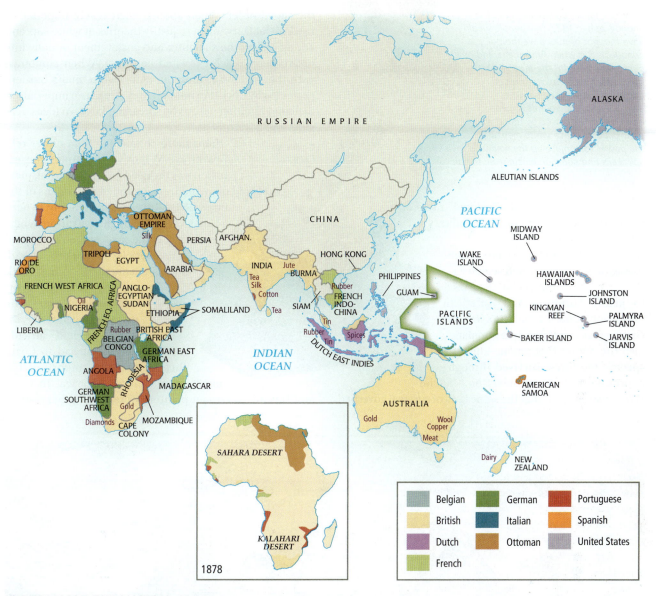

IMPERIALIST EXPANSION, 1900

*A comparison of Africa in 1878 (inset) and 1900 shows how quickly Europeans extended their colonial empires. Often resource-poor countries like Japan and England saw colonies as a way to acquire raw materials, such as South African diamonds and tin from Southeast Asia. Closer scrutiny shows that four of the most rapidly industrializing countries—Germany, Japan, Russia, and the United States—had few if any overseas possessions, even in 1900. And while China appears to be undivided, all the major powers were eagerly establishing spheres of influence there. **What geographic factors explain the location of U.S. possessions? Which countries were winning the race for empire? On what grounds should we make that judgment?***

protect foreign markets, Mahan reasoned, was with large cruisers and battleships. Operating far from American shores, these ships would need coaling stations and other resupply facilities throughout the world.

Mahan's logic was so persuasive and the profits to be reaped from foreign trade were so great that in the 1880s Congress launched a program to rebuild the old wood-and-sail navy with steam vessels made of steel. By 1900 the U.S. Navy ranked third in the world. With a modern navy, the country had the means to become an imperial power.

MISSIONARIES Protestant missionaries provided a spiritual rationale for imperialism that complemented Mahan's military and economic arguments. Because missionaries often encountered people whose cultural differences often made them unreceptive to the Christian message, many of them believed that natives first had to become Western in culture before turning Christian in belief. Missionaries introduced Western goods, schools, and systems of government administration—any "civilizing medium," as one minister remarked. They eagerly took up what they called the "white man's burden" of introducing

When Thomas Edison invented the phonograph in 1877, few people would have thought of it as a weapon of conquest. But when Americans and Europeans brought the machine to less technologically advanced societies, native peoples were awestruck by the sounds it made and sometimes cowed by those who controlled it. These white men, it appeared, had the power to conjure up the voices of invisible speakers and summon music from the air.

Western civilization to the "colored" races of the world but opposed outright military or political intervention.

"SOCIAL DARWINISM"

From scholars, academics, and scientists came racial theories to justify European and American expansion. Charles Darwin's *On the Origin of Species* (1859) had popularized the notion that among animal species, the fittest survived through a process of natural selection. "Social Darwinists" argued that the same laws of survival governed

the social order. When applied aggressively, imperialists used social Darwinism to justify theories of white supremacy as well as the slaughter and enslavement of nonwhite native peoples who resisted conquest. When combined with the somewhat more humane "white man's burden" professed by Christian missionaries, American imperialism included uplifting natives by spreading Western ideas, religion, and government.

COMMERCIAL FACTORS

Perhaps more compelling than either religious or racial motives for American expansion was the need for trade. The business cycle of boom and bust reminded Americans of the unpredictability of their economy. In hard times, people sought salvation wherever they could, and one obvious road to recovery lay in markets abroad. Entrepreneurs such as Minor Keith and his Tropical Fruit Company (later the mammoth United Fruit Company) had already constructed a railroad in Costa Rica and begun importing bananas from Central America. In Cuba and Hawaii, American planters were reaping harvests of

Missionaries often viewed the Chinese as uncivilized "heathen" whose souls needed saving and whose culture needed civilizing. This cartoon, published around 1900, pokes fun at the common stereotype by suggesting what the Chinese must think of American "heathen." "Contributions Received Here to Save the Foreign Devils," reads the sign of the Chinese "preacher," who laments the uncivilized behavior of corrupt American city governments, feuding backwoodsmen, rioting laborers, and mobs tormenting Chinese and black Americans.

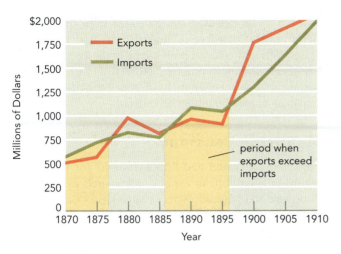

Balance of U.S. Imports and Exports, 1870–1910

After the depression of 1893 both imports and exports rose sharply, suggesting one reason why the age of imperialism was so closely linked with the emerging global industrial economy.

sugarcane, pineapples, and other commercial crops to be processed and sold in domestic and foreign markets. By 1900 the Singer Sewing Machine Company was sending some 60,000 sales agents across the globe to hawk the virtues of their "iron tailor." It is no wonder, then, that as American companies extended their investments abroad and the depression of 1893 deepened at home, the National Association of Manufacturers insisted that the "expansion of our foreign trade is [the] only promise of relief."

Dreams of a Commercial Empire

WILLIAM HENRY SEWARD No one had done more to initiate the idea of a "new empire" for the United States than William Henry Seward, secretary of state (1861–1869) under Lincoln and Andrew Johnson. Seward believed that "empire has . . . made its way constantly westward . . . until the tides of the renewed and decaying civilizations of the world meet on the shores of the Pacific Ocean." The United States must thus be prepared to win supremacy in the Far East—not by planting colonies or sending troops but by pursuing trade. The idea that a commercial empire could be gained by demanding equal access to foreign markets was what made Seward's strategy truly revolutionary.

ACQUISITION OF MIDWAY AND ALASKA While he pursued ties to Japan, Korea, and China, Seward promoted a transcontinental railroad at home and a canal across Central America. Link by link, he was trying to connect eastern factories to western ports in the United States and, from there, to markets and resources in Asia. In pursuit of these goals Seward made two acquisitions in 1867: Midway Island in the Pacific and Alaska. Unimportant by itself, the value of Midway lay as a way

station to Asia not far from Hawaii, where missionary planters were already establishing an American presence. Critics called Alaska "Seward's Folly," but he paid only about 2 cents an acre for a mineral-rich territory twice the size of Texas.

Seward's conviction that the future of the United States lay in the Pacific and Asia produced little in his lifetime. But it flourished in the 1890s, when Mahan provided the naval theory necessary to make the leap and the vanishing American frontier supplied an economic rationale for extending Manifest Destiny beyond the nation's continental borders. In the 1880s Secretary of State James G. Blaine had already began to look for ways to expand American trade and influence southward into Central and South America, where Great Britain had interests of its own to protect.

BLAINE'S PAN-AMERICAN UNION Blaine launched a campaign to cancel the Clayton-Bulwer Treaty (1850), which shared with Great Britain rights to any canal built in Central America. Only in 1901, when the two nations signed the Hay-Pauncefote Treaty (named for the American Secretary of State John Hay and British ambassador Julian Pauncefote), did Blaine's efforts have the desired results. Great Britain ceded its interest in building a canal across the Central American isthmus in

Sugar was the key to Hawaii's English- and American-dominated plantations. Polynesians were culturally ill suited to the backbreaking labor that sugar cultivation demanded. Planters filled their labor needs by recruiting Japanese workers like this one.

return for a U.S. promise to leave such a canal open to ships of all nations. Blaine also tried to shift Central American imports from British to U.S. goods by proposing the creation of a "customs union" to reduce trade barriers in the Americas. His plan resulted in only a weak Pan-American Union to foster peaceful understanding in the region. Latin American nations balked at his more important aim of lowering their tariffs.

If American expansionists wanted to extend trade across the Pacific to China, Hawaii was the crucial link. It afforded a fine naval base and a refueling station along the route to Asia. In 1893 American sugar planters overthrew the recently enthroned Queen Liliuokalani, a Hawaiian nationalist eager to rid the island of American influence. Their success was ensured when a contingent of U.S. marines arrived ashore on the pretext of protecting American lives.

Eager to avoid the McKinley Tariff's new tax on sugar imported into the United States, planters lobbied for the annexation of Hawaii, but President Cleveland refused. He was no foe of expansion but was, as his secretary of state noted, "unalterably opposed to stealing territory, or of annexing people against their consent, and the people of Hawaii do not favor annexation." The idea of incorporating the nonwhite population also troubled Cleveland. For a time, matters stood at a stalemate.

> ✓ **REVIEW**
>
> What social, economic, and cultural factors drew the United States into the race for empire?

THE IMPERIAL MOMENT

**CUBA IN REVOLT** IN 1895, AFTER ALMOST 15 years of planning from exile in the United States, José Martí returned to Cuba to renew the colony's struggle for independence from Spain. With cries of "Cuba libre," Martí and his rebels cut railroad lines, destroyed sugar mills, and set fire to the cane fields. Within a year, rebel forces controlled more than half the island. But even as they fought the Spanish, the rebels worried about the United States. Their island, just 90 miles off the coast of Florida, had long been a target of American expansionists and business interests. Martí had no illusions. "I have lived in the bowels of the monster," he explained of his exile in the United States, "and I know it."

The Spanish struck back at Martí and his followers with brutal force. Governor-General Valeriano Weyler herded half a million Cubans from their homes into fortified camps where filth, disease, and starvation killed perhaps 200,000. Outside these "reconcentration" camps, Weyler chased the rebels across the countryside, polluting drinking water, killing farm animals, burning crops.

The revolt in Cuba was only the first round in a struggle that would eventually end in a war between the United States and Spain. By the time it was over the Spanish-American War left Spain defeated and banished from the Western Hemisphere, Cuba free of Spanish rule, and the United States with new colonial possessions in the Pacific and the Caribbean. The knotty problem of what to do with them soon became the subject of a national debate. For better or worse, America's imperial moment had arrived.

Mounting Tensions

President Cleveland had little sympathy for the Cuban revolt, but Republican expansionists such as Theodore Roosevelt and Massachusetts senator Henry Cabot Lodge wanted to recognize Cuban independence—a step that if taken would likely provoke war with Spain. William McKinley, however, was only a moderate expansionist. As president, he lobbied Spain privately to stop cracking down on the rebels and destroying American-owned property. With over $50 million invested in Cuban sugar and an annual trade of over $100 million, American business interests had much to lose in a war with Spain.

In October 1897 Spain promised to remove the much-despised Weyler, end the reconcentration policy, and offer Cuba greater autonomy. The shift encouraged McKinley to resist pressure at home for more hostile action. But leaders of the Spanish army in Cuba had no desire to compromise. Although Weyler was removed, the military renewed efforts to quash the rebellion. Early in 1898, McKinley dispatched the battleship *Maine* to show that the United States meant to protect its interests and its citizens.

Then in February 1898 the State Department received a stolen copy of a letter to Cuba sent by the Spanish minister in Washington, Enrique Dupuy de Lôme. So did William Randolph Hearst, a pioneer of sensationalist, or **yellow, journalism,** who was eager for war with Spain. "WORST INSULT TO THE UNITED STATES IN ITS HISTORY," screamed the headline of Hearst's *New York Journal.* What had de Lôme actually written? After referring to McKinley as a "would-be politician," the letter admitted that Spain had no intention of changing policy in Cuba. The Spanish planned to crush the rebels. Red-faced Spanish officials recalled de Lôme, but most Americans now believed that Spain had deceived the United States.

SINKING OF THE *MAINE* On February 15, 1898, as the USS *Maine* lay peacefully at anchor in the Havana harbor, explosions ripped through its hull. Within minutes the ship sank to the bottom, killing some 260 American sailors. Much later, an official investigation concluded that the explosion was the result of spontaneous combustion in a coal bunker aboard ship. Most Americans at the time, inflamed by hysterical news accounts, concluded that Spanish agents had sabotaged the ship. McKinley sought a diplomatic solution but also a $50 million appropriation "to get ready for war."

TELLER AMENDMENT Pressures for war proved too great to resist, and on April 11, McKinley asked Congress to authorize "forceful intervention" in Cuba. Nine days later Congress recognized Cuban independence,

An investigation years later concluded that the sinking of the Maine resulted from a spontaneous explosion aboard ship, but at the time fervent patriots turned the event into a call for war and, as can be seen in the lower-right corner, memorabilia, here in the form of a button carrying the famous rallying cry, "Remember the Maine." The peaceful arrival of the Maine in Havana harbor is depicted in the upper-left corner of the painting, the grisly aftermath of the explosion in the large painting.

insisted on the withdrawal of Spanish forces, and gave the president authority to use military force. In a flush of idealism, legislators also adopted the Teller Amendment, renouncing any aim to annex Cuba. Certainly both idealism and moral outrage led many Americans down the path to war. But in the end, the "splendid little war" (as Secretary of State Hay called it) resulted from less lofty ambitions— empire, trade, glory.

The Imperial War

For the 5,462 men who died there was little splendid about the Spanish-American War. Only 379 gave their lives in battle. The rest suffered from accidents, disease, and the mismanagement of an unprepared army. As war began, the American force totaled only 30,000, none of whom had been trained for fighting in tropical climates. The sudden expansion to 60,000 troops and 200,000 volunteers overtaxed the army's graft-ridden supply system. Rather than tropical uniforms, some troops were issued winter woolens, and some fed on rations that were diseased, rotten, or even lethally spoiled. Others found themselves fighting with weapons from the Civil War.

DEWEY AT MANILA The navy fared better. Decisions in the 1880s to modernize the fleet now paid off handsomely (see Daily Lives, "The New Navy"). Naval battles largely determined the outcome of the war. As soon as war was declared, Admiral George Dewey ordered his Asiatic battle squadron from China to the Philippines. Just before dawn on May 1, he began shelling the Spanish ships in Manila Bay. Five hours later the entire Spanish squadron lay at the bottom of the bay. Three

hundred eighty-one Spaniards were killed, but only one American died, a ship's engineer who succumbed to a heart attack. Dewey had no plans to follow up his stunning victory with an invasion. His fleet carried no marines with which to take the city of Manila. So ill-prepared was President McKinley for war, let alone victory, that only after learning of Dewey's success did he order 11,000 American troops to the Philippines.

Halfway around the globe, another Spanish fleet had slipped into Santiago harbor in Cuba just before the arrival of the U.S. Navy. Under Admiral William Sampson, the navy blockaded the island, expecting the Spanish to flee under the cover of darkness. Instead, on July 3, the Spanish fleet made a desperate daylight dash for the open seas. So startled were the Americans that several of their ships nearly collided as they rushed to attack their exposed foes. All seven Spanish ships were sunk, with 474 casualties. Only one American was killed and one wounded. With Cuba now cut off from Spain, the war was virtually won.

War in Cuba

Few Americans had heard of the Philippine Islands; fewer still could locate them on a globe. But most Americans knew that Cuba lay barely 90 miles off the Florida coast.

RACIAL TENSIONS Before the outbreak of hostilities, Tampa, Florida, was a sleepy coastal town with a single railroad line. When it became the port of embarkation for the Cuban expeditionary force, the town exploded. Some 17,000 troops arrived in the spring of 1898 alone. Tampa's overtaxed facilities soon broke down, spawning disease, tension, and finally racial violence. President

DAILY LIVES

THE NEW NAVY

In the era after the Civil War, technology transformed the navies of Europe into modern weapons of war. Compound engines, improved armor plating, self-propelled torpedoes, and large rifled guns revolutionized naval warfare. The U.S. Navy, in contrast, sailed into the past. With 3,000 miles of ocean as protection and no colonies to defend, a large blue-water fleet seemed unnecessary. Even steamships seemed impractical because the United States had no coaling stations in foreign waters to fuel them. By 1878 the navy had just 6,000 sailors, the smallest force since the presidency of Andrew Jackson.

In 1873, as the U.S. Navy fell into disrepair, the British launched the *Devastation*, a single-masted, steam-driven vessel with heavy armor and powerful twin turrets. A forerunner of the modern battleship, it could steam across the Atlantic and back without stopping for coal. Less than a decade later, a British fleet smashed Alexandria, Egypt, whose fortifications were sturdier than those of American ports.

The battle convinced Congress that the American coast was no longer safe. In 1883 it appropriated $1.3 million for four new, steel-hulled vessels. By the turn of the century, the paltry effort had produced a major commitment to modernizing the navy. The new fleet included the navy's first full-sized battleships—the *Indiana, Massachusetts*, and *Oregon*. Each displaced more than 10,000 tons. (Soon after 1900, giant battleships were displacing 20,000 tons; on the eve of World War I they reached more than 30,000 tons.) With five more first-class battleships commissioned by 1896, the U.S. Navy rose to fifth place in the world. The prestige of naval service had risen, too, and with it the number of sailors to nearly 10,000 in uniform.

The new navy, unlike the civilian world, was not a democratic culture. Privileges of rank were everywhere apparent. Commanders lived in wood-paneled luxury

Passengers on riverboats and yachts saluted the new steel-hulled, steam-powered American fleet as it made its way triumphantly up the Hudson River after naval victories in the Spanish-American War. Within a few years, these modern ships would be obsolete due to the international arms race, which forced rapid innovation in naval design.

and dined on specially prepared cuisine, capped by coffee, brandy, and cigars. The crew ate salted meats, beans, and potatoes. Officers had private quarters, while enlisted men, so the saying went, lived under the place where they slept and slept under the place where they ate. At night the tables and benches used for dining in the common quarters were stowed between overhead beams from which hammocks were hung as they had been in the days of sail ships. These cramped quarters could be damp and foul-smelling. But more modern ventilation systems, steam radiators and even refrigerators for keeping food fresh made life at sea more tolerable for sailors in the new navy. Most navies followed the ancient tradition of permitting mascots on board including parrots and other birds but also dogs, cats, goats, chimps, and even kangaroos. They were said to bring good fortune.

In 1907 President Theodore Roosevelt put American naval power on display. He sent 16 battleships on a 46,000-mile, 14-month world tour. Ironically, the Great White Fleet (named for the gleaming white hulls of its ships) was already out of date. In 1906 Great Britain commissioned the *Dreadnought*, a warship whose new guns rendered all others, including the U.S. navy, virtually obsolete and set off a naval arms race that would help to lead the world to the carnage of World War I.

Thinking Critically

Why was a modern navy so critically important to the United States in the late nineteenth and early twentieth centuries?

McKinley had authorized the army to raise five volunteer regiments of black soldiers. By the time war was declared over 8,000 African Americans had signed up, half of them stationed around segregated Tampa. They found that although they could sail off to die freeing the peasants of Cuba, they were forbidden from buying a soda at the local drugstore. "Is America any better than Spain?" one dismayed black chaplain wondered. After drunken white troops shot at a black child, black troops in Tampa rioted. Three white and 27 black Americans were wounded in the melee.

Matters were scarcely less chaotic as 17,000 disorganized troops and hundreds of reporters finally scrambled

Black veterans of the Indian Wars of the American West along with volunteers, segregated and commanded by white officers, made up almost a quarter of the U.S. force that invaded Cuba. Members of the Tenth Cavalry, shown here, were clearly in no mood to be subjected to the harassment they and other black troops encountered around Tampa. Later the Tenth Cavalry supported a charge by Colonel Teddy Roosevelt's Rough Riders at the battle of San Juan Hill.

aboard ship early in June 1898. There they sat for a week, until sailing on June 14 for Santiago and battle. By June 30 the Americans had landed to challenge some 24,000 Spanish, many equipped with modern rifles. The following day 7,000 Americans—including the black soldiers of the Ninth and Tenth Cavalry regiments—stormed up heavily fortified San Juan Hill and nearby Kettle Hill.

THE ROUGH RIDERS   Among them Lieutenant Colonel Theodore Roosevelt thrilled at the experience of battle. He had raised a cavalry troop of cowboys and college polo players, originally called "Teddy's Texas Tarantulas." By the time they arrived in Cuba, the volunteers were answering to the nickname "Rough Riders." As they charged toward the high ground, Roosevelt yelled: "Gentlemen, the Almighty God and the just cause are with you. Gentlemen, charge!" The withering fire drowned out his shrill, squeaky voice, so he repeated the call to his troops. Charge they did and conquer the enemy, though the battle cost more than 1,500 American casualties. (See After the Fact, pages 588–591.)

Without a fleet for cover or way to escape, the Spanish garrison surrendered on July 17. In the Philippines a similar brief battle preceded the American capture of Manila on August 13. The "splendid little war" was over in less than four months.

Peace and the Debate over Empire

Conquering Cuba and the Philippines proved easier than deciding what to do with the islands. The Teller Amendment had renounced any American claim to Cuba. But clearly the United States had not freed the island to see chaos reign or American business and military interests excluded. And what of the Philippines—and Spanish Puerto Rico, which American forces had taken without a struggle? Powerful public and congressional sentiment pushed McKinley to claim empire as the fruits of victory.

ANNEXING HAWAII   The president himself favored such a course. The battle in the Pacific highlighted the need for naval bases and coaling stations. "To maintain our flag in the Philippines, we must raise our flag in Hawaii," New York's *The Sun* insisted. On July 7, 1898, McKinley signed a joint congressional resolution annexing Hawaii, as planters wanted for nearly a decade. The Philippines presented a more difficult problem. Filipinos greeted the American forces as liberators, not new colonizers.

AGUINALDO   The popular leader of the rebel forces fighting Spain, Emilio Aguinaldo, had returned to the islands from exile in Hong Kong on an American ship. To the rebels' dismay, McKinley insisted that the islands were under American authority until the peace treaty settled matters. Such a settlement, McKinley knew, would have to include American control of the Philippines. He had no intention of leaving Spain in charge or of seeing the islands fall to other European rivals. American military advisers warned that without control of the entire island of Luzon, its capital, Manila, would be indefensible as the naval base McKinley wanted. Nor, McKinley felt certain, were the Filipinos capable of self-government. Aguinaldo and his rebels thought otherwise, and in June Aguinaldo declared himself president of a new Philippine republic.

ANTI-IMPERIALISTS   Many influential Americans—former president Grover Cleveland, steel baron Andrew Carnegie, novelist Mark Twain—opposed annexation of the Philippines. Yet even these anti-imperialists favored expansion, if only in the form of trade that would benefit the nation without the costs of maintaining the Philippines as a colony. Annexation would mire the United States too deeply in the quicksands of Asian politics, many business leaders argued. More important, a large, costly fleet would be necessary to defend the islands. To the imperialists that was precisely the point: a large fleet was crucial to the interests of a powerful commercial nation.

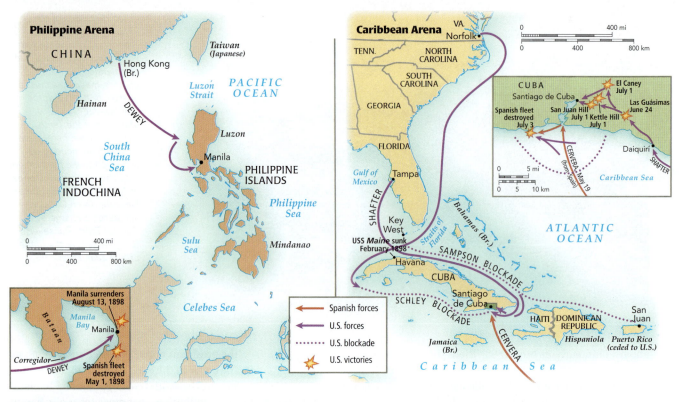

THE SPANISH-AMERICAN WAR

Had the Spanish-American War depended largely on ground forces, the ill-prepared U.S. Army might have fared poorly. But the key to success, in both Cuba and the Philippines, was naval warfare, in which the recently modernized American fleet had a critical edge. Proximity to Cuba also gave the United States an advantage in delivering troops and supplies and in maintaining a naval blockade that isolated Spanish forces.

THE ROLE OF RACE

Racial ideas shaped both sides of the argument. Imperialists believed that the racial inferiority of nonwhites made occupation of the Philippines necessary, and they were ready to assume the "white man's burden" by governing the islands. Filipinos, they said, would gradually be taught the virtues of Western civilization, Christianity, democracy, and self-rule. (In fact, most Filipinos were already Catholic after many years under Spanish rule.) Anti-imperialists feared racial intermixing and the possibility of Filipino and other Asian workers flooding the American labor market. They also maintained that dark-skinned people would never develop the capacity for self-government. An American government in the Philippines could be sustained only at the point of bayonets—yet the U.S. Constitution made no provision for governing people without representation or equal rights. Such a precedent abroad, the anti-imperialists warned, might one day threaten American liberties at home.

Still, when the Senate debated the Treaty of Paris ending the Spanish-American War in 1898, the imperialists had the support of the president, most of Congress, and the majority of public opinion. Even a sturdy anti-imperialist such as William Jennings Bryan, defeated by McKinley in 1896, endorsed the treaty. In it Spain surrendered title to Cuba, ceded Puerto Rico and Guam to the United States, and in return for $20 million turned over the Philippines as well.

From Colonial War to Colonial Rule

 PHILIPPINE-AMERICAN WAR

Managing an empire turned out to be even more devilish than acquiring one. As the Senate debated annexation of the Philippines in Washington, rebels fought with an American patrol outside of Manila. The few Americans who paid attention to the ensuing clash called it the "Filipino insurrection," but to those who fought, it was the brutal Philippine-American War. When it ended more than three years later, nearly 5,000 Americans, 25,000 rebels, and perhaps as many as 200,000 civilians lay dead.

Environment shaped the conduct of the war. After a series of conventional battles ended in their defeat, Filipino *insurrectos* quickly learned to take advantage of the mountainous, jungle terrain of the Philippine archipelago. From his hideaway in Bayombong, Aguinaldo ordered his men to employ "guerrilla" (literally "little war" in Spanish) tactics. Hit-and-run ambushes by lightly armed rebels perfectly suited the dense landscape. As *insurrectos* melted into tropical forests and friendly villages, Americans could barely distinguish between enemies and friends. It was the first instance of jungle warfare the United States had ever encountered.

Jungle warfare aggravated racial antagonisms and spurred savage fighting on both sides. Rebel resistance to

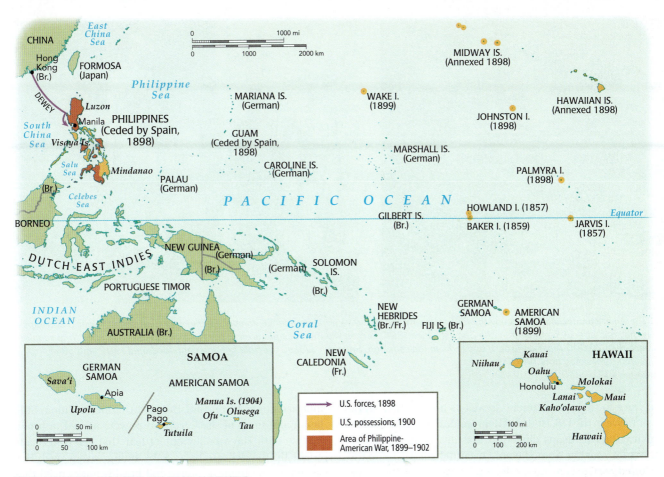

THE UNITED STATES IN THE PACIFIC

In the late nineteenth century both Germany and the United States emerged as major naval powers and as contestants for influence and commerce in China. The island groups of the central and southwest Pacific, though of little economic value, had potential strategic significance as bases and coaling stations along the routes to Asia. Rivalry (as in the case of Samoa) sometimes threatened to erupt into open conflict. Control of Hawaii, Midway, Samoa, Guam, and the Philippines gave the United States a string of strategic stepping-stones to Asia.

foreign occupation was accompanied by reports of *insurrectos* treating American prisoners in "fiendish fashion," burying some alive, dismembering others, and slaughtering even Filipinos who opposed them. For their part American soldiers dismissed Filipinos as nearly subhuman in ways that evoked the Indian Wars of the American West. "The only good Filipino is a dead one," declared one U.S. soldier, echoing the infamous anti-Indian cry. Indeed, many Americans in the Philippines had fought Indians in the Dakota Badlands and northern New Mexico.

In such a climate the frustrations of ordinary troops sometimes boiled over into brutality, torture, and executions. To avenge a rebel attack, one officer promised to turn the countryside into a "howling wilderness." Another, later court-marshaled for the order, exhorted his troops to shoot any Filipino over the age of 10. To combat the insurgents, General Arthur MacArthur—father of Douglas MacArthur—imposed a brutal campaign of "pacification" late in 1899. Filipinos were herded into concentration camps for their protection, while food and crops in the nearby countryside were seized or torched to starve the rebels into surrender.

The strategy was embarrassingly reminiscent of the actions of "Butcher" Weyler in Cuba. Only after the capture of Aguinaldo himself and the last gasps of rebel resistance did the war finally come to a close in 1902. It marked the end of the westward march of American empire that began nearly a century earlier with the Louisiana Purchase in 1803.

In contrast to the bitter guerrilla war, the United States ruled the Philippines with relative benevolence. Under William Howard Taft, the first civilian governor, the Americans built schools, roads, sewers, and factories and instituted modern farming techniques. The aim, said Taft, was to prepare the island territory for independence, and in keeping with it, he granted great authority to local officials. These advances—social, economic, and political—benefited the Filipino elite and thus earned their support. Decades later, on July 4, 1946, the Philippines were finally granted independence.

PUERTO RICO   The United States played a similar role in Puerto Rico. As in the Philippines, executive authority resided in a governor appointed by the U.S. president. Under the Foraker Act of 1900, Puerto Ricans received

The American decision to occupy the Philippines rather than give it independence compelled Filipino nationalists to fight U.S. troops, as they had already been fighting the Spanish since 1896. Forces like the ones pictured at the right were tenacious enough to require more than 70,000 Americans (left) to put down the rebellion. Sporadic, bloody guerrilla fighting continued until 1902, and other incidents persisted until 1906.

a voice in their government as well as a nonvoting representative in the U.S. House of Representatives. All the same, many Puerto Ricans chafed at the idea of such second-class citizenship. Some favored eventual admission to the United States as a state; others advocated independence. The division of opinion persists even today.

An Open Door in China

Like a reciprocal equation, interest in Asia drove the United States to annex the Philippines, and annexation of the Philippines only whetted American interest in Asia. The possibility of markets in China—whether for Christian souls or consumer goods—proved irresistible.

Both the British, who dominated China's export trade, and the Americans, who wanted to, worried that China might soon be carved up by other powers. Japan had defeated China in 1895, encouraging Russia, Germany, and France to join in demanding trade concessions. Each nation sought to establish an Asian **sphere of influence** in which its commercial and military interests reigned. Often such spheres resulted in restrictions against rival powers. Since Britain and the United States wanted the benefits of trade rather than actual colonies, they tried to limit foreign demands while leaving China open to all commerce.

THE OPEN-DOOR NOTES   In 1899, at the urging of the British, Secretary of State John Hay circulated the first of two "open-door" notes among the imperial powers. He did not ask them to give up their spheres of influence in China, only to keep them open to free trade with other nations. The United States could hardly have enforced even so modest a proposal, because it lacked the

military might to prevent the partitioning of China. Still, Japan and most of the European powers agreed in broad outline with Hay's policy out of fear that the Americans might tip the delicate balance by siding with a rival. Hay seized on the tepid response and brashly announced that the open door in China was international policy.

BOXER REBELLION   Unrest soon threatened to close the door. Chinese nationalists, known to Westerners as Boxers for their clenched-fist symbol, formed secret societies to drive out the *fon kwei*, or foreign devils. Encouraged by the Chinese empress, Boxers murdered hundreds of Christian missionaries and their followers and set siege to foreign diplomats and citizens at the British Embassy in Beijing. European nations quickly dispatched troops to quell the uprising and free the diplomats, while President McKinley sent 2,500 Americans to join the march to the capital city. Along the way, the angry foreign armies plundered the countryside and killed civilians before reaching Beijing and breaking the siege.

Hay feared that once in control of Beijing the conquerors might never leave. So he sent a second open-door note in 1900, this time asking foreign powers to respect China's territorial and administrative integrity. They endorsed the proposal in principle only. In fact, the open-door notes together amounted to little more than an announcement of American desires to maintain political stability and commercial trade in Asia. Yet they reflected a fundamental purpose to which the United States dedicated itself across the globe: to open closed markets and to keep open those markets that other empires had yet to close. The new American empire would have its share of colonies, but in Asia as elsewhere it would be built primarily on trade.

To expansionists such as Alfred Thayer Mahan, Theodore Roosevelt, and John Hay, American interests would be secure only when they had been established worldwide, a course of action they believed to be blessed by divine providence. Americans were "trustees under God of the civilization of the world," declared Senator Albert Beveridge. But to one French diplomat, more accustomed to wheeling and dealing in the corridors of international power, it seemed that the Americans were tempting fate. With a whiff of Old World cynicism or perhaps a prophet's eye, he remarked, "The United States is seated at the table where the great game is played, and it cannot leave it."

The United States chose to stay at the table. In the coming century, the "great game" of global power would pay handsomely for those who envisioned the country as a world leader. The game had already settled one account. The divisive shadow of the Civil War finally faded. Despite the concerns of critics, the Spanish-American War and the quest for empire united the North and South and revitalized a generation of Americans who longed to demonstrate their prowess in an age of imperialism.

✓ REVIEW

Why did imperialists launch their quest for empire, and why did anti-imperialists oppose them?

CONCLUSION

THE WORLD AT LARGE

In the end, the Chicago World's Fair of 1893 proved an apt reflection of the world at home and abroad. Though the fair showed off its exhibits within gleaming white buildings the political system was cracking under the strain of a depression. As the fair gathered exhibits from all over the globe, the scramble for resources and markets culminated in an age of imperialism. It seemed that national greatness went hand in hand with empire. Employing the gendered language of the day, the German historian Heinrich von Treitschke proclaimed, "Every virile people has established colonial power."

As in the United States, European imperialists sometimes justified their rule over nonwhite peoples in Darwinian fashion. "The path of progress is strewn with the wreck . . . of inferior races," proclaimed one English professor in 1900. British poet Rudyard Kipling even suggested that Europeans were making a noble sacrifice on behalf of their colonial subjects. "Take up the White Man's Burden," he exhorted his fellow Britons in 1899. "Send forth the best ye breed—/ Go bind your sons to exile/To serve your captives' need."

European critics, like those in the United States, rejected imperialism on the grounds that it delivered few economic benefits, compromised the moral standing of the colonizers, and distracted the public from undertaking much-needed reforms at home. Just as Populists in the United States called on "toilers" to band together and on government to play a more active role in managing the excesses of the new industrial order, radicals in Europe such as the German-born Karl Marx exhorted "workers of the world" to unite and "throw off your chains" by abandoning capitalism and embracing socialism. ∞∞∞

CHAPTER SUMMARY

THE END OF THE NINETEENTH century witnessed a crisis arising from political stalemate at home and the drive for empire abroad.

■ Republicans and Democrats ground politics into near-gridlock over the well-worn issues of regional conflict, tariff, and monetary reform.

■ Discontented Americans often fashioned political instruments of their own, whether for women's suffrage, temperance, monetary change, antilynching and civil rights, or farm issues.

■ The political deadlock finally came to an end in the turbulent 1890s, when depression-spawned labor strife and a revolt of farmers produced the People's, or Populist, Party and a political realignment that left the Republicans in control of national politics.

■ By the 1890s, too, the tradition of Manifest Destiny combined powerfully with the needs of the new industrial order for raw materials and markets and the closing of the American frontier to produce a powerful drive toward empire, which rested on these two principles of American foreign policy:

• The old Monroe Doctrine (1823), which warned European powers to stay out of the Americas.

• The newer open-door notes of Secretary of State John Hay (1899–1900), which stressed the importance of equal commercial access to the markets of Asia.

- Most Americans favored an overseas empire for the United States but disagreed over whether it should be territorial or commercial.

- In the end America's overseas empire was both territorial and commercial. A victory in the Spanish-American War (1898) capped an era of territorial and commercial expansion by furnishing colonial possessions in the Caribbean and the Pacific and at the same time providing more stepping-stones to the markets of Asia.

ADDITIONAL READING

SEAN DENNIS CASHMAN, *America in the Gilded Age* (1984), and Heather Richardson, *West from Appomattox: The Reconstruction of America after the Civil War* (2007), are good overviews of the era. In *Rebirth of a Nation: The Making of Modern America, 1877–1920* (2009), Jackson Lears offers a sweeping revision, stressing the legacy of Civil War brutality and the growing importance of race in shaping modern America. For presidential politics, see H. Wayne Morgan, *From Hayes to McKinley: National Party Politics, 1877–1896* (1969), but for the importance of ethnicity and religion, consult Paul Kleppner, *The Cross of Culture* (1970). The traditional view of the rise of the welfare state is set forth in Harold Wilensky and Charles N. Lebeaux, *Industrial Society and Social Welfare* (1958). Revising that approach, Theda Skocpol, *Protecting Soldiers and Mothers* (1994), stresses nineteenth-century origins and the interplay between the state and nongovernmental political groups.

For Populism, John Hicks's classic *The Populist Revolt* (1931) stresses poverty as a motivating force, and Lawrence Goodwyn, *Democratic Promise* (1976), highlights the movement's push for radical democratic change. Also useful are Robert C. McMath Jr., *American Populism* (1993), and Charles Postel, *The Populist Vision* (2007). The latter sees Populists as democratic modernizers who crossed lines of color and gender, reaching not only farmers but miners and railroad workers as well. On the issue of race in the South before and after slavery, Steven Hahn's *Under Our Feet* (2003) provides a broad and detailed panorama. On the spread of segregation after Reconstruction, see C. Vann Woodward's classic *The Strange Career of Jim Crow* (3rd rev. ed., 1974) and John Cell's *The Highest Stage of White Supremacy* (1982). Contrasting approaches to race relations can be seen in Louis Harlan's two-volume biography, *Booker T. Washington* (1972 and 1983), and David Levering Lewis, *W. E. B. DuBois: Biography of a Race* (1993). James West Davidson uses Ida B. Wells to provide a cultural portrait of the first generation of freed African Americans during these years in *"They Say": Ida B. Wells and the Reconstruction of Race* (2007).

Walter Nugent's *Habits of Empire* (2008) offers a schematic study of the creation of an American empire in the nineteenth and twentieth centuries. For other broad views of American foreign policy, see Michael Hunt, *Ideology and American Foreign Policy* (1984), John Dobson, *America's Ascent* (1978), and Walter LaFeber, *The American Age* (1989). LaFeber's *Inevitable Revolutions* (3rd ed., 1993) is good on Central America. For Sino-American relations, consult Michael Hunt, *The Making of a Special Relationship* (1983), and for the role of missionaries, especially women, Jane Hunter, *The Gospel of Gentility* (1984). For the Spanish-American War, see Ivan Musicant, *Empire by Default* (1998). Kristin Hoganson's *Fighting for American Manhood* (1998)

offers the best account of how gender helped to shape the Spanish-American and Philippine-American Wars. Brian McAlister Linn, *The Philippine War* (2000), presents a well-researched account, as does David J. Silbey's briefer *A War of Frontier and Empire* (2007).

For a fuller list of readings, see the Bibliography at www.mhhe.com/eh8e.

SIGNIFICANT EVENTS

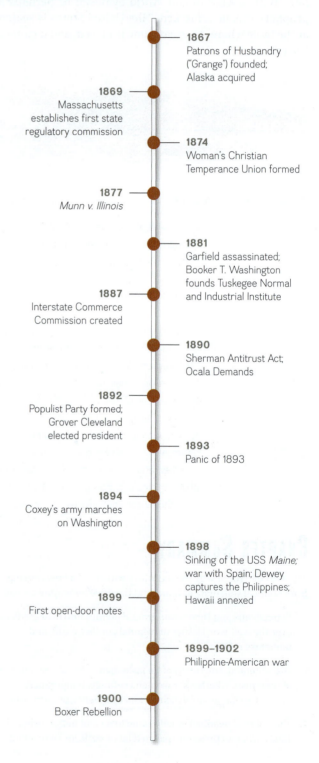

1867
Patrons of Husbandry ("Grange") founded; Alaska acquired

1869
Massachusetts establishes first state regulatory commission

1874
Woman's Christian Temperance Union formed

1877
Munn v. Illinois

1881
Garfield assassinated; Booker T. Washington founds Tuskegee Normal and Industrial Institute

1887
Interstate Commerce Commission created

1890
Sherman Antitrust Act; Ocala Demands

1892
Populist Party formed; Grover Cleveland elected president

1893
Panic of 1893

1894
Coxey's army marches on Washington

1898
Sinking of the USS *Maine;* war with Spain; Dewey captures the Philippines; Hawaii annexed

1899
First open-door notes

1899–1902
Philippine-American war

1900
Boxer Rebellion

REVIEW
Acquiring an Empire, 1860–1900

MAJOR ACQUISITIONS	DATE	MEANS	STATUS
Alaska	1867	Purchased from Russia	Territory*
Hawaiian Islands	1898	Annexed	Territory*
Midway Island	1898	Annexed	Territory
Guam	1898	Ceded by Spain	Territory
Philippines	1898	Ceded by Spain	Territory**
Puerto Rico	1898	Ceded by Spain	Territory
American Samoa	1899	Annexed	Territory
Wake Island	1899	Annexed	Territory

*Granted statehood in 1959.
**Granted independence in 1946.

Rose Schneiderman, a union activist, protested "the firetrap structures that will destroy us the minute they catch on fire. This is not the first time girls have been burned alive in the city."

frustration boiled over into an industrywide strike for better wages and working conditions. Despite a union victory, the only change visible at Triangle was that every morning the doors were locked to keep workers in and union organizers out.

The fire broke out in the lofts as the workers were leaving for home. In minutes the top stories were ablaze. Terrified seamstresses groped through the black smoke, only to find exits locked or clogged with bodies. All but one of the few working fire escapes collapsed. When the fire trucks arrived, horrified firefighters discovered that their ladders could not reach the top stories. "Spectators saw again and again pitiable companionships formed in the instant of death—girls who placed their arms around each other as they leaped," read one news story. Their bodies hit the sidewalk with a sickening thud or were spiked on the iron guard rails. One hundred forty-six people died.

A few days later 80,000 New Yorkers joined the silent funeral procession snaking slowly up Fifth Avenue in the rain. A quarter of a million watched. At the Metropolitan Opera House, union leader Rose Schneiderman told a rally, "This is not the first time that girls have been burned alive in the city. Every year thousands of us are maimed." A special state commission investigated the tragedy. Over the next four years its recommendations produced 56 state laws regulating fire safety, hours, machinery, and home work. They amounted to the most far-reaching labor code in the country.

The Triangle fire shocked the nation and underscored a widespread fear: modern industrial society had created profound strains, widespread misery, and deep class divisions. Men, women, and children worked around the clock in unsafe factories for barely enough to support themselves. Corporations grew to unimagined size, bought and sold legislators, dictated the terms of their own profit. In cities across America, tenement-bred diseases took innocent lives. Criminals threatened people and property, while saloons tied the working poor to dishonest political bosses. In the 1890s, workers and managers fought pitched battles that threatened to break the country apart. Inflation shrank middle-class wallets at the rate of 3 percent a year. "It was a world of greed," concluded one garment worker; "the human being didn't mean anything."

Human beings did mean something to followers of a reform movement sweeping the country. Progressivism emerged as a political force in the mid-1890s and continued to shape politics through World War I. The movement sprang from many impulses, mixing a liberal concern for the poor and working class with conservative efforts to stabilize business and avoid class warfare. Above all, progressives shared a desire to soften the harsher aspects of industrialization, urbanization, and immigration.

Progressivism began in the cities, where those forces converged. It was organized by an angry, idealistic middle class and percolated up from neighborhoods to city halls, state capitals, and, finally, Washington. Though usually pursued through politics, the goals of progressives were broadly social—to create a "good society" where people could live decently, harmoniously, and prosperously, along middle-class lines.

Unlike past reformers progressives saw government as a protector, not an oppressor. Only government possessed the resources for the broad-based reforms they sought. Progressivism spawned the modern activist state, with its capacity to regulate the economy and manage society. And because American society had become so interdependent, progressivism became the first nationwide reform movement. It flowered in the presidencies of Republican Theodore Roosevelt and Democrat Woodrow Wilson. In 1912 it even gave birth to its own party, the Progressive, or "Bull Moose," Party. By then progressivism had filtered well beyond politics into every realm of American life. ∞∞∞

THE ROOTS OF PROGRESSIVE REFORM

FAMILIES TURNED FROM THEIR HOMES; an army of unemployed on the roads; hunger, strikes, and bloody violence across the country—the wrenching depression of 1893 forced Americans to take a hard look at their new industrial order. They saw a society increasingly divided by class, race, and ethnicity. They also found common complaints that cut across those same lines. If streetcar companies raised fares while service deteriorated, if food processors doctored their canned goods with harmful additives, if politicians skimmed money from the public till, everyone suffered.

AIMS OF PROGRESSIVES — The result was not a coherent progressive movement but a set of loosely connected goals that has made progressivism difficult to categorize. Some progressives fought to make government efficient and honest. Others called for greater regulation of business and a more orderly economy. Some sought social justice for the poor and working classes; others, social welfare to protect children, women, and consumers. Still other progressives looked to purify society by outlawing alcohol and drugs, stamping out prostitution and slums, and restricting the flood of new immigrants. And all tried to make business and government more responsive to the will of the people.

Paternalistic by nature, progressives often imposed their solutions, no matter what the less "enlightened" poor or oppressed saw as their own best interests. Reformers also acted out of nostalgia. In a rapidly changing world, they wanted to redeem such traditional American values as democracy, opportunity, and the spirit of public service. And finally progressives sought to save the nation from a second civil war born of class conflict. Yet if the ends of progressives were traditional, their means were distinctly modern. They used the systems and methods of the new industrial order—the latest techniques of organization, management, and science—to fight its excesses and soften its impact.

The Progressive System of Beliefs

Progressives were moderate modernizers—reformers, not revolutionaries. They accepted the American system as sound, only in need of improvement. Many drew on the increasingly popular Darwinian theories of evolution to buttress this gradual approach to change. With its notion of slowly changing species, evolution undermined the acceptance of fixed principles that had guided social thought in the Gilded Age. Progressives saw an evolving landscape and ever-shifting values. They denied the old Calvinist doctrine of inborn sinfulness and instead saw people as having a greater potential for good than for evil.

Progressives had seen the mean side of industrialism and somehow had to explain the existence of evil and wrongdoing. Most agreed that human beings were "largely, if not wholly, products of society or environment." People went wrong, wrote one progressive, because of "what happens to them." By changing what happened, the human potential for good could be released. As reformer Jane Addams explained, "what has been called 'the extraordinary pliability of human nature'" made it "impossible to set any bounds to the moral capabilities which might unfold under ideal civic and educational conditions."

PRAGMATISM — With an eye to results, progressives asked not "Is it true?" but "Does it work?" Philosopher Charles Peirce called this new way of thinking **pragmatism.** William James, a Harvard psychologist, became its most famous popularizer. For James, pragmatism meant "looking towards last things, fruits, consequences, facts."

The Pragmatic Approach

Pragmatism led educators, social scientists, and lawyers to adopt new approaches to reform. John Dewey, the master educator of the Progressive Era, believed that environment shaped the patterns of human thought. Instead of demanding mindless memorization of abstract and unconnected facts, Dewey tried to "make each one of our schools an embryonic community life." At his School of Pedagogy, founded in 1896 with his wife, Alice, he let students unbolt their desks from the floor, move about, and learn by doing so they could train for real life.

Psychologist John B. Watson believed that human behavior could be shaped at will. "Give me a dozen healthy infants," he wrote, ". . . and my own specified world to bring them up in, and I'll guarantee to take any one at random and train him to become any specialist I might select, doctor, lawyer, artist, merchant, chief, and yes, even beggarman and thief." **Behaviorism** swept the social sciences and later advertising, where Watson himself eventually landed.

Lawyers and legal theorists applied their own blend of pragmatism and behaviorism. Justice Oliver Wendell Holmes Jr., appointed to the Supreme Court in 1902, rejected the idea that the traditions of law were constant and universal. "Long ago I decided I was not God," said Holmes. Law was a living organism to be interpreted according to experience and the needs of a changing society.

SOCIOLOGICAL JURISPRUDENCE — This environmental view of the law, known as **sociological jurisprudence,** found a skilled practitioner in Louis Brandeis. Shaken by the brutal suppression of the Homestead steel strike of 1892, Brandeis quit his corporate practice and proclaimed himself the "people's lawyer." The law must "guide by the light of reason," he wrote, by which he meant bringing everyday life to bear in any court case. Older court opinions had been based largely on legal precedent. Progressives asked courts to look at the world around them and realize society had undergone changes so fundamental that many precedents of the past no longer applied. Past and present must stand on equal footing in interpreting the law.

BRANDEIS BRIEF   Brandeis had a chance to test his practical principles when laundry owner Curt Muller challenged an Oregon law that limited his laundresses to working 10 hours a day. Brandeis defended the statute before the Supreme Court in 1908. His famous legal brief in *Muller v. Oregon* contained 102 pages describing the damaging effects of long hours on working women and only 15 pages of legal precedents. The Supreme Court upheld Oregon's right to limit the working hours of women and thus legitimized the "Brandeis Brief."

The Progressive Method

Seeing the nation riven by conflict, progressives tried to restore a sense of community through the ideal of a single public interest. Christian ethics were their guide, to be applied after using the latest scientific methods to gather and analyze data about a social problem. The modern corporation furnished an appealing model for organization. Like corporate executives, progressives relied on careful management, coordinated systems, and specialized bureaucracies to carry out reforms.

Between 1902 and 1912 a new breed of journalists investigated wrongdoers, named them in print, and described their misdeeds in vivid detail. Most of their exposés began as articles in mass-circulation magazines. *McClure's* magazine stirred controversy and boosted circulation when it sent reporter Lincoln Steffens to uncover the crooked ties between business and politics. Steffens's "Tweed Days in St. Louis" appeared in the October 1902 issue of *McClure's* and was followed in the November issue by Ida M. Tarbell's *History of the Standard Oil Company,* another stinging, well-researched indictment. Soon a full-blown literature of exposure was covering every ill from unsafe food to child labor.

MUCKRAKERS   A disgusted Theodore Roosevelt called the new reporters "muckrakers," after the man who raked up filth in the seventeenth-century classic *Pilgrim's Progress.* Still, by documenting dishonesty and blight, muckrakers not only aroused people but also educated them. No broad reform movement of American institutions would have taken place without them.

VOLUNTARY ORGANIZATIONS   To solve the problems that muckrakers exposed, progressives stressed volunteerism, civic responsibility, and collective action. They drew on the organizational impulse that seemed everywhere to be bringing people together in new interest groups. Between 1890 and 1920 nearly 400 organizations were founded, many to combat the ills of industrial society. Some, such as the National Consumers' League, grew out of efforts to promote general causes—in this case protecting consumers and workers from exploitation. Others, such as the National Tuberculosis Association, aimed at a specific problem.

When voluntary action failed, progressives looked to government to protect the public welfare. They mistrusted legislators, who might be controlled by corporate interests or political machines. So they strengthened the executive branch by increasing the power of individual mayors, governors, and presidents. Then they watched those executives carefully.

PROFESSIONALS   Progressives also drew on the expertise of the newly professionalized middle class. Confident, cosmopolitan professionals—doctors, engineers, psychiatrists, city planners—mounted campaigns to stamp out sexually transmitted disease and dysentery, reform prisons and asylums, and beautify cities. At all levels—local, state, federal—new agencies and commissions staffed by impartial experts began to investigate and regulate lobbyists, insurance and railroad companies, public health, even government itself.

✅ REVIEW

What ills did progressives see in society, what solutions did they propose, and what ideas shaped those solutions?

THE SEARCH FOR THE GOOD SOCIETY

IF PROGRESSIVISM ENDED IN POLITICS, it began with social reform: the need to reach out, to do something to bring the "good society" a step closer. Ellen Richards had just such ends in mind in 1890 when she opened the New England Kitchen in downtown Boston. Richards, a chemist and home economist, designed the Kitchen to sell cheap, wholesome food to the working poor.

The New England Kitchen promoted social as well as nutritional reform. Women freed from the drudgery of cooking could seek gainful employment. And as a "household experiment station" and center for dietary information, the Kitchen tried to educate the poor and Americanize immigrants by showing them how the middle class prepared meals. According to philanthropist Pauline Shaw, it was also a "rival to the saloon." A common belief was that poor diets fostered drinking, especially among the poor and working classes.

PATTERN OF REFORM   In the end, the New England Kitchen served more as an inexpensive eatery for middle-class working women and students than as a resource for the poor or an agency of Americanization. Still, Ellen Richards's experiment reflected a pattern typical of progressive social reform: the mix of professionalism with uplift of the needy, socially conscious women entering the public arena, the hope of creating a better world along middle-class lines.

Poverty in a New Light

During the 1890s crime reporter and photographer Jacob Riis launched a campaign to introduce middle-class audiences to urban poverty. Writing in rich detail in *How the Other Half Lives* (1890), Riis brought readers into the teeming tenement. Accompanying the text were shocking photos of poverty-stricken Americans—Riis's "other half." He also publicized their plight with slide shows of his photographs. His pictures of slum life appeared artless, merely recording the desperate poverty before the camera. But Riis used them to tell a moralistic story, much the way the earlier English novelist Charles Dickens had employed his melodramatic tales to attack the abuses of industrialism in England. People began to see poverty in a new, more sympathetic light, the result less of flawed individuals than unwholesome environments.

SOCIAL WORK   A new profession—social work—proceeded from this new view of poverty. Social work developed out of the old settlement house movement (see pages 540–541). Like the physicians from whom they drew inspiration, social workers studied hard data to diagnose the problems of their "clients." Unlike nineteenth-century philanthropists they refused to do things to or for people. Instead, they worked with their "clients," enlisting their help to solve their own problems. A social worker's "differential casework" attempted to treat individuals case by case, each according to the way the client had been shaped by environment.

In reality, poverty was only one symptom of many personal and social ills. Most progressives continued to see it as a by-product of political and corporate greed, slum neighborhoods, and "institutions of vice" such as the saloon. Less

clear to them was how complex and deeply rooted poverty had become.

Expanding the "Woman's Sphere"

Progressive social reform attracted a great many women seeking what Jane Addams called "the larger life" of public affairs. In the late nineteenth century, women found that protecting their traditional sphere of home and family forced them to move beyond it. Bringing up children, making meals, keeping house, and caring for the sick now involved community decisions about schools, public health, and countless other matters.

WOMEN'S ORGANIZATIONS   In the nineteenth century, many middle- and upper-middle-class women received their first taste of public life from women's organizations, including mothers' clubs, temperance societies, and church groups. By the turn of the century some 500 women's clubs boasted over 160,000 members. Through the General Federation of Women's Clubs, they funded libraries and hospitals and supported schools, settlement houses, compulsory education, and child labor laws. Eventually they moved beyond the concerns of home and family to endorse such controversial causes as woman suffrage, unionization, and the fight against the lynching of African Americans.

NEW WOMAN   The dawn of the century saw the rise of a new generation of women. Longer lived, better educated, and less often married than their mothers,

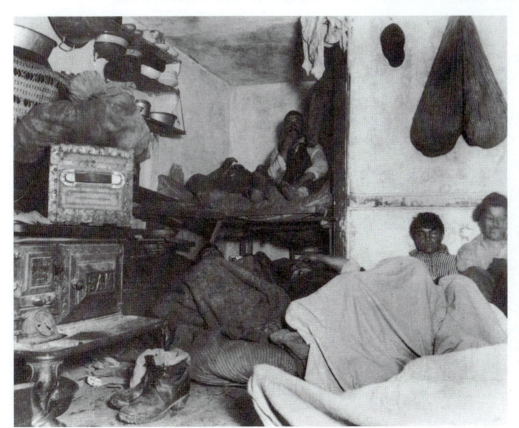

Jacob Riis, a Danish-born reporter and photographer, stalked the streets of New York, meticulously recording the squalor in which many slum dwellers lived. Here we have a Riis photograph of a cramped tenement on Bayard Street, where for "5 cents a spot" a lodger could find a place to sleep for the night. The room, Riis wrote in How the Other Half Lives, was "not thirteen feet either way" and housed "twelve men and women, two or three in bunks in a sort of alcove, the rest on the floor." What originally had been a lifeless engraving in the first edition of the book appeared as this sharp photograph in later editions, adding detail and poignancy to its sleepy-eyed subjects.

they were also willing to pursue careers for fulfillment. Usually they turned to professions that involved their traditional role of nurturers—nursing, library work, teaching, and settlement house work.

Custom and prejudice still restricted women. The faculty at the Massachusetts Institute of Technology refused to allow Ellen Richards to pursue a doctorate. Instead, they hired her to run the gender-segregated "Woman's Laboratory" for training public school teachers. At the turn of the century only about 1,500 women practiced law, and in 1910 women made up barely 6 percent of licensed physicians. That figure rapidly declined as male-dominated medical associations grew in power and discouraged the entry of women.

MARGARET SANGER AND BIRTH CONTROL Margaret Sanger took on one medical problem as a personal crusade: freeing women from the bonds of chronic pregnancy. Sanger, a visiting nurse on the Lower East Side of New York City, had seen too many poor women overburdened with children, pregnant year after year, with no hope of escaping the cycle. The consequences were often crippling and sometimes deadly. "Women cannot be on equal footing with men until they have complete control over their reproductive functions," she argued.

The insight came as a revelation one summer evening in 1912 when Sanger was called to the home of a dis-

| Two women post bills promoting "Votes for Women" in Cincinnati, Ohio, in 1912.

traught immigrant family on Grand Street. Sadie Sachs, mother of three, had accidentally killed herself while trying to terminate yet another pregnancy. Sanger vowed that night "to do something to change the destiny of mothers whose miseries were as vast as the sky." Her own mother had had 18 pregnancies in 22 years. Sanger became a champion of what she called "birth control." By distributing information on contraception, she hoped to free women from unwanted pregnancies and illegal "back alley" abortions that claimed lives. In 1916 she founded the first family planning and birth control clinic in the country. Nine days later, she was arrested and later convicted of distributing contraceptive information, then considered a crime.

Single or married, militant or moderate, professional or nonprofessional, white or black, more and more middle-class urban women thus became "social housekeepers." From their own homes they turned to the homes of their neighbors and from there to all of society.

Social Welfare

In the "bigger family of the city," as one woman reformer called it, settlement house workers soon concluded that private acts of charity would have to be supplemented by government action to make progress. Laws had to be passed and agencies created to promote social welfare, including improved housing, workplaces, parks, and playgrounds; the abolition of child labor; and the enactment of eight-hour-day laws for working women.

KEATING-OWEN ACT By 1910 the more than 400 settlement houses across the nation had organized into a loose affiliation, with settlement workers ready to help shape government policy. Often it was women who led the way. Julia Lathrop, a Vassar College graduate, spent 20 years at Jane Addams's Hull House before becoming the first head of the new federal Children's Bureau in 1912. By then two-thirds of the states had adopted some legislation limiting child labor, although loopholes exempted countless youngsters from coverage. Under Lathrop's leadership, Congress was persuaded to pass the Keating-Owen Act (1916), forbidding goods manufactured by children from crossing state lines.*

Florence Kelley, who had also worked at Hull House, spearheaded a similar campaign in Illinois to protect women workers by limiting their workday to eight hours. As general secretary of the National Consumers' League, she also organized boycotts of companies that treated employees inhumanely. Eventually most states enacted laws restricting the number of hours women could work.

---

*The Supreme Court struck down the law in 1918 as an improper regulation of local labor; nonetheless, the law focused greater attention on the abuses of child labor.

Women's Suffrage

No one had ever seen pickets in front of the White House before, let alone picketing women. But starting on January 10, 1917, from ten in the morning until half past five in the evening, there they stood, stiff and silent at the front gates, six days a week, rain or shine. The "Silent Sentinels," as they called themselves, let their banners speak for them. One quoted the words of Inez Milholland, who had collapsed at a suffrage rally in Los Angeles. "Mr. President," she had said with her dying breath, "how long must women wait for liberty?"

Ever since the conference for women's rights held at Seneca Falls in 1848, women reformers had pressed for the right to vote on the grounds of equal opportunity and simple justice. Progressives embraced women's suffrage by stressing what they saw as the practical results: reducing political corruption, protecting the home, and increasing the voting power of native-born whites. The "purer sensibilities" of women—an ideal held by conservatives and progressives alike—would help cleanse the political process of selfishness and corruption, while their sheer numbers would keep the political balance tilted away from immigrant newcomers.

The suffrage movement benefited, too, from new leadership. In 1900 Carrie Chapman Catt became president of the National American Woman Suffrage Association, founded by Susan B. Anthony in 1890. Politically astute and a skilled organizer, Catt mapped a grassroots strategy of education and persuasion from state to state. She called it "the winning plan." As the map on page 600 shows, victories came first in the West, where women had already forged a more equal partnership with men to overcome the hardships of frontier life. By 1914, 10 western states (and Kansas) had granted women the vote in state elections, as Illinois had in presidential elections.

 MILITANT SUFFRAGISTS The slow pace of progress drove some suffragists to militancy. The shift began in England after 1900, when Emmeline Pankhurst, her daughters, and several of their followers chained themselves to the visitors' gallery in the House of Commons. They smashed department-store windows and broke up political meetings, even burned the

THE AWAKENING

| "The Awakening," a 1915 cartoon, offers a more graphic and emotion-laden map of women's suffrage than the one on page 600. Here, a torch-bearing woman in classical dress carries the franchise from western states, where women's suffrage has already been enacted, to the eastern states, where desperate women eagerly reach out. A poem by suffragist Alice Duer Miller, later collected in Are Women People? (1915), appears below the map. The title of Miller's book became a slogan of the women's suffrage movement.

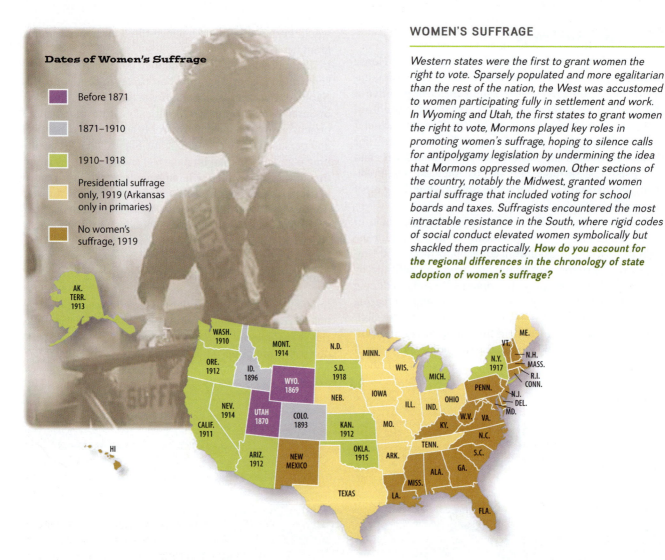

WOMEN'S SUFFRAGE

Dates of Women's Suffrage

- Before 1871
- 1871–1910
- 1910–1918
- Presidential suffrage only, 1919 (Arkansas only in primaries)
- No women's suffrage, 1919

Western states were the first to grant women the right to vote. Sparsely populated and more egalitarian than the rest of the nation, the West was accustomed to women participating fully in settlement and work. In Wyoming and Utah, the first states to grant women the right to vote, Mormons played key roles in promoting women's suffrage, hoping to silence calls for antipolygamy legislation by undermining the idea that Mormons oppressed women. Other sections of the country, notably the Midwest, granted women partial suffrage that included voting for school boards and taxes. Suffragists encountered the most intractable resistance in the South, where rigid codes of social conduct elevated women symbolically but shackled them practically. **How do you account for the regional differences in the chronology of state adoption of women's suffrage?**

AK. TERR. 1913

WASH. 1910
ORE. 1912
ID. 1896
MONT. 1914
N.D.
MINN.
S.D. 1918
WIS.
ME.
VT.
N.H.
MASS.
R.I.
CONN.
N.Y. 1917
NEV. 1914
UTAH 1870
WYO. 1869
NEB.
IOWA
MICH.
PENN.
N.J.
DEL.
MD.
CALIF. 1911
COLO. 1893
KAN. 1912
ILL.
IND.
OHIO
W.V.
VA.
KY.
MO.
ARIZ. 1912
NEW MEXICO
OKLA. 1915
ARK.
TENN.
N.C.
S.C.
ALA.
GA.
MISS.
HI
TEXAS
LA.
FLA.

houses of members of Parliament. British authorities threw many of the protesters in jail, Emmeline Pankhurst included. When the women went on hunger strikes, wardens tied them down and fed them by force.

Among the British suffragists was a small American with large, determined eyes. In 1907, barely out of her teens, Alice Paul had gone to England to join the suffrage crusade. When asked why she had enlisted, she recalled her Quaker upbringing. "One of their principles . . . is equality of the sexes," she explained. Paul marched arm-in-arm with British suffragists and more than once was imprisoned and refused to eat. In 1910 she returned to the United States and brought the aggressive tactics with her. Three years later, in 1913, Paul organized 5,000 women to parade in protest at the inauguration of

| *In Austin township in Illinois, although women got the right to vote, their ballots were deposited in a separate ballot box from the men's.*

President Woodrow Wilson, who favored a state-by-state approach to women's suffrage. Half a million people watched as a near riot ensued. Paul and other suffragists were hauled to jail, stripped naked, and thrown into cells with prostitutes.

In 1914 Paul broke with the moderate National American Woman Suffrage Association and formed the Congressional Union, dedicated to enacting national women's suffrage at any cost through a constitutional amendment. She allied her organization with western women voters in the militant National Woman's Party in 1917. It was Paul who organized the Silent Sentinels at the White House, when President Wilson refused to see any more delegations of women urging a constitutional amendment. She was arrested at the gates of the White House and dragged off to a cellblock in the Washington jail, where she and others refused to eat. Prison officials declared her insane, but a public outcry soon led to her release.

NINETEENTH AMENDMENT
Such repression only widened public support for women's suffrage. So did the contributions of women to World War I (see Chapter 23). In the wake of the war, Great Britain granted women (over age 30) the right to vote in 1918, Germany and Austria in 1919, and the United States in 1920 through the Nineteenth Amendment. Overnight the number of eligible voters in the country doubled.

> ✓ **REVIEW**
>
> Why were women so deeply involved in the "search for the good society," and what were some of their chief accomplishments?

CONTROLLING THE MASSES

"OBSERVE IMMIGRANTS," WROTE ONE AMERICAN in 1912. "You are struck by the fact that from ten to twenty percent are hirsute, low-browed, big-faced persons of obviously low mentality. . . . They clearly belong in skins, in wattled huts at the close of the Ice Age." The writer was neither an uneducated fanatic nor a stern opponent of change. He was Professor Edward A. Ross, a progressive from Madison, Wisconsin, who prided himself on his scientific study of sociology.

Faced with the chaos and corruption of urban life, more than a few progressives feared they were losing control of their country. Saloons and dance halls lured youngsters and impoverished laborers; prostitutes walked the streets; vulgar amusements pandered to the uneducated. Strange Old World cultures clashed with "all-American" customs, and immigrant groups jostled uneasily. The city challenged middle-class reformers to convert this riot of diversity into a more uniform society. To maintain control, progressives sometimes moved beyond education and regulation and sought restrictive laws to control the masses.

Stemming the Immigrant Tide

A rising tide of immigrants from southern and eastern Europe especially troubled native-born Americans, including reformers anxious over the changing ethnic complexion of the country. In northern cities progressives often succeeded in reducing immigrant voting power by increasing residency requirements.

EUGENICS
A new science called "eugenics" lent respectability to the idea that newcomers were biologically inferior. Eugenicists believed that heredity largely shaped human behavior, and they therefore advocated selective breeding for human improvement. By 1914 more magazine articles discussed eugenics than slums, tenements, and living standards combined. In *The Passing of the*

Great Race (1916), upper-crust New Yorker and amateur zoologist Madison Grant helped popularize the notion that the "lesser breeds" threatened to "mongrelize" America. So powerful was the pull of eugenics that it captured the support of some progressives, including Margaret Sanger, who saw contraception as a way of reducing birthrates among those deemed physically and mentally "unfit." It also helped to promote the passage of forced sterilization laws in 30 states, the first in Indiana in 1907.

AMERICANIZATION
Most progressives, however, believed in the shaping impact of environment and so favored either assimilating immigrants into American society or restricting their entry into the country. Jane Addams, for one, stressed the cultural "gifts" immigrants brought with them: folk rituals, dances, music, and handicrafts. With characteristic paternalism, she and other reformers hoped to "Americanize" the foreign-born (the term was newly coined) by teaching them middle-class ways. Education was one key. Progressive educator Peter Roberts, for example, developed a lesson plan for the Young Men's Christian Association that taught immigrants to dress, tip, buy groceries, and vote.

LITERACY TEST
Less-tolerant citizens sought to restrict immigration as a way of reasserting control and achieving social harmony. Though white, Protestant, and American-born, these nativists were only occasionally progressives themselves, but they did employ progressive methods of organization, investigation, education, and legislation. The first solid victory for restrictionists came in 1882, when they succeeded in barring the entry of Chinese laborers into the country. After the turn of the century, restrictionists gained strength as the tidal wave of eastern and southern European immigrants crested. Active since the 1890s the Immigration Restriction League pressed Congress in 1907 to require a literacy test for admission into the United States. Presidents Taft and Wilson vetoed it in 1913 and 1915, but Congress overrode Wilson's second veto in 1917, when war fever raised defensive nationalism to a new peak.

The Curse of Demon Rum

Tied closely to concern over immigrants was an attack on saloons. Part of a broader crusade to clean up cities, the antisaloon campaign drew strength from the century-old drive to lessen the consumption of alcohol. Women made up a disproportionate number of alcohol reformers. The temperance movement reflected their growing campaign to storm male domains—in this case the saloon—and to contain male violence, particularly wife and child abuse associated with drinking.

By 1900 the dangers of an alcoholic republic seemed all too real. Alcohol consumption had risen to an annual rate of more than two gallons per person. Often political bosses owned saloons or conducted their business there. To alcohol reformers, taverns and saloons seemed at the center of many social problems—gambling and prostitution, political

"AMUSING THE MILLION"

On a sunny May morning in 1903, 45,000 people poured through the gates of Luna Park at Coney Island, just south of Brooklyn. What they saw on opening day amazed them: "a storybook land of trellises, columns, domes, minarets, lagoons, and lofty aerial flights." Barkers beckoned them into a Venetian city, a Japanese garden, and a bustling Asian Indian celebration. They could hop aboard the "Switchback" Railroad, a forerunner of the roller coaster, or careen on flat-bottomed boats down a steep incline into the "Shoot-the-Chutes" lagoon.

Coney Island was but one of a host of similar parks that popped up across the country at the turn of the century. Soaring urban populations, increases in leisure time, more spending money, and new trolley systems that made for cheap excursions from the city led to the opening of Boston's Paragon Park, Cleveland's Euclid Beach, Atlanta's Ponce de Leon Park, and Los Angeles's Venice Beach.

All traded in entertainment, but of a sort new to city dwellers. Gilded Age reformers had promoted two models of public entertainment: the spacious city park and the grand public exposition. Both were meant to instruct as well as amuse. Their planners hoped to reduce urban disorder by raising public taste and refining public conduct. When it opened in 1858, New York City's Central Park became a model pastoral retreat in the midst of the city. Its rustic paths, tranquil lakes, and woodsy lookouts were designed as respites from the chaos of urban life. Some amusement parks, like Venice Beach's, mimicked the neoclassical European style of the World's Columbian Exposition (see Chapter 21).

But it did not escape the amusement park operators that people wanted to have fun. At the Columbian Exposition the amusements

Gondolas in Venice Canal, Venice, California

The Venice Amusement Park in California was meant to conjure up Venice, Italy, complete with a network of canals and gondolas. The founders dubbed Venice Amusement Park "the Coney Island of the Pacific."

section, a mile-long strip of theaters, restaurants, sideshows, and rides, had lured more people than did the free public exhibits. As one owner put it, parks were in the business of "amusing the million." Coney Island's Luna Park drew 5 million paying customers in a single season.

Jostling with crowds, eating ice cream and hot dogs, riding Shoot-the-Chutes, young working men and working women, even the newest immigrant, could feel gloriously free and independent, gloriously American. A sense of solidarity drew the mostly working-class crowds together, and the zaniness of the setting loosened social restraints. The

Victorian values of sober industry, thrift, and orderly conduct could hardly compete with the democratic abandon and gaiety of the new amusement parks. The parks heralded the rise of mass culture, invading public space with the private dreams of ordinary people.

Thinking Critically

How did amusement parks foster a vision of society different from public parks?

---

corruption, drug trafficking, unemployment, and poverty. Few reformers recognized the complex cycle of social decay that produced such problems, fewer still the role of saloons as "workingmen's clubs." The saloon was often the only place to cash a check, find out about jobs, eat a cheap meal, or take a bath.

ANTI-SALOON LEAGUE   Reformers considered a national ban on drinking unrealistic and intrusive. They concentrated on prohibiting the sale of alcohol at local and state levels and attacked businesses that profited from it. Led by the Anti-Saloon League (1893), a massive publicity campaign bombarded citizens with pamphlets and advertisements. Doctors cited scientific evidence linking alcohol to cirrhosis, heart disease, and insanity. Social workers connected alcohol consumption with the deterioration of the family; employers, to accidents on the job and lost efficiency.

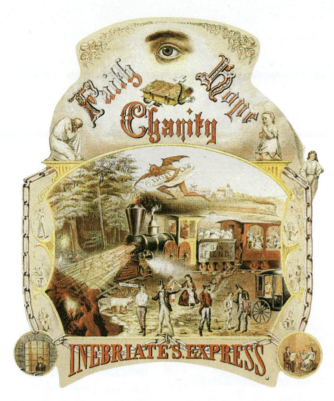

The "Inebriate's Express," loaded with drunken riders, is heading straight for hell. This detail from a chromolithograph, published around 1900, was typical of Victorian-era responses to the problems posed by alcohol. To the all-seeing eye of the omnipotent God, faith, hope, charity, and the Bible are sufficient to cure the problems of drinking.

By 1917 three out of four Americans lived in "dry" counties. Nearly two-thirds of the states had adopted laws outlawing the manufacture and sale of alcohol. Not all progressives were prohibitionists, but the many who were sighed with relief at having taken the profit out of human pain and corruption.

Prostitution

In 1910 the Chicago Vice Commission estimated that 5,000 full-time and 10,000 occasional prostitutes plied their trade in the city. Other cities, small and large, reported similar numbers. An unlikely group of reformers united to fight this vice: feminists who wanted husbands to be as faithful as their wives, public health officials worried about the spread of sexually transmitted disease, and immigration restrictionists who regarded the growth of prostitution as yet another sign of corrupt newcomers. Progressives condemned prostitution but saw the problem in economic and environmental terms. "Poverty causes prostitution," concluded the Illinois Vice Commission in 1916. On average, prostitutes earned five times the income of factory workers.

Some reformers saw more active agents at work. Rumors spread of a vast and profitable "white slave trade." Men armed with hypodermic needles and drinks filled with "knockout drops" were said to be lurking about streetcars, amusement parks, and dance halls in search of young women. Although the average female rider of the streetcar was hardly in danger of abduction, in every city women were held captive and forced into prostitution. By conservative estimates, such women made up some 10 percent of all prostitutes.

As real abuses blended with sensationalism, Congress passed the Mann Act (1910), prohibiting the interstate transport of women for immoral purposes. By 1918 reformers succeeded in banning previously tolerated **red-light districts** in most cities. Once again, progressives went after those businesses that, like the liquor trade, made money from misery.

"For Whites Only"

Most progressives paid little attention to the misery suffered by African Americans. The 1890s had been a low point for black citizens, most of whom still lived in the South. Across the region, the lynching of African Americans increased dramatically, as did restrictions on black voting and the use of segregated facilities to separate the races. Signs decreeing "For Whites Only" appeared on drinking fountains and restrooms and in other public places.

Black boxing champion Jack Johnson's performance in and out of the ring exposed cultural fault lines. In a segregated society, not only did he beat—and taunt—white opponents, Johnson used his celebrity to violate racial conventions. He paraded his sexuality. He consorted with white women. He drank hard and drove fast. "I always take a chance on my pleasures," he boasted. Trespassing boundaries was one way of declaring independence, not merely in pursuit of equality but defiant superiority.

MEMENTOS OF MURDER

Jesse Washington

Could this be "Joe"?

Men face the camera without making any effort to mask their faces.

Young boys are present.

No stamp or postmark indicating that the card was sent. Did "Joe" keep it?

Katy Electric Studio Temple Texas H. Lippe Prop.

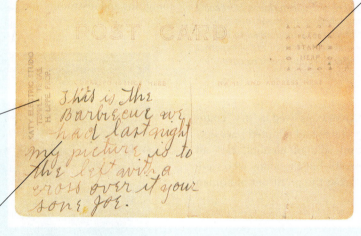

This is the Barbecue we had last night[.] My picture is to the left with a cross over it[.] your son, Joe.

Not all historians are professionals but even amateurs can help us see the past in a new light. James Allen described himself as a "picker," rummaging through other people's junk for things he might sell. Postcards hadn't much interested him until he came on one that bore the photograph of a lynching. "It wasn't the corpse that bewildered me but the canine-thin faces of pack," he recalled. Collected and later published by Allen, such postcards memorializing lynchings were one segment of a larger industry that flourished in the late nineteenth and early twentieth centuries. For a penny in postage the cards might be of hotels or city streets or even just photos of individuals taken by photographers, which could be sent to friends and relatives as souvenirs. But the cards Allen came across over the years were of a different order: grisly mementos of a ritualized murder. The one above—of the lynching and burning of an African American named Jesse Washington in 1916—appears not to have been mailed.

Source: James Allen, *Without Sanctuary: Lynching Photography in America* (Santa Fe, NM: Twin Palms Publishers, 2000).

Thinking Critically

Why might people have their photographs taken for postcards at a lynching and then send the cards to parents and other relatives? What does that practice tell us about the racial environment in which such events occurred?

A few progressives, such as muckraker Ray Stannard Baker and settlement-house worker Lillian Wald, decried racial discrimination, but most ignored it—or used it to their political advantage. Throughout the South, white progressives and even old-guard politicians, including Senator Ben Tillman of South Carolina and Governor James K. Vardaman of Mississippi, used the rhetoric of reform to support white supremacy. Such "reformers" won office by promising to disenfranchise African Americans in order to break the power of corrupt political machines that rested on the black vote, much as northern machines marshaled the immigrant vote.

W. E. B. Du Bois

In the face of such discrimination African Americans fought back. After the turn of the century, black critics in the North rejected the cautious accommodation of Booker T. Washington's "Atlanta Compromise," which counseled African Americans to accept segregation and work their way up the economic ladder (see page 573). W. E. B. Du Bois, a professor at Atlanta University, leveled the most stinging attack in *The Souls of Black Folk* (1903). Du Bois saw no benefit for African Americans in sacrificing intellectual growth for narrow vocational training. Nor would he accept the South's discriminatory caste system. A better future would come only if black citizens struggled politically to achieve suffrage and equal rights.

NAACP

Instead of exhorting African Americans to pull themselves up slowly from the bottom, Du Bois called on the "talented tenth," a cultured black vanguard, to blaze a trail of protest against segregation, **disenfranchisement,** and discrimination. In 1905 he founded the Niagara Movement for political and economic equality. In 1909 a coalition of blacks and white reformers transformed the Niagara Movement into the National Association for the Advancement of Colored People (NAACP) after an ugly race riot rocked Springfield, the capital of Illinois, in the summer of 1908. At least seven people died as whites and blacks fought pitched battles after marauding white mobs torched black homes and businesses. For the first time, however, more whites than blacks perished.

The resulting civil rights organization was biracial, drawing members from both the white and black communities. At first predominantly white, the group included Lincoln Steffens, Jane Addams, and John Dewey as well as African Americans W. E. B. Du Bois and Ida B. Wells-Barnett. As with other progressive organizations, NAACP membership was largely limited to the middle class. It worked to extend the principles of tolerance and equal opportunity in a color-blind fashion by publicizing discrimination through its journal, *The*

Jane Addams founded her settlement at Hull House in Chicago because she was convinced, like many progressives, that reform must be practical, arising out of the needs of individuals within a community. As Addams continued her campaigns, she also looked beyond the local neighborhood to reform political structures of municipal and state governments.

Crisis, and mounting legal challenges to segregation and bigotry. In *Buchanan v. Worley* (1917), for example, NAACP lawyers persuaded the Supreme Court to outlaw residential segregation sponsored by state and local governments. By 1919 the NAACP boasted some 90,000 members in 300 local branches. Accommodation was giving way to new combative organizations and new forms of protest.

✓ **REVIEW**

Which "masses" did progressives want to control, why did they want to control them, and what instruments did they employ?

THE POLITICS OF MUNICIPAL AND STATE REFORM

REFORM THE SYSTEM. IN THE end, so many urban problems seemed to return to the premise that government had to be overhauled. Jane Addams learned as much outside the doors of her beloved Hull House in Chicago. For months during the early 1890s, garbage piled up in the streets. The filth and stench drove Addams and her fellow workers to city hall in protest—700 times in one summer—but to no avail. In Chicago, as elsewhere, corrupt city bosses had made garbage collection a plum awarded to the company that paid them the most for it.

In desperation Addams herself submitted a bid for garbage removal in her neighborhood. When it was thrown out on a technicality, she won an appointment as garbage inspector. For almost a year she dogged collection carts, but boss politics kept things dirty. So Addams ran candidates in 1896 and 1898 against the local ward boss. They lost, but Addams kept up the fight for honest government and social reform—at city hall, in the Illinois legislature, and finally in Washington, D.C. Politics turned out to be the only way to clean things up.

The Reformation of the Cities

In the smokestack cities of the Midwest, where the frustrations of industrial and agricultural America fed each other, the urban battleground furnished the middle class with its first test of political reform. A series of colorful and independent mayors demonstrated that cities could be run humanely without changing the structure of government.

In Detroit, shoe magnate Hazen Pingree turned the mayor's office into an instrument of reform when elected in 1889. By the end of Pingree's fourth term, Detroit had new parks and public baths, fairer taxes, ownership of the local light plant, and a work-relief program for victims of the depression of 1893. In 1901 Cleveland mayor Tom Johnson launched a similar reform campaign. Before the end of his campaign, municipal franchises had been limited to a fraction of their previous 99-year terms and the city ran the utility company. By 1915 nearly two out of three cities in the nation had copied some form of this "gas and water socialism" to control the runaway prices of utility companies.

Tragedy dramatized the need to alter the very structure of government. On a hot summer night in 1900 a hurricane storm surge from the Gulf of Mexico smashed the port city of Galveston, Texas. Floods killed one of every six residents. The municipal government sank into confusion and political wrangling. In reaction, business leaders won approval of a new charter that replaced the mayor and city council with a powerful commission. Each of five commissioners controlled a municipal department, and together they ran the city. By 1920 nearly 400 cities had adopted the plan. Expert commissioners enhanced efficiency and helped to check party rule in municipal government.

CITY-MANAGER PLAN

In other cities elected officials appointed an outside expert, or "city manager," to run things. The first was hired in Staunton, Virginia, in 1908. Within a decade, 45 cities had them. At lower levels experts took charge of services: engineers oversaw utilities; accountants, finances; doctors and nurses, public health; specially trained firefighters and police, the safety of citizens. Broad civic reforms attempted to break the corrupt alliance between companies doing business with the city and the bosses who controlled the wards. Citywide elections replaced the old ward system, and civil service laws helped create a nonpartisan bureaucracy based on merit. Political machines and ethnic voters lost power, while city government gained efficiency.

Progressivism in the States

WEAKNESSES OF CITY GOVERNMENT

"Whenever we try to do anything, we run up against the charter," complained the reform mayor of Schenectady, New York. Charters granted by state governments defined the powers of cities. The rural interests that generally dominated state legislatures rarely gave cities adequate authority to levy taxes, set voting requirements, draw up budgets, or legislate reforms. State legislatures found themselves under the influence of business interests, party machines, and county courthouse rings. Reformers therefore tried to place their candidates where they could do some good—in governors' mansions.

State progressivism, like urban reform, enjoyed its greatest success in the Midwest, under the leadership of Robert La Follette of Wisconsin. A mainstream Republican until a party boss offered him a bribe in a railroad case, La Follette turned about and pledged to break "the power of this

believes in the American people. He believes that YOU should know the TRUTH about the inside workings of YOUR government and the records of your representatives at Washington.

So with the help and approval of a score of other fighters for the common good, Senator La Follette established

La Follette's Magazine

devoted to fearless discussion of the most important public questions, and has departments for the home, special articles, stories, a Farm Department, fiction, humor, important news of the world.

Published monthly. Regular price $1.00 per year. To permit you to get acquainted with the magazine we will send it to you on trial

3 Months for 25c.

Simply send a quarter with your name and address to

LA FOLLETTE'S, Box 45, Madison, Wis.

On the state level progressives made their greatest impact in Wisconsin, where Robert La Follette led the fight to regulate railroads, control corruption, and expand the civil service. In trying to do an end run around political party bosses, he used his publication, La Follette's Magazine, to reach ordinary Americans directly.

corrupt influence." In 1900 he won the governorship of Wisconsin as an uncommonly independent Republican.

Over the next six years "Battle Bob" La Follette made Wisconsin, in the words of Theodore Roosevelt, "the laboratory of democracy." La Follette's **Wisconsin idea** produced the most comprehensive set of state reforms in American history. There were new laws regulating railroads, controlling corruption, and expanding the civil service. His direct primary weakened the hold of party bosses by transferring nominations from the backrooms of party conventions and caucuses to the voters at large. Among La Follette's notable "firsts" were a state income tax, a state commission to oversee factory safety and sanitation, and a Legislative Reference Bureau at the University of Wisconsin. University-trained experts poured into state government.

Other states copied the Wisconsin idea or hatched their own programs of reform. In the West, with its scanty population, strong, independent women had the opportunity to play a larger role in shaping politics, and progressivism thrived. Western states were the nation's first to grant women the right to vote beginning with Wyoming in 1869. In Oregon the legislature limited the number of hours women could work to protect their health from harm. The middle class of heavily urban California supported progressive Hiram Johnson's drive to oust political machines from cities and the statehouse. Colorado governor John Shafroth fought the local political machine and pressed a balky legislature to regulate railroad rates, insure commercial bank deposits, and create a public service commission. Like other progressives, he supported the direct primary. By 1916 all but three states had such laws.

To cut the power of party organizations and make office-holders directly responsible to the public, Shafroth and other progressives worked for three additional reforms: initiative (voter introduction of legislation), referendum (voter enactment or repeal of laws), and recall (voter-initiated removal of elected officials). By 1912 a dozen states had adopted initiative and referendum, and seven, recall. A year later the Seventeenth Amendment to the Constitution permitted the direct election of senators, previously selected by state legislatures.

Almost every state established regulatory commissions with the power to hold public hearings and to examine company books and question officials. Some could set maximum prices and rates. Yet it was not always easy to define, let alone serve, the "public good." All too often commissioners found themselves refereeing battles within industries—between carriers and shippers, for example—rather than between what progressives called "the interests" and "the people." Regulators had to rely on the advice of experts drawn from the business community itself. Many commissions thus became "captured" by the industries they regulated.

Social welfare received special attention from the states. The lack of workers' compensation for injury, illness, or death on the job had long drawn fire from reformers and labor leaders. American courts still operated on the common-law assumption that employees accepted the risks of work. Workers or their families could collect damages only if they proved employer negligence. Most accident victims received nothing. In 1902 Maryland finally adopted the first workers' compensation act. By 1916 most states required insurance for factory accidents and over half had employer liability laws. Thirteen states also provided pensions for widows with dependent children.

SEEDS OF THE WELFARE STATE Despite the progressive attack on machine politics, political bosses survived, in part by adapting the climate of reform to the needs of their working-class constituents. After the Triangle fire of 1911, for example, it was Tammany Democrats Robert F. Wagner and Alfred E. Smith who led the fight for a new labor code to govern conditions in the workplace. This working-class "urban liberalism" also found advocates among women's associations, especially those concerned with mothers, children, and working women. The Federation of Women's Clubs led the fight for mothers' pensions (a forerunner of aid to dependent children). When in 1912 the National Consumers' League and other women's groups succeeded in establishing the Children's Bureau, it was the first federal welfare agency and the only female-run national bureau in the world. At a time when most women lacked the vote, they nonetheless sowed the seeds of the welfare state as they helped to make urban liberalism a powerful instrument of social reform.

 **REVIEW**

What reforms did cities and states enact, and how did those reforms address the problems they faced?

PROGRESSIVISM GOES TO WASHINGTON

ON SEPTEMBER 6, 1901, AT the Pan-American Exposition in Buffalo, New York, Leon Czolgosz stood nervously in line. He was waiting to meet President William McKinley. Unemployed and bent on murder, Czolgosz shuffled toward McKinley. As the president reached out, Czolgosz fired two bullets into his chest. McKinley slumped into a chair. Eight days later the president was dead. The mantle of power passed to Theodore Roosevelt. At 42 he was the youngest president ever to hold office.

Roosevelt's entry into the White House was a political accident. Party leaders had seen the weak office of vice president as a way of removing him from power, but the tragedy in Buffalo foiled their plans. Surely progressivism would have come to Washington without Theodore Roosevelt, and while there he was never its most daring advocate. In many ways he was quite conservative. He saw reform as a way to avoid more-radical change.

TR

TR, as so many Americans called him, was the scion of seven generations of wealthy, aristocratic New Yorkers. A sickly boy, he built his body through rigorous exercise, sharpened his mind through constant study, and pursued a life so strenuous that few could keep up. He learned to ride and shoot, roped cattle in the Dakota Badlands and later climbed the Matterhorn, hunted African game, and explored the Amazon.

In 1880, driven by an urge to lead and serve, Roosevelt won election to the New York State Assembly. In rapid succession he became a civil service commissioner in Washington, New York City police commissioner, assistant secretary of the navy, and the Rough Rider hero of the Spanish-American War. At the age of 40 he won election as reform governor of New York and two years later as vice president. Through it all, TR remained a solid Republican, personally flamboyant but committed to moderate change only.

As president, Roosevelt brought to the Executive Mansion (he formally renamed it the "White House") a passion for order, a commitment to the public, and a sense of presidential possibilities. Most presidents believed the Constitution set limits on their power. Roosevelt thought that the president could do anything not expressly forbidden in the document. Recognizing the value of publicity, he gave reporters the first press room in the White House and favored them with all the stories they wanted. He was the first president to ride in an automobile, fly in an airplane, and dive in a submarine—and everyone knew it.

To dramatize racial injustice, Roosevelt invited black educator Booker T. Washington to lunch at the White House in 1901. White southern journalists called such race mingling treason, but for Roosevelt the gesture served both principle and politics. His lunch with Washington was part of a "black and tan" strategy to build a biracial coalition among southern Republicans. He denounced lynching and appointed black southerners to important federal offices in Mississippi and South Carolina.

BROWNSVILLE INCIDENT
Sensing the limits of political feasibility, Roosevelt went no further. Perhaps his own narrowness on race also stopped him. In 1906, when Atlanta exploded in a race riot that left 12 people dead, Roosevelt said nothing. Later that year he discharged "without honor" three entire companies of African American troops, because some of the soldiers were (unjustly) charged with having "shot up" Brownsville, Texas. All lost their pensions, including six winners of the Medal of Honor. The act stained Roosevelt's record. (Congress acknowledged the wrong in 1972 by granting the soldiers honorable discharges.)

A Square Deal

PHILOSOPHY OF THE SQUARE DEAL
Roosevelt could not long follow McKinley's cautious course. He had more energetic actions in mind. He accepted growth—whether of business, labor, or government—as natural. In the pluralistic system he envisioned, big labor would counterbalance big capital, big farm organizations would offset big food processors, and so on. Standing astride them all, mediating when needed, was a big government that could ensure fair results for all. Later, as he campaigned for a second term in 1904, Roosevelt named this program the "Square Deal."

ANTHRACITE COAL STRIKE
In a startling display of presidential initiative, Roosevelt in 1902 intervened in a strike that idled 140,000 miners and paralyzed the anthracite (hard) coal industry. As winter approached, public frustration with the mine owners mounted. They refused even to recognize the miners' union, let alone negotiate worker demands for higher wages and fewer hours. Roosevelt summoned both sides to the White House. When management refused, Roosevelt leaked word to Wall Street that the army would take over the mines if the owners did not yield.

Seldom had a president acted so boldly and never on behalf of strikers. In late October 1902 the owners settled by granting miners a 10 percent wage hike and a nine-hour day in return for increases in coal prices and no union recognition. Roosevelt was equally prepared to intervene on the side of management, as he did when he sent federal troops to end strikes in Arizona in 1903 and Colorado in 1904. His aim was to establish a vigorous presidency ready to deal squarely with all sides.

U.S. v. E. C. KNIGHT
Roosevelt especially needed to confront the issue of economic concentration. Financial power had become consolidated in giant trusts following a wave of mergers at the end of the century. Government investigations revealed a rash of corporate abuses—rebates, collusion, **"watered" stock,** payoffs to government officials. The conservative courts showed little willingness to break up the giants or blunt their power. In *United States v. E. C. Knight* (1895), the Supreme Court had crippled the Sherman Antitrust Act by ruling that the federal law applied only to **interstate commerce** and not to manufacturing. The decision left the American Sugar Refining Company in control of 98 percent of the nation's sugar-making factories.

In his first State of the Union message in 1901, Roosevelt told Congress that he did not oppose trusts. As he saw it, large corporations were not only inevitable but also capable of producing more goods at lower prices. He wanted to regulate, not destroy, them, to make them fairer and more efficient. Only then would the economic order be humanized, its victims protected, and class violence avoided. Like individuals, trusts had to be held to strict standards of morality. Conduct, not size, was the yardstick TR used to measure "good" and "bad" trusts.

| Bullnecked and barrel-chested, Theodore Roosevelt was "pure act," said Henry Adams. TR may have had the attention span of a golden retriever, as one critic charged, but he also embodied the great virtues of his day— honesty, hard work, constancy, courage, and, while in power, self-control.

With a progressive's faith in the power of publicity and a regulator's need for the facts, Roosevelt moved immediately to strengthen the federal power of investigation. He called for the creation of a Department of Commerce with a Bureau of Corporations that could force companies to hand over their records. Congressional conservatives shuddered at the prospect of putting corporate books on display. Finally, in 1903, after Roosevelt charged that John D. Rockefeller was orchestrating the opposition, Congress enacted the legislation and provided the Justice Department with additional staff to prosecute antitrust cases.

NORTHERN SECURITIES In 1902, to demonstrate the power of government, Roosevelt had Attorney General Philander Knox file an antitrust suit against the Northern Securities Company. The mammoth holding company virtually monopolized railroads in the Northwest. Worse still, it bloated its stock with worthless certificates and gouged consumers. Here, clearly, was a "bad trust." J. P. Morgan, one of the company's founders, rushed to the White House. "Send your man [the attorney general] to my man [Morgan's lawyer] and they can fix it up," he told Roosevelt and Knox. "We don't want to fix it up," replied the attorney general. "We want to stop it." In the end the Supreme Court ordered the company to dissolve in 1904. Ultimately the Roosevelt administration brought suit against 44 giants.

RAILROAD REGULATION Despite his reputation for trustbusting, Roosevelt always preferred continuous regulation. The problems of the railroads, for example, were newly underscored by a recent round of mergers and acquisitions that contributed to higher freight rates. Roosevelt pressed Congress to strengthen the weak Interstate Commerce Commission (ICC), created in 1887. In 1903 Congress enacted the Elkins Act, which gave the ICC power to end rebates. Even the railroads supported the act because it saved them from the costly practice of granting special fee reductions to large shippers.

By the election of 1904 the president's Square Deal had won him broad popular support. He trounced his two rivals, Democrat Alton B. Parker, a jurist from New York, and Eugene V. Debs of the Socialist Party.

Conservatives in his own party opposed Roosevelt's meddling in the private sector. But progressives, goaded by Robert La Follette, demanded still more regulation of the railroads, in particular a controversial proposal for making public the value of all rail property. In 1906 the president finally reached a compromise typical of his restrained approach to reform. The Hepburn Railway Act allowed the ICC to set ceilings on rates and regulate sleeping-car companies, ferries, bridges, and terminals. La Follette did not obtain the provision to disclose company value he wanted, but the Hepburn Act drew Roosevelt nearer to his goal of continuous regulation of business.

Bad Food and Pristine Wilds

Extending the umbrella of federal protection to consumers, Roosevelt belatedly threw his weight behind two campaigns for healthy foods and drugs. In 1905 Samuel Hopkins Adams of *Collier's Weekly* wrote that "Gullible America" was buying over-the-counter patent medicines loaded with "huge quantities of alcohol, an appalling amount of opiates and narcotics," and worse—axle grease, acid, glue. Adams sent the samples he had collected to Harvey Wiley, chief chemist at the Agriculture Department. Wiley's "Poison Squad" produced scientific evidence of Adams's charges.

The appearance of Upton Sinclair's novel *The Jungle* in 1906 spurred Congress to act. Sinclair intended to recruit people to socialism by exposing the plight of workers in the meatpacking industry. *The Jungle* contained a brief but vivid description of the slaughter of cattle infected with tuberculosis, of meat covered with rat dung, and of men falling into cooking vats. Readers paid scant attention to the workers, but their stomachs turned at what they might be eating for breakfast. The Pure Food and Drug Act of 1906 sailed through Congress, and the Meat Inspection Act soon followed.

CONSERVATION THROUGH PLANNED MANAGEMENT Roosevelt had come late to the consumer cause, but on conservation he led the nation. An outdoors enthusiast, he galvanized public concern over the reckless use of natural resources. His chief forester, Gifford Pinchot, persuaded him that planned management under federal guidance was needed to protect the natural domain. Cutting trees must be synchronized with tree plantings, for example, and oil pumped from the ground under controlled conditions.

CONSERVATION VERSUS PRESERVATION In the western states water was the problem, as U.S. Geological Survey director John Welsey Powell had noted years earlier (page 475). Economic growth, even survival, depended on it. Two visions of what to do about Powell's water-starved West emerged. One emphasized the conservation of water (and other scarce resources) through planned use; the

DUELING DOCUMENTS

PRESERVATION VERSUS CONSERVATION

No president is more closely associated with protecting the environment than Theodore Roosevelt. His lifelong love of nature and wilderness only deepened in 1903, when Sierra Club cofounder John Muir took him traipsing through the snow in what became, thanks to Roosevelt and Muir, Yosemite National Park in 1906. Despite their friendship, however, the two men differed on what should be done with wilderness. Muir proposed preservation of the natural world in its most pristine form, while Roosevelt favored conservation for a multitude of uses in the public interest.

DOCUMENT 1   Wilderness Should Be "Unspoiled": Muir

No dogma taught by the present civilization seems to form so insuperable an obstacle in the way of a right understanding of the relations which culture sustains to wildness as that which regards the world as made especially for the uses of man. Every animal, plant, and crystal controverts it in the plainest terms. Yet it is taught from century to century as something ever new and precious, and in the resulting darkness the enormous conceit is allowed to go unchallenged. . . .

The great wilds of our country, once held to be boundless and inexhaustible, are being rapidly invaded and overrun in every direction, and everything destructible in them is being destroyed. How far destruction may go it is not easy to guess. Every landscape, low and high, seems doomed to be trampled and harried. Even the sky is not safe from scath—blurred and blackened whole summers together with the smoke of fires that devour the woods.

The Shasta region [part of the Cascade Mountains in California] is still a fresh unspoiled wilderness, accessible and available for travelers of every kind and degree. Would it not then be a fine thing to set it apart like the Yellowstone and Yosemite as a National Park for the welfare and benefit of all mankind, preserving its fountains and forests and all its glad life in primeval beauty? Very little of the region can ever be more valuable for any other use—certainly not for gold nor for grain. No private right or interest need suffer, and thousands yet unborn would come from far and near and bless the country for its wise and benevolent forethought.

Source: John Muir, *Steep Trails* (Boston, 1918), edited by William Frederic Badé, pp. 11–12, 104.

DOCUMENT 2   Forest Land Has Multiple Uses: Roosevelt

Lands in the forest reserves that are more valuable for agriculture than for fewest purposes are being opened to settlement and entry as fast as their agricultural character can be ascertained. There is therefore no longer excuse for saying that the reserves retard the legitimate settlement and development of the country. On the contrary, they promote and sustain that development, and they do so in no way more powerful than through their direct contributions to the schools and roads. Ten per cent of all the money received from the forest reserves goes to the States for the use of the counties in which the reserves lie, to be used for schools and roads. . . .

The forest policy of the Government in the West has now become what the West desired it to be. It is a national policy, wider than the boundaries of any State, and larger than the interests of any single industry. Of course it cannot give any set of men exactly what they would choose. Undoubtedly the irrigator would often like to have less stock on his watersheds, while the stockman wants more. The lumberman would like to cut more timber, the settler and the miner would often like him to cut less. The county authorities want to see more money coming in for schools and roads, while the lumberman and stockman object to the rise in value of timber and grass. . . .

By keeping the public forests in the public hands our forest policy substitutes the good of the whole people for the profits of the privileged few. With that result none will quarrel except the men who are losing the chance of personal profit at public expense.

Our western forest policy is based upon meeting the wishes of the best public sentiment of the whole West. It proposes to create new reserves wherever forest lands still vacant are found in the public domain, and to give the reserves already made the highest possible usefulness to all the people. . . .

Source: Theodore Roosevelt to Gifford Pinchot, August 24, 1906, reprinted in H. W. Brands, ed., *The Selected Letters of Theodore Roosevelt* (New York, 2001), pp. 432–433.

Thinking Critically

What does wilderness mean to John Muir? What are its benefits? What does Theodore Roosevelt have in mind for "forest reserves," and what does he mean by "the good of the whole people"? How do their different positions help to shape their points of view?

William Howard Taft (on the far right) was big, good-natured, modest, and reluctant to run for the presidency in 1908. At the outset of the campaign President Roosevelt sent him pointed advice: "Photographs on horseback, yes, tennis, no, and golf is fatal." But Taft played anyway. He loved golf despite its reputation as a "dude's game."

The Election of 1912

In June 1910 Roosevelt came home from Africa laden with hunting trophies and exuberant as ever. He found Taft unhappy and progressive Republicans threatening to defect. Party loyalty kept Roosevelt quiet through most of 1911, but in October Taft pricked him personally on the sensitive matter of busting trusts. Like TR, Taft accepted trusts as natural but demanded, more impartially, that all trusts—"good" or "bad" ones—be prevented from restraining trade. In four years as president, Taft brought nearly twice the antitrust suits Roosevelt had in seven years.

NEW NATIONALISM Already, in a speech at Osawatomie, Kansas, in 1910, Roosevelt had sharpened his differences with Taft by outlining a program of sweeping reform. His "New Nationalism" stressed the interests of the nation as a whole and the value of government as an agent of reform. It accepted consolidation in the economy—whether big business or big labor—but insisted on protecting the interests of individuals through big government. The New Nationalism promised government planning and efficiency under a powerful executive, "a steward of the public welfare." It promoted taxes on incomes and inheritances and greater regulation of industry. And it embraced social justice, specifically workers'

Cannon's power without Taft's help, they scorned the president. And Taft's compromise was wasted. Senate protectionists peppered the tariff bill with so many amendments that rates jumped nearly to their old levels.

Late in 1909 the rift between Taft and the progressives reached the breaking point in a dispute over conservation. Taft had appointed Richard Ballinger secretary of the interior over the objections of Roosevelt's old friend and mentor Chief Forester Pinchot. When Ballinger opened a million acres of public lands for sale, Pinchot charged that shady dealings had led Ballinger to transfer Alaskan public coal lands to a syndicate that included J. P. Morgan. Early in 1910, Taft fired Pinchot for insubordination. Angry progressives saw the Ballinger-Pinchot controversy as another betrayal by Taft. They began to look longingly across the Atlantic, where TR was stalking big game in Africa.

TAFT'S ACCOMPLISHMENTS Despite his failures Taft was no conservative pawn. He ended up protecting more land than Roosevelt, and he pressured Congress to enact a progressive program regulating safety standards for mines and railroads, creating a federal children's bureau, and setting an eight-hour workday for federal employees. Taft's support of a **graduated income tax**—sometimes staunch, sometimes mild—was finally decisive. Early in 1913 it became the Sixteenth Amendment. Historians view it as one of the most important reforms of the century, for it eventually generated the revenue for many new social programs.

Yet no matter what Taft did, he managed to alienate conservatives and progressives alike. That spelled trouble for the Republicans as the presidential election of 1912 approached.

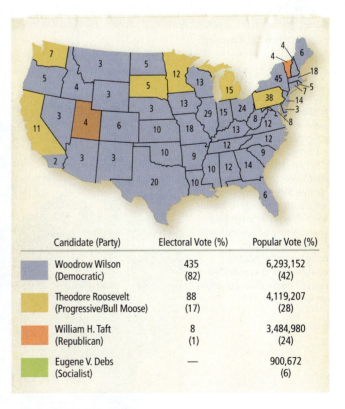

Candidate (Party)	Electoral Vote (%)	Popular Vote (%)
Woodrow Wilson (Democratic)	435 (82)	6,293,152 (42)
Theodore Roosevelt (Progressive/Bull Moose)	88 (17)	4,119,207 (28)
William H. Taft (Republican)	8 (1)	3,484,980 (24)
Eugene V. Debs (Socialist)	—	900,672 (6)

ELECTION OF 1912

compensation for accidents, minimum wages and maximum hours, child labor laws, and "equal suffrage"—a nod to women and loyal black Republicans. Roosevelt, a cautious reformer as president, grew daring as he campaigned for the White House.

PROGRESSIVE, OR "BULL MOOSE," PARTY

"My hat is in the ring!" Roosevelt announced in February 1912. The enormously popular Roosevelt won most of the primaries, but by the time Republicans met in Chicago in June 1912, Taft had used presidential patronage and promises to secure his renomination. A frustrated Roosevelt bolted and took progressive Republicans with him. Two months later, amid choruses of "Onward Christian Soldiers," delegates to the newly formed Progressive Party nominated Roosevelt for the presidency. "I'm feeling like a bull moose!" he bellowed. Progressives suddenly had a symbol for their breakaway party.

WOODROW WILSON'S NEW FREEDOM

The Democrats chose as their candidate Woodrow Wilson, the progressive governor of New Jersey. Wilson wisely concentrated his fire on Roosevelt. He countered the New Nationalism with his "New Freedom." It rejected the economic consolidation that Roosevelt embraced. Bigness itself was a sin, no matter how big corporations acted, because they crowded out competition, thereby promoting inefficiency and reducing economic opportunity. Only by strictly limiting the size of business enterprises could the free market be preserved and Americans be released from the control of the wealthy and powerful. And only by keeping government small could individual liberty be protected. "Liberty," Wilson cautioned, "has never come from government," only from the "limitation of governmental power."

Increasingly, voters found the Republican Taft beside the point. In an age of reform even the Socialists looked good. Better led, financed, and more organized than ever, the Socialist Party had enlarged its membership to nearly 135,000 by 1912. Socialist mayors ran 32 cities. The party also had an appealing candidate in Eugene V. Debs, a homegrown Indiana radical. He had won over 400,000 votes in the last of his three previous bids for president in 1908. Now, in 1912, he summoned voters to make "the working class the ruling class."

On Election Day, voters gave progressive reform a resounding endorsement. Wilson won 6.3 million votes, Roosevelt 4.1 million, Taft just 3.6 million. Debs received almost a million votes. Together the two progressive candidates amassed a 3-to-1 margin. The Republican split, moreover, broke the party's hold on national politics. For the first time since 1896, a Democrat would sit in the White House with his party in control of Congress.

✓ **REVIEW**

How did President Roosevelt's reform agenda reflect his promise of a "Square Deal" for Americans?

WOODROW WILSON AND THE POLITICS OF MORALITY

SOON AFTER THE ELECTION WILSON confessed to William McCombs, chairman of the Democratic National Committee: "God ordained that I should be the next President of the United States." To the White House he brought a

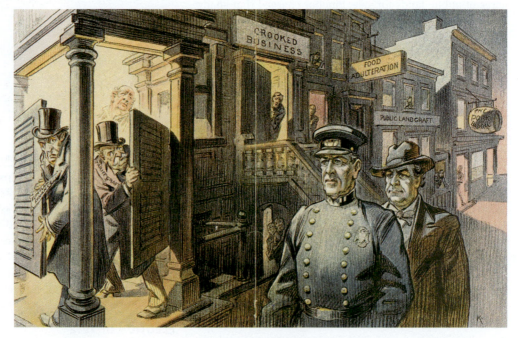

| Woodrow Wilson came to the White House with promises to reform government. In this 1913 cartoon titled "A New Captain in the District," the newly elected president strides through corrupt Washington, ready to police such abuses as easy land grants and pork barreling, the much-criticized congressional practice of voting for projects that benefit home districts and constituents.

passion for reform and the conviction that he was meant to accomplish great things. Under him, progressivism peaked.

Early Career

From the moment of his birth in 1856, Thomas Woodrow Wilson could not escape a sense of destiny. In the family's Presbyterian faith, in the sermons of his minister father, in dinnertime talk ran the unbending belief in a world predetermined by God and ruled by saved souls, the "elect." Wilson ached to be one of them and behaved as if he were.

Like most southerners, he grew up loving the Democratic Party and small government, hating the tariff, and accepting racial segregation. (Under his presidency, segregation returned to Washington for the first time since Reconstruction.) An early career in law bored him, so he turned to political science and became a professor. His studies persuaded him that a modern president must act as a "prime minister," directing and uniting his party, shaping legislation and public opinion, exerting continuous leadership. In 1910, after a stormy tenure as head of Princeton University, Wilson was helped by Democratic Party bosses to win the governorship of New Jersey. In 1912 they helped him again, this time to the presidency of the country.

The Reforms of the New Freedom

As governor Wilson led New Jersey on the path of progressive reform. As president he was a model of executive leadership. More than Theodore Roosevelt he shaped policy and legislation. He went to Congress to let members know he intended to work personally with them. He kept party discipline tight and mobilized public opinion when Congress refused to act.

Lowering the high tariff was Wilson's first order of business. Progressives had long attacked the tariff as another example of the power of trusts. By protecting American manufacturers, Wilson argued, such barriers weakened the competition he cherished. When the Senate threatened to raise rates, the new president appealed directly to the public. "Industrious" and "insidious" lobbyists were blocking reform, he cried to reporters. A "brick couldn't be thrown without hitting one of them."

UNDERWOOD-SIMMONS TARIFF The Underwood-Simmons Tariff of 1913 marked the first downward revision of the tariff in 19 years and

the biggest since before the Civil War. To compensate for lost revenue, Congress enacted a graduated income tax under the newly adopted Sixteenth Amendment. It applied solely to corporations and the tiny fraction of Americans who earned more than $4,000 a year. It nonetheless began a momentous shift in government revenue from its nineteenth-century base—public lands, alcohol taxes, and customs duties—to its twentieth-century base—personal and corporate incomes.

Wilson turned next to the perennial problems of money and banking. Early in 1913 a congressional committee revealed that a few powerful banks controlled the nation's credit system. They could choke Wilson's free market by raising interest rates or reducing the supply of money. As a banking reform bill moved through Congress in 1913, Wall Street conservatives lobbied for a privately controlled, centralized banking system that could issue currency and set interest rates. Rural Democrats favored a decentralized system of regional banks run by local bankers. Populists and progressives—including William Jennings Bryan and Robert La Follette—wanted government control.

FEDERAL RESERVE ACT Wilson split their differences in the Federal Reserve Act of 1913. The new Federal Reserve System contained 12 regional banks scattered across the country. It also created a central Federal Reserve Board in Washington, appointed by the president, to supervise the system. The board could regulate credit and the money supply by setting interest rates charged member banks, by buying or selling government bonds, and by issuing paper currency called Federal Reserve notes.

FEDERAL TRADE COMMISSION When Wilson finally took on the trusts, he moved closer to the New Nationalism of Theodore Roosevelt. The Federal Trade Commission Act of 1914 created a bipartisan executive agency to oversee business activity. The end—to enforce orderly competition—was distinctly Wilsonian, but the means—an executive commission to regulate commerce—were pure Roosevelt.

CLAYTON ANTITRUST ACT Roosevelt would have stopped there, but Wilson made good on his campaign pledge to attack trusts. The Clayton Antitrust Act (1914) barred some of the worst corporate practices—price discrimination, holding companies, and interlocking directorates (directors of one corporate board sitting on others). Despite Wilson's bias against size, the advantages of large-scale production and distribution were inescapable. In practice his administration chose

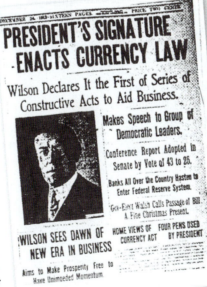

DECEMBER 24, 1913—SIXTEEN PAGES PRICE TWO CENTS

PRESIDENT'S SIGNATURE ENACTS CURRENCY LAW

Wilson Declares It the First of Series of Constructive Acts to Aid Business.

Makes Speech to Group of Democratic Leaders.

Conference Report Adopted in Senate by Vote of 43 to 25.

Banks All Over the Country Hasten to Enter Federal Reserve System.

Gov.-Elect Walsh Calls Passage of Bill A Fine Christmas Present.

WILSON SEES DAWN OF NEW ERA IN BUSINESS

HOME VIEWS OF CURRENCY ACT FOUR PENS USED BY PRESIDENT

Aims to Make Prosperity Free to Have Unimpeded Momentum.

Justice Louis Brandeis, who dropped his corporate law practice to become "the people's lawyer," continued to apply progressive principles after Wilson appointed him to the Supreme Court in 1916.

to regulate rather than break up bigness. Wilson's Justice Department filed fewer antitrust suits than under the Taft administration and negotiated more "gentlemen's agreements" (voluntary agreements by companies to change practices) than under Roosevelt.

Labor and Social Reform

For all of Wilson's impressive accomplishments, voters turned lukewarm toward the New Freedom. In the elections of 1914, Republicans cut Democratic majorities in the House and won important industrial and farm states. To strengthen his hand in the presidential election of 1916,

Wilson began edging toward the social reforms of the New Nationalism he had once criticized as paternalistic and unconstitutional. Early in 1916 he signaled the change when he nominated his close adviser Louis D. Brandeis to the Supreme Court. The progressive Brandeis had fought for the social reforms lacking on Wilson's agenda. His appointment also broke the anti-Semitic tradition of keeping Jews off the Court.

In a host of other ways Wilson revealed his willingness to intervene more actively in the economy. He helped pass laws improving the working conditions of merchant seamen and setting an eight-hour day for workers on interstate railroads. He endorsed the Keating-Owen Child Labor Act (see page 598) and threw his support to legislation providing farmers with low-interest loans. Just before the election Wilson intervened to avert a nationwide strike of rail workers.

Woodrow Wilson's first administration capped a decade and a half of heady reform. Seeing chaos in the industrial city, progressives worked to reduce the damage of poverty and the hazards of factory work, control the rising tide of immigration, and spread a middle-class ideal of morality. In city halls and state legislatures they tried to break the power of corporate interests and political machines. In Washington they enlarged government and broadened its mission from caretaker to promoter of public welfare.

Inevitably they fell short. Progressive reform was a patchwork affair, uneven and incomplete. Reformers sometimes betrayed their high ideals by denying equality to African Americans, Asians, Latinos, and other minorities. Too often government commissions designed as watchdogs found themselves captured by the interests they were supposed to oversee. Well-meaning but cumbersome regulation crippled businesses such as the railroads, while other reforms weakened political machines and corruption without fully eliminating bosses and dishonesty. Still, under progressivism the modern state—active and interventionist—was born. Public policy began to address the inequities of the age. A sense of mastery replaced the disheartening feeling of drift.

 **REVIEW**

Compare and contrast Theodore Roosevelt's approach to reform with that of Woodrow Wilson.

CONCLUSION

THE WORLD AT LARGE

The United States was hardly first among reformers. The Machine Age triggered a wave of reform across the industrialized world. Movements for social justice and social welfare sprang up first in Great Britain, where the Industrial Revolution began. The Factory Act of 1833 outlawed child labor in textile mills for those under the age of nine. The Mines Act of 1842 made it illegal to employ all women as well as children younger than ten in work underground. In comparison, the United States failed even to enact a law prohibiting child labor until 1916. In 1884 Toynbee Hall, the world's first social settlement house, opened in London's East End to minister to the needs of the poor. It became the model for Jane Addams's Hull House in Chicago.

In political reforms the world sometimes lagged behind the United States. Except in Scandinavia, most European women did not receive the vote until after World War I. And despite the democratic revolutions that swept across Latin America in the nineteenth century, national women's suffrage was opposed by the Catholic Church and did not come to Ecuador until 1929, Brazil until 1932, and El Salvador until 1939. Asia was slower still, often because colonial rulers denied or limited suffrage or because patriarchal Asian societies looked on women as subordinate to men. Only in 1950, for example, after India achieved independence, did women receive the right to vote. In Japan, although Japanese suffragists founded the *Fusen Kakutoku Domei* (Women's Suffrage League) in 1924, Japanese militarists crushed the fledgling Japanese democracy in the 1930s, as well as any women's suffrage until 1946. ∞∞∞

CHAPTER SUMMARY

PROGRESSIVISM WAS A BROAD-BASED REFORM movement, the first truly national reform movement in American history, that attempted to address problems arising from industrialization, urbanization, and immigration.

■ Progressive reform sprang from many impulses:

- Desires to curb the advancing power of big business and to end political corruption.

- Efforts to bring order and efficiency to economic and political life.

- Attempts by new interest groups to make business and government more responsive to the needs of ordinary citizens.

- Moralistic urges to rid society of industries such as the liquor trade that profited from human misery, to bridge the gap between immigrants and native-born Americans, and to soften the consequences of industrialization through social justice and social welfare.

■ Led by members of the urban middle class, progressives were moderate modernizers, supporting traditional American values such as democracy, Judeo-Christian ethics, and the spirit of volunteerism and public service while employing the new techniques of management and planning, coordinated systems, and bureaucracies of experts.

■ Progressive women extended their traditional sphere of home and family to become "social housekeepers" and crusaders for women's rights, especially the right to vote.

■ Increasingly, progressivism animated politics, first at the local and state levels, then in the presidencies of Theodore Roosevelt and Woodrow Wilson.

■ In the end, the weaknesses of progressivism—the fuzziness of its conception of the public interest, the exclusion of African Americans and other minorities, the ease with which its regulatory mechanisms were "captured" by those being regulated—were matched by its accomplishments in establishing the modern, activist state.

ADDITIONAL READING

THE LONG INTERPRETIVE DEBATE OVER progressivism is best covered in Arthur Link and Richard L. McCormick, *Progressivism* (1985). Benchmarks in that debate include George Mowry, *The California Progressives* (1951), and Richard Hofstadter, *The Age of Reform* (1955), both of which see progressives as a small elite seeking to recapture its fading status and influence. Gabriel Kolko, *The Triumph of Conservatism* (1963), makes the controversial case that business "captured" reform to control competition and stave off stricter federal regulation. Michael McGerr's *A Fierce Discontent: The Rise and Fall of the Progressive Movement* (2003), sees progressivism as a daring middle-class movement to transform society in four classically progressive ways: "to change other people; to end class conflict; to control big business; and to segregate society." David Traxel examines the reforming spirit of the Progressive Era and the First World War he sees it spawning in *Crusader Nation* (2006). Jackson Lears, *Rebirth of a Nation: The Making of Modern America, 1877–1920* (2009), places progressivism in the longer context of what Lears sees as a search for regeneration in the decades after the Civil War.

The social history of progressivism is the focus of Steven J. Diner's *A Very Different Age: Americans of the Progressive Era* (1998). Eric Rauchway's *Murdering McKinley: The Making of Theodore Roosevelt's America* (2003) presents a revisionist account of American politics and society ranging from criminal psychology to nativism, tariff and currency reform, and ideological conflict. James Chace provides a deft narrative in *1912: Wilson, Roosevelt, Taft, and Debs and the Election That Changed the Country* (2004).

John M. Blum, *The Republican Roosevelt* (1954), remains the most incisive rendering of TR, and Lewis L. Gould, *The Presidency of Theodore Roosevelt* (1991), is the best single-volume study of the White House years. In *The Wilderness Warrior: Theodore Roosevelt and the Crusade for America* (2009), Douglas Brinkley puts TR in the thick of the conservation movement and examines his environmental legacy. Unsurpassed for its detail and depth is Arthur Link, *Woodrow Wilson*, 5 vols. (1947–1965). Robert Crunden, *Ministers of Reform* (1982), emphasizes the cultural origins and impact of progressivism, and Ellen Chesler, *Woman of Valor* (1992), looks through a feminist lens at the life and times of social reformer Margaret Sanger. Melvyn Urofsky's *Louis D. Brandeis: A Life* (2009) is an admiring and authoritative biography of "the people's lawyer." In *Triangle: The Fire That Changed America* (2004), David Von Drehle offers the fullest account yet of that calamity.

For a fuller list of readings, see the Bibliography at www.mhhe.com/eh8e.

SIGNIFICANT EVENTS

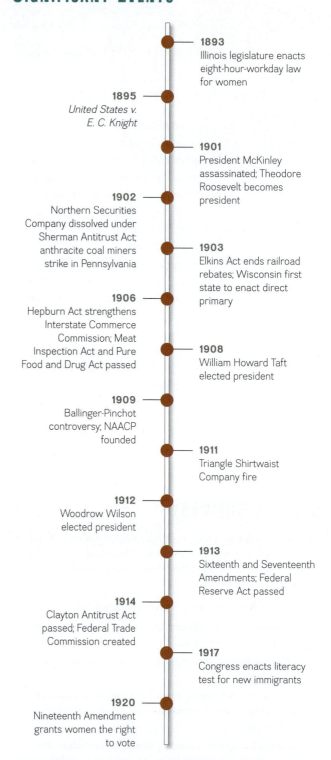

1893
Illinois legislature enacts eight-hour-workday law for women

1895
United States v. E. C. Knight

1901
President McKinley assassinated; Theodore Roosevelt becomes president

1902
Northern Securities Company dissolved under Sherman Antitrust Act; anthracite coal miners strike in Pennsylvania

1903
Elkins Act ends railroad rebates; Wisconsin first state to enact direct primary

1906
Hepburn Act strengthens Interstate Commerce Commission; Meat Inspection Act and Pure Food and Drug Act passed

1908
William Howard Taft elected president

1909
Ballinger-Pinchot controversy; NAACP founded

1911
Triangle Shirtwaist Company fire

1912
Woodrow Wilson elected president

1913
Sixteenth and Seventeenth Amendments; Federal Reserve Act passed

1914
Clayton Antitrust Act passed; Federal Trade Commission created

1917
Congress enacts literacy test for new immigrants

1920
Nineteenth Amendment grants women the right to vote

REVIEW
[The Progressive Amendments]

AMENDMENT	YEAR ADOPTED	WHAT IT DID	WHAT IT ADDRESSED
16th Amendment	1913	Income tax	Tax inequities
17th Amendment	1913	Direct election of U.S. senators	Political corruption through elections by state legislatures
18th Amendment	1918	Prohibition of manufacture, sale, transportation, and importation of alcohol	Reduced consumption of alcohol; liquor business profiting from "human misery"; alcoholism
19th Amendment	1920	Vote to all citizens	Women barred from voting in most elections

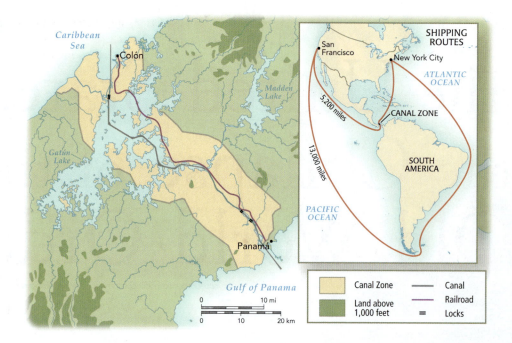

worst. But the *Oregon* passed into the Atlantic and steamed north until finally, after 68 days and 13,000 miles at sea, it reached Cuba and helped win the Battle of Santiago Bay.

The daring voyage electrified the nation but worried its leaders. Since the defeat of Mexico in 1848, the United States had stretched from the Atlantic to the Pacific without enough navy to go around. The country needed a "path between the seas"—a canal across the narrow isthmus of Colombia's Panamanian province in Central America—to defend itself and to promote its growing trade.

"I took the isthmus," Theodore Roosevelt later told a cheering crowd. In a way he did. As president, in 1903 he negotiated an agreement with Colombia to lease the needed strip of land. Holding out for more money and greater control over the canal, the Colombian senate refused to ratify the pact.

Privately TR talked of seizing Panama. But when he learned of a budding independence movement in Panama, he welcomed a revolt. On schedule and without bloodshed, the Panamanians rebelled late in 1903. The next day a U.S. cruiser dropped anchor offshore to prevent Colombia from landing troops. The United States quickly recognized the new Republic of Panama and signed a treaty for a renewable lease on a canal zone 10 miles wide. Panama received $10 million plus an annual rent of $250,000 (the same terms offered to Colombia).

Critics called the treaty "a rough-riding assault upon another republic" but TR never blinked. Arriving in Panama in 1906 he spent three days traveling the canal site in the pouring rain, his panama hat and white suit sagging about his body. He sloshed through the labor camps, asked workers for their complaints, and took the helm of a giant steam shovel. He never apologized for his nation's conduct, although in 1921, after oil had been discovered in the Canal Zone, Congress voted $25 million to Colombia.

The Panama Canal embodied Roosevelt's muscular foreign policy of respect through strength. He modernized the army and tripled its size, enlarged the navy, created a general staff for planning and mobilization, and established the Army War College. As a pivot point between the two hemispheres, his canal allowed the United States to flex its strength across the globe.

These expanding horizons came about largely as an outgrowth of American commercial and industrial expansion, just as the imperialist empires of England, France, Germany, Russia, and Japan were expanding, too. Americans, steeped in democratic ideals, frequently seemed uncomfortable with the naked ambitions of European empire-builders. Roosevelt's embrace of the canal, however, showed how far some progressives had come in being willing to shape the world.

Expansionist diplomats assured each other that global order could be maintained by balancing power through carefully crafted military alliances. But that system did not hold. In 1914, the year the Panama Canal opened, this old world order collapsed in a terrible war. ∞∞∞

Progressive Diplomacy

FOUNDATIONS OF PROGRESSIVE DIPLOMACY

As the Panama Canal was being built, progressive diplomacy was taking shape. Like progressive politics, it stressed moralism and order as it stretched presidential power to new limits in an effort to mold and remake the international environment. It rested on faith in the superiority of Anglo-American stock and institutions. "Of all our race, [God] has marked the American people as His chosen nation to finally lead in the redemption of the world," said one senator in 1900. In this global vision of Manifest Destiny, few progressives questioned the need to uplift the "darker peoples" of the tropical zones.

Economic expansion underlay the commitment to a "civilizing" mission. The depression of 1893 had encouraged American manufacturers and farmers to look overseas for markets, and that expansion continued after 1900. Every administration committed itself to opening doors of trade and keeping them open. By 1918, at the end of World War I, the United States had become the largest creditor in the world.

Big Stick in the Caribbean

PLATT AMENDMENT

Theodore Roosevelt liked to invoke the old African proverb "Walk softly and carry a big stick." In the Caribbean he nonetheless moved loudly and mightily. The Panama Canal gave the United States a commanding position in the Western Hemisphere. Its importance required the country to "police the surrounding premises," explained Secretary of State Elihu Root. Before granting Cuba independence in 1902, the United States reorganized its finances and attached the Platt Amendment to the Cuban constitution. The amendment gave American authorities the right to intervene in Cuba if the independence or internal order of the country were threatened. Claiming that power, U.S. troops occupied the island twice between 1906 and 1923.

In looking to enforce a favorable environment for trade in the Caribbean, Roosevelt worried about European intentions. The Monroe Doctrine of 1823 declared against further European colonization of the Western Hemisphere, but in the early twentieth century the rising debts of Latin Americans to Europeans invited intrusion. "If we intend to say hands off to the power of Europe, then sooner or later we must keep order ourselves," Roosevelt warned. In his balance-of-power system it was the obligation of great powers to avoid the spheres of others while keeping order in their own. Across the globe, great powers would thus check each other, much as big government held big business in check at home.

ROOSEVELT COROLLARY TO THE MONROE DOCTRINE

Going well beyond Monroe's concept of resisting foreign intrusions into the Western Hemisphere, Roosevelt tightened his grip on the region. In 1904, when the Dominican Republic defaulted on its debts, he added the "Roosevelt Corollary" to the Monroe Doctrine by claiming the right to intervene directly if Latin Americans failed to keep their finances in order. Invoking its sweeping and self-proclaimed power, the United States assumed responsibility for several Caribbean states, including the Dominican Republic, Cuba, and Panama.

A "Diplomatist of the Highest Rank"

In the Far East, Roosevelt exercised ingenuity rather than force. He realized that few Americans would support armed intervention half a world away. Like President McKinley, TR committed himself only to maintaining an "open door" of equal access to trade in China and to protecting the Philippines, which he saw as "our heel of Achilles."

TREATY OF PORTSMOUTH

The key to success lay in offsetting Russian and Japanese ambitions in the region. When Japan attacked Russian holdings in the Chinese province of Manchuria in 1904, Roosevelt offered to mediate. He worried that if unchecked, Japan might threaten American interests in China and the Philippines. At the U.S. Naval Base near Portsmouth, New Hampshire, Roosevelt guided the Russians and the Japanese to the Treaty of Portsmouth in 1905. It recognized the Japanese victory, the first by an Asian power over a European country, and ceded to Japan Port Arthur, the southern half of Sakhalin Island, and, in effect, control of Korea. Japan promised to leave Manchuria as part of China and keep trade open to all foreign nations. The balance of power in Asia and the open door in China thus had been preserved. For his contributions, Roosevelt received the Nobel Peace Prize in 1906.

GENTLEMEN'S AGREEMENT

Japanese nationalists resented the peace treaty for curbing Japan's ambitions in China. Their anger surfaced in a protest lodged, of all places, against the San Francisco school board. In 1906 rising Japanese immigration led San Francisco school authorities to place the city's 93 Asian students in a separate school. In Japan citizens talked of war over the insult. Roosevelt, furious at the "infernal fools in California," summoned the mayor of San Francisco and seven school board members to the White House. In exchange for an end to the segregation order, Roosevelt offered to arrange a mutual restriction of immigration between Japan and the United States. In 1907 all sides accepted his "gentlemen's agreement."

GREAT WHITE FLEET

The San Francisco school crisis sparked wild rumors that Japan was bent on taking Hawaii, or the Philippines, or the Panama Canal. In case Japan or any other nation thought of upsetting the Pacific balance, Roosevelt sent 16 gleaming white battleships on a world tour. "By George, isn't it magnificent!" he crowed as the "Great White Fleet" steamed out of Hampton Roads, Virginia, in 1907 (see page 580). The fleet made its most conspicuous stop in Japan, where a group of Japanese children stood on the docks of Yokohama and sang "The Star-Spangled Banner" in English. The show of force heralded a new age of American naval might but had an unintended consequence that haunted Americans for decades: it spurred Japanese admirals to expand their own navy.

Watching Roosevelt in his second term, an amazed London's *The Morning Post* honored him as a "diplomatist of

The Destruction of Russian Torpedo destroyers by Japanese torpedo destroyers at Port Arthur.
The Illustration of the war between Japan and Russia. (NO. 5)

Sailors from the Japanese torpedo boat, Sazanami, board a Russian torpedo boat during a heated sea battle off Port Arthur during the Russo-Japanese War. Japan's victory, the first of an Asian over a European power, signaled Japan's new status as a great world power, as well as the country's success in "modernizing" along Western lines.

WOODROW WILSON AND MORAL DIPLOMACY

THE LIGHTFOOT CLUB HAD BEEN meeting in the Reverend Wilson's hayloft for months when the question of whether the pen was mightier than the sword came up. Young Tommy Wilson, who had organized the debating society, jumped at the chance to argue that written words were more powerful than armies. But when the boys drew lots, Tommy ended up on the other side. "I can't argue that side," he protested. "I can't argue for something I don't believe in."

Thomas Woodrow Wilson eventually dropped his first name, but he never gave up his boyhood conviction that morality, at least as he defined it, should guide all conduct. To the diplomacy of order, force, and finance, Wilson added a missionary's commitment to spreading what he saw as the American system of beliefs—justice, democracy, and the Judeo-Christian values of harmony and cooperation.

the highest rank." Abroad as at home, his brand of progressivism was grounded in an enthusiastic nationalism that mixed force with finesse to achieve balance and order.

Dollar Diplomacy

Instead of force or finesse, Roosevelt's successor in the White House turned to money to advance U.S. interests abroad. William Howard Taft stressed private investment to promote economic stability, keep peace, and tie debt-ridden nations to the United States. "Dollar diplomacy" simply amounted to "substituting dollars for bullets," Taft explained. He and Philander Knox, his prickly secretary of state, treated the restless nations of Latin America like ailing corporations, injecting capital and reorganizing management. By the time Taft left office in 1913, half of all American investments abroad were in Latin America.

Failure dogged Taft overseas as it did at home. In the Caribbean his dollar diplomacy was linked so closely with unpopular regimes, corporations, and banks that his successor, Woodrow Wilson, scrapped it when he entered the White House. Taft's efforts to strengthen China with investments and trade only intensified rivalry with Japan and made China more suspicious of all foreigners, including Americans. In 1911 the southern Chinese provinces rebelled against foreign intrusion and overthrew the monarchy. Only persistent pressure from the White House kept dollar diplomacy alive in Asia.

 **REVIEW**

How did Theodore Roosevelt's policies in Latin America and Asia differ from William Howard Taft's?

Missionary Diplomacy

Although Wilson's missionary diplomacy was deeply idealistic, it had a practical side. In the twentieth century, foreign markets would serve as America's new frontier. American industries "will burst their jackets if they cannot find free outlets in the markets of the world," Wilson cautioned in 1912. His special genius lay in reconciling this commercial self-interest with a global idealism. In his eyes, exporting American democracy and capitalism would promote peace, prosperity, and human advancement throughout the world.

Solitary and self-assured, Wilson conducted foreign policy on his own. Bypassing the State Department, he sent personal emissaries to foreign leaders and often typed his own dispatches. Sometimes Secretary of State William Jennings Bryan had no idea of what was happening. In rare moments of doubt Wilson turned to his trusted friend, Edward M. House. The honorary "Colonel" House had yoked himself to Wilson in the early days of his political career and wielded power behind the scenes.

TWENTY-ONE DEMANDS

In Asia and the Pacific, Wilson moved to put "moral and public considerations" ahead of the "material interests of individuals." He pulled American bankers out of a railroad project in China backed by President Taft. The scheme encouraged foreign intervention and undermined Chinese sovereignty, said Wilson. The United States became the first major power to recognize the new Republic of China in 1911 when nationalists overthrew the last Manchu emperor. And in 1915 Wilson strongly opposed Japan's "Twenty-One Demands" for control of China. At the end of his first administration, the Philippines gained limited self-government, the first step toward independence finally granted in 1946.

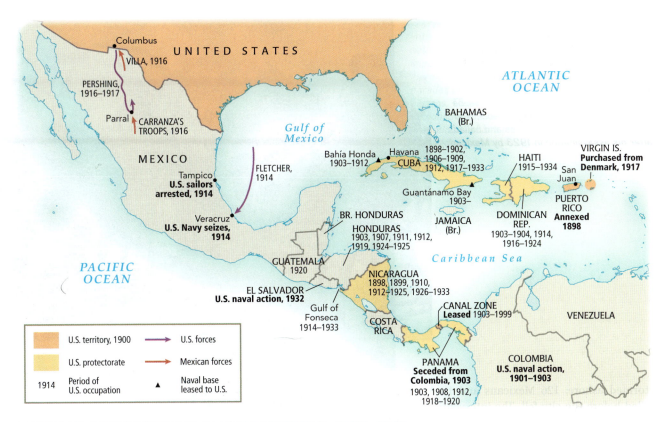

AMERICAN INTERVENTIONS IN THE CARIBBEAN, 1898–1930

In the first three decades of the twentieth century, U.S. diplomacy transformed the Caribbean into an American lake as armed and unarmed intervention became part of the country's diplomatic arsenal. **On what grounds did the United States intervene in the region?**

In the Caribbean and Latin America, Wilson discovered that interests closer to home could not be pursued through high-minded words alone. In August 1914 he convinced Nicaragua, already occupied by American troops, to yield control of a naval base and grant the United States an alternate canal route. Upheavals in Haiti and the Dominican Republic brought in the U.S. Marines. By the end of his administration, American troops were still stationed there and also in Cuba. All four nations were economically dependent on the United States and were virtual protectorates. Missionary diplomacy, it turned out, could spread its gospel with steel as well as cash.

Intervention in Mexico

MEXICAN REVOLUTION A lingering crisis in Mexico turned Wilson's "moral diplomacy" into a mockery. A common border, 400 years of shared history, and millions of dollars in investments made what happened in Mexico of urgent importance to the United States.

In 1910 a revolution overthrew the aged dictator Porfirio Díaz and plunged the country into turmoil. Just as Wilson was entering the White House in 1913, the ruthless general Victoriano Huerta emerged as head of the government. Wealthy landowners and foreign investors endorsed Huerta, a conservative likely to protect their

holdings. Soon a bloody civil war was raging between Huerta and his rivals.

Most European nations recognized the Huerta regime immediately, but Wilson refused to accept the "government of butchers." Huerta had murdered the popular leader Francisco Madera with the approval of the Taft administration. When Huerta proclaimed himself dictator, Wilson banned arms shipments to Mexico. He threw his support to rebel leader Venustiano Carranza, on the condition that Carranza participate in American-sponsored elections. No Mexican was ready to tolerate such foreign interference. Carranza and his "constitutionalists" rejected the offer. With few options, Wilson armed the rebels anyway.

Wilson's distaste for Huerta was so great that he used a minor incident as a pretext for an invasion. In April 1914 the crew of the USS *Dolphin* landed without permission in the Mexican port city of Tampico. Local police arrested the sailors, only to release them with an apology. Unappeased, their squadron commander demanded a 21-gun salute to the American flag. Agreed, replied the Mexicans, but only if American guns returned the salute to Mexico. Learning of a German shipload of weapons about to land at Veracruz, Wilson broke the impasse by ordering American troops to take the city. Instead of the bloodless occupation they expected, U.S. marines encountered stiff resistance as they

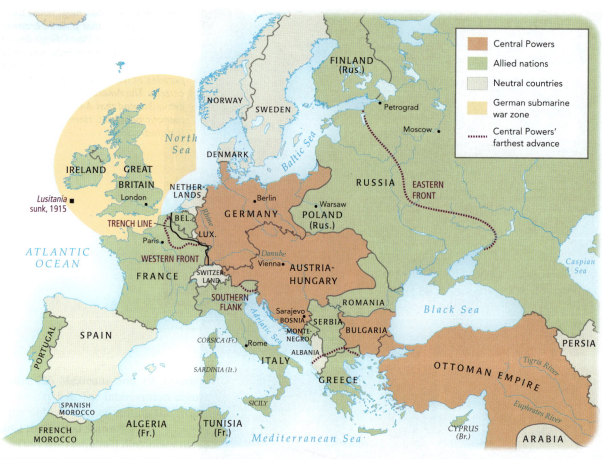

THE COURSE OF WAR IN EUROPE, 1914–1917

When World War I erupted between the Central and Allied Powers in 1914, few countries in Europe remained neutral. The armies of the Central Powers penetrated as far west as France and as far east as Russia, but by 1917, the European war had settled into a hideous standoff along the deadly line of trenches on the western front that stretched from the North Sea to the border of Switzerland. **What does the map tell us about why the British blockade of Germany was so effective?**

Powers" of Germany and Austria-Hungary. Armies fought from the deserts of North Africa to the plains of Flanders in Belgium. Fleets battled off the coasts of Chile and Sumatra. Soldiers came from as far away as Australia and India. Nearly 8 million never returned.

Neutral but Not Impartial

The outbreak of war shocked most Americans. Few knew Serbia as anything but a tiny splotch on the map of Europe. Fewer still were prepared to go to war in its defense. President Wilson issued an immediate declaration of neutrality and approved a plan for evacuating Americans stranded in Belgium.

WILSON'S NEUTRAL IDEALS Wilson came to see the calamity as an opportunity. America could lead warring nations to a new world order. Selfish nationalism would give way to cooperative internationalism, power politics to collective security and Christian charity. Progressive faith in reason would triumph over irrational violence. Only if the United States remained neutral could it lead the way to this higher peace. Americans must be "impartial in thought as well as action," Wilson insisted in 1914.

In a country as diverse as the United States, true impartiality was impossible. Americans of German and Austrian descent naturally sympathized with the Central Powers, as did Irish Americans, on the grounds of England's centuries-old domination of Ireland. The bonds of language, culture, and history tied most Americans to Great Britain. And gratitude for French aid during the American Revolution still lived. When the first American division marched through Paris, its commander stopped to salute the tomb of the Marquis de Lafayette, who served as a general in the Continental army: "Nous voilà, Lafayette!"—"Lafayette, we are here!"

American economic ties to Britain and France also created a financial investment in Allied victory. The American economy boomed with the flood of war orders. The commanding British navy ensured that the Atlantic trade went mostly to the Allies. Between 1914 and 1916, business with the Allies rocketed from $800 million to $3 billion. The Allies eventually borrowed more than $2 billion from American banks to finance their purchases. In contrast, a British naval blockade reduced American **contraband** commerce with the Central Powers to a trickle.

Few Americans cared. Although some progressives admired German social reforms, Americans generally saw Germany as an iron military power bent on conquest. Americans read British propaganda about spike-helmeted "Huns" raping Belgian women, bayoneting their children, pillaging their towns. Some of the stories were true, some embellished, some utterly false, but all worked against Germany in the United States.

The Diplomacy of Neutrality

Though Wilson insisted that all warring powers respect the right of neutrals to trade with any nation, he hesitated to retaliate against Great Britain's blockade of Germany. He recognized that the key to strangling Germany, a land power, was Britain's powerful navy and its iron blockade. Breaking it would cripple the Allied war effort. Meanwhile, Great Britain tightened its noose around Germany with caution where the Americans were concerned. When Britain forbade the sale of cotton to the Central Powers in 1915, the British government bought American surpluses. It also agreed to compensate American firms for their losses when the war was over. By the end of 1915 the United States had all but accepted the British blockade of Germany, while American supplies continued to flow to England. True neutrality was dead.

SUBMARINE WARFARE · Early in 1915 Germany turned to a dreadful new weapon to even the odds at sea. It mounted a counterblockade of Great Britain with two dozen submarines, or *Unterseeboote,* called U-boats. Before submarines, sea raiders usually gave crews and passengers the chance to escape. But if thin-skinned U-boats surfaced to obey these conventions, they risked being rammed or blown from the water. So submarines attacked without warning and spared no lives. Invoking international law and national honor, President Wilson threatened to hold Germany to "strict accountability" for any American losses. Germany promised not to sink any American ships, but soon a new issue grabbed the headlines: the safety of American passengers on belligerent vessels.

LUSITANIA · On the morning of May 7, 1915, the British passenger liner *Lusitania* appeared out of a fog bank off the coast of Ireland on its way from New York to England. The commander of the German U-20 could hardly believe his eyes: the giant ship filled the viewfinder of his periscope. He fired a single torpedo. A tremendous roar followed as one of the *Lusitania*'s boilers exploded. The ship stopped dead in the water and listed so badly that lifeboats could barely be launched before the vessel sank. Nearly 1,200 men, women, and children perished, including 128 Americans.

Wilson, horrified at this "murder on the high seas," did little more than send notes of protest to Germany. Secretary of State William Jennings Bryan advocated what he called "real neutrality" and wanted equal protests lodged against both German submarines and British blockaders. He suspected that the *Lusitania* carried munitions as well as passengers and was thus a legitimate target. (Much later, evidence proved him right.) Relying on passengers for protection against attack, Bryan

J. H. Cassel's 1915 cartoon "Without Warning!" captures the horror of the submarine attack on the Lusitania. A bloody saber in the hand of a spike-helmeted German knifes through the ship from beneath the waves. Flag-waving Americans fall helplessly into the sea and drown.

argued, was "like putting women and children in front of an army." Rather than endorse Wilson's policy, Bryan resigned.

Battling on two fronts in Europe, Germany wanted to keep the United States out of the war. But in February 1916 a desperate Germany declared submarine warfare on all *armed* vessels, belligerent or neutral. A month later a U-boat commander mistook the French steamer *Sussex* for a mine layer and torpedoed the unarmed vessel as it ferried passengers and freight across the English Channel. Several Americans were injured.

SUSSEX PLEDGE · In mid-April Wilson issued an ultimatum in the aftermath of the *Sussex* sinking. If Germany refused to stop sinking nonmilitary vessels, the United States would break off diplomatic relations. War would surely follow. Without enough U-boats to control the seas, Germany agreed to Wilson's terms, all but abandoning its counterblockade. This *Sussex* pledge gave Wilson a diplomatic victory but carried a grave risk. If German submarines resumed unrestricted attacks, the United States would have to go to war. "Any little German [U-boat] commander can put us into the war at any time," the president admitted.

Peace, Preparedness, and the Election of 1916

While hundreds of young Yanks slipped across the border to enlist in the Canadian army, most Americans agreed neutrality was the wisest course. Before the war a peace movement had taken seed in the United States, nourished in 1910 by a gift of $10 million from Andrew Carnegie. In 1914 social reformers Jane Addams, Charlotte Perkins Gilman, and Lillian Wald founded the Women's International League for Peace and Freedom and the American Union Against Militarism. Calling on Wilson to convene a peace conference, they lobbied for open diplomacy, disarmament, an end to colonial empires, and an international organization to settle disputes. In time these aims became the core of Wilson's peace plan.

Pacifists might condemn the war, but Republicans and corporate leaders argued that the nation was woefully unprepared to keep peace. The army numbered only 80,000 men in 1914, the navy just 37 battleships and a handful of new "dreadnoughts," or supercruisers. Advocates of "preparedness" called for a navy larger than Great Britain's, an army of millions of reservists, and universal military training.

By the end of 1915, frustration with German submarines led Wilson to join the preparedness cause. He toured the country promoting preparedness and promised a "navy second to none." In Washington, he pressed Congress to double the army, increase the National Guard, and begin construction of the largest navy in the world. To foot the bill, progressives pushed through new graduated taxes on higher incomes and on estates as well as additional levies on corporate profits.

"HE KEPT US OUT OF WAR" Whoever paid for it, most Americans in 1916 were thinking of preparedness for peace, not war. The Democrats discovered the political power of peace early in the presidential campaign. As their convention opened in St. Louis in June, the keynote speaker began what he expected to be a dull description of Wilson's recent diplomatic maneuvers—only to have the crowd roar back in each case, "What did we do? What did we do?" The speaker knew the answer and shouted it back: "We didn't go to war! We didn't go to war!" The next day Wilson was renominated by acclamation. "He Kept Us Out of War" became his campaign slogan.

The Republicans had already nominated Charles Evans Hughes, the former governor of New York. He endorsed "straight and honest" neutrality and peace. Despite that moderate stand, Democrats succeeded in painting Hughes as a warmonger, partly because Republican Theodore Roosevelt had rattled his own sabers so loudly. As the election approached, Democrats took out full-page advertisements in newspapers across the country: "If You Want WAR, Vote for HUGHES! If You Want Peace with Honor VOTE FOR WILSON!"

As the polls closed on Election Day, Wilson squeaked out a victory. He carried the South and key states in the Midwest and West on a tide of prosperity, progressive reform, and, most of all, promises of peace.

Wilson's Final Peace Offensive

Twice since 1915 Wilson had sent his trusted adviser Edward House to Europe to negotiate a peace among the warring powers, and twice House had failed. With the election over, Wilson opened his final peace offensive. When he

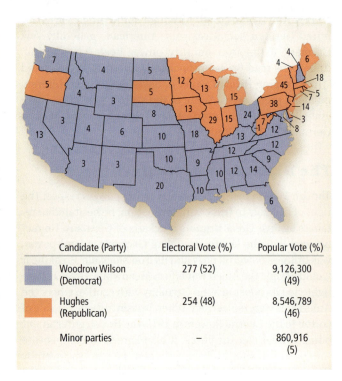

Candidate (Party)	Electoral Vote (%)	Popular Vote (%)
Woodrow Wilson (Democrat)	277 (52)	9,126,300 (49)
Hughes (Republican)	254 (48)	8,546,789 (46)
Minor parties	–	860,916 (5)

ELECTION OF 1916

asked the belligerents to state their terms for a cease-fire, neither side responded. Frustrated, fearful, and genuinely agonized, Wilson called for "peace without victory": no victor, no vanquished, no embittering division of the spoils of war, only "a peace among equals," he said in January 1917.

As Wilson spoke, a fleet of U-boats was cruising toward the British Isles. Weeks earlier German military leaders had persuaded the Kaiser to take one last desperate gamble to starve the Allies into submission. On January 31, 1917, the German ambassador in Washington announced that unrestricted submarine warfare would resume the next day.

ZIMMERMANN TELEGRAM Wilson's dream of neutrality collapsed. He asked Congress for authority to arm merchant ships and early in February severed relations with Germany. Then British authorities handed him a bombshell—an intercepted telegram from the German foreign secretary, Arthur Zimmermann, to the Kaiser's ambassador in Mexico. In the event of war with the United States, the ambassador was instructed to offer Mexico guns, money, and its "lost territory in Texas, New Mexico, and Arizona" to attack the United States. Already frustrated by Pancho Villa's raids across the U.S.-Mexican border, Wilson angrily released the Zimmermann telegram to the press. Soon after, he ordered gun crews aboard merchant ships and directed them to shoot U-boats "on sight."

The momentum of events now propelled a reluctant United States toward war. On March 12 U-boats torpedoed the American merchant vessel *Algonquin.* On March 15 a revolution in Russia toppled Czar Nicholas II. A key ally was crumbling from within. By the end of the month U-boats had sunk nearly 600,000 tons of Allied and neutral shipping.

For the first time Washington received reports of cracking morale in the Allied ranks.

On April 2, 1917, accompanied by armed cavalry, Wilson rode down Pennsylvania Avenue and trudged up the steps of the Capitol. He delivered to Congress a stirring war message, full of idealistic purpose. "We shall fight for the things we have always carried nearest our hearts—for democracy, for the right of those who submit to authority to have a voice in their own governments, for the rights and liberties of small nations."

Pacifists blocked the war resolution until it finally passed on April 6, Good Friday. Six senators and 50 House members opposed it, including the first woman to be elected to Congress, Jeannette Rankin of Montana. Cultural, economic, and historical ties to the Allies, along with the German campaign of submarine warfare, had tipped the country toward war. Wilson had not wanted it, but now the battlefield seemed the only path to a higher peace.

✓ REVIEW

What steps did Woodrow Wilson take to avoid World War I, and why did they fail?

WAR AND SOCIETY

IN 1915 THE GERMAN ZEPPELIN LZ-38, hovering at 8,000 feet, dropped a load of bombs that killed seven Londoners. For the first time in history, civilians died in an air attack. Few such aerial bombardments occurred during World War I, but they signaled the growing importance of the home front in modern combat. Governments not only fielded armies but also mobilized industry, controlled labor, even rationed food. In the United States traditions of cooperation and volunteerism helped government to organize the home front and the battle front, often in ways that were peculiarly progressive.

🌐 The Slaughter of Stalemate

TRENCH WARFARE While the United States debated entry into the Great War, the Allies were close to losing it. Following the German assault in 1914, the war had settled into a grisly stalemate. A continuous, immovable front stretched from Flanders in the north to the border of Switzerland in the south. Troops dug ditches, 6 to 8 feet deep and 4 to 5 feet wide, to escape bullets, grenades, and artillery. Twenty-five thousand miles of these "trenches"—enough to circle the globe—cut a muddy scar across Europe. Men lived in them for years, prey to disease, lice, and a plague of rats.

War in the machine age gave the advantage to the defense. When soldiers bravely charged "over the top" of the trenches, they were shredded by machine guns that fired 600 rounds a minute. Poison gas choked them in their tracks. Giant howitzers lobbed shells on them from positions too distant to see. In the Battle of the Somme River in

1916 a million men were killed in just four months of fighting, all to enable the British army to advance barely 7 miles. Only late in the war did new armored "landships"—codenamed "tanks"—return the advantage to the offense by surmounting the trench barriers with their caterpillar treads.

By then Vladimir Lenin was speeding home to Russia aboard a special train provided by the Germans. Lenin had been exiled to Switzerland during the early stages of the Russian Revolution but returned to lead his Bolshevik ("majority" in Russian) party to power in November 1917. Soon the Bolshevik-controlled government negotiated a separate peace with Germany, which promptly transferred a million of its soldiers to the western front for the coming spring offensive.

"You're in the Army Now"

The Allies' plight forced the U.S. Army into a crash program to send a million soldiers to Europe by the spring of 1918. The United States had barely 180,000 men in uniform. Volunteers rushed to recruitment offices, especially in ethnic communities, where Mexican Americans enlisted in numbers proportionally higher than any other group.

They were not enough. To raise the necessary force, Congress passed the Selective Service Act in May 1917. Men

Trench warfare, wrote one general, was "marked by uniform formations, the regulation of space and time by higher commands down to the smallest details . . . fixed distances between units and individuals." The reality was something else again.

between the ages of 20 and 30 would be conscripted into the armed forces. Feelings over forced military service ran high. "There is precious little difference between a conscript [draftee] and a convict," protested the Speaker of the House in 1917. Progressives disagreed. They saw military service as an opportunity to unite America and promote democracy. "Universal [military] training will jumble the boys of America all together," exclaimed progressive journalist George Creel, ". . . smashing all the petty class distinctions that now divide, and prompting a brand of real democracy."

At ten in the morning on July 20, 1917, Secretary of War Newton Baker tied a blindfold over his eyes, reached into a huge glass bowl, and drew the first number in the new draft lottery. Some 24 million men were already registered. Almost 3 million were drafted; another 2 million volunteered. Most were white and young, between the ages of 21 and 31. Some 20,000 women served as clerks, telephone operators, and nurses. In a nation of immigrants, nearly one draftee in five had been born abroad. Training often aimed at educating and Americanizing ethnic recruits. In special "development battalions," drill sergeants barked out orders while volunteers from the YMCA taught American history and English.

With hostility remaining high between Mexico and the United States after President Wilson sent U.S. troops into Mexico, many Mexican laborers returned to Mexico rather than be drafted into a foreign army whose goals they did not share. However, Mexican Americans, especially those whose families had long lived in the United States, enlisted in the U.S. Army.

Like Mexican Americans, African Americans volunteered in disproportionately high numbers. They quickly filled the four all-black army and eight National Guard units already in existence. They were also granted fewer exemptions from the draft than white Americans were. Only 10 percent of the population, blacks made up 13 percent of all draftees. Overseas, where 200,000 black troops served in France, just one in five was permitted in combat compared with two of three whites. Southern Democrats in Congress had opposed training African Americans to arms, fearful of the prospect of putting "arrogant, strutting representatives of black soldiery in every community." But four regiments of the all-black 93rd Division, brigaded with the French army, were among the first Americans in the trenches and the most decorated units in the U.S. Army.

HOUSTON RIOT Racial violence sometimes flared among the troops. In the summer of 1917 it turned deadly in Houston, Texas. Harassed by white soldiers and by the city's Jim Crow laws, seasoned black regulars rioted and killed 17 white civilians. Their whole battalion was disarmed

Felix Sanchez, a Mexican American recruit from New Mexico.

and sent under arrest to New Mexico. Thirteen troopers were condemned to death and hanged within days, too quickly for appeals even to be filed.

Bias also surfaced as progressive reformers enlisted the social sciences in army testing. Most recruits had fewer than seven years of education, yet they had to be classified and assigned quickly to units. Psychologists saw the chance to use new intelligence tests to help the army and prove their own theories about the value of "IQ" (intelligence quotient) in measuring the mind. In fact, these new "scientific" IQ tests often measured little more than class and cultural origins. Questions such as "Who wrote 'The Raven'?" exposed background rather than intelligence. More than half the Russian, Italian, and Polish draftees and almost 80 percent of blacks showed up as "inferior." The army stopped IQ testing in January 1919, but schools across the country adopted it after the war, reinforcing many ethnic and racial prejudices.

On the home front moral crusaders waged a war against sin, often pursuing old reforms through the prism of patriotism. Temperance leaders pressured the War Department to prohibit the sale of liquor to anyone in uniform in the vicinity of training camps. Alcohol would only impair a soldier's ability to fight. The army also declared war on venereal disease. "A Soldier who gets a dose is a Traitor!" warned one poster. The drive against sexually transmitted diseases constituted the first serious sex education many young Americans had ever received.

Mobilizing the Economy

To equip, feed, and transport an army of nearly 5 million demanded a national effort. The production of even a single ammunition shell brought components from every section of the country, in addition to vital nitrates from Chile, to assembly plants in New Jersey, Virginia, and Pennsylvania and from there to military installations or Atlantic ports.

WAR COSTS At the Treasury Department, Secretary William Gibbs McAdoo fretted over how to finance the war, which cost, finally, $32 billion. New taxes paid about a third of all war costs. The rest came from the sale of "Liberty" and "Victory" bonds and war savings certificates. At huge bond drives, movie stars Douglas Fairbanks, Mary Pickford, and other celebrities exhorted Americans to buy bonds. Boy Scouts sold them under the slogan "Every Scout to Save a Soldier." More than money was at stake. The fund-raising campaign was also designed to raise patriotism. "Every person who refuses to subscribe," McAdoo warned, "is a friend of Germany." The **national debt,** which had stood at $2 billion in 1917, soared to $20 billion only three years later.

SOUNDING THE TIMES: "OVER THERE"

William J. Reilly was a popular sailor who performed this song and others.

What language is this? Why include this version of the lyrics?

Leo Feist paid the original publisher of the music $25,000 for the rights to the song, a record amount at that time. What other ways does the sheet music show that Feist was hoping to make money?

Music has always sounded the times and given historians a feel for the emotional temper of the moment. When George M. Cohan set out to put the martial spirit of the country to music in 1917, the United States had just entered the First World War. Cohan, the son of Irish Catholics, claimed to have written the song on a train ride from New Rochelle to New York City. "I read those war headlines," he later recalled, "and I got to thinking and humming to myself and for a minute, I thought I was going to dance." The song became a popular hit, a powerful recruiting tool for the armed services, and a measure of the innocence of Americans who blithely marched "over there" to save war-torn Europe, only to enter the inferno of industrialized warfare. The song begins with a rhythmic drumbeat and a call to arms: "Johnnie get your gun / Get your gun, get your gun," and builds to its famous chorus, "Over there, over there / Send the word, send the word, over there / That the Yanks are coming / The Yanks are coming / The drums rum-tumming / Ev'rywhere." (To read the entire text of the song and to hear recordings from 1917, see www.firstworldwar.com/audio/overthere.htm.)

The preceding image and text come from the Duke University Library. (Accessed on February 11, 2013, at http://scriptorium.lib.duke.edu/sheetmusic/n/n09/n0967/.)

Thinking Critically

What is the message of the lyrics of the song? How does the music affect the message? How does it help to have so many of the lines repeated? During the Second World War, songs of nostalgia for the home front such as "White Christmas" replaced martial songs such as "Over There." Why might that have been the case?

With sweeping grants of authority provided by Congress, President Wilson constructed a massive bureaucracy to direct the home front. What emerged was a more **managed economy** than had existed before the war, one ironically similar to the federal management of Theodore Roosevelt's New Nationalism. Nearly 5,000 new executive agencies employed business leaders from mammoth machinery makers John Deere and Evinrude to other corporate giants, the readiest source of expert managers. For a nominal "dollar a year," these executives served their country and built a partnership between big business and government. Industrial and **trade associations** as well as professional organizations of engineers and scientists tied industry and science to a network of federal agencies. Antitrust suits, recalled one official, were simply put "to sleep until the war was over."

WAR INDUSTRIES BOARD Under the leadership of Wall Street wizard Bernard Baruch, a War Industries Board (WIB) coordinated production through industrial and trade associations. Though it had the authority to force compliance, the WIB relied instead on persuasion through publicity and "cost-plus" contracts that covered all company expenses, plus a guaranteed profit. When businesses balked—as when Henry Ford refused to accept government curbs on manufacturing automobiles—Baruch could twist arms. In this case, he threatened to have the army run Ford's factories. Ford quickly reversed himself. Overall, corporate profits tripled and production skyrocketed during the war years.

The Food Administration encouraged farmers to grow more and citizens to eat less-wastefully. Herbert Hoover, who had saved starving refugees as chairman of the Commission for Relief in Belgium in 1914, was appointed administrator. Like the WIB, the Food Administration mobilized what Hoover called "the spirit of self-sacrifice." Huge publicity campaigns promoted "wheatless" and "meatless" days each week and encouraged families to plant "victory" gardens. Stirred by high commodity prices, farmers brought more marginal lands into cultivation. Their real income and thus their purchasing power jumped 25 percent.

A Fuel Administration met the army's energy needs by increasing production and limiting domestic consumption. Transportation snarls required more drastic action. In December 1917 the U.S. Railroad Administration took over rail lines for the duration of the war. Government coordination, together with a new system of permits, got freight moving and kept workers happy. Federally imposed "daylight saving time" stretched the workday and saved fuel as well. Rail workers saw their wages grow overall by $300 million. Railroad unions won recognition, an eight-hour day, and a grievance procedure. For the first time in decades, labor unrest subsided and the trains ran on schedule.

BUREAUCRATIC STATE The modern **bureaucratic state** received a powerful boost during the 18 months of American participation in the war. Accelerating trends already under way, hundreds of federal agencies centralized authority as they cooperated with business

During World War I, the federal government became involved in the everyday lives of citizens. In this poster produced by the National War Garden Commission, Lady Liberty sows "seeds of victory," showing every citizen how to transform their gardens into "a Munitions Plant." How would planting vegetables help to win the war?

and labor to mount an unprecedented war effort. The number of federal employees more than doubled between 1916 and 1918, to over 850,000. The wartime bureaucracy was quickly dismantled at the end of the war, but it set an important precedent for the growth of government.

War Work

The war benefited working men and women, though not as much as their employers. Government contracts guaranteed high wages, an eight-hour day, and equal pay for comparable work. To encourage people to stay on the job, federal contracting agencies set up special classes to teach employers the new science of personnel management, which sought to supervise workers more efficiently and humanely. American industry moved one step closer to the **welfare capitalism** of the 1920s, with its promises of profit sharing, company unions, and personnel departments to forestall worker discontent.

| *Movie idol Douglas Fairbanks, brandishing a megaphone, works a huge crowd during this rally in New York City to sell war bonds. When bond sales slacked, the Treasury created a publicity campaign to promote the idea that buying the bonds was a citizen's patriotic duty.*

NATIONAL WAR LABOR BOARD

Personnel management was not always enough to guarantee industrial peace. In 1917 American workers called over 4,000 strikes, the largest annual outbreak in American history. To keep factories running, President Wilson created the National War Labor Board (NWLB) early in 1918. The NWLB arbitrated more than 1,000 labor disputes, helped to increase wages, established overtime pay, and supported the principle of equal pay for women. In return for no-strike pledges, the board guaranteed the rights of unions to organize and bargain collectively. Membership in the American Federation of Labor jumped from 2.7 million in 1914 to nearly 4 million by 1919.

WOMEN IN THE WORKFORCE

The war brought nearly a million more women into the labor force to make up for men in service. Most were young and single. Sometimes they took over jobs once held by men as railroad engineers, drill press operators, and electric lift truck drivers. Here, too, government tried to mediate between labor and management. In 1917 the Labor Department opened the Women in Industry Service (WIS) to recommend guidelines for using female labor. Among its most important proposals were an eight-hour day, rest periods and breaks for meals, and equal pay for equal work. Most women never worked under such conditions, but for the first time, the federal government tried to upgrade their working conditions.

The prewar trend toward higher-paying jobs for women intensified. Most still earned less than the men they replaced as they moved into clerical and light industrial work. And some of the most spectacular gains in defense and government work evaporated after the war as male veterans returned. Tens of thousands of army nurses, defense workers, and war administrators lost their jobs. Agencies such as the Women's Service Section of the Railroad Administration, which fought sexual harassment and discrimination, simply closed down.

War work nonetheless helped to energize a number of women's causes and organizations. Radical suffragist Alice Paul and others who had protested against the war now argued for women's rights, including the right to vote, on the basis of it. As women worked side by side with men in wartime factories and offices, in nursing stations at home or at the front, they could argue more convincingly for both economic and political equality. One step in that direction came after the war with the ratification of the Nineteenth Amendment in 1920 granting women the right to vote (see page 601).

Great Migrations

LATINO MIGRATIONS

War work sparked massive migrations of laborers. As the fighting abroad choked off immigration and the draft depleted the workforce, factory owners and large-scale farmers scoured the country and beyond for willing workers. Congress waived immigration requirements in 1917 for agricultural workers from Mexico and in 1918 for workers on railroads, in mines, and on government construction projects.

Industrial cities soon swelled with newcomers, many of them Mexican and Mexican American. Between 1917 and 1920 some 50,000 Mexicans legally crossed the border into Texas, California, New Mexico, and Arizona. At least another 100,000 entered illegally. Some Mexican Americans left the segregated barrios and farmlands of the West, pushed out by this cheaper labor from Mexico, and migrated to Chicago, Omaha, and other midwestern cities. Mexican *colonias,* or communities, sprang up across the industrial heartland. But most Mexicans and Mexican Americans continued to work on the farms and ranches of the Southwest, where they were freed from military service by the deferment granted to all agricultural labor.

AFRICAN AMERICANS

Northern labor agents fanned out across the rural South to recruit young African Americans, while black newspapers such as *The Chicago Defender* summoned them north to the "Land of Hope." Over the war years more than 400,000 moved to the booming industrial centers of the North. Largely unskilled and semiskilled, they worked in the steel mills of Pennsylvania, the war plants of Massachusetts, the brickyards of New Jersey. Southern towns were decimated by the drain of workers. Finally, under pressure from southern politicians, the U.S. Employment Service suspended its program to assist blacks moving north.

These migrations—of African Americans into the army as well as into the city—aggravated racial tensions. Lynching parties murdered 38 black southerners in 1917 and 58 in 1918. In 1919, after the war ended, more than 70 African Americans were hanged, some still in uniform. Housing shortages and job competition helped spark race riots across the North.

In almost every city black citizens, stirred by war rhetoric of freedom and democracy, showed new militancy by fighting back. In mid-1917 some 40 black and 9 white Americans died when East St. Louis erupted in racial violence. During the "red summer" of 1919, blood flowed in the streets of Washington, D.C., Omaha, Nebraska, New York City, and Chicago, where thousands of African Americans were burned out of their homes and hundreds injured. "The Washington riot gave me the *thrill that comes once in a life time*," wrote a young black woman in 1919. "At last our men had stood like men, struck back, were no longer dumb driven cattle."

Propaganda and Civil Liberties

COMMITTEE ON PUBLIC INFORMATION
"Once lead this people into war," President Wilson warned before American entry into World War I, "and they'll forget there ever was such a thing as tolerance." Americans succumbed to war hysteria, but they had help. Wilson knew how reluctant Americans had been to enter the war, and he created the Committee on Public Information (CPI) to boost their commitment to the war.

Under George Creel, a California journalist, the CPI launched "a fight for the *minds* of men, for the conquest of their convictions." A zealous publicity campaign produced 75 million pamphlets, patriotic "war expositions" attended by 10 million people in two dozen cities, and colorful war posters, including James Flagg's famous "I Want *You* for the U.S. Army." Seventy-five thousand fast-talking "Four-Minute Men" invaded movie theaters, lodge halls, schools, and churches to keep patriotism at "white heat" with four minutes of war tirades. The CPI organized "Loyalty Leagues" in ethnic communities and sponsored parades and rallies, among them a much-publicized immigrant "pilgrimage" to the birthplace of George Washington.

100 PERCENT AMERICANISM
The line between patriotism and intolerance proved all too easy to cross. As war fever rose, voluntary patriotism blossomed into an orgy of "100 percent Americanism" that distrusted all aliens, radicals, pacifists, and dissenters. German Americans became special targets. In Iowa the governor made it a crime to speak German in public. Hamburgers were renamed "Salisbury steak"; German measles, "liberty measles." When a mob outside St. Louis lynched a naturalized German American who had tried to enlist in the navy, a jury found the leaders not guilty.

ESPIONAGE AND SEDITION ACTS
Congress gave concern about espionage and **sedition** more legal bite by passing the Espionage and Sedition Acts of 1917 and 1918. Both set out harsh penalties for any actions that hindered the war effort or that could be viewed as even remotely unpatriotic. Following their passage, 1,500 citizens were arrested for offenses that included denouncing the draft, criticizing the Red Cross, and complaining about wartime taxes.

Radical groups received especially severe treatment. The Industrial Workers of the World (IWW), a militant labor union centered in western states, saw the war as a battle among capitalists and fought by workers. They threatened to strike mining and lumber companies in protest. Federal agents raided the Chicago headquarters of the IWW—familiarly known as the "Wobblies"—and arrested 113 of its leaders in September 1917. The crusade destroyed the union. Similarly, the Socialist Party opposed the "capitalist" war. In response, the postmaster general banned a dozen Socialist publications from the mail, though the party was a legal organization that had elected mayors, municipal officials, and members of Congress. In June 1918 government agents arrested Eugene V. Debs, the Socialist candidate in the presidential election of 1912, for attacking the draft. A jury found him guilty of sedition and sentenced him to 10 years in jail. Running for the presidency from his jail cell in 1920, Debs received nearly 1 million votes.

SCHENCK V. UNITED STATES
The Supreme Court endorsed such actions. In *Schenck v. United States* (1920) the Court unanimously affirmed the use of the Espionage Act to convict a Socialist Party officer who had mailed pamphlets urging resistance to the draft. Free speech had limits, wrote Justice Oliver Wendell Holmes, and the pamphlets created "a clear and present danger" to a nation at war.

Over There

The first American doughboys landed in France in June 1917, but General John Pershing held back his raw troops for nearly six months, until they received more training. He also separated them in a distinct American Expeditionary Force to preserve their identity and avoid Allied disagreements over strategy.

In the spring of 1918, as the Germans pushed within 50 miles of Paris, Pershing rushed 70,000 American troops to the front. American units helped block the Germans both at the town of Château-Thierry and a month later, in June, at Belleau Wood. At Belleau, it cost the Americans half their force to drive the enemy from the woods. Two more German attacks, one at Amiens, the other just east of the Marne River, ended in disastrous German retreats. On September 12, 1918, half a million American soldiers and a smaller number of French troops overran the German stronghold at Saint-Mihiel in four days.

WILSON'S FOURTEEN POINTS
With their army in retreat and civilian morale low, Germany's leaders sought an **armistice.** They hoped to negotiate terms along the lines laid out by Woodrow Wilson in a speech to Congress in January 1918. Wilson's bright vision of peace encompassed his "Fourteen Points." The key provisions called for open diplomacy, free seas and free trade, disarmament, democratic self-rule, and an "association of nations" to guarantee collective security. It was nothing less than a new world order to end selfish nationalism, imperialism, and war.

Allied leaders were not impressed. "President Wilson and his Fourteen Points bore me," French prime minister premier Georges Clemenceau said. "Even God Almighty has

THE LIMITS OF FREE SPEECH

When the Socialist Party printed and distributed 15,000 leaflets attacking the Conscription Act (1917), authorities charged the party's Secretary General Charles Schenck with having violated the newly enacted Espionage Act by opposing conscription (drafting men into military service). In ruling against Schenck, Justice Oliver Wendell Holmes, writing for the majority of the Supreme Court, outlined the limits of free speech in wartime.

DOCUMENT 1   Flyer Distributed by Socialist Party

ASSERT YOUR RIGHTS!

The Constitution of the United States is one of the greatest bulwarks of political liberty. It was born after a long, stubborn battle between king-rule and democracy. . . . In this battle the people of the United States established the principle that freedom of the individual and personal liberty are the most sacred things in life. Without them we become slaves. . . .

The Thirteenth Amendment of the Constitution of the United States . . . embodies this sacred idea. The Socialist Party says this idea is violated by the Conscription Act. When you conscript a man and compel him to go abroad to fight against his will, you violate the most sacred right of personal liberty, and substitute for it what Daniel Webster called "despotism of the worst form."

A conscript is little better than a convict. He is deprived of his liberty and of his right to think and act as a free man. A conscripted citizen is forced to surrender his right as a citizen and become a subject. He is forced into involuntary servitude. He is deprived of the protection given him by the Constitution of the United States. He is deprived of all freedom of conscience in being forced to kill against his will. . . .

In a democratic country each man must have the right to say whether he is willing to join the army. Only in countries where uncontrolled power rules can a despot force his subjects to fight. Such a man or men have no place in a democratic republic. This is tyrannical power in its worst form. It gives control over the life and death of the individual to a few men. There is no man good enough to be given such power.

Conscription laws belong to a bygone age. Even the people of Germany, long suffering under the yoke of militarism, are beginning to demand the abolition of conscription. Do you think it has a place in the United States? Do you want to see unlimited power handed over to Wall Street's chosen few in America? If you do not, join the Socialist Party in its campaign for the repeal of the Conscription Act. Write to your congressman and tell him you want the law repealed. Do not submit to intimidation. You have a right to demand the repeal of any law. Exercise your rights of free speech, peaceful assemblage and petitioning the government for a redress of grievances. Come to the headquarters of the Socialist Party . . . and sign a petition for the repeal of the Conscription Act. Help us wipe out this stain upon the Constitution!

> Help us re-establish democracy in America. Remember, "eternal vigilance is the price of liberty."
> Down with autocracy!
> Long live the Constitution of the United States!
> Long live the Republic!

Source: Nancy Cornwell, *Freedom of the Press: Rights and Liberties under the Law* (Santa Barbara, CA, 2004), pp. 261–265.

DOCUMENT 2   Justice Holmes on Free Speech in Wartime

We admit that, in many places and in ordinary times, the defendants, in saying all that was said in the circular, would have been within their constitutional rights. But the character of every act depends upon the circumstances in which it is done. The most stringent protection of free speech would not protect a man in falsely shouting fire in a theatre and causing a panic. It does not even protect a man from an injunction against uttering words that may have all the effect of force. The question in every case is whether the words used are used in such circumstances and are of such a nature as to create a clear and present danger that they will bring about the substantive evils that Congress has a right to prevent. It is a question of proximity and degree. When a nation is at war, many things that might be said in time of peace are such a hindrance to its effort that their utterance will not be endured so long as men fight, and that no Court could regard them as protected by any constitutional right. It seems to be admitted that, if an actual obstruction of the recruiting service were proved, liability for words that produced that effect might be enforced. The statute of 1917, in §4, punishes conspiracies to obstruct, as well as actual obstruction. If the act (speaking, or circulating a paper), its tendency, and the intent with which it is done are the same, we perceive no ground for saying that success alone warrants making the act a crime. Indeed, that case might be said to dispose of the present contention if the precedent covers all *media concludendi*. But, as the right to free speech was not referred to specially, we have thought fit to add a few words.

It was not argued that a conspiracy to obstruct the draft was not within the words of the [Conscription] Act of 1917. The words are "obstruct the recruiting or enlistment service," and it might be suggested that they refer only to making it hard to get volunteers. Recruiting heretofore usually having been accomplished by getting volunteers, the word is apt to call up that method only in our minds. But recruiting is gaining fresh supplies for the forces, as well by draft as otherwise. It is put as an alternative to enlistment or voluntary enrollment in this act.

Source: *Schenck v. United States*, 249 U.S. 47 (1919).

Thinking Critically

What actions does the leaflet call for and on what grounds? According to Justice Holmes, what are the limits of free speech in peacetime and wartime? Why are they different? Do you think that there are ever instances in war when citizen protest is permissible under the Constitution?

only ten!" But Wilson's idealistic platform was also designed to save the Allies embarrassment. Almost as soon as it came to power in 1917, the new Bolshevik government in Moscow began publishing secret treaties from the czar's archives. They revealed that the Allies had gone to war for territory and colonies, not the high principles they claimed. Wilson's Fourteen Points now gave their cause a nobler purpose.

Wilson's ideals also stirred German liberals. On October 6, 1918, the liberals gave him the chance to put his principles into action when a telegram arrived from Berlin requesting an immediate truce on the basis of the Fourteen Points. Within a month Turkey and Austria surrendered. Early in November the Kaiser was overthrown and fled to neutral Holland. On November 11, 1918, just before dawn, German officers filed into Allied headquarters in a converted railroad car near Compiègne, France, and signed the armistice.

Of the 2 million Americans who served in France, some 116,500 died. Over 200,000 were wounded. By comparison, the war claimed 1.8 million Germans, 1.7 million Russians, 1.4 million French, 1.2 million Austro-Hungarians, and nearly a million Britons. The American contribution had nonetheless been crucial, providing vital convoys at sea and fresh, confident troops on land. The United States emerged from the war stronger than ever. Europe, in contrast, looked forward—as one newspaper put it—to "Disaster . . . Exhaustion . . . Revolution."

The Influenza Pandemic of 1918–1919

In the months before the armistice a scourge more lethal than war began to engulf the globe. It started innocently enough. At Fort Riley, Kansas, on the morning of March 11, 1918, company cook Albert Mitchell reported to the infirmary on sick call. His head and muscles ached, his throat was sore, and he had a low-grade fever.

It was influenza, a virus dangerous for infants and the old but ordinarily no threat for robust young men like Mitchell. By noon 107 soldiers had reported symptoms. Within a week, the number jumped to over 500. Cases of the flu were being reported in virtually every state, even on the isolated island of Alcatraz in San Francisco Bay. And healthy young adults Mitchell's age were dying from it.

The first wave of flu produced few deaths in the United States. As the virus mutated over the next year, its victims experienced more distressing symptoms: vomiting, dizziness, labored breathing, incessant sweating. Eventually sufferers drowned in their own bodily fluids from the pneumonia that accompanied the infection.

Soldiers and others living in close quarters were especially vulnerable, and for reasons that are still uncertain, so were young adults 20 to 34 years old, precisely the ages of most in the services. For every 50 people infected, 1 died. In the United States alone, the death toll rose to at least

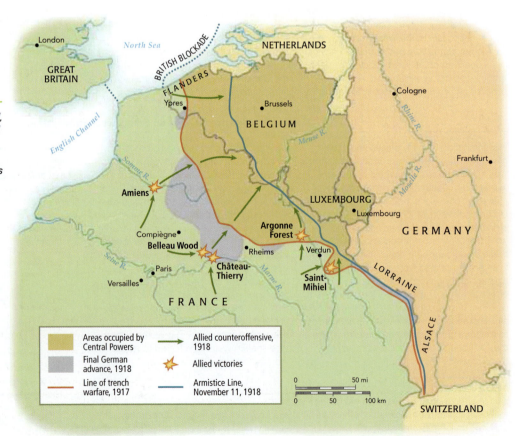

THE FINAL GERMAN OFFENSIVE AND ALLIED COUNTERATTACK, 1918

On the morning of March 21, 1918, the Germans launched a spring offensive designed to cripple the Allies. Sixty-three German divisions sliced through Allied lines for the first time since 1914 and plunged to within 50 miles of Paris. The tide turned in July, when the Germans were stopped at the Marne. The Allied counterattack, with notable American successes at Château-Thierry, Belleau Wood, Saint-Mihiel, and Meuse-Argonne, broke the German war effort.

DAILY LIVES

THE DOUGHBOYS ABROAD

When Secretary of War Newton Baker drew the first number in a new draft lottery on July 20, 1917, the United States had barely 180,000 men in the service. By the time World War I ended in November 1918, nearly 2 million men had donned uniforms and gone off to fight in Europe. For the first time the New World was invading the Old, and for most of those who went, it was their first trip from home.

The "doughboys" marched out of their training camps and up the gangplanks of the "Atlantic Ferry"—the ships that conveyed them to Europe. Some soldiers were fortunate enough to ship out on refitted luxury liners, but most made the voyage below-decks in converted freighters, "the blackest, foulest, most congested hole that I ever set foot into," reported one private. A few died from anthrax in the horsehair of their new shaving brushes. It was a poignant taste of things to come. Disease killed more Americans than enemy fire.

With the United States at war for such a short time, most American soldiers spent more time in training and on leave than in the trenches. To keep the men from becoming restless, company commanders marched their troops against imaginary enemies in never-ending exercises. Soldiers complained about "cooties" (lice) and food (so bad that many reported a 10 percent weight loss within weeks of arriving). Used to freewheeling individualism and equality, they hated military discipline.

Enlisted men groused about army life, but the Old World awed them. Paris was titillating, with women who danced the "Can-Can" and cried "oo-la-la." The antiquity of Europe struck the doughboys even more: "The church here is very, very old. . . . Saint Louis the Crusader, King of France, attended a service there on three occasions and Jeanne d'Arc was there several times." The Europeans seemed both old and old-fashioned. Elderly women in black

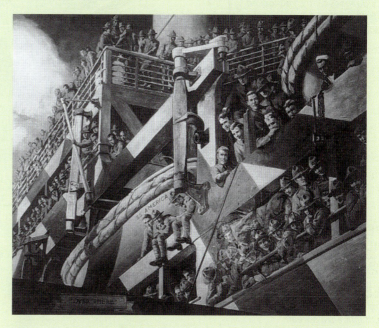

After months of training stateside, the American Expeditionary Force sailed to Europe on the troop ships of the "Atlantic Ferry." Most soldiers departed from Hoboken, New Jersey, and almost half made the journey aboard British vessels.

shawls of mourning often were the only ones left in shattered villages. "They still harvest with cradles and sickles," noted one soldier. Everything endorsed the American myth of the Old World as hidebound and worn and the New as modern and vital.

Disillusion and discontent overcame British and French troops after years in the trenches, but most doughboys never fought long enough to lose their sense of wonder and delight. They returned with a war veteran's sense of dislocation and a new appreciation of the world outside the United States. A year after the war ended a veteran wrote: "I know how we all cried to get

back to the States. But now that we are here, I must admit for myself at least that I am lost and somehow strangely lonesome. These our own United States are truly artificial and bare."

Thinking Critically

How did service overseas affect young American soldiers when they returned home, and what might have been the range of their reactions over the longer term?

600,000, more than the American battle deaths in World War I, World War II, the Korean War, and the war in Vietnam combined.

GLOBAL SPREAD OF THE PANDEMIC Ironically, the United States was the country least affected by this worldwide epidemic, called a **pandemic.** American soldiers seem to have carried the disease to Europe, where it jumped from one country to another

in the spring and summer of 1918. French troops and civilians soon were suffering from it, then British and Germans. General Eric von Ludendorf counted the flu as one of the causes of the failure of the final German offensive in July 1918, which almost won the war for Germany.

With steamships and railroads moving people all over the globe, virtually no place was safe. By the summer of 1918 the virus had leapt from North America and Europe to

In October 1918 artist D. C. Boonzaier drew this grim cartoon of the Spanish flu—Spaanse Griep—when it came to South Africa. In his diary Boonzaier spoke of "the presence of some universal calamity, from which there was no escape. Death stalked by your side incessantly, you looked into its face wherever you turned."

SPREAD OF INFLUENZA PANDEMIC: SECOND STAGE, AUTUMN 1918

After the milder outbreak in the spring of 1918, a more deadly form of influenza spread outward from the coast of France at the beginning of August. The worldwide transportation system quickly dispersed the disease, sending it first to the western coast of Africa (beginning at Freetown, Liberia) and the eastern coast of North America (at Boston). The disease reached virtually all continents, although Australia's strict quarantine delayed entrance of the flu there until 1919. By far, the continent hardest hit was Asia, where anywhere from 12 to 20 million died in India alone. American fatalities, though serious, totaled only about 550,000.

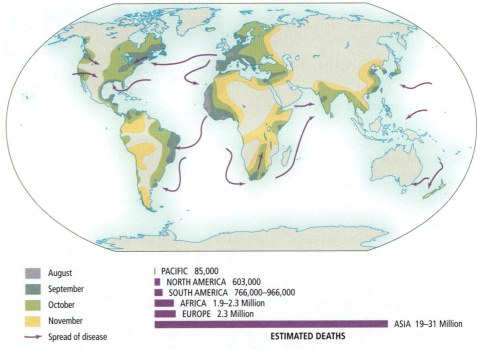

August
September
October
November
→ Spread of disease

	ESTIMATED DEATHS
PACIFIC	85,000
NORTH AMERICA	603,000
SOUTH AMERICA	766,000–966,000
AFRICA	1.9–2.3 Million
EUROPE	2.3 Million
ASIA	19–31 Million

Asia and Japan; by fall, to Africa and South America. As far north as the Russian city of Archangel, officials were reporting 30 influenza deaths a day by October 1918. In densely packed India, one account claimed that at least 12 million perished from influenza.

Sixteen months after Albert Mitchell had first reported to sick call, the flu vanished as quickly as it had appeared. Conservative estimates placed the number of dead worldwide at 50 million, making the influenza pandemic of 1918–1919 the most lethal outbreak of disease on an annual basis in human history.

✓ **REVIEW**

How did progressivism shape the home front during World War I?

THE LOST PEACE

AS THE USS *GEORGE WASHINGTON* approached the coast of France in mid-December 1918 the mist suddenly lifted in an omen of good hope. Woodrow Wilson had come to represent the United States at the Paris peace conference at

Versailles, once the glittering palace of Louis XIV. He was the first sitting president to meet foreign heads of state on foreign soil. A world of problems awaited. Europe had been shelled into ruin and scarred with the debris of war. Some 40 million people lay dead or maimed from the fighting. Millions more had been displaced from their homelands. Throughout the Balkans and the old Turkish Empire, ethnic rivalries, social chaos, and revolution loomed.

With the old world order in shambles, Wilson felt the need for vigorous action. Thus the president handpicked the peace commission of experts that accompanied him. It included economists, historians, geographers, and political scientists—but not a single member of the Republican-controlled Senate. What promised to make peace negotiations easier, however, created a crippling liability in Washington, where Republicans cast a hostile eye on the mirrored halls of Versailles.

The Treaty of Versailles

Everywhere he went, cheers greeted the president. In Paris 2 million people showered him with flowers and called him "Wilson, le Juste" (the Just). In Italy they hailed him as the "peacemaker from America." And Wilson believed them, unaware of how determined the victors were to punish the vanquished Germans. David Lloyd George of England, Georges Clemenceau of France, Vittorio Orlando of Italy, and Wilson made up the Big Four at the conference that included some 27 nations. War had united them; now peacemaking threatened to divide them.

Wilson's sweeping call for reform had taken Allied leaders by surprise. Hungry for new colonies, eager to see Germany crushed and disarmed, they had already drawn up secret treaties dividing the territories of the Central Powers. Germany offered to surrender on the basis of Wilson's Fourteen Points, but the Allies refused to accept them. When Wilson threatened to negotiate peace on his own, Allied leaders finally agreed—but only for the moment.

Noticeably absent when the peace conference convened in January 1919 were the Russians. None of the Western democracies had recognized the Bolshevik regime in Moscow out of fear that the communist revolution might spread. Instead, France and Britain were helping to finance a civil war to overthrow the Bolsheviks. Even Wilson was persuaded to send a small number of American troops to join the Allied occupation of Murmansk in northern Russia and Vladivostok on the Sea of Japan. The Soviets neither forgot nor forgave this invasion of their soil.

Grueling peace negotiations forced Wilson to yield several of his Fourteen Points. Britain, with its powerful navy, refused even to discuss the issues of free trade and freedom of the seas. Wilson's promised "open diplomacy" was conducted behind closed doors by the Big Four. The only mention of disarmament involved Germany, which was permanently barred from rearming. Wilson's call for "peace without victory" gave way to a "guilt clause" that saddled Germany with responsibility for the war. Worse still, the victors imposed an impoverishing debt of $33 billion in reparations on the vanquished.

Wilson did achieve some successes. His pleas for national self-determination led to the creation of a dozen new states in Europe, including Yugoslavia, Hungary, and Austria. (Newly created Poland and Czechoslovakia, however, contained millions of ethnic Germans.) Former colonies gained new status as "mandates" of the victors, who were obligated to prepare them for independence. The old German and Turkish Empires in the Middle East and Africa became the responsibility of France and England, while Japan took over virtually all German possessions in the Pacific north of the equator.

LEAGUE OF NATIONS

Wilson never lost sight of his main goal, his Fourteenth Point calling for a "general association of nations." He had given so much ground precisely because he believed this new world organization would correct any mistakes in the peace settlement. As constituted, what came to be called the "League of Nations" comprised a general Body of Delegates, a select

GOD: Woodrow Wilson, where are your 14 points?
WILSON: Don't get excited, Lord, we didn't keep your Ten Commandments either!

Woodrow Wilson's famous Fourteen Points for establishing a new world order struck some observers, including this cartoonist, as being as idealistic as the Ten Commandments. For Wilson, the Fourteen Points, with their call for a peace based on national self-determination and a League of Nations, had practical political ends. The president hoped to counter the propaganda of Russian revolutionaries about the self-interested aims of the Allies and to bolster German liberals who wanted an end to the war. He also meant to boost sagging morale among the Allies with the promise of peace. Although the Fourteen Points, like the Ten Commandments, set a lofty standard of ideals, Wilson had down-to-earth results in mind.

EUROPE AND THE MIDDLE EAST AFTER WORLD WAR I

The Treaty of Versailles changed the face of Europe and the Middle East. Compare, for example, the map of Europe on page 628 with the one above. **What European countries have been created that did not exist at the start of the war? What Middle Eastern countries?**

Executive Council, and a Court of International Justice. Members vowed to submit all war-provoking disagreements to arbitration and to isolate aggressors by cutting off commercial and military trade. Article X (Wilson called it "the heart of the covenant") bound members to respect one another's independence and territory and to join together against attack. "It is definitely a guarantee of peace," the president told the delegates in February 1919.

The Battle for the Treaty

Wilson left immediately for home to address growing opposition in Congress. In the off-year elections of 1918, voters unhappy with wartime controls, new taxes, and attacks on civil liberties had given both houses to the Republicans. A slim Republican majority in the Senate put Wilson's archrival, Henry Cabot Lodge of Massachusetts, in the chairman's seat of the all-important Foreign Relations Committee. "I never expected to hate anyone in politics with the hatred I feel toward Wilson," Lodge confessed.

While most of the country favored the League, Lodge abhorred it. For decades he had fought to preserve American freedom of action in foreign affairs. He worried that the League would force Americans to subject themselves to "the will of other nations." And he certainly did not want Democrats to win votes by taking credit for the treaty. Securing the signatures of enough senators to block any treaty, Lodge rose in the Senate just before midnight on March 3, 1919, to read a "round robin" resolution against the League. "Woodrow Wilson's League of Nations died in the Senate tonight," concluded New York's *The Sun*.

Wilson formally presented the treaty in July. "Dare we reject it and break the heart of the world?" he asked the senators. His only hope of winning the necessary two-thirds majority for passage of the treaty lay in compromise, but temperamentally he could not abide it. Worn out by the concessions already wrung from him in Paris, afflicted by numbing headaches and a twitch in his left eye, he resisted any more changes. Despite his doctor's warnings, Wilson took his case to the people in a month-long stump across the nation to rally public opinion and bend the Senate to his will.

WILSON'S STROKE — In Pueblo, Colorado, a crowd of 10,000 heard perhaps the greatest oration of Wilson's career. He spoke that evening, utterly exhausted, and collapsed in a spasm of pain. On October 2, four days after being rushed to the White House, the president fell to the bathroom floor, knocked unconscious by a stroke.

For six weeks Wilson could do no work at all and for months after worked little more than an hour a day. His second wife, Edith Bolling Wilson, handled the routine business of government along with the president's secretary and his doctor. The country knew nothing of the seriousness of his condition. Wilson recovered slowly but never fully. More and more the battle for the treaty consumed his fading energies.

In November 1919 Lodge finally reported the treaty out of committee with 14 amendments to match Wilson's Fourteen Points. The most important asserted that the United States assumed no obligation to come to the aid of League members unless Congress consented. Wilson believed Lodge had delivered a "knife thrust at the heart of the treaty" and refused to accept any changes. Whatever ill will Lodge bore Wilson, his objections did not destroy the treaty but only weakened it by protecting the congressional prerogative to declare war.

Under orders from the president, Democrats joined Republicans to defeat the treaty with Lodge's reservations. An attempt to pass the unamended treaty failed. Although four-fifths of the senators favored it in some form, Wilson and Lodge refused to compromise. The Treaty of Versailles was dead, and loyal Democrats were forced to deliver the killing blow. Not until July 1921 did Congress enact a joint resolution ending the war. The United States, which had fought separately from the Allies, made a separate peace as well.

IF WE WERE IN THE LEAGUE OF NATIONS
Copyright, 1920, by Star Company.

HI _ SAM ! SEND ME OVER A NEW ARMY !

"If we were in the League of Nations," warns this cartoon ominously, the United States would see more wounded and dead soldiers coming home by the boatload. Uncle Sam watches silently as the remnants of the American army return, including a flag-draped coffin in the background, while "J[ohn] Bull" (symbol of Great Britain) shouts: "Send over a new army!"

Red Scare

Peace abroad did not bring peace at home. On May Day 1919, six months after the war ended, mobs in a dozen cities broke up Socialist parades, injured hundreds, and killed three people. On the floor of the Senate Kenneth McKellar of Tennessee advocated sending citizens with radical beliefs to a penal colony on the Pacific island of Guam.

RADICALS AND LABOR UNREST — The spontaneous violence and extremism occurred because Americans believed they were under attack. The millions of soldiers who had returned home were now unemployed and looking for work. With prices rising and war regulations lifted, laborers were demanding higher wages and striking when they failed to get them. In Boston even the police walked off their jobs. When a strike by conservative trade unionists paralyzed Seattle for five days in January, Mayor Ole Hanson draped his car in an American flag and led troops through the streets in a show of force. Hanson blamed radicals, while Congress ascribed the national ills to Bolshevik agents inspired by the revolution in Russia.

The menace of radicalism was overblown. With Socialist Eugene Debs in prison, his dwindling party numbered only about 30,000. Radicals at first hoped that the success of the Russian Revolution would help reverse their fortunes in the United States. But most Americans found the prospect of "Bolshevik" agitators threatening, especially after March 1919, when the new Russian government

In September 1919 some 350,000 steelworkers struck for higher wages, recognition of their union, and a reduction in their 70-hour workweeks. Mill owners countered by hiring black strikebreakers and armed guards and by launching a potent publicity campaign that depicted the strike as a plot of "Red agitators." Here, armed police ride down strikers in Philadelphia.

formed the Comintern to spread revolution abroad. Furthermore, the Left itself splintered. In 1919 dissidents deserted the Socialists to form the more radical Communist Labor Party. About the same time, a group of mainly Slavic radicals created a separate Communist Party in the United States. Both organizations together counted no more than 40,000 members.

Terrorism stoked the flames of fear. On April 28 Mayor Hanson received a small brown parcel at his office, apparently another present from an admirer of his tough patriotism. It was a homemade bomb. Within days 20 such packages were discovered, including ones sent to John D. Rockefeller, Supreme Court Justice Oliver Wendell Holmes, and Postmaster General Albert Burleson. On June 2 bombs exploded simultaneously in eight different cities. One of them demolished the front porch of A. Mitchell Palmer, the attorney general of the United States. The bomb thrower was blown to bits, but enough remained to identify him as an Italian anarchist from Philadelphia. Already edgy over Bolshevism and labor militancy, many Americans assumed that an organized conspiracy was being mounted to overthrow the government.

PALMER RAIDS Palmer, a Quaker and a staunch progressive, hardened in the wake of the bombings. In November 1919 and again in January 1920, he launched raids in cities across the United States. In a single night in January, government agents invaded private homes, meeting halls, and pool parlors in 33 cities. They took 4,000 people into custody without warrants, sometimes beating

A. Mitchell Palmer, a Quaker and a progressive, was shocked by the anarchist bombings and took a hard line against the terrorist campaign.

those who resisted. Many were Russians, some were communists, but most were victims of suspicion run amok. Prisoners were marched through streets in chains, crammed into dilapidated jails, and held incommunicado without hearings. Over 200 aliens, most of whom had no criminal records, were deported to the Soviet Union. Arrests continued at the rate of 200 a week through March.

Such abuses of civil liberties finally provoked a backlash. After the New York legislature expelled five elected Socialists in 1919, responsible politicians—from former presidential candidate Charles Evans Hughes to Ohio senator Warren Harding—began to denounce the action. Assistant Secretary of Labor Louis Post refused to issue more deportation orders, and the "deportation delirium" ended early in 1920.

Palmer finally overreached himself by predicting a revolutionary uprising for May 1, 1920. Buildings were put under guard and state militia called to readiness. Nothing happened. Four months later, when a wagonload of bombs exploded on Wall Street, Palmer blamed a Bolshevik conspiracy. Despite over 30 deaths and more than 200 injuries, Americans saw it as the work of a few fanatic anarchists (which it probably was) and went about business as usual.

 **REVIEW**

What were the results of the Paris Peace Conference and the Treaty of Versailles?

CONCLUSION

THE WORLD AT LARGE

In early August 1914 the Panama Canal opened without fanfare, but no one could miss its significance: the new American empire now spanned the globe, stretching from the Caribbean to the Pacific and linked by a waterway between the seas. There were plans for a tremendous celebration in which the battleship *Oregon*, whose 1898 "race around the Horn" had inspired the idea of an American-owned canal, would lead a flotilla of ships through the locks. But the plans were scrapped, for in that fateful month of August, the old world order collapsed into a world war.

World War I was rightly named "the Great War" by Europeans, because it transformed the continent and left a bitter legacy that shaped the rest of the twentieth century. In Europe, France and Great Britain triumphed, only to find their economies enfeebled, their people dispirited and fearful, their empires near collapse. Two other empires—of vanquished Austria-Hungary and Turkey—were dismembered. Revolution toppled the once-mighty czars of Russia, bringing an end to the Russian Empire and the beginning of the Soviet Union under Joseph Stalin. Germany suffered defeat, humiliation, and a crushing burden of debt, which together paved the way for Adolf Hitler and the Nazis.

Elsewhere, a victorious Japan left the Paris peace table shamed by what it regarded as paltry spoils of war and determined to rise to global greatness that equaled the West. Japan's flickering democracy soon crumbled as a cult of militarism and emperor worship took hold. In the Middle East, in Africa, and on the Indian subcontinent, the unfulfilled promises of a world made "safe for democracy" sparked a growing number of nationalist and anticolonialist movements. The twentieth century, a century of global change and violence, was forged in the crucible of the Great War. ∞∞∞

CHAPTER SUMMARY

WORLD WAR I MARKED THE beginning of the end of the old world order of colonial imperialism, military alliances, and balances of power; it also marked a failed effort to establish a new world order based on the progressive ideals of international cooperation and collective security.

■ Progressive diplomacy—whether through Theodore Roosevelt's big stick diplomacy, William Taft's dollar diplomacy, or Woodrow Wilson's missionary diplomacy—stressed moralism and order, championed "uplifting" nonwhites, and stretched presidential authority to its limits.

■ With the outbreak of World War I in 1914, Woodrow Wilson saw an opportunity for the United States to lead the world to a higher peace of international cooperation and collective security by remaining neutral and brokering the peace settlement.

■ However, American sympathy for the Allies, heavy American investments in the Allies, and the German campaign of unrestricted submarine warfare finally drew the United States into the war in 1917.

■ Progressive faith in government, planning, efficiency, and publicity produced a greatly expanded bureaucratic state that managed the war effort on the home front.

• The darker side of progressivism also flourished as the war transformed progressive impulses for assimilation and social control into campaigns for superpatriotism and conformity that helped to produce a postwar Red Scare in 1919 and 1920.

• Meanwhile, changes were already under way, including more women in the labor force and migrations of African Americans and Mexican Americans from rural to urban America, vastly accelerated with the expansion of opportunities for war work.

■ When the war ended, Wilson's hopes for "peace without victory" and a new world order, embodied in his Fourteen Points, were dashed when his European allies imposed a harsh settlement on Germany and the U.S. Senate failed to ratify the Treaty of Versailles.

Additional Reading

For progressive diplomacy, see Howard K. Beale, *Theodore Roosevelt and the Rise of America to World Power* (1956), and Arthur Link, *Woodrow Wilson: Revolution, War, and Peace* (1968). Walter LaFeber's *Inevitable Revolutions* (rev. ed., 1993) presents an incisive account of American foreign policy in Honduras, El Salvador, Guatemala, Nicaragua, and Costa Rica. Julie Green studies the workers who built the Panama Canal and their families, many of them blacks from the Caribbean, and sees the canal as America's springboard to empire in *The Canal Builders: Making America's Empire at the Panama Canal* (2009). Ernest R. May examines American prewar diplomacy and the policies of the Great Powers, especially Germany's U-boat campaign, in *The World War and American Isolation, 1914–1917* (1957).

The debate over American entry into World War I has a long history. Early revisionist accounts emphasizing a financial conspiracy include Charles Beard, *The Open Door to War* (1934), and Charles C. Tansill, *America Goes to War* (1938). A good account from the school of realism, critical of Wilson's moral motives, is George Kennan, *American Diplomacy, 1900–1950* (rev. ed., 1971). David M. Kennedy, *Over Here: The First World War and American Society* (1980), is the definitive account of mobilization and the home front, but see also Maurine W. Greenwald, *Women, War, and Work* (1980), Susan Zeiger, *In Uncle Sam's Service: Women Workers with the American Expeditionary Force, 1917–1919* (1999), and Kathleen Kennedy, *Disloyal Mothers and Scurrilous Citizens: Women and Subversion during World War I* (1999), on the status and role of women during the war. Joe William Trotter, *The Great Migration in Historical Perspective* (1991), is a fine collection of essays that stresses gender and class in the wartime experience of African Americans. Mark Ellis, *Race, War, and Surveillance* (2001), and Mark Robert Schneider, *"We Return Fighting": The Civil Rights Movement in the Jazz Age* (2001), look at the effects of the war on African American civil rights. Frank Freidel re-creates the horrors of trench warfare in *Over There* (1964), while Jennifer D. Keene, *Doughboys, the Great War, and the Remaking of America* (2001), looks at the impact of the war on soldiers and on the country. For African Americans on the battle front, see Arthur E. Barbeau and Henri Florette, *The Unknown Soldiers* (1974). Robert Ferrell, *Woodrow Wilson and World War I* (1985), analyzes Wilson's wartime diplomacy and the fate of the Treaty of Versailles. For the influenza pandemic, see Alfred W. Crosby, *America's Forgotten Pandemic: The Influenza of 1918* (1989), and Dorothy A. Pettit, *A Cruel Wind: Pandemic Flu in America* (2008). For a colorful account of the Paris Peace Conference, see Margaret Macmillan and Richard Holbrooke, *Paris, 1919: Six Months That Changed the World* (2001). Beverly Gage's *The Day Wall Street Exploded* (2009) revisits the unsolved Wall Street bombing of 1920 within the context of class warfare and labor radicalism.

For a fuller list of readings, see the Bibliography at www.mhhe.com/eh8e.

Significant Events

1901
Hay-Pauncefote Treaty

1904
Roosevelt Corollary to Monroe Doctrine

1907
"Gentlemen's agreement" with Japan; "Great White Fleet" embarks on world tour

1910
Mexican Revolution begins

1914
World War I begins; Panama Canal opens

1915
Lusitania torpedoed; Wilson endorses preparedness

1916
General John Pershing invades Mexico in pursuit of Pancho Villa; Wilson reelected

1917
Russian Revolution breaks out; United States enters World War I

1918
Wilson's Fourteen Points; influenza pandemic; armistice declared

1919
Paris Peace Conference; Senate rejects Treaty of Versailles

1920
Palmer raids; Red Scare

POINT	FATE
1. End to secret treaties	rejected
2. Free navigation of seas "alike in peace and in war"	rejected
3. Free trade among nations	rejected
4. Arms reduction "consistent with domestic safety"	rejected
5. Impartial decisions about future of colonies	rejected
6. German army removed from Russia; Russia accepted internationally	rejected
7. Belgium "evacuated and restored" to prewar independence	**accepted**
8. German army removed from France; Alsace-Lorraine returned to France	**accepted**
9. Restoration of Italy's borders "along clearly recognizable lines of nationality"	modified
10. Self-government for peoples of the former Austro-Hungarian Empire	modified
11. Self-government and independence for Balkan states	modified
12. Self-government for peoples of the former Ottoman Empire; sovereignty for Turkey	modified
13. Creation of an independent Poland with access to sea	**accepted**
14. Establishment of a "general association of nations" to guarantee independence and territorial integrity of all members	modified

The automobile, bustling urban centers, the mass media, shorter skirts—these are among the hallmarks of "the New Era" that can be seen in this detail of a fresco depicting downtown San Francisco: *City Life*, by Victor Arnautoff. Who is the star of *City Lights*?

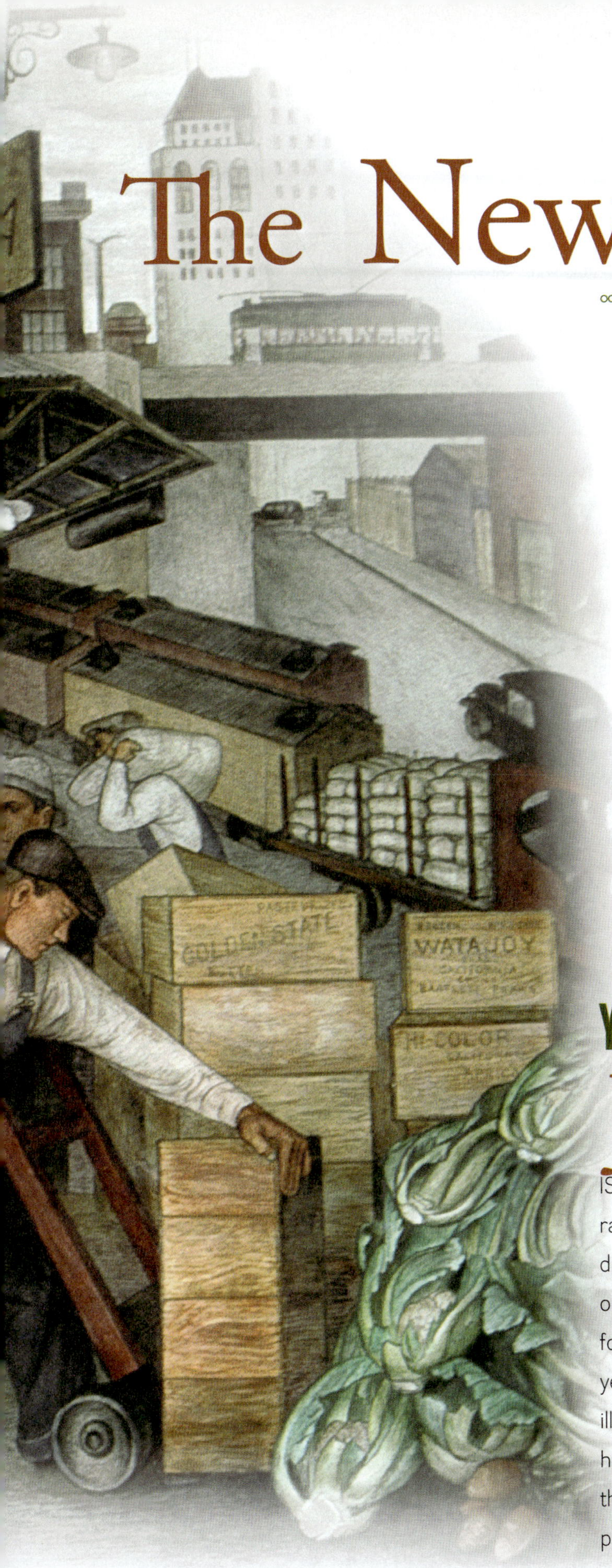

CHAPTER 24

The New Era

1920–1929

Whats to Come

AN AMERICAN STORY

Yesterday Meets Today in the New Era

Just before Christmas 1918 the "Gospel Car" pulled into Los Angeles. Bold letters on the side announced: "JESUS IS COMING—GET READY." Aimee Semple McPherson, the ravishing redheaded driver, had completed a cross-country drive to seek her destiny as an evangelist in the West. With only "ten dollars and a tambourine," Sister Aimee at first found destiny elusive. After wandering the state for three years, she landed in San Diego. With the highest rates of illness and suicide in California, the city was perfect for the healing message of her "Foursquare Gospel." Her revival there attracted 30,000 people, who witnessed her first proclaimed miracle: a paralytic walked.

After the miracle in San Diego, her fame spread. She returned triumphantly to Los Angeles, where nearly three-quarters of a million people, many from the nation's heartland, had migrated in search of opportunity, sun, and perhaps salvation. In heading west, most had lost touch with the traditional Protestant denominations at home. Sister Aimee put her traveling gospel tent away.

To the blare of trumpets on New Year's Day, 1923, she unveiled the $1.5 million Angelus Temple, graced by a 75-foot, rotating electrified cross. It was visible at night from 50 miles away. Inside was a 5,000-seat auditorium, radio station KFSG (Kall Four Square Gospel), a "Cradle Roll Chapel" for babies, and a "Miracle Room" filled with crutches and canes discarded by the cured faithful. Services were not simply a matter of hymns, prayers, and sermons. Sister added pageants, Holy Land slide shows, and healing sessions.

Aimee Semple McPherson succeeded because she was able to blend old and new. Where country preachers menaced their congregations with visions of eternal damnation, Sister Aimee, wrote a reporter, offered "flowers, music, . . . and sex appeal." She had a nose for publicity and understood the booming media industries of the 1920s. Here was one brand of evangelism suited to what contemporaries were calling the "New Era" of prosperity and consumption.

Modernizing the gospel was just one change ushered in by the New Era. Writing in 1931, journalist Frederick Lewis Allen found the changes of the preceding decade so dizzying that he could hardly believe 1919 was *Only Yesterday*, as he titled his best-selling book. To give a sense of the transformation, Allen followed an average American couple, the fictitious "Mr. and Mrs. Smith," through the 1920s. The same revolution in industry and technology that allowed sweet-voiced Sister Aimee to save souls had also transformed the Smiths' home with radios, canned foods, and new electrical gadgets like vacuum cleaners.

Perhaps the most visible changes involved women. By the end of the decade, Mrs. Smith's corset vanished and her hemline jumped from her ankle to her knee. Mimicking stylish young flappers, she bobbed, or cut, her long hair to the popular, near-boyish length. With Prohibition in force, she and other women walked into illegal speakeasy saloons as readily as men. In the trendy hotels she and her husband danced to jazz. But the most striking difference about these "average" Americans was that they lived in the city. The census of 1920 showed that for the first time just over half the population were urbanites.

| Sister Aimee

Yet the city-dwelling Smiths of Frederick Allen's imagination were scarcely average. Nearly as many Americans still lived on isolated farms, in villages, and in small towns as in cities. In fact, many "city" dwellers lived there, too. By defining cities as incorporated municipalities with 2,500 people or more, the Census Bureau had created hundreds of statistical illusions. New York with its millions of inhabitants ranked in the census tables alongside tiny Hyden, located on the Cumberland plateau of eastern Kentucky. In Hyden, Main Street remained unpaved, and God-fearing Baptists still repaired to the Middle Fork of the Kentucky River for an open-air baptism when they declared their new birth in Christ. They would have nothing to do with flapper girls or the showy miracles of Aimee McPherson.

Whether Americans embraced the New Era or condemned it, change came nonetheless, in the form of a mass-produced consumer economy, a culture shaped by mass media, and a more materialistic society. Most Americans believed the New Era of prosperity would last forever and ripple across the globe. Little did they realize that their roaring economy was honeycombed with weaknesses and those who promised to save them turned out to be false saviors. Even Sister Aimee failed: barely three years after her glowing tower lit the skies of Los Angeles, her career had sunk as low as her reputation following her mysterious disappearance (and reappearance) amid charges that she had run away with a married man. ∞∞∞∞

The Roaring Economy

In the 1920s the United States was in the midst of a production boom. Not only did manufacturing increase sharply—by 64 percent over the decade—but so did productivity. Output per worker jumped 40 percent. Between 1922 and 1927 the economy grew by 7 percent a year—the largest peacetime rate ever. If anything roared in the "Roaring Twenties," it was the economy.

Technology and Consumer Spending

Technology was partly responsible. Steam turbines and shovels, electric motors, belt and bucket conveyors, and countless other new machines became common at work sites. Rising demand, especially for new consumer goods, kept the labor force growing at a faster rate than the population, even though machines replaced 200,000 workers annually. Pay improved: between 1919 and 1927, average income climbed nearly $150 for each industrial worker.

As the industrial economy matured, more consumer goods appeared on store shelves—cigarette lighters, wristwatches, radios, panchromatic film. As production of such goods grew, productivity gains helped keep prices down. The cost of a tire and an inner tube, for example, dropped by half between 1914 and 1929. Meanwhile, the purchasing power of wages climbed by 20 percent. Americans enjoyed the highest standard of living any people had ever known.

Yet for all the prosperity, a dangerous imbalance was developing. Most Americans saved little in the mistaken belief that prosperity was here to stay. Falling prices made many items seem cheap, and the rapid expansion of credit allowed consumers to put off paying for what they purchased. As a result, personal debt rose two and a half times faster than personal income, an unhealthy sign of consumers scrambling to spend.

The Booming Construction Industry

Along with technology and consumer spending, new "boom industries" promoted economic growth. In a rebound after the war years, construction soared. Even midsize cities such as Beaumont, Texas, and Memphis, Tennessee, were erecting buildings of 20 stories or more. New York City got a new skyline of tall towers, topped in 1931 when the Empire State Building rose to the world-record height of 86 stories.

Residential construction doubled as people moved from cities to suburbs. Suburban Grosse Point, near Detroit, grew by 700 percent, and Beverly Hills, on the outskirts of Los Angeles, by 2,500 percent. Road construction made suburban life possible and pumped millions of dollars into the economy. In 1919 Oregon, New Mexico, and Colorado hit on a novel idea for financing roads—a tax on gasoline. Within a decade every state had one.

Construction stimulated other businesses: steel, concrete, lumber, home mortgages, and insurance. It even helped change the nation's eating habits. The limited storage space of small "kitchenettes" in new apartments boosted supermarket chains and the canning industry. As shipments of fresh fruits and vegetables sped across new roads, interest in nutrition grew. Vitamins, publicized with new zeal, appeared on breakfast tables.

The Automobile

No industry boomed more than automobile manufacturing. Although cars had first appeared on streets at the turn of the century, for many years they remained little more than expensive toys. By 1929 there were 26 million of them, 1 for every 5 people (compared to 1 for every 43 in Britain and 1 for every 7,000 in Russia). Automakers bought one-seventh of the nation's steel and more rubber, plate glass, nickel, and lead than any other industry. One American in four somehow earned a living from automobiles.

HENRY FORD — Henry Ford helped to make the boom possible by pushing standardization and mass production to such ruthless extremes that the automobiles became affordable. Trading on his fame as a race-car manufacturer, he founded the Ford Motor Company in 1903 with the dream of building a "motor car for the multitude." He believed that the way to succeed was to drive down costs by making all the cars alike, "just like one pin is like another pin." In 1908 Ford perfected the Model T. It had a 20-horsepower engine and a body of steel. It was high enough to ride the worst roads, and it came in only one color: black.

Priced at $845, the Model T was inexpensive by industry standards but still too costly and time-consuming to build. Two Ford engineers suggested copying a practice of Chicago meatpacking houses, where beef carcasses were carried on moving chains past meat dressers. In 1914 Ford introduced the moving assembly line. A conveyor belt, positioned waist high to eliminate bending or walking, propelled the chassis at 6 feet per minute as stationary workers put the cars together. The process cut assembly time in half. In 1925 new Model Ts were rolling off Ford's lines every 10 seconds. At $290, almost anybody could buy one. Within three years, Ford had sold 15 million of his "tin lizzies."

DOCTRINE OF HIGH WAGES — Ford was also a social prophet. Breaking with other manufacturers, he preached a "doctrine of high wages." According to it, workers with extra money in their pockets would buy enough to sustain a booming prosperity. In 1915 Ford's plants in Dearborn established the "Five-Dollar Day," twice the wage rate in Detroit. He reduced working hours from 48 to 40 a week and cut the workweek to five days. By 1926 he also employed 10,000 African Americans, many of whom had advanced far enough to hire and fire their white subordinates.

Yet Ford workers were not happy. Ford admitted that the repetitive operations on his assembly line made it scarcely possible "that any man would care to continue long at the same job." The Five-Dollar Day was designed, in part, to reduce the turnover rate of 300 percent a year at Ford plants. And Ford recouped his profits by speeding up the assembly line and enforcing ruthless efficiencies. Ford workers could not talk, whistle, smoke, or sit on the job. A Sociological Department spied on workers in their homes, and the Education Department taught plant procedures but also Americanization classes where immigrant workers learned English, proper dress, and even etiquette.

General Motors copied Ford's production techniques but not his business strategies. While Ford tried to sell everyone the same car, GM created "a car for every purse and purpose." There were Cadillacs for the wealthy, Chevrolets for the modest. GM cars were painted in a rainbow of colors, and every year the style changed. In a standardized society, such details made automobiles symbols of distinction as well as prestige.

A CAR CULTURE By making automobiles available to nearly everyone, the industry changed the face of America. The spreading web of paved roads fueled urban sprawl, real estate booms in California and Florida, and a new roadside culture of restaurants, service stations, and motels. Thousands of "auto camps" opened to provide tourists with tents and crude toilets. Automobile travel broke down the isolation and provincialism of Americans and helped to standardize dialects and manners.

Across the country the automobile gave the young unprecedented freedom from parental authority. After hearing 30 cases of "sex crimes" (19 had occurred in cars), an exasperated juvenile court judge declared that the automobile was "a house of prostitution on wheels." It was, of course, much more. The automobile was to the 1920s what the railroad had been to the nineteenth century: the catalyst for economic growth, a transportation revolution, and a cultural symbol.

The Future of Energy

The automobile had initially been seen as a clean machine, a more hygienic alternative to horse-drawn vehicles that left mounds of manure on roads and city streets and created breeding grounds for killers such as tuberculosis. The automobile also helped to ensure that the future of energy would be anything but clean. During the 1920s, the consumption of fuel oils more than doubled. But the shift to power based on hydrocarbons such as coal and petroleum was never foreordained. It was the result of several factors—some natural, others economic, still others corporate-made—all converging on the automobile.

One was abundance. Beginning with the great oil strike at Titusville, Pennsylvania, in 1859, drillers tapped into huge pools of petroleum beneath the

| Henry Ford

earth's surface in Ohio, Indiana, Illinois, and other states in the South and the West. The biggest boom came in southeast Texas in 1901 at Spindletop. The first six wells drilled in a field just over a quarter of a square mile produced more oil than all the other wells in the world put together. Crude or unrefined oil from Spindletop retailed at 3 cents a barrel. Coal-driven railroad and steamship companies jumped at the chance to buy new energy at cut-rate costs.

Chemistry abetted abundance. Over the next 20 years, refiners vastly improved the process of turning crude into the light fuel oil needed for automobile engines. With intense pressure and heat, chemists could "crack" or break the string of carbon molecules in oil, more than doubling the gasoline squeezed from unrefined petroleum. In the early 1920s engineers at General Motors discovered that adding certain compounds, including tetraethyl lead, could raise the energy level of new "high-octane" gasoline. The new Ethyl Corporation, the result of a partnership between GM and Standard Oil of New Jersey, manufactured the additive and promoted it as the most economical and efficient means of increasing power.

Among other additives was alcohol. Alcohol from fermented plants was also capable of powering gasoline engines. Peanut oil drove the first diesel engines. By 1925 Henry Ford was calling alcohol "the fuel of the future." Ford was particularly impressed with the availability of fuel alcohol. It could be manufactured, he said, "from fruit like that sumac out by the road, or from apples, weeds, sawdust— almost anything . . . that can be fermented." Hydrocarbons were bound to run out, leaving the United States dependent on foreign oil in the short run and eventually the planet without its most precious source of fuel. But as long as plants grew, alcohol was endlessly renewable. To Ford, it was the energy of tomorrow.

For a time in the 1920s other automobile manufacturers as well as engineers and chemists agreed, but in the end alcohol lost out. For one thing, alcohol provided 30 percent less energy than gasoline. For another, it cost significantly more energy to produce, when growing, harvesting, distilling, and transporting were taken into account. As important, new oil discoveries on the eve of the Great Depression drove down the price of crude to 2 cents a barrel by 1931. Finally, GM and its Ethyl Corporation, which stood to profit from leaded gasoline, waged a relentless campaign against alcohol as a fuel or an additive. Facing such obstacles, alcohol enthusiasts lost out.

The long-term price paid for energy dependence on oil and leaded gasoline was high. Half a century later, long lines at local gas stations and high prices at the pump testified to the power of foreign petroleum producers to vex American consumers and threaten national security by reducing the flow of oil into the country. Even earlier, minute flecks of lead in factories poisoned workers, while lead-laden emissions from automobiles contaminated soil and water. Smog thickened by car exhausts engulfed some cities in a dangerous haze, prompting "smog alerts" and air-quality warnings for residents with respiratory ailments. Pioneered by California, new state and federal laws set limits on harmful auto emissions in the 1960s and 1970s and banned lead in gasoline and other products.

The Business of America

In business, said Henry Ford, the "fundamentals are all summed up in the single word, 'service.'" President Calvin Coolidge echoed the theme of service to society in 1925: "The business of America is business. The man who builds a factory builds a temple. The man who works there worships there." A generation earlier, progressives had criticized business for its social irresponsibility. The wartime contributions of business managers and the return of prosperity in 1922 gained them renewed respect.

CORPORATE CONSOLIDATION Encouraged by federal permissiveness, a wave of mergers swept the country. Between 1919 and 1930 some 8,000 firms disappeared as large gobbled small. Oligopolies (a few firms that dominate whole industries) flourished in steel, meatpacking, cigarettes, and other businesses. National chains began to replace local "mom-and-pop" stores. By 1929 one bag of groceries in ten came from the 15,000 red-and-gold supermarkets of the Great Atlantic and Pacific Tea Company, commonly known as A&P.

MANAGERIAL ELITE This expansion and consolidation meant that the wealth was being controlled not by individuals but by corporations. The model of modern business was the large, bureaucratic corporation, in which those who actually managed the company had little to do with the shareholders who owned it. A salaried bureaucracy of executives and plant managers formed a new elite. They learned the techniques of **scientific management** taught at Harvard and other new schools of business through journals, professional societies, and consulting firms. They channeled earnings back into their companies to expand factories, carry on research, and grow in size and profitability. By the end of the decade, half of all industrial income was concentrated in 100 corporations.

Welfare Capitalism

The new "scientific management" also stressed smooth relations between managers and employees. The rash of postwar strikes had left business leaders as suspicious as

The East Coryell Company marketed ethyl alcohol gasoline as an alternative to hydrocarbon-based fuels. In Lincoln, Nebraska, this gas station touted the virtue of "corn alcohol gasoline" using an eye-catching pump with an ear of corn painted on each of its four sides.

ever of labor unions and determined to find ways to limit their influence.

THE AMERICAN PLAN

Some tactics were more strong-armed than scientific. In 1921 the National Association of Manufacturers, the Chamber of Commerce, and other employer groups launched the "American Plan," aimed at opening "closed shops," factories where only union members could work. Employers made workers sign agreements disavowing union membership. Labor organizers called them "yellow-dog contracts" because they reduced workers to the "level of a yellow dog." Companies infiltrated unions with spies, locked union members out of factories if they protested, and boycotted firms that hired union labor.

The gentler side of the American Plan involved a social innovation called "welfare capitalism." Companies such as General Electric and Bethlehem Steel pledged to care for their employees and give them incentives for working hard. They built clean, safe factories, installed cafeterias, hired trained dietitians, formed baseball teams and glee clubs. Several hundred firms encouraged perhaps a million workers to buy company stock. Millions more enrolled in company unions. Called "Kiss-Me Clubs" for their lack of power, they offered what few independent unions could match: health and safety insurance; a grievance procedure; and representation for African Americans, women, and immigrants.

As it turned out, welfare capitalism affected barely 5 percent of the workforce and often gave benefits only to skilled laborers, the hardest to replace. Most workers lost

ground. In the 1920s a family of four could live in "minimum health and decency" on $2,000 a year. The average industrial wage was $1,304. Thus working-class families often needed more than one wage earner just to get by.

By the end of the decade, labor grievances burst into massive strikes. In 1927, in the most famous strike of the decade, 2,500 mill hands in the textile town of Gastonia, North Carolina, walked off their jobs. Even strikebreakers quit. Eventually, authorities broke the strike, foreshadowing a national trend. A year later there were only 629 strikes, a record low for the nation. Union membership shrank from almost 5 million in 1921 to less than 3.5 million in 1929.

The Consumer Culture

During the late nineteenth century the economy had boomed, too, but much of its growth had gone into producer goods: huge steel factories and rail, telephone, and electric networks. By World War I these industrial networks had penetrated enough of the country to create mass markets for consumer goods such as refrigerators, bicycles, and other products for average Americans. As an increasing percentage of the nation's industries turned out consumer goods, prosperity hinged on consumption. If ordinary buyers purchased more goods, production would increase at the same time that costs would decrease. Lower production costs would allow for lower prices, which would lift sales, production, and employment still higher.

This pen-and-ink drawing depicts a cavernous street in New York City awash in advertising. Its title, Picturesque America, is a play on the growing use of signs to sell products. Already by 1909, when the graphic artist Harry Grant Dart drew the piece, advertising and the consumer culture were overtaking the country—in this case, transforming buildings into billboards for hawking everything from foreign-language courses to cigars, furs, and automobiles. "Electric signs," promises one electrified sign, "make night beautiful." The artist did not agree.

YOUTH IN A JAR

Mirror suggests that what you see is important but also that what others see in you is important, too.

Beauty and youth are both important and closely linked.

Older and younger middle-class women, implying wide reach of product. How might working-class women view this ad?

Source: Duke University Archive.

Historians of popular culture find their sources in the materials of everyday life, including advertisements such as this one for Boncilla's facial creams. It appeared in *Beauty* magazine in 1923. In the 1920s, as mass advertising reached new heights, promoters of products such as this "Pack o' Beauty" shifted strategies from simply listing the advantages of their wares to meeting primary demands for health, love, and in this case youth with splashy advertisements in full color. More and more they targeted women. All reflected the new emphasis on gaining personal contentment not through hard work, achievement, or even religion but through consumption. How might modern psychology, then a new social science, have played a role in creating this ad?

Thinking Critically

What other primary demands do advertisers seek to stimulate? Through what products might these demands be satisfied then and now? Why were women a growing target of advertisers in the 1920s?

ROLE OF ADVERTISING Consumption was the key, and increased consumption rested on two innovations: advertising to help people buy and credit to help them pay. Around the turn of the century, advertisers began a critical shift from emphasizing *products* to stressing a consumer's *desires:* health, popularity, social status. Albert Lasker, the owner of Chicago's largest advertising firm, Lord and Thomas, created modern advertising in America. His eye-catching ads were hard-hitting, positive, and often preposterous. To expand the sales of Lucky Strike cigarettes, Lord and Thomas claimed smoking made people slimmer and more courageous. "Luckies" became one of the most popular brands in America. Bogus doctors and dentists lent an air of authority to ad campaigns by endorsing all kinds of products, including toothpaste containing potassium chloride—8 grams of which was lethal.

Advertisers encouraged Americans to borrow against tomorrow to purchase what advertising convinced them they wanted today. Installment buying had once been confined to sewing machines and pianos. In the 1920s it grew into the tenth biggest business in the United States. In 1919 Alfred Sloan created millions of new customers by establishing the General Motors Acceptance Corporation, the nation's first consumer credit organization. By 1929 Americans were buying most of their cars, radios, and furniture on the installment plan. Consumer debt surged to $7 billion, almost twice the federal budget.

✓ REVIEW

What factors produced unprecedented economic growth in the 1920s?

A MASS SOCIETY

IN THE EVENING AFTER A day's work in the fields—perhaps in front of an adobe house built by one of the western sugar-beet companies—Mexican American workers might gather to chat or sing a *corrido* or two. The *corrido* was a traditional Mexican folk ballad whose lyrics chronicled daily life, good and bad. One *corrido,* written during the 1920s, told of a field laborer distressed that his family had rejected old Mexican customs in favor of new American fashions. His wife, he sang, now had "a bob-tailed dress of silk" and, wearing makeup, went about "painted like a *piñata.*" As for his children:

> My kids speak perfect English
> And have no use for our Spanish
> They call me "fader" and don't work
> And are crazy about the Charleston.

It was enough to make him long for Mexico.

For Americans from all backgrounds the New Era was witness to "a vast dissolution of ancient habits," commented columnist Walter Lippmann. Mass marketing and mass distribution led not simply to a higher standard of living but also to a life less regional and diverse. In the place of moral standards set by local communities and churches came "modern"

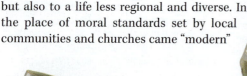

| *The vibrant energy of the New Woman is reflected in the geometric designs of these fashionable slippers, manufactured around 1925, whose jagged shapes suggested the forms of avant-garde Cubist art.*

fashions and attitudes, spread by the new mass media of movies, radio, and magazines. In the place of "ancient habits" came the forces of mass society: independent women, freer love, standardized culture, urban energy and impersonality, and sometimes alienation.

A "New Woman"

In the tumultuous 1890s a "New Woman" appeared, one who was more assertive, athletic, and independent than her Victorian peers. By the 1920s more modern versions of this New Woman were being charged with nothing less than leading what Frederick Lewis Allen called the "revolution in manners and morals." The most flamboyant of them wore close-fitting felt hats and makeup, long-waisted dresses and few undergarments, strings of beads, and unbuckled galoshes (which earned them the nickname "flappers"). Dripping with cocktails, footloose and economically free, the New Woman became a symbol of liberation and sexuality to some, of decadence and decline to others.

World War I served as a social catalyst, continuing the prewar trend of an increase in the female percentage of the workforce and changing many attitudes. Before the war, women were arrested for smoking cigarettes openly, using profanity, and driving automobiles without men beside them. With women bagging explosives, running locomotives, and drilling with rifles during the war, the old taboos often seemed silly.

MARGARET SANGER

Disseminating birth control information by mail had also been a crime before the war and still was after it. But by the armistice there was a birth control clinic in Brooklyn, a National Birth Control League, and later an American Birth Control League led by Margaret Sanger. Sanger's crusade had begun as an attempt to save poor women from the burdens of unwanted pregnancies (see page 598) and, less nobly, to reduce births among those considered "unfit," including many of the immigrants flooding the country. In the 1920s her message found a receptive middle-class audience. Surveys showed that by the 1930s nearly 90 percent of college-educated couples practiced contraception.

Being able to a degree to control the matter of pregnancy, women felt less guilt about enjoying sex and less fear over the consequences. In 1909 Sigmund Freud had come to America to lecture on his theories of coping with the unconscious and overcoming harmful repressions. Some of Freud's ideas, specifically his emphasis on childhood sexuality, shocked Americans, while most of his complex theories sailed blissfully over their heads. As popularized in the 1920s, however, Freudian psychology stamped sexuality as a key to health.

Sexuality became more important in the new model of marriage emerging during the decade. No longer were couples duty-bound to marry for procreation alone and, once married, to keep to separate male and female spheres. As old conventions crumbled and women became more assertive, love replaced duty as the bond holding a couple

April 17, 1929: "A feature at the meeting will be the attendance of Mrs. Margaret Sanger, fresh from [the] raid on her New York clinic. Adhesive tape will seal her lips that they may not preach birth control while in Boston, Mass., but she will be permitted to write on the blackboard." Sanger had been threatened with arrest by Mayor James Curley of Boston, which she put to good use to publicize her appearance. As she stood, her speech was read by a Harvard historian at the meeting, Arthur Schlesinger, Sr.

together. Companionship—spending time with each other and sharing interests (including sex)—became the key to marital bliss. This new "companionate" marriage afforded women greater freedom and equality by breaking down gendered spheres and strengthening ties between husbands and wives. It also gave well-heeled Americans another way to feel superior. Without the money and leisure often needed for companionate marriages, the working class and working poor continued to play traditional married roles.

Such changes in the social climate were real enough, but the life of a flapper girl, as free and independent as a man, hardly mirrored the lives of most American women. Relatively few worked outside of their homes, and pay for those who did never equaled a man's. Over the decade the female labor force grew but only by 2 percent. The paltry gain did little to change the profile of working women. As late as 1930 nearly 60 percent were African American or foreign-born and generally held low-paying jobs in domestic service or the garment industry.

The New Era did spawn new careers for women. The consumer culture capitalized on a preoccupation with appearance and led to the opening of some 40,000 beauty parlors staffed by hairdressers, manicurists, and cosmeticians. Progressive reformers expanded opportunities in education, libraries, and social welfare, all within the bounds of nurturing "women's fields." Women earned a higher percentage of doctoral degrees (from 1 percent in 1910 to 15.4 percent in 1930) and held more college teaching posts than ever (32 percent). But in most areas, professional men resisted the "feminization" of the workforce. The number of female doctors dropped by half as medical schools imposed restrictive quotas and hospitals rejected female interns.

In 1924 two women—Nellie Ross in Wyoming and Miriam ("Ma") Ferguson in Texas—were elected governors, the first female chief executives. But most women continued to be marginalized in party politics, though still involved in educational and welfare programs. Operating outside male-dominated political parties, women activists succeeded in winning passage of the Sheppard-Towner Federal Maternity and Infancy Act in 1921 to fight infant mortality with rural prenatal and baby-care centers. It was the first federal welfare statute. Yet by the end of the decade the Sheppard-Towner Act had lapsed.

EQUAL RIGHTS AMENDMENT   In the wake of their greatest success, the hard-won vote for women, feminists splintered. The National Woman Suffrage Association disbanded in 1920. In its place the new League of Women Voters encouraged informed voting with nonpartisan publicity. For the more militant Alice Paul and her allies, that was not enough. Their National Woman's Party pressed for a constitutional Equal Rights Amendment (ERA). Social workers and others familiar with the conditions under which women labored opposed it. Death and injury rates for women were nearly double those for men. To them the ERA meant losing the protection as well as the benefits women derived from mothers' pensions and maternity insurance. Joined by most men and a majority of Congress, they fought the amendment to a standstill.

Mass Media

MOTION PICTURES   In balmy California, where movies could be made year-round, Hollywood helped give the New Woman notoriety as a temptress and trendsetter. When sexy Theda Bara appeared in *The Blue Flame* in 1920, crowds mobbed theaters. And just as Hollywood dictated standards of physical attraction, it became the judge of taste and fashion in countless other ways because motion pictures were a near-universal medium. There was no need for literacy or fluency, no need even for sound, given the power of the images parading across the screen.

Motion pictures, invented in 1889, had first been shown in tiny neighborhood theaters called "nickelodeons." For a nickel, patrons watched a silent screen flicker with moving images as an accompanist played music on a tinny piano. The audience was anything but silent. The theater reverberated with the cracking of Indian nuts, the day's equivalent

THE BEAUTY CONTEST

Early in September 1921 eight young women stood nervously on the board-walk at Atlantic City, New Jersey. All were white, the picture of middle-class whole-someness and eager to be crowned the first "Miss America."

The American beauty contest drew on an old heritage. In colonial times the traditional May Day celebration crowned a Queen of the May as a symbol of fertility. Though physical beauty mattered in the selection, qualities such as civic leadership and popularity also counted.

In 1854 showman P. T. Barnum conceived of a competition among women to judge their beauty. The idea spread quickly. When the promoters of the St. Louis Exposition advertised a beauty contest in 1905, 40,000 women applied.

Even babies were judged for their beauty. "Baby parades" of costumed infants drew huge crowds in the 1890s. When Coney Island held its first baby parade in 1906, 1,200 children showed up, half of whom entered a contest for the "most beautiful baby."

Starting in Louisiana in 1908, citizens concerned about high rates of infant mortality began holding "Better Babies" contests at state fairs and flower shows. Bright-eyed infants and toddlers were judged on the basis of health, strength, and intellectual development, not beauty. Judges measured naked children as if they were livestock. The slightest deviation from what was perceived as "normal" could lead to point deductions. The intent was to advance infant health, but by the 1920s the contests often ended up promoting drives for "race betterment" through "Fitter Family" campaigns that popularized eugenic ideas of Anglo-Saxon superiority.

Promoters of the Miss America pageant were more concerned with money. They conceived of their pageant as a way of extending the summer vacation season past September 1 and so line the pockets of local merchants and hotel operators with more money. The contest measured physical beauty alone, with the high point being a bathing suit competition. (Only later did the pageant add a talent show.) After the turn of the century, bathing suits had grown alarmingly scant, exposing arms and discarding billowy bloomers in favor of revealing tights.

Aware of such perils, pageant officials depicted entrants as wholesome, conventional, and unsophisticated. The contestants were not permitted to wear short bobbed hair or makeup—both symbols of the racy modern woman.

As the contestants waited anxiously, officials announced the winner—Margaret Gorman of Washington, D.C. She radiated wholesomeness and athletic vigor. "She represents the type of womanhood America needs," observed Samuel Gompers of the American Federation of Labor, "—strong, red-blooded, able to shoulder the responsibilities of homemaking and motherhood."

Miss America and other beauty contests evolved as commercialism and advertising took hold and Gilded Age codes of decorum declined. But the lengths to which pageant organizers went to gain respect demonstrated the strength of the older social ideals. The Miss America pageant in particular came to symbolize the middle-class ideal of womanhood. Physical beauty remained the chief component, marriage and motherhood the chief ends. The message was graphic: men competed in sports gear, business attire, and professional garb; women, in bathing suits.

Margaret Gorman of Washington, D.C., crowned in 1921 as the first Miss America.

Thinking Critically

What roles might race, class, and ethnicity have played in defining beauty and fitness in contests for Miss America and Better Babies?

---

of popcorn, while young cowboys shot off their Kilgore repeating cap pistols during dramatic scenes. Often children read the subtitles aloud to their immigrant parents, translating into Italian, Yiddish, and German.

After the first feature-length film, *The Great Train Robbery* (1903), productions became rich in spectacle, attracted middle-class audiences, and turned into America's favorite form of entertainment. By 1926 more than 20,000 movie houses offered customers lavish theaters with overstuffed

seats, live music, and a celluloid dream world—all for 50 cents or less. At the end of the decade, these picture palaces were drawing over 100 million people a week, roughly the equivalent of the national population.

In the spring of 1920 Frank Conrad of the Westinghouse Company in East Pittsburgh rigged up a research station in his barn and started transmitting phonograph music and baseball scores to local wireless operators. Local stores began selling equipment to "be used by those who

The Roxy, the largest theater in the world when it opened in 1926, in all its palatial glory. Such lavish movie houses sought to attract more prosperous middle-class audiences with splendor reminiscent of European cathedrals. On opening night, pealing chimes heralded the entrance of a man dressed as a monk who pointed to the balcony and declaimed, "Let there be light!" Blazing spotlights then set the orchestra aglow. "Does God live here?" asked a little girl in a New Yorker cartoon.

listen to Dr. Conrad's programs." Six months later Westinghouse Broadcast Company opened the first licensed radio station in history, KDKA, to stimulate sales of its supplies. By 1922 the number of licensed stations had jumped to 430. By the end of the decade nearly one home in three had a radio ("furniture that talks," comedian Fred Allen called it).

At first radio was seen as a civilizing force. "The air is your theater, your college, your newspaper, your library," exalted one ad in 1924. But with the growing number of sets came commercial broadcasting, catering to common tastes. By 1931 advertisers were paying $10,000 an hour for a national hookup, and the most popular show on radio was *Amos 'n' Andy,* a comedy about African Americans created by two white vaudevillians in 1926. It borrowed its style from black comedians Aubrey Lyles and Flournoy Miller, who occasionally wrote dialogue for the show. A slice of black culture, usually stereotyped, entered mainstream American life.

At night families gathered around the radio instead of the hearth, perhaps listening to a concert or a comedian rather than going out. Ticket sales at vaudeville theaters collapsed as a vast national audience emerged, linked by nothing but airwaves.

NEWSPAPER CHAINS

Print journalism also broadened its reach during the 1920s. In 1923 Yale classmates Henry R. Luce and Briton Hadden rewrote news stories in a snappy style, mixed them with photographs, and created the country's first national weekly, *Time* magazine. By 1927, 55 giant newspaper chains distributed 230 newspapers with a combined circulation of 13 million. Though they controlled less than 10 percent of all papers, the chains pioneered modern mass news techniques. Editors relied on central offices and syndicates to prepare editorials, sports, gossip, and Sunday features for a national readership.

The Cult of Celebrity

In a world in which Americans were rapidly being reduced to anonymous parts of mass, industrialized society, media offered them a chance to identify with the achievements of individuals by creating a world of celebrities and heroes. Sports figures, business executives, and movie stars found their exploits splashed across the front pages of newspapers and magazines and followed on radio by millions hungry for excitement and eager to project their own dreams onto others.

CHARLES LINDBERGH

No hero attracted more attention than a shy, reed-thin 25-year-old named Charles Lindbergh. Early on the morning of May 20, 1927, "Lucky Lindy" streaked into the skies above Long Island aboard a silver-winged monoplane called the *Spirit of St. Louis,* headed east, and 33 hours 30 minutes later, landed just outside Paris. Lindbergh was the first flier to cross the Atlantic alone; eight others had died trying. An ecstatic mob swamped him and nearly tore his plane to pieces in search of souvenirs.

Lindbergh, dubbed by reporters the "Lone Eagle," returned with his plane aboard the warship USS *Memphis.* In New York City alone, he was greeted by nearly 4 million cheering fans. Lindbergh had "fired the imagination of mankind," observed one newspaper. Never had one person mastered a machine so completely or conquered nature so courageously. To Americans ambivalent over mass society and worried about being overwhelmed by technology and bureaucracy, Lindbergh's accomplishment signaled salvation. Perhaps they could control the New Era without losing their cherished individualism.

"Ain't We Got Fun?"

SPECTATOR SPORTS

"Ev'ry morning, ev'ry evening, ain't we got fun?" ran the 1921 hit song. As the average hours on the job each week decreased from 47.2 in 1920 to 42 by 1930, spending on amusement and recreation tripled. Spectator sports came of age. In 1921 some 60,000 fans paid $1.8 million to see Jack Dempsey, the "Manassas Mauler," knock out French champion Georges Carpentier. Millions more listened as radio took them ringside for the first time in sports history. Universities constructed huge stadiums for football—a 60,000-seater at Berkeley, a 64,000-seater at Ohio State. By the end of the decade, college football games were outdrawing major league baseball.

Baseball remained the national pastime but became a bigger business. An ugly World Series scandal in 1919 led owners to appoint Judge Kenesaw Mountain Landis as "czar" of the sport to avoid the possibility of more stringent government regulation. His iron-fisted rule reformed the game enough to ward off federal intervention. In 1920 the son of immigrants revolutionized it. George Herman "Babe" Ruth hit 54 home runs and made the New York Yankees the first club to attract a million fans in one season. A heroic producer in an era of consumption, Ruth was also baseball's bad boy: he smoked, drank, cursed, and chased every skirt in sight. Under the guidance of the first modern sports agent, Christy Walsh, Ruth became the highest-paid player in the game and made a fortune endorsing everything from clothing to candy bars.

At parties old diversions—charades, card tricks, recitations—faded in popularity as dancing took over. The ungainly camel walk, the sultry tango, and in 1924 the frantic Charleston were the urban standards. A cultural counterweight to what some regarded as such unseemingly displays, square dancing enjoyed a revival with music provided by Detroit's WBZ, courtesy of Henry Ford.

JAZZ

The new energy could not be contained. From the turn-of-the-century brothels and gaming houses of New Orleans, Memphis, and St. Louis came a rhythmic, compelling music that swept into nightclubs and over the airwaves: jazz. Jazz was a remarkably complex blend of several older African American musical traditions, combining the soulfulness of the blues with the brighter syncopated rhythms of ragtime

| Charles Lindbergh

music. The distinctive style of jazz bands came from a marvelous improvising as the musicians embellished melodies and played off one another. The style spread when the all-white "Original Dixieland Jazz Band" recorded a few numbers for the phonograph. The music business, dominated by white publishers, recording studios, and radio stations, seized on the sound. The music became a sensation in New York in 1917 and spread across the country. Black New Orleans stalwarts like Joe "King" Oliver's Creole Jazz Band began touring. In 1924 Paul Whiteman inaugurated respectable "white" jazz in a concert at Carnegie Hall. When self-appointed guardians of good taste denounced such music as "intellectual and spiritual debauchery," Whiteman disagreed: "Jazz is the folk music of the machine age."

The Art of Alienation

EXPATRIATES

Before World War I a generation of young writers had begun to rebel against Victorian purity. The savagery of the war drove many of them even farther from any faith in reason or progress. Instead, they embraced a "nihilism" that denied all meaning in life. When the war ended, they turned their resentment against American life, especially its small towns and big businesses, its conformity, technology, and materialism. Some led unconventional lives in New York City's Greenwich Village. Others, called **expatriates,** left the country for the artistic freedom of London and Paris. Their alienation helped produce a literary outpouring unmatched in American history.

On the eve of World War I the poet Ezra Pound had predicted an "American *Risorgimento*" that would "make the Italian Renaissance look like a tempest in a teapot." From Europe the expatriate Pound began to make it happen. Abandoning rhyme and meter in his poetry, he decried the "botched civilization" that had produced the war. Another voluntary exile, T. S. Eliot, bemoaned the emptiness of modern life in his epic poem *The Waste Land* (1922). Ernest Hemingway captured the disillusionment of the age in *The Sun Also Rises* (1926) and *A Farewell to Arms* (1929), novels in which resolution came as it had in war—by death.

At home Minnesota-born Sinclair Lewis, the first American to win a Nobel Prize in literature, sketched a scathing vision of midwestern small-town life in *Main Street* (1920). The book described "savorless people . . . saying mechanical things about the excellence of Ford automobiles, and viewing themselves as the greatest race in the world." His next novel, *Babbitt* (1922), dissected small-town businessman George Follansbee Babbitt, a peppy realtor from the fictional city of Zenith. Faintly absurd and supremely dull, Babbitt was the epitome of average.

| Blues, *painted in 1929 by African American artist Archibald Motley Jr., evokes the improvised rhythms of the Jazz Age. New Orleans–born Motley was one of a group of black genre painters in the 1920s who became part of the Harlem Renaissance.*

The novels of another Minnesotan, F. Scott Fitzgerald, glorified youth and romantic individualism but found redemption nowhere. Fitzgerald's heroes, like Amory Blaine in *This Side of Paradise* (1920), spoke for a generation "grown up to find all Gods dead, all wars fought, all faiths in man shaken." Like most writers of the decade, Fitzgerald saw life largely as a personal affair—opulent, self-absorbing, and ultimately tragic.

A "New Negro"

MARCUS GARVEY

As World War I seared white intellectuals, so, too, did it galvanize black Americans. Wartime labor shortages had spurred a migration of over a million African Americans out of the rural South into northern industrial cities. But postwar unemployment and racial violence quickly dashed black hopes for equality. Common folk in these urban enclaves found an outlet for their alienation in a charismatic black nationalist from Jamaica named Marcus Garvey.

Garvey brought his organization, the Universal Negro Improvement Association (UNIA), to America in 1916 in hopes of restoring black pride by returning African Americans to Africa and Africa to Africans. Whereas Booker T. Washington had counseled accommodation of segregated America and W. E. B. Du Bois and the NAACP had pursued racial integration, Garvey urged separation of the races. Yet he stood not entirely apart from these other activists. Garvey relied, like Washington, on a message of self-help and demanded, like Du Bois, an end to colonialism.

"Up you mighty race," Garvey told his followers, "you can accomplish what you will." When Garvey spoke at the first national UNIA convention in 1920, over 25,000 supporters jammed Madison Square Garden in New York City to listen. Even his harshest critics admitted there were at least half a million UNIA members in more than 30 branches of his organization. It was the first mass movement of African Americans in history. But in 1925 Garvey was convicted of mail fraud and sentenced to prison for having oversold stock in his Black Star Line, the steamship company founded to return African Americans to Africa. His dream shattered, but not the image of a proud black man standing up against racial bigotry and intolerance. The memory of Garvey and his movement nurtured budding black nationalism for decades to come.

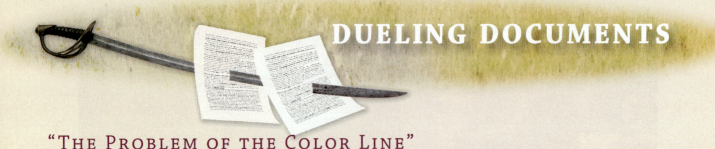

DUELING DOCUMENTS

"THE PROBLEM OF THE COLOR LINE"

"The problem of the twentieth century," wrote African American scholar and activist W. E. B. Du Bois (see page 605), "is the problem of the color-line." For Jamaican-born Marcus Garvey, the charismatic leader of a "Back to Africa" movement, that color-line was so unyielding that the only solution for blacks was returning to Africa (Document 1). For Du Bois, the answer lay in eradicating the line by creating a color-blind society (Document 2).

DOCUMENT 1   "Go Back to Africa": Garvey

The thoughtful and industrious of our race want to go back to Africa, because we realize it will be our only hope of permanent existence. We cannot all go in a day or year, ten or twenty years. It will take time under the rule of modern economics, to entirely or largely depopulate a country of a people, who have been its residents for centuries, but we feel that, with proper help for fifty years, the problem can be solved. We do not want all the Negroes in Africa. Some are no good here, and naturally will be no good there. The no-good Negro will naturally die in fifty years. The Negro who is wrangling about and fighting for social equality will naturally pass away in fifty years, and yield his place to the progressive Negro who wants a society and country of his own. . . .

Africa is the legitimate, moral and righteous home of all Negroes, and now, that the time is coming for all to assemble under their own vine and fig tree, we feel it our duty to arouse every Negro to a consciousness of himself.

White and black will learn to respect each other when they cease to be active competitors in the same countries for the same things in politics and society. Let them have countries of their own, wherein they aspire and climb without rancor. The races can be friendly and helpful to each other, but the laws of nature separate us to the extent of each and every one developing by itself.

We want an atmosphere all our own. We would like to govern and rule ourselves and not be encumbered and restrained. We feel now just as the white race would feel if they were governed and ruled by the Chinese. If we live in our own districts, let us rule and govern those districts. If we have a majority in our communities, let us run those communities. We form a majority in Africa and we should naturally govern ourselves there. No man can govern another's house as well as himself. Let us have fair play. This is the appeal we make to white America.

Source: Marcus Garvey, Speech Delivered at Madison Square Garden, New York City (March 16, 1924), reprinted in Amy Garvey, *Philosophy and Opinions of Marcus Garvey: African for the Africans* (New York, 2nd ed., 1967), pp. 118–123.

DOCUMENT 2   "We Must Oppose All Segregation": Du Bois

My grandfather left a passage in his diary expressing his indignation at receiving an invitation to a "Negro" picnic. Alexander Du Bois, born in the Bahamas, son of Dr. James Du Bois of the well-known Du Bois family of Poughkeepsie, N.Y., had been trained as a gentleman in the Cheshire School of Connecticut, and the implications of a Negro picnic were anathema to his fastidious soul. It meant close association with poverty, ignorance and suppressed and disadvantaged people, dirty and with bad manners.

This was in 1856. Seventy years later, Marcus Garvey discovered that a black skin was in itself a sort of patent to nobility, and that Negroes ought to be proud of themselves and their ancestors, for the same or analogous reasons that made white folk feel superior.

Thus, within the space of three-fourths of a century, the pendulum has swung between race pride and race suicide, between attempts to build up a racial ethos and attempts to escape from ourselves. In the years between emancipation and 1900, the theory of escape was dominant. We were, by birth, law, and training, American citizens. We were going to escape into the mass of Americans in the same way that the Irish and Scandinavians and even the Italians

were beginning to disappear. The process was going to be slower on account of the badge of color; but then, after all, it was not so much the matter of physical assimilation as of spiritual and psychic amalgamation with the American people.

For this reason, we must oppose all segregation and all racial patriotism; we must salute the American flag and sing "Our Country 'Tis of Thee" with devotion and fervor, and we must fight for our rights with a long and carefully planned campaign; uniting for this purpose with all sympathetic people, colored or white. . . .

A new organized group action along economic lines, guided by intelligence and with the express object of making it possible for Negroes to earn a better living and, therefore, more effectively to support agencies for social uplift, is without the slightest doubt the next step. . . . This organization is going to involve deliberate propaganda for race pride. That is, it is going to start out by convincing American Negroes that there is no reason for their being ashamed of themselves; that their record is one which should make them proud; that their history in African and the world is a history of effort, success and trial, comparable with that of any other people. . . .

There is no other way; let us not be deceived. American Negroes will be beaten into submission and degradation if they merely wait unorganized to find some place voluntarily given them in the new reconstruction of the economic world. They must themselves force their race into the new economic set-up and bring with them the millions of West Indians and Africans by peaceful organization for normative action or else drift into greater poverty, greater crime, greater helplessness until there is no resort but the last red alternative of revolt, revenge and war.

Source: W. E. B. Du Bois, "On Being Ashamed of Oneself: An Essay on Race Pride," *The Crisis* (May 1933), reprinted in David Levering Lewis, ed., *W. E. B. Du Bois: A Reader* (New York, 1995), pp. 76–80.

Thinking Critically

Why in Garvey's view do "thoughtful and industrious" African Americans want to return to Africa? What is Du Bois's solution to the "problem of the color-line"? What is the difference between "racial pride" and "racial patriotism," and why does Du Bois favor one over the other?

As Garvey rose to prominence a renaissance of black literature, painting, and sculpture was brewing in Harlem at the northern end of Manhattan. Since the completion of Manhattan's subway system in 1904, Harlem had grown black after eagerly expected white renters failed to appear. By the end of World War I, Harlem had become the cultural capital of black America.

The first inklings of a renaissance in Harlem came in 1922 when Claude McKay, another Jamaican immigrant, published a book of poems titled *White Shadows*. His most famous poem, "If We Must Die," called for defiance and dignity: "Like men we'll face the murderous, cowardly pack / Pressed to the wall, dying but fighting back!" Often supported by white patrons, or "angels," the young black writers and artists of Harlem found their subjects in the street life of cities, the folkways of the rural South, and the primitivism of preindustrial cultures. They wrote without embarrassment of prostitution and pimping, celebrated sex and alcohol, and reveled in the joys of life and love on the streets of Harlem.

Middle-class reformers such as Du Bois often shuddered at such frank depictions, bent as they were on demonstrating the moral equivalency of the races. McKay's colorful descriptions of "brown lips full and pouted for sweet kissing" and "brown breasts throbbing with love" seemed only to reinforce the stereotypes of unbridled black sexuality and made Du Bois, for one, feel "like taking a bath." Renaissance writers did not care. For them, vitality and instinct were among the hallmarks of the New Negro. So, too, were these hallmarks for painters such as Aaron Douglas. His vibrant murals and illustrations fused geometric designs with African myth and everyday African American life and religion. Poet Langston Hughes reminded his readers of the ancient heritage of African Americans in "The Negro Speaks of Rivers," while Zora Neale Hurston collected folktales, songs, and prayers of black southerners.

Though generally not a racial protest, the Harlem Renaissance drew on the new assertiveness of African Americans as well as on the alienation of white intellectuals. In 1925 Alain Locke, a black professor from Howard University, collected a sampling of African American works in *The New Negro*. The New Negro, Locke wrote, was "not a cultural foundling without his own inheritance" but "a conscious contributor ... collaborator and participant in American civilization." The title of the book reflected not only a distinctively black artistic movement but also a new racial consciousness: militant, uncompromising, and self-consciously proud.

Zora Neale Hurston

✓ REVIEW

How did mass media and mass culture reshape American life in the 1920s?

DEFENDERS OF THE FAITH

AS MASS SOCIETY PUSHED THE country into a future of machines, organization, middle-class living, and urbanized diversity, not everyone approved. Dr. and Mrs. Wilbur Crafts, the authors of *Intoxicating Drinks and Drugs in All Lands and Times*, set forth a litany of sins that tempted young people in this depraved "age of cities." "Foul pictures, corrupt literature, leprous shows, gambling slot machines, saloons, and Sabbath breaking. . . . *We are trying to raise saints in hell.*"

The changing values of the New Era seemed especially threatening to traditionalists like the Crafts. Their deeply held beliefs reflected the rural roots of so many Americans: an ethic that valued neighborliness, small communities, and a sameness of race, religion, and ethnicity. Improvements in mass media—radio, movies, magazines—made it impossible for isolated communities to avoid national trends, even when they disapproved of them. Opponents of the new ways could be found among countryfolk and rural migrants to cities as well as an embattled Protestant elite, who felt as if they were drowning in a sea of modern ways and new immigrants. All were determined to defend their older faiths against the modern age of urban anonymity, moral fluidity, diverse races and ethnicities, and religious pluralism. In the 1920s a full-scale culture war erupted pitting these traditionalists against the forces of modern life.

Nativism and Immigration Restriction

In 1921 two Italian immigrants, who freely admitted to being radical anarchists, presented a dramatic challenge to those older faiths. Nicola Sacco and Bartolomeo Vanzetti were sentenced to death—on the face of it, for a shoe company robbery and murder in South Braintree, Massachusetts, committed a year earlier. The evidence against them was controversial, and critics charged that Sacco and Vanzetti were convicted primarily because they were foreign-born radicals. During the trial the presiding judge had scorned them in private as "anarchist bastards" and later refused all motions for a retrial, in spite of a confession to the robbery by a well-known gang member. For protesters around the world, Sacco and Vanzetti's execution in 1927 was a symbol of American bigotry and prejudice.

By then nativism—a rabid hostility to foreigners—had produced the most restrictive immigration laws in American history. In the aftermath of World War I immigration was running close to 1 million a year, almost as high as prewar levels. Most immigrants came from eastern and southern Europe and from Mexico; most were Catholics and Jews.

| Sacco and Vanzetti

Alarmed white native-born Protestants warned that if the flood continued, Americans might become "a hybrid race of people as worthless and futile as the good-for-nothing mongrels of Central America and Southeastern Europe." Appreciating the potential for higher wages in a shrunken labor pool, the American Federation of Labor supported restriction.

MEXICAN AMERICANS In the Southwest, Mexicans and Mexican Americans became a target of concern. The Spanish had inhabited the region for nearly 400 years, producing a rich blend of European and Indian cultures. By 1900 about 300,000 Mexican Americans lived in the United States. In the following decade Mexicans fleeing poverty and a revolution in 1910 almost doubled the Latino population of Texas and New Mexico. In California it quadrupled. During World War I labor shortages led authorities to relax immigration laws, and in the 1920s American farmers opened a campaign to attract Mexican farmworkers.

Thousands of single young men, known as *solos,* also crossed the border to catch trains for northern industrial cities. By the end of the 1920s thriving communities of Mexicans could be found in the "barrios"—Mexican neighborhoods—of Kansas City, Detroit, and elsewhere. Spanish-speaking newcomers settled into an immigrant life of family and festivals, churchgoing, hard work, and slow adaptation. As with other immigrants, some returned home, but some brought their families. The census of 1930 listed nearly 1.5 million Mexicans living in the United States, not including an untold number who had entered the country illegally.

NATIONAL ORIGINS ACTS Mexicans were just one target of the first National Origins Act, passed in 1921. It capped all immigration at 350,000 and parceled out entry by admitting up to 3 percent of each nationality living in the United States as of 1910. The new system of quotas privileged "races" commonly believed to be superior—"Nordics" (from northern and western Europe)—over those considered inferior—"Alpines" and "Mediterraneans" (from southern and eastern Europe). Asian immigration was virtually banned. In 1924 a second National Origins Act cut the quota to 150,000, reduced the percentage to 2, and pushed the base year back to 1890, before the bulk of southern and eastern Europeans had arrived. To control the flow of illegal aliens, Congress also created the Border Patrol. Its tiny force of 450 agents, stationed along the boundaries with Canada and Mexico, constituted nothing more than a symbolic statement of restrictionist sentiment.

The National Origins Act fixed the pattern of immigration for the next four decades. Immigration from southern and eastern Europe was reduced to a trickle. The free movement of Europeans to America, a migration of classes and nationalities unimpeded for 300 years, came to an end.

The "Noble Experiment"

EIGHTEENTH AMENDMENT For nearly a hundred years reformers had tried—with sporadic success—to reduce the consumption of alcohol. In the heated atmosphere of the 1920s, when fear of immigrants from drinking cultures peaked, their most ambitious campaign climaxed. In January 1920 the Eighteenth Amendment went into effect, sanctioning the prohibition of liquor. Prohibition was not total: private citizens could still drink. They simply could not make, sell, transport, or import any "intoxicating beverage" containing 0.5 percent alcohol or more. The aim was to take the profit out of the liquor trade and reduce alcohol consumption without trampling too heavily on the rights of individuals. By some estimates, the consumption of liquor was cut in half.

CONSEQUENCES OF PROHIBITION The consequences of so vast a social experiment were significant and often unexpected. Prohibition reversed the prewar trend toward beer and wine, because hard liquor brought greater profits to bootleggers. Prohibition also advanced women's rights. Whereas saloons had discriminated against "ladies," either barring any but prostitutes or having them enter by a separate door, speakeasies—taverns operating under cover—welcomed them and inadvertently helped to level the playing field between the sexes. Prohibition lined the pockets and boosted the fame of gangsters, including "Scarface" Al Capone. Like Capone, thousands of poor immigrants looked to illegal **bootlegging** to move them out of the slums. Rival gangs fought over territory, and cities erupted in violence. To

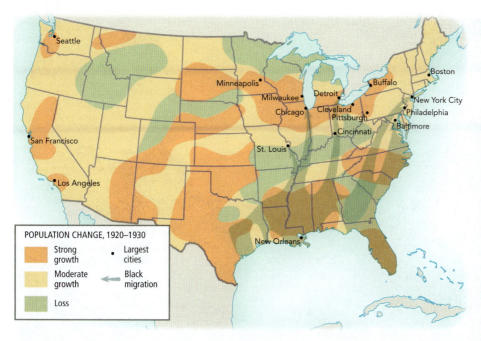

In the 1920s the population of urban America grew by some 15 million people, at the time the greatest 10-year jump in American history. For the first time, more people lived in urban than in rural areas of the United States. Spurred first by the industrial demands of World War I and then by declining farm income, cities grew largely by depopulating rural areas. The biggest gains were in the South and the West, where farmers followed opportunity to cities in climates similar to their own. In the most dramatic manifestation of the overall trend, more than a million African Americans migrated from the rural South to the urban North in hopes of escaping poverty and discrimination. Why did the South and West grow so dramatically?

save lives and profits, gangsters organized crime as if it were a business by dividing their operations and territory and imposing a hierarchy of management.

For all its unhappy consequences, Prohibition enjoyed wide backing. The liquor industry hurt itself with a terrible record of corrupting legislatures and, worse still, corrupting minors, who were one target of its aggressive campaign to recruit new drinkers in the competitive saloon business. The best science of the day taught that alcohol was bad for health; the best social science, that it corroded family life and weakened society. Corporate executives and labor leaders supported Prohibition to promote an efficient and healthy workforce. So did many Catholics, who saw the road to perdition lined with liquor bottles.

Prohibition can also be understood as cultural and class legislation. Support had always run deepest in Protestant churches, especially among the evangelical Baptists and Methodists. And there had always been a strong antiurban and anti-immigrant bias among reformers. As it turned out, the steepest decline in drinking occurred among working-class ethnics. Only the well-to-do had enough money to drink regularly without risking death or blindness, the common effects of cheap, tainted liquor. Traditionalists might celebrate the triumph of the "noble experiment," but modern urbanites either ignored or resented it.

Fundamentalism versus Darwinism

Although Aimee Semple McPherson embraced the fashions and technology of the New Era, many Protestants, especially in rural areas, felt threatened by the secular aspects of modern life. Beginning in the late nineteenth century, scientists and intellectuals spoke openly about the relativity of moral values, questioned the possibility of miracles, and analyzed the Bible as if it were nothing more than a historical document. Darwinism, pragmatism, and other philosophical and scientific theories left traditional religious teachings open to skepticism and scorn. Pastors noted that despite an increase of nearly 13 million in church membership, church attendance was slipping.

Among Protestants, conservatives of various sects worried that their liberal brethren had wandered too far from their faith. As early as the 1870s, liberal Protestants had sought to make Christianity more relevant to contemporary life. Their movement became known as "Modernism," defined by one leader as "the use of scientific, historical and social methods in understanding and applying evangelical Christianity to the needs of living persons."

THE FUNDAMENTALS Conservatives disagreed with this updating of orthodoxy, nowhere more publicly than in a series of pamphlets called *The Fundamentals* published between 1910 and 1915 and subsidized by two wealthy oilmen from Los Angeles, Lyman and Milton Stewart. The 3 million copies distributed nationwide called for a return to what they considered to be the fundamentals of belief, among them the virgin birth and resurrection of Jesus, a literal reading of the Creation account in Genesis, and the divinely inspired authorship of the Bible. Whereas liberal theologians saw the Bible as the product of human beings observing and interpreting godly action within their historical and cultural context, conservatives insisted the Bible was the timeless, revealed word of God. After 1920 a wide variety of conservative Protestants began calling themselves "Fundamentalists."

The Fundamentalist movement grew dramatically in the first two decades of the twentieth century. It fed on fears of Protestant Modernism but also of the Catholic and Jewish immigrants flooding into the country. Fundamentalists

The artist, John Steuart Curry, recalled: "This baptism was on the farm of our neighbor, Will McBride. . . . [Immersion baptisms] were usually held in the creeks, but at this particular time the creeks were dry and the only available water suitable was in the [farm watering] tanks. It was not considered a strange procedure. . . . At that time, the setting, the ceremony, the flying pigeons, the emotional crowd affected me, and years later I put down what my poor abilities permitted me." But like many in the New Era, Curry began to question his devout faith, especially after his brother died while still in college.

maintained effective ministries nationwide but especially among Southern Baptists. Nothing disturbed them more than Darwinian theories of evolution that called into question the divine origins of humankind. In 1925 what began as an in-house fight among Protestants became a national brawl when the Tennessee legislature made it illegal to teach that "man has descended from a lower order of animals." Oklahoma, Florida, Mississippi, and Arkansas passed similar statutes.

SCOPES TRIAL Encouraged by the newly formed American Civil Liberties Union, a number of skeptics in the town of Dayton, Tennessee, decided to test the law by arresting a bespectacled biology teacher named John T. Scopes for teaching evolution. Behind the scenes, Scopes's sponsors were as much preoccupied with boosting their town's commercial fortunes as with the defense of academic freedom.

When the Scopes trial opened in July, millions listened over the radio to the first court case ever broadcast. Clarence Darrow, the renowned defense lawyer from Chicago and a professed agnostic, acted as co-counsel for Scopes. Serving as a co-prosecutor was William Jennings Bryan, the three-time presidential candidate who had recently joined the antievolution crusade. It was urban Darrow against rural Bryan in what Bryan described as a "duel to the death" between Christianity and evolution.

As Bryan saw it, nonbelievers as well as believers had a stake in the trial's outcome, at least if they lived in small-town America. The Industrial Revolution, he argued, had brought unprecedented organization to society and had concentrated power in big business and big government. The result was the erosion of community control and personal autonomy. Thus, for Bryan, the teaching of evolution became another battlefield in the struggle between localities and centralized authority, whether in business or government or even science, that was far removed from ordinary citizens.

The presiding judge ruled that scientists could not be used to defend evolution. He considered their testimony "hearsay" because they had not been present at the Creation. The defense virtually collapsed until Darrow called Bryan to the stand as an "expert on the Bible." Under withering examination Bryan admitted, to the horror of his followers, that the Earth might not have been made "in six days of 24-hours." Even so, the Dayton jury took only eight minutes to find Scopes guilty of violating the law and fine him $100. Scopes never paid the fine after a later court ruling overturned the verdict on a technicality.

By then the excesses of the Scopes trial had transformed it into more of a national joke than a confrontation between darkness and light. Yet the debate over evolution raised a larger issue that continues to reverberate. As scientific, religious, and cultural standards clash, how much should religious beliefs and local standards influence public education?

In the wake of the Scopes trial, the question was resolved in favor of secular over religious instruction, at least in public

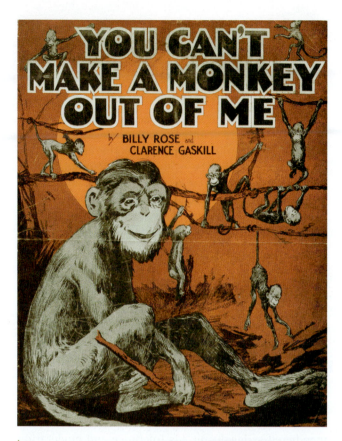

The antievolution campaign wove its way into popular culture, as this sheet music for the lampooning 1925 song "You Can't Make a Monkey Out of Me" attests. Along with music, the Scopes trial brought radio and newspaper coverage that marked a new age of media-driven ballyhoo in politics and advertising.

schools. Before the trial, public education had always contained explicitly religious—indeed, Protestant—components. Now it became increasingly nonreligious. Fundamentalism collapsed into the single image of the Bible-thumping southern redneck clinging to outmoded beliefs. The faith of these true believers never wavered, however. They spent the next two decades spreading their word over the radio and through Bible study and other parachurch groups outside of traditional denominations, biding their time and growing in numbers.

KKK

On Thanksgiving Day 1915, just outside Atlanta, 16 men trudged up a rocky trail to the crest of Stone Mountain. There, as night fell, they set ablaze a large wooden cross and swore allegiance to the Invisible Empire, Knights of the Ku Klux Klan. The KKK was reborn.

NEW KLAN   The modern Klan, a throwback to the hooded order of Reconstruction days (page 456), reflected the insecurities of the New Era. Klansmen worried about the changes and conflicts in American society, which they attributed to the rising tide of new immigrants, "uppity women," and African Americans who refused to "recognize their place." Whereas any white man could join the old Klan, the new one admitted only "native born, white, gentile [Protestant] Americans." And the reborn Klan was not confined to the rural South, like the hooded nightriders of Reconstruction. In Texas, Klansmen fed off hatred of Mexicans; in California, of Japanese; in New York, of Jews and other immigrants. By the 1920s the capital of the Klan was Indianapolis, Indiana. More than half of its leadership

RUNNING THE NEGRO OUT OF TULSA
JUNE. TH.1.1921

As the Ku Klux Klan grew in influence after World War I, race riots erupted in over 25 cities beginning in 1919, including Chicago; Longview, Texas; Knoxville, Tennessee; and Omaha, Nebraska. More than 70 African Americans were lynched in the first year after the end of the war, and 11 were burned alive. Many blacks fought back, their experience in World War I having made them determined to resist repression. In June 1921 rioting in Tulsa left 21 African Americans as well as 11 whites dead. As the billowing smoke in this photograph indicates, white mobs burned down entire neighborhoods belonging to the black community. The National Guard was called out to reestablish order.

and over a third of its members came from cities of more than 100,000 people.

The new Klan drew on the culture of small-town America and responded to some of its anxieties about lost personal independence and waning community control. It was patriotic, gave to local charities, and boasted the kind of outfits and rituals adopted by many fraternal lodges. Klansmen (and Klanswomen) wore white hoods and satin robes. A typical gathering brought the whole family to a barbecue with fireworks and hymn singing, capped by the burning of a giant cross. Members came mostly from the middle and working classes: small businesspeople, clerical workers, independent professionals, farmers, and laborers with few skills. The Klan offered them status, security, and the promise of restoring an older America where white supremacy, chastity, and virtuous Protestantism reigned. When boycotts and whispering campaigns failed to cleanse communities of Jews, Mexicans, Japanese, "uppity women," or others who offended their social code, the Klan resorted to floggings, kidnappings, acid mutilations, and murder.

Using modern methods of promotion, the Klan enrolled perhaps 3 million dues-paying members by the early 1920s. Moving into politics, Klan candidates won control of legislatures in Indiana, Texas, Oklahoma, and Oregon. The organization was instrumental in electing six governors, three senators, and thousands of local officials. In the end, like Aimee Semple McPherson, the Klan was undone by the personal excesses of its leaders that shattered its claim to righteous virtue. In November 1925, amid charges of financial corruption, Grand Dragon David Stephenson of the Indiana Klan and the most powerful leader in the Midwest was sentenced to life imprisonment for rape and second-degree murder. The KKK never fully recovered.

✔ REVIEW

Along what fronts did traditionalists fight the culture war of the 1920s, and with what weapons?

Republicans Ascendant

"THE CHANGE IS AMAZING," WROTE a Washington reporter shortly after the inauguration of Warren G. Harding on March 4, 1921. Sentries disappeared from the gates of the White House, tourists again walked the halls, and reporters freely questioned the president. The reign of "normalcy," as Harding called it, had begun. "By 'normalcy,'" he explained, "...I mean normal procedure, the natural way, without excess."

The Politics of "Normalcy"

"Normalcy" turned out to be anything but normality. After eight years of Democratic rule, Republicans

controlled the White House from 1921 to 1933 and both houses of Congress from 1918 to 1930. Fifteen years of bold reform gave way to eight years of cautious probusiness governing. A strengthened executive fell into weak hands. The cabinet and the Congress set the course of the nation.

WARREN G. HARDING

Harding and his successor, Calvin Coolidge, were content with delegating power. Harding appointed to the cabinet some men of quality, what he called the "best minds": jurist Charles Evans Hughes as secretary of state, farm leader Henry C. Wallace as secretary of agriculture, and Herbert Hoover, savior of Belgian war refugees and former head of the Food Administration, as secretary of commerce. He also made, as one critic put it, some "unspeakably bad appointments": his old crony Harry Daugherty as attorney general and New Mexico senator Albert Fall as interior secretary. Daugherty sold influence for cash and resigned in 1923. Only a divided jury saved him from jail. In 1929 Albert Fall became the first cabinet member to be convicted of a felony. In 1922 he had accepted bribes of more than $400,000 for secretly leasing naval oil reserves at Elk Hills, California, and Teapot Dome, Wyoming, to private oil companies.

Harding died suddenly in August 1923, before most of the scandals came to light. Though he would be remembered as lackluster, his tolerance and moderation had a calming influence on the strife-ridden nation. Slowly he had even begun to lead. In 1921 he created a new Bureau of the Budget, which brought modern accounting techniques to the management of federal revenues. Toward the end of his administration he cleared an early scandal from the Veterans' Bureau and set an agenda for Congress that included expanding the merchant marine.

CALVIN COOLIDGE

To his credit Calvin Coolidge handled Harding's unfavorable legacy with skill and dispatch. He created a special investigatory commission, prosecuted the wrongdoers, and restored public confidence. Decisiveness, when he chose to exercise it, was one of Coolidge's hallmarks. He believed in small-town democracy and minimalist government. "One of the most important accomplishments of my administration has been minding my own business," he boasted. Above all Coolidge worshiped wealth. "Civilization and profits," he once said, "go hand in hand."

Coolidge had been in office barely a year when voters returned him to the White House by a margin of nearly 2 to 1 in the election in 1924. It was another sign that Americans had wearied of reform and delighted in surging prosperity. Whether the business-dominated policies served the economy or the nation well in the long term is open to question.

| Warren G. Harding

The Policies of Mellon and Hoover

Coolidge retained most of Harding's cabinet, including his powerful treasury secretary, Andrew Mellon. The former president of aluminum giant Alcoa, Mellon believed that prosperity "trickled down" from rich to poor through investment, which would raise production, employment, and wages. For more than a decade Mellon devoted himself to encouraging investment by reducing taxes on high incomes and corporations. By the time he was through, Congress had nearly halved taxes.

ASSOCIATIONALISM Unlike Mellon, Commerce Secretary Herbert Hoover (another Harding holdover) was not a traditional Republican. Hoover promoted a progressive brand of capitalism called "associationalism." It involved cooperation between business and government through trade associations, groups of private companies organized industry by industry. Approximately 2,000 trade associations had come into being by 1929, many of them nurtured in the heyday of business-government cooperation during World War I. The role of government, as Hoover saw it, was to promote cooperation among businesses, to advise them on how best to act in the public interest, and to ensure that everyone obeyed the rules. Through associationalism, Hoover married the individualism of the past with what progressives had seen as the efficiency, organization, and cooperation of the future. As such, he represented the best of the New Era.

Both Hoover and Mellon ended up placing government in service of business. Mellon's tax policies helped concentrate wealth in the hands of fewer individuals and corporations, while Hoover's associationalism, for all its faith in the ability of businesses to act for public good, helped them consolidate their power at the expense of the public. By the end of the decade, 200 giant corporations controlled almost half the corporate wealth and nearly a fifth of national wealth. In keeping with this government-sponsored trend, the Antitrust Division of the Justice Department offered few objections and brought few antitrust suits, while the Supreme Court affirmed the constitutionality of trade

Andrew Mellon, secretary of the Treasury and the millionaire head of an aluminum monopoly, is flanked by Grace and Calvin Coolidge on the lawn of the White House. A disciple of business, President Coolidge believed that what was of "real importance to wage-earners was not how they might conduct a quarrel with their employers but how the business of the country might be so organized as to insure steady employment at a fair rate of pay. If that were done there would be no occasion for a quarrel, and if it were not done a quarrel would do no good."

associations. And for all the talk of limiting government, its role in the economy grew. So did its size, by more than 40,000 employees between 1921 and 1930. Building on their wartime partnership, government and business dropped all pretense of a laissez-faire economy. "Never before, here or elsewhere, has a government been so completely fused with business," noted the *Wall Street Journal*.

Problems and Some Solutions at Home and Abroad

Some economic groups remained outside the magic circle of Republican prosperity. Ironically, they included those people who made up the biggest business in America: farmers.

In 1920 farming still had an investment value greater than manufacturing, all utilities, and all railroads combined. A third of the population relied on farming for a living. Yet the farmers' portion of the national income shrank by almost half during the 1920s. The government withdrew wartime price supports for wheat and ended its practice of feeding refugees with American surpluses. As European farms began producing again, the demand for American exports dropped. New dietary habits meant that average Americans of 1920 ate 75 fewer pounds of food annually than they had 10 years earlier. New synthetic fibers drove down demand for natural wool and cotton fibers.

In 1921 a group of southern and western senators organized the "farm bloc" in Congress to coordinate relief for farmers. Over the next two years they succeeded in bringing stockyards, packers, and grain exchanges under federal

supervision. Other legislation exempted farm cooperatives from antitrust actions and created a dozen banks for low-interest farm loans. But regulation and credit were not enough, and over the decade the purchasing power of farmers continued to slide. Over the decade farm foreclosures mounted, eventually exceeding even those during the Great Depression.

For the five years that Coolidge ran a "businessman's government," workers reaped few gains in wages, purchasing power, and bargaining rights. Although welfare capitalism promised workers profit-sharing and other benefits, only a handful of companies put it into practice. Those that did often used it to weaken independent unions. As dangerous imbalances in the economy developed, Coolidge ignored them.

 **THE GREAT FLOOD OF 1927** One problem no one could ignore: the great Mississippi flood of 1927. After years of deforestation and months of heavy rain, the Mississippi River burst through its levees, rampaging across an area roughly the size of New England from southern Missouri to Louisiana. Floodwaters reached 100 feet in some places and did not recede for three months.

A network of private agencies was quickly knit together and placed under the control of Secretary of Commerce Herbert Hoover. An army of local citizens, many of them black and some conscripted at gunpoint, erected a series of refugee camps to cope with the 700,000 people displaced by the flood, but relief efforts were hardly equal to the task. Nearly 250 people died, and 130,000 homes were destroyed. Property damage ran to $350 million ($5 billion in today's

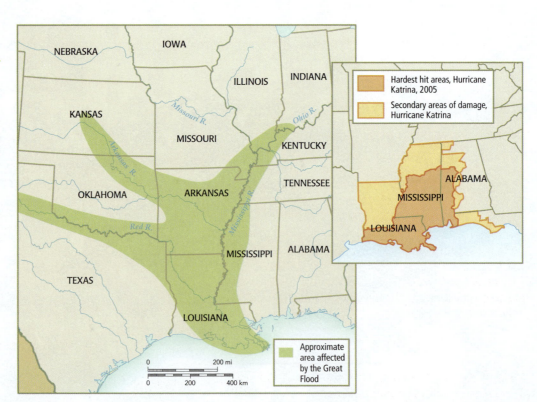

THE GREAT FLOOD OF 1927

Hurricane Katrina scarred the Gulf Coast at the start of the twenty-first century, but the Great Flood of 1927 actually stretched across more states. **How do regional natural disasters affect federal policy?**

Hardest hit areas, Hurricane Katrina, 2005

Secondary areas of damage, Hurricane Katrina

Approximate area affected by the Great Flood

dollars). Before the end of 1928 half the African American population of the Mississippi delta's Black Belt had fled the region. For the rest of the decade commerce throughout the central United States suffered. Still, federal legislation had been passed—for the first time—giving the government responsibility for controlling such disasters along the Mississippi.

If Americans paid little attention to many of the problems at home, most completely disregarded economic unrest abroad. At the end of World War I, Europe's victors had forced Germany to take on $33 billion in war costs or reparations, partly to repay their own war debts to the United States. When Germany defaulted in 1923, French forces occupied the Ruhr valley, the center of German industry. Germany struck back by printing more money to cope with the crushing burden of debt. Runaway inflation soon wiped out the savings of the German middle class, shook confidence in the new democratic Weimar Republic, and eventually threatened the economic structure of all Europe.

THE DAWES PLAN In 1924 American business leader Charles G. Dawes took a stab at solving the problem by persuading victorious Europeans to scale down reparations. In return the United States promised to help stabilize the German economy. Encouraged by the State Department, American bankers made large loans to Germany, with which the Germans paid their reparations. The European victors then used those funds to repay *their* war debts to the United States. It amounted to taking money out of one American vault and depositing it in another. In 1926 the United States also reduced European war debts. Canceling them altogether would have made more sense, but few Americans were so forgiving.

KELLOGG-BRIAND PACT Two grand, if finally futile, gestures reflected the twin desires for peace and prudent budgeting in a world chastened by war, arms races, and military spending. In 1921, in a conference held in Washington, the sea powers of the world agreed to freeze battleship construction for 10 years and to set ratios on the tonnage of each navy. The Five-Power Agreement was the first disarmament treaty in modern history. A more extravagant gesture came in 1928, when the major nations of the world (except the Soviet Union) signed the Kellogg-Briand Pact outlawing war. "Peace is proclaimed," announced Secretary of State Frank Kellogg as he signed the document with a foot-long pen of gold.

What seemed so bold on paper proved timid in practice. The French and Japanese resented the lower limits set on their battleships under the Five-Power Agreement and touched off a new arms race by building smaller warships such as submarines, cruisers, and destroyers. And with no means of enforcement, the Kellogg-Briand Pact remained a hollow proclamation.

The Election of 1928

On August 2, 1927, in a small classroom in Rapid City, South Dakota, Calvin Coolidge handed a terse, typewritten message to reporters: "I do not choose to run for President in nineteen twenty-eight." Republicans honored the request and nominated Herbert Hoover. Hoover was not a politician but an administrator who had never once campaigned for public office. It did not matter. Republican prosperity made it difficult for any Democrat to win. Hoover, perhaps the most admired public official in America, made it impossible.

The Democratic Party continued to fracture between its rural supporters in the South and West and ethnic laborers in the urban Northeast. The two factions had clashed during the 1924 convention, scuttling the presidential candidacy of New York governor Al Smith. By 1928 the shift in population toward cities had given an edge to the party's urban wing. Al Smith won the nomination on the first ballot, even though his handicaps were evident. When the New York City–bred Smith spoke "poysonally" on the "rha-dio," his accent made voters across America wince. Though he pledged to enforce Prohibition, he campaigned against it and even took an occasional drink (which produced the false rumor that he was a hopeless alcoholic). Most damaging of all, Smith was Catholic at a time when anti-Catholicism remained strong in many areas of the country.

In the election of 1928 nearly 60 percent of the eligible voters turned out to give all but eight states to Hoover. The solidly Democratic South cracked for the first time. Still, the stirrings of a major political realignment lay buried in the returns. The 12 largest cities in the country had gone to the Republicans in 1924; in 1928 the Democrats won them.

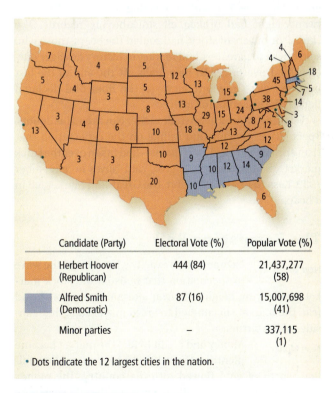

Candidate (Party)	Electoral Vote (%)	Popular Vote (%)
Herbert Hoover (Republican)	444 (84)	21,437,277 (58)
Alfred Smith (Democratic)	87 (16)	15,007,698 (41)
Minor parties	–	337,115 (1)

• Dots indicate the 12 largest cities in the nation.

ELECTION OF 1928

Western farmers, ignored by Republicans for a decade, also voted for Smith. The Democrats were becoming the party of the cities, of immigrants, and of the long-ignored. Around this core, they would build the most powerful vote-getting coalition of the twentieth century.

As important, a new kind of electorate was emerging. No longer were voters part of a vast partisan army whose loyalties were tied to the party year in and year out by barbecues, rallies, and torchlight parades. The reforms of the Progressive Era had restricted the power of political machines and the discipline they could exert over voters. The culture of consumption that shaped American life in the 1920s also shaped politics. Increasingly, parties courted voters with newspaper advertisements and radio "spots." In 1929 the Democrats created the first public relations department in American politics. Paradoxically, the twentieth century would witness a deterioration of party loyalty and election voting as the growing reliance on the media to communicate with "consumer/voters" weakened traditional party networks.

 REVIEW
What public policies did Presidents Harding and Coolidge pursue during the 1920s?

THE GREAT BULL MARKET

STROLLING ACROSS THE FELT-PADDED FLOOR of the New York Stock Exchange, Superintendent William Crawford greeted the New Year with swaggering confidence. Nineteen twenty-eight had broken all stock-buying records. The "bulls," or buyers of stock, had routed the bears, those who sell. It was the greatest bull market in history as eager purchasers drove prices to new highs. At the end of the last business day, Crawford surveyed the floor and declared flatly, "The millennium's arrived."

Veteran financial analyst Alexander Noyes had his doubts. Speculation—buying and selling on the expectation that rising prices will yield quick gains—had taken over the stock market. "Something has to give," said Noyes in September 1929. Less than a month later, the Great Bull Market fell in a heap.

The Rampaging Bull

NEW BREED   No one knows exactly what caused the wave of speculation that boosted the stock market to dizzying heights. Driven alternately by greed and fear, the market succumbed to greed in a decade that considered it a virtue.

NEW MONEY   Money and credit to fuel the market became plentiful. From 1922 to 1929 some $900 million worth of gold flowed into the country. The money supply expanded by $6 billion. Over the decade corporate profits grew by 80 percent. At interest rates as high as 25 percent, more could be made from lending money to brokers (who then made "brokers' loans" to clients for stock purchase) than from constructing new factories. By 1929 brokers' loans had almost tripled from two years earlier.

"Margin requirements," the cash actually put down to purchase stock, hovered around 50 percent for most of the decade. Thus buyers had to come up with only half the price of a share. The rest came from credit furnished by brokers' loans. As trading reached record heights in August 1929, the Federal Reserve Board tried to dampen speculation by raising the interest rates. Higher interest rates made borrowing more expensive and, authorities hoped, would rein in the galloping bull market. They were wrong. It was already too late.

The Great Crash

At the opening bell on Thursday, October 24, 1929, a torrent of sell orders flooded the New York Stock Exchange, triggered by nervous speculators who had been selling for the past week. Prices plunged as panic set in. By the end of "Black Thursday" nearly 13 million shares had been traded— a record. Losses stood at $3 billion, another record.

Prices rallied for the rest of the week, buoyed by a bankers' buying pool organized at the House of Morgan. The following Tuesday, October 29, 1929, the bubble burst. Stockholders lost $10 billion in a single day. And the downward slide continued for almost four years. At their peak in 1929, stocks had been worth $87 billion. In 1933 they bottomed out at $18 billion.

ROLE OF THE CRASH   The Great Crash did not cause the Great Depression, but it did damage the economy and break the unbounded optimism on which the New Era rested. Although only about 500,000 people were actually trading stocks by the end of the decade, their investments had helped to sustain prosperity. Thousands of middle-class investors lost their savings and their futures. Commercial banks—some loaded with corporate stocks, others financing brokers' loans—reeled in the wake of the crash.

🌐 The Sickening Slide in Global Perspective

The Great Crash signaled the start of the greatest depression in the history of the modern world. In the United States, the gains of the 1920s were wiped out in a few years. In the first three years after the crash, national income fell by half, factory wages by almost half. By some estimates 85,000 businesses failed.

Although the Great Depression was less prolonged in other countries, the shock waves from the United States rippled across the globe, helping to topple already fragile economies in Europe. American loans, investments, and purchases had propped up Europe since the end of World War I. When American resources dried up, European governments defaulted on war debts. More European banks

ON THE FLOOR — N.Y. STOCK EXCHANGE   REGINALD MARSH

failed; more businesses collapsed; unemployment surged to at least 30 million worldwide by 1932. Workers in industrialized European nations experienced jobless rates between 20 and nearly 40 percent.

Europeans scrambled to protect themselves. Led by Great Britain in 1931, 41 nations abandoned the gold standard. Foreign governments hoped to devalue their currencies by expanding their supplies of money. Exports would be cheaper and foreign trade would increase. But several countries did so at once, while each country raised tariffs to protect itself from foreign competition. Devaluation failed, and the resulting trade barriers only deepened the crisis. Between 1929 and 1933 world exports declined by two-thirds, from a high of nearly $3 billion to less than $1 billion. (See the chart on the right.)

In Latin America and other regions where countries depended on exporting raw materials, the slide varied. Shrinking sales of metallic minerals, timber, and hides crippled Chile, Bolivia, Peru, and Malaya, while exports of fuel oils still needed to warm homes and run factories shielded Venezuela. Only the Soviet Union escaped catastrophe, with its limited exports and a command economy that had launched a breakneck campaign of industrialization. Even in the Soviet Union, however, bumper crops of Russian wheat forced onto the world market at deflated prices led millions of peasants to starve to death in 1932–1933. Virtually everywhere else economies cracked under the weight of slackening demand and contracting world trade.

In the United States declining sales abroad sent crop prices to new lows. Farm income dropped by more than half. The epidemic of rural bank failures spread to the cities. Nervous depositors rushed to withdraw their cash. Even healthy banks could not bear the strain. In August 1930 every bank in Toledo but one closed its doors. Between 1929 and 1933, collapsing banks took more than $20 billion in assets with them. The economy was spiraling downward, and no one could stop it.

The Causes of the Great Depression

What, then, caused the Great Depression in the United States? In the months before the crash, with national attention riveted on the booming stock market, hardly anyone paid attention to existing defects in the American economy. But by 1928 the booming construction and automobile industries began to lose vitality as demand sagged. In fact, increases in consumer spending for all goods and services slowed to a lethargic 1.5 percent for 1928–1929. Warehouses began to fill as business inventories climbed, from $500 million in 1928 to $1.8 billion in 1929.

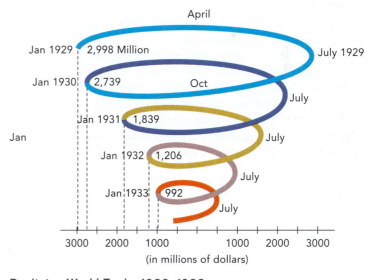

Declining World Trade, 1929-1933

As the Great Depression deepened, world trade spiraled downward. Here the imports of 75 countries are tracked from 1929 to 1933. (The amounts are measured in millions of U.S. gold dollars.) The greatest annual decline occurred between 1930 and 1931 as production plummeted and nation after nation began to erect high tariff barriers to protect their domestic markets from cheaper imports. Over the four-year period, world import trade fell by almost two-thirds, only underscoring the growing interdependence of the global economy.

OVEREXPANSION AND RELATIVE DECLINE IN PURCHASING POWER

In one sense, businesses had done all too well. Corporations had boosted their profits by some 80 percent during the 1920s by keeping the cost of labor and raw materials low as well as by increasing productivity. Businesses used the profits to expand factories rather than to pay workers higher wages. Without strong labor unions or government support, real wages increased (largely because of falling prices) but never kept pace with productivity, which led to a paradox. As consumers, workers did not have enough money to buy the products they were making more efficiently and at lower cost.

CONSUMER DEBT AND UNEVEN DISTRIBUTION OF WEALTH

People made up the difference between earnings and purchases by borrowing. Consumers bought "on time," paying for merchandise a little each month. During the decade, consumer debt rose by 250 percent. Few could afford to keep spending at that rate. Nor could the distribution of wealth sustain prosperity. By 1929, 1 percent of the population owned 36 percent of all personal wealth. The wealthy had more money than they could possibly spend and saved too much. The working and middle classes had not nearly enough to keep the economy growing, spend though they might.

BANKING SYSTEM

Another problem lay with the banking system. Mismanagement, greed, and the emergence of a new type of executive—half banker, half broker—led banks to divert more funds into speculative investments. The uniquely decentralized American banking system left no way to set things right if a bank failed. At the end of the decade, half of the 25,000 banks in America lay outside the Federal Reserve System. Its controls even over member banks were weak, and during the decade, 6,000 banks failed.

CORPORATE STRUCTURE AND PUBLIC POLICY

A shaky corporate structure only made matters worse. No government agency monitored the stock exchanges, while big business operated largely unchecked. Insider stock trading, shady stock deals, and outright stock fraud ran rampant. Meanwhile, public policy encouraged corporate consolidation and control because the government filed few antitrust suits. High profits and the Mellon tax program helped make many corporations wealthy enough to avoid borrowing. Thus changes in interest rates—over which the Federal Reserve exercised some control—had little influence on such corporations. Free from government regulation, fluctuating prices, and the need for loans, big businesses ruled the economy. And they ruled badly.

"SICK" INDUSTRIES

Unemployment began to increase as early as 1927, a sign of growing softness in the economy. By the fall of 1929 some 2 million people were out of work. Many of them were in textiles, coal mining, lumbering, and railroads. All were "sick" industries during the decade because they suffered from overexpansion, killing competition, reduced demand, and weak management. Farmers were in trouble too. As European agriculture revived after World War I, farm prices tumbled. American farmers earned 16 percent of the national income in 1919 but only 9 percent in 1929. As more farmers went bust, so did many of the rural banks that had lent them money.

ECONOMIC IGNORANCE

Finally, plain economic ignorance contributed to the calamity. High tariffs protected American industries but discouraged European business from selling to the world's most profitable market. Because Europeans weren't profiting, they lacked the money for American goods being shipped to Europe. Only American loans and investments supported demand abroad. When the American economy collapsed, those vanished and with them went American foreign trade. Furthermore, the Federal Reserve had been stimulating the economy both by expanding the money supply and by lowering interest rates. Those moves only fed the speculative fever by furnishing investors with more money at lower costs. A decision finally to raise interest rates in 1929 to stem speculation ended up speeding the slide by making it more expensive to borrow when investments with borrowed money would have slowed the decline.

 REVIEW

What caused the Great Depression?

CONCLUSION

THE WORLD AT LARGE

"Everyone ought to be rich," proclaimed one enthusiastic investment adviser in *Ladies' Home Journal*—at a time when the economy was still bubbling and the stock market was setting new highs. Americans like him had nothing but faith in their New Era: in its capacity to produce abundance and spread wealth, in its promise of technological freedom from toil and want, in its ability to blend the vast differences among Americans into a mass culture in which individuals would nonetheless retain their identities. They put their money, some quite literally, on this modernism. Others objected to the price being paid in lost community and independence. They wanted to resurrect a world less organized, less bureaucratized, less complex and varied—a world less modern. In the 1920s, the tensions between these contrasting ideals sparked the first culture wars of the twentieth century.

The mix of exuberance, hedonism, and anxiety was mirrored in other nations. As the postwar recession lifted, many of the world's political systems seemed to sustain Woodrow Wilson's dream of a world made safe for democracy. A Germany ruled by Hohenzollern monarchs transformed itself into the Weimar Republic, whose constitution provided universal suffrage and a bill of rights. The new nations carved out of the old Russian and Austro-Hungarian Empires attempted to create similarly democratic governments, while in Turkey, Kemal Ataturk abolished the sultanate and established the Turkish Republic. In India, the Congress Party formed by Mohandas K. Gandhi united socialists and powerful industrial capitalists and pushed the British to grant them greater political representation. Even where the political mix was more volatile, as in China and Indochina (Vietnam), nationalism mixed with communism as a means of liberating colonial peoples from imperialist rule.

The Great Crash and the Great Depression rocked these fragile beginnings. Fledgling democracies in Japan and Germany gave way to authoritarian states, while dire economic straits strengthened the hands of dictators in Italy and the Soviet Union. Japan, too, departed from its peaceful path of trade and foreign investment toward aggressive militarism and expansion. No one—not the brokers of Wall Street, not the captains of industry, not the diplomats at the League of Nations—could predict the future in such an unstable world. ∞∞∞

CHAPTER SUMMARY

THE NEW ERA OF THE 1920s brought a booming economy and modern times to America, vastly accelerating the forces of change—bureaucracy, productivity, technology, advertising and consumerism, mass media, peer culture, and suburbanization. Urban-rural tensions peaked with shifts in population that gave cities new power. But as the decade wore on, weaknesses in the economy and a new ethos of getting and spending, too much of it on credit, proved to be the New Era's undoing.

- Technology, advertising and consumer spending, and such boom industries as automobile manufacturing and construction fueled the largest peacetime economic growth in American history.

- Key features of modern life—mass society, mass culture, and mass consumption—took hold, fed by mass media in the form of radio, movies, and mass-circulation newspapers and magazines.

- Modern life unsettled old ways and eroded social conventions that had limited life especially for women and children, leading to the emergence of a New Woman and a youth culture.

- Great migrations of African Americans from the rural South to the urban North and of Latinos from Mexico to the United States reshaped the social landscape.

- Traditional culture, centered in rural America, hardened and defended itself against change through immigration restriction, Prohibition, Fundamentalism, and a reborn Ku Klux Klan.

- A galloping bull market in stocks reflected the commitment of government to big business and economic growth.

- When the stock market crashed in 1929, weaknesses in the economy—overexpansion, declining purchasing power, uneven distribution of wealth, weak banking and corporate structures, "sick" industries, and economic ignorance—finally brought the economy down, and with it the New Era came to a close.

ADDITIONAL READING

FOR YEARS, FREDERICK LEWIS ALLEN, *Only Yesterday: An Informal History of the 1920s* (1931), shaped the stereotyped view of the decade as a frivolous interlude between World War I and the Great Depression. William Leuchtenburg, *The Perils of Prosperity, 1914–1932* (1958), began an important reconsideration by stressing the serious conflict between urban and rural America and the emergence of modern mass society. Lynn Dumenil updates Leuchtenburg in her excellent *The Modern Temper: American Culture and Society in the 1920s* (1995). Ann Douglas, *Terrible Honesty: Mongrel Manhattan in the 1920s* (1995), puts Manhattan at the core of the cultural transformation, especially its success at bringing African American folk and popular art into the mainstream. On immigration restriction beginning in 1882 and ending with debates sparked by 9/11, see Roger Daniels, *Guarding the Golden Door* (2004). Paul Avrich, *Sacco and Vanzetti* (1991), covers the two men, as both victims and militant anarchists. For another sympathetic treatment, see Bruce Watson, *Sacco and Vanzetti: The Men, the Murders, and the Judgment of Mankind* (2007). On the Scopes trial, see Edward J. Larson, *Summer for the Gods* (1997). Michael Lienesch's *In the Beginning* (2007) focuses on the rise of Fundamentalism and its continuing role in the battle over "creationism." Matthew Sutton, *Aimee Semple McPherson and the Resurrection of Christian America* (2009), places McPherson and her International Church of the Foursquare Gospel at the center of the religious movement that eventually moved Pentecostals and Evangelicals into the cultural limelight.

Roland Marchand, *Advertising the American Dream* (1985), analyzes the role of advertising in shaping mass consumption, values, and culture, and Ellis Hawley, *The Great War and the Search for a Modern Order* (1979), emphasizes economic institutions. For women in the 1920s, see Kathleen M. Blee, *Women of the Klan* (1991); Virginia Scharff, *Taking the Wheel: Women and the Coming of the Motor Age* (1991); and Jacqueline Jones, *Labor of Love, Labor of Sorrow: Black Women, Work, and Family, from Slavery to the Present* (1985). In a penetrating and gendered discussion of Garveyism and of the Harlem Renaissance, Martin Summers profiles evolving notions of what it meant to be a black man in the early years of the twentieth century in *Manliness and Its Discontents* (2004).

The most readable examination of the stock market and its relation to the economy and public policy is still Robert Sobel, *The Great Bull Market: Wall Street in the 1920s* (1968). See also Maury Klein's colorful *Rainbow's End: The Crash of 1929* (2001). The best books on the disintegration of the American economy remain Lester Chandler, *America's Greatest Depression, 1929–1941* (1970), and, from a global standpoint, Charles Kindleberger, *The World in Depression, 1929–1939* (1973). For an analysis of the Great Depression, from the perspective of Keynesian economics, see John Kenneth Galbraith, *The Great Crash* (rev. ed., 1988). For the argument of monetarists, who see the roots of the Depression in the shrinking money supply, see Milton Friedman and Anna Jacobson Schwartz, *Monetary History of the United States* (1963), and Peter Temin, *Did Monetary Forces Cause the Great Depression?* (1976). John M. Barry, *Rising Tide: The Great Mississippi Flood of 1927 and How It Changed America* (1997), is especially good in describing the fate of African Americans and the failure of government and private aid organizations.

For a fuller list of readings, see the Bibliography at www.mhhe.com/eh8e.

SIGNIFICANT EVENTS

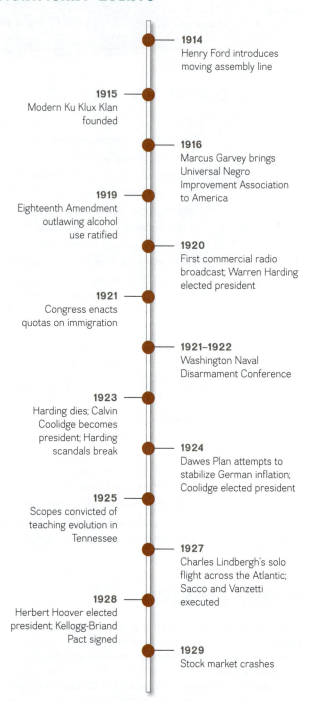

1914
Henry Ford introduces moving assembly line

1915
Modern Ku Klux Klan founded

1916
Marcus Garvey brings Universal Negro Improvement Association to America

1919
Eighteenth Amendment outlawing alcohol use ratified

1920
First commercial radio broadcast; Warren Harding elected president

1921
Congress enacts quotas on immigration

1921–1922
Washington Naval Disarmament Conference

1923
Harding dies; Calvin Coolidge becomes president; Harding scandals break

1924
Dawes Plan attempts to stabilize German inflation; Coolidge elected president

1925
Scopes convicted of teaching evolution in Tennessee

1927
Charles Lindbergh's solo flight across the Atlantic; Sacco and Vanzetti executed

1928
Herbert Hoover elected president; Kellogg-Briand Pact signed

1929
Stock market crashes

The Culture Wars of the 1920s

OPPONENTS	WHAT THEY BELIEVED IN	WEAPONS THEY USED
TRADITIONALISTS 	Small-town life; small government; small business; local control; superiority of white Anglo-Saxons; traditional, home-centered roles for women; traditional Protestantism	Immigration restriction; prohibition of alcohol; antievolution legislation; Ku Klux Klan
MODERNISTS 	Urban life; big government; big business; racial, ethnic, and religious diversity; liberated women	Opposition to restrictions of traditionalists through court cases, legislation, and public media

During the Dust Bowl, "black blizzards" dwarfed the landscape and everything human in it. The drought that helped bring them about lasted from 1932 to 1936. In a single day in 1934, dust storms dumped 12 million tons of western dirt on Chicago. In a moment caught by Farm Security Administration photographer Edward Rothstein, this automobile flees the approaching clouds on a road stretching across the Texas Panhandle.

The Great Depression and the New Deal

1929–1939

∞∞∞ AN AMERICAN STORY ∞∞∞

LETTERS FROM THE EDGE

Winner, South Dakota, November 10, 1933. "Dammit, I don't WANT to write to you again tonight. It's been a long, long day, and I'm tired." All the days had been long since Lorena Hickok began her cross-country trek. Four months earlier Harry Hopkins, the new federal relief administrator, hired the journalist to report on the relief efforts of the New Deal. "Talk with the unemployed," he told her, ". . . and when you talk to them, don't ever forget that but for the grace of God you, I, any of our friends might be in their shoes."

The unemployed, New York City, 1930

In 1933 and 1934, Hickok found that Roosevelt's relief program was falling short. Its half-billion-dollar subsidy to states, localities, and charities was still leaving out too many Americans, like the sharecropper Hickok discovered near Raleigh, North Carolina. He and his daughters had been living in a tobacco barn for two weeks on little more than weeds and table scraps. "Seems like we just keep goin' lower and lower," said the 16-year-old. To Hickok's surprise, hope still flickered in her eyes. Hickok couldn't explain it until she noticed a pin on the girl's chest. It was a campaign button from the 1932 election—"a profile of the President." Hope sprang from the man in the White House.

Before Franklin D. Roosevelt and the New Deal, the White House was far removed from ordinary citizens. The only federal agency with which they had any contact was the post office. And these days it usually delivered bad news. But as Hickok traveled across the country in 1933, she detected a change. People were talking about government programs. Perhaps it was long-awaited contributions to relief or maybe reforms in securities and banking or the new recovery programs for industry and agriculture. Just as likely it was Franklin Roosevelt. People, she wrote, were "for the President."

The message was clear: Franklin Roosevelt and the New Deal had begun to restore national confidence. Though it never brought full recovery, the New Deal did improve economic conditions and provided relief to millions of Americans. It reformed the economic system and committed the federal government to managing its busts and booms. In doing so it extended the progressive drive to soften industrialization and translated decades of growing concern for the disadvantaged into a federal aid program. For the first time, Americans believed Washington would help them through a terrible crisis. The liberal state came of age: active, interventionist, and committed to social welfare. ∞∞∞

The Human Impact of the Great Depression

LONG BREADLINES SNAKED AROUND CORNERS. Vacant-eyed apple-sellers stood shivering in the wind. A man with his hat in his hand came to the back door asking for food in exchange for work. Between 1929 and 1932 an average of 100,000 people lost their jobs every week until some 13 million Americans were jobless. At least one worker in four could find no employment.

The Great Depression was a great leveler that reduced differences in the face of common want. The Baltimore laundress without enough wash to pay her rent felt the same pinch of frustration and anger as the UC Berkeley student whose college education was cut short when the bank let her father go. Not everyone was devastated. Most Americans survived by cooperating with one another and scrimping to make ends meet. As one Depression victim recalled, "We lived lean."

Hard Times

Hard times lasted for a decade. Even before the Great Crash many Americans were having trouble making a living. In 1929 a family of four required $2,000 a year for bare necessities—more money than 60 percent of American families earned.

Unable to pay mortgages or rent, many families lived off the generosity of forgiving landlords. Some traded down to smaller quarters or simply lost their homes. By 1932 between 1 and 2 million Americans were homeless wanderers, among them an estimated 25,000 nomadic families. For the first time, emigration out of the country exceeded immigration into it because Americans could find no work at home. Despite official claims that no one had died of hunger, the New York City Welfare Council reported 29 victims of starvation and 110 dead of malnourishment in 1932 alone.

MARRIAGE AND THE FAMILY

Marriages and births, symbols of faith in the future, plummeted. For the first time in three centuries the curve of population growth began to level, as many young couples postponed having children. Experts worried about an impending "baby crop shortage." Strong families hung together and grew closer; weak ones languished or fell apart. Although divorce declined, desertion—the "poor man's divorce"—mushroomed. Under the strain, rates of mental illness and suicide rose as well.

Many fathers, whose lives had been defined by work, suddenly had nothing to do. They grew listless and depressed. Most mothers stayed home and found their traditional roles as nurturer and household manager less disrupted than the breadwinning roles of their husbands. Between 1929 and 1933 living costs dropped 25 percent, but family incomes tumbled by 40 percent.

Homemakers watched household budgets with a closer eye than ever. They canned more food and substituted less expensive fish for meat. When they earned extra money, they often did so within the confines of the "woman's sphere" by taking in boarders, laundry, and sewing, opening beauty parlors in their kitchens, and selling baked goods.

For those women who worked outside the home, prejudice still relegated them to so-called "women's work." Over half the female labor force continued to work in domestic service or the garment trades, while others found traditional employment as schoolteachers, social workers, and secretaries. Only slowly did the female proportion of the workforce reach pre-Depression levels, until it rose finally to 25 percent by 1940, largely because women were willing to take almost any job.

PSYCHOLOGICAL IMPACT

Whether in the renewed importance of homemaking or the reemergence of home industries, the Great Depression sent ordinary Americans scurrying for the reassuring shelter of past practices and left many of them badly shaken. Shame, self-doubt, and pessimism became epidemic as people blamed themselves for their circumstances. "I would go stand on the relief line [and] bend my head low so nobody would recognize me," recalled one man. The lasting legacy of humiliation and fear—that you had caused your own downfall; that the bottom of the economy would drop out again—was what one writer called an "invisible scar."

The Golden Age of Radio and Film

By the end of the decade almost 9 out of 10 families owned radios. People depended on radios for nearly everything—news, sports, and weather; music and entertainment; recipes for meals or finding salvation. Some programming

In the shantytowns or "Hoovervilles" that sprang up during the Great Depression, housing was makeshift, with the homeless living in crude tin and wood shacks or tents. This young boy in Seattle is asleep in a cardboard box.

helped change national habits. When *The Sporting News* conducted a baseball poll in 1932, editors were surprised to discover that a "new crop of fans has been created by radio . . . the women." Many women were at home during the day when most games were played, and broadcasters went out of their way to educate these new listeners. Night games soon outran day games in attendance, in part because husbands began taking wives and daughters, whose interest was sparked by radio.

Radio entered a golden age of commercialism. Advertisers hawked their products on variety programs like Major Bowes's *Amateur Hour* and comedy shows with entertainers such as George Burns and Gracie Allen. Daytime melodramas (called "soap operas" because they were sponsored by soap companies) aimed at women with stories of the personal struggles of ordinary folk.

RADIO'S UNIFYING EFFECT Radio continued to bind the country together. A teenager in Splendora, Texas, could listen to the same wisecracks from Jack Benny, the same music from Guy Lombardo, as kids in New York City and Los Angeles. In 1938 Orson Welles broadcast H. G. Wells's classic science fiction tale *The War of the Worlds*. Americans everywhere listened to breathless reports of an "invasion from Mars," and many believed it. In Newark, New Jersey, cars jammed roads as families rushed to evacuate the city. The nation, bombarded with reports of impending war in Europe and accustomed to responding to radio advertising, was prepared to believe almost anything, even reports of invaders from Mars.

In Hollywood an efficient but autocratic studio system churned out a record number of feature films. Eight motion picture companies produced more than two-thirds of them. Color, first introduced to feature films in *Becky Sharp* (1935), soon complemented sound, which had debuted in the 1927 version of *The Jazz Singer*. Neither alone could keep movie theaters full. As attendance dropped early in the Depression, big studios such as Metro-Goldwyn-Mayer and Universal lured audiences back with films that shocked, titillated, and just plain entertained.

MASS MEDIA AT HOME AND ABROAD By the mid-1930s more than 60 percent of Americans were going to the movies at least once a week. They saw tamer films as the industry began regulating movie content in the face of growing criticism. In 1933 the Catholic Church created the Legion of Decency to monitor features. To

Art Deco Radio, 1930

Art Deco, popularized in the 1920s, relied on the geometrical patterns of machines arranged in decorative designs.

avoid censorship and boycotts, studios stiffened their own regulations. Producers could not depict homosexuality, abortion, drug use, or sex. (Even the word "sex" was banned, as was all profanity.) Middle-class morality reigned on the screen, and most Depression movies, like most of popular culture, preserved traditional values.

In Europe the "mass aspects" of media could cut more than one way politically and culturally. While Hollywood produced films that affirmed popular faith in democratic government, a capitalist economy, and the success ethic, totalitarian Nazi Germany broadcast the fiery rallies and speeches of Adolf Hitler, which seemed bent on encouraging racist fears and inflaming public hysteria. In *Triumph of the Will* (1935), German director Leni Riefenstahl used her cinematic gifts to combine myth, symbol, and documentary into an image of Hitler as the Führer, a national savior with the power of a pagan god and the charisma of cult leader.

"Dirty Thirties": An Ecological Disaster

DUST BOWL Each year between 1932 and 1939 an average of nearly 50 dust storms, or "black blizzards," turned 1,500 square miles between the Panhandle of western Oklahoma and western Kansas into a gigantic "Dust Bowl," whose baleful effects were felt as far north as the Dakotas and as far south as Texas. It was one of the worst ecological disasters in modern history. Nature played its part, scorching the earth and whipping the winds. But human beings were mostly responsible for the "dirty thirties." The semiarid lands west of the 98th meridian were unsuitable for agriculture or livestock. Sixty years of intensive farming and grazing had stripped the prairie of its natural vegetation and rendered it defenseless against the elements. When the dry winds came, one-third of the Great Plains simply vanished into the air.

EFFECT OF COMMERCIAL FARMING Some 3.5 million plains people abandoned their farms. Landowners or corporations forced off about half of them as large-scale commercial farming slowly spread into the heartland of America. Commercial farms were more common in California, where 10 percent of the farms grew more than 50 percent of the crops. As in industrial America, the strategy in agricultural America was to consolidate and mechanize. In most Dust Bowl counties, people owned less than half the land they farmed. American agriculture was turning from a way of life into an industry. As the economy contracted, owners followed the common industrial strategy of cutting costs by cutting workers.

Relief offices around the country reported a change in migrant families. Rather than black or brown, more and more were white and native-born, typically a young married couple with one child. Long-distance migrants from Oklahoma, Arizona, and Texas usually set their sights on California. If they were like the Joad family in John Steinbeck's classic

SUPERHEROES AS CULTURAL ICONS

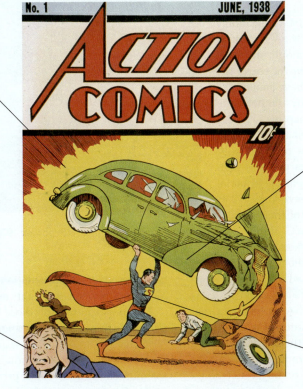

Bold primary colors explode from the page.

Super strength is only one of Superman's powers. Others?

Do you think this man is a villain or a bystander? In interpreting the cover, how would the distinction matter?

Superman's creators originally conceived of him as a bald madman who used his telepathic powers to create chaos.

Comic book heroes may appear to be nothing more than child's play, but to historians they can serve as windows on the values and mores of a culture. When American-born writer Jerry Siegel and Canadian-born artist Joe Shuster created "Superman" in 1932, they never imagined they were conjuring up a cultural icon. Neither did the publishers who initially rejected the comic strip. Not until 1938 did the character appear in comic book form. Part of a long line of mythic heroes dating back to Hercules and the biblical Samson, Superman is also an American invention. He is, after all, the quintessential immigrant, trying (in the form of his alter ego Clark Kent) to fit in as an ordinary American committed to social justice. He springs from the industrial age; in Siegel's words, "Faster than a speeding bullet! More powerful than a locomotive! Able to leap tall buildings in a single bound!" And he is rooted in the anxieties of the Great Depression. At a time when many Americans had lost faith in prevailing institutions and worried over a world spinning out of control, Superman promised to restore order, bring lawbreakers to justice, and rehabilitate the "American way."

Thinking Critically

How does Superman transcend conventional institutions of law enforcement? How might he restore faith in authority? Does the comic book cover suggest he could be subversive of authority? In what ways might a superhero both bolster and undermine authority in Depression-era America?

Source: All DC Comics characters and the distinctive likeness(es) thereof are Trademarks & Copyright © 1938 DC Comics, Inc. ALL RIGHTS RESERVED.

novel *The Grapes of Wrath* (1939), they drove west along Route 66 through Arizona and New Mexico, their belongings piled high atop rickety jalopies, heading for the West Coast and the promise of jobs picking fruit and harvesting vegetables.

More than 350,000 Oklahomans migrated to California—so many that "Okie" came to mean any Dust Bowler, even though most of Oklahoma, including the home of the fictional Joads, lay outside the Dust Bowl. According to one government study, between 1935 and 1940 only a third of migrants from the Southwest to California had lived on farms before leaving. More than half had resided in cities. Unlike the Joads, most ended up in one California city or another.

Wherever they landed, only one in two or three migrants actually found work. The labor surplus allowed growers to cut wages to less than a third the subsistence level.

Families that did not work formed wretched enclaves called "little Oklahomas." The worst were located in California's fertile Imperial Valley. There, at the end of the decade, relief officials discovered a family of 10 living in a 1921 Ford.

Mexican Americans and Repatriation

CÉSAR CHÁVEZ The Chávez family lost their family farm in Arizona in 1934. César, barely six years old at the time, remembered only images of their departure: a "giant tractor" leveling the corral; the loss of his room and bed; a beat-up Chevy hauling the family west; his father promising to buy another farm. But the elder Chávez could never keep his promise. Instead, he and his family "followed the crops" in California. In eight years César went to 37 schools. When they found work, his family earned less than $10 a week. His father joined strikers in the Imperial Valley in the mid-1930s, only to have the strikes crushed. "Some people put this out of their minds," said César Chávez years later. "I don't." Thirty years later he founded the United Farm Workers of America, the first union of migrant workers in the country.

Immigration station near U.S. border, 1938

REPATRIATION A deep ambivalence had always characterized American attitudes toward Mexicans and Mexican Americans like the Chávezes, but the Great Depression turned most Anglo communities against them. Cities such as Los Angeles, fearing the burden of relief, found it cheaper to ship Mexicans home. Some migrants left voluntarily. Frustrated officials or angry neighbors drove out others. Beginning in 1931 the federal government launched a series of deportations, or **"repatriations,"** of Mexicans back to Mexico. These deportations included the Mexicans' American-born children, who by law were citizens of the United States.

During the decade the Latino population of the Southwest dropped by 500,000. In Chicago the Mexican community shrank by almost half. Staying in the United States often turned out to be as difficult as leaving. The average income of Mexican American families in the Rio Grande valley of Texas was $506 a year. Following the harvest made schooling particularly difficult: fewer than two Mexican-American children in ten completed five years of school.

LULAC AND ETHNIC IDENTITY For Americans of Mexican descent, the Great Depression only deepened anxiety over identity. Were they Mexicans, as many Anglos regarded them, or were they Americans, as they regarded themselves? In the 1920s such questions produced several organizations founded to assert the American identity of native-born and naturalized Mexican Americans and to pursue their civil rights. In 1929, on the eve of the Depression, many of these organizations were consolidated into the League of United Latin American Citizens (LULAC). By the early 1940s, "Flying Squadrons" of LULAC organizers

had created 80 chapters nationwide, making it the largest Mexican American civil rights association in the country.

LULAC permitted only those Latinos who were American citizens to join, excluding hundreds of thousands of ethnic Mexicans who nonetheless regarded the United States as their home. It pointedly conducted meetings in English. An assimilated middle class provided its leadership and stressed desegregation of public schools, voter registration, and an end to discrimination in public facilities and on juries.

African Americans in the Depression

Hard times were nothing new to African Americans. "The Negro was born in depression," opined one black man. "It only became official when it hit the white man." Still, when the Depression struck, black unemployment surged. By 1932 it reached 50 percent, twice the national level. By 1933 several cities reported between 25 and 40 percent of their black residents with no support except relief payments.

Migration out of the rural South, up 800,000 during the 1920s, dropped by 50 percent in the 1930s. As late as 1940 three of four African Americans still lived in rural areas; yet conditions there were just as bad as in cities. In 1934 one study estimated the average income for black cotton farmers at under $200 a year.

FATHER DIVINE AND ELIJAH MUHAMMAD Like many African Americans, George Baker refused to be victimized by the Depression. Baker had moved from Georgia to Harlem in 1915. He changed his name to M. J. Divine and founded a religious cult that promised followers an

"Juke joints" like this one in Belle Glade, Florida, provided a temporary haven, and sometimes living quarters, for migratory workers who came to drink and dance to the songs played on a jukebox.

afterlife of full equality. In the 1930s "Father Divine" preached economic cooperation and opened shelters, or "heavens," for regenerate "angels," black and white. In Detroit, Elijah Poole began calling himself Elijah Muhammad and in 1931 established the Black Muslims, a blend of Islamic faith and black nationalism. He exhorted African Americans to celebrate their African heritage, to live lives of self-discipline and self-help, and to strive for a separate all-black nation.

SCOTTSBORO BOYS

The Depression inflamed racial prejudice. Lynchings tripled between 1932 and 1933. In 1932 the Supreme Court ordered a retrial in the most celebrated racial case of the decade. A year earlier nine black teenagers had been accused of raping two white women on a train bound for Scottsboro, Alabama. Within weeks all-white juries sentenced eight of them to death. The convictions rested on the testimony of the women, one of whom later admitted the boys had been framed. Appeals kept the case alive for almost a decade. In the end, charges against four of the "Scottsboro boys" were dropped. The other five received substantial prison sentences.

 REVIEW

What were the human costs of the Great Depression for Anglos, Latinos, and African Americans?

THE TRAGEDY OF HERBERT HOOVER

THE PRESIDENCY OF HERBERT HOOVER began with great promise but soon became a nightmare both personal and professional. "I have no fears for the future of our country," he announced at his inauguration in March 1929. But within seven months a "depression" struck. (Hoover used the word instead of the traditional "panic" to downplay the emergency.) Despite more effort than any of his predecessors to restore a damaged economy, he failed to turn the economic tide. For all of Hoover's promise and innovative intelligence, he was a transitional figure, important as a break from the do-nothing policies of past depression presidents and a herald of more active presidents to come.

The Failure of Relief

By the winter of 1931–1932 the picture was bleak: relief organizations with too little money and too few resources to make much headway against the Depression. Once-mighty private charity dwindled to 6 percent of all relief funds.

Ethnic charities tried to stave off disaster for their own. Over the years Mexican Americans and Puerto Ricans turned to *mutualistas*, traditional societies that provided members with social support, life insurance, and sickness benefits. In San Francisco, the Chinese Six Companies offered food and clothing to needy Chinese Americans. But as the head of the Federation of Jewish Charities warned, private efforts were failing. The government would be "compelled, by the cruel events ahead of us, to step into the situation and bring relief on a large scale."

CITY SERVICES An estimated 30 million needy people nationwide quickly depleted city treasuries, already pressed because nearly 30 percent of city taxpayers had fallen behind in what they owed. In Philadelphia relief payments to a family of four totaled $5.50 a week, the highest in the country. Some cities gave nothing to unmarried people or childless couples, no matter how impoverished they were.

Cities clamored for help from state capitals, but after a decade of extravagant spending and sloppy bookkeeping, many states were already in debt. As businesses and property values collapsed, tax bases shrank and with them state revenues. Until New York established its Temporary Emergency Relief Administration (TERA) in 1931, no state had an agency to handle the unemployed.

The Hoover Depression Program

Beginning in 1930 President Hoover assumed leadership in combating the Depression with more vigor and compassion than any other executive. It was a mark of his character. Orphaned at nine, he became one of Stanford University's first graduates and, before the age of 40, the millionaire head of one of the most successful mine engineering firms in the world. As a good Quaker he balanced private gain with public service, saving starving Belgian refugees in 1915 after war broke out in Europe. He worked 14 hours a day, paid his own salary, and convinced private organizations and businesses to donate food, clothing, and other necessities. In his honor, Finns coined a new word: to "hoover" meant to help.

When the Depression struck, Hoover was no passive executive. Past presidents feared that any intervention by government would upset the natural workings of the economy. They saw their sole responsibility as keeping the federal budget balanced. But Hoover understood the vicious cycle in which rising unemployment drove down consumer demand and appreciated the need for stimulating investment. He set in motion an unprecedented program of government activism.

PROGRAM FAILURES Despite all his work, Hoover's program failed. At first he rallied business leaders, who pledged to maintain employment, wages, and prices—only to back down as the economy sputtered. He pushed a tax cut through Congress in 1930 in order to increase the purchasing power of consumers. When cuts unbalanced the federal budget, Hoover reversed course. At bottom he firmly believed that capitalism would generate its own recovery and that a balanced federal budget was required in order to restore the confidence of business. So he agreed to tax increases in 1932, further undermining investment and consumption.

Equally disastrous, the president endorsed the Smoot-Hawley Tariff (1930) to protect the United States from cheap foreign goods. That bill brought a wave of retaliation from countries abroad, which choked world trade and reduced American sales overseas. Even the $1 billion that Hoover spent on **public works**—more than the total spent by all his predecessors combined—did not approach

| Louis Ribak's Home Relief Station *grimly portrays the failing relief efforts of private charities and the humiliation of applying for relief. A crowd of broken men and women sits anxiously as a burly administrator interrogates a frail relief applicant. To go on relief, said one man, was to endure a "crucifixion."*

the $10 billion needed to employ only half the jobless. Spending such huge sums seemed unthinkable when the entire federal budget was only $3.2 billion.

RECONSTRUCTION FINANCE CORPORATION

Under pressure from Congress, Hoover took his boldest action to save the banks. Between 1930 and 1932 some 5,100 banks failed as panicky depositors withdrew their funds. Without loans from sound banks for investment, the economy would never recover. Hoover agreed to permit the creation of the Reconstruction Finance Corporation (RFC) in 1932, an agency that could lend money to banks. Modeled on a similar agency created during World War I, the RFC had a capital stock of $500 million and the power to borrow four times that amount. Within three months bank failures dropped from 70 a week to 1 every two weeks.

In spite of this success Hoover drew criticism for rescuing banks and not people. From the start he rejected the idea of federal relief for the unemployed for fear that a "dole," or giveaway program, would damage the initiative of recipients, perhaps even produce a permanent underclass. The bureaucracy that would be needed to police recipients would inevitably meddle in the private lives of citizens and bring a "train of corruption and waste," Hoover said. He assumed neighborliness and cooperation would be enough.

UNEMPLOYMENT RELIEF

As unemployment worsened, Hoover softened his stand on federal relief. In 1932 he allowed Congress to pass the Emergency Relief and Construction Act. It authorized the RFC to lend up to $1.5 billion for "reproductive" public works that paid for themselves—like toll bridges and slum clearance. Another $300 million went to states as loans for the unemployed. It barely mattered. When the governor of Pennsylvania requested loans to furnish the destitute with 13 cents a day for a year, the RFC sent only enough for 3 cents a day.

Stirrings of Discontent

Despite unprecedented action, Hoover could not stem rising discontent. "The word revolution is heard at every hand," one writer warned in 1932. Some wondered if capitalism itself had gone bankrupt.

In 1932 anger erupted into violence. Wisconsin dairy farmers overturned tens of thousands of milk cans in a fruitless effort to increase prices. A 48-mile-long "coal caravan" of striking miners drove through southern Illinois in protest. Three thousand marchers stormed Henry Ford's plant in Dearborn, only to have Ford police turn power water hoses and guns on them. When it was over, four marchers lay dead and over 20 more wounded.

In the early years of the Depression, demonstrations by the unemployed, some organized by Communists and other radicals, broke out all over the country. On March 6, 1930, a Communist-led protest at Union Square in New York City turned into an ugly riot. In 1935 Communist parties, under orders from Moscow, allied with democratic and socialist groups against fascism, proclaiming in the United States that "Communism is twentieth-century Americanism."

For all the stirrings of discontent, revolution was never a danger. In 1932 the Communist Party of the United States had 20,000 members—up from 6,500 only three years earlier but hardly enough to constitute a political force. Deeply suspicious of Marxist doctrine, most Americans rejected the Communists' calls for collectivism and an end to capitalism. Despite its strong support for civil rights, fewer than 1,000 African Americans joined the party in the early 1930s.

At first hostile to established politics, the Communists adopted a more cooperative strategy to contain Adolf Hitler when his Nazi Party won control of Germany in 1933. Two years later, the Soviet Union ordered Communist parties in Europe and the United States to join with liberal politicians in a "popular front" against Nazism. Thereafter Communist Party membership in the United States peaked in the mid-1930s at about 80,000.

The Bonus Army

Less radical was the "Bonus Army," a scruffy collection of World War I veterans who marched on Washington in the summer of 1932. They were hungry and looking to cash in the bonus certificates they had received from Congress in 1924 as a reward for wartime service. By the time they reached the Capitol in June, their numbers had swelled to nearly 20,000. It was the largest protest in the city's history. President Hoover sympathized with them but only to a point, as the veterans learned when he dismissed them as a special-interest lobby and refused to meet with their leaders. When the Senate blocked the bonus bill, most veterans left.

About 2,000 stayed to dramatize their plight, camping with their families and parading peaceably. Despite eviction orders, the protesters refused to leave. By the end of July, the president had had enough. He called in the U.S. Army under the command of Chief of Staff General Douglas MacArthur. MacArthur arrived with four troops of saber-brandishing cavalry, six tanks, and a column of infantry with fixed bayonets. By the time the smoke cleared the next morning, only 300 wounded veterans remained.

Though he had intended that the army only assist the police, Hoover accepted responsibility for the action. The sight of unarmed and unemployed veterans under attack by American troops soured most Americans. In Albany, New York, Governor Franklin D. Roosevelt exploded at the president's failure: "There is nothing inside the man but jelly."

The Election of 1932

In 1932 Republicans stuck with Hoover and endorsed his Depression program. Democrats countered with Franklin D. Roosevelt, the charismatic New York governor. As a sign of change, Roosevelt broke precedent by flying to Chicago and addressing the delegates in person. "I pledge you,

I pledge myself to a new deal for the American people," he told them.

Without a national following, Roosevelt zigged and zagged in an effort to appeal to the broadest possible bloc of voters. One minute he called for a balanced budget, the next for costly public works and aid to the unemployed. He promised to help business, then spoke of remembering the "forgotten man" and "distributing wealth and products more equitably." For his part, Hoover denounced Roosevelt's New Deal as a "dangerous departure" from tradition that would destroy American values and institutions and "build a bureaucracy such as we have never seen in our history."

On Election Day, Roosevelt captured a thundering 58 percent of the popular vote and carried large Democratic majorities into the Congress. Just as telling as the margin of victory were its sources. Industrial workers in the North, poor farmers in the South and West, immigrants and big-city dwellers everywhere were being galvanized into a broad new coalition. These people had experienced first-hand the savage effects of the boom-and-bust business cycle and wanted change. They turned to Roosevelt and the Democrats, who recognized that in a modern industrial state it was not enough to rally round business and hope that capitalism would right itself. Over 30 years of nearly unbroken Republican rule came to an end.

✓ REVIEW

In what ways did Herbert Hoover actively seek to counteract the Great Depression? What discouraged him from doing more?

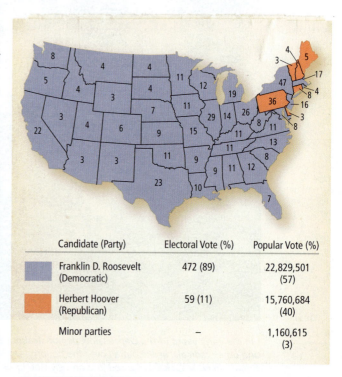

Candidate (Party)	Electoral Vote (%)	Popular Vote (%)
Franklin D. Roosevelt (Democratic)	472 (89)	22,829,501 (57)
Herbert Hoover (Republican)	59 (11)	15,760,684 (40)
Minor parties	–	1,160,615 (3)

ELECTION OF 1932

THE EARLY NEW DEAL (1933–1935)

ON MARCH 4, 1933, AS the clocks struck noon, Eleanor Roosevelt wondered if it were possible to "do anything to save America now." She looked at her husband, who had just been sworn in as thirty-second president of the United States. Franklin faced the audience of over 100,000. He told them the nation had "nothing to fear but fear itself." Heeding the call for "action, and action now," he promised to exercise "broad Executive power to wage a war against the emergency." The crowd cheered. Eleanor was terrified: "One has the feeling of going it blindly because we're in a tremendous stream, and none of us know where we're going to land."

RECOVERY, RELIEF, REFORM
The early New Deal unfolded in the spring of 1933 with a chaotic 100-day burst of legislation. It stressed recovery through planning and cooperation with business but also tried to provide relief for the unemployed and reform the economic system. Above all, the early New Deal broke the cycle of despair. With Roosevelt in the White House, most Americans believed that they were in good hands, wherever they landed.

The Democratic Roosevelts

From the moment they entered it in 1933, Franklin and Eleanor—the Democratic Roosevelts—transformed the White House. No more seven-course meals as Hoover had served in an effort to show that nothing was really wrong. Instead, visitors got fare fit for a boardinghouse. Roosevelt's lunches of hash and a poached egg cost 19 cents. The gesture was symbolic, but it made the president's point of ending business as usual.

Such belt-tightening was new to Franklin Roosevelt. Born of an old Dutch family in New York, he grew up rich and pampered. He idolized his Republican cousin Theodore Roosevelt and mimicked his career, except as a Democrat. Like Theodore, Franklin graduated from Harvard University (in 1904), won a seat in the New York State legislature (in 1910), secured an appointment as assistant secretary of the navy (in 1913), and ran for the vice presidency (in 1920). Then disaster struck. On vacation in the summer of 1921, Roosevelt fell ill with poliomyelitis. The disease paralyzed him from the waist down.

Roosevelt emerged from the ordeal to win the governorship of New York in 1928. When the Depression struck he created the first state relief agency in 1931, the Temporary Emergency Relief Administration. Aid to the jobless "must be extended by Government, not as a matter of charity, but as a matter of social duty," he explained. He considered himself a progressive but moved well beyond the cautious federal activism of most progressives. He adopted no single ideology. He cared little about economic principles. He wanted results. Experimentation became a hallmark of the New Deal.

Eleanor Roosevelt redefined what it meant to be First Lady. Never had a president's wife been so visible, so much of a crusader, so cool under fire. She was the first First Lady to hold weekly press conferences. Her column, "My Day," appeared in 135 newspapers, and her twice-weekly broadcasts made her a radio personality rivaling her husband. She became his eyes, ears, and legs, traveling 40,000 miles a year. Secret Service men code-named her "Rover."

Eleanor believed she was only a spur to presidential action. But she was active in her own right, as a teacher and social reformer before Franklin became president and afterward as a tireless advocate of the underdog. In the White House, she pressed him to hire more women and minorities, supported antilynching and anti-poll-tax measures when he would not, and pressed for experimental towns for the homeless. By 1939 more Americans approved of her than of her husband.

Franklin Roosevelt contracted polio in 1921 and remained paralyzed from the waist down for the rest of his life. Out of deference to Roosevelt, photographers rarely showed him wearing heavy leg braces or sitting in a wheelchair. This photograph, snapped outside his New York City brownstone in September 1933 during his first year as president, is one of the few in which Roosevelt's braces are visible (just below the cuffs of his trousers). Note the wooden ramp and railings constructed specifically to help him navigate the stairs.

TWO VIEWS OF THE "FORGOTTEN MAN"

When President Franklin Roosevelt promised to help the "forgotten man" during the Great Depression, not everyone agreed that such poverty-stricken Americans needed it. Two views of forgotten men and women follow, one from an Indiana farmwoman critical of any form of assistance (Document 1), the other from a reporter stressing the necessity for more aid and the danger of failing to provide it (Document 2).

DOCUMENT 1   Aid Rewards the "Shiftless"

We have always had a shiftless, never-do-well class of people whose one and only aim in life is to live without work. I have been rubbing elbows with this class for nearly sixty years and have tried to help some of the most promising and have seen others try to help them, but it can't be done. We cannot help those who will not try to help themselves and if they do try, a square deal is all they need, and by the way that is all this country needs or ever has needed: a square deal for all and then, let each paddle their own canoe, or sink. . . .

The women and children around here have had to work at the fields to help save the crops and several women fainted while at work and at the same time we couldn't go up or down the road without stumbling over some of the reliefers, moping around carrying dirt from one side of the road to the other and back again, or else asleep. I live alone on a farm and have not raised any crops for the last two years as there was no help to be had. I am feeding the stock and have been cutting the wood to keep my home fires burning. There are several reliefers around here now who have been kicked off relief, but they refuse to work unless they can get relief hours and wages, but they are so worthless no one can afford to hire them.

As for the clearance of the real slums, it can't be done as long as their inhabitants are allowed to reproduce their kind. I would like for you to see what a family of that class can do to a decent house in a short time. Such a family moved into an almost new, neat, four-room house near here last winter. They even cut down some of the shade trees for fuel, after they had burned everything they could pry loose. . . . I will not try to describe their filth for you would not believe me. They paid no rent while there and left between two suns [sic] owing everyone from whom they could get nickels worth of anything. They are just a fair sample of the class of people on whom so much of our hard earned tax money is being squandered and on whom so much sympathy is being wasted. . . .

Is it any wonder the taxpayers are discouraged by all this penalizing of thrift and industry to reward shiftlessness, or that the whole country is on the brink of chaos?

Source: Minnie A. Hardin (Columbus, Ind.) to Mrs. F. D. Roosevelt, December 14, 1937, reprinted in Andrew Carroll, ed., *Letters of a Nation: A Collection of Extraordinary American Letters* (New York, 1997), pp. 196–199.

DOCUMENT 2   Aid Helps the Truly Needy

. . . One hears a good deal about "relief psychology" these days—that if it were all direct relief, with no work, thousands would never apply. No social worker out in the field would deny this. Through work the stigma has to some extent been removed from relief. Into every relief office in the country have come applicants, not for relief, but for jobs. More of them than you would perhaps believe have shaken their heads and turned away when informed that it was really relief. Without doubt there are many thousands of families on work relief in this country who would not have applied had they not been able to call it—to themselves at any rate—"a job." But when one hears the testimony of clinical doctors, school nurses, teachers, and social workers that the "marginal families"—those who haven't yet come on relief—are really worse off than those on relief, one wonders how long these people could have held out after all. . . . This from a doctor in a mental hygiene clinic in Providence, R. I.: "most people we see are not on relief, but are starving. Many of these are white collar people and people in the skilled labor class who avoid relief, whose pride remains stronger than hunger. The result on the children is malnutrition and a neurotic condition produced by hearing and being constantly part of parental fear. The child grows obsessed with the material problems of the home and mentally shoulders them, and the nervous system cracks."

. . . a FERA (Federal Emergency Relief Administration) investigator a few weeks ago sent this poem from a town in Ohio. It was written by an 18-year-old boy:

Prayer of Bitter Men

We are the men who ride the swaying freights,
We are the men whom Life has beaten down,
Leaving for Death nought but the final pain
Of degradation. Men who stand in line
An hour for a bowl of watered soup,
Grudgingly given, savagely received.
We are the Ishmaels, outcasts of the earth,
Who shrink before the sordidness of Life
And cringe before the filthiness of Death.

Will there not come a great, a glittering Man,
A radiant leader with a heavier sword
To crush to earth the enemies who crush
Those who seek food and freedom on the roads?
We care not if their flag be white or red,
Come, ruthless Savior, messenger of God,
Lenin or Christ, we follow Thy bright sword.

Source: Report Summary, Lorena Hickok to Harry Hopkins, January 1, 1935, reprinted in Richard Lowitt and Maurine Beasley, eds., *One Third of a Nation: Lorena Hickok Reports on the Great Depression* (Urbana, IL, 1981), pp. 351–365.

Thinking Critically

What complaints does the woman in the first letter make to the First Lady and why does she make them? What picture emerges from the field report, including the poem of the young man appended to the end of the report? How do you account for the differences between the two views?

Saving the Banks

Before the election Roosevelt had gathered a group of economic advisers called the "Brains Trust." Out of their recommendations came the early, or "first," New Deal of government planning, intervention, and experimentation. Although Brains Trusters disagreed over the means, they agreed over ends: economic recovery, relief for the unemployed, and sweeping reform to ward off future depressions. The first step was to save the banks. By the eve of the inauguration, governors in 38 states had temporarily closed their banks to stem the withdrawal of deposits.

On March 5, the day after his inauguration, Roosevelt ordered every bank in the country closed for four days. He shrewdly called it a "bank holiday." On March 9 the president introduced emergency banking legislation. The House passed the measure, sight unseen, and the Senate endorsed it later in the day. Roosevelt signed it that night.

EMERGENCY BANKING ACT Rather than nationalizing the banks as radicals wanted, the Emergency Banking Act followed the modest course of extending federal assistance to them. Sound banks would reopen immediately with government support. Troubled banks would be handed over to federal "conservators," who would guide them to solvency. In plain and simple language, Roosevelt explained what was happening in the first of his many informal "fireside chat" radio broadcasts. When banks reopened the next day, deposits exceeded withdrawals.

FEDERAL DEPOSIT INSURANCE CORPORATION To guard against another stock crash, financial reforms gave government greater authority to manage the currency and regulate stock transactions. In April 1933 Roosevelt dropped the gold standard and began experimenting with the value of the dollar to boost prices. Later that spring the Glass-Steagall Banking Act restricted speculation by banks and, more important, created federal insurance for bank deposits of up to $2,500. Despite Roosevelt's objections that the Federal Deposit Insurance Corporation would preserve weak banks at the expense of strong ones, fewer banks failed for the rest of the decade than in the best year of the 1920s. The Securities Exchange Act (1934) established a new federal agency, the Securities and Exchange Commission, to oversee the stock market.

Relief for the Unemployed

Saving the banks and financial markets meant little if human suffering continued. Mortgage relief for the millions who had lost their homes came eventually in 1934 in the Home Owners' Loan Act. The need to alleviate starvation led Roosevelt to propose a bold new giveaway program. The Federal Emergency Relief Administration (FERA) opened its door in May 1933. Sitting amid unpacked boxes, gulping coffee and chain-smoking, former social worker Harry Hopkins spent $5 million in his first two hours as head of the new agency. In its two-year existence, FERA furnished more than $1 billion in grants to states, local areas, and private charities.

WORK RELIEF Hopkins persuaded Roosevelt to expand relief with an innovative shift from government giveaways to a work program to see workers through the winter of 1933–1934. Paying someone "to do something socially useful," Hopkins explained, "preserves a man's morale." The Civil Works Administration (CWA) employed 4 million Americans. Alarmed at the high cost of the program, Roosevelt disbanded the CWA in the spring of 1934. Its program of work relief nonetheless created a new weapon against unemployment and an important precedent for future aid programs.

Another work relief program established in 1933 proved even more creative. The Civilian Conservation Corps (CCC) was Roosevelt's pet project. It combined his concern for conservation with compassion for youth. The CCC took unmarried 18- to 25-year-olds from relief rolls and sent them into the woods and fields to plant trees, build parks, and fight soil erosion. During its 10 years, the CCC provided 2.5 million young men with jobs (which prompted some critics of the all-male program to chant, "Where's the she, she, she?").

TENNESSEE VALLEY AUTHORITY New Dealers intended relief programs to last only through the crisis. But the Tennessee Valley Authority (TVA)—a massive public works project created in 1933—helped to relieve unemployment but also made a continuing contribution to regional planning. For a decade planners had dreamed of transforming the flood-ridden basin of the Tennessee River, one of the poorest areas of the country, with a program of regional development and social engineering. The TVA constructed a series of dams along the seven-state basin to control flooding, improve navigation, and generate cheap hydroelectric power. In cooperation with state and local officials, it also launched social projects to stamp out malaria, provide library bookmobiles, and create recreational lakes.

Like many New Deal programs the TVA produced a mixed legacy. It saved 3 million acres from erosion, multiplied the average income in the valley tenfold, and repaid its original investment in federal taxes. Its cheap electricity helped to bring down the rates of private utility companies. But the experiment in regional planning also pushed thousands of families from their land, failed to end poverty, and created an agency that became one of the worst polluters in the country.

Planning for Industrial Recovery

Planning, not just for regions but for the whole economy, seemed to many New Dealers the key to recovery. Some held that if businesses planned and cooperated with each another, the ruthless competition that was driving down prices, wages, and employment could be controlled and the riddle of recovery solved. Business leaders had been urging such a course since 1931, and in his fashion President Hoover had tried to do as much. In June 1933, under the National Industrial Recovery Act (NIRA), Roosevelt put planning to work for industry.

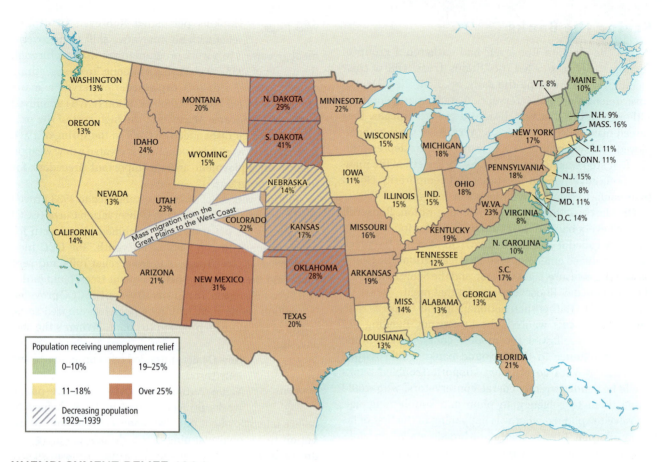

UNEMPLOYMENT RELIEF, 1934

Population receiving unemployment relief

- 0–10%
- 11–18%
- 19–25%
- Over 25%
- Decreasing population 1929–1939

The percentage of those receiving unemployment relief differed markedly throughout the nation. The farm belt of the plains was especially hard-hit, with 41 percent of South Dakota's citizens receiving federal benefits. In the East, the percentage dropped as low as 8 percent in some states. **What factors might have contributed to South Dakota having the highest percentage of those receiving unemployment relief and Vermont and Virginia being among the lowest?**

PUBLIC WORKS ADMINISTRATION The legislation created two new agencies. The Public Works Administration (PWA) was designed to boost industrial activity and consumer spending with a $3.3 billion public works program. The companies put under contract and the workers they employed would help stimulate the economy through their purchases and leave a legacy of capital improvement. Harold Ickes, the prickly interior secretary who headed PWA, built the Triborough Bridge and Lincoln Tunnel in New York, the port city of Brownsville, Texas, and two aircraft carriers. But because he worried so much about waste and corruption, he never spent enough money quickly enough to jump-start the economy.

NATIONAL RECOVERY ADMINISTRATION A second federal agency, the National Recovery Administration (NRA), aimed directly at controlling competition among businesses. Under NRA chief Hugh Johnson, representatives from government and business (and also from labor and consumer groups) drew up "codes of fair practices." Industry by industry, the codes established minimum prices, minimum wages, and maximum hours. No company could seek a competitive edge by cutting prices or wages below certain levels or by working a few employees mercilessly and firing the rest. It also required business to accept key demands of labor, including union rights to organize and bargain with management (thus ensuring that if prices jumped, so, too, might wages). Each code promised improved working conditions and outlawed such practices as child labor and sweatshops.

No business was forced to comply because New Dealers feared that government coercion might be ruled unconstitutional. The NRA relied on voluntary participation. A publicity campaign of parades, posters, and public pledges exhorted businesses to join the NRA and consumers to buy only NRA-sanctioned products. More than 2 million employers eventually signed up. In store windows and on merchandise, shiny decals with blue-eagle crests alerted customers that "We Do Our Part."

For all the hoopla, the NRA failed to spark recovery. Big businesses shaped the codes to their advantage and frequently limited production to maintain or even raise prices. Not all businesses joined, and those that did often found the codes too complicated or costly to follow. Even NRA support for labor tottered, for it had no means of enforcing

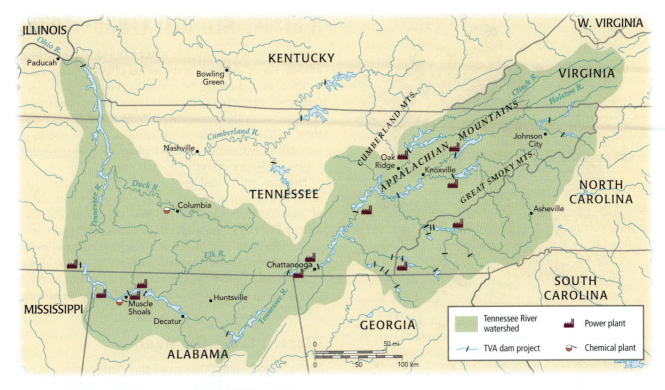

THE TENNESSEE VALLEY AUTHORITY

*The Tennessee River basin encompassed parts of seven states. Rivers honeycombed the area, which received some of the heaviest rainfall in the nation. A longtime dream of Senator George Norris, the Tennessee Valley Authority, created in 1933, constructed some 20 dams and improved 5 others over the next 20 years to control chronic flooding and erosion and to produce cheap hydroelectric power and fertilizers. **Why was this project considered an exercise in regional planning?***

its guarantee of union rights. Business survived under the NRA, but without increasing production there was no incentive for the expansion and new investment needed to end hard times. The NRA soon produced little but evasion and criticism.

SCHECTER DECISION   On May 27, 1935, the Supreme Court struck down the floundering NRA in *Schecter Poultry Corp. v. United States.* The justices unanimously ruled that the NRA had exceeded federal power over commerce among the states by regulating the Schecter brothers' poultry business in a single state, New York. Privately, Roosevelt was relieved to be rid of the NRA. But he and other New Dealers were plainly shaken by the grounds of the decision. Their broad view of the commerce clause to fight the Depression suffered a grave blow. Distress inside the administration only grew when Justice Benjamin Cardozo added a chilling afterthought: the NRA's code making represented "an unconstitutional delegation of legislative power" to the executive branch. Without the ability to make rules and regulations, all the executive agencies of the New Deal might flounder.

Planning for Agriculture

Like planning for industry, New Deal planning for agriculture relied on private interests—the farmers—to act as the principal planners. Under the Agricultural Adjustment Act of 1933, farmers limited their own production. The government, in turn, paid them for leaving their fields fallow, while a tax on millers, cotton ginners, and other processors financed the payments. In theory, production limits would reduce surpluses, demand for farm commodities would rise (as would prices), and agriculture would recover.

AGRICULTURE ADJUSTMENT ADMINISTRATION   In practice, the Agricultural Adjustment Administration (AAA) did help to increase prices. Unlike the code-ridden NRA, the AAA wisely confined coverage to seven basic commodities. As a way to push prices even higher, the new Commodity Credit Corporation gave loans to farmers who stored their crops rather than sold them—a revival of the Populists' old subtreasury plan (see page 567). Farm income rose from $5.5 billion in 1932 to $8.7 billion in 1935.

Not all the gains in farm income were the result of government actions or free from problems. In the mid-1930s dust storms, droughts, and floods helped reduce harvests and push up prices. The AAA, moreover, failed to distribute its benefits equally. Large landowners controlled decisions over which plots would be left fallow. In the South these decisions frequently meant cutting the acreage of tenants and sharecroppers or forcing them out. Even when they reduced the acreage that they themselves

"OF COURSE WE MAY HAVE TO CHANGE REMEDIES IF WE DONT GET RESULTS"

F.D.R.

NEW DEAL REMEDIES

CONGRESS

NRA

Anti-Roosevelt cartoonists had a field day with the New Deal's many agencies created to provide relief during the Depression. Here the president, attended by a willing Congressional nursemaid, supplies an overabundance of patent medicines, which the doctor cheerfully acknowledges may not work. How many bottles of the medicine can you decipher? Are any of the agencies still in existence today? Why is the bottle marked NRA the largest?

plowed, big farmers could increase yields through intensive cultivation.

In 1936 the Supreme Court voided the Agricultural Adjustment Act. In *Butler v. U.S.*, the six-justice majority concluded that the government had no right to regulate agriculture, either by limiting production or by taxing processors. A hastily drawn replacement, the Soil Conservation and Domestic Allotment Act (1936), addressed the complaints. Farmers were now subsidized for practicing "conservation"—taking soil-depleting crops off the land—and paid from general revenues instead of a special tax. A second Agricultural Adjustment Act in 1938 returned production quotas.

Other agencies tried to help impoverished farmers. The Farm Credit Administration refinanced about a fifth of all farm mortgages. In 1935 the Resettlement Administration gave struggling farmers a fresh start by moving them to more productive land. Beginning in 1937 the Farm Security Administration furnished low-interest loans to help tenants buy family farms. In no case, however, did the rural poor have enough political clout to obtain sufficient funds from Congress. Fewer than 5,000 families of a projected 500,000 were resettled, and less than 2 percent of tenant farmers received loans.

✓ REVIEW

What measures did the early New Deal take to relieve the Depression, and how successful were they?

A SECOND NEW DEAL (1935–1936)

"BOYS—THIS IS OUR HOUR," CROWED the president's closest adviser, Harry Hopkins, in the spring of 1935. A year earlier voters broke precedent by returning the party in power to Congress, giving the Democrats their largest majorities in decades. With the presidential election only a year away, time was short and Hopkins knew it: "We've got to get everything we want—a works program, social security, wages and hours, everything—now or never."

Hopkins calculated correctly. In 1935 politics, swept along by a torrent of protest, led to a "second hundred days" of lawmaking and a "Second New Deal." The emphasis shifted from planning and cooperation with business to greater regulation of business, broader relief, and bolder reform. A limited welfare state emerged in which the government was finally committed, at least symbolically, to guaranteeing the material well-being of needy Americans.

Dissent from the Deal

In 1934 a mob of 6,000 stormed the Minneapolis city hall, demanding more relief and higher pay for government jobs. In San Francisco longshoremen walked off the job, igniting a citywide strike. By year's end 1.5 million workers had joined in 1,800 strikes. Conditions were improving but not quickly enough, and across the country dissent grew.

LIBERTY LEAGUE   From the right came the charges of a few wealthy business executives and conservatives that Roosevelt was an enemy of private property and a dictator in the making. In August 1934 they founded the American Liberty League. Despite spending $1 million in anti–New Deal advertising, the league won little support and only helped to convince the president that cooperation with business was failing.

"END POVERTY IN CALIFORNIA"   In California discontented voters took over the Democratic Party and turned sharply to the left by nominating novelist Upton Sinclair, a Socialist, for governor. Running under the slogan "End Poverty in California" (EPIC), Sinclair proposed to confiscate idle factories and land and permit the unemployed to produce for their own use. Republicans mounted a no-holds-barred counterattack, including fake newsreels depicting Sinclair as a Bolshevik, atheist, and free-lover. He lost the election but won nearly 1 million votes.

HUEY LONG   Huey P. Long, the flamboyant Democratic senator from Louisiana, had ridden to power on a wave of rural discontent against banks, corporations, and political machines. As governor of Louisiana, he pushed through reforms regulating utilities, building roads and schools, even distributing free schoolbooks. Opponents called him a "dictator"; most Louisianans simply called him the "Kingfish." Breaking with Roosevelt in 1933, Long pledged to bring about recovery by making "every man a king." His "Share Our Wealth" plan was a drastic but simple program for recovery: the government would limit the size

Louisiana governor and one-time U.S. senator Huey Long promised to make "every man a king," but critics predicted that only Long would wear the crown. Power-hungry and charismatic, the Kingfish made no secret of his presidential aspirations.

of all fortunes and confiscate the rest. Every family would be guaranteed an annual income of $2,500 and an estate of $5,000, enough to buy a house, an automobile, and a radio (over which Long had already built a national following).

By 1935, one year after its founding, Long's Share Our Wealth organization boasted 27,000 clubs with files containing nearly 8 million names. Democratic National Committee members shuddered at polls showing that Long might capture up to 4 million votes in 1936, not enough to win but enough to put a Republican in the White House. Late in 1935, in the corridors of the Louisiana State Capitol, Long was shot to death by a disgruntled constituent whose family had been wronged by the Long political machine.

CHARLES COUGHLIN — Father Charles Coughlin was Long's urban counterpart. Where Long explained the Depression as the result of bloated fortunes, Coughlin blamed banks. In weekly broadcasts from the Shrine of the Little Flower in suburban Detroit, the "Radio Priest" told his working-class, largely Catholic audience that international bankers had toppled the world economy by manipulating gold-backed currencies.

Coughlin promised to end the Depression with simple strokes: nationalizing banks, inflating the currency with silver, spreading work. (None would have worked because each would have dampened investment, the key to recovery.) Across the urban North, 30 to 40 million Americans—the largest audience in the world—huddled around their radios to listen. In 1934 Coughlin organized the National Union for Social Justice to pressure both parties. As the election of 1936 approached, the Union loomed on the political horizon.

FRANCIS TOWNSEND — A less ominous challenge came from Dr. Francis Townsend. The 67-year-old physician had recently retired from California's public health service. Moved by the plight of elderly Americans without pensions or medical insurance, Townsend created Old Age Revolving Pensions, Limited, in 1934. He proposed to have the government pay $200 a month to those 60 years or older who quit their jobs and spent the money within 30 days. By 1936 Townsend clubs counted 3.5 million members, most of them small business-people and farmers at or beyond retirement age.

For all their differences, Sinclair, Long, Coughlin, Townsend, and other critics struck similar chords. Although the solutions they proposed were simplistic, the problems they addressed were serious: a maldistribution of goods and wealth, inadequacies in the money supply, the plight of the elderly. They attacked the growing control of corporations, banks, and government over individuals and communities. And they created mass political movements based on social as well as economic dissatisfaction. When Sinclair supporters pledged to produce for their own use and Long's followers swore to "share our wealth," when Coughlinites damned the "monied interests" and elderly Townsendites bemoaned foul-ups in Washington, they were also trying to protect their freedom and their communities from the intrusion of big business and big government.

The Second Hundred Days

By the spring of 1935 the forces of discontent were pushing Roosevelt to more action. So was Congress. With Democrats accounting for more than two-thirds of both houses, they were prepared to outspend the president in extending the New Deal. A "second hundred days" produced a legislative barrage that moved the New Deal toward Roosevelt's ultimate destination—"a little to the left of center," where government could soften the impact of industrialism, protect the needy, and compensate for the boom-and-bust business cycle.

WORKS PROGRESS ADMINISTRATION — To help the many Americans who were still jobless, Roosevelt proposed the Emergency Relief Appropriation Act of 1935, with a record $4.8 billion for relief and employment. Some of the money went to the new National Youth Administration (NYA) for more than 4.5 million jobs for young people. The lion's share went to the new Works Progress Administration (WPA), where Harry Hopkins mounted the largest work relief program in history. Before its end in 1943, the WPA employed at least 8.5 million people.

Constrained from competing with private industry, Hopkins showed remarkable ingenuity. WPA workers pulled libraries on the backs of horses through the foothills of Kentucky and drafted a map in Braille for sightless citizens in Massachusetts. They taught art in a Cincinnati psychiatric ward and built the handcrafted Timberline Lodge near the peak of Mount Hood in Oregon. In 1938 alone the WPA put 3.3 million Americans to work. Before its demise in 1943, it spent 80 percent of its budget on wages.

The ambitious Social Security Act, passed in 1935, sought to help those who could not help themselves: the aged poor, the infirmed, dependent children. In this commitment to the destitute it laid the groundwork for the modern welfare state. Social Security also acted as an economic stabilizer by furnishing pensions for retirees and insurance for those who lost their jobs. A payroll tax on both employer and employee underwrote pensions after age 65, while an employer-financed system of insurance made possible government payments to unemployed workers.

Social Security marked a historic reversal in American political values. A new social contract between the government and the people replaced the gospel of self-help and the older policies of laissez faire. At last government acknowledged a broad responsibility to protect the social rights of citizens. The welfare state, foreshadowed in the aid given veterans and their families after the Civil War, was institutionalized, though its coverage was limited. To win the votes of southern congressmen hostile to African Americans, the legislation excluded farmworkers and domestic servants, doubtless among the neediest Americans but often black and disproportionately southern.

NATIONAL LABOR RELATIONS ACT Congress whittled down Roosevelt's plan for "cradle-to-grave" social insurance, but its labor legislation pushed the president well beyond his goal of providing paternalistic aid for workers, such as establishing pension plans and

unemployment payments. New York senator Robert Wagner, the son of a janitor, wanted workers to fight their own battles. In 1933 he had included union recognition in the NRA. When the Supreme Court killed the NRA in 1935, Wagner introduced what became the National Labor Relations Act. So important had labor support become to Roosevelt that he gave the bill his belated blessing. The "Wagner Act" created a National Labor Relations Board (NLRB) to supervise the election of unions and ensure union rights to bargain. Most vital, the NLRB had the power to enforce these policies. By 1941 the number of unionized workers had doubled.

Roosevelt responded to the growing hostility of business by turning against the wealthy and powerful in 1935. The popularity of Long's tirades against the rich and Coughlin's against banks sharpened his points of attack. The Revenue Act of 1935 (called the "Wealth Tax Act") threatened to "soak the rich." By the time it worked its way through Congress, however, it levied only moderate taxes on high incomes and inheritances. The Banking Act of 1935 centralized authority over the money market in the Federal Reserve Board. By controlling interest rates and the money supply, government increased its ability to compensate for swings in the economy and reduced the power of banks. The Public Utilities Holding Company Act (1935) limited the size of utility empires. Long the target of progressive reformers, the giant holding companies produced nothing but higher profits for speculators and higher prices for consumers. Diluted like the wealth tax, the utility law was still a political victory for New Dealers.

The Election of 1936

In June 1936 Roosevelt traveled to Philadelphia to accept the Democratic nomination for a second term as president. "This generation of Americans has a rendezvous with destiny," he told a crowd of 100,000. Whatever destiny had in store, Roosevelt knew that the coming election would turn on a single issue: "It's myself."

Roosevelt ignored his Republican opponent, Governor Alfred Landon of Kansas. Despite a bulging campaign chest of $14 million, Landon lacked luster as well as issues. He favored the regulation of business, a balanced budget, and much of the New Deal. For his part Roosevelt turned the election into a contest between haves and have-nots. The forces of "organized money are unanimous in their hate for me," he told a roaring crowd at New York City's Madison Square Garden, "and I welcome their hatred."

The strategy deflated Republicans, discredited conservatives, and stole the thunder of the newly formed Union Party of Townsendites, Coughlinites, and old Long supporters. The election returns shocked even experienced observers. Roosevelt won the largest electoral victory ever—523 to 8—and a whopping 60.8 percent of the popular vote. The margin of victory came from those at the bottom of the economic ladder, grateful for help furnished by the New Deal.

Social Security poster, 1935

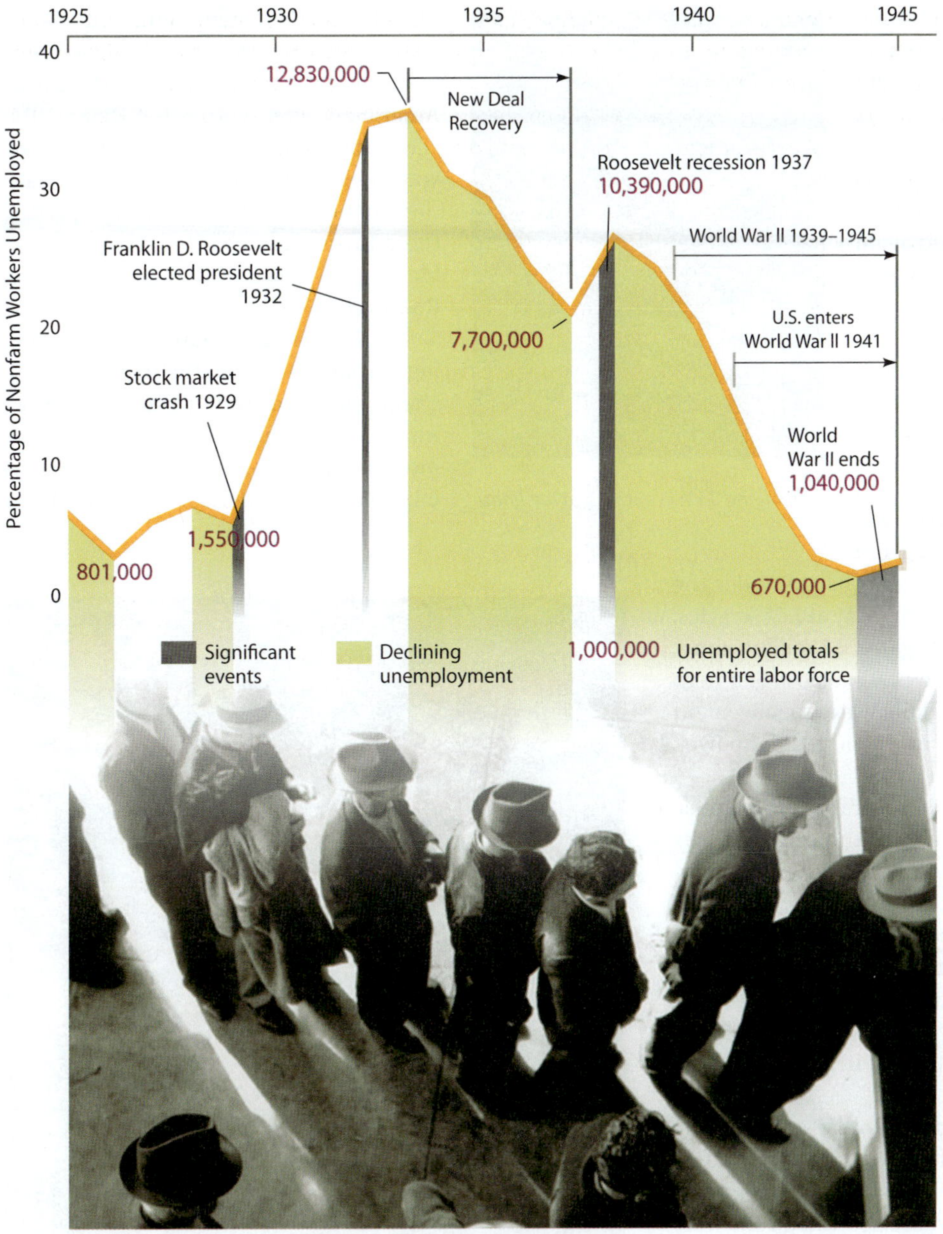

1925 1930 1935 1940 1945

40

12,830,000

New Deal
Recovery

30

Franklin D. Roosevelt
elected president
1932

Roosevelt recession 1937
10,390,000

World War II 1939–1945

20

Stock market
crash 1929

7,700,000

U.S. enters
World War II 1941

World
War II ends
1,040,000

Percentage of Nonfarm Workers Unemployed

10

1,550,000

0

801,000

670,000

■ Significant
events

▨ Declining
unemployment

1,000,000 Unemployed totals
for entire labor force

Unemployment mushroomed in the wake of the stock market crash of 1929. It did not drop to 1929 levels until American entry into the Second World War in 1941. The yellow bands indicate periods of declining unemployment. Note that unemployment begins to rise in 1945 as the military services begin to stand down, wartime industries begin the slow shift to peacetime production, and returning veterans begin to flood the labor force.

ROOSEVELT COALITION A dramatic political realignment was now clearly in place, as important as the Republican rise to power in 1896. The Democrats reigned as the new majority party for the next 30 years. The "Roosevelt coalition" rested on three pillars: traditional Democratic support in the South; citizens of the big cities, particularly ethnics and African Americans; and labor, both organized and unorganized. The minority Republicans became the party of big business and small towns.

✓ REVIEW

What were the differences between the "first" and "second" New Deals?

THE NEW DEAL AND THE AMERICAN PEOPLE

BEFORE 1939, FARMERS IN THE Hill Country of Texas spent their evenings in the light of 25-watt kerosene lamps. Their wives washed eight loads of laundry a week, all by hand. Every day, they hauled home 200 gallons—about 1,500 pounds—of water from nearby wells. Farms had no milking machines, no washers, no automatic pumps or water heaters, no refrigerators, and no radios.

RURAL ELECTRIFICATION ADMINISTRATION The reason for this limited life was simple: the Hill Country had no electricity. Thus no agency of the Roosevelt administration changed the way people lived more dramatically than the Rural Electrification Administration (REA), created in 1935. At the time, less than 10 percent of American farms had electricity. Six years later 40 percent did, and by 1950, 90 percent. The New Deal did not always have such a marked impact, and its overall record was mixed. But time and again it changed the lives of ordinary people as government never had before.

The New Deal and Western Water

| Stringing TVA electric power lines

In September 1936, President Roosevelt pushed a button in Washington, D.C., and sent electricity pulsing westward from the towering Hoover Dam in Colorado (begun under the Hoover administration) to cities as far away as Los Angeles. The waters diverted by the dam irrigated 2.5 million acres, while its floodgates protected millions of people in Southern California, Nevada, and Arizona. In its water management programs, the New Deal further extended federal power, literally across the country.

The Hoover Dam was one of several multipurpose dams completed under the New Deal in the arid West. The aim was simple: to control whole river systems for regional use. Buchanan Dam on the lower Colorado River, the Bonneville and Grand Coulee dams on the Columbia, and many smaller versions curbed floods, generated cheap electricity, and developed river basins from Texas to Washington State. Beginning in 1938 the All-American Canal channeled the Colorado River to irrigate the Imperial Valley in California.

The environmental price of such rewards soon became evident. The once-mighty Columbia River, its surging waters checked by dams, flowed sedately from human-made lake to lake, but without the salmon whose spawning runs were also checked. Blocked by the All-American Canal from its path to the sea, the Colorado River slowly turned salty, until by 1950 its waters were unfit for drinking or irrigation.

The Limited Reach of the New Deal

In the spring of 1939 the Daughters of the American Revolution refused to permit the black contralto Marian Anderson to sing at Constitution Hall in Washington, D.C. Eleanor Roosevelt quit the DAR in protest, and Secretary of the Interior Harold Ickes began looking for another site. On a nippy Easter Sunday, in the shadow of the Lincoln Memorial, Anderson finally stepped to the microphone and sang to a crowd of 7,500. Lincoln himself would not have missed the irony.

AFRICAN AMERICANS

In 1932 most African Americans cast their ballots as they had since Reconstruction— for Republicans, the party of Abraham Lincoln and emancipation. But disenchantment with decades of broken promises was spreading, and by 1934 African Americans were voting for Democrats. "Let Jesus lead you and Roosevelt feed you," a black preacher told his congregation on the eve of the 1936 election. When the returns were counted, three of four black voters had cast their ballots for Roosevelt.

The New Deal accounted for this voting revolution. Sympathetic but never a champion, Roosevelt regarded African Americans as one of many groups whose interests he brokered. Even that was an improvement. Federal offices had been

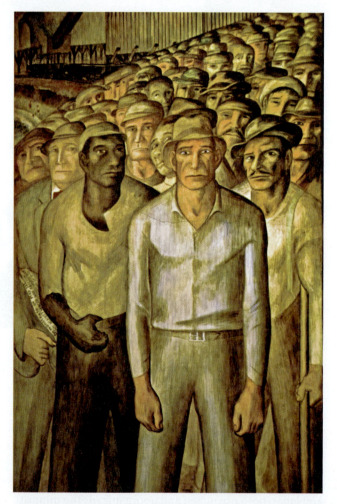

| California's multiethnic workforce is captured in this detail from one of the murals that adorn Coit Tower, built in 1933 on San Francisco's Telegraph Hill. Like other American muralists, John Langley Howard drew on the work of Mexican artists such as Diego Rivera and David Alfaro Siqueiros to paint murals and frescoes with political themes. Here Howard shows resolute workers rallying on May Day, an international labor holiday commemorating, among other things, the Haymarket Square Riot of 1886.

segregated since Woodrow Wilson's day. In the 1920s black leaders called Hoover "the man in the lily-White House." Under Roosevelt racial integration slowly returned to government. Supporters of civil rights such as Eleanor Roosevelt and Harold Ickes brought economist Robert C. Weaver and other African American advisers into the administration, forming a "Black Cabinet" to help design federal policy. Mary McLeod Bethune, a sharecropper's daughter and founder of Bethune-Cookman College, ran a division of the National Youth Administration.

Outside of government the Urban League continued to lobby for economic advancement, and the NAACP pressed to make lynching a federal crime. (Though publicly against lynching and privately in favor of an antilynching bill, Roosevelt refused to make it "must" legislation to avoid losing the white southern members of Congress he needed "to save America.") In New York's Harlem, the Reverend John H. Johnson organized the Citizens' League for Fair Play in 1933 to persuade white merchants to hire black clerks. After picketers blocked storefronts, hundreds of African Americans got jobs with Harlem retailers and utility companies. Racial tension over employment and housing continued to run high, and in 1935 Harlem exploded in the only race riot of the decade.

Discrimination persisted under the New Deal. Black newspapers reported hundreds of cases of NRA codes resulting in jobs lost to white workers or wages lower than white rates of pay. Disgusted editors renamed the agency "Negroes Ruined Again." Federal efforts to promote grassroots democracy often gave control of New Deal programs to local governments, where discrimination went unchallenged. New Deal showplaces such as the TVA's model town of Norris, Tennessee, and the homestead village of Arthurdale, West Virginia, were closed to African Americans.

African Americans reaped some benefits from the New Deal. The WPA hired black workers for almost 20 percent of its jobs, even though African Americans made up less than 10 percent of the population. When it was discovered that the WPA was paying black workers less than whites, Roosevelt issued an executive order to halt the practice. Public Works administrator Ickes established the first quota system for hiring black Americans. By 1941 the percentage of African Americans working for the government exceeded their proportion of the population.

MEXICAN AMERICANS   Civil rights never became a serious aspect of the New Deal, but for the nearly 1 million Mexican Americans in the United States, Latino culture sometimes frustrated meager federal efforts to help. Mexican folk traditions of self-help inhibited some from seeking aid; others remained unfamiliar with claim procedures. Still others failed to meet residency requirements. Meanwhile, low voter turnout hampered their political influence, and discrimination limited economic advancement.

In the Southwest and California the Civilian Conservation Corps and the Works Progress Administration furnished some jobs, though fewer and for less pay than average. On Capitol Hill Dennis Chávez of New Mexico, the only Mexican American in the Senate, channeled what funds he could into Spanish-speaking communities. But like African Americans, most Latinos remained mired in poverty. The many Mexican Americans who worked the fields as migratory laborers lay outside the reach of most New Deal programs.

Tribal Rights

The New Deal renewed federal interest in Indians. Among the most disadvantaged Americans, Indian families on reservations rarely earned more than $100 a year. Their infant mortality rate was the highest in the country; their life expectancy the shortest; their education level the lowest. Their rate of unemployment was three times the national average.

| *During the wave of agricultural strikes in California in 1933, Mexican laborers who had been evicted from their homes settled in camps such as this one in Corcoran. The camp held well over 3,000 people, each family providing an old tent or burlap bags for habitation. Makeshift streets were named in honor of Mexican towns and heroes. By chance the field had been occupied previously by a Mexican circus, the Circo Azteca, which provided nightly entertainment.*

In the 1930s Indians had no stronger friend in Washington, D.C., than John Collier. For years he had fought as a social worker among the Pueblos to restore tribal culture.

As the new commissioner of Indian affairs, he reversed the decades-old policy of assimilation and promoted tribal life. Under the Indian Reorganization Act of 1934, elders were urged to celebrate festivals, artists to work in native styles, children to learn the old languages. A special Court of Indian Affairs removed Indians from state jurisdiction. Tribal governments ruled reservations. Perhaps most important, tribes regained control over Indian land. Since the Dawes Act of 1887 the land had been allotted to individual Indians, who were often forced by poverty to sell to whites. By the end of the 1930s Indian landholding had increased.

Indians split over Collier's policies. The Pueblos, with a strong communal spirit and already functioning communal societies, favored them. The tribes of Oklahoma and the Great Plains tended to oppose them. Individualism, the profit motive, and an unwillingness to share property with other tribe members fed resistance. So did age-old suspicion of all government programs. And some Indians such as the Navajos genuinely desired assimilation and saw tribal government as a step backward.

A New Deal for Women

As the tides of change washed across the country, a new deal for women was unfolding in Washington. The New Deal's welfare agencies offered unprecedented opportunity for social workers, teachers, and other women who had spent their lives helping the downtrodden. They were already experts on social welfare. Several were friends with professional ties, and together they formed a network of activists in the New Deal promoting women's interests and social reform. Women served on the consumers' advisory board of the NRA, helped to administer the relief program, and won appointments to the Social Security Board.

Women also became part of the Democratic Party machinery. Under the leadership of social worker Mary W. "Molly" Dewson, the Women's Division of the Democratic National Committee played a critical role in the election of 1936. Thousands of women mounted a "mouth-to-mouth" campaign, traveling from door to door to drum up support for Roosevelt and other Democrats. When the ballots were tallied, women formed an important part of the new Roosevelt coalition.

Federal appointments and party politics broke new ground for women, but in general the New Deal abided by existing social standards. Gender equality, like racial equality, was never high on its agenda. One-quarter of all NRA codes permitted women to be paid less than men, while WPA wages averaged $2 a day more for men. The New Deal gave relatively few jobs to women, and when it did, they were often in gender-segregated trades such as sewing. Government employment patterns for women fell were less equitable than even those in the private sector.

Reflecting old conceptions of reform, New Dealers placed greater emphasis on aiding and protecting women

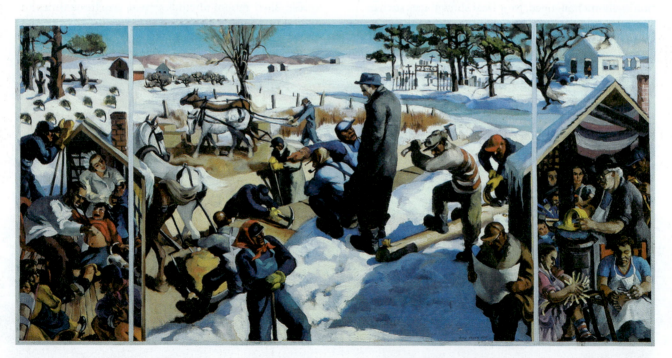

In 1937 artist Amy Jones painted life on an Iroquois reservation in the Adirondack Mountains. Indian rates for tuberculosis were high; a doctor and a nurse examine an Indian child for the disease (left side of the painting). On the right, Iroquois women and children weave baskets from wooden splints while Indian workers split logs to be made into splints for baskets. These themes of public health, manual labor, and Indian crafts formed powerful points of emphasis in the New Deal.

than on employing them. The Federal Emergency Relief Administration built 17 camps for homeless women in 11 states. Social Security furnished subsidies to mothers with dependent children, and the WPA established emergency nursery schools (which also became the government's first foray into early childhood education). But even federal protection fell short. Social Security, for example, did not cover domestic servants, most of whom were women.

The Rise of Organized Labor

Although women and minorities discovered that the New Deal had limits to the changes it promoted, a powerful union movement arose in the 1930s by taking full advantage of the new climate. At the outset of the Depression barely 6 percent of the labor force belonged to unions. By the end of the decade, nearly a third were union members.

CAWIU FARM STRIKE Though the New Deal left farmworkers outside its coverage, its promise of support encouraged these workers to act on their own. In California, where large agribusinesses employed migrant laborers to pick crops, some 37 strikes involving over 50,000 workers swept the state after Roosevelt took office. The most famous strike broke out in the cotton fields of the San Joaquin Valley under the auspices of the Cannery and Agricultural Workers Industrial Union (CAWIU). Most of the strikers were Mexican, supported more by a complex network of families, friends, and coworkers than by the weak CAWIU. The government finally stepped in to arbitrate a wage settlement. The strike ended but at a fraction of the pay the workers sought.

Such government support was not enough to embolden the cautious American Federation of Labor (AFL), the nation's premier union. Historically bound to skilled labor and organized on the basis of craft, it ignored unskilled workers, who made up most of the industrial labor force, and virtually ignored women and black workers. The AFL also avoided major industries like rubber, automobiles, and steel, long hostile to unions and employing many workers with few skills.

CONGRESS OF INDUSTRIAL ORGANIZATIONS In 1935 John L. Lewis of the United Mine Workers and the heads of seven other AFL unions announced the formation of the Committee for Industrial Organization (CIO). The AFL suspended the rogue unions in 1936. The CIO, later rechristened the Congress of Industrial Organizations, turned to the unskilled. CIO representatives concentrated on the mighty steel industry, which had clung to the "open," or nonunion, shop since 1919.

In other industries the rank and file did not wait. Emboldened by the recent passage of the Wagner Act, a group of rubber workers in Akron, Ohio, simply sat down on the job in early 1936. Since the strikers occupied the plants, managers could not replace them with strikebreakers. Nor could the rubber companies call in the military or police without risk to their property. The leaders of the United Rubber Workers Union opposed the "sit-downs," but when the Goodyear Tire & Rubber Company laid off 70 workers, 1,400 rubber workers struck on their own. An 11-mile picket line sprang up outside. Eventually Goodyear settled by recognizing the union and accepting its demands on wages and hours.

Men looking through the broken windows of an automobile plant during the wave of sit-down strikes in 1937. The windows were smashed not by the men in this photograph but by women of the newly established "Emergency Brigade" when they heard that the workers inside were being gassed. Women played a vital role in supporting the strikes, collecting and distributing food to strikers and their families, setting up a first-aid station, and furnishing day care. Women of the Emergency Brigade wore red tams and armbands with the initials "EB" as shown here.

DAILY LIVES

POST OFFICE MURALS

Could a citizen be properly cultured or "finished" if he lived in "an artless town"? That was the question asked by the postmaster of Depression-plagued Pleasant Hill, Missouri, in 1939. Such weighty matters as citizenship and art might have seemed beyond an ordinary postmaster, but he did not think so.

Neither did New Dealers in Washington, D.C. They had just made his post office the recipient of a new painting titled *Back Home: April 1865*. Pleasant Hill, like so many other towns across America, had been "wholly without objects of art." Now it had a piece of art that showed common people at an epic moment in their history, the end of the Civil War. Townsfolk saw it every day, and every day it made them a bit more comfortable with art, more appreciative of the heritage of democracy, more secure in the knowledge that the Republic had endured other crises as it would endure this one.

The Fine Arts Section (FAS) of the Treasury Department sponsored artwork for Pleasant Hill. It was only one of the New Deal programs for artists. The largest and most famous, the Works Progress Administration's Federal Art Project (1935–1943), produced 18,000 easel paintings, 17,000 sculptures, and 2,500 murals. It employed thousands of needy artists and placed their work in state and municipal institutions.

The Treasury Department had a similar mission but focused on federal buildings. During its nine-year existence, the FAS hired 850 artists and authorized nearly 1,400 works. Most were for the 1,100 new post offices built during the New Deal. Post offices were the ideal venue for democratizing art, because they were often at the center of

Back Home: April 1865, *presented to the Pleasant Hill, Missouri, post office in 1939, was commissioned by the Fine Arts Section of the Treasury Department as part of its program to democratize American art by adorning public buildings with it.*

town and almost everyone used them. The rectangular buildings reflected the solidity, permanence, and service for which government stood.

Unlike the renowned muralist Diego Rivera, whose controversial murals adorned public spaces in the United States and Mexico and often glorified workers and revolution, post office muralists were encouraged to avoid controversy. Artists were rarely permitted to deal with inflammatory subjects such as war, radicalism, and poverty.

In a decade of fear and insecurity, the murals stressed the continuity of past and present. Grand themes were distilled into simple, timeless symbols embodied in everyday experiences: picnicking on Sunday, picking fruit, ice-skating across a frozen pond. Family, work, community—these lasting values bound Americans together in good times and bad. Regionalism often influenced

subject matter. Colonial and urban scenes dominated in New England and the mid-Atlantic states; agriculture and country life in the South; the frontier and Indian and Spanish culture in the West.

The quality of the murals varied, but in the end they achieved their aim. They reached millions of common folk, combining daily life and inspiriting themes by filling "artless towns" with fine art and finishing citizens with values needed to see them through troubled times.

Thinking Critically

Why might murals have had such a powerful impact, especially when placed on the walls of post offices? How can we assess their effect?

The biggest strikes erupted in the automobile industry. A series of spontaneous strikes at General Motors plants in Atlanta, Kansas City, and Cleveland spread to Fisher Body No. 2 in Flint, Michigan, late in December 1936. Singing the unionists' anthem, "Solidarity Forever," workers took over the plant while wives, friends, and fellow union members handed food and clothing through the windows. Local police tried to break up supply lines, only to be driven off by a hail of nuts, bolts, coffee mugs, and bottles.

In the wake of this "Battle of Running Bulls" (a reference to the retreating police), Governor Frank Murphy finally called out the National Guard, not to arrest but to protect strikers. General Motors surrendered in February 1937. Less than a month later U.S. Steel capitulated without a strike. By the end of the year every automobile manufacturer except Henry Ford had negotiated with the United Auto Workers.

UNION GAINS   Bloody violence accompanied some drives. On Memorial Day 1937, 10 strikers lost their lives when Chicago police fired on them as they marched peacefully toward the Republic Steel plant. And sit-down strikes often alienated an otherwise sympathetic middle class. (In 1939 the Supreme Court outlawed the tactic.) Yet a momentous transfer of power had taken place. Union membership swelled, and the unskilled now had a powerful voice in the form of the CIO. Women's membership in unions tripled between 1930 and 1940, and African Americans also made gains. Independent unions had become a significant part of industrial America.

"Art for the Millions"

No agency of the New Deal touched more Americans than Federal One, the bureaucratic umbrella of the WPA's arts program. For the first time, thousands of unemployed writers, musicians, painters, actors, and photographers went on the federal payroll. Public projects—from massive murals to tiny guidebooks—would make "art for the millions."

A Federal Writers Project (FWP) produced about a thousand publications. Its 81 state, territorial, and city guides were so popular that commercial publishers happily printed them. A Depression-bred interest in American history prompted the FWP to collect folklore, study ethnic groups, and record the reminiscences of 200 former slaves. Meanwhile, the Federal Music Project (FMP) employed some 15,000 out-of-work musicians. For a token charge, Americans could hear the music of Bach and Beethoven. In the Federal Art Project (FAP), artists taught sculpture, painting, and carving while watercolorists and drafters painstakingly prepared the Index of American Design with elaborate illustrations of American material culture, from skillets to cigar-store Indians.

RIVERA AND OROZCO

The most notable contribution of the FAP came in the form of murals. Under the influence of Mexican muralists Diego Rivera and José Clemente Orozco, American artists covered the walls of thousands of airports, post offices, and other government buildings with wall paintings glorifying local life and work. (See, for example, the mural on page 702.) The rare treatment of class conflict later opened the FAP to charges of communist infiltration, but most of the murals stressed the enduring qualities of American life: family, work, community.

The Federal Theater Project (FTP) reached the greatest number of people—some 30 million—and aroused the most controversy. As its head, Hallie Flanagan made government-supported theater vital, daring, and relevant. *Living Newspapers* dramatized headlines of the day. Occasionally, frank depictions of class conflict riled congressional conservatives, and, beginning in 1938, the House Un-American Activities Committee investigated the FTP as "a branch of the Communistic organization." A year later Congress slashed its budget and brought government-sponsored theater to an end.

DOCUMENTARY REALISM

The documentary impulse to record life permeated the arts in the 1930s. Novels such as Erskine Caldwell's *Tobacco Road*, feature films such as John Ford's *The Grapes of Wrath*, and such federally funded documentaries as Pare Lorentz's *The River* stirred the social conscience of the country. Photographers produced an unvarnished pictorial record of the Great

"Look in her eyes" read the caption of the photograph on the left, snapped by photojournalist Dorothea Lange in 1936. Titled Migrant Mother, the photo became an icon of the era, depicting the anxiety and desperation of so many Americans as well as the perseverance of 32-year-old peapicker Florence Thompson. Her worry-worn face is framed by her children as they turn away from the camera and lean on their mother for support. Lange took at least six photographs of Thompson and her family for the Farm Security Administration. Other poses were less haunting, as can be seen from the photo on the right where the little girl smiles almost reflexively into the camera. FSA administrators chose the more moving photograph to show the human costs of the Depression and to justify the cost of government programs to help the dispossessed.

Depression. Their raw, haunting photographs turned history into propaganda and art. New Dealers had practical motives for promoting documentary realism. They wanted to blunt criticism of New Deal relief measures by documenting the distress.

REVIEW

How did the New Deal help minorities and workers?

THE END OF THE NEW DEAL (1937–1940)

"I SEE ONE-THIRD OF A nation ill-housed, ill-clad, ill-nourished," the president lamented in his second inaugural address on January 20, 1937 (the first January inauguration under a new constitutional amendment). Industrial output had doubled since 1932; farm income had almost quadrupled. But full recovery remained elusive. Over 7 million Americans were still out of work, and national income was only half again as large as it had been in 1933, when Roosevelt took office. At the height of his popularity, with bulging majorities in Congress, Roosevelt planned to expand the New Deal. Within a year, however, the New Deal was largely over, drowned in a sea of economic and political troubles—many of them Roosevelt's own doing.

Packing the Courts

As Roosevelt's second term began, only the Supreme Court clouded the political horizon. A conservative majority spearheaded a new judicial activism. It rested on a narrow view of the constitutional powers of Congress and the president. As the New Deal broadened those powers, the Supreme Court unleashed a torrent of nullifications.

In 1935 the Court wiped out the NRA on the grounds that manufacturing was not involved in interstate commerce and thus lay beyond federal regulation. In 1936 it canceled the AAA, arguing that the Constitution did not permit the government to tax one group (processors) to pay another (farmers). In *Moorehead v. Tipaldo* (1936) the Court ruled a New York minimum-wage law invalid because it interfered with the right of workers to negotiate a contract. A frustrated Roosevelt complained that the Court had created a "'no-man's land,' where no government— State or Federal" could act.

ROOSEVELT'S PLAN
Roosevelt was the first president since James Monroe to serve four years without making a Supreme Court appointment. Among federal judges Republicans outnumbered Democrats by more than two to one in 1933. Roosevelt intended to redress the balance with legislation that added new judges to the federal bench, including the Supreme Court. The federal courts were overburdened and too many judges "aged or infirm," he declared in February 1937. In the interests of efficiency, he proposed to "vitalize" the judiciary with new members. When a 70-year-old judge who had served at least 10 years failed to retire, the president could add another, up to 6 to the Supreme Court and 44 to the lower federal courts.

Roosevelt badly miscalculated. He regarded courts as political, not sacred, institutions and had ample precedent for altering even the Supreme Court. As recently as 1869 Congress had increased its size to nine. But in the midst of the Depression-spawned crisis, most Americans clung to the courts as symbols of stability. Few accepted Roosevelt's efficiency argument, and no one on Capitol Hill—with its share of 70-year-olds—believed that seven decades of life necessarily made one too infirm to work. Worse still, the proposal ignited conservative-liberal antagonisms within the Democratic Party, where many conservatives abandoned him.

THE COURT REVERSES DIRECTION
Suddenly the Court reversed itself. In April, *N.L.R.B. v. Jones and Laughlin Steel Corporation* upheld the Wagner Act by one vote. A month later the justices sustained the Social Security Act as a legitimate exercise of the commerce power. When Justice Willis Van Devanter, the oldest and most conservative justice, retired later that year, Roosevelt at last made his first appointment to the Supreme Court.

With Democrats deserting him, the president accepted a substitute measure that ignored his proposal to appoint new judges. Roosevelt nonetheless claimed victory. After all, the Court shifted course. And eventually he appointed nine Supreme Court justices. But victory came at a high price. The momentum of the 1936 election was squandered and the unity of the Democratic Party destroyed. Opponents learned that Roosevelt could be beaten. A conservative coalition of Republicans and rural Democrats had come together around the first of several anti–New Deal causes.

The End of the New Deal

As early as 1936 Secretary of the Treasury Henry Morgenthau began to plead for fiscal restraint. With productivity rising and unemployment falling, it was time to reduce spending, balance the budget, and permit business to lead the recovery. "Strip off the bandages, throw away the crutches," and let the economy "stand on its own feet," he said.

Morgenthau was preaching to the converted. Although the president had been willing to run budget deficits in the crisis, he was never comfortable with them. Still, some experts believed he was on the right track. In a startling new theory British economist John Maynard Keynes called on government not to balance the budget but to spend its way out of depression, even if it meant running up deficits. When prosperity returned, Keynes argued, government could pay off its debts through taxes. This deliberate policy of "countercyclical" action (spending in bad times, taxing in good) would compensate for swings in the economy.

 **THE DEPRESSION ABROAD** Keynes's theory was precisely the path chosen by several industrial nations in which recovery came more quickly than in the United States. Germany for one built its rapid recuperation on spending. When Adolf Hitler and his National Socialist (Nazi) Party came to power in 1933, they went on a spending spree, constructing huge highways called *Autobahns*, enormous government buildings, and other public works. Later they spent lavishly as they armed for war. Between 1933 and 1939 the German national debt almost quadrupled, while in the United States it rose by barely 50 percent. For Germans the price in lost freedoms was incalculable, but by 1936 their depression was over.

Not all nations relied on military spending. And many of them, such as Great Britain and France, had not shared in the economic expansion of the 1920s, which meant their economies had a shorter distance to rise in order to reach pre-Depression levels. Yet spending of one kind or another helped light the path to recovery in country after country. In Great Britain, for example, low interest rates plus government assistance to the needy ignited a housing boom, while government subsidies to the automobile industry and to companies willing to build factories in depressed areas slowed the slide. By 1937 Britain had halved unemployment.

THE ROOSEVELT RECESSION In the United States, Roosevelt ordered cuts in federal spending early in 1937. Within six months the economy sputtered. At the end of the year, unemployment stood at 10.5 million as the "Roosevelt recession" deepened. Finally, with the jobless rate approaching 20 percent of the labor force, spenders convinced him to propose a $3.75 billion omnibus measure

in April 1938. Facing an election, Congress happily reversed spending cuts, quadrupled farm subsidies, and embarked on a new shipbuilding program. The economy revived but never recovered. Keynesian economics was vindicated, though it would take decades before becoming widely accepted.

With Roosevelt vulnerable, conservatives in Congress struck. They trimmed public housing programs and minimum wage guarantees in the South. The president's few successes came where he could act alone, principally in a renewed attack on big business. At his urging the Justice Department opened investigations of corporate concentration. Even Congress responded by creating the Temporary National Economic Committee to examine corporate abuses and recommend revisions in the antitrust laws. These were small consolations. The president, wrote Interior Secretary Harold Ickes in August 1938, "is punch drunk from the punishment."

Vainly, Roosevelt fought back in the arena of campaign politics. In the off-year elections of 1938 he tried to purge Democrats who had deserted him. The five senators he targeted for defeat all won. Republicans posted gains in the House and Senate and won 13 governorships. Democrats still held majorities in both houses, but conservatives now had the votes to block new programs. The New Deal passed into history.

The Legacy of the New Deal

The New Deal lasted only five years, from 1933 to 1938, and it never spent enough to end the Depression. Though it pledged itself to the "forgotten" Americans, it failed the neediest among them: sharecroppers, tenant farmers, migrant workers. In many ways it was quite conservative. It left capitalism intact and overturned few cultural conventions. Even its reforms followed the old progressive formula of softening industrialism by strengthening the state.

For all its conservatism and continuities the New Deal left a legacy of change. Government assumed a broader role in the economy. To regulation was now added the complicated task of maintaining economic stability—compensating for swings in the business cycle. In its securities and banking regulations, unemployment insurance, and requirements for wages and hours, the New Deal created stabilizers to avoid future breakdowns.

Franklin Roosevelt and the New Dealers modernized the presidency. They turned the White House into the heart of government. Americans looked to the president to set the public agenda, spread new ideas, initiate legislation, and assume responsibility for fixing the nation. The power of Congress diminished, but the scope of government grew. In 1932 there were 605,000 federal employees; by 1939 there were nearly a million (and by 1945, after World War II, some 3.5 million). The many programs of the New Deal touched the lives of ordinary Americans as government never had done before, made them more secure, bolstered the middle class, and formed the outlines of a new welfare state.

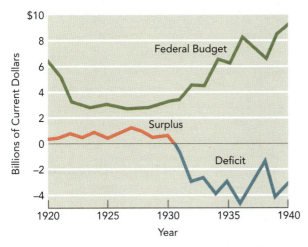

Federal Budget and Surplus/Deficit, 1920–1940

During the 1920s the federal government ran a modest surplus as spending dropped sharply after World War I. Deficits grew steadily as Franklin Roosevelt's New Deal spent boldly and as revenues from taxes and tariffs continued to shrink. In 1937 federal spending cuts to balance the budget reduced the deficit but brought on a recession that was quickly followed by renewed federal spending and increasing deficits.

At a time when dictators and militarists came to power in Germany, Italy, Japan, and Russia, the New Deal strengthened democracy in America. Roosevelt acted as a political broker, responding first to one group, then to another. His "broker state" embraced groups previously spurned: unions, farm organizations, ethnic minorities, women. During the 1930s the United States found a middle way to avoid the extremes of communism and fascism. The broker state had limits. The unorganized, whether in city slums or in sharecroppers' shacks, often found themselves on their own.

Under the New Deal the Democratic Party dominated politics. In a quiet revolution African Americans came into the party, joining workers and farmers. Political attention shifted to from cultural battles over Prohibition and immigration restriction to bread-and-butter issues of economic security—unemployment, labor relations, tax reform, public housing, and the TVA. Perhaps most important of all, Americans now assumed that in hard times government would help them, in Roosevelt's words, "not as a matter of charity but as a matter of social duty."

✓ **REVIEW**

What did the New Deal accomplish, and what did it fail to accomplish?

CONCLUSION

THE WORLD AT LARGE

The Depression shook both the political and material pillars of democratic culture—even more turbulently around the world than at home. By 1939, on the eve of World War II, the Soviet Union, Germany, and Italy were firmly under the control of dictators bent on expanding both their powers and their nations' territory. The number of European democracies shrank from 27 to 10. Latin America was ruled by a variety of dictators and military juntas, little different from the new despots of Europe. China suffered not only from invasion by Japan's militarists but also from the corrupt and ineffectual one-party dictatorship of Chiang Kai-shek.

The New Deal attempted to combat the Depression through the methods of parliamentary democracy, expanding government to humanize industrial society and generate prosperity. New Dealers from the president down nonetheless recognized that the federal government could not do everything. But "it bought us time to think," commented Eleanor Roosevelt in 1939. Even as she spoke those words a measure of doubt crept into her voice. "Is it going to be worthwhile?" With the threat of war on the horizon, only future generations would know for certain. ∞∞∞

CHAPTER SUMMARY

THE GREAT DEPRESSION OF THE 1930s was the longest in the history of the nation; it forced virtually all Americans to live leaner lives, and it spawned Franklin Roosevelt's New Deal.

- The Great Depression acted as a great leveler that reduced differences in income and status and left many Americans with an "invisible scar" of shame, self-doubt, and lost confidence.

  - Unemployment and suffering were especially acute among agricultural migrants, African Americans, Latinos, and American Indians.

  - Rates of marriage and birth declined in all social classes, and many women found themselves working additional hours inside and outside the home to supplement family incomes.

  - Popular culture rallied to reinforce basic tenets of American life: middle-class morality, family, capitalism, and democracy.

- President Herbert Hoover represented a transition from the old, do-nothing policies of the past to the interventionist policies of the future. In the end, his program of voluntary cooperation and limited government activism failed, and in 1932 he lost the presidency to Franklin Roosevelt.

- Roosevelt's New Deal attacked the Great Depression along three broad fronts: recovery for the economy, relief for the needy, and reforms to ward off future depressions.

- The New Deal failed to achieve full recovery but did result in lasting changes:

  - The creation of economic stabilizers such as federal insurance for bank deposits, unemployment assistance, and greater control over money and banking that were designed to compensate for swings in the economy.

  - The establishment of a limited welfare state to provide minimum standards of well-being for all Americans.

  - The revitalization of the Democratic party and the formation of a powerful new political coalition of labor, urban ethnics, women, African Americans, and the South.

  - The modernization of the presidency.

ADDITIONAL READING

THE BEST OVERALL EXAMINATION OF the Great Depression and the Second World War is David M. Kennedy's *Freedom from Fear: The American People in Depression and War, 1929–1945* (1999). For a comparative look at responses to the Great Depression, see John A. Garraty, *The Great Depression* (1987), and Wolfgang Schivelbusch, *Three New Deals: Reflections on Roosevelt's America, Mussolini's Italy, and Hitler's Germany, 1933–1939* (2006). Robert Sobel, *The Great Bull Market: Wall Street in the 1920s* (1968), is a brief, evenhanded study. Caroline Bird, *The Invisible Scar* (1966), remains the most sensitive treatment of the human impact of the Great Depression, but see also Studs Terkel, *Hard Times: An Oral History of the Great Depression* (1970), and Robert McElvaine, *The Great Depression: America, 1929–1941* (1984). Joan Hoff Wilson, *Herbert Hoover: Forgotten Progressive* (1975), makes clear Hoover's progressive impulses.

Frank Freidel, *Franklin D. Roosevelt: A Rendezvous with Destiny* (1990), is the best single-volume biography and William Leuchtenburg, *Franklin D. Roosevelt and the New Deal, 1932–1940* (1963), the best single-volume study of the New Deal. Both fall within the liberal tradition of New Deal scholarship and are admiringly critical of Roosevelt's use of power. Jean Edward Smith's *FDR* (2007) offers a positive, if critical, reinterpretation with greater emphasis on his personal life. For sharp criticism of New Left historians, see Paul Conkin, *The New Deal* (1967). Stephen Lawson's *A Commonwealth of Hope* (2006) argues that the New Deal was less a makeshift reaction to the Great Depression and more a part of a longer tradition of planning and reform. Amity Shlaes, *The Forgotten Man: A New History of the Great Depression* (New York, 2007), provides a conservative critique of the New Deal that rests on stories of "forgotten" men and women and argues that its policies actually prolonged the Great Depression.

Eleanor Roosevelt is analyzed in rich detail and from a frankly feminist viewpoint in Blanche Wiesen Cook, *Eleanor Roosevelt* (1999). Susan Ware, *Beyond Suffrage: Women and the New Deal* (1981), locates a women's political network within the New Deal, and Harvard Sitkoff, *A New Deal for Blacks* (1978), studies a similar network of blacks and whites. The culture and politics of working men and women during the Great Depression are the subject of Lisabeth Cohen, *Making a New Deal: Industrial Workers in Chicago, 1919–1939* (1990). Morris Dickstein's *Dancing in the Dark: A Cultural History of the Great Depression* (2009) evokes the era's pure fantasy on the one hand and its penetrating social criticism on the other. Linda Gordon, *Dorothea Lange: A Life Beyond Limits* (2009), depicts this pioneering photojournalist as a searing social critic with a camera eye for the downtrodden but no heart for revolution. For a probing analysis of New Deal liberalism and its retreat from reform, see Alan Brinkley, *The End of Reform* (1995).

For a fuller list of readings, see the Bibliography at www.mhhe.com/eh8e.

SIGNIFICANT EVENTS

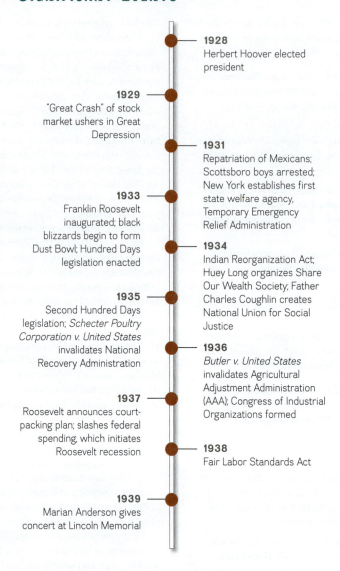

1928
Herbert Hoover elected president

1929
"Great Crash" of stock market ushers in Great Depression

1931
Repatriation of Mexicans; Scottsboro boys arrested; New York establishes first state welfare agency, Temporary Emergency Relief Administration

1933
Franklin Roosevelt inaugurated; black blizzards begin to form Dust Bowl; Hundred Days legislation enacted

1934
Indian Reorganization Act; Huey Long organizes Share Our Wealth Society; Father Charles Coughlin creates National Union for Social Justice

1935
Second Hundred Days legislation; *Schecter Poultry Corporation v. United States* invalidates National Recovery Administration

1936
Butler v. United States invalidates Agricultural Adjustment Administration (AAA); Congress of Industrial Organizations formed

1937
Roosevelt announces court-packing plan; slashes federal spending, which initiates Roosevelt recession

1938
Fair Labor Standards Act

1939
Marian Anderson gives concert at Lincoln Memorial

[What the New Deal Did . . .]

	RELIEF	RECOVERY	REFORM
FOR THE FARMER  	Rural electrifification Administration (1936) Farm Security Administration (1937)	Agriculture Adjustment Act (1933)	
FOR THE WORKER 		National Industrial Recovery Act (1933)	National Labor Relations Act (1935) Fair Labor Standards Act (1938)
FOR THE MIDDLE CLASS	Home Owner's Loan Act (1934)		Revenue ("Wealth Tax") Act (1935) Public Utilities Holding Company Act (1935)
FOR THE NEEDY 	Federal Emergency Relief Act (1933) Civilian Conservation Corps (1933) Civil Works Administration (1933) National Public Housing Act (1937) Emergency Relief Appropriation Act (1935)		
FOR PROTECTION AGAINST FUTURE DEPRESSIONS			Federal Deposit Insurance Corporation (1933) Securities Exchange Act (1934) Social Security Act (1935)

The vast war theater of the Pacific posed immense logistical problems for the United States, even after Americans recovered from the surprise of Pearl Harbor. At Guam, where rains came and went many times a day, the navy had to develop a base and a harbor to move thousands of tons of heavy equipment. This painting by Tom Lovell depicts a landing at Tarawa Atoll in the Pacific.

CHAPTER 26

America's Rise to Globalism

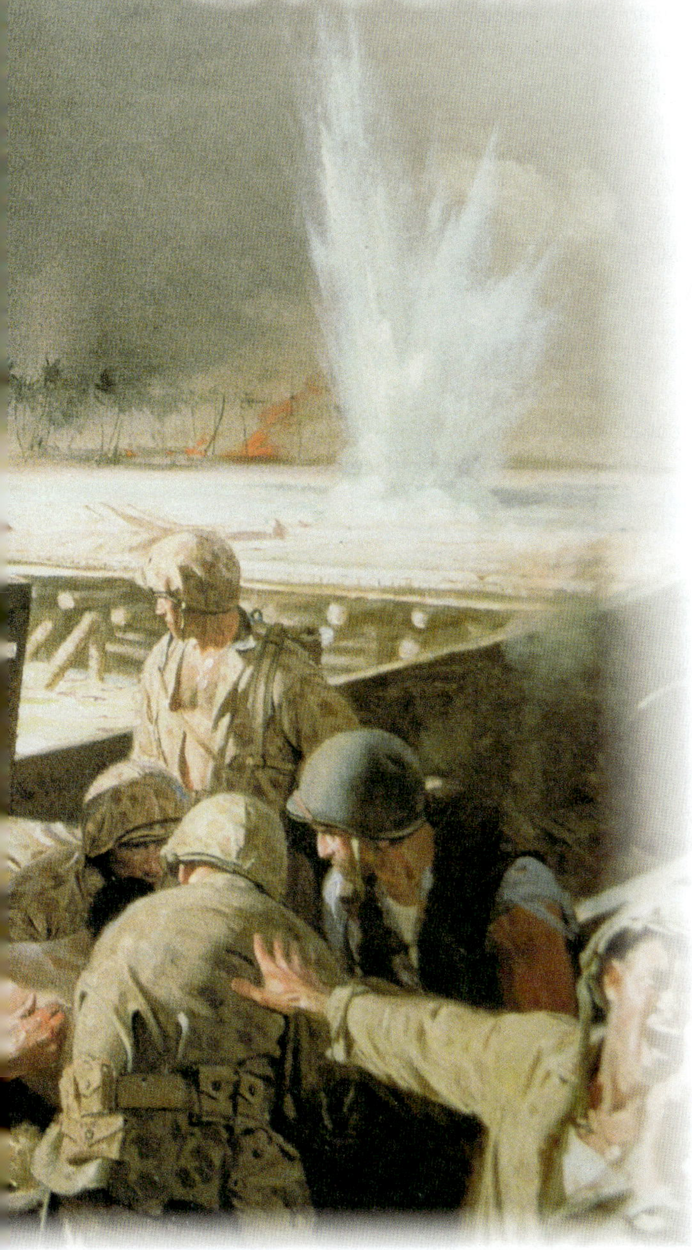

1927–1945

What's to Come

AN AMERICAN STORY

"Oh Boy"

John Garcia, a native Hawaiian pipe fitter's apprentice at the Pearl Harbor Navy Yard in Honolulu, planned a lazy Sunday for December 7, 1941. By the time his grandmother rushed in to wake him that morning at eight, he had already missed the worst of it. "The Japanese were bombing Pearl Harbor," he recalled her yelling at him. John listened in disbelief. "I said, 'They're just practicing.'" "No," his grandmother replied. It was real. He catapulted his huge frame from the bed, ran to the front porch, and caught sight of the antiaircraft fire in the sky. "Oh boy" were his only words.

Hopping on his motorcycle, Garcia sped the 4 miles to the harbor in 10 minutes. "It was a mess," he remembered. The USS *Shaw* was in flames. The battleship *Pennsylvania*, a bomb nesting one deck above the powder and ammunition, was about to blow. When ordered to put out its fires, he refused. "There ain't no way I'm gonna go down there," he told the navy officer. Instead, he spent the rest of the day pulling bodies from the water. There were so many, he lost count. Surveying the wreckage the following morning, he noted that the battleship *Arizona* "was a total washout." So was the *West Virginia*. The *Oklahoma* had "turned turtle, totally upside down." It took two weeks to get all the fires out.

The battleship West Virginia *in flames at Pearl Harbor*

The World War, spreading since 1937, had largely spared the United States until December 7. Suddenly the surprise attack at Pearl Harbor transformed the Pacific into an avenue of potential assault. Dennis Keegan, a young college student at the University of San Francisco, could not believe the radio reports on Pearl Harbor. "These places were so far away from us," he remembered. "It just didn't seem possible that we were at war."

All along the West Coast panic spread. That night downtown San Francisco was "bedlam." "The United Artists Theater had a huge marquee with those dancing lights, going on and off," Keegan recalled, "People were throwing everything they could to put those lights out, screaming Blackout! Blackout!" The next day a false army report of 30 Japanese planes flying toward the coast triggered air-raid sirens throughout the city. Los Angeles turned trigger happy. A young police officer named Tom Bradley (who later served as mayor of the city) heard "sirens going off, aircraft guns firing." "Here we are in the middle of the night," he said; "there was no enemy in sight, but somebody thought they saw the enemy." In January 1942 worried officials moved the Rose Bowl from Pasadena, California, to Durham, North Carolina. Though overheated, their fears were not entirely imaginary. Japanese submarines shelled an oil facility near Santa Barbara and Fort Stevens in Oregon. Balloons carrying incendiary devices caused several deaths in Oregon.

Although the Japanese would never invade the mainland, in a world with long-range bombers and submarines no place seemed safe. The global scale of this war was unprecedented. Arrayed against the Axis powers of Germany, Italy, and Japan were the Allies—Great Britain, the Soviet Union, the United States, China, and the Free French. Their armies fought from the Arctic to the southwestern Pacific, in the great cities of Europe and Asia and the small villages of North Africa and Indochina, in malarial jungles and scorching deserts, on six continents and across four oceans. Perhaps as many as 100 million people took up arms; some 40 to 50 million lost their lives.

Tragedy on such a scale taught a generation of Americans that they could no longer isolate themselves from any part of the world, no matter how remote. Manchuria, Ethiopia, and Poland had once seemed far away to many Americans, yet the road to war had led from those distant places to the United States. Retreat into isolation had not cured the worldwide depression or preserved the peace. To avoid other such disasters, the United States eventually assumed a far wider role in managing the world's geopolitical and economic systems. ◌◌◌◌

THE UNITED STATES IN A TROUBLED WORLD

THE OUTBREAK OF WORLD WAR II had its roots in the aftermath of World War I. So vast was the devastation of the Great War that the victors suffered almost as much as the vanquished. Some of the victorious as well as most of the defeated nations were deeply dissatisfied with the peace terms adopted at Versailles. Over the next two decades Germany, the Soviet Union, Italy, Poland, and Japan all sought to achieve unilaterally what Allied leaders had denied them at Versailles. In central and eastern Europe rivalry among fascists, communists, National Socialists, and other political factions led to frequent violence and instability. Reparations imposed at Versailles shackled Germany's economy. As Germany struggled to recover, so did all of Europe. Although the United States possessed the resources to ease international tensions, it declined to lead in world affairs. It even rejected membership in the League of Nations.

Pacific Interests

A preference for isolation did not mean the United States could simply ignore events abroad. In assuming colonial control over the Philippines, Americans acquired a major interest in the western Pacific that created a potentially dangerous rivalry with Japan. The United States had also committed itself to an open-door policy (page 584) to prevent foreign powers from dividing China. That temptation seemed especially great during the 1920s, because China was wracked by civil war. In 1927 the Nationalist Party, led by Chiang Kai-shek, consolidated power by attacking their former Communist Party allies.

The Japanese had long dominated Korea, and during the 1920s they expanded their influence on the Chinese mainland. In 1931 Japanese agents staged an explosion on a rail line in Manchuria (meant to appear as if carried out by Chinese nationalists) that provided Japan with an excuse to occupy the whole province. A year later Japan converted Manchuria into a puppet state called Manchukuo.

STIMSON DOCTRINE Here was a direct threat to the Versailles system and the open door. But neither the major powers in Europe nor the United States were willing to risk a war with Japan over China. President Hoover would allow Secretary of State Henry Stimson only to protest that the United States would refuse to recognize Japan's takeover of Manchuria. The policy of "nonrecognition" became known as the Stimson Doctrine, even though Stimson himself doubted its worth. He was right to be skeptical. Three weeks later Japan's imperial navy shelled the Chinese port city of Shanghai. When the League of Nations condemned Japan in 1933, the Japanese withdrew from the League. The seeds of war in Asia had been sown.

Becoming a Good Neighbor

GOOD NEIGHBOR POLICY Trouble abroad encouraged the United States to improve relations with nations closer to home. By the late 1920s the United States had intervened in Latin America so often that the Roosevelt Corollary (page 623) had become an embarrassment. Slowly, Washington began to abandon some of its high-handed policies. In 1927, when Mexico confiscated American-owned properties, President Coolidge sent an ambassador, instead of the marines, to settle the dispute. In 1933, when some critics compared the American position in Nicaragua to Japan's in Manchuria, Secretary Stimson ordered U.S. troops to withdraw. In those gestures and in President Hoover's efforts to cultivate goodwill south of the border lay the roots of a "Good Neighbor" policy.

Franklin Roosevelt pushed the good neighbor idea. To Roosevelt that meant correcting the political inequities between the United States and Latin America. At the seventh Pan-American Conference in 1933, his administration accepted a resolution denying any country "the right to intervene in the internal or external affairs of another." The following year he negotiated a treaty with Cuba that

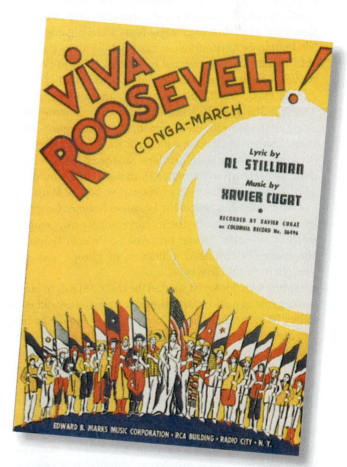

The Good Neighbor policy made Franklin Roosevelt unusually popular in Latin America, as this sheet music suggests. Roosevelt was the first American president to visit South America, and his diplomacy paid dividends when a largely united Western Hemisphere faced the world crisis.

renounced the American right to intervene under the Platt Amendment (page 623). Moving forward, the United States would replace direct military presence with indirect (but still substantial) economic influence.

As the threat of war increased during the 1930s, the United States found that its new sense of Pan Americanism promoted cooperation in matters of common defense. In the first visit of an American president to the capital of Argentina, Roosevelt opened the Pan-American Conference in 1936 by declaring that outside aggressors "will find a Hemisphere wholly prepared to consult together for our mutual safety and our mutual good." By the end of 1940 the administration had defense agreements in place with every Latin American country but Argentina. The United States faced the threat of war with the American hemisphere largely secured.

The Diplomacy of Isolationism

 THE RISE OF FASCISM During the 1920s Benito Mussolini had appealed to Italian nationalism and fear of communism to gain power in Italy. Spinning dreams of a new Roman empire, Mussolini embodied the rising force of fascism. Mussolini's *Fasci di Combattimento,* or fascists, used terrorism and murder to create an "all-embracing" single-party state, outside which "no human or spiritual values can exist, let alone be desirable." Italian fascists rejected the liberal belief in political parties in favor of a glorified nation-state dominated by the middle class, small businesspeople, and small farmers. Then, on March 5, 1933, one day after the inauguration of Franklin Roosevelt, the German legislature gave Adolf Hitler control of Germany. Riding a wave of anticommunism and anti-Semitism, Hitler's Nazi party promised to unite all Germans in a Greater Third Reich that would last a thousand years. Just over a week earlier, Yosuke Matsuoka had led the Japanese out of the League of Nations. Governed by militarists, Japan began to carve out its own empire, which it called the Greater East Asia Co-Prosperity Sphere. The rise of fascism and militarism in Europe and Asia brought the world to war.

As much as Roosevelt wanted the United States to play a leading role in world affairs, the nation proved unwilling to follow. "It's a terrible thing to look over your shoulder when you are trying to lead—and to find no one there," he commented during the mid-1930s. Programs to pull the economy out of the Great Depression gained broad support; efforts to resolve crises abroad provoked controversy.

NYE COMMITTEE American involvement in foreign affairs became more difficult in 1935 after Senator Gerald P. Nye of North Dakota held hearings on the role of bankers and munitions makers in World War I. These so-called **merchants of death,** Nye's committee revealed, had made enormous profits during World War I. The Nye Committee report implied, but could not prove, that business interests had even steered the United States into war. "When Americans went into the fray," declared Senator

Nye, "they little thought that they were there and fighting to save the skins of American bankers who had bet too boldly on the outcome of the war and had two billions of dollars of loans to the Allies in jeopardy."

INTERNATIONALISTS VERSUS ISOLATIONISTS Such charges provoked debate over how the United States should respond to the growing threats to peace. Internationalists such as the League of Women Voters and former secretary of state Henry Stimson favored a policy of collective security—working actively with other nations. "The only certain way to keep out of a great war is to prevent war," Stimson declared. "The only hope of preventing war . . . is by the earnest, intelligent, and unselfish cooperation of the nations of the world towards that end."

On the other side stood the **isolationists,** united by their firm opposition to war and the conviction that the United States should avoid entangling alliances. Yet many strange bedfellows made up the isolationist movement. It included liberal reformers such as George W. Norris and conservatives such as Robert A. Taft of Ohio, a concentration of midwesterners as well as major leaders from both coasts, and a number of Democrats as well as leading Republicans. Pacifists added yet another element to the debate.

Neutrality Legislation

Roused by the Nye Committee hearings, Congress debated the Neutrality Act of 1935, which prohibited the sale of arms to all belligerents in time of war. Internationalists protested: the embargo should apply only to aggressor nations. Otherwise, aggressors could strike when they had an advantage over their victims. A troubled Roosevelt argued that, without the power to apply the embargo selectively, the Neutrality Act might "drag us into war rather than keeping us out."

The limitations of the Neutrality Act became immediately apparent. In October 1935 Benito Mussolini ordered Italian forces into the North African country of Ethiopia. Against tanks and planes, the troops of Emperor Haile Selassie fought with spears and flintlock rifles. Roosevelt immediately invoked the act in hopes of depriving Italy of war goods. Unfortunately for Roosevelt, Italy needed not arms but oil, steel, and copper—materials not included under the Neutrality Act. When Secretary of State Cordell Hull called for a "moral embargo" on such goods, hard-pressed American businesses shipped them anyway. With no effective opposition from the League of Nations or the United States, Mussolini quickly completed his conquest. In a second Neutrality Act, Congress added a ban on loans or credits to belligerents.

Neutrality legislation also benefited Nazi dictator Adolf Hitler. In March 1936 German troops thrust into the demilitarized area west of the Rhine River. This flagrant act violated the Treaty of Versailles. As Hitler shrewdly calculated, Britain and France did nothing, while the League of Nations sputtered out a worthless condemnation. Roosevelt

A flag company of Hitler Youth parades past its Führer, Adolf Hitler (centered in the balcony doorway). Hitler's shrewd use of patriotic and party symbols, mass rallies, and marches exploited the possibilities for mass politics and propaganda.

remained aloof. The Soviet Union's lonely call for collective action fell on deaf ears.

SPANISH CIVIL WAR Then came a rebellion against Spain's fledgling democracy. In July 1936 Generalissimo Francisco Franco, made bold by Hitler's success, sought to overthrow the newly elected Popular Front government. The civil war that followed became a staging ground for World War II. Hitler and Mussolini sent supplies, weapons, and troops to Franco's Fascists, while the Soviet Union and Mexico aided the left-leaning government. The war divided opinion in Europe and America. Catholics supported the anticommunist Franco forces. Leftists, including 3,000 Americans who called themselves the Abraham Lincoln brigade, backed the democratic government. In the face of domestic political divisions, Roosevelt refused to take sides in the conflict. By 1939 the Spanish Republic had fallen to Franco.

CASH-AND-CARRY Congress sought a way to allow American trade to continue (and thus to promote economic recovery at home) without drawing the nation into war. Under new "cash-and-carry" provisions in the Neutrality Act of 1937, belligerents could buy supplies other than munitions. But they would have to pay beforehand and carry the supplies on their own ships. If war spread, these terms favored the British, whose navy would ensure that supplies reached England.

AGGRESSION IN CHINA But the policy of cash-and-carry hurt China. In 1937 Japanese forces pushed into its southern regions. In order to give China continued access to American goods, Roosevelt refused to invoke the Neutrality Act, which would have cut off trade with both nations. But Japan had by far a greater volume of trade with the United States. Because the president lacked the freedom to impose a selective embargo, Japan could use American resources to support the invasion.

Inching toward War

QUARANTINE SPEECH With Italy, Germany, and Japan fully armed, war seemed inevitable in both Europe and Asia. The three militant nations signed the Anti-Comintern Pact in 1937. On the face of it, the pact was merely a pledge of mutual support against the Soviet Union. But the Rome-Berlin-Tokyo axis freed those nations for further expansion. Roosevelt groped for a way to contain the Axis powers—these "bandit nations." In his first foreign policy speech in 14 months, he called for an international "quarantine" of aggressor nations. Most newspaper editorials applauded his remarks, yet the American public remained skeptical, and Roosevelt quickly retreated. When Japanese planes sank the American gunboat *Panay* on China's Yangtze River in December, only two months later, he meekly accepted an apology for the unprovoked attack.

APPEASEMENT In Europe the Nazi menace continued to grow as German troops marched into Austria in 1938. Hitler then insisted that the 3.5 million ethnic Germans in the Sudetenland of Czechoslovakia be brought into the Reich. With Germany threatening to invade Czechoslovakia, the leaders of France and Britain flew to Munich in September 1938, where they struck a deal to appease Hitler. Czechoslovakia would give up the Sudetenland in return for German pledges to seek no more territory in

"I believe it is peace in our time," announced Prime Minister Neville Chamberlain, who flourished the agreement he and Hitler signed at Munich, promising to resolve differences peacefully. Hitler overran Czechoslovakia six months later.

Europe. When British prime minister Neville Chamberlain returned to England, he told cheering crowds that the Munich Pact would bring "peace in our time." Six months later, in open contempt for the European democracies, Hitler took over the remainder of Czechoslovakia. "**Appeasement**" became synonymous with betrayal, weakness, and surrender.

Hitler's Invasion

By 1939 Hitler made little secret that he intended to recapture territory lost to Poland after World War I. Russia was the key to his success. If Soviet leader Joseph Stalin joined the Western powers, Hitler might face war on two fronts. But Stalin suspected that the West hoped to turn Hitler against the Soviet Union. On August 24, 1939, the foreign ministers of Russia and Germany signed a nonaggression pact, shocking the rest of the world. The secret protocols of the agreement freed Hitler to invade Poland without having to fight a war with enemies attacking on two fronts. Stalin could extend his western borders by bringing eastern Poland, the Baltic states (Latvia, Estonia, and Lithuania), and parts of Romania and Finland into the Soviet sphere.

GERMANY BEGINS WORLD WAR II   On the hot Saturday of September 1, 1939, German tanks and troops surged into Poland. "It's come at last," Roosevelt sighed. "God help us all." Within days France and England declared war on Germany. Stalin quickly moved into eastern Poland, where German and Russian armor took just three weeks to crush the Polish cavalry. As Hitler consolidated his hold on eastern Europe, Stalin invaded Finland.

Once spring arrived in 1940, Hitler moved to protect his sea lanes by capturing Denmark and Norway. The French retreated behind their Maginot Line, a steel and concrete fortification at the German border. Undeterred, German panzer divisions supported by air power knifed through Belgium and Holland in a blitzkrieg—a "lightning war." The Low Countries fell in 23 days, giving the Germans a route into France. By May a third of a million British and French troops had been driven back onto the Atlantic beaches of Dunkirk. Only a strenuous rescue effort, staged by the Royal Navy and a flotilla of English pleasure craft, saved them. The way was clear for the Germans to march to Paris.

On June 22, less than six weeks after the German invasion, France capitulated. Hitler insisted that the surrender come in the very railway car in which Germany had submitted in 1918. William Shirer, an American war correspondent standing 50 yards away, watched the dictator through binoculars: "He swiftly snaps his hands on his hips, arches his shoulders, plants his feet wide apart. It is a magnificent gesture of defiance, of burning contempt for this place and all that it has stood for in the twenty-two years since it witnessed the humbling of the German Empire."

Retreat from Isolationism

Now, only Britain stood between Hitler and the United States. If the Nazis defeated the British fleet, what would prevent the Atlantic Ocean from becoming a gateway to the Americas? Isolationism suddenly seemed dangerous. By the spring of 1940 Roosevelt was openly aiding the Allied war effort. In May he requested funds to motorize the army (it had only 350 tanks) and build 50,000 airplanes a year (fewer than 3,000 existed, most outmoded). Over isolationist protests he soon persuaded Congress to adopt a bill for the first peacetime draft in history.

BATTLE OF BRITAIN   That summer thousands of German fighter planes and heavy bombers struck targets in England. In the Battle of Britain, Hitler and his air chief, Hermann Goering, sought to soften up England for a German invasion from occupied France. Radio reporters relayed graphic descriptions of London in flames and Royal Air Force pilots putting up a heroic defense. Such tales convinced a majority of Americans that the United States should help Britain win the war, though few favored military involvement.

LEND-LEASE AID   In the 1940 election campaign both Roosevelt and his Republican opponent, Wendell Willkie, favored an internationalist course short of war. In defeating Willkie, Roosevelt promised voters that "your boys are not going to be sent into any foreign wars." He portrayed the United States, instead, as "the great arsenal of democracy." Because the British no longer could pay for arms under the provisions of cash-and-carry, Roosevelt proposed a scheme to "lease, lend, or otherwise dispose of" arms and supplies to countries whose defense was vital to the United States. That meant sending supplies to England on the dubious premise that they would be returned when the war ended. Roosevelt likened "lend-lease" to lending a garden hose to a neighbor whose house was on fire. Isolationist

During World War II President Franklin Roosevelt and British Prime Minister Winston Churchill developed the closest relationship ever between an American president and the head of another government. These distant cousins shared a sense of the continuities of Anglo-American culture and of the global strategy for pursuing the war to a successful end.

senator Robert Taft thought a comparison to "chewing gum" more apt: after a neighbor used it, "you don't want it back." In March 1941 Congress rejected isolationism, passing the Lend-Lease Act by a large majority.

Step by step Roosevelt led the United States to the verge of war in Europe. Then, in June 1941 Hitler, ever audacious, launched a surprise invasion of the Soviet Union. The Allies expected a swift Russian collapse. Soviet armies had fought poorly in the Finnish War, and Stalin in a series of purges three years earlier had executed much of his officer corps. But when the Russians threw up a heroic resistance, Roosevelt extended lend-lease to the Soviet Union.

In August 1941 Roosevelt took a secret voyage to Argentia Bay off the coast of Newfoundland. There he met Britain's new war prime minister, Winston Churchill. Almost every day since England and Germany had gone to war, the two leaders had exchanged phone calls, letters, or cables. The Argentia meetings cemented this partnership—one key to Allied victory. Roosevelt and Churchill also drew up the Atlantic Charter, a statement of principles that the two nations held in common. The charter condemned "Nazi tyranny" and embraced the "Four Freedoms"—freedom of speech and expression, freedom of worship, freedom from want, and freedom from fear. In effect, the Atlantic Charter was an unofficial statement of war aims. It put humanitarian values ahead of narrow interests.

By the time of the Argentia meetings, American destroyers in the North Atlantic were stalking German U-boats and reporting their whereabouts to British commanders. Given the harsh weather and aggressive American policy, incidents were inevitable. In October a U-boat sank the destroyer *Reuben James* with the loss of more than 100 American sailors. That attack increased public support for the Allied cause. Yet as late as September 1941, eight of ten Americans opposed entering the hostilities. Few in the United States suspected that an attack by Japan, not Germany, would bring a unified America into the war.

Disaster in the Pacific

Worried most by the prospect of a German victory in Europe, Roosevelt avoided a showdown with Japan. The navy, the president told his cabinet, had "not got enough ships to go round, and every little episode in the Pacific means fewer ships in the Atlantic." But precisely because American and European attention lay elsewhere, Japan was emboldened to expand militarily into Southeast Asia.

JAPANESE EXPANSION   Japanese leaders viewed their sphere of influence—what they called the Greater East Asia Co-Prosperity Sphere—as an Asian version of the Monroe Doctrine. Japan, the preeminent power in the region, would replace the Europeans as a promoter of economic development. American leaders, however, viewed Japan's invasion of Nationalist China as a threat to the U.S. open-door policy. Even more disturbing, in 1937 and 1938, Japanese soldiers launched a murderous attack on civilians in Nanking, the Chinese capital, leaving hundreds of thousands dead. By the summer of 1941 Japanese forces controlled the Chinese coast and all major cities. When its army marched into French Indochina (present-day Vietnam) in July, Japan stood ready to conquer the entire Southeast Asian peninsula and the oil-rich Dutch East Indies.

Roosevelt believed he had to act. He embargoed trade, froze Japanese assets in American banks, and barred shipments of vital scrap iron and petroleum. Japanese leaders indicated a willingness to negotiate with the United States, but diplomats from both sides were only going through the motions. The two nations' goals were totally at odds. Japan demanded that its conquests be recognized; the United States insisted that Japan withdraw from China and renounce the alliance it had made with Germany and Italy in 1940. As negotiations sputtered on, the Japanese secretly prepared for an attack on American positions in Guam, the Philippines, and Hawaii.

PEARL HARBOR   In late November American intelligence located, and then lost, a Japanese armada in Hitokappu Bay in Japan. Observing strict radio silence, the six carriers and their escorts steamed across the North Pacific toward the American base at Pearl Harbor in Hawaii. On Sunday morning, December 7, 1941, the first wave of Japanese planes roared down on the Pacific Fleet lying at anchor. For more than an hour the Japanese pounded the harbor and nearby airfields. "We were flabbergasted by the devastation," a sailor wrote. Altogether 19 ships—the heart of the Pacific Fleet—were sunk or battered. Practically all of the 200 American aircraft were damaged or destroyed. Only the aircraft carriers, sent to reinforce Midway and Wake Island, escaped the worst naval defeat in American history.

In Washington, Secretary of War Henry Stimson could not believe the news. "My God! This can't be true, this must mean the Philippines." Later that day the Japanese did attack the Philippines, along with Guam, Midway, and British forces in Hong Kong and on the Malay Peninsula. On December 8, Franklin Roosevelt told a stunned nation that "yesterday, December 7, 1941," was "a date which will live in infamy." America, the "reluctant belligerent," was in the war at last. Three days later Hitler declared war on the "half Judaized and the other half Negrified" people of the United States. Italy quickly followed suit.

REVIEW
What were the major turning points that pushed the United States from isolationism to intervention in World War II?

A GLOBAL WAR

PRIME MINISTER CHURCHILL GREETED THE news of Pearl Harbor with shock but, even more, relief. Great Britain would no longer stand alone in the North Atlantic and the Pacific wars. "We have won the war," he thought, and that night he slept "the sleep of the saved and thankful."

Japan's shocking triumph over U.S. forces united Americans in a way Roosevelt never could. And, as Churchill recognized, only with the Americans fully committed to war could the Allies make full use of the enormous matériel and human resources of the United States. Still, the Allies needed to secure an alliance between the Anglo-American democracies and the Soviet Communist dictatorship. And they needed to find a strategy to win both the war and the peace to follow.

 ## Strategies for War

Within two weeks Churchill was in Washington, meeting with Roosevelt to coordinate production schedules for ships, planes, and armaments. The numbers they announced were so large that some critics openly laughed—at first. A year later combined British, Canadian, and American production boards not only met but exceeded the schedules.

DEFEAT GERMANY FIRST   Roosevelt and Churchill also planned grand strategy. Outraged by the attack on Pearl Harbor, many Americans thought Japan should be the primary target. But the two leaders agreed that Germany posed the greater threat. The Pacific war would be fought as a holding action until the Allies defeated the Nazis. In a global war, in which arms and resources had to be allocated carefully, the Allies faced a daunting future indeed.

Gloomy Prospects

U-BOAT WAR   By summer's end in 1942 the Allies faced defeat. The Nazi military, or *Wehrmacht*, had become the world's deadliest fighting force. Nazi troops were massed outside the Soviet Union's three major cities—Leningrad, Moscow, and Stalingrad. In North Africa General Erwin Rommel, the famed "Desert Fox," swept into Egypt with his Afrika Korps and stood within striking distance of the Suez Canal—a crucial link to the resources of the British Empire. German U-boats in the North Atlantic threatened to break the ocean link between the United States and Britain. U-boat sailors called the first six months of 1942 "the American hunting season" as they sank 400 Allied ships in U.S. territorial waters. So deadly were these "wolfpacks" that merchant sailors developed a grim humor about sleeping. Those on freighters carrying iron ore slept above decks because the heavily laden ships could sink in less than a minute. On flammable oil tankers, however, sailors closed their doors, undressed, and slept soundly. If a torpedo hit, no one would survive.

FALL OF THE PHILIPPINES   In the Far East the Allies fared no better. Japanese forces had invaded the Philippines, British Malaya, and the Dutch East Indies. The supposedly impregnable British bastion of Singapore fell in just one week, and at the Battle of Java Sea, the Japanese navy destroyed almost the entire remaining Allied naval force in the western Pacific. In April 1942 General Douglas MacArthur, commander of American forces in the Philippines, fled to Australia. In what appeared to be an empty pledge, he vowed, "I shall return." Left behind with scant arms and food, American and Philippine troops on Bataan and Corregidor put up a heroic but doomed struggle. By summer no significant Allied forces stood between the Japanese and India or Australia.

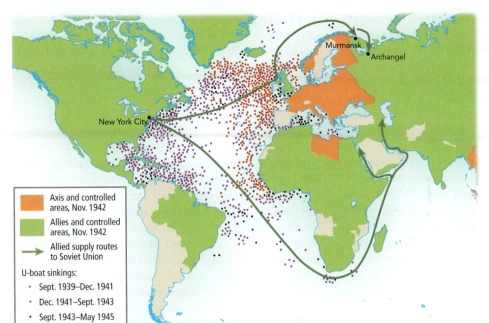

Axis and controlled
areas, Nov. 1942

Allies and controlled
areas, Nov. 1942

Allied supply routes
to Soviet Union

U-boat sinkings:
• Sept. 1939–Dec. 1941
• Dec. 1941–Sept. 1943
• Sept. 1943–May 1945

THE U-BOAT WAR

In the world's first truly global war, the need to coordinate and supply troops and matériel became paramount. But as German U-boats took a heavy toll on Allied shipping, it became difficult to deliver American supplies to Europe. Avoiding the North Atlantic route forced an arduous 12,000-mile journey around Africa to the Persian Gulf and then across Iran by land. The elimination of German submarines greatly eased the shipping problem and, as much as any single battle, ensured victory. **Why did so many U-boat sinkings occur off the north coast of South America?**

The chain of spectacular victories disguised fatal weaknesses within the Axis alliance. Arrogance would lead Hitler into major strategic blunders. Japan and Germany were fighting separate wars, each on two fronts. They never coordinated strategies. Vast armies in China and Russia drained them of both personnel and supplies. Brutal occupation policies made enemies of conquered populations. Axis armies had to use valuable forces to maintain control and move supplies. The Nazis were especially harsh. They launched a major campaign to exterminate Europe's Jews, Slavs, and Gypsies. Resistance movements grew as the victims of Axis aggression fought back. At the war's height 50 countries joined the Allies, who referred to themselves as the United Nations.

A Grand Alliance

Defeat at first obscured the Allies' strengths. Chief among these were the human resources of the Soviet Union and the industrial capacity of the United States. During World War II, Americans would develop a global economy. Safe from the fighting, American farms and factories could produce enough food and munitions to supply two separate wars at once. By the end of the war, American factories had turned out 300,000 airplanes, 87,000 ships, 400,000 artillery pieces, 102,000 tanks and self-propelled guns, and 47 million tons of ammunition.

THE BIG THREE   The Allies benefited too from exceptional leadership. The "Big Three"—Joseph Stalin, Winston Churchill, and Franklin Roosevelt—all had shortcomings but were able to maintain a unity of purpose that eluded Axis leaders. All three understood the global nature of the war. To a remarkable degree, they managed to set aside their differences in pursuit of a common goal—the defeat of Nazi Germany. The staunch anticommunist

Churchill pledged Britain's resources to assist the defense of the world's largest Communist state. The anti-imperialist Roosevelt poured American resources into the war effort of two of Europe's imperial powers, and the Marxist Joseph Stalin allied with two capitalist states.

To be sure, each nation had its own needs. Russian forces faced 3.5 million Axis troops along a 1,600-mile front in eastern Europe. To ease the pressure on those troops, Stalin repeatedly called on the Allies to open a second front in western Europe. So urgent were his demands that one Allied diplomat remarked that Stalin's foreign minister knew only four words in English: *yes, no,* and *second front.* But Churchill and Roosevelt felt compelled to turn Stalin down. In August 1942 the western Allies lacked the massive, well-trained force needed for a successful invasion of Europe. Churchill himself flew to Moscow to give Stalin the bad news: no second front in Europe until 1943. Postponed again until mid-1944, the second front became a source of festering Russian discontent.

OPERATION TORCH   Yet, after his initial anger over the postponement, Stalin accepted Churchill's rationale for a substitute action. British and American forces would invade North Africa by the end of 1942. Codenamed Operation Torch, the North African campaign could be mounted quickly. Equally important, it could bring British and American troops into direct combat with the Germans and stood an excellent chance of succeeding. Here was an example of how personal contact among the Big Three ensured Allied cooperation. The alliance sometimes bent but never broke.

The Naval War in the Pacific

Despite the decision to concentrate on defeating Germany first, the Allies' earliest successes came in the Pacific. At the

Battle of Coral Sea in May 1942, planes from the aircraft carriers *Yorktown* and *Lexington* stopped a large Japanese invading force headed for Port Moresby in New Guinea (see the map on page 735). For the first time in history, two fleets fought without seeing each other. The age of naval aviation had arrived. The Japanese fleet actually inflicted greater damage but decided to turn back to nurse its wounds. Had they captured Port Moresby, the Japanese could have severed Allied shipping routes to Australia.

MIDWAY   To extend Japan's defenses, Admiral Isoruku Yamamoto ordered the capture of Midway, a small island guarding the approach west of Hawaii. The Americans, in possession of decoded messages, knew the Japanese were coming. On June 3, as the Japanese main fleet bore down on Midway, American aircraft sank four enemy carriers, a cruiser, and three destroyers. The Japanese sank only one American aircraft carrier, the *Yorktown*. More important, the Japanese lost many of their best carrier pilots, who were more difficult to replace than planes. The Battle of Midway broke Japanese naval supremacy in the Pacific. In August 1942 American forces launched their first offensive—on the Solomon Islands, east of New Guinea. With the landing of American marines on the key island of Guadalcanal, the Allies started on the bloody road to Japan and victory.

Turning Points in Europe

By the fall of 1942 the Allies had their first successes in the European war. At El Alamein, 75 miles from the Suez Canal, British forces under General Bernard Montgomery broke through Rommel's lines. Weeks later, the Allies launched Operation Torch, the invasion of North Africa. Under the command of General Dwight D. Eisenhower, Allied forces swept eastward through Morocco and Algeria. They were halted in February 1943 at the Kasserine Pass in Tunisia, but General George S. Patton regrouped them and masterminded an impressive string of victories. By May 1943 Rommel had fled from North Africa, leaving behind 300,000 German troops.

STALINGRAD   Success in North Africa provided a stirring complement to the Russian stand at Stalingrad. From August 1942 until February 1943, Axis and Soviet armies threw into battle more than a million troops. In one of the bloodiest engagements in history, each side suffered more casualties than the Americans did during the entire war. When it was over, the Germans had lost an army and their momentum. Stalin's forces went on the offensive, moving south and west through the Ukraine toward Poland and Romania. By the fall of 1942 the Allies had also gained the edge in the war for the Atlantic. Supplies moved easily after antisubmarine forces sank 785 out of the nearly 1,200 U-boats the Germans built.

Mobilizing for a Global War

Assembling an army brought together Americans from all regions, social classes, and ethnic backgrounds. "The first time I ever heard a New England accent," recalled a midwesterner, "was at Fort Benning. The southerner was an exotic creature to me." More than any other social institution the army acted as a melting pot. It also offered educational opportunities and job skills or suggested the need for them. "I could be a technical sergeant only I haven't had enough school," reported one Navajo soldier in a letter home to New Mexico. "Make my little brother go to school even if you have to lasso him."

In waging the world's first global war, the U.S. armed forces swept millions of Americans into new worlds and new experiences. When Pearl Harbor came, the army had 1.6 million men in uniform. By 1945 it had more than 7 million; the navy, 3.9 million; the army air corps, 2.3 million; and the marines, 600,000. Nineteen-year-olds who had never left home found themselves swept off to Europe or to the South Pacific. At basic training new recruits were subjected to forms of regimentation—the army haircut, foul-mouthed drill sergeants, and barracks life—they had seldom experienced in other areas of America's democratic culture.

In this war, as in most wars, the infantry bore the brunt of the fighting and dying. They suffered 90 percent of the battlefield casualties. In all, almost 400,000 Americans died and more than 600,000 were wounded. But service in the military did not mean constant combat. Most battles were reasonably short, followed by long periods of waiting and preparation. The army used almost 2 million soldiers just to move supplies. Yet even during the lull in battle, the soldiers' biggest enemy, disease, stalked them: malaria, dysentery, typhus, and even plague. In the Pacific theater, the thermometer sometimes rose to over 110 degrees Fahrenheit.

Wherever they fought, American soldiers usually lived in foxholes dug by hand with small shovels. Whenever possible they turned a hole in the ground into a home. "The American soldier is a born housewife," observed war correspondent Ernie Pyle. Between battles, movies were about the only entertainment many troops had. Each film was a tenuous link to a more comfortable world at home, a place American soldiers yearned for with special intensity. It was not a country or an idea for which they fought so much as a set of memories—a house, a car, Mom and Pop.

Minorities at War

AFRICAN AMERICANS   Minorities enlisted in unusually large numbers because the services offered training and opportunities unavailable in civilian life. Still, prejudice against African Americans and other minorities remained high. The army was strictly segregated and generally assigned black soldiers to noncombatant roles. The navy accepted them only as cooks and servants. At first the air corps and marines would not take them at all. The American Red Cross even kept "black" and "white" blood plasma separated, as if there were a difference. (Ironically, a black physician, Charles Drew, had invented the process for storing plasma.)

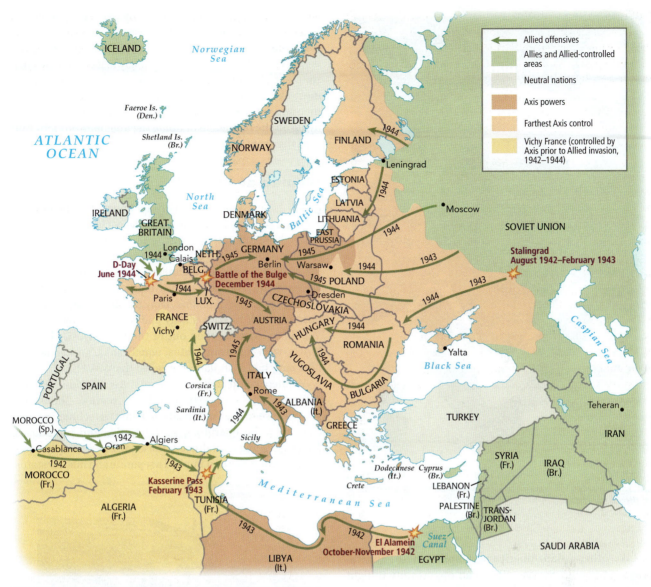

WORLD WAR II IN EUROPE AND NORTH AFRICA

Coordination of Allied strategy was crucial to victory. Until 1944 Soviet forces engaged the bulk of the Axis armies across a massive front. The Battle of Stalingrad prevented Hitler from reinforcing Rommel against the British in North Africa. After winning North Africa, the Allies turned north to knock Italy out of the war. The final key to defeating the Nazis was the invasion of western Europe at Normandy. D-Day would not have been possible had the Allies been unable to use England as a base to gather their forces. Stalin supported D-Day with a spring offensive in eastern Europe. **Why did the first Anglo-American ground campaigns occur in North Africa?**

Despite the persistence of prejudice more than a million black men and women served. As the war progressed, leaders of the black community pressured the military to ease segregation and allow black soldiers a more active role. The army did form some black combat units, usually led by white officers, as well as a black air corps unit. By mid-1942 black officers were being trained and graduated from integrated officer candidate schools at the rate of 200 a month. More than 80 black pilots won the Distinguished Flying Cross.

For both Mexican Americans and Asian Americans the war offered an opportunity to enter the American mainstream.

Putting on a uniform was an essential act of citizenship. Mexican Americans had a higher enlistment rate than the general population. A California congressional representative observed that "as I read the casualty list from my state, I find that anywhere from one-fourth to one-third of these names are names such as Gonzales and Sanchez." Chinese Americans served at the highest rate of all population groups. As Harold Liu of New York's Chinatown recalled, "for the first time Chinese were accepted as being friends. . . . All of a sudden we became part of an American dream." Korean Americans were especially valuable in the Pacific theater because many could translate Japanese.

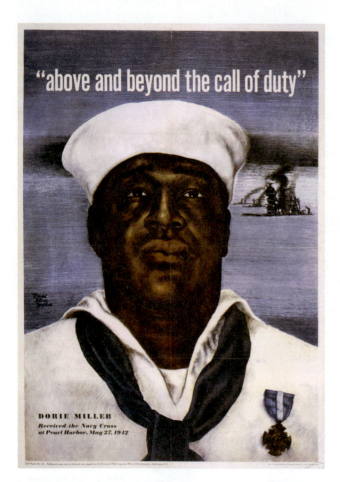

"above and beyond the call of duty"

DORIE MILLER
Received the Navy Cross
at Pearl Harbor, May 27, 1942

| Dorie Miller, an African American soldier, served in World War II and was awarded the Navy Cross. He was killed during the invasion of the Gilbert Islands in 1943.

a time of great national emergency by virtue of some stupid regulation about being gay." Homosexuals who did pass the screening test found themselves in gender-segregated bases, where life in an overwhelmingly male or female environment allowed many, for the first time in their lives, to meet like-minded gay men and women. Like other servicemen and women, they served in a host of roles, fighting and dying on the battlefield or doing the unglamorous jobs that kept the army going.

Women at War

WACs

World War II brought an end to the military as an exclusive male enclave that women entered only as nurses. During the prewar mobilization, Eleanor Roosevelt and other female leaders had campaigned for a regular military organization for women. The War Department came up with a compromise that allowed women to join the Women's Army Auxiliary Corps (WAAC), but only with inferior status and lower pay. By 1943 the "Auxiliary" had dropped out of the title: WAACs became WACs, with full army status, equal ranks, and equal pay. (The navy had a similar force called the WAVES.)

Women could look with a mixture of pride and resentment on their wartime military service. Thousands served close to the battlefields, working as technicians, mechanics, radio operators, postal clerks, and secretaries. Although filling a vital need, these jobs were largely traditional female ones that implied a separate and inferior status.

Like other Asian Americans, Filipinos had powerful reasons to enlist. Service offered an opportunity to fight for the liberation of their homeland from Japanese invaders. And, like other minorities, Filipino Americans realized that in fighting for freedom abroad they were fighting for freedom at home. A Filipino soldier commented that he was doing something he had never before been allowed to do: serve "as an equal with American boys." Such loyalty had its rewards. Filipinos who volunteered became citizens. The California attorney general reinterpreted laws that had once prevented Filipinos from owning land. Now they could buy their own farms. Jobs opened in war factories. The status of other Asian Americans and Mexican Americans improved in similar ways. After the war, minority veterans would provide new leadership in their communities.

CHOICES FOR HOMOSEXUALS

Homosexuals who wished to join the military faced a dilemma. Few Americans of the day had any knowledge of gays in their midst, and fewer had much tolerance for homosexuality. Still, many gays risked exposure. Charles Rowland, from Arizona, recalled that he and other gay friends "were not about to be deprived the privilege of serving our country in

| In the face of Japanese occupation, many Filipinos actively supported the American war effort. Valentine Untalan survived capture by the Japanese and went on to serve in the American army's elite Philippine Scouts. Like a growing number of Filipinos, he moved to the United States after the war ended.

NOSE ART AND GENDER RELATIONS

Other subjects of nose art included a shark face with gaping teeth (to make the plane look like a marauder) as well as cowboys, dragons or kicking mules, to name only a few.

What is Rose doing?

Would you consider this imagery masculine, feminine or both? Why, and in what ways?

During World War I and even more in World War II, fighter planes began sporting "nose art," decorative images painted on the nose cone. The images helped to identify friendly planes but also expressed their crews' individual identities. Military regulations sometimes forbade such decorations, but commanders looked the other way, fearing protests or lowered morale. The paintings portrayed a variety of subjects, but "pin-up" art was always the favorite. It derived first from paintings of scantily clad models in *Esquire* magazine (often pinned on walls near bunks). Original designs, like "Rose's Raiders," were created by amateurs among the ground crews. Nose art made a come-back during the Persian Gulf and Iraq Wars, allowed (always unofficially) so long as the female models were clothed. How to interpret the cultural effects of this folk art? No doubt the decorations eased homesickness and brought to mind memories of female companionship for soldiers caught in the brutal world of combat. But the stereotyping and objectification also made life more difficult for women in the service.

Thinking Critically

What wartime conditions led men to create nose art? What social functions did such art perform? Do popular perceptions of what is offensive change over time? Have they here? Would it be relevant to consider the Secretary of Defense's more recent estimate that in 2012 approximately 26,000 female and male service members had been sexually assaulted?

Until 1944 women were prevented by law from serving in war zones, even as noncombatants. There were female pilots, but they were restricted to shuttling planes behind the lines. At many posts WAVEs and WACs lived behind barbed wire and could move about only in groups under armed escort.

 REVIEW

What strategy did the "Big Three" adopt in fighting the war, and what were the first turning points of that strategy in Europe and in the Pacific?

WAR PRODUCTION

WHEN PEARL HARBOR BROUGHT THE United States into the war, Thomas Chinn sold his publishing business and devoted himself full-time to war work. Like many other Chinese Americans, he was working for the first time outside Chinatown. He served as a supervisor in the Army Quartermaster Market Center, which was responsible for supplying the armed forces with fresh food as it was harvested across California. Chinn found himself coordinating a host of cold storage warehouses all the way from the

To fight inflation the Office of Price Administration (OPA) imposed rationing on products in short supply. Consumers received coupons to trade for goods such as meat, shoes, and gasoline. The program was one of the most unpopular of the war.

Oregon border as far south as Fresno. "At times," he recalled, "in order to catch seasonal goods such as fresh vegetables, as many as 200 or 300 railroad cars would be shuttling in and out" of the warehouses.

Food production and distribution were only two of the many areas that demanded attention from the government. After Pearl Harbor, steel, aluminum, and electric power were all in short supply, creating bottlenecks in production lines. Roosevelt saw a need for more-direct government management of the economy.

Although the conversion from peace to war came slowly at first, the president used a mix of compulsory and voluntary programs to control inflation and guarantee an ever-increasing supply of food, munitions, and equipment. In the end the United States worked a miracle of production that proved every bit as important to victory as any battle fought overseas.

Coordinating Production

Roosevelt first attempted to coordinate the production effort by setting up a War Production Board (WPB). In one of its first acts the WPB ordered an end to all civilian car and truck production. The American people would have no new cars until the war ended.

In practice, the WPB was hindered by other federal agencies with their own czars in control of petroleum, rubber, and labor resources. To end the bottlenecks once and for all, the president in 1943 installed Supreme Court Justice James F. Byrnes as director of the new Office of War Mobilization (OWM). A canny politician, Byrnes became the dictator the economy needed. By assuming control over vital materials such as steel, aluminum, and copper, the OWM made the bottlenecks disappear.

Such centralized planning helped ease the conversion to war production of industries both large and small. While the "Big Three" automakers—Ford, General Motors, and Chrysler—generated some 20 percent of all war goods, small business also played a vital role. A manufacturer of model trains, for example, made bomb fuses.

WEST COAST WAR INDUSTRIES

The aircraft industry transformed the industrial landscape of the West Coast. When production of aircraft factories peaked in 1944, the industry had 2.1 million workers. Most of the new factories were located around Los Angeles, San Diego, and Seattle, where large labor pools, temperate climates, and available land made the locations attractive. The demand for workers opened opportunities for many Asian workers who had been limited to jobs within their own ethnic communities. By 1943, 15 percent of all shipyard workers around San Francisco Bay were Chinese.

As the military relied on large, established firms to turn out planes, ships, and tanks, big corporations increased their dominance over the American economy. Workers in companies with more than 10,000 employees amounted to just 13 percent of the workforce in 1939; by 1944 they made up more than 30 percent. In agriculture a similar move toward bigness occurred, as small farms were consolidated into larger ones. Large commercial farming by corporations rather than individuals (later called "agribusiness") came to dominate agriculture.

Productivity increased for a less tangible but equally important reason: pride in work done for a common cause. Civilians volunteered for civil defense, hospitals, and countless scrap drives. Children became "Uncle Sam's Scrappers" and "Tin-Can Colonels" as they scoured vacant lots for valuable trash. One teenager in Maywood, Illinois, collected more than 100 tons of paper between Pearl Harbor and D-Day. Backyard "victory" gardens added 8 million tons of food to the harvest in 1943; car-pooling conserved millions of tires. Morale ran high because people believed that every contribution, no matter how small, helped defeat the Axis.

Science, the War, and the Environment

Victory gardens and recycling drives reshaped the environment at home in order to project a war reaching into every corner of the globe. The war's physical damage to the environment was obvious, of course, and vast: buildings leveled; fields and forests pockmarked by bomb craters; millions of gallons of oil, steel, and other natural resources extracted from the earth, refined and recast, and thrown into battle. But changes to the environment were not merely monumental in size, they were new in kind. And science was at the center of those alterations.

When the Japanese and American fleets met in the Coral Sea and Midway, new technology affected how the Americans fought. In both battles weather conditions and great distances prevented direct observation of the enemy. The Americans used radar gunnery and airplanes to spot and sink enemy ships. Elsewhere, improved fighter planes and long-range bombers allowed Allied air forces to take the war to the Axis homelands. As a result, the idea of a front line lost its meaning. New offensive weapons inspired better defensive weapons such as radar and sonar, which detected enemy aircraft and submarines.

Applied mathematics and game theory helped the U.S. Navy find and destroy the U-boats that preyed on Allied shipping. The electronic calculators used to designate search patterns became a basis for future computers. One of the most critical technical advances—developed with as much secrecy as the atomic bomb—produced the proximity fuse. A small radio device placed in an antiaircraft shell could detect nearby metal and then detonate the shell without having to hit the target.

METEOROLOGY AND CLIMATE CHANGE

In their quest to defeat fascism, scientists began to explore some of the basic forces of nature. Because the fortunes of battle could turn on the weather, the navy and the Massachusetts Institute of Technology created a professional program in meteorology, using the principles of physics to better understand the patterns of climate. Meteorology and other fields of geophysics provided the military with information on the winds, ocean currents, and tides in far-flung theaters of the war. These efforts laid the foundation for future understanding of climate change.

No scientific quest did more to alter the relationship between humans and the natural world than the effort to build an atomic bomb. In 1938 German scientists discovered the process of nuclear **fission.** Atoms of uranium-235 when split released enormous energy. Leading American physicists, many of them refugees from fascist Europe, understood that a fast fission reaction might be used to build a bomb. In 1939 Albert Einstein, Enrico Fermi, and Leo Szilard warned President Roosevelt that the Germans might be well on the way to creating a weapon, the use of which might determine the war.

MANHATTAN PROJECT

Immediately, Roosevelt authorized what became an enormous research and development effort, code named the Manhattan Project. Over 100,000 scientists, engineers, technicians, and support staff from Canada, England, and the United States worked at 39 installations in a concerted effort to build an atomic bomb. Yet even as they spent over $2 billion in their quest, leaders of the project feared the Germans might succeed before they did.

Applied science was not simply about destruction. Production of war matériel mattered as well. With so many farmers at war, increased agricultural productivity became vital. In the 1930s plant geneticists had learned to cross-pollinate corn to create new varieties. These hybrids greatly increased yields per acre. Plastics offered an alternative to natural materials such as glass, rubber, wood, steel, and copper, all in short supply. For example, commercial production of polyvinyl chloride (PVC) began modestly in 1933. Given its stability and flexibility, PVC was ideal for use in construction, plumbing, packaging, and flooring. Production jumped from 1 million pounds a year before 1941 to 120 million by 1945.

ENVIRONMENTAL BENEFITS AND RISKS

Some scientific advances increased health and life expectancy. Antibiotics were first used widely during the war. Infectious diseases such as tuberculosis, syphilis, and pneumonia, once the scourge of armies, could now be contained. Pesticides such as DDT controlled insects that spread malaria and other deadly and debilitating diseases. With the use of these chemicals, the health of the nation actually improved. Life expectancy increased an average of three years over all and jumped by five years for African Americans. Infant mortality fell by a third.

The atomic bomb, DDT, PVC, and hybrid seeds symbolized for many Americans humankind's ability to improve on nature. What they did not anticipate were the environmental dangers those discoveries posed. Atomic bombs spewed clouds of radiation into the atmosphere. DDT controlled insect pests but killed beneficial insects and proved harmful to wildlife. PVC production produced carcinogens dangerous to humans. And the products existed nowhere in nature and, once discarded, took ages to degrade. The widespread use of hybrid seeds created through artificial pollination greatly reduced genetic variety. Some scientists anticipated these dangers, but any concerns were brushed aside in the determination to win the war.

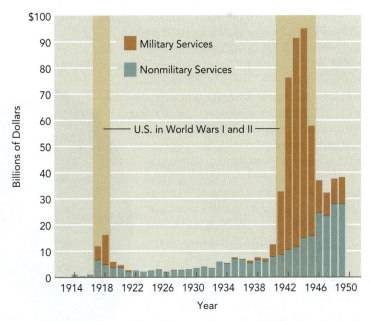

The Impact of World War II on Government Spending

As the chart shows, the war spurred government spending more than the New Deal, even on nonmilitary sectors. Note that after both world wars, nonmilitary spending was higher than in the prewar years.

War Work and Prosperity

Not only did war production end the Depression, it revived prosperity. As late as 1940 unemployment stood at almost 7 million. By 1944 it had virtually disappeared. Jeff Davies, president of Hoboes of America, reported in 1942 that 2 million of his members were "off the road." Employers, eager to overcome the labor shortage, welcomed disabled workers. The hearing-impaired found jobs in deafening factories; very short people became aircraft inspectors because they could crawl inside wings and other cramped spaces. By the summer of 1943, nearly 3 million children aged 12 to 17 were working.

TAX REFORM Roosevelt had to find some means to pay the war's enormous cost without undermining prosperity. His approach mixed both conservative and liberal elements. The Treasury Department raised money voluntarily, by selling war bonds through advertising campaigns. To raise more funds, Secretary of the Treasury Henry Morgenthau proposed a tax structure that was highly progressive—that is, it taxed higher income at a higher rate. Conservatives in Congress balked at sweeping tax reforms. After six months of wrangling, Congress passed a compromise, the Revenue Act of 1942, which levied a flat 5 percent tax on all annual incomes over $624. That provision struck hardest at low-income workers: in 1942 almost 50 million citizens paid taxes compared with 13 million the year before.

Organized Labor

WAR LABOR BOARD Wartime prosperity did not end the tug-of-war between business and labor. In 1941 alone more than 2 million workers walked off their jobs in protest over wages and working conditions. To end labor strife, Roosevelt established the War Labor Board (WLB) in 1942. Like the agency Woodrow Wilson had created during World War I, the new WLB had authority to impose arbitration in any labor dispute. Its most far-reaching decision established a compromise between employers and unions that gave workers 15 days to leave the union after a contract was signed. Any worker who remained a member had to pay union dues for the life of the contract. That policy led to an almost 40 percent growth in union membership between 1941 and 1945, when a record 14.75 million workers held union cards.

LEWIS LEADS A COAL STRIKE Despite the efforts of the WLB, strikes did occur. Dissatisfied railroad workers tied up rail lines in a wildcat strike in 1943. General George C. Marshall cursed it as the "damnedest crime ever committed against America." To break the impasse the government seized the railroads and then granted wage increases.

That same year the pugnacious John L. Lewis allowed his United Mine Workers to go on strike. "The coal miners of America are hungry," he charged. "They are ill-fed and undernourished." Roosevelt seized the mines and ran them for a time; he even considered arresting union leaders and drafting striking miners. But as Secretary of the Interior Harold Ickes noted, a "jailed miner produces no more coal than a striking miner." In the end the government negotiated a settlement that gave miners substantial new benefits.

Most Americans were unwilling to forgive Lewis or his miners. A huge coal shortage along the East Coast had left homes dark and cold. "John L. Lewis—Damn your coal black soul," wrote the military newspaper *Stars and Stripes.* In reaction, Congress easily passed the Smith-Connolly Act of 1943. It gave the president more authority to seize vital war plants shut by strikes and required union leaders to observe a 30-day "cooling-off" period before striking. Roosevelt vetoed the bill, only to be overridden in both houses.

Despite these incidents, workers remained dedicated to the war effort. Stoppages actually accounted for only about one-tenth of 1 percent of total work time during the war. When workers did strike, it was usually in defiance of their union leadership, and they left their jobs for just a few days.

In other ways, however, the workforce was transformed by the turmoil of war. In the years after Pearl Harbor, over 15 million civilians changed their addresses. "The war dispersed the reservation people as nothing ever had," recalled Vine DeLoria, an Indian activist. "Every day, it seemed, we would be bidding farewell to families as they headed west to work in defense plants on the coast." So many African Americans left the South that cotton growers began to buy mechanical harvesters to replace their labor. So many Appalachian hill people traveled back and forth from Kentucky to Detroit that the bus company added an express service. Western states that had deported Mexican workers during the Depression now welcomed a contract labor program set up by the Department of Agriculture, which brought in several hundred thousand *braceros,* or farm laborers. Their labor was vital to the war effort.

Women Workers

WOMANPOWER FILLS THE LABOR SHORTAGE With as many as 12 million men in uniform, women (especially married women) became the nation's largest untapped source of labor. During the high-unemployment years of the Depression, both government and business had discouraged women from competing with men for jobs. Now, suddenly, magazines and government bulletins began trumpeting "the vast resource of womanpower." The percentage of female workers grew from around a quarter in 1940

John L. Lewis

| Viola Sievers was one of many women during the war who took jobs traditionally performed by men. Here she cleaned a locomotive using a scalding hot stream of steam.

to more than a third by 1945. These women were no longer mostly young and single, as female workers of the past had been. A majority were either married or between 55 and 64 years old.

Beyond patriotism, many women preferred the relative freedom of work and wages to the confines of home. With husbands off at war, millions of women needed additional income and had more free time. Black women in particular realized dramatic gains. Once concentrated in low-paying domestic and farm jobs with erratic hours and tedious labor, some 300,000 rushed into factories that offered higher pay and more-regular hours. Given the chance to learn skills like welding, aircraft assembly, and electronics, women shattered many stereotypes about their capabilities. The diary of a ship welder in Oregon recorded both amazement and pride at what she accomplished:

> I, who hates heights, climbed stair after stair after stair till I thought I must be close to the sun. I stopped on the [tanker's] top deck. I, who hate confined spaces, went through narrow corridors, stumbling my way over rubber-coated leads. . . . I welded in the poop deck lying on the floor while another welder spattered sparks from the ceiling and chippers like giant woodpeckers shattered our eardrums. . . . I did overhead welding, horizontal, flat, vertical. . . . I made some good welds and some frightful ones. But now a door in the poop deck of an oil tanker is hanging, four feet by six of solid steel, by my welds. Pretty exciting!

Although the demand for labor improved the economic status of women, it did not alter conventional views about gender roles. Most Americans assumed that when the war ended, veterans would pick up their old jobs and women would return to the home. The birthrate, which had fallen during the Depression, began to rise in 1943 as prosperity returned. And other traditional barriers continued to limit women's opportunities, even in wartime. As women flooded into government bureaucracies, factory production lines, and corporate offices, few became managers. Supervision remained men's work. In short, the war inspired a change in economic roles for women without fomenting a revolution in attitudes about gender. That would come later.

✓ REVIEW

How did advances in science help the Allied war effort, and what environmental problems were overlooked in the process?

A QUESTION OF RIGHTS

FRANKLIN ROOSEVELT HAD BEEN A government official during World War I. Now, presiding over a bigger world war, he was determined to avoid many of the patriotic excesses he had witnessed then: mobs menacing immigrants, the patriotic appeals to spy on neighbors, the raids on pacifist radicals. Even so, the conflicts arising over race, ethnic background, and class differences could not be avoided. In a society in which immigration laws discriminated against Asians by race, the war with Japan made life difficult for loyal Asian Americans of all backgrounds. Black and Latino workers faced as much discrimination in shipyards and airplane factories as they had in peacetime industries.

Little Italy

Aliens from enemy countries fared far better in World War II than in World War I. When the war began, about 600,000 Italian aliens and 5 million Italian Americans lived in the United States. Most still resided in Italian neighborhoods centered around churches, fraternal organizations, and clubs. Some had been proud of Mussolini and supported *fascismo*. "Mussolini was a hero," recalled one Italian American. "A superhero. He made us feel special." Those attitudes changed abruptly after Pearl Harbor. During the war, Italian Americans pledged their loyalties to the United States.

At first the government treated Italians without citizenship (along with Japanese and Germans) as "aliens of enemy nationality." They could not travel without permission, enter strategic areas, or possess shortwave radios, guns, or maps. By 1942 few Americans believed that German Americans or Italian Americans posed any real danger. Eager to keep the support of Italian voters in the 1942 congressional elections, Roosevelt chose Columbus Day 1942 to lift restrictions on Italian aliens.

Concentration Camps

Americans showed no such tolerance to the 127,000 Japanese living in the United States, whether they were aliens or citizens. Ironically, tensions were least high in Hawaii, where the war with Japan had begun. Local newspapers there expressed confidence in the loyalty of Japanese Americans, who in any case were crucial to Hawaii's economy.

ISSEI On the mainland, Japanese Americans remained largely separated from the mainstream of American life. State laws and local custom threw up complex barriers to integration. In the western states, where they were concentrated around urban areas, most Japanese could not vote, own land, or live in decent neighborhoods. Approximately 47,000 Japanese aliens, known as **Issei,** were ineligible for citizenship under American law. Only their children could become citizens. Despite such restrictions, some Japanese achieved success in small businesses like landscaping, while many others worked on or owned farms that supplied fruits and vegetables to growing cities.

NISEI West Coast politicians pressed the Roosevelt administration to evacuate the Japanese from their communities. It did not seem to matter that about 80,000 were American citizens, called **Nisei,** and that no evidence indicated that they posed any threat. "A Jap's a Jap," commented Lieutenant General John L. DeWitt, commander of West Coast defenses. "It makes no difference whether he is an American citizen or not." In response, the War Department in February 1942 drew up Executive Order 9066, which allowed the exclusion of any person from designated military areas. Under De Witt's authority, the order was applied only on the West Coast against Japanese Americans. By late February, Roosevelt had agreed that both Issei and Nisei would be evacuated. But where would they go?

The army began to ship the entire Japanese community to "assembly centers." Most Nisei incurred heavy financial losses as they sold property at far below market value. Their distress became a windfall for people who had long resented their economic competition. "We've been charged with wanting to get rid of the Japs for selfish reasons," admitted the Grower-Shipper Vegetable Association. "We might as well be honest. We do. It's a question of whether the white man lives on the Pacific Coast or the brown man." At the assembly centers—racetracks, fairgrounds, and similar temporary locations—the army had not prepared basic sanitation, comfort, or privacy. "We lived in a horse stable," remembered one young girl. "We filled our cheesecloth with straw—for our mattress." The authorities at least had the decency to keep families together.

INTERNMENT CAMPS Most Japanese were interned in 10 camps in remote areas of seven western states. No claim of humane intent could change the reality—these were concentration camps. Internees were held in wire-enclosed compounds by armed guards. Temporary tar-papered barracks housed families or small groups in single rooms. Each room had a few cots, some blankets, and a single lightbulb. That was home.

Some Japanese within the camps protested. Especially offensive was a government loyalty questionnaire that asked Nisei if they would be willing to serve in the armed forces. "What do they take us for? Saps?" asked Dunks Oshima, a camp prisoner. "First, they . . . run me out of town, and now they want me to volunteer for a suicide squad so I could get killed for this damn democracy. That's going some, for sheer brass!" Yet thousands of Nisei did enlist, and many distinguished themselves in combat.

KOREMATSU AND HIRABAYASHI Other Japanese Americans challenged the government through the courts. Fred Korematsu in California and Gordon Hirabayashi in Washington State were arrested when they refused to report for relocation. "As an American citizen, I wanted to uphold the principles of the Constitution," recalled Hirabayashi. But the Supreme Court let stand military policies aimed specifically at Japanese Americans. The majority opinion stated that "residents having ethnic affiliations with an invading enemy may be a greater source of danger than those of different ancestry," even though the army had never demonstrated that any danger existed. And in *Korematsu v. United States* (1944), the Court upheld the government's relocation program as a wartime necessity. Three justices dissented, criticizing relocation as the "legalization of racism."

Concentration camps in America did not perpetuate the horror of Nazi death camps, but they were built on racism and fear. Worse, they violated the traditions of civil rights and liberties for which Americans believed they were fighting.

Heart Mountain, Wyoming, was the site of one of ten "relocation centers" set up to hold interned Japanese Americans. This photo of the camp was taken by Bill Manbo, an auto mechanic and amateur photographer from California who was one of the internees. Despite the drab surroundings, prisoners did bring Japanese and American traditions into the camps, holding Boy Scout parades, sumo wrestling matches, and pickup games of baseball. The child grabbing the barbed wire is Manbo's son.

At War with Jim Crow

When World War II began, Americans lived in a society deeply segregated along racial lines. Three-quarters of the 12 million black Americans lived in the South. Hispanic Americans, then numbering around 1 million, resided largely in a belt along the U.S.-Mexican border. Though separated by geography, religion, language, and history, these two groups shared many common experiences. Both were segregated in housing and in public places. Neither had much access to health care, decent educations, or good jobs. Both found employment primarily as low-wage agricultural workers.

Hispanic and black leaders recognized the irony of a war their government fought in the name of freedom. That same government denied them basic civil rights and liberties, including the right to vote. "A jim crow army cannot fight for a free world," the NAACP declared. Several barriers stood in the way of the freedom to seek higher-wage work and improved housing. For one, many unions simply refused to allow minorities to join. For another, most employers refused to hire minorities or restricted them to unskilled jobs such as janitor. Finally, residential segregation was deeply embedded in the South by law and throughout the country by common practice.

A. PHILIP RANDOLPH These were inequities A. Philip Randolph was determined to eliminate. Randolph had developed organizing skills as a leader of the Brotherhood of Sleeping Car Porters, the most powerful black labor organization. Now, he looked to bring down the wall of discrimination that blocked minority workers from skilled jobs in defense industries and segregated them in government agencies, unions, and the armed forces. "The Administration leaders in Washington will never give the Negro justice," Randolph argued, "until they see masses— ten, twenty, fifty thousand Negroes on the White House lawn." To that end, he began in 1941 to organize a march on Washington.

FEPC President Roosevelt wished to avoid any show of racial discontent. He had the power to issue an executive order banning workplace segregation within the government and within companies receiving federal contracts, as Randolph demanded. Fearful of alienating southerners and union members, Roosevelt refused to act until confronted by the threat of the march. Only then, in June 1941, did he issue Executive Order 8802 barring discrimination in the hiring of government or defense industry workers. To enforce the order, he established the Fair Employment Practices Commission (FEPC).

While it never fulfilled Randolph's hopes, the FEPC was in some ways the boldest step toward racial justice since the era of Reconstruction. The commission opened jobs in California's shipyards and aircraft factories that had previously refused to hire Hispanics. Thousands of workers migrated to the coast from Texas, where job discrimination was the most severe. Facing acute labor shortages, the United States joined with the Mexican government to create a guest worker, or *bracero*, program. It guaranteed laborers from Mexico both better wages and improved working conditions. Despite the need for labor, opposition to the program from nativists in Texas remained severe.

Black Americans encountered similar resistance. More than half of all defense jobs were closed to minorities. In the aircraft industry, blacks held just 200 janitorial positions

"WHO DO YOU WANT TO WIN THIS WAR?"— JUSTIFYING INTERNMENT

In June 1943, Lieutenant General John L. DeWitt submitted a report on the evacuation of Japanese Americans from the West Coast, justifying his actions (Document 1). Mary Suzuki Ichino grew up in Los Angeles, California and was interned at Camp Manzanar, about 230 miles northeast of there. Document 2 is a transcript of an interview with her, made decades later.

DOCUMENT 1   Sabotage on a Mass Scale

The Department of Justice had agreed to authorize its special field agents of the Federal Bureau of Investigation to undertake spot raids without warrant to determine the possession of arms, cameras and other contraband by Japanese. . . . In the Monterey area in California a Federal Bureau of Investigation spot raid made about February 12, 1942, found more than 60,000 rounds of ammunition and many rifles, shotguns and maps of all kinds. . . .

The combination of spot raids revealing hidden caches of contraband, the attacks on coastwise shipping, the interception of illicit radio transmissions, the nightly observation of visual signal lamps from constantly changing locations, and the success of the enemy offensive in the Pacific, had so aroused the public along the West Coast against the Japanese that it was ready to take matters into its own hands. . . .

Because of the ties of race, the intense feeling of filial piety and the strong bonds of common tradition, culture and customs, this population presented a tightly-knit racial group. It included in excess of 115,000 persons deployed along the Pacific Coast. Whether by design or accident, virtually always their communities were adjacent to very vital shore installations, war plants, etc. . . . It could not be established, of course, that the location of thousands of Japanese adjacent to strategic points verified the existence of some vast conspiracy to which all of them were parties. Some of them doubtless resided there through mere coincidence. It seems equally beyond doubt, however, that the presence of others was not mere coincidence. It was difficult to explain the situation in Santa Barbara County, for example, by coincidence alone.

Throughout the Santa Maria Valley in that County, including the cities of Santa Maria and Guadalupe, every utility, air field, bridge, telephone and power line or other facility of importance was flanked by Japanese. They even surrounded the oil fields in this area. Only a few miles south, however, in the Santa Ynez Valley, lay an area equally as productive agriculturally as the Santa Maria Valley and with lands equally available for purchase and lease, but without any strategic installations whatever. There were no Japanese in the Santa Ynez Valley. . . . It was certainly evident that the Japanese population of the Pacific Coast was, as a whole, ideally situated with reference to points of strategic importance, to carry into execution a tremendous program of sabotage on a mass scale should any considerable number of them have been inclined to do so.

Source: Lieutenant General John L. DeWitt, Final Report: Japanese Evacuation from the West Coast 1942 (Washington, DC: Government Printing Office, 1943), chap. 2.

---

out of over 100,000 new jobs created. The FEPC had the authority to investigate these conditions, but when faced with powerful employers and unions the commission acted reluctantly if at all. In most sections of the country it honored "whites only" hiring practices. "Hitler has not done anything to the colored people," one worker told the president, "—it's people right here in the United States who are keeping us out of work and keeping us down." In the end, labor shortages more than government action improved the job situation. By 1944 African Americans, who made up 10 percent of the nation's population, held 8 percent of its jobs.

DETROIT RACE RIOT   As blacks and Hispanics moved into urban areas, they also competed with whites for the diminishing supply of housing. The government tried to ease the problem by building new developments. In Detroit, housing authorities picked a site along the edge of a Polish neighborhood. When the first black family moved into the new development, Detroit authorities

sent in the National Guard to protect the newcomers from a band of the Ku Klux Klan. As summer approached, tensions rose with the heat. Sporadic rioting broke out until, in June 1943, white mobs began beating blacks riding the trolley lines or going to movies. In retaliation, black rioters looted white stores. It took 6,000 regular army soldiers to impose a troubled calm, but not before violence claimed the lives of 24 blacks and 9 whites.

The situation in Southern California was no less volatile. There Hispanics were frustrated by the persistence of white racism, job and housing discrimination, and high unemployment even amid a booming economy. Whites, in turn, blamed the rapid growth in the Hispanic population for an increase in crime. Their particular hostility focused on pachucos, or "zoot suiters." These were young Hispanic men and boys who adopted the style of Harlem hipsters: oiled hair swept back into a ducktail; broad-shouldered, long-waisted suit coats; baggy pants pegged at the ankles,

RP [Richard Potashin]: Tell us about what your attitude, where your attitude was at, or your opinions about this based on the rumors and the opinions that you were hearing. Did you form your own ideas about the injustice of this, the unconstitutionality of it? Was that something you were thinking about?

MI [Mary Ichino]: I think I was a little bit naïve that way. I didn't, I think, understand that depth of the, you know, the situation. You just kind of wonder, and then you follow on. I think as you mature, and I realized as I go— well, I told you about that letter I wrote to General DeWitt. It took me until I got in camp for me to realize, "What was I doing in this place?" And I go, "Why didn't that hit me before this as a question?"

RP: So your attitude changed—

MI: My attitude changed because—

RP: —when you got into camp?

MI: —I thought, it's sort of like an adventure, you know, for a teenager, when you think about it. You're moving, you're going, you know. But when I started seeing that my dad is losing his business, we're losing all our property, he lost his new car that he worked so darn hard for— What for? We're not from Japan. You know? Then when finally we went to camp is when I realized the injustice of the whole thing. And you're always taught in civics in high school that we're all equal under the law, and I said, "But how can you be equal when you haven't had a hearing as to whether you're guilty or not guilty?" And that's when I wrote that letter to General DeWitt.

RP: There was another friend that you—

MI: Yeah, Marie Hisamune. She was my classmate at Sacred Heart. And we decided to put our—well, she and I, in order to keep busy,

decided to write—first we started writing a murder mystery. And we came to a point where we couldn't figure out how to end the darn thing. And then, so then the next thing was, "You know what? We ought to write to General DeWitt." Says, "You know what, I don't know what we're doing in here." And so Marie and I put our heads together and we wrote, and we said, "We haven't gotten our constitutional hearing before we're declared guilty to be put into this place. Why is it? How is it? And how could it be?" And then we wanted an explanation. And then we're getting a little bit smarter, you know, at that age. "Okay, we better send it to General DeWitt." "Oh," somebody says, "They'll throw it out." "No they won't. We're going to make it registered directly to him." And so he must have gotten it because we never got the letter back, anything. No answer—

RP: No reply?

MI: No, never got a letter back.

RP: How long had you been in camp before you decided to take this course of action?

MI: Not quite six months, I bet. It dawned on us real quick.

RP: You just looked around and—

MI: Says, "Oh my God, can't get out of camp, you can't do this, you can't do that. The food is lousy. The physical facility's lousy. What did I do to deserve this?" You know.

RP: Right.

MI: And then it turned out to be, at that age we were realizing that it was hysteria. We figured that out.

RP: Did you have any second thoughts about writing that letter after you'd sent it? You know, like, "Are they going to, you know, are we going to be—

MI: No.

RP: —on a blacklist or anything or—

MI: Nope.

RP: You felt—

MI: Fearless.

RP: Let's—what have you got to lose?

MI: The reason, we're only sixteen. What are they going to do with us? You know? I mean, 'cause, yeah. Mmhmm. I'd been told more that once, "Oh, you're probably on the blacklist." I said, "So?" In a way, it's sort of a compliment, you know?

RP: Right. Yeah, it took a lot of courage to do that.

MI: It's either your courage, or you're so darned innocent. If you're worried about what's going to happen or what will happen to you, you're not going to do a thing. If you think you're right and you need an explanation, it's as simple as that. That was it. So there was no gaman there. Tell it like it is.

Source: 16. Item # Acc-196 (letter to Mary Ichino); Mary Suzuki Ichino [MI], MANZ 1216A, interviewed by Richard Potashin [RP] Disc 1, Part 2 (DVD), 22:41–27:53.

Thinking Critically

What contraband items does DeWitt cite to indicate Japanese disloyalty? Do they substantiate his case? What elements Mary Ichino cites throw doubt on DeWitt's arguments? What do you think gave Ichino the courage to write directly to General Dewitt? Why might she be proud to be on a blacklist?

---

the whole outfit polished off with a knee-length, gold chain. For most "zooters" this style expressed a modest form of rebellion; for a few it was the uniform of a criminal culture; for many whites it was a racial affront. The all-white Los Angeles city council even made it a crime to wear a zoot suit.

ZOOT SUIT RIOTS   In June 1943 navy shipmen stationed at the local base invaded Hispanic neighborhoods in search of zooters who had allegedly assaulted their comrades. These self-styled vigilantes grabbed any zooters they saw, ripped their clothes, shaved their heads, and beat their victims. Only when Hispanics retaliated did the Los Angeles police respond, all the while ignoring white violence. The local press added to the hysteria with irresponsible and inaccurate headlines such as "Zooters Threaten L.A. Police." An investigatory commission appointed by California governor Earl Warren rejected the press charges and placed the blame more properly on

white racism and the daily indignities faced by the Hispanic community.

CORE   Despite their many frustrations, minority leaders recognized the war effort as an opportunity to develop new strategies to confront old grievances. For example, the Congress of Racial Equality (**CORE**) found inspiration in the nonviolent passive resistance adopted by the leader of India's independence movement, Mohandas K. Gandhi. In northern cities CORE used sit-ins, boycotts, and picketing in an effort to desegregate movie theaters, restaurants, and other public places. In 1944 the Supreme Court indicated that it was reconsidering issues of racial inequality when, in *Smith v. Allwright*, it struck down the "all-white" primary used in southern states to disenfranchise black voters. In the one-party South the candidate who won the primary usually ran without major opposition in the general election. Unable to participate in the primaries, black voters had no meaningful influence. In

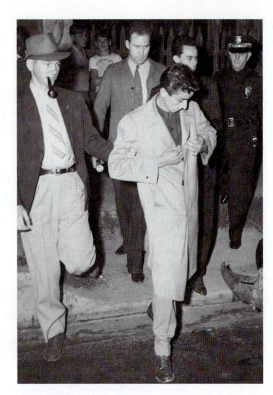

| A "zoot suiter" gets escorted by the police.

rejecting this practice the Court indicated another way in which wartime experiences had opened new approaches to confronting racial discrimination.

The New Deal in Retreat

After Pearl Harbor, Roosevelt told reporters that "Dr. New Deal" had retired so that "Dr. Win-the-War" could get down to business. Political opposition, however, could not be eliminated even during a global conflict. The increasingly powerful anti–New Deal coalition of Republicans and rural Democrats saw in the war an opportunity to attack programs they had long resented. They quickly ended the Civilian Conservation Corps and the National Youth Administration, reduced the powers of the Farm Security Administration, and blocked moves to extend Social Security and unemployment benefits. Seeming to approve such measures, voters in the 1942 elections sent an additional 44 Republicans to the House and another 9 to the Senate. The GOP began eyeing the White House.

ROOSEVELT WINS A FOURTH TERM — By the spring of 1944 no one knew whether Franklin Roosevelt would seek an unprecedented fourth term. The president's health had declined noticeably. Pallid skin, sagging shoulders, and shaking hands seemed obvious signs that he had aged too much to run. In July, one week before the Democratic Convention, Roosevelt announced his decision: "All that is within me cries out to go back to my home on the Hudson River. . . . But as a good soldier . . . I will accept and serve." Conservative Democrats, however, made sure to remove Roosevelt's liberal vice president, Henry Wallace, from the ticket. In his place they settled on

Harry S Truman of Missouri, a loyal New Dealer and party stalwart. The Republicans chose the moderate governor of New York, Thomas E. Dewey, to run against Roosevelt, but the stiff and formal Dewey never had much of a chance. At the polls, voters gave Roosevelt 25.6 million popular votes to Dewey's 22 million, a clear victory, although the election was tighter than any since 1916. Like its aging leader, the New Deal coalition was showing signs of strain.

REVIEW

How did the war affect the rights of Italian Americans, Japanese Americans, African Americans, and Mexican Americans?

WINNING THE WAR AND THE PEACE

TO IMPRESS UPON NEWLY ARRIVED officers the vastness of the war theater in the Pacific, General Douglas MacArthur laid out a map of the region. Over it he placed an outline map of the United States. Running the war from headquarters in Australia, MacArthur pointed out, the distances were about the same as if, in the Western Hemisphere, the center was located in South America. On the same scale Tokyo would lie far up in northern Canada, Iwo Jima somewhere in Hudson Bay, Singapore in Utah, Manila in North Dakota, and Hawaii off the coast of Scotland.

In a war that stretched from one end of the globe to the other, the Allies had to coordinate their strategies on a grand scale. Which war theaters would receive equipment in short supply? Who would administer conquered territories? Inevitably, the questions of fighting a war slid into discussions of the peace that would follow. What would happen to occupied territories? What peace terms would the Allies offer? If a more stable world order could not be created, the cycle of violence might never end. So, as Allied armies struggled mile by mile to defeat the Axis, Allied diplomacy concentrated winning the peace as well as the war.

The Fall of the Third Reich

After pushing the Germans out of North Africa in May 1943, Allied forces looked to drive Italy from the war. Late in July, two weeks after a quarter of a million British and American troops had landed on Sicily, Mussolini fled to German-held northern Italy. Although Italy surrendered early in September, Germany continued to pour in reinforcements. It took the Allies almost a year of bloody fighting to reach Rome, and at the end of the campaign they had yet to break German lines. Along the eastern front, Soviet armies steadily pushed the Germans out of Russia and back toward Berlin.

D-DAY — General Dwight D. Eisenhower, fresh from battle in North Africa and the Mediterranean, took command of Allied preparations for Operation Overlord, a massive invasion of Europe striking from across the English Channel. By June 1944 all attention focused on the coast of France, for Hitler, of course, knew the Allies were

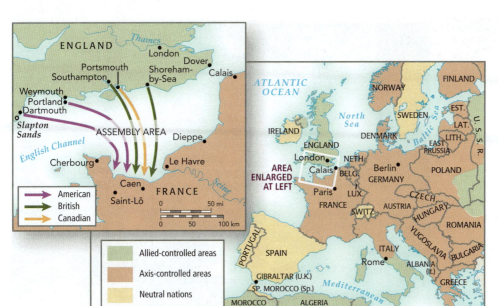

The final key to defeating the Nazis was the invasion of western Europe at Normandy. D-Day for the invasion was June 6, 1944, and the massive undertaking would not have been possible had the Allies been unable to use England as a base to gather their forces. Stalin supported D-Day with a spring offensive in eastern Europe. **Why might Hitler have assumed Calais was the Allies' likely target?**

preparing to invade. He suspected they would hit Calais, the French port city closest to the British Isles. Allied planners did their best to encourage this belief, even deploying fake armaments across the channel. On the morning of June 6, 1944, the invasion began—not at Calais but on the less fortified beaches of Normandy. Almost 3 million men, 11,000 aircraft, and more than 2,000 vessels took part in D-Day.

As Allied forces hit the beaches, luck and Eisenhower's meticulous planning favored their cause. Persuaded that the Allies still wanted Calais, Hitler delayed sending in two reserve divisions. His indecision allowed the Allied forces to secure a foothold. Over the next few days more than 1.5 million soldiers landed on the beaches—but they still had to move inland. The Allied advance from Normandy took almost two months, not several weeks as expected. But once Allied tanks broke through German lines, their progress was spectacular. In August Paris was liberated, and by mid-September the Allies had driven the Germans from France and Belgium.

All went well until December 1944, when Hitler threw his reserves into a last, desperate gamble. The unexpected German onslaught drove the Allied lines back along a 50-mile bulge. There the Germans trapped the 101st Airborne Division. When asked to surrender, General Tony MacAuliffe sent back a one-word reply: "Nuts!" His troops held, General George Patton raced to the rescue, and the last German offensive collapsed. Little stood between the Allies and Berlin.

Two Roads to Tokyo

In the bleak days of 1942 General Douglas MacArthur—flamboyant and jaunty with his dark sunglasses and corncob pipe—had emerged as America's only military hero. MacArthur believed that the future of America lay in the Far East. The Pacific theater, not the European, should have top priority, he argued. In March 1943 the Combined Chiefs of Staff agreed to his plan for a westward advance along the northern coast of New Guinea toward the Philippines and

Tokyo. Naval forces directed by Admiral Chester Nimitz used amphibious warfare to move up the island chains of the Central Pacific (see the map on page 735).

By July 1944 the navy's leapfrogging campaign had reached the Marianas, east of the Philippines. From there B-29 bombers could reach the Japanese home islands. As a result, Admiral Nimitz proposed bypassing the Philippines in favor of a direct attack on Formosa (present-day Taiwan). MacArthur insisted on keeping his promise "to eighteen million Christian Filipinos that the Americans would return." Roosevelt himself came to Hawaii to resolve the impasse, giving MacArthur the green light. Backed by more than 100 ships of the Pacific Fleet, the general splashed ashore on the island of Leyte in October 1944 to announce his return.

BATTLE OF LEYTE GULF The decision to invade the Philippines led to savage fighting until the war ended. As retreating Japanese armies left Manila, they tortured and slaughtered tens of thousands of Filipino civilians. The United States suffered 62,000 casualties redeeming MacArthur's pledge. But a spectacular U.S. Navy victory at the Battle of Leyte Gulf spelled the end of the Japanese Imperial Navy as a fighting force. MacArthur and Nimitz prepared to tighten the noose around Japan's home islands.

Big Three Diplomacy

While the Allies cooperated to gain military victories in both Europe and the Pacific, negotiations over the postwar peace proved knottier. Churchill believed that only a stable European balance of power, not an international agency, could preserve peace. In his view the Soviet Union was the greatest threat to upsetting that balance of power. Premier Joseph Stalin left no doubt that an expansive notion of Russian security defined his war aims. For future protection Stalin expected to annex the Baltic states, once Russian provinces, along with bits of Finland and Romania and about half of prewar Poland. In eastern Europe and

The Normandy landing involved complex problems of moving troops and matériel. The Rhino ferry allowed the landing forces to improvise docking facilities soon after the invasion forces landed. Sailors described these awkward craft as "ugly as hell, cranky as hell—but efficient as hell."

other border areas such as Iran, Korea, and Turkey, he wanted "friendly" neighbors. It soon became apparent that "friendly" meant regimes dependent on Moscow.

Early on Franklin Roosevelt had promoted his own version of an international balance of power, which he called the "Four Policemen." Under its framework the Soviet Union, Great Britain, the United States, and China would guarantee peace through military cooperation. But by 1944 Roosevelt was seeking an alternative both to this scheme and to Churchill's wish to return to a balance of power that safely hemmed in the Russians. He preferred to bring the Soviet Union into a peacekeeping system based on an international organization similar to the League of Nations. This time Roosevelt intended that the United States, as well as all the great powers, would participate. Whether Churchill and Stalin—or the American people as a whole—would accept the idea was not yet clear.

The Road to Yalta

TEHERAN CONFERENCE The outlines—and the problems—of a postwar settlement became clearer during several summit conferences among the Allied leaders. In November 1943, with Italy's surrender in hand and the war against Germany going well, Churchill and Roosevelt agreed to make a hazardous trip to Teheran, Iran. There, the Big Three leaders had their chance to take a personal measure of each other. ("Seems very confident," Roosevelt said of Stalin, "very sure of himself, moves slowly—altogether quite impressive.") The president tried to charm the Soviet premier, teasing Churchill for Stalin's benefit, keeping it up "until Stalin was laughing with me, and it was then that I called him 'Uncle Joe.'"

Teheran was the high point of cooperation among the Big Three. There Roosevelt and Churchill committed to the D-Day invasion Stalin had so long sought, although Churchill's promise was halfhearted at best. The British hoped to delay D-Day as long as possible, largely to minimize British casualties. Stalin, for his part, promised to launch a spring offensive to keep German troops occupied on the eastern front. He also reaffirmed his earlier pledge to declare war against Japan once Germany was beaten.

YALTA CONFERENCE But thorny disagreements over the postwar peace had not been resolved. That was clear in February 1945, when the Big Three met one last time, at the Russian resort city of Yalta, on the Black Sea. By then, Russian, British, and American troops were closing in on Germany. Roosevelt arrived tired, ashen. At 62, limited by his paralysis, he had visibly aged. He came to Yalta mindful that although Germany was all but beaten, Japan still held out in the Pacific. Under no circumstances did he want Stalin to withdraw his promises to enter the fight against Japan and to join a postwar international organization. Churchill remained profoundly mistrustful of Soviet intentions. As Germany and Japan disintegrated, he saw power vacuums opening up in both Europe and Asia. These the Russians appeared only too eager to fill. Most diplomats in the American State Department and a growing number of military officers and politicians shared Churchill's fears.

DISPUTE OVER POLAND Allied differences were most clearly reflected in the disagreements over Poland. For Britain, Hitler's invasion of Poland had been the flashpoint for war. It was fighting, in part, to ensure that Poland survived as an independent nation. For Stalin, Poland was the historic corridor of invasion used by Russia's enemies. After

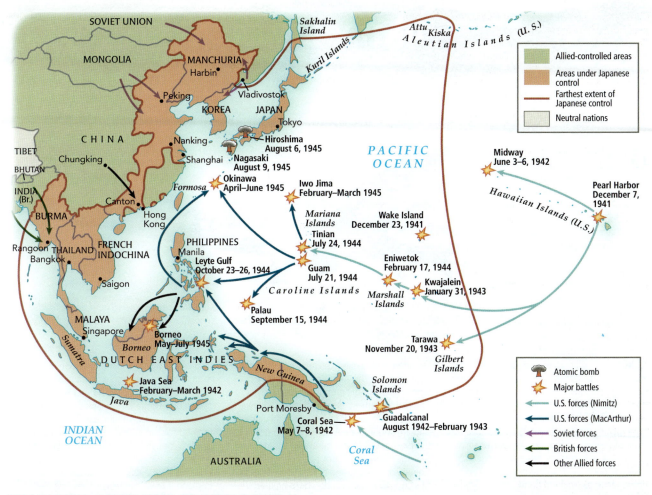

THE PACIFIC CAMPAIGNS OF WORLD WAR II

*The extraordinary distances of the Pacific spurred the United States to devise a two-front strategy to defeat Japan. MacArthur's army forces used Australia as a base of operations, aiming for the Philippines and the southeast coast of China. Once those areas were secured, forces could then launch air attacks on Japan. The navy, under command of Admiral Nimitz, set out to destroy the Japanese fleet and to conduct a series of amphibious landings on island chains in the Central Pacific. Meanwhile, British forces launched separate operations in Burma, forces under Chiang Kai-shek occasionally engaged Japanese forces on China's mainland, and in August 1945 Soviet troops attacked northern China. **After you read Daily Lives: "Air Power Shrinks the Globe" (page 736), explain why MacArthur's invasion of the Philippines was no longer a military necessity.***

Soviet troops reentered Poland, he insisted that he would recognize only the Communist-controlled government at Lublin. Stalin also demanded that Russia receive territory in eastern Poland, for which the Poles would be compensated with German lands. That was hardly the **self-determination** called for in the Atlantic Charter. Roosevelt proposed a compromise. For the time being, Poland would have a coalition government; after the war, free elections would settle the question of who should rule. The Soviets would also receive the territory they demanded in eastern Poland, and the western boundary would be established later.

Similarly, the Allies remained at odds about Germany's postwar future. Stalin was determined that the Germans would never invade Russia again. Many Americans shared his desire to have Germany punished and its war-making capacity eliminated. At the Teheran Conference, Roosevelt and Stalin had proposed that the Third Reich be drastically dismembered, split into five powerless parts. Churchill was

much less eager to bring low the nation that was the most natural barrier to Russian expansion. The era after World War I, he believed, demonstrated that a healthy European economy required an industrialized Germany.

DIVIDING GERMANY

Again, the Big Three put off making a firm decision. For the time being, they agreed to divide Germany into separate occupation zones (France would receive a zone carved from British and American territory). These four powers would jointly occupy Berlin, while an Allied Control Council supervised the national government.

When the Big Three turned their attention to the Far East, Stalin held a trump card. Roosevelt believed that only a bloody invasion of Japan itself could force a surrender. He thus secured from Stalin a pledge to enter the Pacific war within three months of Germany's defeat. His price was high. Stalin wanted to reclaim territories that Russia had lost in the Russo-Japanese War of 1904–1906,

AIR POWER SHRINKS THE GLOBE

During World War I short flying ranges and an inability to carry heavy loads limited what airplanes could do. Between the two wars, however, airframes grew stronger, engines more powerful, and payloads greater. Air-power strategists believed strategic bombing would prove decisive in war. Concerted waves of planes could attack industrial and military targets deep in enemy territory, devastate the economy, and undermine civilian morale.

The B-29 bombers gave the American air force much greater range, speed, and bomb loads. The Enola Gay (above), named after the pilot's mother, was modified to carry the first atom bomb, dropped on Hiroshima.

During the blitzkriegs against Poland and France in the opening campaigns of the war, Hitler's air attacks terrorized civilian populations and disrupted enemy forces. Air Marshal Hermann Goering predicted that bombers from the German Luftwaffe would soon bring England to its knees. The Battle of Britain, fought during the winter of 1940–1941, signaled the start of the age of modern air warfare. For the first time in history, one nation tried to conquer another from the skies. Goering's boast failed as England continued doggedly to resist.

Despite the Luftwaffe's failure, Allied air-power strategists believed heavy bombers could cripple Germany and Japan. The first test of such "strategic bombing" came in 1942, when more than 1,100 planes of the British Royal Air Force (RAF) destroyed some 20,000 homes, 1,500 stores and offices, and about 60 factories around Cologne, Germany. Horrific as that sounds, the attack did not level the city, as RAF planners had predicted. Indeed, later studies indicated that for all the damage done, Axis productivity actually increased until the last months of the war. Still, strategic bombing disrupted Japanese and German industry, brought the war home to the civilian population, and diverted enemy forces from the front to home defense.

Raids on Dresden and on Tokyo dramatized the horrors of the new technology.

Dresden, a charming German city almost untouched by the twentieth century, had largely been ignored until February 1945. The RAF hit it first; then, with fires still raging, the American bombing wave struck (see photograph above). A huge inferno drew all the oxygen out of the center of the city, so that victims who did not burn suffocated. Some 60,000 citizens of Dresden died. In March 340 American bombers hit Tokyo with incendiary bombs. The resulting firestorms, whipped by strong winds, leveled 16 square miles, destroyed 267,000 homes, left 83,000 dead, and injured 41,000. The heat was so intense that the water in canals boiled.

To ensure the success of aerial warfare, aircraft designers on both sides raced to make their planes bigger and faster. The first English raids used the Wellington bomber, a plane 65 feet long with a wing span of 86 feet and a bomb load of 1,500 pounds. In contrast, the American B-29s that bombed Hiroshima and Nagasaki carried up to 10 tons on a plane that was about 50 percent larger than the heaviest bombers. They could travel faster—more than 350 miles an hour, fly higher—up to 30,000 feet, and travel some 5,000 miles. Such technical improvement did not come cheaply. The United States spent a billion dollars more

to develop the B-29 than it did on the atomic bomb. German scientists took an even more radical step. To increase the speed and range of their weaponry, they produced a new V-1 pilotless "buzz bomb" (named for the sound of its jet engine) and the V-2 rocket, the first true missile used as a weapon. Launched from bases in Europe, V-1s and V-2s easily reached targets in England. For all the terror they inspired, however, they were inaccurate and the Germans nerer launched enough of them to mount a decisive threat.

Long-range air power eliminated the "front line" of traditional war. Every civilian became a potential combatant, every village a potential target. Although air power was not decisive in the war, the creation of longer-range aircraft with heavier payloads forced Americans to rethink their place in the world. The nation was now a matter of hours, not days, away from both friends and potential enemies.

Thinking Critically

What impact would the development of long-range bombers have on Americans' sense of their national security?

---

including islands north of Japan as well as control over the Chinese Eastern and South Manchurian railroads.

The agreements reached at Yalta depended on Stalin's willingness to cooperate. In public Roosevelt put the best face on matters. He argued that the new world organization (which Stalin had agreed to support) would "provide the greatest opportunity in all history" to secure a lasting peace. As if to lay to rest the isolationist sentiments that had destroyed Woodrow Wilson's dream, Roosevelt told Congress, "We shall take responsibility for world collaboration, or we shall have to bear the responsibility for another world conflict." Privately the president was less optimistic.

He confessed to one friend that he doubted that, "when the chips were down, Stalin would be able to carry out and deliver what he had agreed to."

The Fallen Leader

The Yalta Conference marked one of the last and most controversial chapters of Franklin Roosevelt's presidency. Critics charged that the concessions to Stalin had left American national interests unprotected. Poland had been betrayed; China sold out; the United Nations crippled at birth. Yet Roosevelt gave to Stalin little that Stalin had not liberated with Russian blood and could have taken anyway. Four out of five Nazi soldiers killed in action died on the eastern front.

What peace Roosevelt might have achieved can never be known. He returned from Yalta visibly ill. On April 12, 1945, while sitting for his portrait at his vacation home in Warm Springs, Georgia, he complained of a "terrific headache," then suddenly fell unconscious. Two hours later he was dead, the victim of a cerebral hemorrhage. Not since the assassination of Lincoln had the nation so grieved. Under Roosevelt's leadership government had become a protector, the president a father and friend, and the United States the leader in the struggle against Axis tyranny. Eleanor Roosevelt recalled how many Americans later told her that "they missed the way the President used to talk to them. . . . There was a real dialogue between Franklin and the people."

TRUMAN BECOMES PRESIDENT Harry S Truman faced the awesome task of replacing Roosevelt. "Who the hell is Harry Truman?" the chief of staff had asked when Truman was nominated for the vice presidency in 1944. In the brief period he served as vice president, Truman had met with Roosevelt fewer than 10 times. He knew almost nothing about the president's postwar plans and promises. When a reporter now addressed him as "Mr. President," he winced. "I wish you didn't have to call me that," he said. Sensing his own inadequacies, Truman adopted a tough pose and made his mind up quickly. People welcomed the new president's decisiveness as a relief from Roosevelt's evasive style. Too often, though, Truman acted before the issues were clear. He at least knew victory in Europe was near as Allied troops swept into Germany.

The Holocaust

The horror of war in no way prepared the invading armies for the liberation of the concentration camps. Hitler, they discovered, had ordered the systematic extermination of all European Jews, as well as Gypsies, homosexuals, and others considered deviant. The SS, Hitler's security force, had constructed six extermination centers in Germany and Poland. By rail from all over Europe, the SS shipped Jews to die in the gas chambers.

No issue of World War II more starkly raised questions of human good and evil than what came to be known as the Holocaust. Tragically, the United States could have done more to save some of the 6 million Jews that were killed.

Until the autumn of 1941 the Nazis permitted Jews to leave Europe, but few countries would accept them—including the United States. Americans haunted by unemployment feared that a tide of new immigrants would make competition for jobs even worse. Tales of persecution from war refugees had little effect on most citizens: opinion polls showed that more than 70 percent of Americans opposed easing quotas. After 1938 the restrictive provisions of the 1924 Immigration Act were made even tighter.

American Jews wanted to help, especially after 1942, when they learned of the death camps. But they worried that highly visible protests might only aggravate American **anti-Semitism.** They were also split over support for Zionists working to establish a Jewish homeland in Palestine. The British had blocked Jewish emigration to Palestine and, to avoid alienating the Arabs, opposed Zionism. Roosevelt and his advisers ultimately decided that the best way to save Jews was to win the war quickly, but that strategy still does not explain why the Allies did not do more. They could have bombed the rail lines to the camps, sent commando forces, or tried to destroy the death factories.

A Lasting Peace

BRETTON WOODS ECONOMIC STRATEGIES After 15 years of depression and then war, the Allies sought a new international framework for cooperation among nations. That system, many believed, needed to be economic as well as political. At a 1944 meeting at Bretton Woods, a resort in New Hampshire, Americans led the way in creating two new economic organizations: the International Monetary Fund (IMF) and the International Bank for Reconstruction and Development, later known as the World Bank. The IMF hoped to promote trade by stabilizing national currencies, and the World Bank was designed to stimulate economic growth by investing in projects worldwide. Later that summer the Allies met **DUMBARTON OAKS AND THE UNO** at Dumbarton Oaks, a Washington, D.C., estate, to lay out the structure for the proposed United Nations Organization (UNO, later known simply as the UN). An 11-member Security Council would oversee a General Assembly composed of delegates from all member nations. By the end of the first organizational meeting, held in San Francisco in April 1945, it had become clear that the United Nations would favor the Western powers in most postwar disputes.

While the United Nations was organizing itself in San Francisco, the Axis powers were collapsing in Europe. As Mussolini attempted to escape to Germany, antifascist mobs in Italy captured and slaughtered him like a pig. Adolf Hitler committed suicide in his Berlin bunker on April 30. Two weeks later General Eisenhower accepted the German surrender.

POTSDAM SUMMIT In one final summit meeting, held in July 1945 at Potsdam (just outside Berlin), President Truman met Churchill and Stalin for the first time. Two issues dominated the meeting: Germany's

In April 1945, at the concentration camp in Buchenwald, Germany, Senator Alben Barkley of Kentucky viewed a grisly reminder of the horrors of the Nazis' "final solution." As vice president under Harry Truman, Barkley urged the administration to support an independent homeland in Israel for Jews.

political fate and how much the defeated nation would pay in reparations. The three leaders agreed that Germany should be occupied and demilitarized. Stalin insisted that Russia receive a minimum of $10 billion, regardless of how much it might hurt postwar Germany or the European economy. A complicated compromise allowed Britain and the United States to restrict reparations from their zones. But in large part Stalin had his way. For the foreseeable future, Germany would remain divided into occupation zones and without a central government of its own.

Atomic Diplomacy

The most crucial factor affecting postwar relations never even reached the bargaining table in Potsdam. On July 16, 1945, the first atomic fireball rose from the desert in Alamogordo, New Mexico. Scientists at the Manhattan Project had successfully detonated their first explosive device. On receiving the news, Truman returned to the negotiations a changed man—firmer, more confident. He "told the Russians just where they got on and off and generally bossed the whole meeting," observed Churchill. Several questions loomed: Should the United States now use the bomb? Should it warn Japan before dropping it? And perhaps equally vital, should Truman inform Stalin?

SHOULD THE BOMB BE DROPPED?

Some scientists recommended not using the bomb or at least attempting to convince Japan to surrender by demonstrating the new weapon's power. A high-level committee considered but then dismissed that idea, though some committee members later regretted they did so. Nor did Truman choose to tell Stalin about the bomb. He mentioned

only obliquely that the United States possessed a weapon of "awesome destructiveness." Stalin, whose spies had already informed him of the bomb, showed no surprise. He remarked casually that he hoped the Americans would use their new weapon to good effect against Japan. Atomic diplomacy had failed its first test. Stalin immediately stepped up the Russian program to build an atom bomb. After Potsdam the nuclear arms race was on.

Finally, Truman and Churchill decided to drop the first bomb with only an implied warning to the Japanese. In an ultimatum issued at Potsdam, they demanded unconditional surrender and threatened Japan with "inevitable and complete destruction" using the "full application of our military power" if it did not comply. Unaware of the warning's full meaning, officials in Tokyo made no formal reply.

THE BOMB AS A THREAT TO THE SOVIETS

Truman and Churchill knew Japan was on the verge of defeat. Japan's leaders had even sent peace feelers to the Russians. Why, then, did the Allies insist on unconditional surrender? Some historians have charged that Secretary of State James Byrnes, a staunch anticommunist, wanted a dramatic combat demonstration of the bomb that would serve to persuade Stalin to behave less aggressively in negotiations with the British and Americans. However much Byrnes had Soviet diplomacy on his mind, most evidence indicates that Truman decided to drop the bomb in order to end the war quickly.

Before leaving Potsdam, Truman ordered crews on Tinian Island in the South Pacific to proceed to their first target as soon as weather permitted. On August 6 the *Enola Gay,* a B-29 bomber, dropped a uranium bomb nicknamed "Little Boy" that leveled 4 square miles of Hiroshima, an industrial and military center. The blast immediately killed

This aerial view of Hiroshima gives stark testimony to the destructive force of the atomic blast. In one of the many bitter ironies, only the shells of the Western-style buildings survived.

nearly 80,000 people (including 20 American prisoners of war). A German priest came upon soldiers who had looked up as the bomb exploded. Their eyeballs had melted from their sockets. Another eyewitness spoke of survivors "so broken and confused that they moved and behaved like automatons." Two days later the Soviet Union declared war on Japan, and on August 9 a second atomic bomb (a plutonium weapon nicknamed "Fat Man") exploded over the port of Nagasaki. Another 60,000 people were killed instantly. In both cities many who lived through the horror began to sicken and die as radiation poisoning claimed tens of thousands of additional lives.

The two explosions left the Japanese stunned. Breaking all precedents, the emperor intervened and declared openly for peace. On September 3 a humiliated Japanese delegation boarded the battleship *Missouri* in Tokyo Bay and signed the document of surrender. World War II had ended.

✓ **REVIEW**

In what ways did Allied diplomacy deal with the postwar world in terms of Germany, international stability, and the role of atomic weapons?

CONCLUSION

THE WORLD AT LARGE

"World War II changed everything," observed an admiral long after the war. The defeatism of the Depression gave way to the exhilaration of victory. Before the war Americans seldom exerted leadership in international affairs. After, the world looked to the United States to rebuild the economies of Europe and Asia and to maintain peace. World War II had not only shown the global interdependence of economic and political systems; it had also increased that interdependence. Out of the war developed a truly international economy. At home the trends toward bigness and centralization vastly accelerated. Advances in electronics, communications, and aviation brought the world closer to every home. Government grew, too. The size of the national debt alone guaranteed that Washington, D.C., would continue to dominate the economy. Americans had come to believe in a strong defense, even if that meant a large federal bureaucracy and a generous military budget.

Still, a number of fears loomed, despite the victory parades snaking down the nation's main streets. Would the inevitable cutbacks in spending bring on another depression? Would Soviet ambitions undo the new global peace, much as fascism and economic instability had undone the peace of Versailles? And then there was the shadow of the atomic bomb looming over the victorious as well as the defeated. As a sobered Robert Oppenheimer, Director of the bomb project at Los Alamos, told a group of scientists: "If atomic bombs are to be added to the arsenals of warring nations . . . then the day will come when mankind will curse the names of Los Alamos and Hiroshima." With the advent of the atomic age, no one in the world, not even in the United States, was safe anymore. ∞∞∞∞

Chapter Summary

WORLD WAR II DEEPENED THE global interdependence of nations and left the United States as the greatest economic and military power in the world.

- As fascism spread in Europe and as militarism spread in Asia, Franklin Roosevelt struggled to help America's allies by overcoming domestic political isolation and the fervor for neutrality.

- Despite German aggression against Poland in 1939, France and the Low Countries in 1940, and the Soviet Union in 1941, the United States did not enter the war until the Japanese surprise attack on Pearl Harbor in December 1941.

- The alliance forged among British prime minister Winston Churchill, Soviet premier Joseph Stalin, and President Franklin Roosevelt did not swerve from its decision to subdue Germany first, even though early defeats and America's lack of preparation slowed the war effort until 1943.

- At home America's factories produced enough goods to supply the domestic economy and America's allies.
  - Demands for labor created opportunities for women and minorities.
  - War hysteria aggravated old prejudices and led to the internment of Japanese Americans.
  - New Deal reform ended as "Dr. Win-the-War" replaced "Dr. New Deal."

- Although the successful landings in France on D-Day and the island-hopping campaign in the Pacific made it clear that the Allies would win the war, issues over Poland, Germany, and postwar boundaries raised doubts about the peace.

- The war ended with the atomic bombings of Hiroshima and Nagasaki, but not soon enough to limit the horrors of the Holocaust.

Additional Reading

A COMPREHENSIVE TREATMENT OF THE war years is David Kennedy, *The American People in World War II: Freedom from Fear: Part II* (2003). Robert Divine, *The Reluctant Belligerent* (2nd ed., 1979), is still excellent on the prewar diplomacy. Andrew Roberts, *Masters and Commanders: How Four Titans Won the War for the West, 1941–1945* (2009), explains the dynamics of Anglo-American relations. Perhaps the most powerful single volume on the war is Max Hastings, *Inferno: The World at War, 1939–1945* (2011), while Martin Gilbert, *The Second World War: A Complete History* (2004), captures the vast scale. Richard Lingeman, *Don't You Know There's a War On? The Home Front, 1941–1945* (updated ed., 2003), is a classic study. Emily Yellin, *Our Mothers' War: American Women at Home and at the Front during World War II* (2005), explores the many roles women played. Tetsuden Kashmia, *Judgment without Trial: Japanese American Imprisonment during World War II* (2003), examines the diverse experiences of those in the camps and reveals that planning for internment of the Japanese began well before the war.

The decision to drop two atomic bombs on Japan remains one of the most controversial legacies of the war. To better understand the racial dimension, see John Dower, *War without Mercy: Race and Power in the Pacific War* (1986). Richard Rhodes, *The Making of the Atomic Bomb* (1987), re-creates the history of the Manhattan Project. Gar Alperowitz, *The Decision to Use the Atomic Bomb* (1995), extends an interpretation he first advanced in *Atomic Diplomacy* (1965) that the Soviet Union was the planners' real target. Martin Sherwin, *A World Destroyed* (rev. ed., 1985), and, with Kai Bird, *American Prometheus: The Triumph and Tragedy of J. Robert Oppenheimer* (2005), discusses the process of designing and using the bomb. David Holloway, *Stalin and the Bomb: The Soviet Union and Atomic Energy, 1939–1956* (1994), uses Russian sources to trace the origins of atomic diplomacy. Students who wish to work with some of the original documents should see Michael Stoff et al., *The Manhattan Project: A Documentary Introduction to the Atomic Age* (1991).

For a fuller list of readings, see the Bibliography at www.mhhe.com/eh8e.

Significant Events

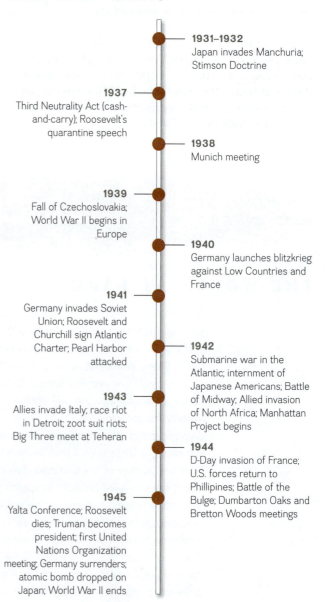

1931–1932 Japan invades Manchuria; Stimson Doctrine

1937 Third Neutrality Act (cash-and-carry); Roosevelt's quarantine speech

1938 Munich meeting

1939 Fall of Czechoslovakia; World War II begins in Europe

1940 Germany launches blitzkrieg against Low Countries and France

1941 Germany invades Soviet Union; Roosevelt and Churchill sign Atlantic Charter; Pearl Harbor attacked

1942 Submarine war in the Atlantic; internment of Japanese Americans; Battle of Midway; Allied invasion of North Africa; Manhattan Project begins

1943 Allies invade Italy; race riot in Detroit; zoot suit riots; Big Three meet at Teheran

1944 D-Day invasion of France; U.S. forces return to Phillipines; Battle of the Bulge; Dumbarton Oaks and Bretton Woods meetings

1945 Yalta Conference; Roosevelt dies; Truman becomes president; first United Nations Organization meeting; Germany surrenders; atomic bomb dropped on Japan; World War II ends

[Pivotal Events in World War II]

	MILITARY/DIPLOMATIC	HOME FRONT	SOCIOECONOMIC
1941	Germany invades Russia "Four Freedoms" states war principles Japanese attack Pearl Harbor	Labor unrest Lend-Lease Act Roosevelt creates FEPC to fight discrimination	Increased war production boosts economy
1942	Battle of Midway breaks Japanese naval superiority Invasion of North Africa Battle of Stalingrad	Japanese aliens and Japanese Americans placed in internment camps New Deal in retreat	Industry converts to war production; auto manufacturing halted
1943	Allies invade Sicily and Italy Central Pacific island-hopping campaign Teheran Conference	Detroit race riot Zoot suit riots Coal miners strike	Women flood into war industries Prosperity returns
1944	D-Day: Allies invade France Battle of the Bulge MacArthur invades the Philippines	Roosevelt reelected to fourth term Supreme Court upholds Japanese internment	International Monetary Fund and World Bank created
1945	Yalta Conference Holocaust revealed Germany surrenders Potsdam Conference Atomic bombs dropped on Japan; war ends	Roosevelt dies; Harry Truman becomes president	

The Honest John rocket was the first nuclear armed surface-to-surface missile manufactured by the United States in the early 1950s. It could carry either a conventional explosive or a 20-kiloton nuclear warhead. As World War II gave way to a cold war between two new superpowers, the United States and the Soviet Union, American military planners began to rely increasingly on nuclear weapons.

Cold War America

1945–1954

∞∞∞ **AN AMERICAN STORY** ∞∞∞

GLAD TO BE HOME?

The war had been over for almost five months and still troopships steamed into New York and other ports. Timuel Black was packing his duffel belowdecks when he heard some of the white soldiers shout, "There she is! The Statue of Liberty!" Black felt a little bitter about the war. He'd been drafted in Chicago in 1943, just after race riots ripped the city. His father, a strong supporter of civil rights, was angry. "What the hell are you goin' to fight in Europe for? The fight is here." He wanted his son to go with him to demonstrate in Detroit, except the roads were blocked and the buses and trains screened to prevent more African Americans from coming in.

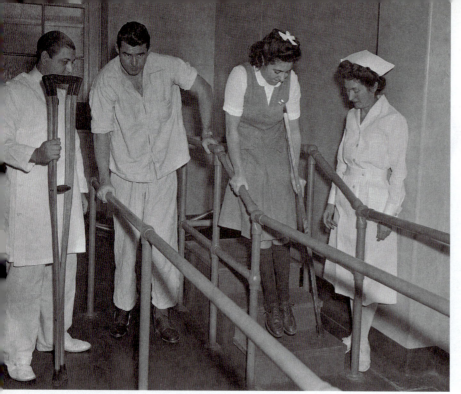

| A rehabilitation center

Instead, Black went off to fight the Nazis, serving in a segregated army. He'd gone ashore during the D-Day invasion, survived the Battle of the Bulge, and marched through one of the German concentration camps. "The first thing you get is the stench," he recalled. "Everybody knows that's human stench. You begin to realize something terrible had happened. There's quietness. You get closer and you begin to see what's happened to these creatures. And you get—I got more passionately angry than I guess I'd ever been." He thought: if it could happen here, to the Germans, it could happen anywhere. It could happen to black folk in America. So when the white soldiers called to come up and see the Statue of Liberty, Black's reaction was, "Hell, I'm not goin' up there. Damn that." But after all, he went up. "All of a sudden, I found myself with tears, cryin' and saying the same thing [the white soldiers] were saying. Glad to be home, proud of my country, as irregular as it is. Determined that it could be better."

At the same time, Betty Basye was working across the continent as a nurse in a burn-and-blind center at Menlo Park, California. Her hospital treated soldiers shipped back from the Pacific: "Blind young men. Eyes gone, legs gone. Parts of the face. Burns—you'd land with a firebomb and be up in flames." She'd joke with the men, trying to keep their spirits up, talking about times to come. She liked to take Bill, one of her favorites, for walks downtown. Half of Bill's face was gone, and civilians would stare. It happened to other patients, too. "Nicely dressed women, absolutely staring, just standing there staring." Some people wrote the local paper, wondering why disfigured vets couldn't be kept on their own grounds and off the streets. Such callousness made Basye indignant. The war was over—"and we're still here." After a time, she started dating a soldier back from the South Pacific. "I got busy after the war," she recalled, "getting married and having my four children. That's what you were supposed to do. And getting your house in suburbia."

Yet as Basye and Black soon discovered, the return to "normal" life was filled with uncertainties. The first truly global war had left a large part of Europe in ruins and the old balance of power shattered. The dramatic events occurring month after month during 1945 and 1946 made it clear that whatever new world order emerged, the United States would have a central role in building it. Isolation seemed neither practical nor desirable in an era in which the power of the Soviet Union and communism seemed on the rise.

To blunt that threat, the United States converted not so much to peace as to a "cold war" against its former Soviet ally. This undeclared war came to affect almost every aspect of American life. Abroad, it justified a far wider military and economic role for the United States in areas like the Middle East and the Pacific Rim nations of Asia, from Korea to Indochina. At home it sent politicians scurrying across the land in a search for Communist spies and **"subversives,"** from the State Department to the movie studios of Hollywood and even into college classrooms.

Preparing for war in times of peace dramatically increased the role of the military-industrial-university complex formed during World War II. A nation that had traditionally followed an isolationist foreign policy would come to deploy military forces across the globe. A people who had once kept government intrusion into the economy at a minimum now voted to maintain programs that ensured an active federal role. That economy produced prosperity beyond anything Americans had known before. ∞∞∞

THE RISE OF THE COLD WAR

WORLD WAR II DEVASTATED LANDS and people almost everywhere outside the Western Hemisphere. Once the war ended the world struggled to rebuild. Power that had once been centered in Europe shifted to nations on its periphery. In place of Germany, France, and England, the United States and the Soviet Union emerged as the world's two reigning superpowers—and as enemies. Their rivalry was not altogether an equal one. The United States ended the war with a booming economy, a massive military establishment, and the atomic bomb. In contrast, much of the Soviet Union lay in ruins.

AMERICANS FEAR SOVIET INTENTIONS

But the defeat of Germany and Japan left no power in Europe or Asia to block the still-formidable Soviet army. And many Americans feared that desperate, war-weary peoples would find the appeal of communism irresistible. If Stalin intended to extend the Soviet Union's dominion, only the United States had the economic and military might to block him. Events in the critical years of 1945 and 1946 persuaded most Americans that Stalin did have such a plan. The Truman administration concluded that "the USSR has engaged the United States in a struggle for power, or 'cold war,' in which our national security is at stake and from which we cannot withdraw short of national suicide." What had happened that led

Western leaders to such a dire view of their former Soviet allies? How did such a wide breach open between the two nations?

American Suspicions

ROOTS OF THE COLD WAR

Even before postwar events deepened American suspicions of the Soviets, an ideological gulf had separated the two nations. The October Revolution of 1917 shocked most Americans. They had come to view Lenin's Bolshevik revolutionaries with a mixture of fear, suspicion, and loathing. As the Communists grasped power, they had often used violence and terror to achieve their ends. As Marxists they rejected both religion and the notion of private property, two institutions central to the American way of life. Furthermore, Soviet propagandists had made no secret that they intended to export revolution throughout the world, including the United States.

MUNICH ANALOGY

One event leading to World War II taught Western leaders to resist "appeasement." In 1938 British prime minister Neville Chamberlain's attempt to satisfy Hitler's demands on Czechoslovakia only emboldened the Nazis to expand further. After the war, Secretary of the Navy James Forrestal applied the Munich analogy to the new Europe. Appeasing Russian demands, he believed, would only seem like an attempt "to buy their understanding and sympathy. We tried that once with Hitler. . . . There are no returns on appeasement." To many of Truman's advisers, the Soviet dictator seemed as much bent on conquest as Hitler had been.

Communist Expansion

During the war Stalin did make numerous demands to control territory along the Soviet borders. And with the coming of peace, he continued to push for greater influence. He asked for a role in controlling the Dardanelles, the narrow strait linking Soviet ports on the Black Sea with the Mediterranean Sea. Soviet forces occupying northern Iran backed a rebellion against the Iranian government. In Greece, local Communists led the fighting to overturn the traditional monarchy.

Asia, too, seemed a target for Communist ambitions. Russian occupation forces in Manchuria were turning over captured Japanese arms to Chinese Communists under Mao Zedong. Russian troops controlled the northern half of Korea. In Vietnam leftist nationalists were fighting against the return of French colonial rule.

Despite Russian actions, many historians have argued, American policy makers consistently exaggerated Stalin's ambitions. At war's end, much of the farmland and industry in the Soviet Union lay in ruins. When Stalin looked outward, he saw American occupation forces in Europe and Asia ringing the Soviet Union, their military might backed by a newly developed atomic arsenal. American corporations owned or controlled vast oil fields in the Middle East.

Churchill, Truman, and Stalin met at Potsdam in July 1945. Their smiles masked serious disagreements about the shape of the postwar world.

Along with the French and the British, the United States was a strong presence in Southeast Asia. Given that situation, many historians have argued, Stalin's actions after the war were primarily defensive, designed to counter what appeared to him a threatening American-European alliance.

More recent evidence from once-secret files of the Soviet Union suggests that despite the ravages of war, Stalin recognized that in 1945 the Soviet Union was emerging as a more powerful state. With Germany and Japan defeated, Soviet borders to the east and west were secure from invasion. Only to the south did Stalin see a problem, along the border with Iran. Further, he recognized that the people of Britain and the United States were tired of war. Their leaders were not about to attack the Soviet Union, at least not in the near term. Equally significant, Soviet spies had informed Stalin in 1946 that the United States possessed only a few atomic bombs. For the time being, the nuclear threat was more symbolic than real. As a political realist, Stalin saw an opportunity to advance the interests of the Soviet state and his own regime—as long as his actions did not risk war.

The tensions arising from the conflicting Soviet and American points of view came to a head in the first months of 1946. Stalin announced in February that the Soviet Union would act vigorously to preserve its national security. In a world dominated by capitalism, he warned, future wars were inevitable. The Russian people had to ensure against "any eventuality" by undertaking a new five-year plan for economic development.

THE MOVE TO "GET TOUGH" Although some Americans thought Stalin was merely rallying Russian support for his domestic programs, others agreed with *Time* magazine, an early voice for a "get tough" policy, when it called Stalin's speech "the most warlike pronouncement uttered by any top-rank statesman since V-J day." "I'm tired of babying the Soviets," remarked President Truman, who in any case seldom wore kid gloves. Truman's advisers spelled out the political advantages of taking this tough line toward the Soviet Union. "The worse matters get . . . ," they told him, "the more there is a sense of crisis. In times of crisis, the American citizen tends to back up his president." In March, Winston Churchill warned that the Soviets had dropped an "Iron Curtain" between their satellite nations and the free world. Poland, East Germany, Romania, and Bulgaria lay behind it. Iran, Greece, Turkey, and much of Europe seemed at risk.

A Policy of Containment

As policy makers groped for an effective way to deal with these developments, the State Department received a diplomatic cable, extraordinary for both its length (8,000 words) and its impact in Washington. The author was George Kennan, chargé d'affaires in Moscow and long a student of Soviet conduct. Kennan argued that Russian leaders, including Stalin, were so paranoid that it was impossible to reach any useful accommodations with them. This temperament could best be explained by "the traditional and instinctive Russian sense of insecurity." That insecurity, when combined with Marxist ideology that viewed capitalism as the enemy, created a potent force for expansion. Soviet power, Kennan explained, "moves inexorably along a prescribed path, like a toy automobile wound up and headed in a given direction, stopping only when it meets some unanswerable force."

GEORGE KENNAN DEFINES CONTAINMENT The response Kennan recommended was "containment." The United States must apply "unalterable counterforce at every point where [the Soviets] show signs of encroaching upon the interests of a peaceful and stable world." The idea of containment was not particularly novel, but Kennan's historical analysis provided leaders in Washington with a framework for analyzing Soviet behavior. By applying firm diplomatic, economic, and military counterpressure, the United States could block Russian aggression. Truman wholeheartedly adopted the doctrine of containment.

The Truman Doctrine

At first it appeared that Iran, lying along the Soviet Union's southern border, would provide the first test. An independent Iran seemed crucial in protecting rich fields of petroleum in the Persian Gulf region. Stalin had pledged to

As American fears of Soviet intentions increased, journalists often described communism as though it were a disease, an inhuman force, or a savage predator. In April 1946 Time magazine, a particularly outspoken source of anticommunist rhetoric, portrayed the spread of "infection" throughout Europe and Asia as the "Red Menace."

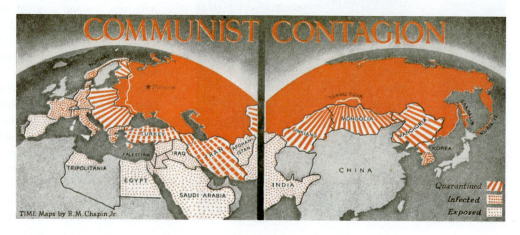

withdraw Russian troops from Iran after the war, but did not, hoping to force Iran to grant the Soviets economic and political concessions. In March 1946 Secretary of State James Byrnes went to the United Nations, determined to force a showdown over continued Soviet occupation of northern Iran. But before he could extract his pound of Russian flesh, the Soviets reached an agreement with Iran to withdraw.

AID TO GREECE AND TURKEY The face-off in Iran only intensified American suspicions. In Europe severe winter storms and a depressed postwar economy threatened to encourage domestic Communist movements. A turning point in the cold war came in early 1947, when Great Britain announced that it could no longer support the governments of Greece and Turkey. Without British aid, the Communists seemed destined to win critical victories. Truman decided that the United States should provide $400 million in military and economic aid. He went before Congress in March, determined to "scare hell out of the country." The world was now divided into two hostile camps, the president warned. To preserve the American way of life the United States must now step forward and help "free people" threatened by **totalitarian** regimes." This rationale for aid to Greece and Turkey soon became known as the Truman Doctrine.

The Truman Doctrine marked a new level of American commitment to a cold war. Just what responsibility the Soviets had for unrest in Greece and Turkey remained unclear. But Truman had linked communism with rebel movements all around the globe. That committed Americans to a relatively open-ended struggle. In the battle between communism and freedom, the president gained expanded powers to act when unrest threatened. Occasionally, Congress would regret giving the executive branch so much power, but by 1947 anticommunism had become the dominant theme in American policy, both foreign and domestic.

The Marshall Plan

For all its importance, the Truman Doctrine did not address the area of primary concern to Washington, Western Europe. Across Europe desperate people scrounged for food and coal to heat their homes. Streets stood dark at night. National treasuries had neither capital nor credit needed to reopen idled factories. American diplomats warned that without aid to revive the European economy, Communists would seize power in Germany, Italy, and France.

In June 1947 Secretary of State George C. Marshall stepped before a Harvard commencement audience to announce a recovery plan for Europe. He invited all European nations, East and West, to request assistance to rebuild their economies. Unlike Truman, Marshall did not emphasize the Communist menace. All the same, his massive aid plan was designed to eliminate conditions that produced the discontent Communists often exploited. Humanitarian

| Few cities suffered as severely during World War II as Dresden in Germany. The Allies subjected it to systematic firebombing that provoked Kurt Vonnegut to write Slaughterhouse Five. In 1946 little had been done to rebuild the city. Much of Europe suffered widespread destruction, and the Marshall Plan provided aid to rebuild.

aid also had its practical benefits. As Europe recovered, so would its ability to buy American goods. The secretary did not rule out Soviet participation, but he gambled that fears of American economic domination would lead the Soviets and their allies to reject his offer.

COMMUNISM IN CZECHOSLOVAKIA At first **neo-isolationists** in Congress argued that the United States could not afford such generosity. But when Communists expelled the non-Communists from Czechoslovakia's government, the cold war seemed to spread. Congress then approved the Marshall Plan, as it became known. And as the secretary anticipated, the Soviets blocked the efforts of Czechoslovakia and Poland to participate. The blame for dividing Europe fell, as Marshall guessed it would, on the Soviet Union, not the United States.

The Fall of Eastern Europe

American efforts to stabilize Europe and the eastern Mediterranean led Stalin to take countermeasures. Most shocking to the Western nations were his steps to consolidate Soviet political and military domination over Eastern

COLD WAR EUROPE

By 1956 the postwar occupation of Europe had hardened into rigid cold war boundaries. The United States reacted to the presence of Soviet conventional forces in Eastern Europe by rearming West Germany and creating the NATO alliance (1949) for the defense of nations from the North Atlantic through the Mediterranean basin. The U.S.S.R. formed a counteralliance under the Warsaw Pact (1955). Although Bonn became the de facto capital of West Germany, Berlin remained the official capital and into the 1960s the focus of the most severe cold war tensions. **In what ways does the map suggest geographically why Greece and Turkey were early cold war trouble spots?**

Europe. In 1947 he moved against Hungary, run since 1945 by a moderate government chosen under relatively free elections. Soviet forces imposed a Communist regime dependent on Moscow. In February 1948 Communists toppled the duly elected government of Czechoslovakia. Shortly after, news came that the popular Czech foreign minister, Jan Masaryk, had fallen to his death from a small bathroom window. Suicide was the official explanation, but many suspected murder. In response to the Marshall Plan, the Soviet foreign ministry initiated a series of trade agreements tightly linking the Soviet and Eastern European economies. It also established the Cominform, or Communist

Information Bureau, to assert greater political control over foreign Communist parties.

BERLIN AIRLIFT The spring of 1948 brought another clash between the Soviets and their former allies, this time over Germany. There, the United States, Great Britain, and France decided to transform their occupation zones into an independent West German state. The Western-controlled sectors of Berlin, however, lay over 100 miles to the east, well within the Soviet zone. On June 24 the Soviets reacted by blockading land access to Berlin. Truman did not hesitate to respond. "We are going to stay, period." But he did say no when General Lucius Clay proposed to shoot his way through the blockade. Instead, the United States began a massive airlift of supplies that lasted almost a year. In May 1949 Stalin lifted the blockade, conceding that he could not prevent the creation of West Germany.

NATO FORMED Stalin's aggressive actions accelerated the American effort to use military means to contain Soviet ambitions. By 1949 the United States and Canada had joined with Britain, France, Belgium, the Netherlands, and Luxembourg to establish the North Atlantic Treaty Organization (NATO) as a mutual defense pact. For the first time since George Washington had warned against the practice in his Farewell Address of 1793, the United States during peacetime entered into entangling alliances with European nations.

ISRAEL RECOGNIZED Truman's firm handling of the Berlin crisis won him applause from both Democrats and Republicans. They were equally enthusiastic about another bold presidential action. Minutes after the Israelis announced their independence in May 1948, Truman recognized the new state of Israel. He had previously supported the immigration of Jews into Palestine despite the opposition of oil-rich Arab states and diplomats in the State Department. The president sympathized with Jewish aspirations for a homeland. He also faced a tough campaign in 1948 in which Jewish votes would be critical. As British prime minister Clement Attlee observed, "There's no Arab vote in America, but there's a heavy Jewish vote and the Americans are always having elections."

The Atomic Shield versus the Iron Curtain

The Berlin crisis forced Truman to consider the possibility of war. If it came, would atomic weapons again be used? That dilemma raised two other difficult questions: Should the decision to use atomic weapons rest in civilian or military hands? And was it possible to create an international system to control nuclear power?

ATOMIC ENERGY COMMISSION On the question of civilian or military control of the bomb, Truman's response was firm. He was not going to have "some dashing lieutenant colonel decide when would be the proper time to drop one." In 1946 Congress seemed to have decided the issue in Truman's favor when it passed the McMahon Act. This bill established the Atomic Energy Commission (AEC), with control of all fissionable materials for both peacetime and military applications. The AEC was a civilian, not a military, agency.

But civilian control was not as complete as Truman had demanded. The wartime head of the Manhattan Project, General Leslie Groves, had been working behind the scenes to give the military a decisive voice in atomic policy. During debate over the bill, Groves had leaked information about a Canadian atomic spy ring delivering secrets to the Soviet Union. That news spread doubts that scientists and civilians could be trusted with key secrets. Thus Groves persuaded Congress to allow the military to review many civilian decisions and even severely limit their actions.

BARUCH PLAN The idea of international control of atomic energy also fell victim to cold war fears. Originally, a high-level government committee proposed to Truman that the mining and use of the world's atomic raw materials be supervised by an agency of the United Nations. The committee argued that in the long run the United States would be more secure under a system of international control than relying on its temporary nuclear monopoly. But Truman chose Bernard Baruch, a staunch cold warrior, to draw up the recommendations to the United Nations in June 1946. Baruch's proposals ensured that the United States would dominate any international atomic agency. The Soviets countered with a plan calling for destruction of all nuclear bombs and a ban on their use. But Baruch had no intention of bargaining. It was either his plan or nothing, he announced. And so it was nothing. The Truman administration never seriously considered giving up the American nuclear monopoly. Stalin, for his part, gave top priority to the Soviet atomic bomb program. Failure at the United Nations thus promoted an arms race, not nuclear supremacy.

NUCLEAR DETERRENCE As the cold war heated up, American military planners were forced to adopt a nuclear strategy in face of the overwhelming superiority of Soviet forces. The Soviet army had at its command over 260 divisions. In contrast, the United States had reduced its forces by 1947 to little more than a single division. That meant that only the prospect of a devastating atomic counterattack was likely to deter any Soviet threat.

At first, this strategy of nuclear **deterrence** was little more than a makeshift doomsday scenario to incinerate vast areas of the Soviet Union. A 1946 war plan, "Pincher," proposed obliterating 20 Soviet cities if the Soviets attacked Western Europe. But, by 1949, the Joint Chiefs of Staff had fully committed themselves to a policy of nuclear deterrence in an indefinitely extended cold war. Western Europe was on

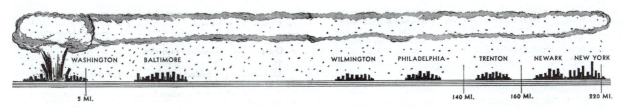

As this diagram of a hypothetical bombing of Washington suggests, Americans began to understand that radioactive fallout was a grave danger as well.

DUCK AND COVER

Sound track and music: ". . . and Bert the Turtle was very alert. When danger threatened him, he never got hurt, He knew just what to do . . ."

What tone is set by using "Bert the Turtle" and a monkey for teaching students the tactic of "Duck and Cover" in an atomic attack?

Go to YouTube and search for "Duck and Cover." Play the film. How do the sound track, animation, music and script contribute to the impression the film gives of an atomic bomb?

Narrator: "Now, [laughs] you and I don't have shells to crawl into like Bert the Turtle so, we have to cover up in our own way. First you duck . . ."

". . . and then you cover! And very tightly, you cover the back of your neck . . ." How do you react to the idea that "ducking and covering" would protect these children in case of a nuclear attack?

The Soviet Union's explosion of an atomic bomb in 1949 confronted American civil defense planners with a delicate task. On the one hand, they had to warn citizens that a nuclear attack against the United States was a distinct possibility. On the other, in order to avoid panic and hysteria, they had to reassure Americans that an atomic war did not mean certain death and destruction. The film "Duck and Cover," a collaboration of civil defense officials and educators in 1951, was designed to convey to students the message that government had plans in place to protect them. Did the message get across? And perhaps just as interesting to consider, did the officials making the film believe what they were teaching? If not, why teach the techniques? In the end, *Time* magazine concluded that while Americans feared the bomb, they accepted "the idea they must live with it."

its way to economic recovery, thanks to the Marshall Plan. Soviet pressure on Iran, Greece, and Turkey had abated.

Yet these tentative successes brought little comfort. The Soviet Union was not simply a major power seeking to protect its interests and expand where opportunity permitted. In the eyes of many Americans, the Soviets were determined, if they could, to overthrow the United States from either without or within. This war was being fought not only around the globe but right in America, by unseen agents using subversive means. In this way, the cold war mentality soon came to shape the lives of Americans at home much as it did American policy abroad.

 REVIEW

What were Soviet and American strategies after World War II, and what were the hot spots where these strategies clashed?

POSTWAR PROSPERITY

AT WAR'S END MANY BUSINESS leaders feared that a sudden drop in government purchases would bring back the hard times of the 1930s. Instead, despite a rocky year or two adjusting to the peacetime economy, Americans entered into the longest period of prosperity in the nation's history, lasting until the 1970s. Even the fear of communism could not dampen the simple joys of getting and spending.

SOURCES OF PROSPERITY — Two forces drove the postwar economic boom. One was unbridled consumer and business spending that followed 16 years of depression and war. High war wages had piled up in savings accounts and war bonds. Eager consumers set off to find the new cars, appliances, and foods unavailable during the war. Second, government expenditures at the local, state, and federal levels provided a boost to prosperity. The three major growth industries in the decades after World War II were health care, education, and government programs. Each of these was spurred by public spending. Equally important, the federal government poured billions of dollars into the military-industrial sector. The defense budget, which fell to $9 billion in 1947, reached $50 billion by the time Truman left office. Over the longer term, these factors promoting economic growth became clearer. In 1946, though, the road from war to peace seemed more uncertain, especially for Americans at the margins of the economy.

Postwar Energy and the Environment

Fighting World War II made many planners in government all too aware that modern economies depended heavily on fossil fuels, especially coal and petroleum products. Faced with decreasing oil reserves at home, Petroleum Administrator for War Harold Ickes wondered if the United States "could fuel another war." Rather than consider alternate energy sources, planners looked to the Middle East, which had cheap and seemingly unlimited supplies. But the Middle East also faced political unrest as nationalists challenged their colonial rulers. To protect the Middle East's energy, the United States would have to influence the region's political future.

Having lived through 12 years of depression, Americans placed jobs at the top of their postwar domestic agenda. The Employment Act of 1946 shifted responsibility for a full-employment economy from the private sector to the federal government.

Art © Estate of Ben Shahn/Licensed by VAGA, New York, NY

At home, manufacturers began producing automobiles and other consumer goods again, as well as taking advantage of a wide array of new materials and technologies developed during the war. Among them were pesticides such as DDT, hybrid seeds, and synthetic fertilizers for farming, plastics to replace natural products, and long-range airplanes for transportation. Chemical giant DuPont caught the spirit of the American fascination with these new wonders as it promised "Better Things for Better Living . . . through Chemistry." Since hydrocarbons from petroleum formed the basis for many fertilizers and plastics, cheap oil made increased production possible.

But the ideal of a full-blown consumer society contained a serious flaw: it largely ignored the impact that synthetic goods and the burning of fossil fuels would have on the environment. The factories producing plastics so essential to automobiles, homes, and appliances emitted toxic substances into the air, land, and water. Because plastic did not degrade naturally, it added mountains of trash to the nation's landfills. The dangers that "miracle" chemicals posed was seen in the small industrial town of Donora, Pennsylvania, outside Pittsburgh, in 1948. During a five-day period an inversion layer over the town trapped a toxic brew of sulfur dioxide, carbon monoxide, and metal dust spewing from the metal smelters there. Some 20 people died, and half the town's 7,000 residents were hospitalized.

Industry officials viewed the accident as unfortunate but argued that the atmosphere was a "useful natural resource" to be used "for the dispersion of wastes within its capacity to do so without harm to the surroundings." A few critics charged that such ideas ignored the fundamental principles of ecology. Fairfield Osborn in *Our Plundered Planet* (1948) warned that humans had to recognize the interdependence of life and cooperate with nature, rather than dominate it. Aldo Leopold, a pioneering ecologist, proposed in *A Sand Country Almanac* (1949) what he called a "land ethic." He observed that "we abuse the land because we see it as a commodity belonging to us." Instead, Leopold believed, "When we see land as a community to which we belong, we may use it with love and respect."

But most Americans in the postwar years were not ready to heed such warnings. They believed that cheap energy, new technologies, and a growing economy would keep the depression wolf from their doors.

Postwar Adjustments

Despite these hopes the transition from wartime to the new consumer economy was far from smooth.

With millions of veterans looking for peacetime jobs, workers on the home front, especially women and minorities, found themselves out of work. As peace came, almost 75 percent of the working women in one survey indicated that they hoped to continue their jobs. But male social scientists stressed how important it was for women to accept "more than the wife's usual responsibility for her marriage" and offer "lavish—and undemanding—affection" on returning GIs. One marriage counselor urged women to let their husbands know "you are tired of living alone, that you want him now to take charge."

Congress debated over how much it should do to ease the transition to peace and bring down unemployment. Organized labor, led by the CIO, argued that "all Americans able to work and seeking work have the right to a useful and remunerative job." Congress, especially conservative Republicans, was unwilling to go so far, but the Employment Act of 1946 at least created the Council of Economic Advisers to guide the president's policies. The bill thus established the principle that the government, not the private sector, was responsible for managing unemployment.

For minorities, the end of the war brought the return of an old labor practice, "last hired, first fired." At the height of the war over 200,000 African Americans and Hispanics worked in shipbuilding. By 1946 that number had dwindled to fewer than 10,000. The influx of Mexican laborers under the *bracero* program temporarily halted. In the South, where the large majority of black Americans lived, wartime labor shortages had become surpluses, leaving few jobs available.

AMERICAN G.I. FORUM

At the same time, many Hispanic and black veterans who had fought for their country during the war resented returning to a deeply segregated society. Such GIs "have acquired a new courage, have become more vocal in protesting the restrictions and inequalities with which they are confronted," noted one white Texan. When a funeral director in Three Rivers, Texas, refused to open its segregated cemetery for the burial of Felix Longoria, a Mexican American soldier killed in battle, his supporters organized. Led by Dr. Hector Garcia, a former army medical officer, the American G.I. Forum was founded in 1948 to campaign for civil rights. Longoria was finally buried in Arlington National Cemetery after the G.I. Forum convinced Congressman Lyndon Baines Johnson to intervene.

BLACK VETERANS AND CIVIL RIGHTS

Black veterans had a similar impact on the civil rights movement. Angered by violence, frustrated by the slow pace of desegregation, they breathed new energy into civil rights organizations such as the NAACP and CORE (the Congress of Racial Equality). Some voting registration drives in the South had success in urban centers such as Atlanta. Other black leaders pressed for improved education.

TO SECURE THESE RIGHTS

Out in the countryside, however, segregationists used economic intimidation, violence, and even murder, to preserve the Jim Crow system. President Truman, who saw civil rights as a key ingredient in his reform agenda, was especially disturbed when he learned that police in South Carolina had gouged out the eyes of a recently discharged black veteran. In December 1946 he appointed a Committee on Civil Rights, which published its report, *To Secure These Rights,* a year later.

Discovering inequities for minorities, the committee exposed a racial caste system that denied African Americans

JACKIE ROBINSON INTEGRATES BASEBALL

After World War II, Branch Rickey of the Brooklyn Dodgers was determined to break the color line in baseball. For years he had wanted to give black players the opportunity to play in the majors. Equally to the point, he was convinced that integration would improve his team. "The greatest untapped reservoir of raw material in the history of the game is the black race," he explained, adding, "The Negroes will make us winners for years to come."

In the early years of professional baseball, African Americans had played on several major league teams. In 1887, however, as Jim Crow laws spread across the South, the threat of a boycott by some white players caused team owners to adopt an unwritten rule barring black players. That ban stood for 60 years.

World War II created a new climate. The hypocrisy of fighting racism abroad while promoting it at home was becoming harder for team owners to ignore. "If a black boy can make it on Okinawa and Guadalcanal," Commissioner Albert "Happy" Chandler told reporters in April 1945, "hell, he can make it in baseball." Economic factors played a role as well. The African American migration to northern cities during World War II created a new, untapped audience for major league baseball. Growing cold war tensions added yet another factor. Even a Mississippi newspaper saw blacks in the major leagues as "a good answer to our communist adversaries who say the Negro has no chance in America."

Rickey recognized the enormous hostility that the first black player would face. He found the ideal prospect in Jackie Robinson, a World War II veteran and a remarkable athlete who had lettered in four

Jackie Robinson and his teammates celebrating a key win in the 1948 pennant race. Though Robinson had made the Dodgers a much better team, full integration of major league sports took many more years.

sports at UCLA. Rickey told Robinson in 1945, "I need a man that will take abuse, insults." Robinson would be carrying "the flag for [his] race."

Robinson was willing. He had risked court-martial during the war to fight segregation. "Nobody's going to separate bullets and label them 'for white troops' and 'for colored troops,'" Robinson told a superior officer. But he assured Rickey, "If you want to take this gamble, I will promise you there will be no incident." Rickey assigned him to Montreal, where he led the Dodgers' farm team to a championship.

When the Dodgers invited Robinson to spring training, several southern-born players circulated a petition stating their opposition to playing with a black man. But manager Leo Durocher bluntly warned them they would be traded if they refused to cooperate. Robinson would make them all rich, Durocher insisted.

On April 15, 1947, Robinson made his debut with the Dodgers at Ebbets Field. A black newspaper, the Boston *Chronicle,* proclaimed, "TRIUMPH OF WHOLE RACE SEEN IN JACKIE'S DEBUT IN MAJOR LEAGUE BALL."

But the abuse heaped on Robinson was worse than Rickey had anticipated. Robinson received death threats, his family was harassed, and some hotels barred him from staying with the team. He secretly wore a protective lining inside his hat in case he was beaned (he was hit a record nine times during the season, 65 times in seven years). Through it all, Robinson kept his temper, though not without difficulty. Once when a Cubs player kicked him, Robinson started to swing, then stopped. "I knew I was kind of an experiment," he recalled; " . . . the whole thing was bigger than me."

In Robinson's first year the Dodgers won the pennant and he was named Rookie of the Year. Two years later he was named the Most Valuable Player in the National League. After he retired in 1957 the skill and dignity he brought to the game earned him a place in baseball's Hall of Fame.

In the wake of his success, other teams added African Americans. Professional basketball and football followed baseball's lead. Still, the pace of integration was slow, and it was not until 1959 that all major league teams had at least one black member. Thanks to the vision of Branch Rickey and the courage of Jackie Robinson, America's pastime had become truly a national game.

Thinking Critically

In what other ways did the experience of World War II lead to greater integration in American life?

The Liga Pro Defensa Escolar, or Pro Schools Defense League, pushed to abolish segregated schooling, which affected Latinos as well as African Americans. No doubt deliberately, the league's emblem was written in English.

PRO SCHOOLS DEFENSE LEAGUE

TO BALANCE THE SCALE IS OUR AIM

employment opportunities, equal education, voting rights, and decent housing. But every time Truman appealed to Congress to implement the committee's recommendations, southern senators threatened to filibuster. So the president resorted to executive authority to achieve some modest results. In his most direct attack on segregation, he issued an **executive order** in July 1948 banning discrimination in the armed forces. Segregationists predicted disaster, but integrated units fought well and exhibited minimal racial tension.

ORGANIZED LABOR

For organized labor, reconversion brought an abrupt drop in hours worked and overtime paid. As wages declined and inflation ate into paychecks, strikes spread. Autoworkers walked off the job in the fall of 1945; steelworkers, in January 1946; miners, in April. In 1946 some 5 million workers struck, a rate triple that of any previous year. Antiunion sentiment soared. The crisis peaked in May 1946 with a national rail strike, which temporarily paralyzed the nation's transportation network. An angry President Truman asked, "What decent American would pull a rail strike at a time like this?"

At first Truman threatened to seize the railroads and then requested from Congress the power to draft striking workers into the military. He planned a speech in which he would say, "Let's put transportation and production back to work, hang a few traitors, and make our country safe for democracy." More-temperate aides persuaded him to revise the speech, but he still insisted on congressional action to authorize drafting strikers. The strike was settled before the threat was carried out, but few people, whether conservative or liberal, approved the idea of using the draft to punish political foes.

Truman under Attack

In September 1945 Harry Truman had boldly claimed his intention to extend the New Deal into the postwar era. He called for legislation to guarantee full employment, subsidized public housing, national health insurance, and a peacetime version of the Fair Employment Practices Commission to fight job discrimination. Instead of promoting his liberal agenda, he found himself fighting a conservative backlash. Labor unrest was just one source of his troubles. The increased demand for consumer goods temporarily in short supply triggered a sharp inflation. For two years prices rose as much as 15 percent annually.

With Truman's political stock falling, conservative Republicans and Democrats blocked the president's attempts to revive and extend the New Deal. As the congressional elections of 1946 neared, Republicans pointed to production shortages, the procession of strikes, the mismanagement of the economy. "To err is Truman," proclaimed the campaign buttons—or, more simply, "Had Enough?" Many voters had. The Republicans gained control of both houses of Congress. Not since 1928 had the Democrats fared so poorly.

TAFT-HARTLEY ACT

Leading the rightward swing was Senator Robert A. Taft of Ohio, son of former president William Howard Taft. Bob Taft not only wanted to halt the spread of the New Deal—he wanted to dismantle it. "We have to get over the corrupting idea we can legislate prosperity, legislate equality, legislate opportunity," he said in dismissing the liberal agenda. Taft especially wished to limit the power of the unions. In 1947 he pushed the Taft-Hartley Act through Congress, over Truman's veto. In the event of a strike, the bill allowed the president to order workers back on the job during a 90-day cooling-off period while collective bargaining continued. It also permitted states to adopt right-to-work laws, which banned the closed shop by eliminating union membership as a prerequisite for many jobs. Union leaders criticized the new law as a slave-labor act but discovered they could live with it, though it did hurt union efforts to organize, especially in the South.

A Welfare Program for GIs

THE GI BILL

Despite Republican gains, most Americans still supported the New Deal's major accomplishments: Social Security, a minimum wage law, and a more active role for government in reducing unemployment. The administration maintained its commitment to setting a minimum hourly wage, raising it again in 1950, from 45 to 75 cents. Social Security coverage was broadened to cover an additional 10 million workers. Furthermore, a growing list of welfare programs benefited not only the poor but also veterans, middle-income families, the elderly, and students. The most striking of these was the GI Bill of 1944, designed to reward soldiers for their service during the war.

For veterans the "GI Bill of Rights" created unparalleled opportunity. Those with more than two years of service received all tuition and fees plus living expenses for three years of college education. By 1948 the government was paying the college costs of nearly half of all male students as more than 2 million veterans took advantage of the GI Bill. Increased educational levels encouraged a shift from blue- to white-collar work and self-employment. Veterans

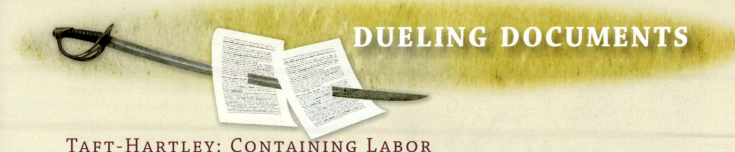

Taft-Hartley: Containing Labor

Widespread strikes involving over 5 million workers sparked conservative efforts to curb union power, leading to the Taft-Hartley or Labor Management Relations Act of 1947. The act forbid wildcat strikes, solidarity or political strikes, secondary boycotts, closed shops, and donations to federal political campaigns. John L. Lewis, the outspoken president of the United Mine Workers, warned the American Federation of Labor to fight Taft-Hartley (Document 1). Lewis especially disliked a clause that required union officers, but not business officials, to sign noncommunist affidavits. Senator Robert A. Taft defended his bill (Document 2).

DOCUMENT 1   John L. Lewis Condemns the Taft-Hartley Act

The question of signing the anti-Communist affidavit, which is only one small feature of the abrogations of this act, has occupied the minds of our leaders and the columns of the public press now for more than six weeks, and at last we come to the fatal and unhappy day when men who purport to lead the mighty hosts within the American Federation of Labor cry aloud and say, "There is nothing else for us to do—nothing else for us to do!"

I will tell you what you should do at least once in your lives—you should do your duty by your membership.

I suppose it is hardly necessary for me to say that I am not a Communist. I suppose it is hardly necessary for me to say that I was fighting Communism in America, with the other members of my organization, before many people in this country knew what Communism stood for in America and throughout the world. . . . The United Mine Workers of America has been in the vanguard of our citizenship in opposing the cast iron Oriental philosophy of Communism or any other damned kind of ism in this country. And we expect to remain in that position. We don't expect to change our principles too often; and we do expect some support from the American labor movement, because we think that our attitude reflects the attitude of the rank and file in these great organizations of labor who work for a living and who want a country tomorrow in which their children and their grandchildren can live.

The signing of the affidavit isn't the only thing that an organization has to do to conform to this Act. This Act is a trap, a pitfall for the organizations of labor, and I am surprised that those who have been attempting to analyze it haven't looked down the road just a few months or a year to find out some of the things that are inherent in this Act. This Act was passed to oppress labor, to make difficult its current enterprises for collective bargaining, to make more difficult the securing of new members for this labor movement, without which our movement will become so possessed of inertia that there is no action and no growth, and in a labor movement where there is no growth there is no security for its existence, because deterioration sets in and unions, like men, retrograde.

Source: John L. Lewis, *Speech Delivered before the AFL Convention*, October 14, 1947; www.laborstandard.org/ Vol4No2/John_L_Lewis_Speech.htm.

DOCUMENT 2   Taft Defends His Act

In the last few weeks the air has been filled with the raucous cries of union officials that every Congressman and Senator who voted for the Taft-Hartley law, or voted against its repeal, shall be liquidated in 1950. . . . The CIO is to collect more millions and apparently Ohio [Taft's home state] is to get more than its share of these millions. Labor officials . . . accused me of opposing every interest of the working man on housing, welfare, education, wages and prices . . . [overlooking] the fact that I blocked Truman's real slave labor bill to draft railroad workers and miners into the army, that I was for continuing price control and that Truman was the one who brought it to an end. . . .

As for the Taft-Hartley law . . . for a while they called it a slave labor law but that has become so ridiculous they have dropped the epithet. It is hard to see how it could be a slave labor law when the unions have gained a million members since its enactment and enjoy the best contracts, welfare services, and pensions they have ever had. The Taft-Hartley Act had only one purpose, to protect and strengthen collective bargaining by restoring equality between management and labor. . . . Before the passage of this act previous laws [like the Wagner Act of 1935], while giving the unions many rights to which they were entitled, completely relieved them from any responsibility to the public, to employers, or even to their own members. . . .

The Act protects the people. The number of strikes has been cut in half since the passage of the Act as compared to the period between the end of the war and the passage of the Act. . . . The Act gives equal treatment to employers and penalizes unfair labor practices on the part of the labor union officials, retaining, of course, the prohibition of unfair practices on the part of employers just as provided by the Wagner Act. . . .

In the third place, the Act protects the union member. It makes it an unfair labor practice for a union to coerce employees. It prohibits the use of the dues of union members for political purposes, to be used perhaps against their best friends. It requires a non-communist affidavit so that they may know whether their officers are communists. It requires financial reports so they may know what their officers are doing with their money. It require written consent before their dues can be deducted from their wages. It prohibits excessive and discriminatory initiation fees.

Source: Robert A. Taft, *Speech to Smaller Businessmen of America*, September 7, 1949, in Clarence E. Wunderlin, ed., *The Papers of Robert A. Taft: 1949–1953* (Kent, OH, 2006), pp. 99–100.

Thinking Critically

Why would Congress call for a loyalty oath—the noncommunist affidavit—in 1947? Besides the loyalty oath provision, why did Lewis oppose Taft-Hartley? Why does Robert Taft believe his act is fair to labor? What is he referring to when he mentions Truman's "slave labor law to draft railroad workers"?

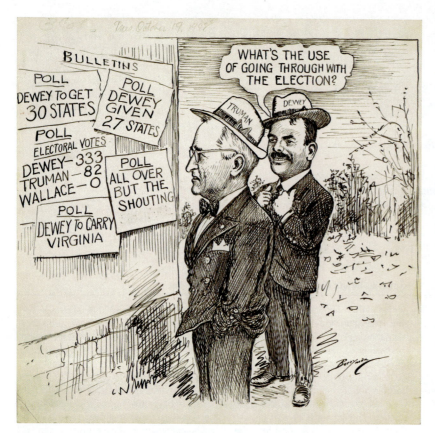

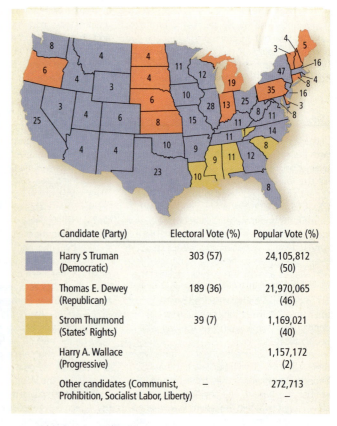

moderate civil rights proposals for a voting rights bill and an antilynching law. When the liberal wing of the party passed a civil rights plank as part of the Democratic platform, delegates from several Deep South states stalked out of the convention. They banded together to create the States' Rights, or "Dixiecrat," Party, with J. Strom Thurmond, the segregationist governor of South Carolina, as their candidate.

With the Democrats divided, Republicans smelled victory. They moved toward the political center by rejecting the conservative Taft in favor of the more moderate former New York governor Thomas Dewey. Dewey proved so aloof that he inspired scant enthusiasm. "You have to know Dewey well to really dislike him," quipped one Taft supporter. Still, most observers assumed that Dewey would walk away with the race.

TRUMAN FIGHTS BACK Truman, did not meekly roll over and play dead. He launched a stinging attack against the "reactionaries" in Congress: that "bunch of old mossbacks . . . gluttons

Everyone, including opinion pollsters, assumed Dewey would easily defeat Truman.

also received low-interest loans to start businesses or farms of their own and to buy homes. The GI Bill accelerated trends that would transform American society into a prosperous, heavily middle-class suburban nation.

Less fortunately, the bill did little to help minorities and females. Few women received benefits under the bill. African Americans and Hispanics, even those eligible for veterans' benefits, were hampered by Jim Crow restrictions in segregated universities and in jobs in both the public and private sectors. The Federal Housing Administration even helped draw up "model" restrictive housing covenants. In order to "retain stability," neighborhoods were allowed to use the covenants to segregate according to "social and racial classes."

The Election of 1948

HENRY WALLACE AND THE PROGRESSIVES As the election of 1948 approached, the New Deal coalition that Franklin Roosevelt had held together for so long seemed to be coming apart. On the left Truman was challenged by Henry Wallace, a progressive who had been vice president under Roosevelt and who wanted to pursue New Deal reforms even more vigorously than Truman did. Disaffected liberals bolted the Democratic Party to support Wallace on a third-party Progressive ticket.

DIXIECRATS Within the southern conservative wing of the party, archsegregationists resented Truman's

	Candidate (Party)	Electoral Vote (%)	Popular Vote (%)
	Harry S Truman (Democratic)	303 (57)	24,105,812 (50)
	Thomas E. Dewey (Republican)	189 (36)	21,970,065 (46)
	Strom Thurmond (States' Rights)	39 (7)	1,169,021 (40)
	Harry A. Wallace (Progressive)		1,157,172 (2)
	Other candidates (Communist, Prohibition, Socialist Labor, Liberty)	–	272,713 –

ELECTION OF 1948

of privilege . . . all set to do a hatchet job on the New Deal." From the rear platform of his campaign train, he made almost 400 speeches in eight weeks. Over and over he hammered away at the "do-nothing" 80th Congress, which, he told farmers, "had stuck a pitchfork" in their backs. Hours before the polls closed, the archconservative Chicago *Tribune* happily headlined "Dewey Defeats Truman." But the experts were wrong. Not only did the voters return Truman by over 2 million popular votes, but they also gave the Democrats commanding majorities in the House and Senate.

THE FAIR DEAL As he began his new term, Harry Truman expressed his conviction that all Americans were entitled to a "Fair Deal" from their government. He called for a vigorous revival of New Deal programs such as national health insurance and regional TVA-style projects. Echoing an old Populist idea, Truman hoped to keep his working coalition together by forging stronger links between farmers and labor. But the conservative coalition of Democrats and Republicans in Congress blocked any significant new initiatives. On the domestic front, Truman remained largely the conservator of Franklin Roosevelt's legacy.

REVIEW

What government policies encouraged postwar prosperity?

THE COLD WAR AT HOME

BOB RAYMONDI, A MOBSTER SERVING a prison term in the late 1940s, was no stranger to extortion, racketeering, or gangland killings. In fact, he was so feared that he dominated the inmate population at Dannemora Prison. Raymondi began to make the acquaintance of a group of Communists who had been jailed for advocating the overthrow of the government. He enjoyed talking with people who had some education. When Raymondi's sister learned about his new friends, she was frantic. "My God, Bob," she told him. "You'll get into trouble."

Was something amiss? Most Americans judged it riskier to associate with Communists than with hardened criminals. Out of a population of 150 million, the Communist Party in 1950 could claim a membership of only 43,000. (More than a few of those were FBI undercover agents.) But Americans did worry about Communists. In part, conscientious citizens were appalled by party members who excused Stalin's violent crimes against his own people. Millions of Russians had been executed or sent to Siberian labor camps; under those circumstances, most Americans found it outrageous to hear American Communists dismiss civil liberties as "bourgeois."

CONSERVATIVE ANTICOMMUNISM Conservatives were especially outspoken about the Communist menace. Some honestly feared the New Deal as "creeping socialism." The president's advisers, it seemed to them, were either Communist agents or their unwitting dupes. Leftists, they believed, controlled labor unions, Hollywood, and other interest groups sympathetic to the New Deal. Conservative outrage grew as Stalin extended Soviet control in Eastern Europe and Asia. Many conservatives charged that a conspiracy within Roosevelt's administration had sold out America to its enemies. More-cynical conservatives used Red baiting simply to discredit people and ideas they disliked.

The Shocks of 1949

THE H-BOMB Truman won in 1948 in large part because of his strong leadership in foreign affairs. In 1949 a series of foreign policy shocks allowed Republicans to seize the anticommunist issue. In August, American scientists reported that rains monitored in the Pacific contained traces of hot nuclear waste. Only one conclusion seemed possible: the Soviet Union had exploded its own atomic bomb. When Truman announced the news, Congress was debating whether to spend $1.5 billion for military aid to the newly formed NATO alliance. The House stopped debating and passed the bill, while Truman decided to accelerate research into a newer, more powerful fusion, or hydrogen, bomb. Senator Arthur Vandenberg, a Republican leader in international affairs, summed up the reaction of many officials to the end of the American nuclear monopoly: "This is now a different world."

CHINA FALLS TO COMMUNISTS Then in December came more disturbing news. The long-embattled Nationalist government of Chiang Kai-shek had fled mainland China to the offshore island of Formosa (present-day Taiwan). By January, Communist troops under Mao Zedong were swarming into Beijing, China's capital city. Chiang's defeat came as no surprise to State Department officials, who had long regarded the Nationalists as hopelessly corrupt and inefficient. Despite major American efforts to save Chiang's regime, full-scale civil war had broken out in 1947. Mao's triumph was hardly unexpected.

But Republicans, who had up until 1949 supported the president's foreign policy, now broke ranks. For some time, many conservatives had resented the administration's preoccupation with Europe. Time-Life publisher Henry Luce used his magazines to campaign for a greater concern for Asian affairs and especially more aid to defeat Mao Zedong. Luce and his associates, known as the "China Lobby," were supported in part with funds from the Chinese embassy. When Chiang at last collapsed, his American backers charged that Democrats had let the Communists win.

THE HISS CASE Worries that subversives had sold out the country were heightened when former State Department official Alger Hiss was brought to trial in 1949 for perjury. Hiss, an adviser to Roosevelt at the Yalta Conference, had been accused by former Communist Whittaker Chambers of passing secrets to the Soviet Union during the 1930s. Though the evidence in the case was far from conclusive, the jury convicted Hiss for lying about his association with Chambers. And in February 1950 the nation was further shocked to learn that a high-ranking British physicist, Klaus Fuchs, had spied for the Russians while working on the Manhattan Project. Here was clear evidence of conspiracy at work.

The Loyalty Crusade

President Truman sought to blunt Republican accusations that he was "soft" on communism. Ten days after proposing the Truman Doctrine in March 1947, the president signed an executive order establishing a Federal Employee Loyalty Program designed to guard against the possible disloyalty of "Reds, phonies, and 'parlor pinks.'" Since the FBI could hardly find time to examine all of the 2 million government employees, the order required supervisors to review and certify the loyalties of those who worked below them, reporting to a system of federal loyalty review boards.

LOYALTY REVIEW BOARD — The system quickly got out of hand. Seth Richardson, the conservative head of the Loyalty Review Board, argued that the government could "discharge any employee for reasons which seem sufficient to the Government, and without extending to such employee any hearing whatsoever." After several years the difficulty of proving that employees were actually disloyal became clear, and Truman allowed the boards to fire those who were "potentially" disloyal or "bad security risks," such as alcoholics, homosexuals, and debtors. Suspect employees, in other words, were assumed guilty until proven innocent. After some 5 million investigations, the program identified a few hundred employees who, though not Communists, had at one time been associated with suspect groups. Rather than calm public fears, the loyalty program gave credibility to the growing Red Scare.

HUAC, Hollywood, and Unions

About the same time Truman established the Loyalty Review Board, the House Committee on Un-American Activities (HUAC) began to investigate Communist influence in the film industry. Hollywood, with its wealth, glamour, and highly visible Jewish and foreign celebrities, had long aroused a mixture of attraction and suspicion among traditional Americans. "Large numbers of moving pictures that come out of Hollywood carry the Communist line," charged committee member John Rankin of Mississippi. Indeed, during the Depression some Hollywood figures

The fall of China to the Communist forces of Mao Zedong was one of two great cold war shocks of 1949. Anticommunists joined members of the China Lobby in blaming Truman for "losing China."

THE SATURDAY EVENING POST SERIAL THAT JOLTED MILLIONS!

WARNER BROS. BRING IT TO THE SCREEN!

I WAS A COMMUNIST FOR THE F.B.I.
FRANK LOVEJOY

| Many Hollywood films exploited anticommunist fears.

and Ronald Reagan, were considered "friendly" because they supplied names of suspected leftists. Others refused to inform on their colleagues. Eventually, 10 uncooperative witnesses, known as the "Hollywood Ten," refused on First Amendment grounds to say whether they were or ever had been Communists. They served prison terms for contempt of Congress.

BLACKLISTING For all its probing, HUAC never offered convincing evidence that filmmakers were in any way subversive. About the most damning evidence presented was that one eager left-leaning extra, when asked to "whistle something" during his walk-on part, hummed a few bars of the Communist anthem the "Internationale." The investigations did, however, inspire nervous Hollywood producers to turn out films such as *I Was a Communist for the FBI* (1950). The studios also adopted a blacklist that prevented admitted or accused Communists from finding work. Because no judicial proceedings were involved, victims of false charges, rumors, or spiteful accusations found it nearly impossible to clear their names.

McCARRAN ACT Suspicion of aliens and immigrants led finally to the passage, over Truman's veto, of the McCarran Act (1950). It required all Communists to register with the attorney general, forbade the entry of anyone who had belonged to a totalitarian organization, and allowed the Justice Department to detain suspect aliens indefinitely during deportation hearings. That same year a Senate committee began an inquiry designed to root out homosexuals holding government jobs. Even one "sex pervert in a Government agency tends to have a corrosive influence upon his fellow employees," warned the committee.

had developed ties to the Communist Party or had become sympathetic to party causes. To generate support for the Allies during the war, Hollywood (with Roosevelt's blessing) produced films with a positive view of the Soviet Union such as *Mission to Moscow* and *Song of Russia*.

HOLLYWOOD TEN HUAC called a parade of movie stars, screenwriters, and producers to sit in the glare of its public hearings. Some witnesses, such as Gary Cooper

| The energetic and opportunistic Roy Cohn (left) served as a key strategist in the inquisition that made Senator Joseph McCarthy a figure to fear. He and fellow staffer David Schine (right) helped McCarthy turn a minor Senate subcommittee into a major power center.

The campaign had effects beyond government offices: the armed forces stepped up their rates of dismissal for sexual orientation, while city police more frequently raided gay bars and social clubs.

The Ambitions of Senator McCarthy

By 1950 anticommunism had created a climate of fear in which legitimate concerns mixed with irrational hysteria. Joseph R. McCarthy, a Senate nonentity from Wisconsin, saw in that fear an issue with which to build his political fortunes. To an audience in Wheeling, West Virginia, in February 1950 he waved a sheaf of papers in the air and announced that he had a list of 205—or perhaps 81, 57, or "a lot of"—Communists in the State Department. (No one, including the senator, could remember the number, which he continually changed.) In the following months McCarthy leveled charge after charge. He had penetrated the "iron curtain" of the State Department to discover "card-carrying Communists," the "top Russian espionage agent" in the United States, "egg-sucking phony liberals," and "Communists and queers" who wrote "perfumed notes."

It didn't seem to matter that McCarthy never substantiated his charges. When examined, his lists contained names of people who had left the State Department long before or who had been cleared by the FBI. When forced into a corner, McCarthy simply lied and went on to another accusation. No one seemed beyond reach. In the summer of 1950 a Senate committee headed by Millard F. Tydings of Maryland concluded that McCarthy's charges were "a fraud and a hoax." Such candor among those in government did not last long, as "Jolting Joe" (one of McCarthy's favorite macho nicknames) in 1952 helped defeat Tydings and several other Senate critics.

McCarthy served as a blunt instrument that some conservative Republicans used to damage the Democrats. Without this support McCarthy would have had little credibility. Many of his accusations came from information secretly (and illegally) funneled to him by FBI director J. Edgar Hoover. But McCarthyism was also the bitter fruit Truman and the Democrats reaped from their own attempts to exploit the anticommunist mood. McCarthy, more than Truman, tapped the fears and hatreds of a broad coalition of Catholic leaders, conservatives, and neo-isolationists who harbored suspicion of things foreign, liberal, internationalist, European, or a touch too intellectual. They saw McCarthy and his allies as the protectors of a deeply felt spirit of Americanism.

By the time Truman left office in 1953, 32 states had laws requiring teachers to take loyalty oaths and government loyalty boards were asking employees what newspapers they subscribed to or phonograph records they collected. A library in Indiana had banned *Robin Hood* because the idea of stealing from the rich to give to the poor seemed too leftish. As one historian commented, "Opening the valve of anticommunist hysteria was a good deal simpler than closing it."

REVIEW

How did the Truman administration contribute to the Red Scare?

FROM COLD WAR TO HOT WAR AND BACK

AS THE COLD WAR HEATED up in 1949, the Truman administration searched for a more assertive foreign policy. The new policy was developed by the National Security Council (NSC), an agency created by Congress in 1947 as part of a plan to help the executive branch respond more effectively to cold war crises. Rather than merely "contain" the Soviets, as George Kennan had suggested, the National Security Council wanted the United States to "strive for victory." In April 1950 it sent Truman a document, NSC-68, which came to serve as the framework for American policy over the next 20 years.

NSC-68 NSC-68 called for an immediate increase in defense spending from $13 billion to $50 billion a year, to be paid for with a large tax increase. Most of the funds would go to rebuild conventional forces, but the NSC urged that the hydrogen bomb be developed to offset the Soviet nuclear capacity. Efforts to carry out NSC-68 at first aroused widespread opposition as too expensive, too simplistic, and too militaristic. But all such reservations were swept away on June 25, 1950. "Korea came along and saved us," Secretary of State Dean Acheson later remarked.

Police Action

In 1950 Korea was about the last place in the world Americans might have imagined themselves fighting a war. Since World War II the country had been divided along the 38th parallel, the north controlled by the Communist government of Kim Il Sung, the south by the dictatorship of Syngman Rhee. Preoccupied with China and the rebuilding of Japan, the Truman administration's interest had dwindled steadily after the war. When Secretary of State Acheson discussed American policy in Asia before the National Press Club in January 1950, he did not even mention Korea.

NORTH KOREAN INVASION On June 24 Harry Truman was enjoying a leisurely break from politics at the family home in Independence, Missouri. In Korea it was already Sunday morning when Acheson called the president. North Korean troops had crossed the 38th parallel, Acheson reported, possibly to fulfill Kim Il Sung's proclaimed intention to "liberate" the South. A full-scale invasion was in progress. The United Nations, meeting in emergency session, had ordered a cease-fire, which the North Koreans were ignoring. Truman flew back to Washington, convinced that Stalin and his Chinese Communist allies had ordered the invasion. The threat of a third world war, this one atomic, seemed agonizingly real. The president wanted to respond firmly enough to deter aggression but without provoking a larger war with the Soviet Union or China.

Truman did not hesitate; American troops would fight the North Koreans, though the United States would not declare war. The fighting in Korea would be a "police action" supervised by the United Nations. On June 27 the Security Council passed a U.S. resolution to send United Nations forces to Korea. That move succeeded only because the Soviet delegate, who possessed veto power, had walked out six months earlier in protest over the council's refusal to seat mainland China. Stalin had secretly approved North Korea's attack, but he promised only supplies. Neither Russian troops nor prestige would be involved, he warned Kim.

Americans of almost all political persuasions supported Truman's forceful response. Congress quickly voted the huge increase in defense funds needed to carry out the recommendations of NSC-68. American allies were less committed to the action. Though 16 nations contributed to the war effort, the United States provided half of the ground troops, 86 percent of the naval units, and 93 percent of the air force. By the time the UN forces could be marshaled, North Korean forces had pinned the South Koreans within a small defensive perimeter centered on Pusan. Then Douglas MacArthur, commander of the UN forces, launched a daring amphibious attack behind North Korean lines at Inchon, near the western end of the 38th parallel. Fighting eastward, MacArthur's troops threatened to trap the invaders, who fled back to the North.

The Chinese Intervene

MacArthur's success led Truman to a fateful decision. With the South liberated, he gave MacArthur permission to cross the 38th parallel, drive the Communists from the North, and reunite the country under Syngman Rhee. With Senator Joe McCarthy on the attack at home, the 1950 elections nearing, and the McCarran Act just passed, Truman

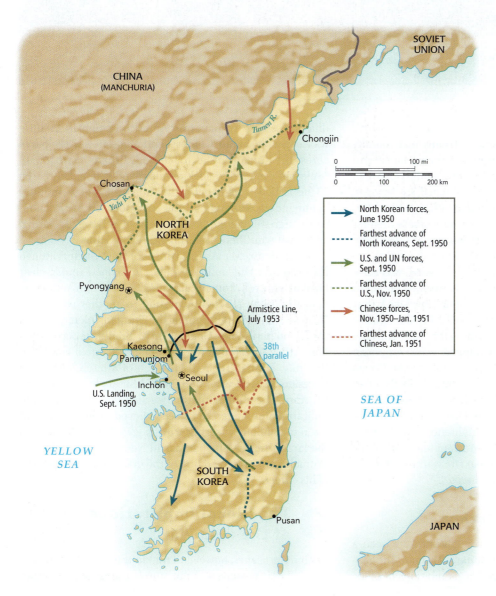

THE KOREAN WAR

In their opening offensive, North Korean troops almost pushed South Korean and American forces into the sea at Pusan. After MacArthur rallied UN forces, he commanded a successful landing at Inchon behind North Korean lines and then crossed the 38th parallel into North Korea. Red Chinese troops counterattacked, inflicting one of the most humiliating defeats on U.S. troops in American military history. Fighting continued for another two years. **How did Korea's geographic location increase the risk of escalating the scale of the war?**

An American soldier interrogates two boys taken prisoner in 1950. Both were in the North Korean army.

was glad enough for the chance to vanquish the North Koreans. By Thanksgiving American troops had roundly defeated northern forces and were advancing on several fronts toward the frozen Yalu River, the boundary between Korea and China. MacArthur, emboldened by success, promised that the boys would be home by Christmas.

Throughout the fall offensive, however, Chinese premier Zhou Enlai warned that his country would not tolerate an American presence on its border. Washington officials belittled the warning. Mao Zedong, they assumed, was a Soviet puppet, and Stalin had declared the Korean conflict to be merely a "civil war" and off-limits. But after MacArthur launched his end-the-war offensive, some 400,000 Chinese troops poured across the Yalu, smashing through lightly defended UN lines. At Chosan they trapped 20,000 American and South Korean troops, inflicting one of the worst defeats in American military history. Within three weeks they had driven UN forces back behind the 38th parallel. So total was the rout that Truman wondered publicly about using the atomic bomb. That remark sent a frightened British prime minister Clement Attlee flying to Washington to dissuade the president. He readily agreed that the war must remain limited and withdrew his nuclear threat.

Truman versus MacArthur

The military stalemate in Korea brought into the open a simmering feud between MacArthur and Truman. The general had made no secret of his political ambitions or of his differences with Truman over American policy in Asia. He was eager to bomb Chinese and Russian supply bases across the Korean border, to blockade China's coast, and to "unleash" Chiang Kai-shek on mainland China. On March 23 he issued a personal ultimatum to Chinese military commanders demanding total surrender. To his Republican congressional supporters he sent a letter declaring, "We must win. There is no substitute for victory."

To Truman, MacArthur's insubordination threatened the tradition that military policy remained under clear civilian control. Equally alarming, MacArthur's strategy appeared to be an open invitation to another world war. Despite the general's popularity, Truman made plans to discipline him. When General Omar Bradley reported that MacArthur threatened to resign before Truman could act, the irate Truman replied, "The son of a bitch isn't going to resign on me. I want him fired!" Military leaders agreed. On April 11 a stunned nation learned that the celebrated military commander had been relieved of his duties. On his return home, cheering crowds gave MacArthur one of the largest ticker-tape parades in New York City's history. Truman's move seemed one of the great political mistakes of his career.

The Global Implications of the Cold War

Behind the scenes, however, Truman was winning this personal clash. At stake was not simply the issue of whether

THE SPHINX

WHAT DO YOU THINK OF THE KOREAN TRUCE, GENERAL?

THE PUBLIC

General Douglas MacArthur, who was lionized when Truman fired him, became a more ambiguous figure after his bid for the presidency fizzled. Here, in 1953, he is portrayed as the silent Sphinx of Egypt, unwilling to give his opinion on the Korean armistice agreement.

Reinhold Niebuhr put it, using American cold war weapons against the ideology of communism would be "like the spears of the knights when gunpowder challenged their reign."

Secretary of State Acheson agreed with the Eurocentrists. Korea was to Acheson but a small link in a global "collective security system." The wider war in Asia that MacArthur favored would threaten American interests in Europe because American resources would be stretched too thinly. Or, as General Bradley told Congress, a war in Asia would lead to "the wrong war, at the wrong place, at the wrong time, and with the wrong enemy." In this debate the Eurocentric faction prevailed. Congressional leaders agreed with Truman that the war in Korea should remain limited and that American resources should go to rebuilding Europe's defenses.

Meanwhile, the war in Korea bogged down in stalemate. As peace negotiators argued over how to reunify Korea, the United States suffered another 32,000 casualties in an ugly war of attrition. By March 1952 Truman's popularity had sunk so low that he lost the New Hampshire presidential primary to Senator Estes Kefauver of Tennessee. With that defeat, he announced he would not run for reelection in 1952.

The Election of 1952

With Truman out of the race, the war in stalemate, and the Fair Deal agenda blunted by anticommunist crusades, the Republicans were determined to triumph in the 1952 elections. Rather than choose Senator Robert Taft from the party's conservative wing, they tapped General Dwight Eisenhower, a World War II hero. Eisenhower was less ideological: in fact, no one even knew whether he was a Republican or Democrat until he announced he was joining the Republican Party. Although the Democratic candidate, Senator Adlai Stevenson of Illinois, was an eloquent speaker, he lacked Eisenhower's common touch. "I like Ike!" proclaimed his campaign posters. A pledge that if elected, he would go to Korea personally to help end the conflict, highlighted Eisenhower's stature as a leader.

The election outcome was never much in doubt. Eisenhower's broad smile and confident manner won him more than 55 percent of the popular vote. A carefully staged television advertising campaign revealed the power of the new media to influence political outcomes. "The great problem of America today," Eisenhower had said during the campaign, "is to take that straight road down the middle." Most Americans who voted for him were comforted to think that was just where they were headed.

EISENHOWER IN KOREA — Even before taking office, Eisenhower traveled to Korea to appraise the situation firsthand. Once in office, he renewed negotiations but warned that unless the talks made speedy progress, the United States might retaliate "under circumstances

he or MacArthur would prevail. Rather, the outcome would determine the future direction of American foreign policy. The cold war crisis forced American leaders to think globally. Where in the world did the nation's interests lie? What region was most critical to the future? MacArthur believed that the Pacific basin would "determine the course of history in the next ten thousand years." To avoid being swept aside, the United States should make an all-out effort, not just to contain the Communist onslaught in Korea, but to play a major role throughout Asia. "What I advocate is that we defend every place, and I say that we have the capacity to do it," insisted MacArthur. Many conservative Republicans and groups like the China Lobby shared MacArthur's view.

EUROPE, NOT ASIA, FIRST — Truman and his advisers continued to see Europe as the key to American foreign policy. Western Europe in particular, they believed, remained the center of the world's economic and military power. Political scientist Hans Morgenthau argued that "he who controls Europe is well on his way toward controlling the whole world." Further, Eurocentric Americans felt that the cultural differences between the United States and Asia were so great that the battle for Asia could not be won by military might. As theologian

With the rise of a cold war between the United States and the Soviet Union, the fears of an atomic war that might leave the world in ashes became a part of everyday life—and of popular culture. This poster advertising Invasion U.S.A., a film first released in 1953, conjured up a New York City in ruins. Hollywood studios made a number of such low-budget movies that reflected American fears of the Communist menace.

of our choosing." The carrot-and-stick approach worked. On July 27, 1953, the Communists and the UN forces signed an armistice ending a "police action" in which 54,000 Americans had died. Korea remained divided, almost as it had been in 1950. Communism had been "contained," but at a high price in human lives.

The Fall of McCarthy

It was less clear, however, whether domestic anticommunism could be contained. Eisenhower boasted that he was a "modern" Republican, distinguishing himself from what he called the more "hidebound" members of the GOP. Their continuing anticommunist campaigns caused him increasing embarrassment. Senator McCarthy's reckless antics, at first directed at Democrats, began to hit Republican targets as well.

By the summer of 1953 the senator was on a rampage. He dispatched two young staff members, Roy Cohn and David Schine, to investigate the State Department's overseas information agency and the Voice of America radio stations. Behaving more like college pranksters, the two conducted a whirlwind 18-day witch hunt through Western Europe, condemning government libraries for possessing "subversive" books, including volumes by John Dewey and Foster Rhea Dulles, a conservative historian and cousin of Eisenhower's secretary of state. Some librarians, fearing for their careers,

burned a number of books. That action drove President Eisenhower to denounce "book burners," though soon afterward he reassured McCarthy's supporters that he did not advocate free speech for Communists.

THE ROSENBERGS EXECUTED The administration's own behavior contributed to the hysteria on which McCarthy thrived. The president launched a loyalty campaign, which he claimed resulted in 3,000 firings and 5,000 resignations of government employees. It was a godsend to McCarthyites: What further proof was needed that subversives were lurking in the federal bureaucracy? Furthermore, a well-publicized spy trial had led to the conviction of Ethel and Julius Rosenberg, a couple accused of passing atomic secrets to the Soviets. Although the evidence against Ethel was not conclusive, the judge sentenced both Rosenbergs to the electric chair, an unusually harsh punishment even in cases of espionage. When asked to commute the death sentence to life imprisonment, Eisenhower refused, and the Rosenbergs were executed in June 1953.

McCARTHY VERSUS THE ARMY In such a climate—where Democrats remained silent for fear of being called leftists and Eisenhower cautiously refused to "get in the gutter with *that* guy"—McCarthy lost all sense of proportion. When the army denied his aide David Schine special treatment, McCarthy decided to investigate communism in the army. The new American Broadcasting Company network, eager to fill its afternoon program slots, televised the hearings. For three weeks, the public had an opportunity to see McCarthy badger witnesses and make a mockery of Senate procedures. Soon after, his popularity began to slide, and the anticommunist hysteria ebbed as well. In 1954 the Senate finally moved to censure him. He died three years later, destroyed by alcohol and the habit of throwing so many reckless punches.

 REVIEW

How did differences over strategy during the Korean War lead to the firing of General MacArthur?

CONCLUSION

THE WORLD AT LARGE

With the Democrats out of the White House for the first time since the Depression and with right-wing McCarthyites in retreat, Eisenhower did indeed seem to be leading the nation on a course "right down the middle." Still, it is worth noting how much that sense of "middle" had changed.

Both the Great Depression and World War II made most Americans realize that the nation's economy was firmly tied to the international order. The crash in 1929, with its worldwide effects, illustrated the closeness of the links. The New Deal demonstrated that Americans were willing to give the federal government power to influence American society in major new ways. And the war led the government to intervene in the economy even more actively.

So when peace came in 1945, it became clear that the "middle road" did not mean a return to the laissez-faire economics of the 1920s or the isolationist politics of the 1930s. Supporters of the Marshall Plan recognized that the economic recovery of Europe should be an American priority for reasons of self-interest as much as of charity. Gone were the policies of the 1920s, under which the United States sternly demanded repayment of European war debts. ("They hired the money, didn't they?" President Coolidge allegedly complained in 1926.) Encompassing the liberal theories of John Maynard Keynes, the Marshall Plan assumed that American intervention in the world economy would promote not only prosperity but also international security. At home, "moderate Republicans" supported social welfare programs such as Social Security and granted that the federal government had the power to lower unemployment, control inflation, and manage the economy in a variety of ways.

Finally, the shift from war to peace demonstrated that it was no longer possible to make global war without making a global peace. Under the new balance of power in the postwar world, the United States and the Soviet Union stood alone as superpowers, with the potential capability to annihilate each other and the rest of the world. ∞∞∞∞

CHAPTER SUMMARY

IN THE POSTWAR PERIOD, THE cold war between the Soviet Union and the United States affected every aspect of American domestic and foreign policy and overshadowed American life.

■ The cold war had roots in American suspicions of Soviet communism dating back to World War I, but Stalin's aggressive posture toward Eastern Europe and the Persian Gulf region raised new fears among American policy makers.

■ In response, the Truman administration applied a policy of containment through the Truman Doctrine, the Marshall Plan, and NSC-68.

■ Despite a brief period of inflation, labor unrest, and shortages of goods and housing, the transition from war to peace launched the longest period of prosperity in the nation's history.

■ Domestic fear of Communist subversion led the Truman administration to devise a government loyalty program and inspired the witch hunts of Senator Joseph McCarthy.

■ The Soviet detonation of an atomic bomb and the fall of China to the Communists, followed one year later by the Korean War, undermined the popularity of Harry Truman and the Democrats, opening the way for Dwight Eisenhower's victory in the 1952 presidential election.

Additional Reading

A GOOD PLACE TO BEGIN reading on the cold war is Fred Logevall and Campbell Craig, *America's Cold War* (2009). For the science and politics of the H-bomb, see Gregg Herken, *Brotherhood of the Bomb: The Tangled Lives and Loyalties of Robert Oppenheimer, Ernest Lawrence, and Edward Teller* (2003), and Kai Bird and Martin Sherwin, *American Prometheus: The Triumph and Tragedy of J. Robert Oppenheimer* (2006). On the domestic cold war, see David Halberstam, *The Fifties* (1994), and Stephen Whitfield, *The Culture of the Cold War* (1991). Robert Sklar, *Movie Made America: A Cultural History of American Movies* (rev. ed., 1994), offers insight into how the cold war affected Hollywood.

Brian Burnes, *Harry S Truman: His Life and Times* (2003), is a lively account of a president who became more popular with the passage of time. Elizabeth Edwards Spalding, *The First Cold Warrior: Harry Truman, Containment and the Remaking of Liberal Internationalism* (2006), measures Truman as an architect of the postwar world order. The best account of the man who gave his name to the Red Scare is David Oshinsky, *A Conspiracy So Immense: The World of Joe McCarthy* (2005). Two historians have shown how cold war politics and the civil rights movement intersected: Thomas Borstelmann, *The Cold War and the Color Line: American Race Relations in the Global Arena* (2003), and Mary Dudziak, *Cold War Civil Rights: Race and the Image of American Democracy* (2002).

For a fuller list of readings, see the Bibliography at www.mhhe.com/eh8e.

Significant Events

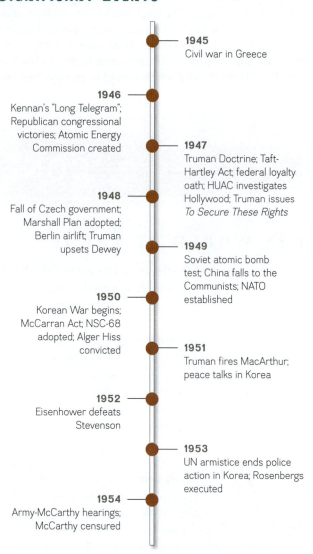

1945
Civil war in Greece

1946
Kennan's "Long Telegram"; Republican congressional victories; Atomic Energy Commission created

1947
Truman Doctrine; Taft-Hartley Act; federal loyalty oath; HUAC investigates Hollywood; Truman issues *To Secure These Rights*

1948
Fall of Czech government; Marshall Plan adopted; Berlin airlift; Truman upsets Dewey

1949
Soviet atomic bomb test; China falls to the Communists; NATO established

1950
Korean War begins; McCarran Act; NSC-68 adopted; Alger Hiss convicted

1951
Truman fires MacArthur; peace talks in Korea

1952
Eisenhower defeats Stevenson

1953
UN armistice ends police action in Korea; Rosenbergs executed

1954
Army-McCarthy hearings; McCarthy censured

Cold War / Red Scare: Mileposts

	FOREIGN	DOMESTIC
1945–1946	Iranian crisis	Labor unrest
1946	Kennan's "Long Telegram" Stalin: future wars inevitable Churchill: "Iron Curtain" Baruch Plan: no international nuclear control	"Red baiting" begins
1947	Truman Doctrine announced	Federal Employee Loyalty Program HUAC investigates Hollywood Taft-Hartley Act
1948	Marshall Plan Fall of governments in Czechoslovakia and Hungary Berlin blockade	Progressive Party's liberal agenda
1949	NATO created Soviets explode an atomic bomb China falls to Communists	Alger Hiss convicted of perjury Klaus Fuchs charged as atomic spy
1950	NSC-68 North Korea invades South Korea: Korean War	McCarthy's list of Communists in the State Department McCarran Act
1953	Armistice signed in Korean War	Rosenbergs executed as spies
1954		Senate censures McCarthy

Just as a nuclear arms race pitted the United States against the Soviet Union in a quest for atomic weapons, so the "Big Three" automakers of the 1950s (General Motors, Ford, and Chrysler) raced to outdo one another in producing sleeker, jet-age-styled cars. Here Ford portrays its 1959 Mercury Monterey as the pride of this ideal suburban family—a young couple, two children, and a dog.

CHAPTER 28

The Suburban Era

1945–1963

What's to Come

∞∞∞ **AN AMERICAN STORY** ∞∞∞

DYNAMIC OBSOLESCENCE (THE WONDERFUL WORLD OF HARLEY EARL)

No company epitomized the corporate culture of the 1950s more than General Motors. GM executives sought to blend in rather than to stand out. They chose their suits in drab colors—dark blue, dark gray, or light gray—to increase their anonymity. Not head car designer Harley Earl. Earl brought a touch of Hollywood into the world of corporate bureaucrats. He had a closet filled with colorful suits. His staff would marvel as he headed off to a board meeting dressed in white linen with a dark blue shirt and *blue suede shoes,* the same shoes that Elvis Presley sang so protectively about.

Mr. Earl—no one who worked for him ever called him Harley—could afford to be a maverick. He created the cars that brought customers into GM showrooms across the country. Before he came to Detroit, engineering sold cars. Advertising stressed the mechanical virtues of reliable brakes or power steering. Earl made style the distinctive feature. Unlike the boxy look other designers favored, an Earl car was low and sleek, suggesting motion even when the car stood still. No feature stood out more distinctively than the fins he first put on the 1948 Cadillac. By the mid-1950s jet planes inspired Earl to design ever more outrageous fins, complemented by huge, shiny chrome grills and ornaments. Critics dismissed the designs as jukeboxes on wheels.

To Earl and GM the criticism hardly mattered. Design sold cars. "It gave [customers] an extra receipt for their money in the form of visible prestige marking for an expensive car," Earl said. The "Big Three" auto manufacturers—General Motors, Ford, and Chrysler—raced one another to redesign their annual models. Earl once joked, "I'd put smokestacks right in the middle of the sons of bitches if I thought I could sell more cars." In the lingo of the Detroit stylists, these designs were "gasaroony," an adjective *Popular Mechanics* magazine translated as "terrific, overpowering, weird." The goal was not a better car but what Earl called "dynamic obsolescence," or change for change's sake. Even a successful style had to go within a year. "We would design a car to make a man unhappy with his 1957 Ford 'long about the end of 1958." Even though the mechanics of cars changed little from year to year, dynamic obsolescence persuaded Americans in the 1950s to buy new cars in record numbers.

| The monstrous tail fins of the 1959 Cadillac

Fins, roadside motels, "gaseterias," drive-in burger huts, interstate highways, shopping centers, and, of course, suburbs—all these were part of a culture of mobility in the 1950s. Americans continued their exodus from rural areas to cities and from the cities to the suburbs. African Americans left the South, heading for industrial centers in the Northeast, Midwest, and West Coast. Mexican Americans concentrated in southwestern cities, while Puerto Ricans came largely to New York. And for Americans in the Snow Belt, the climate of the West and South (at least when civilized by air-conditioning) made the Sun Belt irresistible to ever-larger numbers.

The mobility was social, too. As the economy continued to expand, the size of the American middle class grew. In an era of prosperity and peace, some commentators began to speak of a **"consensus"**—a general agreement in American culture, based on values of the broad middle class. In a positive light, consensus reflected the agreement among most Americans about fundamental democratic values. Most citizens embraced the material benefits of prosperity as evidence of the virtue of "the American way." And they opposed the spread of communism abroad.

But consensus had its dark side. Critics worried that it bred a mindless **conformity.** Were Americans becoming too homogenized? Was there a depressing sameness in the material goods they owned, in the places they lived, and in the values they held? Besides, wasn't any notion of consensus hollow as long as racism and segregation prevented African Americans and other minorities from fully sharing in American life?

The baby boomers born into this era seldom agonized over such issues. In the White House, President Eisenhower radiated a comforting sense that the affairs of the nation and the world were in capable hands. That left teenagers free to worry about what really mattered: a first date, a first kiss, a first job, a first choice for college, and whether or not to "go all the way" in the backseat of one of Harley Earl's fin-swept Buicks. ∞∞∞

THE RISE OF THE SUBURBS

SUBURBAN GROWTH ACCELERATED SHARPLY AT the end of World War II. During the 1950s suburbs grew 40 times faster than cities, so that by 1960 half the American people lived in them. The return of prosperity brought a baby boom and a need for new housing. Automobiles made the suburbs accessible. But the spurt in suburban growth took its toll on the cities, which suffered as the middle class fled urban areas. And the lack of planning regulations saddled suburbanites with the pollution and congestion they hoped to escape.

A Boom in Babies and in Housing

The Depression forced many couples to delay beginning a family. In the 1930s birthrates had reached the low point of American history, about 18 to 19 per thousand. As prosperity returned during the war, birthrates began to rise. In 1946 Americans married in record numbers, twice as many as in 1932. The new brides were also younger, most in their peak years of fertility. In a 10-year period the American population increased by 30 million, giving the United States a rate of growth comparable to that of India. By 1952 the birthrate passed 25 live births per thousand, and it did not peak until 1957. Ten years later it had dropped to under 18.

 THE BOOM WORLDWIDE Historians and demographers have been hard-pressed to explain this extraordinary population bulge. It was not limited to the United States. In several other industrialized nations fertility rates also soared, Australia, New Zealand, Britain, and West Germany prime among them. Yet as the chart below indicates, the long-term trend in American fertility rates was downward, as it was in other

industrialized nations. Fertility rates peaked in Australia and New Zealand in 1961 and, three years later, in Great Britain and West Germany. Hence the baby boom stands as an anomaly, one that remains hard to explain.

Perhaps Americans were indeed "making up for lost time" after the war. Rising income allowed more people to afford marriage and children. But Americans should have caught up by the early 1950s, whereas the baby boom continued into the 1960s. Worldwide, urbanization and higher living standards are linked to lower birthrates. In 1950 the most industrialized and urban nations had a birthrate of 21.8 per thousand, while in less developed and less densely settled sub-Saharan Africa the rate was 49.8. In South Asia it was 44.8.

Whatever factors contributed to the baby boom, it had both immediate and long-term consequences for American society. For one, the boom in marriages and families increased demand for housing. At war's end, 5 million American families were eagerly searching for housing, tired of living in doubled-up conditions with other families, in basements, or even in coal cellars. With the help of the GI Bill and the rising prosperity, the chance to own a house rather than rent became a reality for over half of American families. And it was the suburbs that offered the residence most idealized in American culture: a detached single-family house with a lawn and garden.

LEVITTOWN, U.S.A. After World War II inexpensive, suburban housing became synonymous with the name of William Levitt. From building houses for war workers, Levitt learned how to use mass-production techniques. In 1947 he began construction of a 17,000-house community in the New York City suburb of Hempstead. All the materials for a Levittown house were precut and assembled at a factory, then moved to the site for assembly. If all went according to schedule, a new house was erected on a cement slab every 16 minutes. Buoyed by his success in Hempstead, Levitt later built developments in Bucks County, Pennsylvania, and Willingboro, New Jersey.

The typical early Levitt house, a "Cape Codder," had a living room, kitchen, bath, and two bedrooms on the ground floor and an expansion attic, all for $7,990. None had custom features, insulation, or any amenities that complicated construction. "The reason we have it so good in this country," Levitt said, "is that we can produce lots of things at low prices through mass production." Uniformity in house style extended to behavior as well. Levitt discouraged owners from changing colors or adding distinctive features to the house or yard. Buyers promised to cut the grass each week of the summer and not to hang out wash on weekends. African Americans were expressly excluded. Other suburban communities excluded Jews and ethnic Americans through restrictive covenants that dictated who could take up residence.

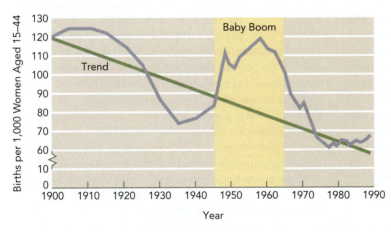

The United States Birthrate, 1900–1989

Despite periods of rapid rise and fall, the nation's birthrate has shown a steady downward trend. The Depression years showed an even sharper decline as financially strapped couples deferred childbearing. Younger marriages and postwar prosperity triggered the baby boom, but in general, affluence encourages lower birthrates.

Here is an aerial view of a typical, Levittown like, suburban tract. Note that almost all the trees are gone.

In California, a state with three cars registered for every four residents, suburbs bloomed across the landscape. By 1962 it had become the nation's most populous state. Growth was greatest around Los Angeles. In 1940 city planners began building a freeway system to lure shoppers into downtown Los Angeles. Instead, white Angelinos saw the road network as an opportunity to migrate to the suburbs. Eventually one-third of the Los Angeles area was covered by highways, parking lots, and interchanges, increasing to two-thirds in the downtown areas.

Cities and Suburbs Transformed

Single-family houses on their own plots of land required plenty of open land, unlike the row houses built side by side in earlier suburban developments. That meant Levitt and other builders chose vacant areas outside major urban areas. With the new houses farther away from factories, offices, and jobs, the automobile became more indispensable than ever.

INTERSTATE HIGHWAY ACT OF 1956

As the population shifted to suburbs, traffic choked old country roads. To ease this congestion, the Eisenhower administration proposed a 20-year plan to build a massive interstate highway system of some 41,000 miles. Eisenhower addressed cold war fears to build support, arguing that the new system would ease evacuation of cities in case of nuclear attack. In 1956 Congress passed the National Interstate and Defense Highway Act, setting in motion the largest public works project in history. The federal government picked up 90 percent of the cost through a Highway Trust Fund, financed by special taxes on cars, gas, tires, lubricants, and auto parts.

The Interstate Highway Act had an enormous impact on American life. Average annual driving increased by 400 percent. Shopping centers, linked by the new roads, sprang up to provide suburbanites with an alternative to the longer trip downtown. Almost every community had at least one highway strip dotted with drive-in movies, stores, bowling alleys, gas stations, and fast-food joints.

DECLINING CITIES

For cities, the interstates created other problems. The new highway system featured beltways—ring roads around major urban areas. Instead of leading traffic downtown, the beltways allowed motorists to avoid the center city altogether. As people took to their cars, intercity rail service and mass transit declined. Seventy-five percent of all government transportation dollars went to subsidize travel by car and truck; only 1 percent was earmarked for urban mass transit. At the same time that middle-class homeowners were moving to the suburbs, many low-paying, unskilled jobs disappeared from the cities, especially in old industrial centers. These trends forced the urban poor into reverse commuting, from city to suburb. All these trends made cities less attractive places to live or do business. With fewer well-to-do taxpayers to draw on, city governments lacked the tax base to finance public services. A vicious cycle ensued that proved most damaging to the urban poor, who had few means of escape.

African Americans and Hispanics replaced much of the white population that left cities for suburbs. These newcomers were part of larger migrations, especially of millions of black families leaving the South to search for work in urban centers. Most headed for the Middle Atlantic, Northeast, and upper Midwest regions. While central cities lost 3.6 million white residents, they gained 4.5 million African Americans. Indeed, by 1960 half of all black Americans were living in central cities.

Earlier waves of European immigrants had been absorbed by the expanding urban economy. During the 1950s, however, the flight of jobs and middle-class taxpayers to the suburbs made it difficult for African Americans and Hispanics to follow the same path. In the cities fewer jobs awaited them, while declining school systems made it harder for newcomers to acculturate. In the hardest-hit urban areas, unemployment rose to over 40 percent.

MINORITIES AND SUBURBS

In contrast, the suburbs remained beyond the reach of most minorities. Because few black or Hispanic families could afford the cost of suburban living, they accounted for less than 5 percent of the population there. The few black suburbs that existed dated from before the war and had little in common with the newer white "bedroom communities." Black suburbanites were poorer, held lower-status jobs, lived in more-ramshackle housing, and had less education than urban African Americans. Even minorities who could afford the suburbs discovered that most real estate agents refused to show them houses; bankers would not provide mortgages. The developers of Levittown did not sell directly to African Americans until 1960.

Suburban Blues

During the suburban boom, homebuilders seldom took the environment into account—until something happened to make residents sit up and take notice. In late summer of 1956 some residents of Portuguese Bend, California, discovered

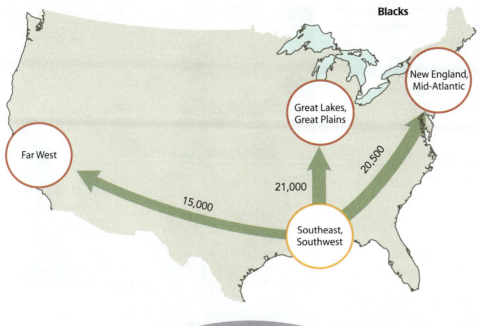

AVERAGE ANNUAL REGIONAL MIGRATION, 1947–1960

In this period, African Americans were moving in significant numbers to urban centers in the Northeast, the Midwest, and the Far West. Whites were being drawn to the increasingly diversified economy of the South as well as to the new industries, stimulated by the war, in the Far West. By the 1970s the trend had become known as the "Sun Belt" phenomenon.

Whites

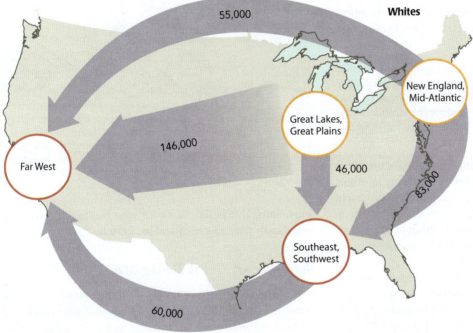

that their houses were actually on the move. By October 156 homes, along with their lawns, gardens, and swimming pools, had "gently slumped downhill as though they were so much custard pudding." Over time, the effluent from septic systems, abetted by lawn watering, slicked the underlying shale that naturally tilted toward the nearby Pacific Ocean. Gravity did the rest of the work.

During the 1950s developers in Los Angeles built two-thirds of all new houses on the region's hills. Such construction was especially popular in California. Powerful bulldozers and other earth-moving equipment made hillside building practical, while lower land prices made it cheaper. The landslides that periodically occurred after

heavy rains soon provoked a move toward stricter building codes. Nor was California alone. Suburbs in Washington, D.C., Cincinnati, and Pittsburgh suffered similar disasters. Other misfortunes occurred when developers built in wetlands and on floodplains. Even on dry level ground, houses built with cheap septic systems often failed, leaving homeowners with large repair bills, sewage stench, and the threat of infectious disease. In the following decades the federal government was forced to spend billions of dollars to replace septic systems with local sewers.

The disappearance of open space confronted many suburbanites with yet another threat to their dreams. "No more sweep of green," mourned William Whyte; "across the hills are splattered scores of random subdivisions, each laid out with the same dreary curves. Gone are the streams, brooks, woods and forests that the subdivisions signs talked about." Gone, too, were habitats for birds, small mammals, fish, and amphibians. Years later, homeowners' desire to preserve a shred of the suburban dream would contribute to the movement to protect the environment.

REVIEW

What factors pushed the growth of suburbs, and what were the environmental costs of pushing too hard?

THE CULTURE OF SUBURBIA

IN SUBURBAN HOUSING TRACTS ACROSS America, a new appetizer began appearing at trendy dinner parties. Named the California Dip, it was the brainchild of the Lipton Company, which was searching for new ways to market its dehydrated onion soup. Homemakers simply mixed Lipton's soup powder with sour cream and served it up with chips. As one commentator has noted,

> Using potato chips as little shovels, you gathered up the deliciously salty but drip-prone liquid and popped it, potato chip and all, into your mouth as quickly and gracefully as possible. There was anxiety in all this—particularly the fear that a great glop of the stuff would land on your tie or the rug—but also immense satisfaction.

As much genius, perhaps, went into the naming of the dip as into the recipe. Sour cream had been a mainstay in ethnic dishes such as blintzes (thin Jewish pancakes) and borscht (an Eastern European beet soup). With the all-American name of "California Dip," sour cream's ethnic associations were left behind. The ingredient went mainstream—into the consensus.

The evolving culture of the suburbs reflected a similar process, a shucking off of ethnic associations. In many city neighborhoods, immigrant parents or grandparents lived on the same block or even in the same apartment with their children. In the suburbs, single-family dwellers often left their relatives and in-laws behind, which meant that ethnic lifestyles were less pronounced. The restrictive immigration policies of the 1920s had also reduced the number of newly arrived foreign-born Americans. Thus suburban culture reflected the tastes of the broad, mostly assimilated middle classes.

SUBURBS AND SOCIAL CLASS   Class distinctions were more pronounced between suburban communities than within them. The upper middle class clustered in older developments, which often revolved around country clubs. Working-class suburbs sprouted on the outskirts of large manufacturing centers, where blue-collar families eagerly escaped the city. Within suburbs a more homogeneous suburban culture evolved. "We see eye to eye on most things," commented one Levittown resident, "about raising

| In Easter Morning, *Norman Rockwell satirized the contrasting conformities of suburban life. The sheepish father, no doubt forced to wear suits all week, prefers a shocking red bathrobe, a cigarette, and the Sunday paper to the gray flannel lockstep of his churchbound family.*

kids, doing things together with your husband . . . we have practically the same identical background."

American Civil Religion

If suburban residents retained less of their ethnic heritages, most held on to their religious beliefs. Religion continued to be a distinctive and segregating factor during the 1950s. Catholics, Protestants, and Jews generally married within their own faiths, and in the suburbs they kept their social distance as well.

THE RELIGIOUS DIVISION   Communities that showed no obvious class distinctions were sometimes deeply divided along religious lines. Many Catholics attended parochial rather than public schools, formed their own clubs, and generally did not socialize with their Protestant neighbors. Protestant and Catholic members of the same country club usually did not play golf or tennis in the same foursomes. As for Jews, social historian Richard Polenberg has remarked that whereas a gulf divided many Catholics and Protestants, Jews and Gentiles "seem to have lived on the opposite sides of a religious Grand Canyon." Even superficial signs of friendliness masked the persistence of old stereotypes.

DAILY LIVES

THE NEW SUBURBIA

When World War II ended, many Americans were happy to find housing of any kind. But prosperity in the 1950s brought a demand for houses that, like automobiles, reflected the status of their owners. No longer would William Levitt's 900-square-foot Cape Cod salt-box satisfy popular demand.

The most renowned of all suburban architectural features, the picture window, traced its roots to architect Frank Lloyd Wright. Wright's turn-of-the-century innovations combined open interior space, wide windows for natural lighting, and a horizontal, single-story layout. California architects translated Wright's ideas into the ranch house, where rooms flowed into each other and indoor spaces opened to the outdoors to take advantage of the mild climate. Houses with fewer walls and defined spaces discouraged formality and even privacy.

Developers across the country seized on the California "fantasy" style to conjure up dreams of glamorous informal living. The use of picture windows allowed them to make small houses seem more spacious. Critics of suburban living suggested that the picture window was a means to ensure conformity. Why, after all, was the window most often placed looking onto the front yard, except to afford homeowners a means to keep an eye on neighbors who were watching them through their own picture windows? In truth, it made sense to have a picture window look onto the street in order to keep an eye on children.

In the wake of the baby boom and a demand for new homes, mass-produced houses soon filled suburban developments all across the United States. By varying styles only slightly, developers were able to construct houses quickly at prices many young couples could afford.

By 1955 surveys showed that three-quarters of all would-be buyers wanted a single-story house. But with soaring land prices and new zoning codes, builders could not fit enough floor space onto typical lots. To build a two-story house without seeming to, they hit upon the split-level, or "raised ranch": something, as one critic wryly noted, that "looked like a ranch-style house that had fallen out of the air and landed on something else." The basic construction, two simple boxes side by side, was cheap to build. By placing half the living space—either the kitchen, dining, and family rooms or the bedrooms—in what would otherwise be a basement, the split level created more habitable living space at little additional cost.

Most of all, homeowners in the 1950s wanted family rooms and "eat-in kitchens." One magazine described the family room as "the newest room in the house, but also the oldest," for the concept originated in the middle-class Victorian front parlor. Like it, the 1950s living room acquired more elegant furnishings for use during holidays or special entertaining. That led to the conversion of what often had been a basement "rumpus" room for the kids into a family room. Here, families sought a cozier feel with pine paneling and furniture designed for comfort and durability, with the television as the focus of the room.

The new, larger eat-in kitchens of the suburbs were designed, one advertiser claimed, to make "mother a member of the family again." Everyone could gather while mom cooked. The same space would also hold appliances such as dishwashers, dual ovens, and televisions, which became common kitchen features.

Clearly, suburban houses were more than "Little boxes on the hillside / Little boxes all the same," as one folk-singing critic of the 1960s complained. To the people who flocked to suburbia, their homes represented a compromise between fantasy and practicality.

Thinking Critically

How did new lifestyles influence suburban architecture?

Although such religious boundaries remained distinct, religion was central to American life. Church membership rose to more than 50 percent for the first time in the twentieth century, and by 1957 the Census Bureau reported that 96 percent of the American people cited a specific affiliation when asked, "What is your religion?" The religious upswing was supported in part by the prevailing cold war mood, because communists were avowedly atheists. Cold war fervor led Congress in 1954 to add the phrase "under God" to the Pledge of Allegiance.

Patriotic and anticommunist themes were strong in the preaching of clergy who pioneered the use of television. Billy Graham, a Baptist revival preacher, first attracted national attention at a tent meeting in Los Angeles in 1949. Following in the tradition of nineteenth-century revivalists like Charles Finney and Dwight Moody, he soon achieved an even wider impact by televising his meetings. Though no revivalist, the Roman Catholic bishop Fulton J. Sheen became a popular television celebrity. In his weekly program he extolled traditional values and attacked communism.

Baptist Billy Graham led the revival of evangelical religion in American culture. While his message emphasized the traditional Fundamentalist themes of sin, redemption, and the Second Coming of Christ, his up-to-date methods took advantage of television, advertising, radio, and paperback books to reach the widest possible audience.

The growing consensus among Americans was that *any* religious belief was better than none. President Eisenhower made the point quite clear: "Our government makes no sense unless it is founded on a deeply religious faith," he proclaimed, "—and I don't care what it is." Children got the message, too. Every Friday afternoon kids watching *The*

Howdy Doody Show were exhorted by Buffalo Bob to worship "at the church or synagogue of your choice."

"Homemaking" Women in the Workaday World

The growth of a suburban culture revealed a contradiction in the lives of middle-class women. Never before were their traditional roles as housewives and mothers so central to American society. Yet never before did more women join the workforce outside the home.

Most housewives found that suburban homes and growing families required increasing time and energy. With relatives less likely to live nearby, mothering became full-time work. Dependence on automobiles made many a suburban housewife the chauffeur for her family. In the 1920s grocers or milkmen had commonly delivered their goods from door to door; by the 1950s delivery services were being replaced by housewives doing "errands."

WORKING WOMEN — Yet between 1940 and 1960 the percentage of wives working outside the home doubled, from 15 to 30 percent. Although some women took jobs simply to help make ends meet, often more than financial necessity was involved. Middle-class married women went to work as often as lower-class wives, and women with college degrees were the most likely to get a job. Two-income families were able to spend far more on extras: gifts, education, recreation, and household appliances. In addition, women found status and self-fulfillment in their jobs, as well as a chance for increased social contacts.

More women were going to college, too, but that increased education did not translate into economic equality. The percentage of women holding professional jobs actually

Once a utilitarian space for food preparation, kitchens became centers of style and even fantasy in the suburban era. They also became larger and brighter. Note that the stainless steel appliances echo the futuristic look of the era's cars.

dropped between 1950 and 1960. And the gap between men's and women's wages was greater than in any other industrial nation. In the United States, the median wage for women was less than half that for men.

When women possessed leverage, they reshaped traditional work roles. Many nurses, for example, left the profession after World War II to start families. As the health care industry grew sharply, an acute nursing shortage occurred. As health administrators (almost all men) sought new recruits, professional nursing associations pressed for increased wages and part-time positions, on-site child care, and maternity leaves so that nurse mothers had flexibility in working. In heavily female jobs such as teaching, stenography, and retail clerking, where fewer shortages existed, women did not achieve comparable gains until much later.

MEDIA IMAGES OF WOMEN Despite women's wider roles in society, the media most often portrayed women either as sex objects or as domesticated housewives and mothers. A typical article appearing in *Redbook* in 1957 made a heroine of Junior, a "little freckle-faced brunette" who had given up work. As the story closed, Junior nursed her baby at two in the morning, crooning "I'm glad, glad, glad I'm just a housewife." In 1950 Lynn White, the president of Mills College for women, advocated a curriculum that displaced traditional academic subjects with those that were "distinctly feminine," such as crafts and home economics.

A Revolution in Sexuality?

Throughout the twentieth century, a trend had been under way deemphasizing the tradition that sex within marriage was primarily for the procreation of children—a duty (especially for women) to be endured rather than enjoyed. During the 1920s reformer Ben Lindsey promoted the idea of "companionate marriage," stressing personal happiness and satisfaction as primary goals. Such a marriage included the enjoyment of sex for both wife and husband. The suburban home of the 1950s encouraged such ideals, symbolizing as it did a place of relaxation and enjoyment. Unlike city apartments, where extended families often lived in crowded conditions, the suburban single-family houses provided greater privacy and more space for intimacy.

THE KINSEY REPORTS Social scientists noted a trend to see sexual pleasure as an integral part of marriage. That idea received additional attention in 1948 with the publication of an apparently dry scientific study, *Sexual Behavior in the Human Male.* Its author, Professor Alfred Kinsey, hardly expected the storm of publicity his study and its companion, *Sexual Behavior in the Human Female* (1953), provoked. Kinsey began his research career as a zoologist with a zest for classifying data. During the 1940s he turned to collecting information on sexual behavior. Based on more than 10,000 interviews, Kinsey reached conclusions that were unorthodox and even startling for his day. Masturbation and premarital petting, he reported,

were widespread. Women did not just endure sex as a wifely duty; they enjoyed it in much the same way men did. Extramarital sex was common for both husbands and wives. About 10 percent of the population was homosexual.

Publicly, Kinsey maintained a posture of scientific objectivity. He argued that he had only published a report "on what people do" and wasn't concerned with "what they should do." But biographers of Kinsey have revealed that, in fact, he was as much interested in social change as in scientific research, believing that many acts treated as deviant should be placed within a normal range of sexual behavior. His personal attitudes influenced that conclusion, for sexual obsessions were central to Kinsey's private life. (He practiced masochism; and he, his wife, and members of his staff filmed themselves engaging in group sex.) Though the public knew nothing about his personal behavior, Kinsey provoked intense controversy. Social scientists objected that his sample was too narrow to produce valid norms, and his most severe critics called him "a menace to society." According to opinion polls, most Americans disagreed. The large majority took comfort (as he had hoped) that behaviors once condemned as sinful or perverse were widely practiced.

The Flickering Gray Screen

In the glow of postwar prosperity, most Americans found themselves with more leisure time and more income. In the suburbs, a yard to tend and a young family to raise determined that much of that free time would be spent around the house. The new medium of television fit perfectly into suburban lifestyles. It provided an ideal way to entertain families at home as well as to sell them consumer goods.

Television viewership boomed after World War II. By 1949 Americans had bought a million sets; by 1960 that number had jumped to 46 million, and by then more Americans had television sets than had bathrooms. Home viewing transformed American entertainment habits, cutting sharply into pastimes like movies and professional sports. In cities around the country, more than 4,000 neighborhood theaters closed. Many were replaced in the suburbs by popular drive-ins, which allowed whole families to enjoy movies in the comfort of their cars.

TELEVISION AND POLITICS In 1948 television began to enter into politics, covering both the Democratic and the Republican Conventions. Two years later, it combined entertainment, politics, and news by televising a series of hearings on organized crime chaired by Senator Estes Kefauver. Some 30 million viewers watched senators grill mobster Frank Costello about his criminal organization and its ties to city governments. Millions more watched Senator Joseph McCarthy's ill-fated crusade against the army in 1954. Clearly, television demonstrated the potential to shape the political life of the nation. By the mid-1950s, however, controversy over news coverage of issues like McCarthyism led the networks to downgrade public affairs programs. As an alternative, the networks turned to Hollywood film

HISTORIAN'S TOOLBOX

THEIR FIRST TELEVISION

In most urban areas, only three channels were available during the 1950s, broadcasting only for a part of the day.

If you were researching this era, what sources might provide information on the age of this television and its cost when new?

Was the occasion of this photograph formal or informal? How can you tell?

Television came to dominate American popular culture in the decade following World War II. In 1945 fewer than 10,000 people owned TV sets. By 1950 about 10 percent of American families did. That percentage jumped to 90 percent by 1960. The arrival of the first family television was

cause for celebration. The photograph above shows Leonor, Virginia, and Angelica Lozano in front of their television, around 1953. While the television provided access to the mainstream of American life, the Lozanos, a Mexican American family living in Los Angeles, would have seen few

images on the gray screen that connected in any meaningful way to their own lives. Most people portrayed on television were white, middle-class, and more often male than female.

Thinking Critically

Does this picture suggest anything about the social class of the family? Why might this apparently celebratory photo have been taken in front of the television? How does the technology of this television compare to current sets? Why did television networks pay so little attention to minority audiences?

studios, which provided them with telefilm series. By selling time to advertisers, the networks, rather than the sponsors, gained ultimate control over program content. By 1959 live television was virtually a thing of the past.

 REVIEW

How were the ideals of a middle-class consensus reflected in religion, the world of the suburban home, and television?

THE POLITICS OF CALM

IN PRESIDING OVER THESE CHANGES in American society, President Dwight David Eisenhower projected an aura of paternal calm. Pursuing "modern Republicanism," the new president sought consensus, not confrontation. Eisenhower declared that he was "conservative when it comes to money and liberal when it comes to human beings."

Eisenhower's Modern Republicanism

Eisenhower had been raised in a large Kansas farm family. His parents, though poor, provided him a warm, caring home steeped in religious faith. A graduate of West Point, "Ike" was neither a scholar nor a flamboyant general like George Patton. Yet his genial ways could not hide his ambition or his ability to judge character shrewdly. In an era of organization men, Eisenhower succeeded by mastering the military's bureaucratic politics. It took a gifted organizer to coordinate the D-Day invasion and to hold together the egocentric generals who pushed east to Berlin. Eisenhower was such a promising candidate that both parties had considered him for the 1948 presidential race.

In pursuing his pragmatic course, Eisenhower resisted conservative demands to dismantle New Deal programs. He even agreed to increases in Social Security, unemployment insurance, and the minimum wage. He accepted a small public housing program and a modest federally supported medical insurance plan for the needy. But as a conservative, Eisenhower remained uncomfortable with big government. Thus he rejected more far-reaching liberal proposals on housing and universal health care through the Social Security system.

Success for the Eisenhower administration depended most on how well it managed the economy. The Democrats of the New Deal had established a tradition of activism. When the economy faltered, deficit spending and tax cuts stimulated it. Eisenhower, in contrast, wanted to reduce federal spending and the government's role in the economy. When a recession struck in 1953–1954, the administration was concerned more with balancing the budget and holding inflation in line than with reducing unemployment through government spending.

Eisenhower was similarly pragmatic in other areas. When major projects called for federal leadership, as with the Highway Act, he supported the policy. In 1954 he signed the St. Lawrence Seaway Act, which joined the United States and Canada in an ambitious engineering project to open the Great Lakes to ocean shipping. Like the highway program, the Seaway was fiscally acceptable because the funding came from user tolls and taxes rather than from general revenues.

EISENHOWER REELECTED — Despite a recession in 1953–1954, Eisenhower remained popular. Even after he suffered a major heart attack in 1955, voters gladly reelected him over Adlai Stevenson in 1956. But poor economic performance took its toll on the Republican Party. In 1958, when recession again dragged down the economy, the Democrats took a commanding 68-seat majority in the House and a 12-vote advantage in the Senate. Modern Republicanism did not put down deep roots outside Eisenhower's White House.

The Conglomerate World

Large corporations welcomed the administration's pro-business attitudes as well as the era's general prosperity.

Eisenhower was a popular president, but his health created widespread public concern. He suffered a heart attack in September 1955, and timely surgery on a bowel obstruction the following June saved his life. Despite his age and ill health, the president was easily reelected in 1956. Here he recuperates after the 1955 heart attack, at an army hospital in Denver.

Wages for the average worker rose over 35 percent between 1950 and 1960. At the same time, the economic distress of the 1930s had led corporate executives to devise new ways to minimize the danger of economic downturns. Each of the approaches expanded the size of corporations in various ways in order to minimize shocks in specific markets.

DIVERSIFICATION — One expansion strategy took the form of diversification. In the 1930s a giant General Electric had concentrated largely in one industrial area: equipment for generating electric power and light. When the Depression struck, GE found its markets evaporating. The company responded by entering markets for appliances, X-ray machines, and elevators—all products developed or enhanced by the company's research labs. In the postwar era General Electric diversified even further to become a **conglomerate,** expanding into nuclear power, jet engines, and television. Diversification was most practical for large industrial firms, whose size allowed them to support extensive research and development.

Conglomeration often turned small companies into giants. Unlike earlier horizontal and vertical combinations, conglomerate mergers could join companies with seemingly unrelated products. Over a 20-year period International Telephone and Telegraph branched out from its basic communications business into baking, hotels and motels, car rental, home building, and insurance. Corporations also became multinational by expanding their overseas operations or buying out potential foreign competitors. Large integrated oil companies like Mobil and Standard Oil of New Jersey (Exxon) developed huge oil fields in the Middle East and markets around the free world.

Many large corporations also decided they could profit more from cooperating with labor unions rather than reviving the pitched battles of the 1930s. As former GM executive Lee Iacocca explained, "Because strikes were so devastating, the leaders of industry would do almost anything to avoid one." He added, "In those days we could afford to be generous. Because we had a lock on the market, we could continually spend more money on labor and simply pass the additional costs on to the consumer in the form of price increases." Unions gladly negotiated higher wages and generous benefits, while their members avoided losing wages to strikes.

One aid to managing these modern corporate giants was the advent of electronic data processing. In the early 1950s computers were virtually unknown in private industry. But banks and insurance companies saw these calculating machines as an answer to their need to manipulate huge quantities of records and statistical data. Manufacturers, especially in the petroleum, chemical, automotive, and electronics industries, began to use computers to monitor their production lines, quality control, and inventory.

Corporations that manufactured consumer goods depended on advertising to reach potential customers. "The only institution which we have for instilling new needs, for training people to act as consumers, for altering men's values, and thus for hastening their adjustment to potential abundance is advertising," historian David Potter concluded in 1954. About the same time, economist John Kenneth Galbraith agreed that advertising "creates desires—to bring into being wants that previously did not exist."

The great "cola war" dramatized Potter's point. The smaller Pepsi corporation touted itself as a David battling Goliath—Coca-Cola. In reality, while the two soft-drink companies cultivated alternative images to gain market share, they did not attack each other nor did either raise the most obvious question: "Which tastes better?" Instead, Pepsi created ads that suggested its drinkers were young, fashionable, and popular:

Be sociable, look smart
Keep up-to-date with Pepsi
Drink light refreshing Pepsi
Stay young and fair and debonair
Be sociable, have a Pepsi!

Pepsi's decision to target the young and women transformed its corporate fortunes. From 1949 to 1959, while Coke's gross profits rose about 50 percent (albeit from a high level), Pepsi's rose 500 percent, enough to make it a formidable rival. Each product had its brand identity—Coke, the cola with a universal appeal that stood the test of time, versus Pepsi, the drink for young, upwardly mobile, suburban families.

✓ REVIEW
How did conglomerates fit into the scheme of Eisenhower's "modern Republicanism"?

CRACKS IN THE CONSENSUS

AS CORPORATIONS MERGED IN ORDER to increase their reach, power, and stability, they saw themselves as a part of the emerging consensus over the American way. ("What's good for the country is good for General Motors.") Yet there were distinct cracks in the consensus. Intellectuals and social critics spoke out against the stifling features of a conformist corporate culture. At the fringes of American society, the "beats" rejected conformity, while the more mainstream rock and roll movement broadcast its own brand of youthful rebellion.

Critics of Mass Culture

In Levittown, New Jersey, a woman who had invited her neighbors to a cocktail party eagerly awaited them dressed in newly fashionable Capri pants—a tight-fitting calf-length style. Alas, one early-arriving couple glimpsed the woman through a window. What on earth was the hostess wearing? *Pajamas?* Who in their right mind would entertain in pajamas? The couple sneaked home, afraid they had made a mistake about the day of the party.

Finally, they mustered enough courage to drop in. But when the hostess later learned of their misunderstanding, she put her Capri pants in the closet. Levittown was not ready for such a change in fashion.

SUBURBAN CONFORMITY

Was America turning into a vast suburban wasteland, where the neighbors' worries over Capri pants would stifle all individuality? Many intellectuals worried openly about the homogenized lifestyle created by mass consumption, conformity, and **mass media.** Critics such as Dwight Macdonald sarcastically attacked the culture of the suburban middle classes: *Reader's Digest* Condensed Books, uplifting film spectacles such as *The Ten Commandments,* television dramas that pretended to be high art but in reality were little more than simplistic pontificating. "Midcult," Macdonald called it, which was his shorthand for middlebrow culture.

DAVID RIESMAN'S *THE LONELY CROWD*

Other critics charged that the skyscrapers and factories of giant conglomerates housed an all-too-impersonal world. In large, increasingly automated workplaces, skilled laborers seemed little more than caretakers of

James Dean in Rebel Without a Cause. *Dean was just 24 when he died in a car crash in 1955, but his screen performances portrayed a youthful rebellion against a conformist society.*

The Rebellion of Young America

JUVENILE DELINQUENCY Young Americans were among suburbia's sharpest critics. Dance crazes, outlandish clothing, strange jargon, rebelliousness toward parents, and sexual precociousness—all these behaviors challenged middle-class respectability. More than a few parents and public figures warned that America had spawned a generation of rebellious juvenile delinquents. Psychiatrist Frederic Wertham told a group of doctors, "You cannot understand present-day juvenile delinquency if you do not take into account the pathogenic and pathoplastic [infectious] influence of comic books." Others laid the blame on films and the lyrics of popular music.

The center of the new teen culture was the high school. Whether in consolidated rural school districts, new suburban schools, or city systems, the large, comprehensive high schools of the 1950s were often miniature melting pots in which middle-class students were exposed to, and often adopted, the style of the lower classes. Alarmed school administrators complained of juvenile delinquents who wore jeans and T-shirts, challenged authority, and defiantly smoked cigarettes, much like the motorcycle gang leader portrayed by Marlon Brando in the film *The Wild One* (1954).

In many ways the argument about juvenile delinquency was an argument about social class and, to a lesser degree, race. Adults who complained that delinquent teenagers dressed poorly, lacked ambition, and were irresponsible and sexually promiscuous were voicing the same arguments traditionally used to denigrate other outsiders—immigrants, the poor, and African Americans. Nowhere were these racial and class undertones more evident than in the hue and cry greeting the arrival of rock and roll.

machines. Large corporations required middle-level executives to submerge their personal goals in the processes and work routines of a large bureaucracy. David Riesman, a sociologist, condemned stifling conformity in *The Lonely Crowd* (1950). In nineteenth-century America, Riesman argued, Americans had been "inner directed." It was their own consciences that formed their values and drove them to seek success. In contrast, modern workers had developed a personality shaped not so much by inner convictions as by the opinions of their peers. The new "other-directed" society of suburbia preferred security to success. "Go along to get along" was its motto.

WILLIAM WHYTE'S THE ORGANIZATION MAN William Whyte carried Riesman's critique from the workplace to the suburb in *The Organization Man* (1956). Here he found rootless families, shifted from town to town by the demands of corporations. (IBM, according to one standard joke, stood for "I've Been Moved.") The typical organization man was sociable but not terribly ambitious. He sought primarily to keep up with the Joneses and the number of consumer goods they owned. He lived in a suburban "split-level trap," as one critic put it, one among millions of "haggard" men, "tense and anxious" women, and "the gimme kids," who, like the cartoon character Dennis the Menace, looked up from the litter under the Christmas tree to ask, "Is that all?"

No doubt such portraits were overdrawn. (Where, after all, did Riesman's nineteenth-century inner-directed Americans get their values, if not from the society around them?) But such critiques indicated the problems of adjustment faced by people working within large bureaucratic organizations and living in suburbs that were decentralized and self-contained.

The King, Elvis Presley

THE RISE OF ROCK AND ROLL Before 1954 popular music had been divided into four major categories: pop, country and western, jazz, and rhythm and blues. A handful of record companies with almost exclusively white singers dominated the pop charts. On one fringe of the popular field was country and western, often split into cowboy musicians such as Roy Rogers and Gene Autry and the hillbilly style associated with Nashville. The music industry generally treated jazz and rhythm and blues as "race music," whose performers and audience were largely black. Each of these musical traditions grew out of regional cultures. As the West and the South merged into the national culture, so too were these musical subcultures gradually integrated into the national mainstream.

By the mid-1950s the distinctiveness of these styles began to blur. Singers on the white pop charts recorded a few songs from country and from rhythm and blues. The popularity of crossover songs such as "Sh-boom," "Tutti-Frutti," and "Earth Angel" indicated that a major shift in taste and market was under way. Lyrics still reflected the pop field's preoccupation with young love, marriage, and happiness, but the music now vibrated with the rawer, earthier style of rhythm and blues. Country and western singer Bill Haley brought the new blend to the fore in 1954 with "Shake, Rattle, and Roll," the first rock song to reach the top ten on the pop charts.

And then—calamity! Millions of middle-class roofs nearly blew off with the appearance in 1955 of the rhythmic and raucous Elvis Presley. By background, Elvis was a country boy whose musical style combined elements of gospel, country, and blues. But it was his hip-swinging, pelvis-plunging performances that electrified teenagers. To conservative adults, Presley's long hair, sideburns, and tight jeans seemed menacingly delinquent, an expression of hostile rebellion. What they often resented but rarely admitted was that Elvis looked lower class, sounded black, and really could sing.

The "Beat" Generation

Beyond the frenetic rhythms of rock and roll, and even farther beyond the pale of suburban culture, flourished a subculture known as the "beat" generation. In run-down urban neighborhoods and college towns this collection of artists, intellectuals, musicians, and middle-class students dropped out of mainstream society. In dress and behavior the beats self-consciously rejected what they viewed as the excessive spiritual bankruptcy of America's middle-class culture. Cool urban hipsters—especially African-American jazz musicians such as John Coltrane and Sonny Rollins—were their models. They read poetry, listened to jazz, explored Asian philosophy, and experimented openly with drugs, mystical religions, and sex.

The beats viewed themselves as being driven to the margins of society, rejecting the culture of abundance, materialism, and conformity. "I saw the best minds of my generation destroyed by madness, starving hysterical naked," wrote Allen Ginsberg in his 1955 poem *Howl*. Jack Kerouac tapped the frenzied energy beneath the beats' cool facade in *On the Road* (1957), a novel based on his travels across the country with his friend Neal Cassady. Kerouac finished the novel in one frenetic three-week binge, spilling out tales of pot, jazz, crazy sex, and all-night raps undertaken in a search for "IT"—the ultimate moment when mind and experience mesh.

 **REVIEW**

Why did social critics worry about "conformity" in the 1950s, and what aspects of American life upset that conformity?

NATIONALISM IN AN AGE OF SUPERPOWERS

TRY AS THEY MIGHT, THE beats could not ignore the atomic menace that overshadowed American society at midcentury. Along the Iron Curtain of Eastern Europe and across the battle lines of northern Asia, Soviet-American rivalry had settled into a stalemate. The American public shared with most foreign policy makers a view of the globe as divided between the "free world" nations and the "Communist bloc." Thus the Eisenhower administration sought ways to contain the Soviets: setting up security and trade agreements, employing covert action to install governments favorable to the United States, and using the threat of nuclear war, if need be.

To the Brink?

JOHN FOSTER DULLES

As a general who had fought in a global war, Eisenhower was no stranger to world politics. Still, he shared the conduct of foreign policy with his secretary of state, John Foster Dulles. Dulles approached his job with a somber enthusiasm. Coming from a family of missionaries and diplomats, he had within him a touch of both. He viewed the Soviet-American struggle in almost religious terms: a fight of good against evil between two irreconcilable superpowers. Admirers praised his global vision; detractors saw him as "the wooliest type of pontificating American." Certainly Dulles did not lack confidence. "With my understanding of the intricate relationship between the peoples of the world," he told Eisenhower, "and your sensitiveness to the political considerations, we will make the most successful team in history."

The administration was determined to make Truman's containment strategy more forceful. Dulles, the more confrontational of the two men, wanted the United States to aid in liberating the "captive peoples" of Eastern Europe and other Communist nations. On the other hand, Eisenhower was equally determined to cut back military spending in order to keep the budget balanced. The president, who understood well how the military services and defense industries competed for government money, was irked at the "fantastic programs" the Pentagon kept proposing. "If we demand too much in taxes in order to build planes and ships," he argued, "we will tend to dry up the accumulations of capital that are necessary to provide jobs for the million or more new workers that we must absorb each year."

THE NEW LOOK IN FOREIGN POLICY

So Eisenhower and Dulles hit on a less costly strategy. Rather than rely on conventional forces, they would contain Soviet aggression by using the threat of massive nuclear retaliation. Dulles insisted that Americans should not shrink from the threat of nuclear war: "If you are scared to go to the brink, you are lost." As Treasury Secretary George Humphrey put it, a nuclear strategy provided "a bigger bang for the buck." Henceforth American foreign policy would have an aggressive "New Look." Behind the more militant rhetoric, however, lay an ongoing commitment to containment.

Brinkmanship in Asia

TAIWAN AND MAINLAND CHINA

Moving from talk of **brinkmanship** to concrete action did not prove easy. When Dulles announced American intentions to "unleash" Chiang Kai-shek to attack mainland China from his outpost on Taiwan (formerly Formosa), China threatened to invade Taiwan. At that, Eisenhower ordered the Seventh Fleet into the area to protect rather than unleash Chiang. If the Communists attacked, he warned bluntly in 1955, "we'll have to use atomic weapons."

Nuclear weapons also figured in the American response to a crisis in Southeast Asia. There, Vietnamese forces led by Ho Chi Minh were fighting the French, who had returned to reestablish their own colonial rule. Between 1950 and 1954, the United States provided France with more than $1 billion in military aid in Vietnam. Eisenhower worried that if Vietnam fell to a communist revolutionary like Ho, other nations of Southeast Asia would soon follow. "You have a row of dominoes set up," the president warned,

"you knock over the first one.... You could have the beginning of a disintegration that would have the most profound influences."

VIETNAMESE VICTORY AT DIEN BIEN PHU

The French in 1954 tried to force a showdown with Ho's forces at Dien Bien Phu. With Vietnamese and Chinese communist troops holding the surrounding hilltops, the French garrison of 12,000 could not have chosen a worse place to do battle. Desperate, the French government pleaded for more American aid and the Joint Chiefs of Staff responded by volunteering to relieve the besieged French forces with a massive American air raid—including the use of tactical nuclear weapons, if necessary. Instead, Eisenhower pulled back. After Korea, the idea of American involvement in another Asian war aroused opposition from both allies and domestic political leaders.

UNITED STATES BACKS DIEM

Collapsing under the siege, the French garrison at Dien Bien Phu surrendered in May 1954. At a peace conference held in Geneva, Switzerland, Ho Chi Minh agreed to withdraw his forces north of the 17th parallel, temporarily dividing the nation into North and South Vietnam. Because of Ho's widespread popularity, he could count on an easy victory in the elections that the peace conference agreed would be held

ASIAN TROUBLE SPOTS

After the Geneva Accords divided Indochina into North and South Vietnam, Secretary of State Dulles organized the Southeast Asia Treaty Organization (SEATO) to resist communist aggression in Southeast Asia. Curiously, Thailand and the Philippines were the only Southeast Asian countries to join, while such trouble spots as Indonesia and Laos did not. In addition to the conflict in Vietnam, tensions were fueled by the mutual hostility between mainland Communist China and Chiang Kai-shek's Taiwan as well as the offshore islands of Quemoy and Matsu. **Why would Thailand be such a critical American ally in the region?**

| The CIA secretly helped overthrow the Guatemalan government in 1954. One plan, apparently never carried out, called for the assassination of 58 Guatemalan officials. But the CIA's chilling "Conference Room Technique" survived, a four-step plan showing how "a room containing as many as a dozen subjects can be 'purified' in about 20 seconds" by two assassins. Step 4 was to "leave propaganda," making it seem as if Communists had carried out the massacre.

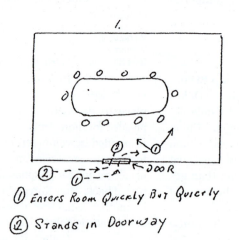

Conference Room Technique

1.

① Enters Room Quickly But Quietly

② Stands in Doorway

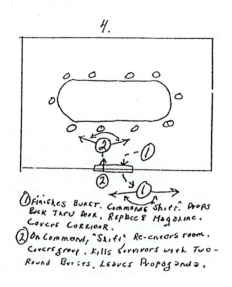

4.

① Finishes Burst. Commands "Shift". Drops Back Thru Door. Replaces Magazine. Covers Corridor.
② On command, "Shift" Re-enters room. Covers group. Kills survivors with Two-Round Bursts. Leaves Propaganda.

within two years. Dulles, however, viewed any communist victory as unacceptable, even if the election was democratic. He convinced Eisenhower to support a South Vietnamese government under Ngo Dinh Diem. Diem, Dulles insisted, was not bound by the agreement signed in Geneva to hold any election. The United States became further involved by sending a military mission to help keep Diem in power.

The Covert Side of the New Look

OVERTHROWING MOSSADEQ

In pursuing their aggressive New Look in foreign policy, Dulles and Eisenhower sometimes authorized the Central Intelligence Agency (CIA) to use **covert operations** against those they saw as sympathetic to Moscow. For example, in Iran in 1951 a nationalist government under Mohammed Mossadeq seized the giant British-owned Anglo-Iranian Oil Company. With the United States boycotting Iranian oil, Dulles worried that Mossadeq would turn to the neighboring Soviet Union for aid. Eisenhower approved a secret CIA operation to topple the Mossadeq government. Led by Teddy Roosevelt's grandson, Kermit, Operation Ajax ousted Mossadeq and returned Iran's monarch, Shah Mohammad Reza Pahlavi, to his throne in August 1953.

INTERVENTION IN GUATEMALA

Dulles looked to use another clandestine mission in Guatemala. Unlike Iran, however, Guatemala had an elected democratic government under Colonel Jacobo Arbenz Guzmán. Arbenz was determined to reduce the poverty in

his country by giving the peasants the idle farmland of large landowners. Guatemala's richest landowner was the Boston-based United Fruit Company. When Arbenz seized 400,000 acres from United Fruit, the company's agents branded him a communist. Arbenz was no communist, but as the American ambassador later explained "the man thought like a communist and talked like a communist, and if not actually one, would do until one came along." A week after a CIA-trained band of Latin American mercenaries entered the country, supported by American warplanes, the leader of the Guatemalan rebels replaced the Arbenz democracy with a military dictatorship that quickly returned the expropriated lands to United Fruit.

Success in Iran and Guatemala convinced American policy makers that covert operations could achieve dramatic results at low cost. But in overthrowing popular governments or defending unpopular ones, the United States gained a reputation in many Third World countries as a foe of national liberation, popular democracy, and social reform. In 1958 the depth of anti-American feeling became obvious when angry crowds in several Latin American countries attacked Vice President Richard Nixon's car, spat at him, and pelted him with eggs and stones.

Rising Nationalism

Korea, Indochina, Iran, Guatemala—to Dulles and Eisenhower, the crises in all these countries could be traced back to the Soviet Union.

| Nikita Khrushchev was by turns bombastic and somber, threatening and conciliatory—a style that both captivated and alarmed Americans.

Yet American policy could not be simply anticommunist. As nationalists in the Middle East, Africa, and Southeast Asia fought to gain independence from their colonial masters, new nations like India proclaimed themselves "nonaligned," independent of the Soviet Union and the United States. As the two superpowers competed for the allegiance of emerging nations, the United States sought to counter the moves of the dynamic Soviet leader who had replaced Joseph Stalin.

NIKITA KHRUSHCHEV Stalin died in March 1953 after becoming increasingly isolated, vengeful, and perhaps simply mad. Nikita Khrushchev, a party stalwart with a formidable intellect and peasant origins in the farm country of the Ukraine, soon gained power. In some ways Khrushchev resembled another farm-belt politician, Harry Truman. Both were unsophisticated yet shrewd, earthy in their senses of humor, energetic, short-tempered, and largely inexperienced in international affairs. Khrushchev kept American diplomats off balance: at times genial and conciliatory, he would suddenly become demanding and boastful.

At home Khrushchev established a more moderate regime, gradually shifting the economy toward production of consumer goods. Internationally, he sought to ease tensions and reduce forces in Europe, hoping to make Western Europeans less dependent on the United States. Yet the growing tide of nationalism made it difficult for either superpower to pursue more conciliatory policies.

When Khrushchev began to ease Stalin's iron ways, nationalists in Soviet-controlled Eastern Europe pushed for greater independence. Riots erupted in Poland, while in Hungary students took to the streets. When the rioting spread, Moscow accepted the new Hungarian government and began to remove Soviet tanks. But Hungary's decision to withdraw from the Warsaw Pact proved too threatening. In October 1956 Soviet tanks rolled back into Budapest to crush the uprising. The U.S. State Department issued formal protests but did nothing to help liberate the "captive nations." For all Dulles's tough talk, the New Look foreign policy recognized that the Soviets possessed a sphere of influence in which the United States would not intervene.

Eastern Europe was not the only nationalist crisis Eisenhower faced in 1956. In Egypt, the nationalist colonel Gamal Abdel Nasser was attempting to modernize his country. Dulles hoped to win Nasser's friendship by offering American aid to build the Aswan Dam, a massive power project on the Nile River. But when Nasser formed an Arab alliance against the young state of Israel and continued to pursue economic ties with the Warsaw bloc, Dulles decided to teach the Egyptian leader a lesson: he withdrew the American pledge on Aswan. Nasser angrily upped the ante by seizing the Suez Canal, through which tankers carried most of Europe's oil.

Events moved quickly. Israel, alarmed at Nasser's Arab alliance, invaded Egypt's Sinai peninsula on October 29—the same day Hungary announced it was leaving the Warsaw Pact. Three days later French and British forces seized the canal in an attempt to restore their own interests and prestige. Eisenhower saw it as colonialism reborn and joined the Soviet Union in supporting a UN resolution condemning Britain, France, and Israel. The two superpowers demanded an immediate cease-fire. By December, American pressures forced Britain and France to remove their forces.

THE EISENHOWER DOCTRINE Given the unstable situation in the Middle East, Eisenhower convinced Congress to grant him the authority to use force against any communist attack in that region. What became known as the Eisenhower Doctrine in effect allowed the president in times of crisis to preempt Congress's power to declare war. In 1958 he used that power to send U.S. marines into Lebanon, a small nation that claimed to have been infiltrated by Nasser's supporters. Since no fighting had yet occurred, sunbathers on the beaches of Beirut, Lebanon's capital, were startled as 5,000 combat-clad marines stormed ashore. In the end the crisis blew over and the American forces withdrew.

Nationalist forces were also in ferment in Latin American countries, where only 2 percent of the people controlled 75 percent of the land. Repressive dictatorships exercised power, and foreign interests—especially American—dominated Latin American economies. Given the unequal distribution of wealth and a rapidly growing population, social tensions were rising. Cuba, only 90 miles south of American shores, was typical.

CASTRO'S REVOLUTION IN CUBA Americans owned many Cuban economic resources, including 80 percent of its utilities, and operated a naval base at Guantánamo Bay. Cuban dictator Fulgencio Batista had close ties both to the American government and to major crime figures who operated gambling, prostitution, and drug rings in Havana. A disgruntled middle-class lawyer, Fidel Castro, gained the support of impoverished peasants in Cuba's mountains and in January 1959 drove Batista from power.

At first many Americans applauded the revolution and welcomed Castro when he visited the United States. But President Eisenhower was distinctly cool to the cigar-smoking Cuban. By summer Castro had filled key positions with communists, launched a sweeping agricultural reform, and confiscated American properties. In retaliation Eisenhower placed an embargo on Cuban sugar and mobilized opposition to Castro in other Latin American countries. Cut off from American markets and aid, Castro turned to the Soviet Union.

The Response to *Sputnik*

Castro's turn to the Soviets seemed all the more dangerous because the Soviet Union in 1957 stunned America by launching the first space satellite, dubbed *Sputnik*. By 1959 the Soviets had crash-landed a much larger payload on the moon. If the Russians could target the moon, surely they could launch nuclear missiles against America. In contrast,

The Kitchen Debate

On July 24, 1959, Vice President Richard Nixon and Soviet Premier Nikita Khrushchev met at an exhibition in Moscow, showcasing American technology and culture. For Nixon the consumer goods on display offered proof of the superiority of the American free-enterprise system. Khrushchev argued forcefully, though defensively, that the Soviet Union could provide equally well for its housewives. While the event appeared to be spontaneous, Nixon had been looking for an opportunity to stand up to the pugnacious Russian leader. In this primary newspaper account, the dueling is within a single document.

DOCUMENT 1   Khrushchev-Nixon Debate

Nixon: "There are some instances where you may be ahead of us, for example in the development of the thrust of your rockets for the investigation of outer space; there may be some instances in which we are ahead of you—in color television, for instance."

Khrushchev: "No, we are up with you on this, too. We have bested you in one technique and also in the other."

Nixon: "You see, you never concede anything."

Khrushchev: "I do not give up."

Nixon: "Wait till you see the picture. Let's have far more communication and exchange in this very area that we speak of. We should hear you more on our televisions. You should hear us more on yours."

Khrushchev: "That's a good idea. Let's do it like this. You appear before our people. We will appear before your people. People will see and appreciate this."

Nixon: "There is not a day in the United States when we cannot read what you say. When Kozlov was speaking in California about peace, you were talking here in somewhat different terms. This was reported extensively in the American press. Never make a statement here if you don't want it to be read in the United States. I can promise you every word you say will be translated into English."

Khrushchev: "I doubt it. I want you to give your word that this speech of mine will be heard by the American people."

Nixon: [shaking hands on it] "By the same token, everything I say will be translated and heard all over the Soviet Union?"

Khrushchev: "That's agreed."

Nixon: "You must not be afraid of ideas."

Khrushchev: "We are telling you not to be afraid of ideas. We have no reason to be

afraid. We have already broken free from such a situation."

Nixon: "Well, then, let's have more exchange of them. We are all agreed on that. All right? All right?". . .

Khrushchev: [after Nixon called attention to a built-in panel-controlled washing machine]: "We have such things."

Nixon: "This is the newest model. This is the kind which is built in thousands of units for direct installation in the houses." He added that Americans were interested in making life easier for their women.

Mr. Khrushchev remarked that in the Soviet Union, they did not have "the capitalist attitude toward women."

Nixon: "I think that this attitude toward women is universal. What we want to do is make easier the life of our housewives." He explained that the house could be built for $14,000 and that most veterans had bought houses for between $10,000 and $15,000. . . .

"Let me give you an example you can appreciate. Our steelworkers, as you know, are on strike. But any steelworker could buy this house. They earn $3 an hour. This house costs about $100 a month to buy on a contract running 25 to 30 years."

Khrushchev: "We have steel workers and we have peasants who also can afford to spend $14,000 for a house." He said American houses were built to last only 20 years, so builders could sell new houses at the end of that period. "We build firmly. We build for our children and grandchildren."

Mr. Nixon said he thought American houses would last more than 20 years, but even so, after 20 years many Americans want a new home or a new kitchen, which would be obsolete then. The American system is designed to

take advantage of new inventions and new techniques, he said.

Khrushchev: "This theory does not hold water." He said some things never got out of date—furniture and furnishings, perhaps, but not houses. He said he did not think houses. He said he did not think that what Americans had written about their houses was all strictly accurate.

Nixon: [pointing to television screen] "We can see here what is happening in other parts of the home."

Khrushchev: "This is probably always out of order."

Nixon: "Da [yes]."

Khrushchev: "Don't you have a machine that puts food into the mouth and pushes it down? Many things you've shown us are interesting, but they are not needed in life. They have no useful purpose. They are merely gadgets. We have a saying, if you have bedbugs you have to catch one and pour boiling water into the ear."

Nixon: "We have another saying. This is that the way to kill a fly is to make it drink whisky. But we have a better use for whisky. [Aside] I like to have this battle of wits with the Chairman. He knows his business."

Source: "The Kitchen Debate," Richard Nixon and Nikita Khruschev, July 24, 1959, Moscow, USSR.

Thinking Critically

How does Khrushchev counter Nixon's explanation of "planned obsolescence"? What is Khrushchev's attitude about high-tech American consumer goods? Why was Nixon so insistent that his ideas be broadcast in the Soviet Union? In what way could women be offended by the two leaders' comments?

Even before the launch of *Sputnik* in 1957, Americans had begun devising fallout shelters for protection from the effects of a nuclear attack. What messages about nuclear war does this photo send?

the American space program suffered so many delays and mishaps that rockets exploding on launch were nicknamed "flopniks" and "kaputniks."

A MISSILE GAP? How had the Soviets managed to catch up with American technology so quickly? Some analysts blamed U.S. schools, especially weak programs in science and math. In 1958 Eisenhower joined with Congress to enact a National Defense Education Act, designed to strengthen graduate education and the teaching of science, math, and foreign languages. At the same time, the administration encouraged a crash program to build basement fallout shelters as protection in case of a nuclear attack. Democrats charged that the United States now faced an unacceptable "missile gap" (an accusation that was not borne out).

Thaws and Freezes

Throughout this series of crises, each superpower found it difficult to interpret the other's motives. The Russians exploited nationalist revolutions where they could—less successfully in Egypt, more so in Cuba. "We will bury you," Khrushchev admonished Americans, though it was unclear whether he meant through peaceful competition or military confrontation.

Rather than adopt a more belligerent course, Eisenhower determined to use the final 18 months of his presidency to improve Soviet-American relations. The shift in policy was made easier after Dulles died and the president learned from American intelligence (but could not admit publicly) that the missile gap was not real. Eisenhower chose to invite Khrushchev to visit the United States in September 1959. The Soviet premier undertook a picturesque tour across America, swapping comments about manure with Iowa farmers, reacting puritanically to movie cancan dancers,

and grousing when his visit to the new capitalist marvel, Disneyland, was canceled for security reasons.

THE U-2 INCIDENT Eisenhower's plans for a return visit to the Soviet Union were abruptly canceled in 1960 after the Russians shot down a high-altitude U-2 American spy plane over Soviet territory. At first Eisenhower claimed that the plane had strayed off course while doing weather research, but Khrushchev sprang his trap: the CIA pilot, Gary Powers, had been captured alive. The president then admitted that for reasons of national security he had personally authorized the U-2 overflights.

That episode ended Eisenhower's hopes that his personal diplomacy might thaw cold war tensions. Yet a less mature president might have led the United States into more severe conflict or even war. Eisenhower was not readily impressed by the promises of new weapons systems or overheated talk about a missile gap between the United States and the Soviet Union. He left office with a warning that too much military spending would lead to "an unwarranted influence, whether sought or unsought" by the **military-industrial complex** at the expense of democratic institutions.

 REVIEW

How did Eisenhower's aggressive policy of the "New Look" play out in Asia, Iran, and Guatemala?

THE COLD WAR ALONG A NEW FRONTIER

THE 1960 ELECTION PROMISED TO bring the winds of change to Washington. The opponents—Vice President Richard Nixon and Senator John F. Kennedy of Massachusetts— were the first major presidential candidates born in the twentieth century. At the age of 43 Kennedy would be the youngest person ever elected to the presidency, and Nixon was only four years older. The nation needed to find new challenges and "new frontiers," Kennedy proclaimed. His rhetoric was noble, but the direction in which he would take the nation was far from clear.

The Election of 1960

THE CATHOLIC ISSUE Jack Kennedy's biggest hurdle to election was social as much as political. He was a Roman Catholic out of Irish Boston, and no Catholic had ever been elected president. Conservative Protestants, many concentrated in the heavily Democratic South, were convinced that a Catholic president would never be "free to exercise his own judgment" if the pope ordered otherwise. Kennedy chose to confront the issue head-on. In September he entered the lions' den, addressing an association of hostile Protestant ministers in Houston. The speech was the best of his campaign. "I believe in an America where the separation of church and state is

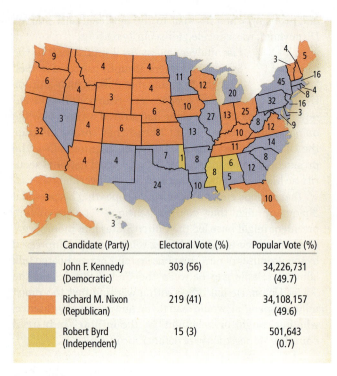

Candidate (Party)	Electoral Vote (%)	Popular Vote (%)
John F. Kennedy (Democratic)	303 (56)	34,226,731 (49.7)
Richard M. Nixon (Republican)	219 (41)	34,108,157 (49.6)
Robert Byrd (Independent)	15 (3)	501,643 (0.7)

ELECTION OF 1960

an experienced leader and staunch anticommunist, but his campaign faltered in October as unemployment rose. Nixon agreed to a series of debates with Kennedy—the first to be televised nationally. Image proved more telling than issues. According to one poll, radio listeners believed Nixon won the debate; but television viewers saw a fatigued candidate with "five o'clock shadow," because Nixon had refused to use television makeup. A relaxed Kennedy convinced many viewers that he could handle the job.

In the end religion, ethnicity, and race played decisive roles in Kennedy's triumph. One voter was asked if he voted for Kennedy because he was a Catholic. "No, because *I* am," he answered; and in key states Catholic support made a difference. "Hyphenated" Americans—Hispanic, Jewish, Irish, Italian, Polish, and German—voted Democratic in record numbers, while much of the black vote that had gone to Eisenhower in 1956 returned to the Democratic fold. Indeed, when civil rights leader Dr. Martin Luther King Jr. was imprisoned during a protest in Georgia, Kennedy attracted the support of black Americans by telephoning his sympathy to Dr. King's wife. Interest in the election ran so high that 64 percent of voters turned out, the largest percentage in 50 years. Out of 68.8 million ballots cast, Kennedy won by a margin of just 119,000.

absolute," he said, "—where no Catholic prelate would tell the President (should he be Catholic) how to act, and no Protestant minister would tell his parishioners how to vote." House Speaker Sam Rayburn, an old Texas pol, was astonished by Kennedy's bravura performance. "My God! . . . He's eating them blood raw."

TELEVISED PRESIDENTIAL DEBATES Both candidates stressed cold war themes. Kennedy lamented the apparent "missile gap" and attacked Eisenhower and Nixon for not better managing tensions between Communist China and the nationalists on Formosa (Taiwan). Vice President Richard Nixon ran on his record as

The Hard-Nosed Idealists of Camelot

Many observers compared the Kennedy White House to Camelot, King Arthur's magical court. With youthful vigor, Kennedy brought into his administration bright, energetic advisers. He and his stylish wife, Jacqueline, invited artists, musicians, and intellectuals to the White House. Impromptu touch football games on the White House lawn displayed a rough-and-tumble playfulness, akin to Arthur's jousting tournaments of old.

In truth, Kennedy was not a liberal by temperament. Handsome and intelligent, he possessed an ironic, self-deprecating humor. In Congress he had led an undistinguished career,

The urbane and energetic John F. Kennedy (center) was associated with both King Arthur (left, played by Richard Burton in the 1960 musical) and the spy James Bond (played by Sean Connery, right). Kennedy and his advisers prided themselves on their pragmatic, hard-nosed idealism. But whereas Bond used advanced technology and covert operations to save the world, in real life such approaches had their downside, as the growing civil war in Vietnam would demonstrate.

supported Senator Joe McCarthy, and earned a reputation as a playboy. Once Kennedy set his sights on the White House, however, he revealed a facility for political maneuvering and organization.

ROBERT McNAMARA Robert Strange McNamara typified the pragmatic, liberal bent of the new Kennedy team. Steely and brilliant, McNamara was one of the postwar breed of young executives known as the "whiz kids." As a Harvard Business School professor and later as president of Ford Motor Company, he specialized in using quantitative tools to streamline business. As the new secretary of defense, McNamara intended to find more flexible and efficient ways of conducting the cold war.

Kennedy liked men such as McNamara—witty, bright, ambitious—because they seemed comfortable with power and not afraid to use it. The president's leisure reading reflected a similar adventurous taste: the popular James Bond spy novels. Agent 007, with his license to kill, was sophisticated, a cool womanizer (as Kennedy himself continued to be), and ready to use the latest technology to dispatch communist villains. Ironically, Bond demonstrated that there could be plenty of glamour in being hard-nosed and pragmatic. That illicit pleasure was the underside, perhaps, of Camelot's high ideals.

The (Somewhat) New Frontier at Home

Despite bold campaign promises, the president's domestic legislative achievements were modest. Once in the White House, Kennedy found himself hemmed in by a Democratic Congress dominated by conservatives. He convinced Congress to raise the minimum hourly wage to $1.25. But on key issues, including aid to education and medical insurance, Kennedy made no headway.

He wavered, too, on how to manage the economy. The president's liberal economic advisers favored increased government spending to reduce unemployment, even if that spending meant a budget deficit. Similarly, they argued that tax cuts could be used to increase consumer spending and so stimulate the economy. Kennedy toyed with both remedies, but conservatives continued to push for a balanced budget. Only in 1963 did he send a tax proposal to Congress, which passed it the following year.

Always pragmatic, Kennedy hoped to work with, not against, the leaders of big business to promote growth for the whole nation. But he did believe that the government should be able to limit wages and prices for large corporations and unions; if not, an inflationary spiral might result. Wage increases would be followed by price increases followed by even higher wage demands.

SHOWDOWN WITH BIG STEEL To prevent inflation, the Council of Economic Advisors proposed to stabilize prices by tying wage increases to improved productivity. In April 1962 the United Steelworkers, like most other major unions, agreed to a contract that followed those guidelines. The large steel corporations, however, broke their part of the informal bargain by raising steel prices substantially. Incensed, Kennedy called for investigations into price fixing, mounted antitrust proceedings, and shifted Pentagon purchases to smaller steel companies that had not raised prices. The pressure caused the big companies to drop the price hikes but soured relations between Kennedy and the business community.

Kennedy's Cold War

During the 1960 race for the White House, Kennedy had pledged to fight the cold war with new vigor. Once elected, the new president was determined not to be seen as soft on communism, as Republicans so often charged the Democrats. The cold war contest, Kennedy argued, had shifted from the struggle over Europe to the developing nations in Asia, Africa, and Latin America. The United States should be armed with a more flexible range of military and economic options.

ALLIANCE FOR PROGRESS AND PEACE CORPS The "Alliance for Progress," announced in the spring of 1961, indicated the course Kennedy would follow. He promised $20 billion in foreign aid to Latin America over 10 years— four times what Truman and Eisenhower had provided. In return, Latin American nations would agree to reform unfair tax policies and begin agricultural land reforms. If successful, the alliance would discourage future Castro-style revolutions. With similar fanfare, the administration set up the Peace Corps. This program sent idealistic young men and women to Third World nations to provide technical, educational, and public health services. Under the alliance, a majority of Peace Corps volunteers were assigned to Latin America.

To give economic programs some military muscle, the Pentagon created jungle warfare schools in North Carolina and the Canal Zone. These schools trained Latin American police and paramilitary groups to fight guerrilla wars. They also trained American special forces such as the Green Berets in the arts of jungle warfare. If the Soviets or their allies promoted "wars of liberation," United States commandos would be ready to fight back.

SPACE PROGRAM Kennedy believed, too, that the Soviets had made space the final frontier of the cold war. Only a few months after the president's inauguration, a Russian cosmonaut orbited the world for the first time. In response, Kennedy challenged Congress to authorize a manned space mission to the moon that would land by the end of the decade. In February 1962 John Glenn circled the earth three times in a "fireball of a ride." The race to the moon was on.

Cold War Frustrations

In down-to-earth ways, high ideals did not translate easily into practical results. In the first five years of the alliance, nine Latin American governments were overthrown by military coups. The Peace Corps, for its part, proved a

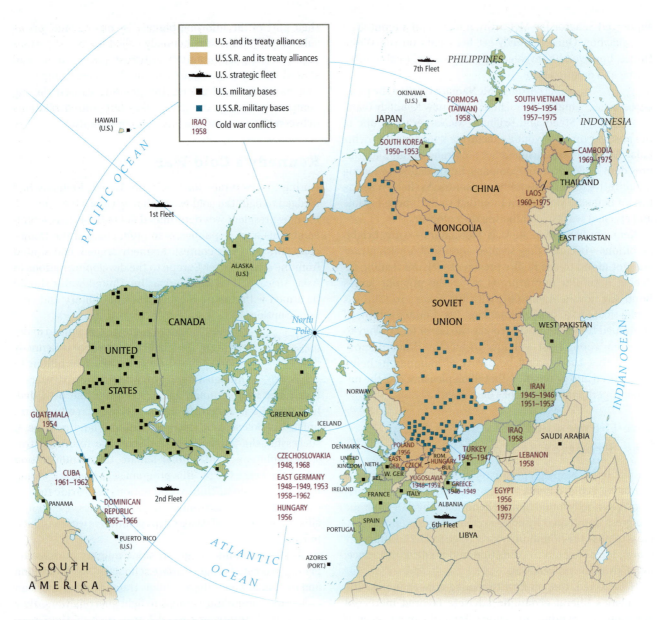

THE WORLD OF THE SUPERPOWERS

This map shows the extent of the cold war Soviet and American military buildup. The United States established a worldwide network of bases and alliances surrounding Soviet bloc nations that extended from Japan and South Korea, South Vietnam, Pakistan, and Turkey in Asia to the nations of the NATO alliance in Europe. Soviet efforts to expand its influence in the Third World led to the creation of an outpost in Cuba. Around these strategic perimeters, hot spots and centers of crisis continued to simmer.

tremendous public relations success and helped thousands of Third World farmers on a people-to-people basis. But individual Peace Corps workers could do little to change corrupt policies on a national level, and more than a few worked for the CIA.

BAY OF PIGS INVASION Nor did Kennedy succeed in countering revolutionary "wars of liberation." His prime target was Fidel Castro's communist regime in Cuba. After breaking diplomatic relations in 1960, the Eisenhower administration had secretly authorized the CIA to organize an invasion of that nation. The CIA assured

Kennedy that its 1,400-member army of Cuban exiles could inspire discontented Cubans to overthrow Castro. Eager to establish his own cold war credentials, the president approved an attack. But the invasion in April 1961 turned into a disaster. The poorly equipped rebel forces landed at the swampy Bay of Pigs with no protective cover for miles. Within two days Castro's army had rounded them up. Taking responsibility for the fiasco, Kennedy suffered a bitter humiliation whose sting goaded the administration to undertake further covert operations. The CIA secretly hatched plans to destabilize the Cuban government or even murder Castro.

KENNEDY AND VIETNAM

Kennedy's advisers took a similar covert approach in South Vietnam. There, a civil war with religious overtones was under way. The unpopular dictator Ngo Dinh Diem remained in power. South Vietnamese communists, known as the Vietcong, waged a guerrilla war against Diem with support from North Vietnam. Buddhist elements also backed the rebellion against Diem, who was a Catholic. In May 1961, a month after the Bay of Pigs invasion, Kennedy secretly ordered 500 Green Berets and military advisers to Vietnam to help Diem. By 1963 the number of "military advisers" had risen to more than 16,000. Increasingly, they were being drawn into combat with the Vietcong.

DIEM FALLS

Diem's corruption, police state tactics, and ruthless campaign against his Buddhist opposition increasingly isolated the regime. As the Kennedy administration lost faith in Diem, it tacitly encouraged a military coup by South Vietnamese military officers. To the surprise of American officials, the coup plotters not only captured Diem but shot him in November 1963. Despite Kennedy's policy of pragmatic idealism, the United States found itself mired in a Vietnamese civil war, which it had no clear strategy for winning.

Confronting Khrushchev

Vietnam and Cuba were just two areas in the Third World where Kennedy sought to battle communist forces. But the conflict between the United States and the Soviet Union soon overshadowed developments in Asia, Africa, and Latin America.

THE BERLIN WALL

June 1961 was the president's first chance to take the measure of Nikita Khrushchev, at a summit meeting held in Vienna. For two long days, Khrushchev was brash and belligerent. East and West Germany must be reunited, he demanded. In the divided capital of Berlin, located deep within East Germany (see map, page 752), citizens from all across East Germany were crossing from the eastern sector of Berlin into the free western zone as a way of escaping communist rule. This "problem" must be settled within six months, Khrushchev insisted. Kennedy tried to stand up to Khrushchev's bullying, but he left Vienna worried that the Soviet leader perceived him as weak and inexperienced. By August events in Berlin confirmed his fears. Under cover of night, the Soviets threw up a wall sealing off any entry into West Berlin. Despite American protests, the heavily guarded Berlin Wall stayed up.

A FLEXIBLE NUCLEAR RESPONSE

Tensions with the Soviet Union led the administration to rethink American nuclear strategy. Under the Dulles doctrine of massive retaliation, almost any incident threatened to trigger a launch of the full arsenal of nuclear missiles. Kennedy and McNamara sought to replace the policy of **mutually assured destruction (MAD)** with a "flexible response doctrine." By limiting the level of a first nuclear strike, they would leave room for negotiation. In that case, however, conventional forces in Europe would have to be built up so that they could better deter aggression. McNamara proposed equipping them with smaller tactical nuclear weapons.

But what if the Soviets launched a first-strike attack to knock out American missiles? McNamara's flexible response policy required that enough missiles survive so that the Americans could retaliate. If the Soviets knew the United States could survive a first strike, they would then be less likely to launch a surprise attack. So McNamara began a program to place missile sites underground and to develop submarine-launched missiles. The new flexible response policies resulted in a 15 percent increase in the 1961 military budget, compared with only 2 percent increases during the last two years of Eisenhower's term. Under Kennedy, the military-industrial complex thrived.

The Missiles of October

The peril of nuclear confrontation became dramatically clear in the Cuban missile crisis of October 1962. President Kennedy had emphasized repeatedly that the United States would treat any attempt to place offensive weapons in Cuba as an unacceptable threat. Khrushchev promised that the Soviet Union had no such intention but bristled privately at what he perceived as a gross inequality in the cold war. "The Americans had surrounded our country with military bases and threatened us with nuclear weapons," he told high Soviet officials in May 1962. In that month he convinced them to begin building a secret nuclear base in Cuba. "Now [the Americans] would learn just what it feels like to have enemy missiles pointing at you."

Throughout the summer the buildup went undetected by Americans. But by October 14, overflights of Cuba by U-2 spy planes had revealed the offensive missile sites. Kennedy was outraged.

For a week, American security advisers met in secret strategy sessions. Hawkish advisers urged air strikes against the missile sites, and at first Kennedy agreed. "We're certainly going to . . . take out these . . . missiles," he said. But more cautious advisers pointed out that the U-2 flights had not photographed all of Cuba. What if there were more concealed bases with missiles ready to fire? The Soviets could then launch an atomic attack on the United States despite the air strikes. Furthermore, if the United States attacked Cuba with no advance warning, the act would appear to the world uncomfortably like the Japanese surprise attack on Pearl Harbor in World War II.

A NAVAL BLOCKADE

Although the Joint Chiefs of Staff continued to press for a large air attack, Kennedy finally chose the more restrained option, a naval blockade to intercept "all offensive military equipment under shipment to Cuba." On October 22, word of the confrontation began to leak out. "CAPITAL CRISIS AIR HINTS AT DEVELOPMENTS ON CUBA; KENNEDY TV TALK IS LIKELY," ran the headline in the *New York Times*. Americans were stunned that evening by the president's television address.

The discovery of Soviet offensive missile sites in Cuba, revealed by low-level American reconnaissance flights, led to the first nuclear showdown of the cold war. For several tense days in October 1962, President Kennedy met with his National Security Council to debate the proper course of action.

Over the next few days, tensions mounted as a Soviet submarine approached the line of American ships. On October 25 the navy stopped an oil tanker. Several Soviet ships reversed course. In Cuba, Soviet general Issa Pliyev felt that he had to assume the worst—that despite all the talk of a blockade, an American invasion of Cuba was being prepared. Pliyev sent a coded message to Moscow that "in the opinion of the Cuban friends [that is, the Castro government] the U.S. air strike on our installations in Cuba will occur in the night between October 26 and October 27 or at dawn on October 27." Equally ominously, he added, "We have taken measures to disperse 'techniki' [the nuclear warheads] in the zone of operations." In other words, Pliyev was making his nuclear missiles operational.

The morning of October 27, alarmed Soviet technicians detected a U-2 plane flying over Cuba. Was this the beginning of the expected attack? General Pliyev had issued strict instructions not to use force without his authorization, but when the air defense command looked to consult him, he could not be found. Soviet officers went ahead and shot it down, killing its pilot.

Meanwhile, Kennedy strove to resolve the crisis through diplomatic channels. On October 26 he had received a rambling message from Khrushchev agreeing to remove the missiles in return for an American promise not to invade Cuba. The following day a second, more troubling message arrived with a new condition, that the United States must also dismantle its missile bases in Turkey, which bordered on the Soviet Union. Then word came of the downed U-2, further heightening tension. If the Soviets launched an attack from their Cuban bases, stated policy called for U.S. retaliation.

Worried that events might spiral out of control, the president put off that decision until the following morning.

Kennedy decided to ignore Khrushchev's second letter and accept the offer in the first: removal of Soviet missiles if the Americans pledged not to invade Cuba. He also gave private assurances that the missiles in Turkey would come out within half a year. In Moscow, Khrushchev agreed reluctantly to the deal, telling his advisers somberly that there were times to advance and times to retreat; and this time, "we found ourselves face to face with the danger of war and of nuclear catastrophe, with the possible result of destroying the human race." Thus the face-off ended on terms that saved either side from overt humiliation.

NUCLEAR TEST BAN TREATY The nuclear showdown prompted Kennedy and his advisers to seek ways to control the nuclear arms race. "We all inhabit this small planet," he warned in June 1963. "We all breathe the same air. We all cherish our children's future. And we are all mortal." The administration negotiated a nuclear test ban with the Soviets, prohibiting all aboveground nuclear tests. Growing concern over radioactive fallout increased public support for the treaty. A telephone hotline was also installed, providing a direct communications link between the White House and the Kremlin for use in times of crisis. At the same time, Kennedy's prestige soared for "standing up" to the Soviets.

✓ **REVIEW**

How did Kennedy confront the Soviet Union at the Bay of Pigs, in Berlin, and during the Cuban missile crisis?

CONCLUSION

THE WORLD AT LARGE

The Cuban missile crisis was the closest the world had come to "destroying the human race," in Khrushchev's words, and it sobered both superpowers. It did not end the cold war, however; indeed, both nations endured long, drawn-out regional wars before scaling back their ambitions—the United States in Vietnam and the Soviet Union in Afghanistan. Yet the intensity of confrontation—with Eisenhower and Dulles's brinkmanship, Khrushchev's provocations, and Kennedy's cold war rhetoric—began to ease. The nuclear anxieties of the 1950s, so much a part of the suburban era, yielded to different concerns in the 1960s.

In large part that change came about because the supposed consensus of the 1950s masked a profound *lack* of consensus concerning the state of equality in America. While the suburbs flourished, urban areas decayed. While more white Americans went to college, more African Americans found themselves out of work on southern farms or desperate for jobs in northern ghettos, and still in segregated schools. As Mexican-American migrant workers picked crops in California or followed the harvest north from Texas, they saw their employers resist every attempt to unionize and improve their wages. To all these Americans, the often-proclaimed "consensus" about opportunity in American life was no longer acceptable. The 1950s sparked a movement pursued by ordinary Americans who acted, despite the reluctance of their leaders, to bring about a civil rights revolution. ∞∞∞

CHAPTER SUMMARY

AT MIDCENTURY, DURING AN ERA of peace and prosperity, the United States began to build a new social and political agenda.

■ Automobiles and the culture of the highways helped bind Americans to one another in a "consensus" about what it meant to be an American.

- Highways made possible rapid suburban growth.

- Suburbs proved popular with the growing white-collar middle class.

- Consensus in suburbs blurred class distinctions and promoted the notion of "civil religion."

- Suburban life nurtured the ideal of the woman who found fulfillment as a homemaker and a mother, even though more women began to work outside the home.

■ President Eisenhower resisted the demands of conservatives to dismantle the New Deal and of liberals to extend it, in favor of moderate, or "middle of the road," Republicanism.

■ Cracks in consensus appeared among discontented intellectuals and among teenagers who, through Elvis Presley and new teen idols, discovered the power of rock and roll.

■ Efforts to contain more vigorously the U.S.S.R. and Communist China, through a policy of "brinkmanship," proved difficult to apply because of growing Third World nationalism.

- Eisenhower held back from using tactical nuclear weapons during crises in Vietnam and Taiwan.

- Successful CIA operations in Iran and Guatemala encouraged American policy makers to use covert operations more frequently.

- Postcolonial nationalism contributed to crises in Hungary, Egypt, and Cuba, where President Kennedy was embarrassed by the failure of an invasion attempt to overthrow Fidel Castro.

■ Relations between the two superpowers thawed gradually but not without recurring confrontations between the United States and the Soviet Union.

- Under Eisenhower, the Soviet success with *Sputnik* increased fears that the United States was vulnerable to missile attacks, while the U-2 spy plane incident worsened relations.

- John F. Kennedy proved willing to use covert operations as well as diplomatic and economic initiatives such as the Peace Corps and the Alliance for Progress.

- The construction of Soviet missile bases 90 miles from American shores triggered the Cuban missile crisis of 1962, the closest the United States and the Soviet Union ever came to nuclear war.

Additional Reading

David Halberstam profiles suburban America engagingly in *The Fifties* (1994); using suburban Orange County, California, as her focus, Lisa McGirr, *Suburban Warriors: The Origins of the New American Right* (2001), explores how conservatives organized at the political grassroots level. An interesting source linking suburbia to a new environmental consciousness is Adam Rome, *The Bulldozer in the Countryside: Suburban Sprawl and the Rise of American Environmentalism* (2001). Karal Ann Marling, *As Seen on TV: The Visual Culture of Everyday Life in the 1950s* (1998), gives insight into the popular aesthetics of the era. Glenn Altschuler, *All Shook Up: How Rock and Roll Changed America* (2003), shows how rock music reshaped American culture. As a corrective response to the view of women in the 1950s popularized by Betty Friedan, *The Feminine Mystique* (1963), see the provocative essays in Joanne Meyerowitz, ed., *Not June Cleaver: Women and Gender in Postwar America* (1994).

Fred Greenstein, *The Hidden Hand Presidency: Eisenhower as Leader* (rev. ed., 1994), contradicted the view of Ike as a bumbling president. Just as historians have refurbished Eisenhower's image, they have also removed some of the tarnish from Kennedy. See, for example, Graham Allison, *The Essence of Decision: Explaining the Cuban Missile Crisis* (2nd ed., 1999), and Warren Bass, *Support Any Friend: Kennedy, the Middle East, and the Making of the U.S.-Israel Alliance* (2003). To do some judging on your own, look at Ernest R. May and Philip Zelikow, eds., *The Kennedy Tapes: Inside the White House during the Cuban Missile Crisis* (1997). Two fine books on Kennedy and Vietnam are Fredrik Logevall, *Choosing War: The Lost Chance for Peace and the Escalation of War in Vietnam* (2003), and David Kaiser, *American Tragedy: Kennedy, Johnson, and the Origins of the Vietnam War* (2002).

For a fuller list of readings, see the Bibliography at www.mhhe.com/eh8e.

Significant Events

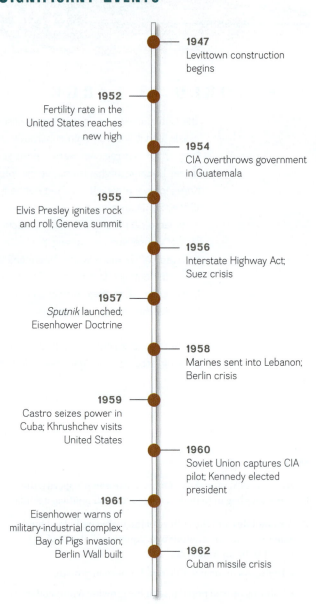

1947 Levittown construction begins

1952 Fertility rate in the United States reaches new high

1954 CIA overthrows government in Guatemala

1955 Elvis Presley ignites rock and roll; Geneva summit

1956 Interstate Highway Act; Suez crisis

1957 *Sputnik* launched; Eisenhower Doctrine

1958 Marines sent into Lebanon; Berlin crisis

1959 Castro seizes power in Cuba; Khrushchev visits United States

1960 Soviet Union captures CIA pilot; Kennedy elected president

1961 Eisenhower warns of military-industrial complex; Bay of Pigs invasion; Berlin Wall built

1962 Cuban missile crisis

ELEMENTS OF CONSENSUS

Suburban life: Uniform styles in suburban housing tracts

Creation of a broad
middle class

Television as a homogeneous medium
of middle-class taste

Civil religion and the emphasis
on religiosity

Growth of a new corporate culture and the
rise of the "organization man"

The feminine ideal of domesticity

Eisenhower's "modern Republicanism"

Widely accepted anticommunism
and support for free-enterprise
democracy

ELEMENTS OF CONFLICT

Discrimination against Jews and
minorities in new suburbs

Undermining of American cities in
favor of suburbs

Opposition to destruction of countryside
by suburban development

Intellectual attacks on conformity, midcult,
organizational behavior, and materialism

Controversy over the Kinsey Reports and
the sexual revolution

New teen culture built around comic books,
movies, and rock and roll

Religious issues during the 1960 election

Eisenhower's warning about the dangers
of the "military-industrial complex"

Debate over the policies of "mutual assured
destruction" and nuclear arms race

On August 28, 1963, more than 250,000 demonstrators joined the great civil rights march on Washington. Although the day belonged to the Reverend Martin Luther King Jr., the movement's most prominent leader, ordinary Americans both black and white played key roles in initiating the civil rights crusade.

CHAPTER 29

Civil Rights and Uncivil Liberties

1947–1969

What's to Come

∞∞∞ **AN AMERICAN STORY** ∞∞∞

TWO ROADS TO INTEGRATION

Six-year-old Ruby knew the drill. She was to look straight ahead—not to one side or the other—and especially not at *them.* She was to keep walking. Above all, she was not to look back once she'd passed, because that would encourage them. Despite her parents' warnings, Ruby still struggled to keep her eyes straight. The first day of school, federal marshals were there along with her mother and father. So were hundreds of nasty white people who came near enough to yell things like "You little nigger, we'll get you and

When Ruby drew pictures for psychologist Robert Coles, her true feelings came out. Her white children had all their features carefully sketched. The black children had body parts missing. "When I draw a white girl, I know she'll be okay," Ruby explained, "but with the colored it's not okay."

kill you." Then she was within the building's quiet halls and alone with her teacher. She was the only person in class: none of the white students had come. As the days went by during that autumn of 1960, the marshals stopped walking with her but the hecklers still waited. And once in a while Ruby couldn't help looking back, trying to see the face of one woman in particular.

Ruby's parents were not social activists. They signed their daughter up for the white school because "we thought it was for all the colored to do, and we never thought Ruby would be alone." Her father's white employer fired him; letters and phone calls threatened the family's lives and home. Ruby seemed to take it all in stride, though her parents worried that she was not eating the way she used to. Often she left her school lunch untouched or refused anything other than packaged food such as potato chips. It was only after a time that the problem was traced to the hecklers. "They tells me I'm going to die, and that it'll be soon. And that one lady tells me every morning I'm getting poisoned soon, when she can fix it." Ruby was convinced that the woman owned the nearby variety store and would carry out her threat by poisoning the family's food.

Over the course of a year white students gradually returned to class and life settled into a new routine. By the time Ruby was 10 she had developed a remarkably clear perception of herself. "Maybe because of all the trouble going to school in the beginning I learned more about my people. Maybe I would have anyway; because when you get older you see yourself and the white kids; and you find out the difference. You try to forget it, and say there is none; and if there is you won't say what it be. Then you say it's my own people, and so I can be proud of them instead of ashamed."

If the new ways were hard for Ruby, they were not easy for white southerners either—even those who saw the need for change. One woman, for years a dedicated teacher in Atlanta, vividly recalled a traumatic summer 10 years earlier, when she went north to New York City to take courses in education. There were black students living in the dormitory, an integrated situation that was new to her. One day as she stepped from her shower, so did a black student from the nearby stall. "When I saw her I didn't know what to do," the woman recalled. "I felt sick all over, and frightened. What I remember—I'll never forget it—is that horrible feeling of being caught in a terrible trap, and not knowing what to do about it. I thought of running out of the room and screaming, or screaming at the woman to get out, or running back into the shower. . . . My sense of propriety was with me, though—miraculously—and I didn't want to hurt the woman. It wasn't *her* that was upsetting me. I knew that, even in that moment of sickness and panic." So she ducked back into the shower until the other woman left.

Summer was almost over before she felt comfortable eating with black students at the same table. And when she returned home, she told no one about her experiences. "At that time people would have thought one of two things: I was crazy (for being so upset and ashamed) or a fool who in a summer had become a dangerous 'race mixer.'" She continued to love the South and to speak up for its traditions of dignity, neighborliness, and honor, but she saw the need for change. And so in 1961 she volunteered to teach one of the first integrated high school classes in Atlanta, even though she had her doubts. By the end of two years she concluded that she had never spent a more exciting time teaching. "I've never felt so useful, so constantly useful, not just to the children but to our whole society. American as well as Southern. Those children, all of them, have given me more than I've given them." ◌◌◌◌◌

THE CIVIL RIGHTS MOVEMENT

FOR AMERICANS IN ALL WALKS of life, the upheavals that swept America in the 1960s were wrenching. From the schoolrooms and lunch counters of the South to the college campuses of the North, from eastern slums to western migrant-labor camps, American society was in ferment. And at the center of that ferment was a battle for civil rights.

On the face of it such agitation seemed to be a dramatic reversal of the placid 1950s. Turbulence and activism had overturned stability and consensus. Yet the events of the 1960s grew naturally out of the social conditions that preceded those years. The civil rights movement was brought about not by a group of farsighted leaders in government but by ordinary folk who sought change, often despite the reluctance or even fierce opposition of people in power. After World War II, grassroots organizations such as the NAACP for blacks and the American GI Forum for Latinos acted with a new determination to achieve the equality of opportunity promised by the American creed.

Thus the 1950s were a seedbed for the more turbulent revolutions of the 1960s. The booming postwar economy held out the possibility of better lives for minorities; yet systematic discrimination and racism, long embedded in American life by custom and law, prevented prosperity from spreading equally. Time and again, activists challenged the political system to deal with what the 1950s had done—and what had been left undone. As one friend of Martin Luther King Jr. predicted in 1958, "If the young people are aroused from their lethargy through this fight, it will affect broad circles throughout the country." And, he might have added, around the world, because a similar spirit of reform existed on a global scale.

The struggle of African Americans for equality during the postwar era is filled with ironies. By the time barriers to legal segregation in the South began to fall, millions of black families were leaving for regions where discrimination was less easily challenged. The South they left behind was in the early stages of an economic boom. The cities to which many migrated had entered a period of decline. Yet, as if to close a circle, the rise of large black voting blocs in major cities created political pressures that helped force the nation to dismantle the worst legal and institutional barriers to racial equality.

The Changing South and African Americans

After World War II the southern economy began to grow significantly faster than the national economy. The remarkable about-face began during the New Deal with federal programs such as the Tennessee Valley Authority. World War II brought even more federal dollars to build and maintain military bases and defense plants. And the South attracted new business because it offered a "clean slate." In contrast to the Northeast and upper Midwest, the South had few unions, little regulation and bureaucracy, and low wages and taxes. Finally, there was the matter of climate, which later caused the region to be nicknamed the **Sun Belt.** Especially with improvements in air-conditioning, the South grew more attractive to skilled professionals, corporate managers, and affluent retirees.

MECHANIZED COTTON FARMING

Before World War II, 80 percent of African Americans lived in the South. Most raised cotton as sharecroppers and tenant farmers. But the war created a labor shortage, as millions of workers went off to fight and others labored in war industries. This shortage gave cotton growers an incentive to mechanize cotton picking. In 1950 only 5 percent of the crop was picked mechanically; by 1960 at least half was. Farmers began to consolidate land into larger holdings. Tenant farmers, sharecroppers, and hired labor of both races, no longer in short supply, left the countryside for the city.

The national level of wages also profoundly affected southern labor. When federal minimum-wage laws forced lumber or textile mills to raise their pay scales, the mills no longer expanded. In addition, steel and other industries with strong national unions and manufacturers with plants around the country set wages by national standards. Those changes brought southern wages closer to the national average by the 1960s. As the southern economy grew, what had for many years been a distinct regional economy became more diversified and more integrated into the national economy.

As wages rose and unskilled work disappeared, job opportunities for black southerners declined. Outside cotton farming, the lumber industry had provided the largest number of jobs for young black men. There, the number of black teenagers hired by lumber mills dropped 74 percent between 1950 and 1960. New high-wage jobs were reserved for white southerners, because outside industries arriving in the South made no effort to change local patterns of discrimination. So the ultimate irony arose. As per capita income rose and industrialization brought in new jobs, black laborers poured out of the region in search of work. They arrived in cities that showed scant tolerance for racial differences and little willingness or ability to hire unskilled black labor.

The NAACP and Civil Rights

In the postwar era the NAACP decided it would use the judicial system to attack Jim Crow laws. That stepped-up attack reflected the increased national political influence that African Americans achieved as they migrated in great numbers out of the South. No longer could northern politicians readily ignore the demands black leaders made for greater equality. Presidents Roosevelt and Truman had taken small but significant steps to address the worst forms of legal and economic discrimination. And across the South black churches and colleges became centers for organized resistance to segregation.

THURGOOD MARSHALL

Thurgood Marshall emerged as the NAACP's leading attorney. Marshall had attended law school in the 1930s at Howard University in Washington, D.C. There, the law school's dean, Charles Houston, was in the midst of revamping the school and turning out sharp, dedicated lawyers, Marshall among them, but with a difference. "Before he came along," one observer noted,

> the principal black leaders—men like Du Bois and James Weldon Johnson and Charles Houston—didn't talk the language of the people. They were upper-class and upper-middle-class Negroes. Thurgood Marshall was *of* the people.... Out in Texas or Oklahoma or down the street here in Washington at the Baptist church, he would make these rousing speeches that would have 'em all jumping out of their seats.... "We ain't gettin' what we should," was what it came down to, and he made them see that.

During the late 1930s and early 1940s Marshall toured the South (in "a little old beat-up '29 Ford"), typing out legal briefs in the backseat, trying to get teachers to sue for equal pay, and defending blacks accused of murder in a Klan-infested county in Florida. He was friendly with whites, not shy, and black citizens who had never even considered the possibility that a member of their race might win a legal battle "would come for miles, some of them on muleback or horseback, to see 'the nigger lawyer' who stood up in white men's courtrooms."

For years NAACP lawyers had worked hard to organize local chapters, to support members of the community willing to risk their jobs, property, and lives in order to challenge segregation. But they waged a moderate, pragmatic campaign. They chose not to attack head-on the Supreme Court decision (*Plessy v. Ferguson,* 1896) that permitted "separate but equal" segregated facilities. They simply demonstrated that a black college or school might be separate, but it was hardly equal if it lacked a law school or even indoor plumbing.

The *Brown* Decision

In 1950 the NAACP determined to attack the separate but equal doctrine itself. Oliver Brown was one of the people who provided a path to the Supreme Court. Brown objected because his daughter Linda had to walk past an all-white school on her way to catch the bus to her segregated black school in Topeka, Kansas. A three-judge federal panel rejected Brown's suit because the schools in Topeka, while segregated, did meet the court's test of equality. But after two years of arguments, the NAACP convinced the Supreme Court to overturn the

| Thurgood Marshall

lower court ruling in *Brown v. Board of Education of Topeka* (1954).

OVERTURNING PLESSY

Marshall and his colleagues succeeded in part because of a change in the Court itself. The year before, President Eisenhower had appointed Earl Warren, a liberal Republican from California, as chief justice. Warren, a forceful advocate, persuaded even the Court's segregationists that segregation as defined in *Plessy* perpetuated racial supremacy. The Court ruled unanimously that separate facilities were inherently unequal. To keep black children segregated by race, it ruled, "generates a feeling of inferiority as to their status in the community that may affect their hearts and minds in a way unlikely ever to be undone."

At the time of the *Brown* decision, 21 states and the District of Columbia operated segregated school systems. All of them had to decide, in some way, how to comply with the new ruling. The Court allowed a certain amount of leeway, handing down a second ruling in 1955 that required that desegregation be carried out "with all deliberate speed." Some border states reluctantly decided to comply, but in the Deep South, many citizens called for die-hard defiance. In 1956, 19 U.S. senators and 81 representatives issued a "Southern Manifesto," which declared their intent to use "all lawful means" to reestablish legal segregation.

Latino Civil Rights

Mexican Americans also considered school desegregation as central to their campaign for civil rights. At the end of World War II, only 1 percent of children of Mexican descent in Texas graduated from high school. Both the American GI Forum and the League of United Latin American Citizens (LULAC; see page 684) supported legal challenges to the system.

DELGADO AND SEGREGATED SCHOOLS

In a 1947 case, *Mendez et al. v. Westminster School District of Orange County,* the courts had ordered several California school districts to integrate. LULAC saw a way to apply that ruling in Texas. The superintendent in the town of Bastrop had refused a request to enroll first-grader Minerva Delgado in a nearby all-white school. Civil rights lawyer and activist Gus Garcia, an adviser to both LULAC and the GI Forum, helped bring a case on Minerva's behalf against the school district. Before *Delgado et al. v. Bastrop et al.* went to trial, a Texas judge ordered an end to segregated schools beyond the first grade (based on the assumption that the youngest Mexican American children needed special classes to learn English). *Delgado* served notice that Mexicans would no longer accept second-class citizenship. It also served as a precedent in *Brown v. Board of Education* in 1954.

Latinos faced a peculiar Jim Crow system that left them segregated in practice, but technically not by law. Throughout

A first-grade class at segregated Washington Elementary School in Topeka, Kansas. To get to her school bus stop, 8-year-old Linda Brown had to dodge through a five-track switching yard, where large engines maneuvered railcars of lumber, eggs, beer, and potatoes; then cross Kansas Street, a busy thoroughfare. In freezing weather, she sometimes became so cold, she cried or turned back. Yet there was a white school located closer to her home. Linda's father, Oliver Brown, sued Topeka's Board of Education in a case that reached the Supreme Court.

the Southwest the states recognized just two races: black and white. That dividing line left Mexican Americans in legal limbo. Though legally grouped with whites, they were by long-standing social custom barred from many public places, they could not serve on juries, and they faced widespread job discrimination. To remedy the situation, Mexican Americans had to establish themselves in the courts as a distinct class of people.

HERNÁNDEZ AND DESEGREGATION An opportunity arose in the case of Pete Hernández, who had been convicted of murder by an all-white jury in Jackson County, Texas. Indeed, as Mexican American lawyer Gus Garcia

realized, no Mexican American had served on a Jackson jury in the previous 25 years. Garcia, one of the leaders of the American GI Forum, saw in the tactics of Thurgood Marshall and the NAACP a way to use the Hernández case to extend to Mexicans the benefits of the Fourteenth Amendment's equal protection clause.

The key to the case was ingenious but direct. The state argued that because Mexicans were white, a jury without Mexicans was still a jury of peers. Yet the courthouse in which Hernández was tried had two men's rooms. One said simply, "MEN." The other, labeled with a crudely hand-lettered sign, said "COLORED MEN" and below that, in Spanish,

Attorney Gus Garcia (left) was one of the key leaders of the American GI Forum, founded by Mexican American veterans to pursue their civil rights. He and his colleagues successfully appealed the conviction of Pete Hernández (center) before the Supreme Court in 1954.

"HOMBRES AQUI [MEN HERE]." As one of Gus Garcia's colleagues recalled, "In the jury pool, Mexicans may have been white, but when it came to nature's functions they were not." This and similar examples of discrimination persuaded the Supreme Court, in *Hernández v. Texas,* to throw out the state's argument. Latinos in south Texas, like African Americans across the South, were held to be a discrete group whose members deserved equal protection under the law. "The Fourteenth Amendment is not directed solely against discrimination due to a 'two-class theory,' that is, based on differences between 'white' and Negro," ruled Chief Justice Earl Warren. Warren's reasoning made it possible for Latinos to seek redress as a group rather than as individuals. After *Hernández,* the Mexican-American community had both the legal basis and the leadership to broaden its attack against discrimination.

A New Civil Rights Strategy

ROSA PARKS   Neither the *Brown* nor the *Hernández* decision ended segregation, but they combined with political and economic forces to usher in a new era of southern race relations. In December 1955 Rosa Parks, a 43-year-old black civil rights activist, was riding the bus home in Montgomery, Alabama. When the driver ordered her to give her seat to a white man, as Alabama Jim Crow laws required, she refused. Police took her to jail and eventually fined her $14.

Determined to overturn the law, a number of women from the NAACP, friends of Parks, met secretly at midnight to draft a letter of protest.

> Another Negro woman has been arrested and thrown into jail because she refused to get up out of her seat on the bus and give it to a white person. . . . Until we do something to stop these arrests, they will continue. The next time it may be you, or you or you. This woman's case will come up Monday. We are, therefore, asking every Negro to stay off the buses on Monday in protest of the arrest and trial.

Thousands of copies of the letter circulated, and the Monday **boycott** was such a success it was extended indefinitely. Buses wheeled around the city virtually empty, losing over 30,000 fares a day. The white community, in an effort to halt the unprecedented black challenge, resorted to various forms of legal and physical intimidation. No local agent would insure cars used to carpool black workers. A bomb exploded in the house of the Reverend Martin Luther King Jr., the key boycott leader. And when that failed to provoke the violence that whites could use to justify harsh reprisals, 90 black leaders were arrested for organizing an illegal boycott. Still, the campaign continued until November 23, 1956, when the Supreme Court ruled that bus segregation was illegal.

MARTIN LUTHER   The triumph was especially sweet for
KING JR.   Martin Luther King Jr., whose leadership in Montgomery brought him national fame.

Before becoming a minister at the Dexter Street Baptist Church, King had little personal contact with the worst forms of white racism. He had grown up in the relatively affluent middle-class black community of Atlanta, Georgia, the son of one of the city's most prominent black ministers. He attended Morehouse College, an academically respected black school in Atlanta, and Crozer Theological Seminary in Philadelphia before entering the doctoral program in theology at Boston University. As a graduate student, King embraced the pacifism and nonviolence of the Indian leader Mohandas Gandhi and the activism of Christian reformers of the Progressive Era. King heeded the call to Dexter Street in 1954 with the idea of becoming a theologian after he served his active ministry and finished his dissertation.

NONVIOLENCE   As boycott leader, King had the responsibil-
AS A STRATEGY   ity to rally black support without triggering violence. Because local officials were all too eager for any excuse to use force, King's nonviolent approach was the ideal strategy. King offered his audience two visions. First, he reminded them of the many injustices they had been forced to endure. The boycott, he asserted, was a good way to seek redress. Then he counseled his followers to avoid the actions of their oppressors: "In our protest there will be no cross burnings. No white person will be taken from his home by a hooded Negro mob and brutally murdered." And he evoked the Christian and republican ideals that would become the themes of his civil rights crusade. "If we protest courageously, and yet with dignity and Christian love," he said, "when the future history books are written, somebody will have to say, 'There lived a race of people, of black people, of people who had the moral courage to stand up for their rights. And thereby they injected a new meaning into the history of civilization.'"

Indeed, the African Americans of Montgomery did set an example of moral courage that rewrote the pages of American race relations. Their firm stand caught the attention of the national news media. King and his colleagues were developing the tactics needed to launch a more aggressive phase of the civil rights movement.

Little Rock and the White Backlash

The civil rights spotlight moved the following year to Little Rock, Arkansas. White officials there had reluctantly adopted a plan to integrate the schools with a most deliberate lack of speed. Nine black students were scheduled to enroll in September 1957 at the all-white Central High School. Instead, the school board urged them to stay home. Governor Orval Faubus, generally a moderate on race relations, called out the Arkansas National Guard on the excuse of maintaining order. President Eisenhower tacitly supported Faubus in his defiance of court-ordered integration by remarking that "you cannot change people's hearts merely by laws."

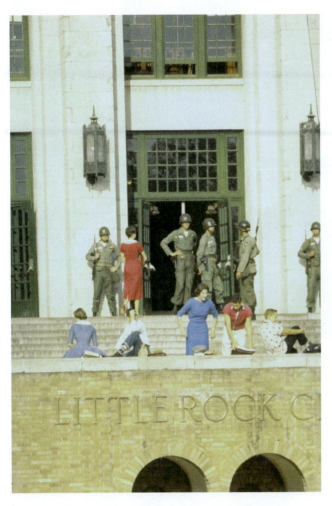

Governor Faubus first called out the National Guard to prevent African-American students from integrating Little Rock's Central High School. Once President Eisenhower federalized the Guard, soldiers stayed at the school to protect the nine students who dared to cross the color line.

Still, the Justice Department could not simply let Faubus defy the federal courts. It won an injunction against the governor, but when the nine blacks returned on September 23 a mob of 1,000 abusive whites greeted them. So great was national attention that President Eisenhower felt compelled to send in federal troops and take control of the National Guard. For a year the Guard preserved order until Faubus, in a last-ditch maneuver, closed the schools. Only in 1959, under pressure of another federal court ruling, did Little Rock schools reopen and resume the plan for gradual integration.

The skirmishes of Montgomery and Little Rock were a beginning, not an end. In fact, segregationist resistance increased in the wake of King's Montgomery success. From 1955 to 1959, civil rights protesters endured over 200 acts of violence in the South. Legislatures and city councils passed scores of laws attempting to either outlaw the NAACP or prevent it from functioning. Black leaders were unable to achieve momentum on a national scale until 1960. Then, a series of demonstrations by young people changed everything.

 REVIEW

How did African American and Latino civil rights cases spark a civil rights movement that went beyond court challenges?

A MOVEMENT BECOMES A CRUSADE

ON JANUARY 31, 1960, Joseph McNeill got off the bus in Greensboro, North Carolina, a freshman on the way back to college. When he looked for something to eat at the lunch counter, the waitress gave the familiar reply: "We don't serve Negroes here."

It was a refrain repeated countless times and in countless places. Yet for some reason this rebuke particularly offended McNeill. He and his roommates had read a pamphlet describing the 1955 bus boycott in Montgomery, Alabama. They decided it was time to make their own protest against segregation. Proceeding the next day to the "whites only" lunch counter at a local store, they sat politely waiting for service. "The waitress looked at me as if I were from outer space," recalled one of the protesters. Rather than serve them, the manager closed the counter. Word of the action spread. A day later—Tuesday—the four students were joined by 27 more. Wednesday, the number jumped to 63; Thursday, to over 300. Come the weekend, 1,600 students rallied to plan further action.

On Monday, February 8, **sit-ins** began in nearby Durham and Winston-Salem. Tuesday it was Charlotte; Thursday, High Point and Portsmouth, Virginia. A news broadcast reassured white residents in Raleigh that black students there would not follow Greensboro's example. In response, angry black students launched massive sit-ins at variety stores in Raleigh. By Lincoln's birthday the demonstrations had spread to Tennessee and Florida; by April to 78 different southern and border communities. By September at least 70,000 African Americans as well as whites had participated. Thousands had been arrested and jailed.

The campaign for black civil rights gained momentum not so much by the power of national movements as through a host of individual decisions by local groups, churches, and citizens. When New Orleans schools were desegregated in 1960, young Ruby's parents had not intended to make a social statement. But once involved, they refused to back down. The students at Greensboro had not been approached by the NAACP, but acted on their own initiative.

In May 1961 a mob in Montgomery, Alabama, surrounded the Negro First Baptist Church where Martin Luther King Jr. was leading an all-night vigil. King put in a call to Attorney General Robert Kennedy, who sent 400 federal marshals to keep order.

Riding to Freedom

NEWER CIVIL RIGHTS ORGANIZATIONS
Of course, organizations channeled these discontents and aspirations. But the new generation of younger activists also shaped and altered the organizations. Beginning in the 1960s, the push for desegregation moved from court actions launched by the NAACP and the Urban League to newer groups determined to take direct action. Since organizing the Montgomery boycott, Martin Luther King Jr. and his Southern Christian Leadership Conference (SCLC) had continued to advocate nonviolent protest: "To resist without bitterness; to be cursed and not reply; to be beaten and not hit back." A second key organization, the Congress of Racial Equality (CORE), was more willing than the SCLC to force confrontations with the segregationist system. Another group, the Student Non-Violent Coordinating Committee (SNCC, pronounced "Snick"), grew out of the Greensboro sit-in. SNCC represented the more militant, younger generation of black activists who grew increasingly impatient with the slow pace of reform.

In May 1961 CORE director James Farmer led a group of black and white "freedom riders" on a bus trip into the heart of the South. They hoped their trip from Washington, D.C., to New Orleans would focus national attention on the inequality of segregated facilities. Violent southern mobs gave them the kind of attention they feared. In South Carolina, thugs beat divinity student John Lewis as he tried to enter an all-white waiting room. Mobs in Anniston and Birmingham, Alabama, assaulted the freedom riders as police ignored the violence. One of the buses was burned.

President Kennedy had sought to avoid forceful federal intervention in the South. When the freedom riders persisted in their plans, he tried to convince Alabama officials to protect the demonstrators so that he would not have to send federal forces. His hopes were dashed. From a phone booth outside the bus terminal, John Doar, a Justice Department official in Montgomery, relayed the horror to Attorney General Robert Kennedy, the president's brother:

> Now the passengers are coming off. They're standing on a corner of the platform. Oh, there are fists, punching! A bunch of men led by a guy with a bleeding face are beating them. There are no cops. It's terrible! It's terrible! There's not a cop in sight. People are yelling, "There those niggers are! Get 'em, get 'em!" It's awful.

FREEDOM RIDERS ATTACKED
Appalled, Robert Kennedy ordered in 400 federal marshals, who barely managed to hold off the crowd. Martin Luther King Jr., addressing a meeting in town, phoned the attorney general to say that the church had been surrounded by an angry mob of several thousand—jeering, throwing rocks, and carrying firebombs. As Kennedy later recalled, "I said that we were doing the best that we could and that he'd be as dead as Kelsey's nuts if it hadn't been for the marshals and the efforts that we made."

Both Kennedys understood that civil rights was the most divisive issue the administration faced. For liberals, civil rights measured Kennedy's credentials as a reformer. Kennedy needed black and liberal votes to win reelection. Yet an active federal role threatened to drive white southerners from the Democratic Party. It was for that reason that Kennedy had hedged on his promise to introduce major civil rights legislation. Through executive orders, he assured black leaders, he could eliminate discrimination in the government civil service and in businesses filling government contracts. He appointed several African Americans to high administrative positions and five, including Thurgood Marshall, to the federal courts. The Justice Department beefed up its civil rights enforcement procedures. But the freedom riders, by their bold actions, forced the Kennedys to do more.

Civil Rights at High Tide

By the fall of 1961 Attorney General Robert Kennedy had persuaded SNCC to shift tactics to voter registration, which he assumed would stir less violence. Voting booths, Kennedy noted, were not like schools, where people would protest, "We don't want our little blond daughter going to school with a Negro."

As SNCC and CORE workers arrived in southern towns in the spring of 1962, they discovered that voting rights was not a peaceful issue. Over two years in Mississippi they registered only 4,000 out of 394,000 black adults. Angry racists attacked with legal harassment, jailings, beatings, bombings, and murders. Terrorized workers who called for protection found it woefully lacking. FBI agents often stood by taking notes while SNCC workers were assaulted. Undaunted, SNCC workers made it clear that they intended to stay. They fanned out across the countryside to speak with farmers who had never before dared to ask for a vote.

JAMES MEREDITH Confrontation increased after a federal court ordered the segregated University of Mississippi to admit James Meredith, a black applicant. When Governor Ross Barnett personally blocked Meredith's registration in September 1962, Kennedy faced a crisis much as Eisenhower did with Little Rock in 1957. The

president ordered several hundred federal marshals to escort Meredith into a university dormitory. Kennedy then announced on national television that the university had been integrated and asked students to follow the law of the land. Instead, a mob moved on campus, shooting out streetlights, commandeering a bulldozer, and throwing rocks and bottles. To save the marshals Kennedy finally sent in federal troops, but not before 2 people were killed and 375 wounded.

"LETTER FROM BIRMINGHAM JAIL" In Mississippi, President Kennedy had begun to lose control of the civil rights issue. The House of Representatives, influenced by television coverage of the violence, introduced a number of civil rights measures. And Martin Luther King Jr. led a group to Birmingham, Alabama, to force a showdown against segregation. From a prison cell there, he produced one of the most eloquent documents of the civil rights movement, his "Letter from Birmingham Jail." Addressed to local ministers who had counseled an end to confrontation, King defended the use of civil disobedience. The choice, he warned, was not between obeying the law and nonviolently breaking it to bring about change; it was between his way and streets "flowing with blood," as restive black citizens turned toward more-militant ideologies.

Once freed, King led new demonstrations. Television cameras were on hand that May as Birmingham police chief "Bull" Connor, a man with a short fuse, unleashed attack dogs, club-wielding police, and fire hoses powerful enough to peel the bark off trees. When segregationist bombs went off in African American neighborhoods, black mobs retaliated with their own riot, burning a number of shops and businesses owned by whites. In the following

In Birmingham, Alabama, firefighters used high-pressure hoses to disperse civil rights demonstrators. The force of the hoses was powerful enough to tear bark off trees. Pictures like this one aroused widespread sympathy for the civil rights movement.

10 weeks, more than 750 riots erupted in 186 cities and towns, both North and South. King's warning of streets "flowing with blood" no longer seemed far-fetched.

Kennedy sensed that he could no longer compromise on civil rights. In phrases that, like King's, drew heavily on Christian and republican rhetoric, he asked the nation, "If [an American with dark skin] cannot enjoy the full and free life all of us want, then who among us would be content to have the color of his skin changed and stand in his place? Who among us would then be content with counsels of patience and delay?" The president threw his support behind a strong civil rights bill to end segregation and protect black voters. When King announced a massive march on Washington for August 1963, Kennedy objected that it would undermine support for his bill. "I have never engaged in any direct action movement which did not seem ill-timed," King replied.

THE MARCH ON WASHINGTON On August 28 some 250,000 people gathered at the Lincoln Memorial to march and sing in support of civil rights and racial harmony. Appropriately, the day belonged to King. In the powerful tones of a southern preacher, he reminded the crowd that the Declaration of Independence was a promise that applied to all people, black and white. "I have a dream," he told them, that one day "all of God's children, black men and white men, Jews and Gentiles, Protestants and Catholics, will be able to join hands and sing in the words of the old Negro spiritual, 'Free at last! Free at last! Thank God Almighty, we are free at last!'" Congress began deliberation of the civil rights bill, which was reported out of the Judiciary Committee on October 23.

The Fire Next Time

TRAGEDY IN DALLAS With civil rights dividing the Democratic Party, the president scheduled a trip to Texas to recoup some southern support. On November 22, 1963, the people of Dallas lined the streets for his motorcade. Suddenly, a sniper's rifle fired several times. Kennedy slumped into his wife's arms, fatally wounded. His assassin, Lee Harvey Oswald, was caught several hours later. Oswald seemed a mysterious figure: emotionally unstable, he had spent several years in the Soviet Union. But his actions were never fully explained, because only two days after his arrest—in full view of television cameras—a disgruntled nightclub operator named Jack Ruby gunned him down.

In the face of such mounting violence, many Americans came to doubt that gradual reform could hold the nation together. A few black radicals believed that the Kennedy assassination was a payback to a system that had tolerated its own racial violence—the "chickens coming home to roost," as separatist Malcolm X put it. Many younger black leaders observed that civil rights received the greatest national coverage when white, not black, demonstrators were killed. They wondered, too, how Lyndon Johnson, a consummate southern politician, would approach the civil rights programs.

LBJ AND THE CIVIL RIGHTS ACT OF 1964 The new president, however, saw the need for action. Just as the Catholic issue had tested Kennedy's ability to lead, Johnson knew that without strong leadership on civil rights, "I'd be dead before I could ever begin." On November 23, his first day in office, he promised civil rights leaders that he would pass Kennedy's bill. Despite a southern filibuster in the Senate, the Civil Rights Act of 1964 became law the following summer. The bill marked one of the great moments in the history of American reform. It barred discrimination in public accommodations such as lunch counters, bus stations, and hotels; it authorized the attorney general to bring suit to desegregate schools, museums, and other public facilities; it outlawed discrimination in employment by race, color, religion, sex, or national origin.

VOTING RIGHTS ACT OF 1965 Still, the Civil Rights Act did not bar the techniques that southern registrars routinely used to prevent black citizens from voting. A coalition of idealistic young black and white protesters had continued the Mississippi voting drive in what they called "Freedom Summer." In 1965 Martin Luther King Jr., in the face of police violence, led a series of demonstrations. The campaign climaxed with a 54-mile walk from Selma to Montgomery, Alabama. As pressure mounted, Johnson sent Congress a strong Voting Rights Act, which was passed in August 1965. The act suspended literacy tests and authorized federal officials to supervise elections in many southern districts. With some justice, Johnson called the act "one of the most monumental laws in the entire history of American freedom." Within a five-year period, black registration in the South jumped from 35 to 65 percent.

Black Power

The civil rights laws did not strike at the **de facto segregation** found outside the South. This segregation was not codified in law but practiced through unwritten custom. In large areas of America, African Americans were locked out of suburbs, kept out of decent schools, barred from exclusive clubs, and denied all but the most menial jobs. Nor did the Voting Rights Act deal with the sources of urban black poverty. The median income for urban black residents was approximately half that for whites.

| Malcolm X

NATION OF ISLAM

In such an atmosphere, militants sharply questioned the liberal goal of integration. Since the 1930s the Nation of Islam, dedicated to complete separation from white society, had attracted as many as 100,000 members, mostly young men. During the early 1960s the sect drew even wider attention through the energetic efforts of Malcolm X. This charismatic leader had learned the language of the downtrodden from his own experience as a former hustler, gambler, and prison inmate. His militancy alarmed whites, though by 1965 Malcolm was in fact moving toward a moderate position. He accepted integration but emphasized black community action. After he broke with Elijah Muhammad, leader of the Black Muslims, Malcolm was gunned down by rivals.

But by 1965–1966, even CORE and SNCC had begun to give up working for nonviolent change. If black Americans were to liberate themselves fully, militants argued, they could not merely accept rights "given" to them by whites—they had to claim them. Some members began carrying guns to defend themselves. In 1966 Stokely Carmichael of SNCC gave the militants a slogan—"Black Power"—and the defiant symbol of a gloved fist raised in the air. In its moderate form, the black power movement encouraged African Americans to recover their cultural roots, their African heritage, and a new sense of identity. African clothes and natural hairstyles became popular. On college campuses, black students pressed universities to hire black faculty, create black studies programs, and provide segregated social and residential space.

BLACK PANTHERS

Among more militant factions, the Black Panther Party of Oakland called on the black community to arm. Because California law forbade carrying concealed weapons, Panther leader Huey Newton and his followers openly brandished shotguns and rifles as they patrolled the streets protecting blacks from police harassment. In February 1967 Newton forced the showdown he had been looking for. "O.K., you big fat racist pig, draw your gun," he shouted while waving a shotgun. A gun battle with police left Newton wounded and in jail.

Eldridge Cleaver, who assumed leadership of the party, attracted the attention of whites with his searing autobiography, *Soul on Ice.* But even at the height of the Black Panthers' notoriety, the group never counted more than 2,000 members nationwide.

Violence in the Streets

No ideology shaped the reservoir of frustration and despair that existed in the ghettos. Often, a seemingly minor incident such as an arrest or an argument on the streets triggered violence. A mob would gather, and police cars and white-owned stores would be firebombed or looted. Riots broke out in Harlem and Rochester, New York, in 1964, the Watts area of Los Angeles in 1965, Chicago in 1966, and Newark and Detroit in 1967. In the riot at Watts, more than

A National Guardsman watches as flames consume large areas of the Watts section of Los Angeles during the 1965 riot. Often, a seemingly trivial event set off such scenes of violence, revealing the depth of explosive rage harbored within urban ghettos.

$200 million in property was destroyed and 34 people died, all of them black. It took nearly 5,000 troops to end the bloodiest rioting in Detroit, where 40 died, 2,000 were injured, and 5,000 were left homeless.

To most whites the violence was unfathomable and inexcusable. Lyndon Johnson spoke for many when he argued that "neither old wrongs nor new fears can justify arson and murder." Martin Luther King Jr., still pursuing the tactics of nonviolence, came to understand the anger behind it. Touring Watts only days after the riots, he was approached by a band of young blacks. "We won," they told him proudly. "How can you say you won," King countered, "when thirty-four Negroes are dead, your community is destroyed, and whites are using the riot as an excuse for inaction?" The youngsters were unmoved. "We won because we made them pay attention to us."

For Johnson, ghetto violence and black militancy mocked his efforts to achieve racial progress. The Civil Rights and Voting Rights Acts were essential parts of the Great Society he hoped to build. In that effort he had achieved a legislative record virtually unequaled by any other president in the nation's history. What Kennedy had promised, Johnson delivered. But the growing white backlash and the anger exploding in the nation's cities exposed serious flaws in the theory and practice of liberal reform.

 REVIEW

What were the different tactics, and where was each used in the civil rights campaigns led by CORE, SCLC, and SNCC?

HISTORIAN'S TOOLBOX

POWER TO WHICH PEOPLE?

White authorities wear coats and ties.

Despite the guns and tense atmosphere, does the black officer look generally at ease? If so, why?

What messages do the protesters' clothing, hairstyles, and gear convey?

News photographs provide journalists with both drama and answers to the basic reporters' questions: Who? What? Where? Why? But historians have ample time to analyze the details and the mixed messages. During Parents' Weekend at Cornell University in April 1969, a burning cross was erected late one night in front of Wari House, a cooperative run by black Cornell students. The next day student members of the Afro-American Society took over the student union, Willard Straight Hall, to protest what they viewed as long-standing racism on campus as well as the slow progress toward establishing a black studies program. During the 36-hour takeover, these armed students emerged from the building with members of the administration. Both consciously and unconsciously, the clothing as well as facial and body expressions send different messages about who has power and who does not in this particular situation.

Thinking Critically

Analyze this photo in terms of the following categories: age, race, gender. Is each category significant? Why would this image, set at a university, have been particularly shocking to many observers?

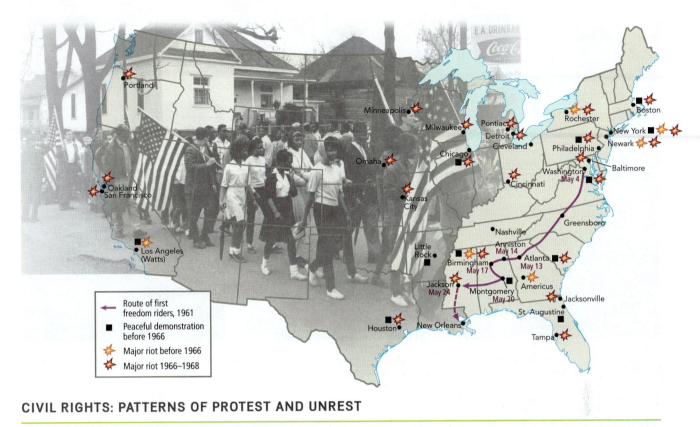

CIVIL RIGHTS: PATTERNS OF PROTEST AND UNREST

*The first phase of the civil rights movement was confined largely to the South, where the freedom riders of 1961 dramatized the issue of segregation. Beginning in the summer of 1964, urban riots brought the issue of race and politics home to the entire nation. Severe rioting followed the murder of Martin Luther King Jr. in 1968, after which the worst violence subsided. **What does this map indicate about the notion that desegregation was a problem focused on the former slave states of the South?**

LYNDON JOHNSON AND THE GREAT SOCIETY

LIKE THE STATE HE HAILED from, Lyndon Baines Johnson was in all things bigger than life. His gifts were greater, his flaws more glaring. Insecurity was his Achilles' heel and the engine that drove him. If Kennedy had been good as president, Johnson would be "the greatest of them all, the whole bunch of them." If FDR won in a landslide in 1936, Johnson would produce an even larger margin in 1964. And to anyone who displeased him, he could be ruthlessly cruel. His scatological language and preoccupation with barnyard sex amused few and offended many. Yet Johnson could not understand why so few people genuinely liked him; one courageous diplomat, when pressed, found the nerve to respond, "Because, Mr. President, you are not a very likable man."

Johnson was born in Stonewall, Texas, in the Hill Country outside Austin, where the dry climate and rough terrain only grudgingly yielded up a living. He arrived in Washington in 1932 as an ardent New Dealer who loved the political game. When he became majority leader of the Senate in 1954, he cultivated an image as a moderate conservative who knew what strings to pull or levers to jog to get the job done. On an important bill, he latched onto the undecided votes until they succumbed to the famous "Johnson treatment," a combination of arguments, threats, emotional or patriotic appeals, and enticing rewards. Florida senator George Smathers likened Johnson to "a great overpowering thunderstorm that consumed you as it closed around you."

JOHNSON'S LIBERAL FAITH Despite his compulsion to control every person and situation, Johnson possessed certain bedrock strengths. No one was better at hammering out compromises among competing interest groups. To those who served him well, he could be loyal and generous. As president, he cared sincerely about society's underdogs. His support for civil rights, aid to the poor, education, and the welfare of the elderly came from genuine conviction. Like Franklin Roosevelt, whom he deeply admired, Johnson shared the liberal belief that the government should play an active role in managing the economy in order to soften the boom-and-bust swings of capitalism. Like progressives from the turn of the century, liberals looked to improve society by applying the intelligence of "experts." Liberals had confidence, at times bordering on arrogance, that poverty could be eliminated and the good society achieved. That faith might prove naive, but during the 1960s such optimism was both infectious and energizing.

Lyndon Johnson applied the "Johnson treatment" (as shown here, in 1957, to Senator Theodore Green) whenever he wanted people to see things his way. Few could say no, as he leaned in and reminded them who dominated the situation.

The Origins of the Great Society

In the first months after the assassination, Johnson acted as the conservator of the Kennedy legacy. "Let us continue," he told a grief-stricken nation. Liberals who had dismissed Johnson as an unprincipled power broker grudgingly came to respect the energy he showed in steering the Civil Rights Act and tax-cut legislation through Congress. Kennedy's advisers believed tax cuts would create economic growth beneficial to the poor. Under Johnson, they did.

DISCOVERING POVERTY

Kennedy had come to recognize that prosperity alone would not ease the plight of America's poor. In 1962 Michael Harrington's book *The Other America* brought attention to the widespread persistence of poverty despite the nation's affluence. Harrington focused attention on the hills of Appalachia that stretched from western Pennsylvania south to Alabama. In some counties a quarter of the population survived on a diet of flour and dried-milk paste supplied by federal surplus food programs. Under Kennedy, Congress had passed a new food stamp program as well as laws designed to revive the economies of poor areas, replacing urban slums with newer housing and retraining the unemployed. Robert Kennedy also headed a presidential committee to fight juvenile delinquency in urban slums by involving the poor in **community action programs.** Direct participation, they hoped, would overcome "a sense of resignation and fatalism" that sociologist Oscar Lewis had found while studying the Puerto Rican community of New York City.

It fell to Lyndon Johnson to fight Kennedy's "War on Poverty." By August 1964 this master politician had driven through Congress the most sweeping social welfare bill since the New Deal. The Economic Opportunity Act addressed almost every major cause of poverty. It included training programs such as the Job Corps, granted loans to rural families and urban small businesses as well as aid to migrant workers, and launched a domestic version of the Peace Corps, known as VISTA (Volunteers in Service to America). Even if the price tag for these programs was high, the scale of the problems dwarfed the almost $1 billion Johnson committed to Sargent Shriver, a Kennedy brother-in-law, who directed the new Office of Economic Opportunity (OEO).

The speed Johnson demanded led inevitably to confusion, conflict, and waste. Officials at OEO often found themselves in conflict with other cabinet departments as well as with state and local officials. For example, OEO workers organized voter registration drives in order to oust corrupt city officials. Others led rent strikes to force improvements in public housing. The director of city housing in Syracuse, New York, reacted typically: "We are experiencing a class struggle in the traditional Karl Marx style in Syracuse, and I do not like it." Such battles for power and bureaucratic turf undermined federal poverty programs.

The Election of 1964

In 1964, however, before these controversies surfaced, Johnson's political stock remained high. To an audience at the University of Michigan in May, he announced his ambition to forge a "Great Society," in which poverty and racial injustice no longer existed. The chance to fulfill his dreams seemed open to him, for the Republicans nominated Senator Barry Goldwater of Arizona as their presidential candidate. Ruggedly handsome, Goldwater was a true son of the West who held a narrow view of what government should do, for he was at heart a **libertarian.** Government, he argued, should not dispense welfare, subsidize farmers, tax incomes on a progressive basis, or aid public education. At the same time, Goldwater was so anti-communist that he championed a large defense establishment.

Goldwater's extreme views allowed Johnson to portray himself as a moderate. He chose Minnesota's liberal senator Hubert Humphrey to balance the ticket. Only the candidacy of Governor George Wallace of Alabama marred Johnson's election prospects. In Democratic primaries Wallace's segregationist appeal won nearly a third or more of the votes in Wisconsin, Indiana, and Maryland—hardly the Deep South. Wallace was persuaded, however, to drop out of the race.

The election produced the landslide Johnson craved. Carrying every state except Arizona and four in the Deep South, he received 61 percent of the vote. Democrats gained better than 2-to-1 majorities in the Senate and the House. Many observers saw the election as a repudiation of Goldwater and his conservative values. In reality, his defeat opened the way for grassroots conservatives to gain control of the Republican Party.

The Great Society

In January 1965 Johnson announced a legislative vision that would extend welfare programs on a scale beyond Franklin

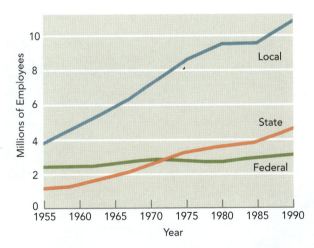

Growth of Government, 1955–1990

Government has been a major growth industry since World War II. Most people think of "big government" as federal government. But even during the Great Society, far more people worked in state and local government.

Roosevelt's New Deal. By the end of 1965, 50 bills had been passed, many of them major pieces of legislation, with more on the agenda for the following year.

PROGRAMS IN EDUCATION
As a former teacher, Johnson made education the cornerstone of his Great Society. Stronger schools would compensate the poor for their disadvantaged homes, he believed. Under the Elementary and Secondary School Act, students in low-income school districts were to receive educational equipment, money for books, and enrichment programs such as Project Head Start for nursery-school-age children.

MEDICARE AND MEDICAID
Johnson also pushed through the Medicare Act to provide the elderly with hospital health insurance. Medicare targeted the elderly, because older people used hospitals three times more than other Americans and generally had incomes only half as large. Because Medicare made no provision for the poor who were not elderly, Congress also passed a program called Medicaid. Participating states received federal matching grants to pay the medical expenses of those on welfare or too poor to afford medical care.

 IMMIGRATION REFORM
The Great Society reformed immigration policy, in ways that reflected the drastic changes in global economics and culture since the last major immigration legislation was passed in 1924. Then, the National Origins Act (see page 664) reflected the deeply Eurocentric orientation of American society and its prejudices against people of color. Virtually all the annual admissions quota of 154,000 went to Northern Europeans. Asians were barred almost entirely. By the 1960s American attitudes were changing, in terms of both race and region. American soldiers, after all, had fought wars to defend Korea, the Philippines, Vietnam, Taiwan, Japan, and other Asian nations. How could it justify discriminating against citizens from those countries?

By 1965, with Asian economies growing, the war in Vietnam expanding, and civil rights sentiments at a peak, the need for reform took on special urgency. The Immigration Act of 1965 abolished the national origins system. It increased annual admissions to 170,000 people and put a cap of 20,000 annually on immigrants from any single nation. The law gave marked preference to reuniting families of those immigrants already in the United States—so much so that some observers nicknamed it the "brothers and sisters act." Asians and Eastern Europeans were among its prime beneficiaries.

The act's liberalization was offset, however, by prejudice toward Central Americans, especially Mexicans. The National Origins Act of 1924 had placed no limit on immigrants from the Americas. But by the 1960s many in Congress feared a massive influx of workers from south of the border. Widespread poverty in Latin American nations had left thousands unemployed and desperate to find work. Hence the new act capped arrivals from the

Western Hemisphere at 120,000 annually. In that way immigration reform reflected the shifting balance of the global economy.

 THE ENVIRONMENT

A mass-consumption economy took an increasing toll on the environment. By the mid-1960s many Americans had become increasingly concerned about acrid smog from factories and automobiles; about lakes and rivers polluted by detergents, pesticides, and industrial wastes; and about the disappearance of wildlife. The woman who most forcefully focused public attention on these issues was biologist and writer Rachel Carson, who published *Silent Spring* in 1962.

More than one observer compared *Silent Spring* to older American muckraking classics: Harriet Beecher Stowe's *Uncle Tom's Cabin* and Upton Sinclair's *The Jungle.* Carson warned that "the contamination of man's total environment with such substances of incredible harm"—most significantly the persistent pesticide DDT—could "alter the very material of heredity upon which the shape of the future depends." Beyond that she challenged the popular belief that humans through science and technology could "improve on nature." The "control of nature," she wrote, was "a phrase conceived in arrogance, born of the Neanderthal age of biology and philosophy when it was supposed that nature exists for the convenience of man...."

Carson's critics dismissed her as hysterical, linking her to "the organic gardeners, the anti-fluoride leaguers, the worshippers of 'natural foods,' . . . and other pseudoscientists and faddists." But a scientific panel appointed by the Kennedy administration essentially vindicated the charges *Silent Spring* made. Equally important, Carson taught Americans to think ecologically. She showed in moving and elegant language the interconnection of living things and the means by which toxic chemicals moved through the food chain. The alarm she sounded helped to inspire a broad movement to protect the environment.

In response, Congress in 1964 passed the National Wilderness Preservation System Act to set aside 9.1 million acres of wilderness as "forever wild." Lady Bird Johnson, the president's wife, campaigned to eliminate the garish billboards and junkyards along many of the nation's roads. Congress first established pollution standards for interstate waterways and a year later provided funds for sewage treatment and water purification. Legislation also tightened standards on air pollution. Environmental reform provoked opposition from such groups as mining companies, cattle-grazers, and the timber industry, who wanted to continue using the public domain for their own purposes. But the public accepted the benefits of the new regulation.

For all he had done, Johnson wanted to do more. In 1966 he pushed through bills to raise the minimum wage, improve auto safety, aid mass transit, and develop "model cities." But opposition mounted. "Doesn't matter what kind of majority you come in with," Johnson predicted early on. "You've got just one year when they treat you right, and before they start worrying about themselves." Yet as late as 1968 Johnson pushed major legislation through Congress to ban discrimination in housing (Fair Housing Act), to build public housing, to protect consumers from unfair credit practices (Truth-in-Lending Act), and to protect scenic rivers and expand the national park system.

EVALUATING THE GREAT SOCIETY

Historians have difficulty measuring the Great Society's impact. It produced more legislation and more reforms than the New Deal. However, economic statistics suggested that general

Convinced that pesticides such as DDT posed no threat to humans, public health and agriculture officials sprayed people and land with a reckless abandon that compelled Rachel Carson to begin efforts to curb pesticide use.

D.D.T.
Powerful Insecticide
Harmless to Humans
Applied By
TODD INSECT FOG APPLICATOR

I was sentenced to the State Penitentiary by The Circuit Court of Bay County, State of Florida. The present proceeding was commenced on a petition for a Writ of Habeus Corpus To The Supreme Court of The State of Florida To vacate The sentence, on the grounds that I was made to stand Trial with out the aid of counsel, and, at all times of my incarseretion. The said Court refused To appoint counsel and therefore deprived me of Due process of law, and violate my rights in The Bill of Rights and the constitution of the United States.

Clarence Earl Gideon Petitioner

5th day of Jan 1962

Lawrence C Sueyco
Notary Public

Gideon's Letter to the Supreme Court
John F. Davis, Clerk, Supreme Court of the United States

| Clarence Earl Gideon (right) used this handwritten letter to bring his appeal to the attention of the Supreme Court. In the Gideon case, the Court ruled that even poor defendants have the right to legal counsel. Such incidents, while rare, restore faith in the idea of a government for the people.

prosperity, accelerated by the tax-cut bill, did more to fight poverty than all the OEO programs. And the inevitable scandals began to surface.

Despite such problems the Great Society established the high-water mark of interventionist government, a trend that began in the Progressive Era and flourished during the Great Depression and in World War II. Although Americans continued to pay lip service to the notion that government should remain small and interfere little in citizens' lives, no strong movement emerged to eliminate Medicare or Medicaid. Few Americans disputed the right of the government to regulate industrial pollution, or to manage the economy, and provide citizens with a safety net of benefits in sickness and in old age. In this sense, the tradition of liberalism prevailed, whatever Johnson's failings.

The Reforms of the Warren Court

Although Lyndon Johnson and the Congress left the stamp of liberalism on federal power during the decade, the third branch of government played a role that, in the long run, proved equally significant. Supreme Court chief justice Earl Warren turned what was traditionally the least activist branch of government into a center of liberal reform. His political skills, compassion, and tact had been instrumental in bringing his colleagues to a unanimous ruling on school desegregation in *Brown v. Board of Education*. Warren continued to use these skills, until his retirement in 1969, to forge a liberal coalition of justices who handed down a series of landmark decisions in broad areas of civil liberties and civil rights.

PROTECTING DUE PROCESS

In 1960 the rights of citizens accused of a crime but not yet convicted were often unclear. Those too poor to afford lawyers frequently faced trial without representation. The police and the courts seldom informed those accused of a crime of their rights under the Constitution. In a series of decisions, the Court ruled that the Fourteenth Amendment provided broad guarantees of **due process** under the law. *Gideon v. Wainwright* (1963), an appeal launched by a Florida prisoner, made it clear that all citizens were entitled to legal counsel in any case involving a possible jail sentence. In *Escobedo v. Illinois* (1964) and *Miranda v. Arizona* (1966), the Court declared that individuals detained for a crime must be informed of the charges against them, of their right to remain silent, and of their right to have an attorney present during questioning. Though these decisions applied to all citizens, they were primarily intended to benefit the poor, who were most likely to be in trouble with the law and least likely to understand their rights.

BANNING SCHOOL PRAYER

In *Engel v. Vitale* (1962), the Court issued a ruling that especially troubled conservative religious groups. The case involved a nonsectarian prayer written by the New York State Board of Regents that public school students were required to recite. Even if dissenting children could be excused, the Court ruled, they faced indirect pressure to recite the prayer. That violated the constitutional separation of church and state. The following year the Court extended the ban on school prayer to cover the reading of the Bible and the Lord's Prayer.

The Court also confronted a segregationist strategy to use libel lawsuits to intimidate newspapers reporting on the civil rights movement. Almost $300 million in libel suits had been filed by 1964, when the Supreme Court heard *New York Times v. Sullivan*. In dismissing the case, the Court established a stricter standard for libel or defamation. A plaintiff had to prove that the publisher of the statement in question knew that it was false or had acted with reckless disregard for the truth. Victory for the *Times* freed the press to report without fear of punitive lawsuits.

Other decisions promoted a more liberal social climate. In *Griswold v. Connecticut* (1964), the Warren Court overturned a nineteenth-century law banning the sale of contraceptives or providing medical advice about their use. The Court demonstrated its distaste for censorship by greatly narrowing the legal definition of obscenity. A book had to be "utterly without redeeming social value" to permit censorship. The combination of decisions reforming criminal rights, prayer, free speech, and morality angered conservatives of almost all social and political backgrounds. These issues would again become a political battleground in the 1980s and beyond.

ONE PERSON, ONE VOTE The Court's most far-reaching decision was probably one of its least controversial, though politically most sensitive. As cities and suburbs grew, few states redrew their legislative districts to reflect the change. Rural (and generally conservative) elements continued to dominate state legislatures. In *Baker v. Carr* (1962) and a series of later cases, the Court ruled that the states must apportion seats not by "land or trees or pastures" but as closely as possible by the principle of "one person, one vote."

✔ **REVIEW**

What were the major legislative achievements of Johnson's Great Society agenda?

THE COUNTERCULTURE

IN 1964 SOME 800 STUDENTS from UC Berkeley, Oberlin, and other colleges met in western Ohio to train for the voter registration campaign in the South. Protest-hardened SNCC coordinators instructed middle-class students who had grown up in peaceful white suburbs on the perils of "Mississippi Freedom Summer." The lessons were sobering. When beaten by police, the SNCC staff advised, assume the fetal position—hands protecting the neck, elbows covering the temples. That minimized injuries from nightsticks. A few days later, grim news arrived. Local police in Philadelphia, Mississippi, had already arrested a volunteer who had left two days earlier. Now he and two others were "missing." Six weeks later, searchers uncovered their

mangled bodies, bulldozed into the earthworks of a freshly finished dam. That did not stop other sobered volunteers from heading to Mississippi.

By the mid-1960s conservatives, civil rights groups, and the poor were not alone in rejecting liberal solutions. The students who returned to campus from the voter registration campaign that summer of 1964 were the shock troops of a much larger movement. Dissatisfied members of the middle class—especially the young—joined a revolt against the conventions of society and politics as usual.

Activists on the New Left and Right

SDS AND PORT HURON More than a few students had become disillusioned with the slow pace of reform. Since the "establishment"—whether it was liberal or conservative—blocked meaningful change, why not overthrow it? Tom Hayden, raised in a working-class family outside Detroit, went to college at the University of Michigan, then traveled to UC Berkeley, and soon joined civil rights workers in Mississippi. Hayden, along with Al Haber, another student at the University of Michigan, was a driving force in forming the radical Students for a Democratic Society (SDS). SDS had little sympathy with an "old left" generation of radicals who grew up in the 1930s and still debated the merits of Marxism. Action was the route to change, Hayden argued: through sit-ins, protest marches, and direct confrontation. At a meeting in Port Huron, Michigan, in 1962 the group condemned the modern bureaucratic society exemplified by the organization man of the 1950s. The Port Huron Statement called for "participatory democracy," in which large organizations run by bureaucrats would be decentralized and turned into face-to-face communities in which individual participation mattered.

THE FREE SPEECH MOVEMENT The Free Speech Movement at the University of California, Berkeley, was a case in point. To most liberals, Berkeley seemed the gem of the California state university system. Like so many other universities, it had educated a generation of GIs following World War II. But to people like Tom Hayden and the SDS, Berkeley was a bureaucratic monster, enrolling more than 30,000 students and marching them into impersonal classrooms to hear lectures from remote professors. In the fall of 1964 Berkeley declared off-limits the one small area in which political organizations had been allowed to advertise their causes. When university police tried to remove a recruiter for CORE, thousands of angry students surrounded the police car for 32 hours. Out of this protest a student named Mario Savio emerged as a spokesperson and leader.

Before traveling south to Freedom Summer in 1964, Savio had been a graduate student in philosophy. Mississippi politicized him. And not just Savio. Twelve of the 21 Freedom Summer veterans at Berkeley were

Jacob Blum was a volunteer who traveled south to be a part of Mississippi Freedom Summer. Here he puts up a voter registration poster outside Mount Zion Baptist Church in Hattiesburg, Mississippi. Many students returned to their campuses in the fall radicalized, ready to convince others to join them in finding alternatives to "the system."

These clean-cut young Americans seldom marched or demonstrated. They wanted instead to limit the power of the federal government that they believed threatened true freedom and liberty. Both Eisenhower's "middle-of-the-road Republicanism" and Kennedy's liberalism, they charged, sapped the "moral and physical strength of the nation." YAF denounced the Peace Corps as "a grand exercise in—self-denial and altruism, paid for by the American taxpayers and administered by the United Nations." Barry Goldwater embodied for YAF members the values they cherished. Although Goldwater went down to defeat, the ranks of the YAF would supply a new generation of conservative activists.

Vatican II and American Catholics

Many conservatives feared that the secular trends of modern life threatened the Christian faith as well. They worried that even the traditions of the Roman Catholic Church seemed under siege when Pope John XXIII summoned church leaders to an ecumenical council, popularly known as Vatican II. It assembled in October 1962.

ECUMENISM   Racing against the cancer that would soon fell him, Pope John bade the council deal with issues of social change engaging the world in the 1960s, including poverty, nuclear war, atheism, and birth control. He wished, as well, to bring the church hierarchy more closely in touch with lay members and with the modern world around it. By the time the council concluded in 1965 Pope John had died, having been succeeded by Pope Paul VI, and the acts of the council had transformed the church. At a superficial level, many changes seemed small, though they affected the everyday lives of Catholics. No longer was it a requirement to go without meat on "fish Fridays" or to say confession on Saturdays. More significant, during services priests would now face the congregation rather than the altar and conduct the mass in the vernacular rather than Latin. Lay members would also have a greater role in implementing the faith. In addition, Vatican II encouraged a spirit of **ecumenism,** in which Catholics would seek greater understanding with other Christians.

The changes of Vatican II energized many American Catholics and led them to embrace further reform within and without the church. Priests such as Fathers Daniel and Philip Berrigan were active in the antipoverty and antiwar movements of the era. Many female Catholics sought a larger role for women in religious life. Yet even those who did not take to the streets or the pulpit felt the effects of Vatican II.

arrested during the protest. "In our free-speech fight," Savio proclaimed, "we have come up against what may emerge as the greatest problem of our nation—depersonalized, unresponsive bureaucracy." When the university's president, Clark Kerr, threatened to expel Savio, 6,000 students took control of the administration building, stopped classes with a strike, and convinced many faculty members to join them. Kerr backed down, placing no limits on free speech on campus except those that applied to society at large. But the rebellious spirit spread to other major universities, such as Michigan, Yale, and Columbia, and then to campuses across the nation.

YOUNG AMERICANS FOR FREEDOM   Not all radicalized students on college campuses were leftists. To the conservative members of Young Americans for Freedom (YAF), those behind the Free Speech Movement at Berkeley were a motley crowd of beats, liberals, and Communists. YAF had a larger (though probably less visible) membership than leftist groups like SNCC or SDS.

DUELING DOCUMENTS

STUDENT VOICES FOR A NEW AMERICA

In 1960 students created three organizations committed to ideals of political and moral regeneration for America. The organizations were the Student Non-Violent Coordinating Committee (SNCC: see page 808), Young Americans for Freedom (YAF: see page 819), and the Students for a Democratic Society (SDS: see page 818). Each organization addressed the issue of justice but in different ways.

DOCUMENT 1   SNCC Statement of Purpose

We affirm the philosophical or religious ideal of nonviolence as the foundation of our purpose, the presupposition of our belief, and the manner of our action. Nonviolence as it grows from the Judaic-Christian tradition seeks a social order of justice permeated by love. Integration of human endeavor represents the crucial first step towards such a society.

Through nonviolence, courage displaces fear; love transcends hate. Acceptance dissipates prejudice; hope ends despair. Peace dominates war; faith reconciles doubt. Mutual regards cancel enmity. Justice for all overthrows injustice. The redemptive community supersedes systems of gross immorality.

Love is the central motif of nonviolence. Love is the force by which God binds man to Himself and man to man. Such love goes to the extreme; it remains loving and forgiving even in the midst of hostility. It matches the capacity of evil to inflict suffering with an even more enduring capacity to absorb evil, all the while persisting in love.

By appealing to conscience and standing on the moral nature of human existence, nonviolence nurtures the atmosphere in which reconciliation and justice become actual possibilities.

Adopted at Raleigh, North Carolina, April, 1960.

Source: John Lewis with Michael D'Orso, *Walking with the Wind: A Memoir of the Movement* (New York, 1998), p. 189. www.crmvet.org/docs/sncc1.htm.

DOCUMENT 2   YAF Sharon Statement

In this time of moral and political crises, it is the responsibility of the youth of America to affirm certain eternal truths.

We, as young conservatives, believe:

That foremost among the transcendent values is the individual's use of his God-given free will, whence derives his right to be free from the restrictions of arbitrary force;

That liberty is indivisible, and that political freedom cannot long exist without economic freedom;

That the purpose of government is to protect those freedoms through the preservation of internal order, the provision of national defense, and the administration of justice;

The Rise of the Counterculture

Spiritual matters also aroused secular rebels, who found their culture too materialistic and shallow. These alienated students, often from conservative backgrounds, began to grope toward spiritual, nonmaterial goals. "Turn on to the scene, tune in to what is happening, and drop out of high school, college, grad school, junior executive," advised Timothy Leary, a Harvard psychology professor who dropped out himself. People who heeded Leary's call to spiritual renewal rejected politics for a lifestyle of experimentation with music, sex, and drugs. Observers labeled their movement a "counterculture."

COMMUNES   The counterculture of the 1960s had much in common with earlier religious revival and utopian movements. It admired the quirky individualism of Henry David Thoreau, and like Thoreau, it turned to Zen Buddhism and other Oriental philosophies. Like Brook Farm and other nineteenth-century utopian communities, the new hippie communes sought perfection along the fringes of society. Communards built geodesic domes based on the designs of architect Buckminster Fuller; they "learned how to scrounge materials, tear down abandoned buildings, use the unusable," as one member of the Drop City commune put it. The introduction of the birth control pill in 1962 ushered in an era of increased sexual freedom. Young rebels embraced the new freedoms as a means to liberate them from the repressive inhibitions that distorted the lives of their "uptight" parents. Drugs appeared to open the inner mind to a higher state of consciousness or pleasure. No longer would people be bound by conventional relationships and the goals of a liberal, bourgeois society.

The early threads of the 1960s counterculture led back to the 1950s and the subculture of the beat generation (page 786). For the beats, unconventional drugs had

That when government ventures beyond these rightful functions, it accumulates power, which tends to diminish order and liberty. . . .

That we will be free only so long as the national sovereignty of the United States is secure; that history shows periods of freedom are rare, and can exist only when free citizens concertedly defend their rights against all enemies;

That the forces of international Communism are, at present, the greatest single threat to these liberties;

That the United States should stress victory over, rather than coexistence with, this menace; and

That American foreign policy must be judged by this criterion: does it serve the just interests of the United States?

Adopted in conference at Sharon, Connecticut, September 11, 1960.

Source: Young Americans for Freedom website, http://www.yaf.org/sharon_statement.aspx.

DOCUMENT 3   SDS Port Huron Statement

INTRODUCTION: AGENDA FOR A GENERATION

We are people of this generation, bred in at least modest comfort, housed now in universities, looking uncomfortably at the world we inherit. . . . Freedom and equality for each individual, government of, by, and for the people—these American values we found good, principles by which we could live as men. Many of us began maturing in complacency.

As we grew, however, our comfort was penetrated by events too troubling to dismiss. First, the permeating and victimizing fact of human degradation, symbolized by the Southern struggle against racial bigotry, compelled most of us from silence to activism. Second, the enclosing fact of the Cold War, symbolized by the presence of the Bomb, brought awareness that we ourselves, and our friends, and millions of abstract "others" we knew more directly because of our common peril, might die at any time. We might deliberately ignore, or avoid, or fail to feel all other human problems, but not these two, for these were too immediate and crushing in their impact, too challenging in the demand that we as individuals take the responsibility for encounter and resolution.

While these and other problems either directly oppressed us or rankled our consciences and became our own subjective concerns, we began to see complicated and disturbing paradoxes in our surrounding America. The declaration "all men are created equal . . ." rang hollow before the facts of Negro life in the South and the big cities of the North. The proclaimed peaceful intentions of the United States contradicted its economic and military investments in the Cold War status quo. . . .

Some would have us believe that Americans feel contentment amidst prosperity—but might it not be better called a glaze above deeply felt anxieties about their role in the new world? And if these anxieties produce a developed indifference to human affairs, do they not as well produce a yearning to believe there is an alternative to the present, that something *can* be done to change circumstances in the school, the workplaces, the bureaucracies, the government? It is to this latter yearning, at once the spark and engine of change, that we direct our present appeal. The search for truly democratic alternatives to the present, and a commitment to social experimentation with them, is a worthy and fulfilling human

enterprise, one which moves us and, we hope, others today. On such a basis do we offer this document of our convictions and analysis: as an effort in understanding and changing the conditions of humanity in the late twentieth century, an effort rooted in the ancient, still unfulfilled conception of man attaining determining influence over his circumstances of life.

Adopted at Port Huron, Michigan, June 15, 1962.

Source: Tom Hayden, *The Port Huron Statement: The Visionary Call of the 1960s Revolution* (New York, Thunder's Mouth Press, 2005), pp. 45–48 (and on the web in numerous places including http://coursesa.matrix.msu.edu/~hst306/documents/huron.html).

Thinking Critically

How would you characterize the tone of each of these statements? What evidence in each suggests that students believed the United States faced a spiritual crisis? In what ways do they disagree about the meaning of such ideals as "freedom," "justice," and "equality"?

long been a part of the scene, but now their use expanded dramatically. Professor Timothy Leary began experimenting with hallucinogenic mushrooms in Mexico and soon moved on to LSD. The drug "blew his mind," as he put it, and he became so outspoken in making converts that Harvard blew him straight out of its hallowed doors.

Whereas Leary's approach to LSD was cool and contemplative, novelist Ken Kesey *(One Flew over the Cuckoo's Nest)* embraced it with antic frenzy. His ragtag company of druggies and freaks formed the "Merry Pranksters" at Kesey's home outside San Francisco. Writer Tom Wolfe chronicled their outrageous style in *The Electric Kool-Aid Acid Test,* a book that pioneered the "New Journalism." Wolfe dropped the rules of reporting that demanded objectivity and distance by taking himself and his readers on a **psychedelic** tour with Kesey and his fellow Pranksters. Their example inspired others to drop out.

| LSD inspired the genre of psychedelic art that adorned this Grateful Dead phonograph album cover, with its freaked-out lettering that seemed to dazzle and dance even if the viewer had not inhaled or ingested hallucinogens. (The album is American Beauty.)

THE POLITICS OF DRESS

Three-piece suits, fur coats, berets, Grateful Dead T-shirts—clothing has always made a statement about the values of the wearer. In the 1950s that statement was conformity. The khaki slacks and brush-cut hair popular with middle-class boys hinted at military regimentation. Rock-and-rollers, lower-class kids, and farm boys often wore dungarees and T-shirts, perhaps with a cigarette pack tucked in the rolled-up sleeve. Beatniks advertised their nonconformity by adopting an exotic look: long hair, goatees, turtlenecks, and sandals.

During the 1960s nonconformity became the norm. The revolution began in earnest with the coming of the Beatles, four British rockers from working-class Liverpool. John, Paul, George, and Ringo hit the United States like a cultural tidal wave. Their longish hair, mod clothes, and zaniness defined a new masculine style. It was youthful rather than macho, irreverent without being overtly rebellious.

The ambiguity of this androgynous image, especially the long hair, disturbed many Americans. While traditional men thought long hair was effeminate, rock stars saw it as sexy. And in the 1960s rock stars displaced movie stars as the public figures who most defined the male image. Mick Jagger of the Rolling Stones rejected the idea that "being masculine means looking clean, close-cropped, and ugly."

New fashions represented a desire to break social constraints in favor of greater sensuality and freedom of expression. Nowhere was that more evident than in the costuming of the counterculture. Middle-class students began to let their hair grow. African American men and women found an alternative way to make long hair into a cultural statement. They gave up wavy processing or short cuts that mirrored Anglo hair and let their hair grow into full Afros. Many whites with naturally curly hair imitated the Afro look.

Fashion had become a function of politics and rebellion. Traditional Americans saw beads, long hair, sandals, drugs, radical politics, and rock and roll as elements of a revolution. To them, hippies and radicals were

The Beatles had a major impact on men's style as well as on popular music. This 1963 photo shows their "mod" look popular first in England. Later they adopted a hippie look.

equally threatening. To restore order, they tried to censor and even outlaw the trappings of the counterculture. Schools expelled boys when their hair was too long and girls when their skirts were too short. It became indecent to desecrate the flag by sewing patches of red, white, and blue on torn blue jeans. Short-haired blue-collar workers harassed long-haired hippies and antiwar protesters. The personal fashions of the youth rebellion came to symbolize a "generation gap" between the young and their elders.

In time, however, that gap narrowed. Men especially, urged on by fashion designers and advertisers, broke with past tradition. Sideburns lengthened and mustaches and beards flourished as they had not since the nineteenth century. Men began to wear jewelry, furs, perfume, psychedelic shirts, and shoulder-length hair. By

the early 1970s, commercial success, not legal repression, had signaled an end to the revolution in fashion. As formerly hostile blue-collar workers and GIs began to sport long hair and hip clothes, fashion no longer made such clear distinctions. Even middle-aged men and women donned boots, let their hair grow a bit fuller, and slipped into modified bell-bottoms. The democratic and eclectic spirit of the 1960s persisted. Informality provided Americans of both sexes with a wider choice in fashions.

Thinking Critically

Besides hairstyles and clothing, how do people use their bodies to make political or cultural statements?

The Rock Revolution

In the 1950s rock and roll defined a teen culture preoccupied with young love, cars, and adult pressures. One exception was the Kingston Trio, which in 1958 popularized folk music that appealed to young adult and college audiences. As the interest in folk music grew, the lyrics increasingly focused on social or political issues. Joan Baez helped define the folk style by dressing simply, wearing no makeup, and rejecting the commercialism of popular music. She joined folksinger Bob Dylan in the civil rights march on Washington in 1963, singing "We Shall Overcome" and "Blowin' in the Wind." Such folksingers reflected the activist side of the counterculture as they sought to provoke their audiences to political commitment.

THE BEATLES In 1964 a new sound from England exploded on the American scene. Within a year the Beatles, four musicians from Liverpool, were driving teen audiences into frenzies as they sang "I Want to Hold Your Hand." With hair that was considered long in the 1960s, modish English clothes, fresh faces, and irreverent wit, they looked and sounded like nothing young Americans had experienced before. Their boyish enthusiasm captured the Dionysian spirit of the new counterculture. But the Beatles' enormous commercial success also reflected the creativity of their music. Along with other English groups such as the Rolling Stones, the Beatles reconnected white American audiences with the rhythm-and-blues roots of rock and roll.

DYLAN Until 1965 Bob Dylan was the quintessential folk artist, writing about nuclear weapons, pollution, and racism. He appeared at concerts with longish frizzy hair, working-class clothes, an unamplified guitar, and a harmonica suspended on a wire support. But then Dylan shocked his fans by donning a black leather jacket and shifting to a "folk-rock" style featuring an electric guitar. His new songs seemed to suggest that the old America was almost beyond redemption. The Beatles, too, transformed themselves. After a pilgrimage to India to study transcendental meditation, they returned to produce *Sergeant Pepper's Lonely Hearts Club Band,* possibly the most influential album of the decade. It blended sound effects with music, alluded to trips taken with "Lucy in the Sky with Diamonds" (LSD), and welcomed the listener into a turned-on world. In San Francisco, bands such as the Grateful Dead pioneered "acid rock" with long pieces aimed at echoing drug-induced states of mind.

SOUL MUSIC The debt of white rock musicians to rhythm and blues led to increased integration in the music world. Before the 1960s, black rhythm-and-blues bands had played primarily to black audiences, in segregated clubs, or over black radio stations. The civil rights movement and a rising black social and political consciousness gave rise to "soul" music. One black disc jockey described soul as "the last to be hired, first to be fired, brown all year round, sit-in-the-back-of-the-bus feeling." Soul was the quality that expressed black pride and separatism. Out of Detroit came the "Motown sound," which combined elements of gospel, blues, and big band jazz. Diana Ross and the Supremes, the Temptations, Stevie Wonder, and other groups under contract to Berry Gordy's Motown Record Company appealed to black and white audiences alike. Yet, although soul music promoted black consciousness, it offered little by way of social commentary. It evoked the traditional blues themes of workday woes, unhappy marriages, and the troubles between men and women.

The West Coast Scene

For all its themes of alienation, rebellion, and utopian quest, the counterculture also signaled the increasing importance of the West Coast in defining American popular culture. In the 1950s the shift of television production from the stages of New York to the film lots of Hollywood helped establish Los Angeles as a communications center. San Francisco became notorious as a home of the beat movement. And then in 1958 the unthinkable happened: the Brooklyn Dodgers and the New York Giants baseball teams fled the Big Apple for Los Angeles and San Francisco. By 1963 the "surfing sound" of West Coast rock groups such as the Beach Boys and Jan and Dean had made Southern California's preoccupation with surfing and cars into a national fad.

THE FIRST BE-IN Before 1967 Americans were only vaguely aware of another West Coast phenomenon, the hippies. But in January a loose coalition of drug freaks, Zen cultists, and political activists banded together to hold the first well-publicized Be-In. The beat poet Allen Ginsberg was on hand to offer spiritual guidance. The Grateful Dead and Jefferson Airplane, acid rock groups based in San Francisco, provided entertainment. A mysterious group called the Diggers somehow managed to supply free food and drink, while the notorious Hell's Angels motorcycle gang policed the occasion. Drugs of all kinds were plentiful. And a crowd attired in a bizarre mix of Native American, circus, Oriental, army surplus, and other costumes came to enjoy it all.

The West Coast had long been a magnet for Americans seeking opportunity, escape, and alternative lifestyles; now the San Francisco Bay Area staked its claim as the spiritual center of the counterculture. Politically conscious dropouts gravitated toward Berkeley; the apolitical "flower children" moved into Haight-Ashbury, a run-down San Francisco neighborhood of apartments, Victorian houses, and "head shops" selling drug paraphernalia, wall posters, Indian bedspreads, and other eccentric accessories. Similar dropout communities and communes sprang up across the country. Colleges became centers of hip culture, offering alternative courses, eliminating strict requirements, and tolerating the new sexual mores of their students.

In the summer of 1969 all the positive forces of the counterculture converged on Bethel, New York, in the Catskill Mountains resort area, to celebrate the promise of peace, love, and freedom. The Woodstock Music Festival attracted 400,000 people to the largest rock concert ever organized. For one long weekend the audience and performers joined to form an ephemeral community based on sex, drugs, and rock and roll. But even then, the counterculture was dying. Violence intruded on the laid-back urban communities that hippies had formed. Organized crime and drug pushers muscled in on the lucrative trade in LSD, amphetamines, and marijuana. Bad drugs and addiction took their toll. Urban slum dwellers turned hostile to the strange middle-class dropouts who, in ways the poor could not fathom, found poverty ennobling. Free sex often became an excuse for rape, exploitation, and loveless gratification.

Much that had once seemed outrageous in the hippie world was readily absorbed into the marketplace. Advertisers were in the forefront of promoting a "hip" style. Rock groups became big business enterprises commanding huge fees. Slick concerts with expensive tickets replaced communal dances with psychedelic light shows. Yogurt, granola, and herbal teas appeared on supermarket shelves. Ironically, much of the world that hippies embraced was generated by the society they had rejected.

 REVIEW

How did the movements of the counterculture develop both politically and socially?

| Some 400,000 people converged on the Woodstock Music Festival in the summer of 1969. These two came with their psychedelic VW Microbus.

CONCLUSION

THE WORLD AT LARGE

By the late 1960s most dreams of human betterment seemed shattered—whether those dreams emanated from the promise of the march on Washington, Lyndon Johnson's Great Society, or the communal society of the hippie counterculture. Recession and inflation brought an end to the easy affluence that made liberal reform programs and alternative lifestyles seem so easily affordable. Poverty and unemployment menaced even middle-class youth who had found havens in communes, colleges, and graduate schools. Racial tensions divided black militants and the white liberals of the civil rights movement into sometimes hostile camps.

But the civil rights movement changed the United States in fundamental ways. Although de facto segregation and racism remained entwined in American life, segregation as a legal system had been overturned. No longer was it enshrined by the decisions of the highest court in the land, as it had been in *Plessy v. Ferguson*. And the rise of black power—in both its moderate and radical forms—reflected a political and cultural current that was international as well as national. Catholics in Northern Ireland, for example, discovered in the civil rights struggle a window into their own status as second-class citizens. In Africa the drive for civil rights revolved around the effort to overthrow the imperial powers of Europe. In colony after colony, African nationalists fought for their independence, with Ghana leading the way in 1957. Too often the new governments devolved into dictatorships; and in South Africa the white regime maintained a system of *apartheid* that strictly segregated the races and smothered black political and economic progress. But colonial empires continued to fall across the globe.

The United States granted independence to its principal Asian colony, the Philippines, in 1946. Yet Americans, too, found themselves ensnared by the conflicts of colonialism. More than any other single factor, a growing war in France's former colony, Vietnam, destroyed the promise of Lyndon Johnson's Great Society and distracted from the campaign for civil rights. After 1965 the nation divided sharply as the American military role in Southeast Asia grew. Radicals on the left looked to rid America of a capitalist system that promoted race and class conflict at home and imperialism and military adventurism abroad. Conservatives who supported the war called for a return to traditional values like law and order. Both the left and the right attacked the liberal center. Their combined opposition helped undermine the consensus Lyndon Johnson had worked so hard to build. ∞∞∞∞

CHAPTER SUMMARY

LARGELY EXCLUDED FROM THE PROSPERITY of the 1950s, African Americans and Latinos undertook a series of grassroots efforts to gain the legal and social freedoms denied them by racism and, in the South, by an entrenched system of segregation.

- Early postwar campaigns focused on legal challenges to the system, culminating with victories in the Supreme Court decisions of *Brown v. Board of Education* and *Hernández v. Texas*.

- Later in the 1950s Martin Luther King Jr. and other civil rights activists used new techniques of protest, such as the boycott, to desegregate the bus system in Montgomery, Alabama.

- Continued resistance by white southerners sparked a school integration dispute in Little Rock, Arkansas.

- Beginning in 1960 widespread grassroots efforts from African American churches, students, and political groups across the South accelerated the drive for an end to segregation.

- Violence against sit-ins, freedom rides, voter registration drives, and other forms of nonviolent protest made the nation sympathetic to the civil rights cause.

- In the wake of the assassination of President Kennedy, Lyndon Johnson persuaded Congress to adopt the Civil Rights Act of 1964 and the Voting Rights Act of 1965.

- The Supreme Court under Chief Justice Earl Warren expanded civil rights and liberties through its *Gideon, Escobedo,* and *Miranda* decisions, while also easing censorship, banning school prayer, and increasing voting rights.

- Lyndon Johnson delivered on the liberal promise of his Great Society through his 1964 tax cut, aid to education, Medicare and Medicaid, wilderness preservation, and urban redevelopment, and through the many programs of his War on Poverty.

- Johnson's liberal reforms did not satisfy student radicals, minority dissidents, gays, and the counterculture whose members sought to transform America into a more just and less materialistic society.

ADDITIONAL READING

STEVEN LAWSON, CHARLES PAYNE, AND James Patterson provide an excellent overview in *Debating the Civil Rights Movement, 1945–1968* (2006). An older, still effective survey is Robert Weisbrot, *Freedom Bound: A History of America's Civil Rights Movement* (1990). Though exhaustive in detail (nearly 3,000 pages in all), Taylor Branch's three-volume biography of Martin Luther King Jr. is superb: *Parting the Waters, America in the King Years, 1954–63* (1988); *Pillar of Fire: America in the King Years, 1963–65* (1998); and *At the Edge of Canaan: America in the King Years, 1965–68* (2006). Given the importance of leaders such as King, the prominent role of women is sometimes underrepresented. As a corrective, see Bettye Collier-Thomas and V. P. Franklin, eds., *Sisters in the Struggle: African-American Women in the Civil Rights–Black Power Movements* (2001). Latino civil rights movements are covered in Henry A. J. Ramos, *American G.I. Forum* (1998), and F. Arturo Rosales, *Chicano! The History of the Mexican-American Civil Rights Movement* (1997).

Todd Gitlin, *The Sixties* (1987), set the early tone for books that are part history and part memoir. Terry Anderson, *The Movement and the Sixties* (1995), offers a view that is both politically engaged and scholarly. For a narrative history of the era, see Mark Hamilton Lytle, *America's Uncivil Wars: The Sixties Era from Elvis to the Fall of Richard Nixon* (2006). Robert Dallek, *An Unfinished Life: John F. Kennedy, 1917–1963* (2003), draws a portrait that balances Kennedy's virtues and vices. The best recent biography of Lyndon Johnson is Randall Woods, *LBJ: Architect of Ambition* (2006).

For a fuller list of readings, see the Bibliography at www.mhhe.com/eh8e.

SIGNIFICANT EVENTS

1954
Hernández v. Texas; Brown v. Board of Education

1955
Montgomery bus boycott begun

1957
Little Rock crisis

1960
Greensboro sit-ins

1961
CORE freedom rides begin

1962
James Meredith desegregates University of Mississippi; *Engel v. Vitale; Baker v. Carr*

1963
March on Washington; *Gideon v. Wainwright;* Kennedy assassinated

1964
Escobedo v. Illinois; Griswold v. Connecticut; Civil Rights Act passed; Economic Opportunity Act; Wilderness Preservation System Act; Johnson defeats Goldwater; Berkeley Free Speech Movement; Beatles introduce British rock

1965
Johnson launches the Great Society; Voting Rights Act; Watts riots; Malcolm X assassinated; Medicare and Medicaid Acts

1967
Black Panthers battle Oakland, California, police; first Be-In

1969
Woodstock Music Festival

The Warren Court: Critical Decisions in an Era of Upheaval

CIVIL RIGHTS AND VOTING RIGHTS

1954 *Brown v. Board of Education of Topeka, Kansas*
Reversed *Plessy v. Ferguson* (1896) and the doctrine of "separate but equal"; ordered lower courts to admit African American students to public schools without discrimination and "with all deliberate speed."

1954 *Hernandez v. Texas*
Ruled that the Fourteenth Amendment's equal protection clause extended to other racial groups besides African Americans.

1962 *Baker v. Carr*
Declared that states must base legislative districts on the principle of "one person, one vote," forcing nearly every state to redraw district lines and increasing the political power of previously underrepresented metropolitan areas.

FREE SPEECH AND CENSORSHIP

1962 *Engel v. Vitali*
Banned school prayer: "It is no part of the business of government to compose official prayers to be recited as part of a religious program carried on by government."

1964 *New York Times v. Sullivan*
Increased protection of freedom of the press; protected newspaper reporting on civil rights campaigns in the South from the threat of libel suits by requiring a strict standard of proving "actual malice." A publisher had to know that a statement was false or had to act in reckless disregard of its truth or falsity.

1964 *Griswold v. Connecticut*
Ruled that a Connecticut law banning the use of contraceptives was unconstitutional because the Constitution protected a citizen's right to privacy.

RIGHTS OF THE ACCUSED

1963 *Gideon v. Wainwright*
Established that defendants have the right to legal counsel in cases that involve a potential jail sentence.

1964 *Escobedo v. Illinois*
Extended its decision in Gideon by ruling that, under the Sixth Amendment, a suspect had the right to an attorney during police questioning.

1966 *Miranda v. Arizona*
Held that statements by a defendant in police custody would be admissible at trial only if the prosecution showed that the defendant was informed of the right to consult with an attorney before and during questioning and of the right against self-incrimination but "waived," or gave up, that right.

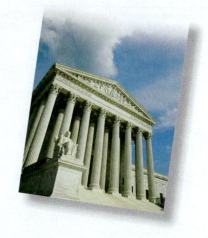

In Vietnam, helicopters gave infantry unusual mobility—a critical element in a war with no real front line, because troops could be quickly carried from one battle to another. Tim Page, who snapped this photo, described the chaos of such warfare: "On the ground it's always confusion, dust, smoke, unfamiliar territory wet or dry. Everyone seems to mill around in mad ant-like patterns waiting for the seething to calm down; maybe it will, maybe it won't, and when it's hot, it's very hot."

The Vietnam Era

1963–1975

What's to Come

∞∞∞ AN AMERICAN STORY ∞∞∞

WHO IS THE ENEMY?

Vietnam from afar: it looked like an emerald paradise. Thomas Bird, an army rifleman sent there in 1965, recalled his first impression: "A beautiful white beach with thick jungle background. The only thing missing was naked women running down the beach, waving and shouting 'Hello, hello, hello.'" Upon landing, Bird and his buddies were each issued a "Nine-Rule" card outlining proper behavior toward the Vietnamese. "Treat the women with respect, we are guests in this country and here to help these people."

But who were they helping and who were they fighting? When American troops searched out Vietcong forces, the VC generally disappeared into the jungle beyond the villages and rice fields. When rifleman John Muir walked into a hamlet, the place looked ordinary, but the Korean lieutenant with him had been in Vietnam a while. "We have a little old lady and a little old man and two very small children," he pointed out. "According to them, the rest of the family has been spirited away. . . . So there's only four of them, and they have a pot of rice that's big enough to feed 50 people. And rice, once it's cooked, will not keep. They gotta be feeding the VC." Muir watched in disbelief as the lieutenant set the house on fire. The roof "started cooking off ammunition, because all through the thatch they had ammunition stored."

GIs soon learned to walk down jungle trails with a cautious shuffle, looking for a wire or a piece of vine that seemed too straight. "We took more casualties from booby traps than we did from actual combat," recalled David Ross, a medic. "It was very frustrating because how do you fight back against a booby trap? You're just walking along and all of a sudden your buddy doesn't have a leg. Or you don't have a leg." Yet somehow the villagers would walk the same paths and never get hurt. Who was the enemy and who the friend?

| Death at Kent State

The same question was being asked half a globe away, on the campus of Kent State University on May 4, 1970. By then the American phase of the Vietnam War had dragged on for more than five years, driving President Lyndon Johnson from office and embroiling his successor, Richard Nixon, in controversy. When Nixon expanded the war beyond Vietnam into Cambodia, opposition to the war had become so intense in this normally apolitical community near Akron, Ohio, that 300 angry students spilled into the nearby town, smashed shop windows, and returned to campus to burn down an old army ROTC building. Governor James Rhodes ordered in 750 of the National Guard. Student dissidents were the "worst type of people we harbor in America," he announced. "We are going to eradicate the problem."

When demonstrators assembled for a rally on the college commons, the Guard ordered them to disperse. The protesters stood their ground. So the guardsmen advanced, wearing full battle gear and armed with M-1 rifles, whose high-velocity bullets had a horizontal range of almost two miles. Some students scattered; a few picked up rocks and threw them. The guardsmen suddenly fired into the crowd, many of whom were students passing back and forth from classes. Incredulous, a young woman knelt over Jeffrey Miller; he was dead. In addition, three other students had been killed and nine more wounded, some caught innocently by the Guard's fire.

As news of the killings swept the nation, antiwar protesters at Jackson State, a black college in Mississippi, seized a women's dormitory. State police surrounding the building opened fire without provocation, killing two more students and wounding a dozen. In both incidents the demonstrators had been unarmed. The events at Kent State and Jackson State turned sporadic protests against the American invasion of Cambodia into a nationwide student strike. Many students believed the forces of law and order sworn to protect them had betrayed the ideals of the United States.

Not since the Civil War had the nation been so deeply divided. As the war dragged on, debate moved off college campuses and into the homes of middle-class Americans, where sons went off to fight and the war came home each night on the evening news. As no other war had, Vietnam seemed to stand the nation on its head. When American soldiers shot at Vietnamese "hostiles," who could not always be separated from "friendlies," or when National Guardsmen fired on their neighbors across a college green, who were the enemies and who were the friends? ∞∞∞

The Road to Vietnam

For several thousand years Vietnam had struggled periodically to fight off foreign invasions. Buddhist culture had penetrated eastward from India. More often Indochina faced invasion and rule by the Chinese from the north. After 1856 the French entered as a colonial power, bringing with them a strong Catholic tradition.

HO CHI MINH   Ho Chi Minh, a Vietnamese nationalist, hoped to free his people of French as well as Chinese domination. Since the end of World War I, he had struggled to create an independent Vietnam. After World War II, he organized a guerrilla war against the French, which finally led to their defeat at Dien Bien Phu in 1954 (see page 787). He agreed at the Geneva Peace Conference to withdraw his forces north of the 17th parallel in return for a promise to hold free elections in both the North and the South. The Americans, having supported the French struggle against Ho, helped install Ngo Dinh Diem in South Vietnam. They then supported Diem's decision not to hold elections, which Ho's followers seemed sure to win. Frustrated South Vietnamese Communists—the Vietcong—renewed their guerrilla war. "I think the Americans greatly underestimate the determination of the Vietnamese people," Ho remarked in 1962, as President Kennedy was committing more American advisers to South Vietnam.

Lyndon Johnson's War

THE DOMINO THEORY   For Kennedy, Vietnam had been just one of many anticommunist skirmishes his activist advisers wanted to fight. As attention focused increasingly on Vietnam, he came to discount President Eisenhower's "domino theory" that if Diem's pro-Western government fell to the Communists, the other nations of Southeast Asia would collapse one after the other. Still, he saw a Communist victory as unacceptable. But what to do? Even 16,000 American "advisers" had been unable to help the unpopular Diem, who was executed after a military coup in November 1963, which had the tacit support of the United States. When Kennedy was assassinated a few weeks later, Lyndon Johnson assumed the burden of Vietnam.

Johnson's political instincts told him to keep the Vietnam War at arm's length. He felt like a catfish, he remarked, who had "just grabbed a big juicy worm with a right sharp hook in the middle of it." Johnson's heart was in his Great Society programs. Yet the political heat Democrats endured after the fall of China to the Communists during the Truman years and the long-stalemated Korean War taught Johnson lessons he never forgot. The political costs of defeat in Vietnam were unacceptable. That conviction led him steadily toward deeper American involvement.

Until August 1964, American advisers had focused on training and supporting the South Vietnamese army, which fought the Vietcong reluctantly. North Vietnam, for its part, infiltrated men and supplies along the Ho Chi Minh Trail, a network of jungle routes threading through Laos and Cambodia into the highlands of South Vietnam. With the Vietcong controlling some 40 percent of South Vietnam, Johnson strategists decided to relieve the South by increasing pressure on North Vietnam itself.

TONKIN GULF INCIDENT   American ships patrolling the Gulf of Tonkin began supporting secret South Vietnamese raids against the North. On August 2, three North Vietnamese patrol boats exchanged fire with the American destroyer *Maddox*. Two nights later, in inky blackness and a heavy thunderstorm, a second incident occurred. But a follow-up investigation could not determine whether enemy ships had even been near the scene. President Johnson was not pleased. "For all I know our navy might have been shooting at whales out there," he remarked privately.

Whatever his doubts, the president publicized both incidents as "open aggression on the high sea" and ordered retaliatory air raids on North Vietnam. He did not disclose that the navy and South Vietnamese forces had been conducting secret military operations. When Johnson then asked for the authority to take "all necessary measures" to "repel any armed attack" on American forces and to "prevent future aggression," Congress overwhelmingly passed what became known as the Tonkin Gulf Resolution.

Nguyen Ai Quoc, who became Ho Chi Minh, once worked at London's posh Carlton Hotel in the pastry kitchen of the renowned chef Escoffier. But he was soon swept up in socialist and nationalist politics, appearing at the Versailles Peace Conference (left) to plead for an independent Vietnam. Ho spent a lifetime in anticolonialist and revolutionary activity and became a revered leader of his people (right). He died in 1969, six years before his dream of a united Vietnam became a reality.

THE WAR IN VIETNAM

For the United States, one strategic problem was to locate and destroy the supply routes known as the Ho Chi Minh Trail. Rugged mountains and triple canopy jungles hid much of the trail from aerial observation and attack. **How many nations does the Ho Chi Minh Trail pass through? How would this pose problems for the United States?**

Senator Ernest Gruening of Alaska, one of only two lawmakers to vote no, objected that the resolution gave the president "a blank check" to declare war, a power the Constitution reserved to Congress. Johnson insisted that he had limited goals. But with his overwhelming victory in the 1964 election, the president felt free to exploit the powers the resolution gave him.

Rolling Thunder

ESCALATION In January 1965 Johnson received a disturbing memorandum from two top advisers. "Both of us are now pretty well convinced that our present policy can lead only to disastrous defeat," they said. The United States should either increase its attack—*escalate* was the term coined in 1965—or simply withdraw. In theory *escalation* would increase military pressure to the point at which further resistance would cost more than the enemy was willing to pay. By taking gradual steps, the United States would demonstrate its resolve to win while leaving the door open to negotiations.

Escalation did not work well in practice. Instead, it hardened the resolve of the Vietcong and North Vietnamese. When a Vietcong mortar attack in February killed seven marines stationed at Pleiku air base, Johnson ordered U.S. planes to begin bombing North Vietnam.

AIR STRIKES Restricted air strikes did not satisfy more-hawkish leaders. Retired Air Force chief of staff Curtis LeMay complained, "We are swatting flies when we should be going after the whole manure pile." In March Johnson ordered Operation Rolling Thunder, a systematic bombing campaign aimed at bolstering confidence in South

The Vietcong often fought in small groups, using the dense vegetation to cover their movements. These suspects faced an arduous interrogation as U.S. soldiers tried to learn more about the location of Vietcong units.

Vietnam and cutting the flow of supplies from the North. Rolling Thunder achieved none of its goals. American pilots could seldom spot the Ho Chi Minh Trail under its dense jungle canopy. Equally discouraging, South Vietnamese leaders quarreled among themselves and jockeyed for power instead of uniting against the Vietcong.

Once the Americans established bases from which to launch the new air strikes, these too became targets for guerrilla attacks. General William Westmoreland, the chief of American military operations in Vietnam, requested combat troops to defend the bases. Johnson's decision to send 3,500 marines proved to be a crucial first step toward Americanizing the war. Another 40,000 soldiers arrived in May and 50,000 more by July.

Defense Secretary McNamara ordered that the escalation be carried out in a "low-keyed manner to avoid undue concern and excitement in the Congress and in domestic public opinion." He worried also about how China and Russia might react. By 1966 almost 185,000 American troops had landed—and the call for more continued. In 1968, at the height of the war, 536,000 American troops were being supported with helicopters, jet aircraft, and other advanced military technologies. This was "escalation" with a vengeance.

> ✓ **REVIEW**
>
> How did Lyndon Johnson justify escalating the war in Vietnam, and what strategies did the United States use in doing so?

SOCIAL CONSEQUENCES OF THE WAR

THE IMPACT OF THE WAR was greatest on the baby-boom generation of the 1950s. As these young people came of age, draft calls for the armed services were rising. At the same time, the civil rights movement and the growing counterculture were encouraging students to question the goals of establishment America. Whether they fought in Vietnam or protested at home, supported the government or demonstrated against it, eventually these baby boomers—as well as Americans of all ages—were forced to take a stand on Vietnam.

The Soldiers' War

EFFECTS OF THE DRAFT

Most Americans sent to Vietnam were drafted. Under the Selective Service System, as it was called, privileged young people could avoid service: college students or those working in "critical" occupations, such as teachers and engineers. As the war escalated, the draft was changed so that some students were called up through a lottery system. Still, those who knew the medical requirements might produce a doctor's affidavit certifying a weak knee, flat feet, or bad eyes—all grounds for flunking the physical. Of the 1,200 men in Harvard's class of 1970, only 56 served in the military, and only 2 of them in Vietnam.

The poorest and least educated were also likely to escape service, because the Armed Forces Qualification Test and the physical often screened them out. Thus the sons of blue-collar America were most likely to accept

Uncle Sam's letter of induction. Once in uniform, Hispanic and black Americans who had fewer skills were more often assigned to combat duty. The draft also made it a relatively young man's war. The average age of soldiers serving in Vietnam was 19, compared with an average of 26 for World War II.

BODY COUNTS Most American infantry came to Vietnam ready and willing to fight. But physical and psychological hardships took their toll. An American search-and-destroy mission would fight its way into a Communist-controlled hamlet, clear and burn it, and move on—only to be ordered back days or weeks later because the enemy had moved in again. Since success could not be measured in territory gained, the measure became the "body count": the number of Vietcong killed. Unable to tell who was friendly and who was hostile, GIs sometimes took out their frustrations on innocent civilians. Officers counted those victims as Vietcong in order to inflate the numbers that suggested their tactics were working.

Before and After

The devastating effects of American bombing and use of defoliants such as Agent Orange on the Vietnamese countryside.

THE AIR WAR AND AGENT ORANGE Most Americans assumed that superior military technology could guarantee success. But technology alone could not tell friend from foe. Since the Vietcong routinely mixed with the civilian population, the chances for deadly error increased. Bombs of napalm (jellied gasoline) and white phosphorus rained liquid fire from the skies, coating everything from village huts to the flesh of fleeing humans. Since the enemy could hide in the jungle, the Americans made war on its vegetation. American planes spread more than 100 million pounds of defoliants, including Agent Orange that destroyed more than one-third of South Vietnam's timberlands—an area approximately the size of the state of Massachusetts. The long-term health and ecological effects were severe; the military benefits minimal.

By 1967 the war cost more than $2 billion a month. To fight it, the United States dropped more bombs on Vietnam than it had during all of World War II. After one air attack on an enemy village, American troops walked into the smoldering ruins. "We had to destroy the town in order to save it," an officer explained. As the human and material costs of the war increased, that statement stuck in the minds of many observers. What sense was there in a war that saved people by destroying their homes?

The War at Home

As the war dragged on, such questions provoked anguished debate among Americans, especially on college campuses. Faculty members held "teach-ins" to explain the issues to concerned students. Scholars familiar with Southeast Asia questioned every major assumption the president used to justify escalation. The United States and South Vietnam had brought on the war, they charged, by violating the Geneva Accords of 1954. The war was a civil war among the Vietnamese, not an effort by Soviet or Chinese Communists to conquer Southeast Asia, as Eisenhower, Kennedy, and Johnson had claimed. Moreover, the Vietcong, as an indigenous rebel force, had legitimate grievances against Saigon's corrupt government.

HAWKS AND DOVES By 1966 national leaders had divided into opposing camps of **"hawks"** and **"doves."** The hawks argued that America must win in Vietnam to save Southeast Asia from communism, to preserve the nation's prestige, and to protect the lives of American soldiers fighting the war. Most Americans supported those views. The doves were nonetheless a prominent minority. African Americans as a group were far less likely than white Americans to support the war. Some resented the diversion of resources from the cities to the war effort. Many black Americans' heightened sense of racial consciousness led them to identify with the Vietnamese people. Martin Luther King Jr., SNCC, and CORE all opposed the war. Heavyweight boxing champion Muhammad Ali, a black Muslim, refused on religious grounds to serve in the army, even though the decision cost him his title.

By 1967 crowds of college students and faculty expressed their outrage: "Hey, hey, LBJ, how many kids have you killed today?" Over 300,000 people demonstrated in April 1967 in New York City. Some college protesters burned their draft cards in defiance of federal law. In the fall more violent protests erupted as antiwar radicals stormed a draft induction center in Oakland, California. The next day 55,000 protesters ringed the Pentagon in Washington. Again, mass arrests followed.

As protests flared, key moderates became increasingly convinced the United States could not win the war. Senator William Fulbright of Arkansas was among them. Having helped President Johnson push the Tonkin Gulf Resolution through the Senate, Fulbright now held hearings sharply critical of American policy.

MCNAMARA LOSES FAITH Defense Secretary Robert McNamara became the most dramatic defector. For years the statistically minded secretary struggled to quantify the success of the war effort. By 1967 McNamara had become skeptical. If Americans had killed 300,000 Vietnamese, enemy forces should be shrinking. Instead, intelligence estimates indicated that North Vietnamese infiltration had risen from 35,000 a year in 1965 to 150,000 in 1967. McNamara came to have deep moral qualms about continuing the war indefinitely. "The picture of the world's greatest superpower killing or seriously injuring 1,000 noncombatants a week, while trying to pound a tiny, backward nation into submission on an issue whose merits are hotly disputed, is not a pretty one," he advised. With Johnson, who did not want to be remembered as the first American leader who lost a war, continuing to side with the hawks, McNamara resigned.

INFLATION The soaring cost of the war fueled a rising inflation. Medicare, education, housing, and other Great Society programs raised the domestic budget

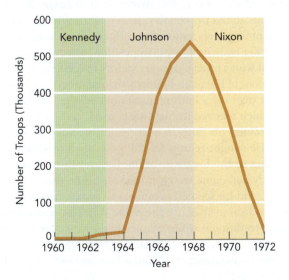

Number of U.S. Troops (Thousands)

The graph suggests one reason why protest against the war increased after 1964, peaked by 1968, and largely ended after 1972.

sharply too. Through it all Johnson refused to raise taxes, even though wages and prices rose rapidly. From 1965 to 1970, inflation jumped from about 2 percent to around 4 percent. The economy was headed for trouble.

REVIEW

How did conditions in Vietnam make it difficult for American soldiers to fight the war, and how did conditions at home lead to dissent over the war?

THE UNRAVELING

ALMOST ALL THE FORCES DIVIDING America seemed to converge in 1968. Until January of that year, most Americans had reason to believe General Westmoreland's estimate of the war. There was, he suggested, "light at the end of the tunnel." Johnson and his advisers, whatever their private doubts, in public painted an optimistic picture. With such hope radiating from Washington, few Americans were prepared for the events of the night of January 30, 1968.

Tet Offensive

As the South Vietnamese began their celebration of Tet, the Vietnamese lunar New Year, Vietcong guerrillas launched a series of concerted attacks. They assaulted Saigon's major airport, the South Vietnamese presidential palace, and Hue, the ancient Vietnamese imperial capital. Most unnerving to Americans, 19 Vietcong commandos blasted a hole in the American embassy compound in Saigon and stormed in. They fought in the courtyard until all 19 lay dead. One reporter, stunned by the carnage, compared the courtyard to a butcher shop.

Tet must rank as one of the great American intelligence failures, on a par with the failure to anticipate Japan's attack on Pearl Harbor or China's intervention in the Korean War. For nearly half a year the North Vietnamese had lured American troops away from Vietnam's cities into pitched battles at remote outposts. As American forces dispersed, the Vietcong infiltrated major population centers. A few audacious VC, disguised as South Vietnamese soldiers, even hitched rides on American jeeps and trucks. Though surprised by the Tet Offensive, American and South Vietnamese troops repulsed most of the assaults. General Westmoreland announced that the Vietcong's "well-laid plans went afoul."

MILITARY SUCCESS AND THE "CREDIBILITY GAP" In a narrow military sense, Westmoreland was right. The enemy had been driven back, sustaining perhaps 40,000 deaths. Only 1,100 American and 2,300 South Vietnamese soldiers had been killed. But Americans at home received quite another message. Tet created a "credibility gap" between the administration's optimistic reports and the war's harsh reality. The president had repeatedly claimed that the Vietcong were on their last legs. Yet as Ho

Chi Minh had coolly informed the French after World War II: "You can kill ten of my men for every one I kill of yours . . . even at those odds, you will lose and I will win." Respected CBS news anchor Walter Cronkite drew a gloomy lesson of Tet for his national audience: "To say that we are mired in stalemate seems the only realistic, yet unsatisfactory, conclusion."

STALEMATE The Tet offensive sobered Lyndon Johnson as well as his new secretary of defense, Clark Clifford. Clifford was a Johnson loyalist and a believer in the war. But as he reviewed the American position in Vietnam, the Joint Chiefs of Staff, who had requested an additional 206,000 troops, offered no satisfactory answers to his questions. "How long would it take to succeed in Vietnam?" Clifford recalled asking them:

> They didn't know. How many more troops would it take? They couldn't say. Were two hundred thousand the answer? They weren't sure. Might they need more? Yes, they might need more. Could the enemy build up [their own troop strength] in exchange? Probably. So what was the plan to win the war? Well, the only plan was that attrition would wear out the Communists, and they would have had enough. Was there any indication that we've reached that point? No, there wasn't.

Clifford decided to build a case for de-escalation. He formed a panel of "wise men," respected pillars of the cold war establishment who concluded the war could not be won. Johnson should thus seek a negotiated settlement.

"CLEAN FOR GENE" Meanwhile, the antiwar forces had found a political champion in Senator Eugene McCarthy from Wisconsin. McCarthy was something of a maverick, who wrote poetry in his spare time. He announced that no matter how long the odds, he intended to challenge Lyndon Johnson in the 1968 Democratic primaries. Idealistic college students got haircuts and shaves in order to look "clean for Gene" as they campaigned for McCarthy in New Hampshire. Johnson won the

| Despite the liberal achievements of the Great Society, antiwar protestors vilified Lyndon Johnson.

primary, but his margin was so slim (300 votes) that it amounted to a defeat. To the anger of McCarthy supporters, Robert Kennedy, John Kennedy's younger brother, announced his own antiwar candidacy.

LBJ WITHDRAWS "I've got to get me a peace proposal," the beleaguered president told Clifford. White House speechwriters put together an announcement that bombing raids against North Vietnam would be halted, at least partially, in hopes that peace talks could begin. They were still trying to write an ending when Johnson told them, "Don't worry; I may have a little ending of my own." On March 31 he supplied it, announcing: "I have concluded that I should not permit the presidency to become involved in the partisan divisions that are developing in this political year. . . . Accordingly I shall not seek, and I will not accept, the nomination of my party for another term as your president."

The announcement shocked nearly everyone. The Vietnam War had pulled down one of the savviest, most effective politicians of the era. North Vietnam responded to the speech by sending delegates to a peace conference in Paris, where negotiations quickly bogged down. And American attention soon focused on the chaotic situation at home, where all the discontent and violence of the 1960s seemed to be coming together.

The Shocks of 1968

KING AND KENNEDY ASSASSINATED On April 4, Martin Luther King Jr. traveled to Memphis to support striking sanitation workers. He was relaxing on the balcony of his motel when James Earl Ray, an escaped convict, fatally shot him with a sniper's rifle. The violent reaction to King's murder eroded his campaign of nonviolence. Riots broke out in ghetto areas of the nation's capital; by the end of the week, disturbances rocked 125 more neighborhoods across the country. Then on the evening of June 5 a disgruntled Arab nationalist, Sirhan Sirhan, assassinated Robert Kennedy. Running in opposition to the war, Kennedy had just won a crucial primary victory in California.

The loss of King and Kennedy pained Americans deeply. In their own ways both men exemplified the liberal tradition, which reached its high-water mark in the 1960s. King had retained his faith in a Christian theology of nonviolence. He sought reform for the poor of all races without resorting to the language of the fist and the gun. Robert Kennedy had come to reject the war his brother had supported, and he seemed genuinely to sympathize with the poor and minorities. At the same time, he was popular among traditional white ethnics and blue-collar workers. Would the liberal political tradition have flourished longer if these two charismatic figures had survived the turbulence of the 1960s?

Though Lyndon Johnson planned to step down, he still dominated his party and chose his loyal vice president, Hubert Humphrey, as his successor. Humphrey had begun his career as a progressive and a strong supporter of civil rights. But as vice president, he was intimately associated with the war and the old-style liberal reforms that could never satisfy radicals. The Republicans had chosen Richard Nixon, a traditional anticommunist now reborn as the "new," more moderate Nixon. As much as radicals disliked Johnson, they truly despised Nixon, "new" or old.

CONVENTION MAYHEM Chicago, where the Democrats met for their convention, was the fiefdom of Mayor Richard Daley, long a symbol of machine politics. Daley was determined that the dissatisfied radicals who poured into Chicago would not disrupt "his" Democratic convention. The radicals were equally determined that they would. For a week the police skirmished with demonstrators: police clubs, riot gear, and tear gas versus the demonstrators' eggs, rocks, and balloons filled with paint and urine. When Daley refused to allow a peaceful march past the convention site, the radicals marched anyway, and then the police, with the mayor's blessing, turned on the crowd in what a federal commission later labeled a police riot. In one pitched battle, many officers took off their badges and waded into the crowd, nightsticks swinging, chanting "Kill, kill, kill." Reporters, medics, and other innocent bystanders were injured; at 3 a.m. police invaded candidate Eugene McCarthy's hotel headquarters and pulled some of his assistants from their beds.

With feelings running so high, President Johnson did not dare appear at his own party's convention. Theodore White, a veteran journalist covering the gathering, scribbled his verdict in a notebook as police chased hippies down Michigan Avenue. "The Democrats are finished," he wrote.

Revolutionary Clashes Worldwide

The clashes in Chicago seemed homegrown, but they took place against the backdrop of a global surge in radical, often violent, student upheavals. In 1966 Chinese students were in the vanguard of Mao Zedong's Red Guards, formed to enforce a Cultural Revolution that sought to purge China of all bourgeois cultural influences. Although that revolution persecuted millions among the educated classes and left the country in economic shambles, Mao became a hero to radicals outside China. Radicals also lionized other revolutionaries who took up arms: Fidel Castro and Che Guevara in Cuba and Ho Chi Minh in Vietnam.

Radical targets varied. In Italy students denounced the official Marxism of the Soviet Union and the Italian Communist Party. French students at the Sorbonne in Paris rebelled against the university's efforts to discipline political activists. Students in Czechoslovakia launched a full-scale rebellion, known as Prague Spring, against the Soviet domination of their nation—until Soviet tanks crushed the uprising. Though the agenda varied from country to country, virtually all student revolutionaries condemned the American war in Vietnam.

Chicago police confront protesters during the 1968 Democratic convention. With provocation on both sides, violence inevitably erupted.

Whose Silent Majority?

GEORGE WALLACE Radicals were not the only Americans alienated from the political system in 1968. Governor George Wallace of Alabama sensed the frustration among the "average man on the street, this man in the textile mill, this man in the steel mill, this barber, this beautician, the policeman on the beat." In running for president, Wallace sought the support of blue-collar workers and the lower middle classes.

Wallace had first come to national attention in 1963, when he barred integration of the University of Alabama. Briefly, he pursued the Democratic presidential nomination in 1964. For the race in 1968 he formed his own American Independent Party. Wallace took on the "liberals, intellectuals, and long hairs [who] have run this country for too long." He did not simply appeal to law and order, militarism, and white backlash; he was too sharp for that. With roots in southern Populism, he called for federal job-training programs, stronger unemployment benefits, national health insurance, a higher minimum wage, and a further extension of union rights. Many Robert Kennedy voters shifted to Wallace. A quarter of all union members backed him.

NIXON'S "SILENT MAJORITY" Richard Nixon, too, sought the votes of disgruntled Democrats, especially those from the once solidly Democratic South. Republicans had long been identified with big business and the money power, but Nixon himself had modest roots. He came from a middle-class family and at Duke Law School was so pinched for funds that he lived in an abandoned toolshed. His dogged hard work earned him the somewhat dubious nickname of "iron pants." And Nixon well understood the disdain ordinary laborers felt for "kids with beards from the suburbs" who seemed always to be insisting, protesting, *demanding*. Nixon believed himself a representative of the **"silent majority,"** as he later described it, not a strident minority.

Candidate (Party)	Electoral Vote (%)	Popular Vote (%)
Richard M. Nixon (Republican)	301 (56)	31,785,480 (44)
Hubert H. Humphrey (Democratic)	191 (36)	31,275,166 (43)
George C. Wallace (American Independent)	46 (8)	9,906,473 (13)

Election of 1968

He thus set two campaign goals: to distance himself from President Johnson on Vietnam and to turn Wallace's "average Americans" into a Republican majority. The Vietnam issue was delicate, because Nixon had generally supported the war. As he told one aide, "I've come to the conclusion that there's no way to win the war. But we can't say that, of course. In fact, we have to seem to say the opposite." During the campaign he hinted that he had a secret plan to end the war but steadfastly refused to disclose it. He pledged only to find an honorable solution. As for Wallace's followers, Nixon promised to promote "law and order" while cracking down on "pot," pornography, protest, and permissiveness.

Hubert Humphrey, facing the ruins of the Chicago convention, undertook a daunting task. All through September, antiwar protesters dogged his campaign with "Dump the Hump" posters. Although Humphrey picked up steam late in the campaign (partly by cautiously criticizing Johnson's war policies), the last-minute surge was not enough. Nixon captured 43.4 percent of the popular vote to 42.7 percent for Humphrey and 13.5 percent for Wallace. The outcome did nothing to close the nation's deep divisions.

 REVIEW

What four or five events in 1968 made that year a turning point for the war at home and abroad?

THE NIXON ERA

IN RICHARD NIXON, AMERICANS HAD elected two men to the presidency. The public Nixon appeared to be a traditional small-town conservative who cherished individual initiative, chamber-of-commerce capitalism, Fourth of July patriotism, and middle-class Victorian values. The private Nixon was a troubled man. His language among intimates was caustic and profane. He waxed bitter toward those he saw as enemies. Never a natural public speaker, he was physically rather awkward—a White House aide once found toothmarks on a "childproof" aspirin cap the president had been unable to pry open. The public Nixon seemed to search out challenges—"crises" to face and conquer.

Vietnamization—and Cambodia

HENRY KISSINGER

A settlement of the Vietnam "crisis" thus became one of Nixon's first priorities. He found a congenial ally in National Security Advisor Henry Kissinger. Kissinger, an intensely ambitious Harvard academic, shared with the new president a global vision of foreign affairs. Like Nixon, Kissinger had a tendency to pursue his ends secretly, circumventing the traditional channels such as the State Department.

Both men wanted to end the war but insisted on "peace with honor." That meant leaving a pro-American South Vietnamese government behind. The strategy Nixon adopted was "Vietnamization," a gradual withdrawal of American troops as a way to advance peace talks in Paris. The burden of fighting would shift to the South Vietnamese army. Critics likened this strategy to little more than "changing the color of the corpses." All the same, as the media shifted their focus to the peace talks, the public had the impression the war was winding down.

At the same time, Nixon hoped to drive the North Vietnamese into negotiating peace on American terms. Quite consciously, he traded on his reputation as a cold warrior who would stop at nothing. As he explained to his chief of staff, Robert Haldeman:

> I call it the Madman Theory, Bob. I want the North Vietnamese to believe that I've reached the point where I might do anything to stop the war. We'll just slip the word to them that, "for God's sake, you know Nixon is obsessed about Communists. We can't restrain him when he's angry—and he has his hand on the nuclear button"—and Ho Chi Minh himself will be in Paris in two days begging for peace.

INVADING CAMBODIA

In the spring of 1969 the president launched a series of bombing attacks against North Vietnamese supply depots inside neighboring Cambodia. Johnson had refused to widen the war in this manner, fearing domestic reaction. Nixon simply kept the raids secret.

Ho Chi Minh's death in 1969 did not weaken the North's resolve. His successors continued to reject any offer that did not end with complete American withdrawal and an abandonment of the South Vietnamese military government. Once again Nixon turned up the heat. Over the opposition of his secretaries of defense and state, he ordered American troops into Cambodia to wipe out reported North Vietnamese bases there. On April 30, 1970, he announced the "incursion" of American troops, proclaiming that he would not allow "the world's most powerful nation" to act "like a pitiful helpless giant."

The wave of protests that followed included the fatal clashes between authorities and students at Kent State and Jackson State as well as another march on Washington by 100,000 protesters. Congress was upset enough to repeal the Tonkin Gulf Resolution, a symbolic rejection of Nixon's invasion. After two months American troops left Cambodia, having achieved little.

Fighting a No-Win War

For a time, Vietnamization seemed to work. As more American troops went home, the South Vietnamese forces improved modestly. But for American GIs still in the country, morale became a serious problem. Why were the "grunts" in the field still being asked to put their lives on the line, when it was becoming clear there would be no victory? The anger surfaced increasingly in incidents known as "fragging," in which GIs threw fragmentation grenades at officers who pursued the war too aggressively.

Nor could the army isolate itself from the trends dividing American society. Just as young Americans "turned on" to marijuana and hallucinogens, so soldiers in Vietnam used drugs. Black GIs brought with them from home the issues of black power. One white medic noticed that when Muhammad Ali refused to be drafted, African Americans in his unit began "to question why they were fighting the Honky's war against other Third World people."

The Move toward Détente

Despite Nixon's insistence on "peace with honor," Vietnam was not a war he had chosen to fight. And both Kissinger and Nixon recognized that by 1968 the United States no longer had the resources to dominate international relations around the globe. The Soviet Union remained their prime concern. Ever since Khrushchev had backed down at the Cuban missile crisis in 1962, the Soviets had steadily expanded their nuclear arsenal. The Vietnam War also diverted valuable military and economic resources making it difficult for Nixon to address instability in the Middle East and other Third World regions.

NIXON DOCTRINE   In what the White House labeled the "Nixon Doctrine," the United States would remain engaged in Asia but shift some of the military burden for containment to other allies: Japan in the Pacific, the shah of Iran in the Middle East, Zaire in central Africa, and the apartheid government in South Africa. At the same time, Nixon and Kissinger looked for new ways to contain Soviet power not simply through nuclear deterrence but through negotiations to ease tensions. This policy was named, from the French, **détente.**

Richard Nixon's trip to China included this visit to the Great Wall. Precisely because he had been so staunch an anticommunist, Nixon appreciated the enormous departure his trip marked in Sino-American relations.

Kissinger and Nixon looked to ease tension by linking separate cold war issues. The arms race burdened the Soviet economy; why not offer American concessions on nuclear missiles? In return, the Soviets would be asked to put pressure on North Vietnam to negotiate an end to the war. Nixon also decided to reach out to Mao Zedong, the Communist Chinese dictator. The Soviets viewed China in some ways as more of a threat than the United States. Nixon thus calculated that they would likely cooperate in order to discourage the Americans from enlarging Chinese power. Playing this "China card" was a significant break from Nixon's conservative past. Republicans had long supported the Nationalists in Taiwan and viewed the Soviet Union and China as part of a Communist monolith. To activate this new strategy, Kissinger slipped off to China on a secret mission and then reappeared to announce the president would travel to China. During that visit in early 1972, Nixon pledged to normalize relations, a move the public enthusiastically embraced.

SALT I   Later that year Nixon advanced his plan for détente. In May he traveled to the Soviet Union to join Premier Leonid Brezhnev in signing the first Strategic Arms Limitation Treaty (SALT I). In the agreement, both sides pledged to limit the number of intercontinental ballistic missiles (ICBMs) each side would deploy, as well as agreeing not to develop a new system of antiballistic missiles (ABMs).

Americans were pleased at the prospect of lower cold war tensions. But it was not clear that the linkages achieved in Moscow and Beijing would help free the United States from its war in Vietnam.

> ✓ **REVIEW**
>
> In what ways did Richard Nixon escalate the war even as he was working to wind it down?

THE NEW IDENTITY POLITICS

THE LIBERAL TRADITION HAD LONG embraced a belief in the common humanity of all Americans. Lyndon Johnson expressed the notion pungently, updating Shakespeare's Shylock with a Texas twang: "They cry the same tears, they feel hungry the same, they bleed the same." Differences among individuals, liberals argued, came not from race or gender but from cultural circumstances and historical experiences. Out of such beliefs, civil rights advocates committed themselves to an integrated America.

PLURALISM VERSUS ASSIMILATION    But just as Vietnam weakened the liberal consensus on the need to contain communism, minority activism challenged liberal assumptions on integration. The emerging politics of the late 1960s substituted a model of **pluralism** for the unified one sought by integrationists. This model hoped to dissolve inequality not by ending divisions of social class, but by raising up the status of formerly disadvantaged groups—women, African Americans, Latinos, and other hyphenated-Americans. Traditionally, Latino civil rights activists such as LULAC and World War II veterans in the American GI Forum had looked to assimilate into American society. Now minorities began to forge identities in opposition to the prevailing culture. By 1970 black nationalists had abandoned integration for the politics of black pride. To these activists the qualities that distinguished black Americans were what made them distinct—their music, clothing, hairstyles, and religion. In similar ways radical feminists, Latinos, Native Americans, and gays demanded that the nation respect and protect their essential differences.

AFFIRMATIVE ACTION   To some degree the Supreme Court had already granted that point in both the *Brown* and *Hernandez* decisions of 1954 (see pages 804–805). In each case the Court declared that Latinos and African Americans had suffered not simply as individuals but as groups. To correct past injustices, identity politics called for positive steps—what the Johnson administration called **affirmative action**—to repair the damage done by past injustices.

Latino Activism

The distinct identities of minorities became more visible owing to a new wave of immigration in the 1950s and 1960s from Puerto Rico, Mexico, and Cuba. Historical and cultural ethnic differences among the three major Latino groups made it difficult to develop a common political agenda. Still, some activists did seek a greater unity.

PUERTO RICANS AND CUBANS   After World War II more than a million Puerto Ricans migrated to New York City. As citizens of the United States, they could move freely to the mainland and back home again. That dual consciousness discouraged many from establishing deep roots stateside. Equally important, the newcomers were startled to discover that, whatever their status at home, on the mainland they faced racial discrimination and segregation in urban slums. Light-skinned migrants escaped those conditions by blending into the middle class as "Latin Americans." The Puerto Rican community thereby lost some of the leadership it needed to advance its political interests.

Still, during the 1960s groups such as *Aspira* adopted the strategies of civil rights activists and organizations such as the Black and Puerto Rican Caucus created links with other minority groups. The Cubans who arrived in the United States after Fidel Castro came to power in 1959—some 350,000 over the course of the decade—forged fewer ties with other Latinos. Most settled around Miami. An unusually large number came from Cuba's professional, business, and government class and were racially white and politically conservative.

Mexican Americans, however, constituted the largest segment of the Latino population. Until the 1940s most were farmers and farm laborers in Texas, New Mexico, and California. But during the 1950s the process of mechanization

FARMWORKERS' ALTAR

The crucifix suggests that the migrant worker is Catholic. Protestant Christians traditionally used the symbol of the cross without Jesus.

This is the flag of the United Farm Workers, designed at the request of César Chávez. To find out more about its symbolism on the web, what key words would you use in your search?

The grape leaves decorating the altar remind people of the UFW's grape boycott.

What do the different skin tones of the arms suggest?

Historians use artworks as a lens through which they can view the beliefs and values of an era. This altar was created by artist Emanuel Martínez at a time when the United Farm Workers were engaged in a campaign for the right to negotiate labor contracts with grape growers. In 1968 César Chávez held a 24-day hunger strike that ended successfully with the celebration of mass. This altar was used at the ceremony, which was attended by farmworkers as well as civil rights supporters, including Senator Robert F. Kennedy. The altar thus had symbolic overtones for the occasion. Most Mexican-American farmworkers were devout Catholics, just as many early African-American civil rights activists shared a Protestant faith. But other symbols suggest the complexity of the movement's belief system, with allegiance to union activity and political struggle, as well as the movement's connection to Aztec and mestizo traditions of Mexico.

Thinking Critically

Why would it be appropriate to end a hunger strike with a mass? What other cultural echoes in this decade resonate from the image of a raised, closed fist? In what ways do those symbols link to the "new identity politics"?

pushed them toward the cities—some 85 percent of the population by 1969. With urbanization came a slow improvement in the quality of jobs held. A body of skilled workers, middle-class professionals, and entrepreneurs emerged.

CÉSAR CHÁVEZ AND THE UFW Yet Mexican agricultural workers continued to face harsh working conditions and meager wages. Attempts to unionize faltered partly because workers migrated from job to job and strikebreakers were easily imported. In 1963 a soft-spoken but determined farmworker, César Chávez, recruited fellow organizers Gil Padilla and Dolores Huerta to make another attempt. Their efforts over the next several years led to the formation of the United Farm Workers labor union.

Chávez, like Martin Luther King, proclaimed an ethic of nonviolence. Also like King, he was guided by a deep religious faith (Roman Catholicism in the case of Chávez and most Mexican American farmworkers). During a strike of Mexican and Filipino grape workers in the summer of 1966, Chávez led a 250-mile march on Sacramento. ("Dr. King had been very successful" with such marches, he noted.) Seeking additional leverage, the UFW organized a consumer boycott of grapes in supermarkets across the nation. Combined with a 24-day hunger strike—a technique Chávez borrowed from Gandhi—the boycott forced growers to negotiate contracts with the UFW beginning in 1970.

CHICANO ACTIVISTS Just as King found his nonviolent approach challenged by radical activists, Chávez saw a new generation of Mexican Americans take

Living conditions were harshest for Mexican Americans among agricultural workers. César Chávez mobilized migrant workers into the United Farm Workers union. Here he meets with Dolores Huerta, his vice president in the UFW in January 1968. Note the three iconic symbols prominently displayed in the office.

college in increasing numbers. In addition, Lyndon Johnson's Educational Opportunity Programs, part of the War on Poverty, brought higher education to thousands more Latinos. By 1968 some 50 Mexican-American student organizations had sprung up on college campuses. Two years later *La Raza Unida* (The Race United) launched a third-party movement to gain power in communities in which Chicanos were a majority. The more militant "Brown Berets" adopted the paramilitary tactics and radical rhetoric of the Black Panthers.

The Choices of American Indians

Ironically, the growing strength of the civil rights movement created a threat to Indian tribal identities. During the 1950s the Bureau of Indian Affairs adopted a policy called "termination." To reduce the reservation system, the bureau would cut federal services, gradually sell off tribal lands, and push the people into the "mainstream" of American life. Although most full-blooded Indians objected to the policy, some of mixed blood and others already assimilated into white society supported the move. The relocation of some 35,000 Indians accelerated a shift from rural areas to cities. The urban Indian population, which had been barely 30,000 in 1940, reached more than 300,000 by the 1970s.

AMERICAN INDIAN MOVEMENT

Still, the activism of the 1960s inspired Indian leaders to shape their own political agenda. In 1968 urban activists in Minneapolis created AIM, the American Indian Movement. A year later like-minded Indians living around San Francisco Bay formed Indians of All Tribes. Because the Bureau of Indian Affairs refused to address the problems of urban Indians, militant members of the organization seized the abandoned federal prison on Alcatraz Island in San Francisco Bay. The Alcatraz action, though short-lived, inspired calls for a national Pan-Indian rights movement.

Then in 1973 AIM organizers Russell Means and Dennis Banks led a dramatic takeover of a trading post at Wounded Knee, on a Sioux reservation in South Dakota. In 1890 white cavalry had gunned down over a hundred Sioux (page 480), at Wounded Knee. Ever since, it symbolized for Indians the betrayal of white promises and the bankruptcy of reservation policy. Even more, Wounded Knee now demonstrated how difficult it was to achieve unity when so many tribes were determined to go their own ways. Other Indians did not support the militant takeover of Wounded Knee, and

up an aggressive brand of identity politics. Many began calling themselves Chicanos. Like blacks, Chicanos saw themselves as a people whose heritage had been rejected, their labor exploited, and their opportunity for advancement denied. In Denver, Rodolfo "Corky" Gonzales laid out a blueprint for a separatist Chicano society, with public housing set aside for Chicanos and the development of economically independent barrios. "We are Bronze People with a Bronze Culture," declared Gonzales. "We are a Nation. We are a union of free pueblos. We are Aztlán."

LA RAZA UNIDA   The new activism came from both college and high school students. Like others of the baby-boom generation, Mexican Americans attended

In 1890 the U.S. cavalry killed 146 Indians at Wounded Knee, South Dakota. In 1973 members of the American Indian Movement seized the hamlet of Wounded Knee, making it once again a symbol of conflict.

federal officers soon forced its occupiers to leave. The movement splintered further as more than 100 different organizations were formed during the 1970s to pursue reform at the local, state, and federal levels.

Asian Americans

In striking down the old quota system, the 1965 Immigration Reform Act led to a sharp increase in the numbers of immigrants from Asia. Asians, who in 1960 made up less than 1 percent of the American population (about a million people), were by 1985 2 percent (about 5 million). This new wave included many middle-class professionals, a lower percentage of Japanese, and far more newcomers from Southeast and South Asia. Earlier civil rights reforms had swept away the legal barriers to full citizenship that had once stigmatized Asians.

Many Americans saw these new immigrants as "model minorities." They possessed skills in high demand, worked hard, were often Christian, and seldom protested. The 1970 census showed Japanese and Chinese Americans with incomes well above the median for white Americans. Such statistics, however, hid fault lines within communities. Although many professionals assimilated into the American mainstream, agricultural laborers and sweatshop workers remained trapped in poverty. And no matter how much Anglos praised their industry, Asian Americans still wore what one sociologist defined as a "racial uniform." They were nonwhites in a white society.

Few Americans were aware of Asian involvement in identity politics. That was in part because the large majority of Asian Americans lived in just three states—Hawaii, California, and New York. Further, Asian Americans were less likely to join the era's vocal protests. Nonetheless, Asian

students did join with African Americans, Chicanos, and Native Americans to advocate a "Third World revolution" against the white establishment. Asian students, too, wanted a curriculum that recognized their histories and cultures.

Gay Rights

In 1972 Black Panther Huey Newton observed that homosexuals "might be the most oppressed people" in American society. Certainly, Newton was qualified to recognize oppression when he saw it. But by then a growing number of homosexuals had embraced liberation movements that placed them among minorities demanding equal rights.

Even during the "conformist" 1950s, gay men founded the Mattachine Society (1951) to fight antihomosexual attacks and to press for wider public acceptance. Lesbians formed a similar organization, the Daughters of Bilitis, in 1955. Beginning in the mid-1960s, more-radical gay and lesbian groups began organizing to raise individual consciousness and to establish a gay culture in which they felt free. One group called for "acceptance as full equals . . . basic rights and equality as citizens; our human dignity; . . . [our] right to love whom we wish."

STONEWALL INCIDENT The movement's defining moment came on Friday, June 27, 1969, when New York police raided the Stonewall Inn, a Greenwich Village bar. Such raids were common enough: the police regularly harassed gays and lesbians by raiding the places where they gathered. This time the patrons fought back, first with taunts and jeers, then with paving stones and parking meters. Increasingly, gay activists called on homosexuals to "come out of the closet" and publicly affirm their sexuality. In 1974 gays achieved a major symbolic victory

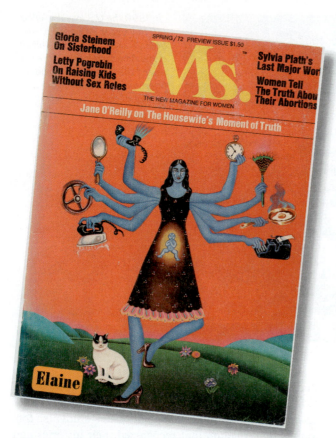

The creation of Ms. magazine in 1972 gave feminists a means to reach a broader audience. The cover of its first issue used the image of a many-armed Hindu goddess to satirize the many roles of the modern housewife.

when the American Psychiatric Association removed homosexuality from its list of mental disorders.

Feminism

Organized struggle for women's rights and equality in the United States began before the Civil War. Sustained political efforts had won women the vote in 1920. But the women's movement of the 1960s and 1970s began to push for equality in broader, deeper ways.

THE FEMININE
MYSTIQUE

Writer Betty Friedan was one of the earliest to voice dissatisfaction with the cultural attitudes that flourished after World War II. Even though more women were entering the job market, the media routinely glorified housewives and homemakers while discouraging those who aspired to independent careers. In *The Feminine Mystique* (1963), Friedan identified the "problem that has no name," a dispiriting emptiness in the midst of affluent lives. "Our culture does not permit women to accept or gratify their basic need to grow and fulfill their potentialities as human beings."

The Feminine Mystique gave new life to the women's rights movement. The Commission on the Status of Women appointed by President Kennedy proposed the 1963 Equal Pay Act and helped add gender to the forms of discrimination outlawed by the 1964 Civil Rights Act. Women also assumed an important role in both the civil rights and antiwar movements. They accounted for half the students who went south for the "Freedom Summers" in 1964 and 1965. But even women who joined the protests of the 1960s often found themselves limited to providing menial services such as cooking and laundry. Casey Hayden, a veteran of SDS and SNCC, told her male comrades that the "assumptions of male superiority are as widespread . . . and every much as crippling to the woman as the assumptions of white superiority are to the Negro."

NATIONAL
ORGANIZATION
FOR WOMEN

By 1966 activist women were less willing to remain silent. Friedan joined a group of 24 women and 2 men who formed the National Organization for Women (NOW). In arguing that "sexism" was much like racism, they persuaded President Johnson in 1967 to include women along with African Americans, Hispanics, and other minorities as a group covered by federal affirmative action programs.

Broader social trends established a receptive climate for the feminist appeal. After 1957 the birthrate began a rapid decline; improved methods of contraception, such as the birth control pill, permitted smaller families. By 1970 an unprecedented 40 percent of all women were employed outside the home. Education also spurred the shift from home to the workplace, since higher educational levels allowed women to enter an economy oriented increasingly toward white-collar service industries rather than blue-collar manufacturing.

Equal Rights and Abortion

As its influence grew, the feminist movement translated women's grievances into a political agenda. In 1967 NOW proclaimed a "bill of rights" that called for maternity leave for working mothers, federally supported day care facilities, child care tax deductions, and equal education and job training. But feminists divided on two other issues: the

DUELING DOCUMENTS

TWO VIEWS OF THE LIBERATION OF WOMEN

The publication of Betty Friedan's The Feminine Mystique *in 1963 triggered a sharp debate about the role of women in society. Gloria Steinem emerged as one of the primary spokespersons for feminists who stressed economic and sexual liberation as crucial to equal standing for women. She created* Ms. *magazine to provide a forum for feminist ideas and interests. Efforts to pass an Equal Rights Amendment inspired Phyllis Schlafly to become an outspoken advocate for traditional family roles and an ardent opponent of feminism and the ERA. Indeed, she received much of the credit for the amendment's ultimate defeat.*

DOCUMENT 1   Gloria Steinem: What Would It Be Like if Women Win?

Women do not want to change places with men. . . . That is not our goal. But we do want to change the economic system to one more based on merit. In Women's Lib Utopia, there will be free access to good jobs—and decent pay for the bad ones women have been performing all along, including housework. Increased skilled labor might lead to a four-hour workday, and higher wages would encourage further mechanization of repetitive jobs now kept alive by cheap labor. . . .

Men will have to give up ruling-class privileges, but in return they will no longer be the only ones to support the family, get drafted, bear the strain of power and responsibility. Freud to the contrary, anatomy is not destiny, at least not for more than nine months at a time. In Israel women are drafted, and some have gone to war. . . . In Sweden, both parents take care of the children. In this country, come utopia, men and women won't reverse roles; they will be free to choose according to individual talents and preferences.

If role reform sounds sexually unsettling, think how it will change the sexual hypocrisy we have now. No more sex arranged on the barter system, with women pretending interest, and men never sure whether they are loved for themselves or for the security few women can get any other way. . . . No more men who are encouraged o spend a lifetime living with inferiors; with housekeepers or dependent creatures who are still children. No more domineering wives, emasculating women, and "Jewish mothers," all of whom are simply human beings with all their normal ambition and drive confined to home. No more unequal partnerships that eventually doom sex and love.

Source: Gloria Steinem, "What It Would Be Like If Women Win," in Alexander Bloom and Wini Breines, eds., *"Takin' It to the Streets": A Sixties Reader* (New York: Oxford University Press, 1995), pp. 475–477.

DOCUMENT 2   Phyllis Schlafly: What "Women's Lib" Really Means

Many women are under the mistaken impression that "women's lib" means more job employment opportunities for women, equal pay for equal work, appointments of women to high positions, admitting more women to medical schools, and other desirable objectives which all women favor. We all support these purposes, as well as any necessary legislation which would bring them about.

But all this is only a sweet syrup which covers the deadly poison masquerading as "women's lib." The women's libbers are radicals who are waging a total assault on the family, on marriage, and on children. Don't take my word for it—read their own literature and prove to yourself what these characters are trying to do. . . .

The women's libbers don't understand that most women want to be wife, mother and homemaker—and are happy in that role. The women's libbers actively resent the mother who stays at home with her children and likes it that way. The principal purpose of *Ms.'s* shrill tirade is to sow seeds of discontent among happy, married women so that all women can be unhappy in some new sisterhood of frustrated togetherness. . . .

Another women's lib magazine, called *Women,* tells the American woman that she is a prisoner in the "solitary confinement" and "isolation" of marriage. The magazine promises that it will provide women with "escape from isolation . . . release from boredom," and that it will "break the barriers . . . that separate wife, mistress and secretary . . . heterosexual women and homosexual women."

These women's libbers do, indeed, intend to "break the barriers" of the Ten Commandments and the sanctity of the family. It hasn't occurred to them that a woman's best "escape from isolation and boredom" is—not a magazine subscription to boost her "stifled ego"—but a husband and children who love her.

Source: Phyllis Schlafly, "What's Wrong with 'Equal Rights' for Women?" in Peter B. Levy, ed., *America in the Sixties— Right, Left, and Center: A Documentary History* (Westport, CT: Praeger, 1998), pp. 221–228.

Thinking Critically

In what ways do both writers deal in stereotypes and generalizations? At what class of women are their appeals aimed? On what points do they most strongly disagree? Could you describe grounds on which the two writers might agree or their views might be reconciled? Which of the two more accurately anticipates the situation in which women find themselves today?

passage of an Equal Rights Amendment to the Constitution and a repeal of state antiabortion laws.

ROE V. WADE At first, support seemed strong for an Equal Rights Amendment that forbade all discrimination on the basis of gender. In 1972 both the House and the Senate passed the Equal Rights Amendment (ERA) virtually without opposition. Within a year, 28 of the necessary 38 states had approved the ERA. It seemed only a matter of time before 10 more state legislatures would complete its ratification. Many in the women's movement also applauded the Supreme Court's decision, in *Roe v. Wade* (1973), to strike down 46 state laws restricting a woman's access to abortion. In his opinion for the majority, Justice Harry Blackmun observed that a woman in the nineteenth century had "enjoyed a substantially broader right to terminate a pregnancy than she does in most states today." As legal abortion in the first three months of pregnancy became more readily available, the rate of maternal deaths from illegal operations, especially among minorities, declined.

But the early success of the Equal Rights Amendment and the feminist triumph in *Roe v. Wade* masked underlying divisions among women's groups. *Roe v. Wade* triggered a sharp backlash from many Catholics, Protestant evangelicals, and socially conservative women. Their opposition inspired a crusade for a "right to life" amendment to the Constitution. A similar conservative reaction breathed new life into the "STOP ERA" crusade of Phyllis Schlafly, an Illinois political organizer. Although a professional herself, Schlafly believed that women should embrace their traditional role as homemakers subordinate to their husbands. "Every change [that the ERA] requires will deprive women of a right, benefit, or exemption that they now enjoy," she argued. By 1979 supporters of ERA were forced to admit that they would not succeed in convincing the necessary three-fourths of the state legislatures to ratify the amendment.

 **REVIEW**

How did each of the following groups work to change their identities and status in American society: Latinos, women, Indians, Asian Americans, and gays?

VALUE POLITICS: THE CONSUMER AND ENVIRONMENTAL MOVEMENTS

AMONG THOSE SEEKING TO CHANGE America were reformers who defined themselves by their ideas and values rather than by personal identity. Where many participants in identity politics viewed themselves as outsiders, consumer advocates and environmentalists generally came from the social mainstream. Still, they shared with the counterculture a worry that excessive materialism wasted resources and generated pollution, while too many corporations exploited the public through misleading advertising and shoddy, even dangerous, products.

Technology and Unbridled Growth

SOURCES OF POLLUTION As early as 1962, marine biologist Rachel Carson had warned in *Silent Spring* against the widespread use of chemical pesticides, especially DDT (see page 816). But pesticides were only one aspect of what environmentalists considered misguided technology. A report issued in 1965 indicated that every river near an urban area in the United States was polluted, save one (the St. Croix near St. Paul, Minnesota). Certainly, anyone with a sense of irony could not help marveling that the industrially fouled Cuyahoga River running through Cleveland, Ohio, burst into flames in 1969. Smog, radioactive fallout, lethal pesticides, and polluted rivers were the by-products of a society wedded to technology and unbridled economic growth.

To consumer advocates, rising fatality rates on American highways signaled another kind of corporate failure. Besides contributing to smog and other forms of pollution, many automobiles were inherently dangerous to their occupants. That was a conclusion announced by reformer Ralph Nader in his 1965 exposé, *Unsafe at Any Speed.* Nader's particular target was the rear-engine Chevrolet Corvair. General Motors' internal studies confirmed crash data that the Corvair tended to flip over during turns or skidded uncontrollably. Though the company fixed the problem, it also hired private investigators to try to discredit Nader.

The company picked the wrong target. Nader was the son of immigrant Lebanese parents who supported their son's success at Princeton and Harvard Law School. He lived simply and had no vices. And when he discovered GM's campaign against him, he successfully sued. GM's embarrassed president publicly apologized, but by then Nader had become a counterculture hero. In 1966 Congress passed the National Traffic and Motor Vehicle Safety Act and the Highway Safety Act. For the first time, the government required seatbelts and set safety standards for cars, tires, and roads.

NADER'S RAIDERS With the money from his lawsuit, Nader founded a consumer advocacy organization in 1969, the Center for the Study of Responsive Law. His staff of low-paid but eager lawyers, student interns, and volunteers investigated a wide range of consumer and environmental issues. "Nader's Raiders," as his staff was called, shared their leader's view that it was time for corporations "to stop stealing, stop deceiving, stop corrupting politicians with money, stop monopolizing, stop poisoning the earth, air and water, stop selling dangerous products, stop exposing workers to cruel hazards." In the tradition of progressive reform, Nader looked to an interventionist government and informed citizen-consumers to regulate corporate behavior.

"Some river! Chocolate brown, oily, bubbling with subsurface gases, it oozes rather than flows." So Time magazine described the Cuyahoga River when it caught fire in 1969. Newspaper photographers arrived too late to record that fire, but Time was able to run a photo of the blazing Cuyahoga anyway—because the river had also caught fire in 1868, 1883, 1887, 1912, 1936, 1941, 1948, and—most disastrously—in 1952, as shown here.

FOCUS ON ECOLOGY

Many environmentalists, too, had links to the Progressive Era and the idea that government action could police corporate irresponsibility and preserve scenic and natural wonders for the benefit of future generations. What made modern environmentalism distinct was a growing focus on the field of ecology. Since the early twentieth century, this biological science had demonstrated how closely life processes throughout nature depended on one another. In condemning the abuse of pesticides, Rachel Carson had called for a **biocentric** approach to nature rather than an anthropocentric, or human-centered, one.

Barry Commoner, a politically active biologist, argued in his book *The Closing Circle* (1971) that modern society courted disaster by trying to "improve on nature." American farmers, for example, greatly increased their crop yields by switching from animal manures to artificial fertilizers. But the change consumed large quantities of energy, raised costs, often left soils sterile, and polluted nearby water. By the 1970s chemical discharges had virtually killed Lake Erie. Technology might prove profitable in the short run, Commoner argued, but in the long run modern methods were bankrupting the environment.

Political Action

ENVIRONMENTAL PROTECTION AGENCY

Although he was no friend of liberal reform, President Nixon sensed that these value movements had broad popular appeal. His administration supported the passage of the National Environmental Policy Act of 1969, which required

Ralph Nader's dogged, ascetic style forced corporations such as General Motors to more seriously examine public safety issues. Nader's organization, Public Citizen, expanded its efforts on behalf of consumers to a wide range of issues.

The first Earth Day, 1970. Although President Nixon created the Environmental Protection Agency, he recognized the costs of environmental regulation did not play well with voters in the "silent majority" and the world of business. So he distanced himself from the environmental movement.

environmental impact statements for all major public projects. And in 1970 Nixon established the Environmental Protection Agency (EPA), whose first major act recognized Rachel Carson's campaign by banning most domestic uses of DDT. The president also signed a bill establishing an Occupational Safety and Health Agency (OSHA) to enforce health and safety standards in the workplace, and the Endangered Species, Clean Water, and Clean Air Acts.

EARTH DAY   On April 22, 1970, millions of Americans demonstrated their commitment to a healthy environment as they celebrated the first Earth Day. Their enthusiasm reflected the movement's dual appeal: it was both practical in seeking to improve the quality of air, water, and earth and spiritual in celebrating the unity of living things. But Senator Gaylord Nelson of Wisconsin, who helped bring Earth Day about, appreciated the occasion's radical implications: "The Establishment sees this as a great big antilitter campaign. Wait until they find out what it really means . . . to clean up our earth."

The Legacy of Identity and Value Politics

Earth Day did not signal a consensus on an environmental ethic. President Nixon, for one, was unwilling to impose regulations that stifled growth, especially when facing a troubled economy. Radical activists "aren't really one damn bit interested in safety or clean air," he commented to one industry group. "What they are interested in is destroying the system." If he faced "a flat choice between jobs and smoke," nature would lose.

NIXON'S SOUTHERN STRATEGY   Nixon's political instincts were shrewd. Rather than fight the popular tides, he rode them, basking, for example, in the triumphant *Apollo 11* moon landing in 1969. At the same time, he resisted those such as affirmative action that offended Republicans and traditional Democrats. Both the 1968 and 1972 presidential elections revealed a shift in political power toward the southern and western rims of the United States where traditional values flourished and where whites, in the wake of the civil rights revolution, were deserting the Democrats. These were the voters Nixon courted, in what he sometimes referred to as his "southern strategy" to replace the old New Deal coalition with a new Republican majority. By the early 1970s his silent majority worried more about job security than clean air and water. As one bumper sticker declared: "Out of work? Hungry? Eat an environmentalist."

The president sought to channel a similar backlash against identity politics. Conservatives opposed many of the era's reforms, including the Equal Rights Amendment, the integration of private clubs, and the use of racial and gender quotas for jobs and college admissions. Merit, not race or gender, should determine an individual's opportunities, they argued. Ethnic identity organizations such as the Italian American Civil Rights League spoke out against affirmative action for minorities.

Most labor leaders also resisted the push for affirmative action. Rising inflation and the erosion of high-wage, union employment in major industries such as automobiles, steel, and consumer technologies left them on the defensive. They worried more about providing older members security and benefits than addressing issues that mattered to younger workers, such as job safety, working conditions, and opportunities for minorities and women. George Meany, head of the powerful AFL/CIO and an anticommunist, remained a strong supporter of the Vietnam War. And when Jock Yablonski led an insurgent movement to oust the corrupt leadership of the United Mine Workers, the union president, Tony Boyle, hired gunmen who murdered Yablonski and his wife and daughter.

Despite the backlash against reform, even critics could not deny that political and social activists had empowered people who had long seen themselves as "other" Americans who had been excluded. The reforms of the 1960s opened doors to jobs, careers, and avenues of success previously closed to all but white males. Inevitably, however, a pluralistic approach to equality tended to fragment rather than unify the nation. The road to equality—whether in the workplace, schools, or even the bedroom—remained a fault line dividing the nation.

The End of the War

Like identity politics the continuing debate over Vietnam continued to divide America. A peace settlement there eluded President Nixon because the North Vietnamese continued to reject any agreement that left the South Vietnamese government in power. Unwilling to send back American troops, in May 1972 Nixon instead mined and blockaded North Vietnam's major port, Haiphong, along with a sustained bombing campaign. In December he launched an even greater wave of attacks, as American planes dropped more bombs in 12 days than they had from 1969 to 1971.

Ironically, South Vietnamese leaders threw up the greatest obstacle to a settlement, for they were rightly convinced that General Thieu's regime would not last once the United States departed. But by January 1973, with Kissinger back in Paris, a treaty was finally arranged. Three months later the last American units were home.

> ✓ **REVIEW**
> How did the environmental movement attempt to change attitudes toward American habits and everyday life?

PRAGMATIC CONSERVATISM

PHILADELPHIA PLAN

IN AUGUST 1969, 4,000 ANGRY white union workers marched on city hall in Pittsburgh, Pennsylvania. There, a confrontation with police turned violent, leaving 50 protestors injured and 200 under arrest. A month later the scene repeated itself in Chicago, where hundreds of construction workers "slugged it out with 400 policemen." In both cases the issue was the "Philadelphia Plan" for affirmative action. Under it, the Nixon administration adopted the rule set forth under Lyndon Johnson in 1967 that government funding would be provided only if contractors' bids had "the result of producing minority group representations in all trades and in all phases of the construction project." The building trades unions wanted to know why they had been singled out when so many other industries did not meet those goals. Race played a role as well. "Why should these guys be given special consideration, just because they happen to be black?" one angry worker asked.

By 1969 affirmative action had become a political hot potato and Richard Nixon knew it. Over the course of his first term the president charted a pragmatic course, preserving and even expanding popular entitlements such as Social Security, seeking a middle ground on civil rights and affirmative action, while following the liberal tides in areas such as environmental protection.

Nixon's New Federalism

Nixon envisioned his New Federalism as a conservative counter to liberal programs run by the federal government.

Passed in 1972, a revenue-sharing act distributed $30 billion over five years in federal block grants to state and local governments. Instead of the funds being earmarked for specific purposes, localities could decide which problems needed attention and how best to attack them. A similar approach influenced aid to individuals. In the past, liberal programs from the New Deal to the Great Society often provided specific services to individuals: job retraining programs, Head Start programs for preschoolers, food supplement programs for nursing mothers. Republicans argued that such a "service strategy" too often assumed that federal bureaucrats best understood what the poor needed. Nixon favored an "income strategy," which gave recipients money to spend as they saw fit. Such grants were meant to encourage initiative and reduce government bureaucracy. Even if Nixon was determined to reverse the liberalism of the 1960s, he was hardly a deep-dyed conservative.

Stagflation

Ironically, a worsening economy forced Nixon to adopt liberal remedies. By 1970 the nation had entered its first recession in a decade. Normally a recession brought a decrease in demand for goods and a rise in unemployment as workers were laid off. Manufacturers then cut prices in order to encourage demand for their goods and cut wages in order to preserve profit margins. But in the recession of 1970, unemployment rose as economists would have expected, yet wages and prices were also rising in an inflationary spiral—a condition described as "stagflation."

Unfriendly Democrats labeled the phenomenon "Nixonomics," although in truth Lyndon Johnson had brought on inflation by refusing to raise taxes to pay for the war and for Great Society social programs. In addition, wages continued to rise partly because powerful unions had negotiated automatic cost-of-living increases into their contracts. Similarly, where a few large corporations dominated an industry, like steel and oil, prices and wages ignored market forces and continued to rise as demand and employment fell. Nixon added inflationary pressures by greatly increasing the numbers eligible for Social Security and pegging benefits to rises in the cost of living.

Mindful that his own "silent majority" were the people most pinched by the slower economy, Nixon decided that unemployment posed a greater threat than inflation. Announcing "I am now a Keynesian," he adopted a deficit budget designed to stimulate the growth of jobs. More surprising, in August 1971 he declared that to provide short-term relief, wages and prices would be frozen for 90 days. For a Republican to advocate wage and price controls was near heresy, almost as heretical as Nixon's overtures to China. For a year federal wage and price boards enforced the ground rules for any increases until the economy grew again. Controls were lifted in January 1973. As in foreign policy, Nixon had reversed long-cherished policies to achieve practical results.

DAILY LIVES

THE RACE TO THE MOON

In campaigning for the presidency in 1960, John F. Kennedy charged the Republicans with creating a missile gap. While the American space program limped along, the Soviet Union had launched *Sputnik*. Only a few months after Kennedy's inauguration, Russian cosmonaut Yuri Gagarin orbited the world in a 5-ton spacecraft. The first American space flight on May 6, 1961, succeeded only in carrying Commander Alan Shepard into a suborbital flight of 300 miles. Kennedy feared that if it lost the space race, the United States might lose the cold war as well.

Thus Kennedy ordered his science advisers "to shift our efforts in space from low to high gear." He announced on national television that the United States would do something truly dramatic: land a man on the moon and bring him back alive "before the decade is out." No matter how great the cost, Kennedy believed the investment was sound. "We must go into space because whatever mankind must undertake, free men must fully share," he proclaimed.

There were skeptics, such as former president Eisenhower, who thought anyone was "nuts" to spend billions for a space spectacular that promised little in the way of scientific discoveries. To many members of Congress, however, the space program was a huge pork barrel, so they voted to fund Kennedy's "great new American enterprise." From then on the space program achieved a string of triumphs. In February 1962 Colonel John Glenn successfully circled the earth three times in "a fireball of a ride"; an unmanned satellite passed Venus later that year; and a Telstar communications satellite began relaying television broadcasts, launching an era of truly global mass communications.

One after another, the space spectaculars continued, much to the public's delight. In March 1965 American astronauts first maneuvered their capsule; in May, Edward White took America's first space walk; the following year two vehicles met and docked for the first time. By Christmas eve 1968 the

Landing on the moon may have been one small step for a man, but NASA spent $25 billion on the project, more than $2 billion for each of the 12 astronauts who took lunar walks.

Apollo 8 mission was circling the moon. It seemed a "vast, lonely and forbidding sight," one astronaut remarked to hundreds of millions in a live telecast.

On July 20, 1969, the lunar module of *Apollo 11* at last touched down on the earth's closest neighbor. Commander Neil Armstrong, moving awkwardly in his bulky space suit, worked his way down a ladder to the white, chalky surface. He was not alone. Besides Edwin Aldrin, who followed him, and Michael Collins, orbiting in the command module, Armstrong brought along a quarter of the world's population, who monitored the moment live on television. "That's one small step for a man, one giant leap for mankind," he proclaimed.

Apollo 11 marked the climax of a phase of exploration, not a beginning. After *Apollo 17* and $25 billion in costs, Richard Nixon predicted "this may be the last time in this century men will walk on the moon." Space travel since then has belonged largely to the space shuttles and to unmanned missions around the solar system and space telescopes to penetrate distant galaxies.

Thinking Critically

What do you see as the greatest significance of the Apollo program?

Social Policies and the Court

SCHOOL BUSING Affirmative action, school prayer, contraception, criminal rights, obscenity, and school busing were all issues on which Supreme Court decisions offended the silent majority. By and large the liberal Court placed rights and liberties ahead of traditional values and law enforcement. The justices recognized, for example, that 15 years after its *Brown v. Board of Education* decision, most school districts remained segregated. In white neighborhoods, parents opposed having their children bused to more distant, formerly all-black schools as part of a plan to achieve racial balance. Although black parents for their part worried about how their children might be treated in hostile white neighborhoods, by and large they supported busing as a means to better education.

THE NIXON COURT

Under Nixon, federal policy on desegregation took a 180-degree turn. In 1969 the Justice Department supported lawyers for Mississippi who asked the Supreme Court to delay an integration plan. The Court not only rejected that proposal but two years later ruled, in *Swann v. Charlotte-Mecklenburg Board of Education* (1971), that busing, balancing ratios, and redrawing school district lines were all acceptable ways to achieve integration. Given the continuing liberal activism of the Court, the president looked to change its direction by filling vacancies with more conservative justices. He replaced Chief Justice Earl Warren in 1969 with Warren Burger, a jurist who had no wish to break new ground. When another vacancy occurred in 1969, Nixon tried twice to appoint conservative southern judges with reputations for opposing civil rights and labor unions. Congress rejected both. In the end, the president nominated Minnesotan Harry Blackmun, a moderate judge of unimpeachable integrity. Two more conservative appointments guaranteed that the Court would no longer lead the fight for minority rights. But neither would it reverse the achievements of the Warren Court.

Triumph and Revenge

MCGOVERN AND LIBERAL DEMOCRATS

As the election of 1972 approached, Nixon's majority seemed to be falling into place, especially after the Democrats nominated Senator George McGovern of South Dakota. McGovern's nomination gave Nixon the split between "us" and "them" he sought. The Democratic platform embraced all the activist causes that the silent majority resented. It called for immediate withdrawal from Vietnam, abolition of the draft, amnesty for war resisters, and a minimum guaranteed income for the poor. By November the only question that remained to be settled was the size of Nixon's majority. He received almost 61 percent of the popular vote.

Yet the overwhelming victory did not relieve the president's urge to settle scores. In his political battles, Nixon exhibited a tendency to see issues in terms of a very personal "us against them." "We have not used the power in the first four years, as you know . . . ," he remarked to his chief of staff, H. R. Haldeman, "but things are going to change now." The administration began compiling an "enemies list"—everyone from television news correspondents to student activists—to be targeted for audits by the Internal Revenue Service or other forms of harassment.

THE "PLUMBERS" AND THE PENTAGON PAPERS

In truth, Nixon had already begun to abuse his presidential powers. In June 1971 the *New York Times* published a secret, often highly critical military study of the Vietnam War, soon dubbed the "Pentagon Papers." Angrily the president authorized a secret group known as "the plumbers" to burglarize the office of a psychiatrist treating the disillusioned official who leaked the study. The burglars hoped to find records that were personally damaging.

Break-In

The president's fall from power began with what seemed a minor event. In June 1972 burglars entered the Democratic National Committee headquarters, located in Washington's plush Watergate apartment complex. The five burglars were an unusual lot. When they were arrested, they wore business suits and carried bugging devices, tear-gas guns, and more than $2,000 in crisp new 100-dollar bills. One had worked for the CIA. Another was carrying an address book whose phone numbers included that of a Howard Hunt at the "W. House." Nixon's press secretary dismissed the break-in as "a third-rate burglary attempt," and Nixon himself announced that "no one on the White House staff . . . was involved in this very bizarre incident. What really hurts in matters of this sort is not the fact that they occur," the president continued. "What really hurts is if you try to cover up."

In January 1973 the burglars were tried along with former White House aides E. Howard Hunt Jr. and G. Gordon Liddy. Judge John Sirica was not satisfied with the defendants' guilty plea. He wanted to know who had directed the burglars and why "these 100-dollar bills were floating around like coupons." Facing a stiff jail sentence, one of the burglars admitted that the defendants had been bribed to plead guilty and were protecting higher government officials. Soon after, the president accepted the resignations of his two closest aides, H. R. Haldeman and John Ehrlichman. He also fired John Dean, his White House counsel, after Dean agreed to cooperate with prosecutors.

To the Oval Office

WHITE HOUSE TAPES

Over the summer of 1973 a string of officials testified at televised Senate hearings. Each witness took the trail of the burglary and its cover-up higher into White House circles. Then John Dean gave his testimony. Young, with a Boy Scout's face, Dean declared in a quiet monotone that the president had personally been involved in the cover-up. Still, it remained Dean's word against the president's until Senate committee staff discovered, almost by chance, that since 1970 Nixon had been secretly recording all conversations and phone calls in the Oval Office.

Obtaining that crucial evidence proved no easy task. Nixon agreed to appoint a special prosecutor, Harvard law professor Archibald Cox, to investigate the new disclosures, but when Cox subpoenaed the tapes of the conversations and phone calls, the president refused to turn them over. As that battle raged and the astonished public wondered if matters could possibly get worse, they did. Evidence unrelated to Watergate revealed that Vice President

Under the leadership of the folksy but razor-sharp Senator Sam Ervin of North Carolina, the Senate committee investigating the Watergate scandal attracted a large television audience. John Dean (center), the former White House legal counsel, provided the most damning evidence linking President Nixon to the cover-up—until the existence of secretly recorded White House tapes became known.

Spiro Agnew had systematically solicited bribes, both as governor of Maryland and while serving in Washington. He resigned the vice presidency in October. Under provisions of the Twenty-Fifth Amendment, Nixon appointed Representative Gerald R. Ford of Michigan to replace Agnew.

Then on Saturday night, October 20, Nixon fired Special Prosecutor Cox. Reaction to this "Saturday Night Massacre" was overwhelming: 150,000 telegrams poured into Washington, and by the following Tuesday, 84 House members had sponsored 16 different bills of impeachment. The beleaguered president turned over the tapes to a new special prosecutor, Texas lawyer Leon Jaworski. Jaworski's investigations led him to request additional tapes and again the president refused, although he grudgingly supplied some 1,200 pages of typed transcripts. Littered with cynicism and profanity, even these edited documents revealed Nixon talking with his counsel John Dean about how to "take care of the jackasses who are in jail." When Dean estimated it might take a million dollars to buy their silence, Nixon replied, "We could get that. . . . You could get a million dollars. And you could get it in cash. I know where it could be gotten." Finally, Special Prosecutor Jaworski petitioned the Supreme Court to order release of the tapes he requested. In *United States v. Nixon,* the Court ruled unanimously in Jaworski's favor.

Resignation

The end came quickly. The House Judiciary Committee adopted three articles of impeachment, charging that Nixon had obstructed justice, had abused his constitutional authority in improperly using federal agencies to harass citizens, and had hindered the committee's investigation.

The tapes showed that on June 23, 1972, only a few days after the break-in, Nixon knew the burglars were tied to the White House staff and knew that his attorney general had acted to limit an FBI investigation. Not willing to be the first president convicted in a Senate impeachment trial, Nixon resigned on August 8, 1974. The following day Gerald Ford became president. "The Constitution works," Ford told a relieved nation. "Our long national nightmare is over."

The Road's End for Vietnam and Liberalism

As an unelected president, Gerald Ford had no popular mandate. Ford hoped to put Watergate behind the nation rather than look backward in recrimination. To that end, only a month into office and without any warning, he granted Richard Nixon a full pardon for any crimes he might have committed. But the pardon succeeded only in deepening the nation's cynicism, because Nixon would never face prosecution nor assume responsibility for his crimes.

And then there was still Vietnam, where in January 1975 North Vietnamese forces renewed their offense against the South. President Ford implored Congress to grant $1 billion in emergency aid, but the nation's political will was exhausted. "My God, we're all tired of it, we're sick to death of it," exclaimed one citizen in Oregon. "55,000 dead and $100 billion spent and for what?" In April 1975 Saigon fell, amid scenes of desperate Americans and South Vietnamese fighting to squeeze onto evacuation helicopters.

By then more than Saigon had fallen; and more than a foreign policy had failed in Vietnam. The liberalism of

Lyndon Johnson's Great Society—of Franklin Roosevelt's New Deal and Harry Truman's Square Deal had reached its high-water mark and was now receding, amid the battles over the war. Like all wars, Vietnam changed more in the nation's society than anyone ever expected.

REVIEW

In which ways did Richard Nixon's domestic policies mark a conservative turn, and in which ways take a more liberal approach to governing?

CONCLUSION

THE WORLD AT LARGE

"The enemy must fight his battles far from his home base for a long time," a Vietnamese strategist once wrote. "We must further weaken him by drawing him into protracted campaigns. Once his initial dash is broken, it will be easier to destroy him." The enemy in question was not the Americans, nor the French, but the Mongol invaders of 1284 CE. The strategy of resistance and attrition that kept the Chinese at bay for centuries also defeated the United States. Between 1961 and 1973, the war cost billions in national treasure and left some 57,000 soldiers dead and over 300,000 wounded. The cost to Southeast Asia was even more incalculable. Much of the land lay devastated, and some 6.5 million South Vietnamese had become refugees along with 3 million Laotians and Cambodians. In excess of 3 million Vietnamese soldiers and civilians died during the war.

Defeat in Vietnam marked the end of liberalism triumphant and offered a stark reminder of the limits of American power. No longer did most Americans believe that the world could be remade in their image. While the United States waged its futile war in Vietnam, power had shifted to the growing economies of Europe and the Pacific Rim and to the members of OPEC. If Richard Nixon had not overreached, he might have replaced the liberal creed with a new conservative approach to government. But Nixon had exceeded the limits of presidential power in his desire for mastery, just as liberalism exceeded its limits in the quagmire of Lyndon Johnson's war. The rise of a new conservative tide would have to wait for a new quest to restore America's power and prestige. ∞∞∞

CHAPTER SUMMARY

THOUGH PRESIDENTS FROM TRUMAN TO Nixon sent American forces to Indochina, Vietnam was Lyndon Johnson's war, and the political divisions it caused ended both his presidency and the consensus on liberal reform.

■ To force the North Vietnamese to negotiate, Johnson escalated the American war effort. By 1966 American soldiers were doing most of the fighting. American warplanes subjected North Vietnam to heavy bombing.

■ As the nation divided into prowar hawks and antiwar doves, the Vietcong's Tet Offensive shocked Americans. Johnson almost lost the New Hampshire presidential primary to Senator Eugene McCarthy, leading the president to abandon his reelection campaign.

■ In the wake of the assassinations of Martin Luther King Jr. and Robert Kennedy, Hubert Humphrey became the Democrats' presidential nominee. But riots at the Chicago convention so damaged Humphrey's candidacy that Richard Nixon won the election, promising a "peace with honor" in Vietnam.

■ A wide range of minorities—Latinos, Indians, Asian Americans, gays, and feminists—adopted identity politics as a way to claim their full rights and opportunities as Americans.

• Mexican American migrant workers led by César Chávez successfully established a farmworkers' union, the UFW, while a rising generation of Latino students adopted militant techniques for establishing a Chicano identity.

• Though often divided by tribal diversity, militant Native Americans called attention to the discrimination faced by Indians in urban settings as well as on reservations.

- Feminists campaigned for civil and political equality as well as to change deep-seated cultural attitudes of a "patriarchal" society.

- In addition to reform movements based on identity, the value politics of environmentalists and consumer advocates extended the spirit of reform.

■ White House involvement in the Watergate break-in and the president's subsequent cover-up led to the first resignation of an American president.

■ President Gerald Ford inherited an office weakened by scandal.

■ The fall of Vietnam after three decades of debilitating war left liberal ideals in disarray, though Nixon's overreaching in the White House temporarily forestalled a resurgence of conservatism in the United States.

ADDITIONAL READING

TWO BOOKS—DAVID KAISER, *American Tragedy: Kennedy, Johnson, and the Origins of the Vietnam War* (2000), and Fredrik Logevall, *Choosing War: The Lost Chance for Peace and the Escalation of War in Vietnam* (1999)—trace the road by which the United States escalated its military commitments in Vietnam. Among those who lay the blame with Lyndon Johnson, see Michael Hunt, *Lyndon Johnson's Cold War Crusade in Vietnam, 1945–1968* (1997), and Lloyd Gardner, *Pay Any Price: Lyndon Johnson and the Wars for Vietnam* (1997). For the soldiers' experience, look at the classic by Michael Herr, *Dispatches* (1977), and David Maraniss, *They Marched into Sunlight: War and Peace, Vietnam and America, October 1967* (2004). Maraniss looks simultaneously at soldiers on the battlefront, protest that tore apart the University of Wisconsin, and policymaking in Washington.

Keith Olsen, *Watergate: The Presidential Scandal That Shook America* (2003), is a lively brief account of Nixon's fall, while Stanley Kutler, *The Wars of Watergate: The Last Crisis of Richard Nixon* (1992), provides more detail. For a look at the politics of division and emergence of identity and value political movements that divided the nation, see Mark Hamilton Lytle, *America's Uncivil Wars* (2006); and for an argument that the 1970s were more significant than the 1960s, see Bruce Shulman, *The Seventies: The Great Shift in American Culture, Society, and Politics* (2002). Gender politics are widely explored in Ruth Rosen, *The World Split Open: How the Modern Women's Movement Changed America* (2001). Union and labor issues are explored in Jefferson Cowie, *Stayin' Alive: The 1970s and the Last Days of the Working Class* (2010). Excellent on the environmental movement is Robert Gottlieb, *Forcing the Spring: The Transformation of the American Environmental Movement* (1996). Mark Hamilton Lytle, *The Gentle Subversive: Rachel Carson,* Silent Spring, *and the Rise of the Environmental Movement* (2007), provides a brief biographical approach to the topic.

For a fresh, nonpartisan look at Richard Nixon, see Melvin Small, *The Presidency of Richard Nixon* (2003), or Richard Reeves, *President Nixon: Alone in the White House* (2002). A dissenter from the camp of Kissinger admirers is Jussi Hanhimaki, *The Flawed Architect: Henry Kissinger and American Foreign Policy* (2004).

For a fuller list of readings, see the Bibliography at www.mhhe.com/eh8e.

SIGNIFICANT EVENTS

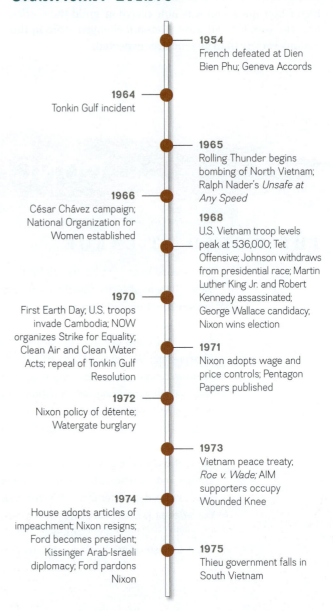

1954 French defeated at Dien Bien Phu; Geneva Accords

1964 Tonkin Gulf incident

1965 Rolling Thunder begins bombing of North Vietnam; Ralph Nader's *Unsafe at Any Speed*

1966 César Chávez campaign; National Organization for Women established

1968 U.S. Vietnam troop levels peak at 536,000; Tet Offensive; Johnson withdraws from presidential race; Martin Luther King Jr. and Robert Kennedy assassinated; George Wallace candidacy; Nixon wins election

1970 First Earth Day; U.S. troops invade Cambodia; NOW organizes Strike for Equality; Clean Air and Clean Water Acts; repeal of Tonkin Gulf Resolution

1971 Nixon adopts wage and price controls; Pentagon Papers published

1972 Nixon policy of détente; Watergate burglary

1973 Vietnam peace treaty; *Roe v. Wade;* AIM supporters occupy Wounded Knee

1974 House adopts articles of impeachment; Nixon resigns; Ford becomes president; Kissinger Arab-Israeli diplomacy; Ford pardons Nixon

1975 Thieu government falls in South Vietnam

The Making of a Quagmire: Vietnam

ENTANGLEMENT

1948 French name Bao Dai head of Vietnam. U.S. begins funding the French war.

1954 French defeated at Dien Bien Phu. Ngo Dinh Diem arrives in South Vietnam.

1955– Diem, with U.S. backing, rejects
1956 Geneva Accord provision for free elections.

1959 Diem's repressive measures provoke armed resistance in the South.

1960 National Liberation Front (NLF) created to oppose Diem.

ESCALATION

1961 President Kennedy orders 3,000 military "advisers" to Vietnam. Number rises to 16,000 by 1963.

1962 Military coup assassinates Diem November 2. Kennedy assassinated November 22.

1964 Tonkin Gulf Resolution gives Johnson authority to take "all necessary measures."

1965 Johnson escalates the U.S. role in the war.

1966 Senate hearings on the war. U.S. troop levels reach 362,000.

1967 March on Washington. U.S. troops at 535,000.

ESCAPE

1968 Tet Offensive. Johnson withdraws from presidential race. Paris peace talks. Nixon claims plan to end the war.

1969 Nixon bombs Cambodia; "Vietnamization." My Lai revealed. Renewed antiwar demonstrations.

1970 Paris peace talks. U.S. invades Cambodia; Kent State and Jackson State shootings.

1971 Pentagon Papers published.

1972 "Christmas bombing" of North Vietnam.

1973 January agreement reached in Paris. Last U.S. combat troops leave South Vietnam.

1974 Nixon resigns over Watergate. Congress rejects new military aid to South Vietnam.

1975 Fall of Saigon. Vietnam War ends.

On June 12, 1987 President Ronald Reagan spoke before the Brandenburg Gate in West Berlin, Germany. He had already made great progress with Soviet Premier Mikhail Gorbachev in easing the nuclear arms race. Now, speaking before German leaders, he invited Gorbachev to "tear down this wall," meaning the Berlin Wall, a vestige of Cold War conflict.

The Conservative Challenge

1976–1992

∞∞∞ AN AMERICAN STORY ∞∞∞

THE NEW AMERICAN COMMONS

In the early 1970s San Diego city officials looked out at a downtown that was growing seedier each year as stores and shoppers fled to suburban malls. Indeed, many once-thriving downtown retail centers across the nation had become virtual ghost towns at the close of the business day. But San Diego found a way to bounce back. The city launched an ambitious redevelopment plan calling for a convention center, a marina, hotels, and apartment complexes.

Minnesota's Mall of America: the ultimate cathedral of consumption

The core of the plan was Horton Plaza, a mall with the look of an Italian hill town. Stores with stucco facades fronted twisting pedestrian thoroughfares where Renaissance arches lured customers to upscale stores selling clothing, jewelry, and sporting goods. Jugglers and clowns wandered the streets, while guitarists serenaded passersby. Horton Plaza soon ranked just behind the zoo and Sea World as San Diego's prime tourist attraction.

With their soaring atriums, lavish food courts, and splashing fountains, malls became the cathedrals of American material culture. Shopping on Sunday rivaled churchgoing as the weekly family ritual. Whereas American youth culture centered on the high school in the 1950s and on college campuses in the 1960s, in the 1970s and 1980s it gravitated toward the malls' fast-food stores and video arcades. For single men and women, malls became a place to find a date. Older people discovered that the controlled climate was ideal for "mall walking."

As cathedrals of consumption, malls reflected a society turning away from social crusades to private paths of personal fulfillment. Some individuals adopted a consumerist or material path. Evangelical religion offered the spiritual prospect of being "born again" and embracing the virtues of traditional family values. Through private charity and volunteerism, these evangelicals proposed to replace the intrusive social policies of the modern welfare state. Along less orthodox paths, the "human potential movement" taught techniques such as yoga, Transcendental Meditation, and "biogenics" as means to inner fulfillment. The search for moral meaning spread out, much as a mall did, along many corridors and past a host of spiritual boutiques, all nestled among the ever-present food courts and the acres of parking arrayed around the new American commons.

Following the twin calamities of Watergate and Vietnam, political leaders addressed the era's spiritual hunger and discontent. On the eve of the nation's bicentennial, opinion polls showed that some 70 percent of those surveyed believed "over the last 10 years, this country's leaders have consistently lied to the people." Jimmy Carter, who followed Gerald Ford into the White House, saw a "crisis of confidence"—a "growing doubt about the meaning of our own lives and in the loss of a unity of purpose for our nation." In 1981 Carter's successor, Ronald Reagan, sought to reverse that pessimism and to restore national confidence. He evoked a vision of the United States as a "city upon a hill" that would inspire the rest of the world through its actions and virtues. In doing so, Reagan deliberately echoed language Puritan leader John Winthrop used to describe the seventeenth-century Massachusetts Bay Colony.

Carter's and Reagan's rhetoric carried strong religious overtones. While Carter evoked a sense of decline and uncertainty (a time of "declension," the Puritans would have said), Reagan's vision was more uplifting. It drew on the nineteenth-century idea that the United States had a "manifest destiny" to spread across the continent and become preeminent on the world's stage. But while the politics of both Carter and Reagan reflected a move to the right, the nation was still very much split between joining the born-again conservative revolution and sticking with secular, centrist politics. Despite the efforts of religious conservatives, popular culture continued to reflect the trends of the 1960s, when sex and violence became standard media fare and tolerance for alternative lifestyles grew. Liberal activists continued to see government, not the private sector, as the best way to clean up the environment, improve schools, reduce urban violence, and solve public health issues such as the AIDS epidemic.

The conservative rebellion thus fed off this secular and liberal vision of society—not simply by opposing it but often by harnessing its techniques in the service of conservative causes. In doing so, the long-brewing rebellion gained the momentum to become a revolution, leaving behind the half-measures of Jimmy Carter and sweeping Ronald Reagan into power. ∞∞∞∞

The Conservative Rebellion

In California, Howard Jarvis, a retired Mormon businessman, had for years promoted tax-cutting referenda on the state ballot. While those measures failed to attract wide support, Jarvis's efforts to reduce property taxes did. In the case of property taxes, the issue was equity, not simply lower taxes. Small homeowners often paid taxes at much higher rates than large property owners and businesses that received breaks from friendly and often corrupt tax assessors. Hence, the extremely conservative Jarvis began to frame his antigovernment agenda in populist terms. His supporters, he claimed, were the small interests and individuals: teachers, blue-collar workers, and "a great number of Negroes." His group, the United Organizations of Taxpayers (UOT), received no money from oil companies, bankers, land speculators, or insurance companies.

Tax Revolt

PROPOSITION 13 By the late 1970s California was ripe for the Jarvis rebellion. Inflation imposed a crushing burden on middle- and lower-class homeowners. At the same time, their taxes rose steadily. One woman complained to California governor Jerry Brown that her hopes to live in a house mortgage-free were not possible, "because our government won't let this happen." An old radical and union organizer described state politicians and bureaucrats as "those leeches who must have more and more taxes." Such mounting anger helped UOT collect 1.25 million signatures to place Proposition 13 on the ballot in 1978. Opponents warned that the loss of revenue would force school closings, job losses, and reduced police and fire protection. Despite those warnings the measure passed easily.

The tax rebellion quickly spread across the nation. The *New York Times* likened it to "a modern Boston Tea Party." Over the next four years 12 states passed similar resolutions, while many legislatures cut public spending and taxes, hoping to avoid the voters' wrath. Even in Massachusetts, where government programs were generally popular, voters capped local property taxes and prevented future increases of more than 2½ percent, no matter how much inflation rose or the population grew. The only state to support the liberal George McGovern in 1972 voted narrowly for Ronald Reagan in 1980. After 1975 Americans no longer embraced the liberal consensus that professional expertise in the service of government could solve the nation's problems and promote progress.

The Diverse Evangelical World

The conservative rebellion was not merely the child of a faltering economy, stagnating wages, and a resistance to paying taxes. The social ferment of the 1960s had taken its toll on spiritual life and on the churches. During that decade mainline Protestant churches struggled over how their religious beliefs should engage with civil rights, the war in Vietnam, issues of sex and gender, and more-liberated lifestyles. As congregations moved to embrace liberal definitions of faith, many found themselves yearning for a traditional religious experience. They moved in large numbers from long-established denominations such as Presbyterians and Congregationalists to evangelical churches. By the mid-1980s some 36 percent of Americans described themselves as "born again." Similar trends occurred among Catholics and Jews, many of whom also resisted the liberalization of their faith.

Among evangelicals the Southern Baptists and Assemblies of God attracted large national memberships, but their real focus was local, centered in church communities. Such congregations insisted that salvation came through a spiritual rebirth (being "born again") after a person had acknowledged sinfulness and embraced Christ's atonement. Evangelical tradition encouraged proselytizing by the faithful, often in the form of revivals and spiritual awakenings. Finally, most evangelicals anticipated the rapture, when Christ would return to transport true believers into his Father's kingdom. These shared beliefs, when combined with a commitment to piety, put evangelicals squarely at odds with modern society. They imposed a strict personal morality, often insisted on the central role of fathers in the family, and in some churches forbade such "worldly evils" as dancing, cosmetics, movies, gambling, and premarital sex.

PAT ROBERTSON Though evangelicals condemned much of modern culture, many preachers advocated a "prosperity theology" that encouraged economic success. They also used the media to spread the word, none more effectively than did Virginia-based Pat Robertson, the son of a Virginia politician. Robertson, a magnetic Southern Baptist, used cable and satellite broadcasts to expand the Christian Broadcast Network into a media empire. His *700 Club* reached an audience of millions and inspired his colleague Jim Bakker to launch the even more popular *Praise the Lord Club*—PTL for short. Although the content featured gospel singing, fervent preaching, faith healing, and speaking in tongues, the format mirrored that of major network talk shows, opening with a Christian monologue, conversations with celebrity guests, and musical entertainment.

The Catholic Conscience

POPE JOHN PAUL II American Catholics faced their own decisions about the lines between religion and politics. In the 1960s a social activist movement had arisen out of the church council known as Vatican II (see page 819). Disturbed by these currents, Catholic conservatives found support for their views when the magnetic John Paul II assumed the papacy in 1979. Pope John Paul reined in the modern trends inspired

During the late 1970s and the 1980s, conservatives increasingly spoke out against abortion and in favor of the right to life for an unborn fetus. Adopting the tactics of protest and civil disobedience once common to radicals in the 1960s, in this photograph they clash with pro-choice demonstrators outside Faneuil Hall in Boston.

by Vatican II. He ruled against a wider role for women in the church hierarchy and stiffened church policy against birth control. These edicts put him at odds with a majority of American Catholics. The American church also faced a crisis as fewer young men and women chose celibate lives as priests and nuns.

Though conservative Catholics and Protestant evangelicals were sometimes wary of one another, they shared certain views. Both groups lobbied for the government to provide federal aid to parochial schools and Fundamentalist academies. But it was the issue of abortion that attracted the greatest mutual support. Pope John Paul reaffirmed the church's teaching that all life begins at conception and that abortion amounts to murder of the unborn. Evangelicals, long skeptical of the power of secular technology and science, attacked abortion as another instance in which science had upset the natural moral order of life.

Moving Religion into Politics

CONSERVATIVES AND *ROE V. WADE*

Since many evangelicals believed that the apocalypse—the end-time of the world—was imminent, before the 1970s they saw little reason to reform society. Many refused even to vote. Gradually that apolitical stance weakened. A number of Supreme Court decisions, beginning with the ban on school prayer in *Engel v. Vitale* (1962), struck conservatives as an attack on their faith, but none more so than *Roe v. Wade*. If an unborn fetus was fully human, was it not necessarily endowed with both a soul and with human rights? Abortion constituted "the slaughter of the innocents." Here was a case where it seemed that the government posed a threat to faith and family. So also did the inclusion of such subjects as Darwinian evolution and sex education in school curricula.

Some conservative parents countered by establishing Christian academies, many of which were racially as well as religiously segregated. The Internal Revenue Service proposed in 1978 to deny tax-exempt status for schools that failed to meet its standards of racial integration. Reacting strongly, conservatives bombarded the IRS, their congressional representatives, and the White House with protests. By 1979 the IRS dropped its desegregation initiative.

JERRY FALWELL AND THE LAHAYES

Having crossed the line into politics, evangelicals began to organize their efforts. In 1977 the Reverend Jerry Falwell from Lynchburg, Virginia, joined his fellow Baptist preacher, Tim LaHaye of San Diego, to fight for the repeal of a gay rights ordinance in Miami, Florida. LaHaye and his wife Beverly, a writer, had formed the Concerned Women of America (CWA), a "pro-family" organization that by the 1980s claimed more members than the National Organization for Women. The LaHayes were outspoken opponents of homosexuality and pornography. Under their leadership, CWA crusaded against abortion, no-fault divorce laws, and the Equal Rights Amendment.

THE MORAL MAJORITY

Their ally, the Reverend Falwell, epitomized the entrepreneurial gifts of many preachers of prosperity theology. His daily radio broadcasts and Sunday television show, the *Old Time Gospel*

Hour, reached an audience of over a million. His home church ran multiple Sunday services to accommodate a congregation of 17,000. In addition, Falwell founded a school, a facility to treat alcoholics, a summer camp, and Liberty University. And when he and LaHaye defeated the gay rights ordinance in Miami, they went on to form the Moral Majority, a political action organization, which Falwell described as "pro-life, pro-family, pro-morality, and pro-American." The Moral Majority also shared the conservative opposition to labor unions, environmental reform, and most government-based social welfare programs.

The Media as Battleground

Evangelicals and political conservatives believed the mass media played a central role in corrupting family values. Its permissive, even positive portrayal of unmarried women, premarital sex and drug use, profanity, homosexuality, nudity, and violence offended their moral sensibilities. The conservative determination to censor media content clashed with a liberal commitment to free speech and toleration for diversity in lifestyles.

ARCHIE BUNKER Hollywood movies had long pushed the boundaries of acceptable content, but by the 1970s television began to introduce more controversial and politicized programming. In 1971 producer Norman Lear introduced *All in the Family,* whose main character, Archie Bunker, embodied the blue-collar backlash against liberal and permissive values. The ultimate male chauvinist, Archie treated his wife Edith like a servant, clashed with his modestly rebellious daughter Gloria, and heaped verbal abuse on his leftist Polish-American son-in-law. All things liberal or cosmopolitan—"Hebes," "Spics," and "Commie Crapola"—became targets for Archie's coarse insults. While millions watched the show, both the left and the right attacked it. Many conservatives who shared Archie's values found the language offensive, while some minority leaders charged that the show legitimized the prejudices it attacked.

SATURDAY NIGHT FEVER If *All in the Family* defined the class anger of blue-collar Americans, the hugely popular disco movie *Saturday Night Fever* revealed their alienation. The film explores the Brooklyn world of Tony Manero, played by John Travolta, who holds a dead-end job as a hardware store clerk during the day, but at night transforms himself into a white-suited disco king. Where his loser friends walk down Brooklyn's mean streets, Tony struts. When his boss counsels him to consider his long-term prospects for getting ahead, he replies angrily, "Fuck the future." To which his boss expresses the declining prospects of blue-collar Americans: No, "the future fucks you."

| Jerry Falwell of the Moral Majority

The glitter of disco offers Tony a world in which he can be somebody. In the end, however, he rejects his suffocating family, loser friends, and blue-collar roots for a future across the Brooklyn Bridge in Manhattan, where his girlfriend is bent on a professional career. He embraces the notion that those with talent and dreams can escape the past and reinvent themselves. In the end, *Saturday Night Fever,* the most popular movie of the 1970s, looked to have its cake and eat it. On the one hand, it glamorized the youthful blue-collar culture with its vulgar language, violence, explicit sexuality, and drug use that so offended conservative critics of the media. But at the same time, its escapist ending offered audiences fantasy rather than a political or spiritual path to salvation.

Perhaps inevitably, the wars for the soul of prime-time entertainment spilled into the political arena. Fearful that the Moral Majority's political pressure would lead television producers to censor themselves, the creator of Archie Bunker, Norman Lear, formed People for the American Way. The organization self-consciously opposed the agenda set by LaHaye and Falwell. People for the American Way campaigned for

| John Travolta, the blue-collar Brooklyn boy with aspirations, dressed to the nines and "Stayin' Alive," to the beat of the Bee Gees.

THE CULTURE WARS

A series of events—including the abortion-rights case Roe v. Wade *(1973), a Miami ordinance adopted protecting the rights of homosexuals, and a move by the Internal Revenue Service to tax racially exclusive Christian schools—prompted evangelical Christian leaders Tim LaHaye and Jerry Falwell to form the Moral Majority, a political action organization. As a counterweight, Norman Lear, a liberal producer of popular TV series such as* All in the Family, Maude, *and* The Jeffersons, *created People for the American Way.*

DOCUMENT 1   Take a Stand on Moral Issues

We must reverse the trend America finds herself in today. Young people between the ages of twenty-five and forty have been born and reared in a different world than Americans of years past. The television set has been their primary baby-sitter. From the television set they have learned situation ethics and immorality—they have learned a loss of respect for human life. They have learned to disrespect the family as God has established it. They have been educated in a public-school system that is permeated with secular humanism. They have been taught that the Bible is just another book of literature. They have been taught that there are no absolutes in our world today. They

have been introduced to the drug culture. They have been reared by the family and the public school in a society that is greatly void of discipline and character-building. These same young people have been reared under the influence of a government that has taught them socialism and welfarism. They have been taught to believe that the world owes them a living whether they work or not.

It is now time to take a stand on certain moral issues, and we can only stand if we have leaders. We must stand against the Equal Rights Amendment, the feminist revolution, and the homosexual revolution. We must have a revival in this country. . . . The

hope of reversing the trends of decay in our republic now lies with the Christian public in America. We cannot expect help from the liberals. They certainly are not going to call our nation back to righteousness and neither are the pornographers, the smut peddlers, and those who are corrupting our youth. Moral Americans must be willing to put their reputations, their fortunes, and their very lives on the line for this great nation of ours. Would that we had the courage of our forefathers who knew the great responsibility that freedom carries with it. . . .

Our Founding Fathers separated church and state in function, but never intended to

---

diversity and tolerance. In turn, conservatives, particularly the religious right, advanced their pro-life and pro-family agenda.

 REVIEW

Why did evangelicals become political in the late 1970s, and what techniques did they use to increase their influence?

THE PRESIDENCY IN TRANSITION: GERALD FORD AND JIMMY CARTER

WAR POWERS RESOLUTION

THE CROSSCURRENTS IN AMERICAN CULTURE shook the political system as well. In the wake of Watergate and the Vietnam War, Congress was determined to place limits on a presidency which, under Nixon, had seemed to grow entirely too imperial. The War Powers Resolution, passed in 1973 before Gerald Ford took office, required that the president consult Congress before committing troops to the battlefield, report within

two days of taking action, and withdraw troops after 60 days unless Congress voted to retain them.

Meanwhile, congressional hearings revealed that the CIA had routinely violated its charter forbidding it to spy on Americans at home. Abroad, the agency had attempted to assassinate foreign leaders in Cuba, the Congo, South Vietnam, and the Dominican Republic. The FBI had also used illegal means to infiltrate and disrupt domestic dissidents. J. Edgar Hoover had authorized an (unsuccessful) operation to drive Martin Luther King Jr. to suicide. Determined to rein in the executive branch, the Senate established committees to oversee intelligence operations.

INFLUENCE OF KISSINGER

Hemmed in by a newly assertive Congress, President Gerald Ford relied on Henry Kissinger's guidance in foreign policy. The secretary of state perceived himself as a realist who offended idealists on the political left and right. Quoting the German writer Goethe, Kissinger explained, "If I had to choose between justice and disorder, on the one hand, and injustice and order, on the other, I would always choose the latter."

establish a government void of God. As is evidenced by our Constitution, good people in America must exert an influence and provide a conscience and climate of morality in which it is difficult to go wrong, not difficult for people to go right in America.

Source: Jerry Falwell, *Listen, America!* (New York: Doubleday, 1980), pp. 17–23.

DOCUMENT 2   Room for a Diversity of Voices

America and television face a new brand of monopolists, not monopolists of money or goods but of truth and values. In times of hardship, voices of stridency and division have always replaced those of reason and unity, and the results have always been a deterioration of free and open dialogue, a tension among races, classes, and religions, and the temptation to grasp at simplistic solutions to complex problems.

In our time of hardship, we find the New Right and the Religious New Right—a new breed of robber barons who have organized to corner the market on morals. . . . As communicators ourselves, it should be interesting to look at how well they are able to spread their absolutist views. There are now over 1,500 Christian radio stations blanketing the country—with approximately one new station being added each week; there are forty-some independent television stations with a full-time diet of religious programming, largely fundamentalist; and three Christian Broadcasting Networks. . . .

There are also scores and scores of local radio and TV evangelicals, espousing the same absolutist fundamentalist points of view while attacking the integrity and character of anyone who does not stand with them. . . . Here is some of what is occurring on the local level across the country:

- In Washington and Virginia, Moral Majoritarians have attempted to secure the names of all those who borrowed books on sex education from the public library.
- Five dictionaries have been banned from use in schools throughout the state of Texas because "concerned parents" objected to such "filth" as the word "bastard" and the word "bed," when used as a verb.
- Textbooks across the country are not being bought by some school boards, under pressure from local groups, until all liberal dogma and secular humanism has been excised by a fundamentalist couple in Texas, the Gablers.
- In North Carolina, a social studies test was found objectionable and removed because seventh graders are not emotionally or intellectually capable of dealing with such complex problems. The problems they didn't want seventh graders dealing with were food shortages, overpopulation, and ecology. . . .

Ironically, this occurs at a time when the communications industry is witnessing an explosion of new technologies, delivery systems, and satellite networks, promising as many as 100 channels to the home. With this overabundance of sources, there will be room for a diversity of voices, a place for the emergence of cultures and subcultures that have not been heard from before. . . .

The First Amendment says that "Congress shall make no law . . . abridging the freedom of speech." It says *"no* law. . . ." It doesn't say that there will be freedom of speech provided that said speech does not run contrary to popular thought. It doesn't say that there will be freedom of speech provided that said speech has no tendency to subvert standing institutions. . . . But, and this is a very big but, this is not the America of the early 1900s—and today the blessings of the First Amendment cannot be realized fully by every segment of our society without access to the mass media.

Source: Norman Lear, "Liberty and Its Responsibilities," in *Broadcast Journalism 1979–1981: The Eighth Alfred I. DuPont Columbia University Survey,* Marvin Barrett, ed. (New York: Everest House, 1982). Also on the web at www.normanlear.com/backstory_writings.html.

Thinking Critically

What does Falwell see as the source of moral decay? What does Lear find threatening in the message of the New Right and New Religious Right? How do their views on the proper role of government compare? What does each see as the proper role of television and the media?

During the final years of Nixon's administration, Kissinger had followed that maxim (with the president's blessing) by ordering the CIA to finance a military coup in Chile in 1973. The coup overthrew the democratically elected socialist leader, Salvador Allende Gossens. Allende died, and a brutally oppressive military regime assumed power. Kissinger argued that the United States had the right to limit democratic disorder in Latin America, in order to guard against the evils of communism.

Energy and the Middle East

Kissinger also looked to manage an energy crisis brought to a head by events in the Middle East. The United States and its allies had long depended on Middle Eastern oil and, so long as the pipelines were full, low oil prices discouraged conservation or the use of alternative energy. Prime among the nation's foreign suppliers were the 13 nations making up the Organization of Petroleum Exporting Countries (OPEC)— and chief among those were seven Arab states and Iran.

The importance of that supply became clear in the autumn of 1973, when on Yom Kippur, the holiest day of the Jewish year, troops from Egypt and Syria launched a surprise attack on Israel. The seven Arab members of OPEC supported Egypt and Syria by imposing a boycott on oil exports to countries seen as friendly to the Israelis. Lasting

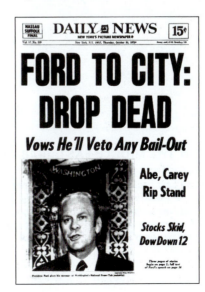

As the energy crisis contributed to New York City's near-bankruptcy, Gerald Ford at first opposed federal assistance. New Yorkers were not amused.

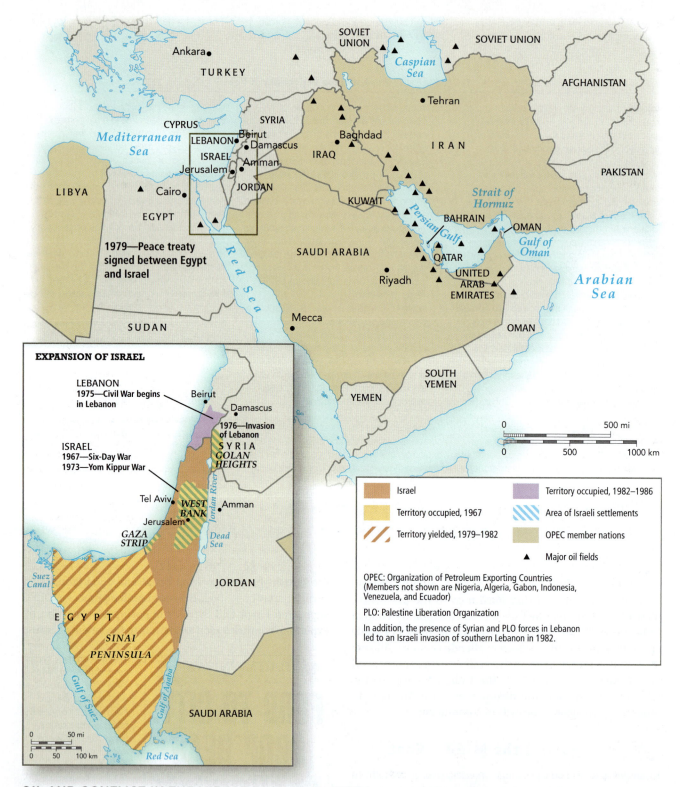

EXPANSION OF ISRAEL

LEBANON
1975—Civil War begins in Lebanon

1976—Invasion of Lebanon

ISRAEL
1967—Six-Day War
1973—Yom Kippur War

1979—Peace treaty signed between Egypt and Israel

Legend:
- Israel
- Territory occupied, 1967
- Territory yielded, 1979–1982
- Territory occupied, 1982–1986
- Area of Israeli settlements
- OPEC member nations
- ▲ Major oil fields

OPEC: Organization of Petroleum Exporting Countries (Members not shown are Nigeria, Algeria, Gabon, Indonesia, Venezuela, and Ecuador)

PLO: Palestine Liberation Organization

In addition, the presence of Syrian and PLO forces in Lebanon led to an Israeli invasion of southern Lebanon in 1982.

OIL AND CONFLICT IN THE MIDDLE EAST, 1948–1988

After World War II the Middle East became a vital geopolitical region beset by big-power rivalry and complicated by local, tribal, ethnic, and religious divisions. Much of the world's oil reserves lie along the Persian Gulf. Proximity to the former Soviet Union and vital trade routes such as the Suez Canal have defined the region's geographic importance. Revolutions in Iran and Afghanistan, intermittent warfare between Arabs and Jews, the unresolved questions of Israel's borders and a Palestinian homeland, the disintegration of Lebanon, and a long war between Iran and Iraq were among the conflicts that unsettled the region. **What makes the Suez Canal and the Strait of Hormuz strategically important?**

from October 1973 to March 1974, the boycott staggered the Western nations and Japan. The price of crude oil had been rising in any case, from under $2 a barrel in 1972 to over $12 by 1976. As the price of petroleum soared, so did the cost of carbon-based plastics used in a huge range of products from phonograph records to raincoats to tires. Inflation rose to an annual rate of 14 percent. Meanwhile, with gasoline scarce, motorists found themselves waiting in line for hours at the pump, in hopes of purchasing a few gallons.

The oil crisis pushed many cities toward financial disaster. In October 1975 New York announced it was near bankruptcy and petitioned the Ford administration for relief. When the president refused, the *New York Daily News* headline blared, "Ford to City: Drop Dead." The administration eventually extended a loan, but the political damage had been done.

To ease the crisis, Kissinger mediated the conflict between Israel and the Arab states. In negotiating he flew back and forth so often between Jerusalem in Israel and Cairo in Egypt that observers nicknamed his efforts "shuttle diplomacy." Eventually the Israelis agreed to withdraw from the west bank of the Suez Canal and to disengage from Syrian troops along the Golan Heights, which overlooked Israel. As an uncertain peace returned, OPEC lifted its boycott. The following year Congress addressed the energy crisis by ordering electric utilities to switch from expensive oil to more abundant and cheaper (though more polluting) coal. The new legislation also ordered the auto industry to improve the efficiency of its cars.

Limits across the Globe

The energy crisis was only one factor limiting American ambitions. The United States also faced mounting competition from industries in Europe and in the emerging economies of the Pacific Rim (Japan, South Korea, Taiwan, Hong Kong, Singapore, and the Philippines). Lower wages there convinced many American manufacturers to move high-wage jobs overseas. The AFL-CIO complained that as skilled union jobs disappeared, what remained would be "a nation of hamburger stands, a country stripped of its industrial capacity . . . a nation of citizens busily buying and selling hamburgers and root beer floats."

Both Ford and Henry Kissinger looked to ease America's economic burdens by further détente with the Soviet Union. The Soviet economy, like the American, was mired in stagnation. In two summit meetings, the second held at Helsinki, Finland, in 1975, the two superpowers established the framework for a second Strategic Arms Limitation Treaty (SALT II). Conservative Republicans, led by presidential contender Ronald Reagan, strongly opposed what they saw as concessions to an untrustworthy enemy. For them, détente spelled weakness. Reagan accused Kissinger and Ford of allowing the United States "to become number two in military power in a world where it is dangerous—if

not fatal—to be second best." That claim exaggerated Soviet strength and American weakness.

Jimmy Carter: Restoring the Faith

In the escalating war between liberal and conservative forces, James Earl "Jimmy" Carter did not fit neatly into either camp. Carter represented a new breed of Southern governors—from the Sun Belt, not the Cotton Belt; they were economic progressives, not segregationists. At the same time, Carter had credentials conservatives could appreciate. He was a former navy man and nuclear engineer, a peanut farmer from the humble town of Plains, Georgia, and had served as Georgia's governor. More unusual still, Carter openly declared his faith as a "born-again" Christian, a term largely unknown outside evangelical circles.

When he began campaigning, only 2 percent of Americans had heard of him. Carter turned his outsider's status to advantage by bringing honesty and openness to Washington. "I will not lie to you," he assured voters. President Ford, for his part, had to fight off a challenge from his party's right wing, led by Ronald Reagan. Reagan grew up as a New Deal Democrat, but as a foe of high income taxes and communism he took up conservative causes. Only by controlling the party's nominating process was Ford able to defeat Reagan at the Republican convention. In the election Carter eked out a slim victory and at his inauguration vowed to bring simplicity and directness to Washington politics. The imperial presidency, he made clear, was a thing of the past. But Congress was equally determined to rein in the executive branch in its own way. To succeed in governing, Carter and his brash Georgia outsiders would have to prove they could swim among the political sharks.

CARTER'S AGENDA Carter brought to the office a mastery of detail, disciplined work habits, and a wealth of plans to address the energy crisis, economic stagnation, the financial woes facing the nation's cities, and a host of foreign policy issues. What he and his advisers had not decided was how to set priorities. Veteran politicians warned not to try too much too soon, but Carter admitted, "it's almost impossible for me to delay something that I see needs to be done." Almost immediately he asked Congress to eliminate 19 expensive pork-barrel water projects as financially wasteful and environmentally destructive. The move stunned even Democrats, who liked bringing home funds to their communities. Their threat to bury his other legislative proposals forced Carter to restore the projects.

Energy and the Environment

The times demanded that the president address two related issues: the environment and skyrocketing energy prices. Those issues were in constant tension, since satisfying energy needs required the use of natural resources, just at the time when the need to protect them had become more evident.

Carter did make progress on a number of environmental fronts. He strengthened the Environmental Protection Agency as well as the clean air and water regulations the EPA enforced. And he championed legislation to create a Superfund that could spend $1 billion a year to clean up hazardous waste sites.

Problems arose, however, when environmental and energy policies clashed. The exceptionally harsh winter that greeted the new administration drove the price of heating oil even higher and pushed Carter to promise a comprehensive new energy policy. His preferred strategy for increasing fuel supplies was the most environmentally friendly: conservation. Americans, after all, were consuming more energy in 1977 than they had been before the OPEC oil boycott spawned gas lines during the Nixon years. But the energy industry lobbied for the opposite solution: instead of cutting back on the demand for energy, they looked to increase the supply, by deregulating the price of natural gas and oil to encourage new production.

Carter's National Energy Program was certainly comprehensive (it contained 113 separate recommendations), but it was also complicated. "Gas guzzler" taxes promoted conservation. So did new efficiency standards for buildings and appliances. Solar tax credits encouraged alternative energy. An almost incomprehensible plan targeted at oil and gas interests proposed deregulation to give energy "its true value." Citing the need to "act quickly," Carter described the fight for a comprehensive plan as "the moral equivalent of war." Unfortunately, few areas of public policy were more subject to the pressure of special interests, and after 18 months of debate Congress managed to approve only deregulation, some energy-conservation tax credits, and a new cabinet-level Department of Energy. No comprehensive policy ever emerged.

Environmentalists and energy producers clashed over climate change and nuclear energy. A 1977 report of the National Academy of Sciences warned that fossil fuel consumption raised the possibility that the world would face catastrophic warming. A *New York Times* headline announced, "Scientists Fear Heavy Use of Coal May Bring Adverse Climate Shift." Neither scientists nor energy companies were yet prepared to recommend specific policies to regulate greenhouse gases.

THREE MILE ISLAND Some utilities favored nuclear power, since fission energy emitted no carbon dioxide. That was an option few environmentalists could abide. No permanent solution yet existed to dispose of the radioactive wastes that were a by-product of nuclear power. Then in March 1979 a plume of radioactive steam spewed from an overheated nuclear reactor at Three Mile Island in Pennsylvania. Local authorities evacuated some 100,000 panicked residents from nearby communities. Whatever support existed for nuclear energy evaporated along with the steam from the overheated reactor. While existing nuclear plants continued to operate, no new ones would be built for decades to come.

The Sagging Economy

Throughout the 1970s wages stagnated, unemployment rose, and so did inflation, spurred upward by rising energy costs, falling industrial productivity, and foreign competition. President Carter at first proposed stimulating the economy with a series of popular tax rebates. And he did win the approval of progressive politicians by finding new funding for federal programs such as food stamps, Social Security, Medicare, and Medicaid.

But the president's fiscal conservatism offset these attempts to cushion the blow of hard times. Confronted by the large deficit from the Nixon and Ford years, Carter canceled his proposed tax rebates. Government could not "eliminate poverty, or provide a bountiful economy, or reduce inflation, or save our cities, or cure illiteracy or provide energy," Carter insisted. That sentiment, spoken by a Democrat, indicated how successful conservatives had been in promoting their ideas.

Foreign Policy: Principled or Pragmatic?

In foreign policy, Jimmy Carter again gravitated between conservative and liberal impulses, between being practical and being idealistic. Like Nixon and Kissinger, he recognized that the United States had neither the strength nor the resources to police a postcolonial world. But unlike his conservative critics Carter viewed the threat of Soviet strength with greater skepticism. Too often, he believed, a knee-jerk fear of Soviet power led Americans to support right-wing dictators, no matter how brutal or corrupt, simply because they professed to be anticommunist.

HUMAN RIGHTS Instead, Carter insisted that the United States should take a moral posture by giving human rights a higher priority. He spoke out publicly on behalf of

| Oil shortages in the 1970s increased American dependence on nuclear power as an alternative energy source. The danger became evident in 1979 when an accident closed a nuclear power plant at Three Mile Island near Harrisburg, Pennsylvania. The large towers pictured here are part of the cooling system in which the accident occurred.

political prisoners and reduced foreign aid to some dictatorships (though strategic allies such as the Philippines under the autocratic Ferdinand Marcos were largely spared). Argentinian Nobel Peace Prize winner Adolfo Pérez Esquivel claimed he owed his life to Carter's policies. Hundreds of other journalists and dissidents, who routinely faced imprisonment, torture, and even murder, benefited as well.

PANAMA CANAL TREATIES Carter also eased decades of animosity against Yankee imperialism by negotiating a treaty to turn over to Panama control of the Canal Zone, a 10-mile-wide strip that the United States administered under a perpetual lease. For many conservatives, Carter's initiative offered further evidence of declining American power. Presidential hopeful Ronald Reagan condemned the proposed treaty as "appeasement," while Senator S. I. Hayakawa of California quipped, "It's ours; we stole it fair and square." Despite such criticisms the Senate ratified the final agreement in 1978.

For conservatives, however, the real test of Carter's mettle would come in relations with the Soviet Union. There, the president's first impulse was to continue the policy of détente scorned so long by the right wing. Soviet premier Leonid Brezhnev accepted Carter's overtures to negotiate, as his nation had been struggling with an economy saddled by inefficient industries and obligations to poor client states such as Cuba, Vietnam, and Bulgaria. The Soviets became even more willing to negotiate after the Carter administration offered diplomatic recognition to Communist China—playing "the China card" as Kissinger and Nixon once had. At a summit meeting held in Vienna in 1979, Carter and Brezhnev followed through on the strategic arms limitation agreement set in motion by President Ford. The agreement, SALT II, was seriously flawed because neither side would agree to scrap major weapon systems. But conservatives who blocked ratification of the treaty in the Senate even attacked Carter's minor concessions. To them, cooperation with the Soviet Union was not an option.

The Middle East: Hope and Hostages

Throughout the cold war, instability in the oil-rich Middle East continually threatened to set off a larger conflict. Secular dictators in Iran, Egypt, Syria, and Iraq vied with autocratic monarchies in Saudi Arabia, Kuwait, Jordan, and the United Arab Emirates. Vast inequality existed between oil-rich sheiks and impoverished peasants and nomadic tribes. Tensions simmered between rival Islamic religious sects, the Sunnis and Shi'ites, while all the Arab nations were united in their hostility toward Israel.

American policy for the region was pulled in two different directions. On the one hand, the United States wanted to ensure the free flow of Middle Eastern oil to the industrial world; on the other, it was committed to the survival of Israel. The energy crises of the 1970s heightened the tensions between these goals, as did Israel's decision to refuse

Palestinian demands for a homeland in the West Bank. The diplomatic impasse eased somewhat when Egyptian president Anwar Sadat traveled to Israel to meet Israeli president Menachem Begin. Sensing an opportunity to promote peace, Carter invited the two leaders to Camp David in September 1978.

CAMP DAVID ACCORDS For 13 days the two antagonists argued, while Carter kept them at the table. Each feared the consequence of giving the other side too much. Finally, they struck a limited compromise: Sadat would recognize Israel; Israel would return the Sinai Peninsula to Egypt. On the question of a Palestinian state in the West Bank and Gaza, Begin would not yield. Even so, the discussions had been historic. Begin and Sadat shared the Nobel Peace Prize for their courageous diplomacy, but it could just as well have gone to Carter, who brokered the peace.

IRANIAN REVOLUTION Amid the turmoil of the Middle East, the shah of Iran had long seemed a stabilizing force. But in the autumn of 1978 Shi'ite fundamentalists rebelled against his dictatorship. Long dismayed by the increasing Westernization of their society, they found the presence of tens of thousands of non-Muslim American military advisers particularly offensive. When the shah's regime collapsed in February 1979, the religious leader Ayatollah Ruhollah Khomeini established an Islamic republic. Later that year the United States admitted the ailing shah to an American hospital for medical treatment, upon which several hundred Iranian students stormed the U.S. Embassy in Tehran and took 53 Americans hostage. Though this act violated every convention of Western diplomacy, the United States had no way to free the hostages.

A President Held Hostage

SOVIETS INVADE AFGHANISTAN At first, American policymakers worried that the Soviet Union might take advantage of the new Khomeini regime. In truth, the Soviets were fearful themselves that Islamic fundamentalists might spread unrest among the Muslim populations living within Soviet borders. In December 1979, the Soviet Union invaded neighboring Afghanistan, where Islamic rebels had toppled a pro-Soviet regime. President Carter condemned the invasion, but in practical terms there was little he could do to counter it. As a symbolic gesture, he announced that the United States would boycott the 1980 Olympics in Moscow.

HYPERINFLATION Once again the problems of energy dependence and the economic instability interacted to create a political crisis. Nightly newscasts aired the spectacle of "America Held Hostage" in Iran. And the turbulence in the Middle East set off another round of OPEC increases in the price of oil. Soaring energy costs soon drove up inflation to near 14 percent and some interest rates above 20 percent. Chrysler Corporation, the nation's third-leading automaker, teetered on the

It was at Camp David, in private talks sponsored by President Jimmy Carter (center), that Egyptian president Anwar Sadat (left) and Israeli prime minister Menachem Begin (right) hammered out a "Framework for Peace in the Middle East" as a first step toward ending decades of war and mutual distrust.

edge of bankruptcy and was saved only by a federally guaranteed loan.

With polls giving Carter a negative rating of 77 percent, the president once again moved to the right. He revived the cold war rhetoric of the 1950s and accelerated the development of new classes of nuclear weapons. But whereas the CIA in 1953 had successfully overthrown an Iranian government, an airborne mission launched in April 1980 to rescue the hostages ended in disaster. Eight marines died when two helicopters and a plane collided in Iran's central desert in the midst of a blinding sandstorm. Carter's secretary of state, Cyrus Vance, who had opposed the mission, resigned in protest. The United States, as even the president admitted, was mired in "a crisis of confidence."

The administration's mistakes had no doubt contributed to that malaise. Yet the obstacles to projecting American power internationally were not simply a result of Carter's mismanagement. Vietnam had demonstrated the clear limits of what U.S. forces could accomplish in distant lands; the long lines for expensive gas rose from an energy crisis decades in the making. The problems in the Middle East had proved intractable over many centuries. Finally, Carter could not be blamed for the reluctance of Americans to sacrifice personal comforts for the general good. American culture had long defined wealth as having more, not wanting less. In 1980 the discouraged electorate discovered in Ronald Reagan a political leader who shared that faith.

 **REVIEW**

In what ways did the issue of energy affect Jimmy Carter's presidency?

PRIME TIME WITH RONALD REAGAN

THE RECESSION OF THE 1970S and the accompanying runaway inflation similarly brought about a major political realignment, only the third since the Civil War. Republicans undermined the Democrats' New Deal coalition and established a conservative majority that would dominate American politics for at least three decades. In the 1980 presidential campaign Ronald Reagan asked Americans, "Are you better off now than you were four years ago?" Many thought not, as Reagan swept the election with an unexpectedly large majority. The fight against inflation and high taxes would be the cornerstone of his administration and would replace unemployment in determining federal economic policy.

 **THE CONSERVATIVE TIDE WORLDWIDE** The United States was not the only nation to experience a resurgence of political conservatism, nationalism, and religious revival. The year before Ronald Reagan became president, Great Britain chose Margaret Thatcher as its first woman prime minister. Under her conservative leadership, "Thatcherism" became a synonym for cutting social programs, downsizing government, and privatizing state-controlled industries. Even within the Soviet bloc, rumblings could be felt as more citizens turned to religion after becoming disillusioned with the communist system. In China, the successors to revolutionary leader Mao Zedong introduced market capitalism into the economy during the 1980s.

As evangelical Christianity surged in the United States, fundamentalist religious revivals elsewhere in the world reflected a questioning of the liberal values that emerged from Europe's eighteenth-century Enlightenment. That

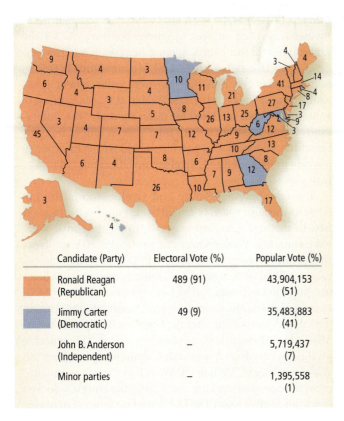

Candidate (Party)	Electoral Vote (%)	Popular Vote (%)
Ronald Reagan (Republican)	489 (91)	43,904,153 (51)
Jimmy Carter (Democratic)	49 (9)	35,483,883 (41)
John B. Anderson (Independent)	–	5,719,437 (7)
Minor parties	–	1,395,558 (1)

ELECTION OF 1980

era's faith in the rational spirit of science and technology had dominated Western thought for 200 years. Increasingly, fundamentalists demanded that traditional religion become the center of public life. The student radicals in Iran who seized the American embassy feared that Western ideas would destroy their Islamic faith. They saw the theocracy of the Ayatollah Khomeini as a way to rid Iran of Western secularism. In Israel religious conservatives became a political force as they, too, resisted secular trends in their society. And as we have seen, leadership of the Roman Catholic Church fell to Pope John Paul II, who rejected calls to liberalize doctrine on such issues as birth control, abortion, and the acceptance of female priests.

The Great Communicator

REAGAN "REVOLUTION" Reagan's message was clear: "It is time to reawaken the industrial giant, to get government back within its means, and to lighten the punitive tax burden." To both liberals and conservatives, he signaled the onset of what came to be called "the Reagan revolution." Liberals feared—and conservatives hoped—that the revolution meant a harder line on cold war issues and an assault on a wide range of social programs and regulations at home. What both groups ignored in the early days of the administration were the moderating forces at work. As governor of California, Reagan had showed a willingness to accommodate his ideas to political

realities. At times he increased both spending and taxes. As president, he appointed to his administration advisers with diverging ideas about how to fix the economy and build American prestige. *The Washington Post* commented that Reagan was not someone to allow rigid ideas to prevent flexible policies. Equally important, noted the *Post,* almost anyone who met him thought he was "a nice guy, a happy secure person who likes himself and most other people."

HANDS-OFF LEADERSHIP In other ways Reagan contradicted expectations. With his jaunty wave and jutting jaw, he projected an aura of physical vitality and movie star good looks. Yet at 69 he was the oldest person to become president, and no one, since Calvin Coolidge, slept as soundly or as much. Such serenity marked his refusal to become bogged down in the details of his job. Outsiders applauded his "hands-off" style after four years under Jimmy Carter, whose obsession with policy details led critics to say he missed the forest for the trees. Reagan set the tone and direction of his administration, leaving the rest to his advisers. Sometimes that left Reagan in the dark about major programs. Donald Regan, his first Treasury secretary, once noted, "The Presidential mind was not cluttered with facts."

The effectiveness of Reagan's message was no accident. The president had honed his public speaking skills as an actor, as a spokesperson for General Electric, and as a politician. His communications staff planned everything from the president's words to a speech's location and camera angles down to the lighting. But the elaborate preparation also depended on Reagan's discipline as a performer. The president understood as well as his staff how to use a battlefield, a classroom, or the flag to communicate a hopeful message.

HOSTAGES FREED Luck played a role as well. Problems that handcuffed Carter seemed to ease on Reagan's watch. The day he took office, Iran announced it would release the American hostages after 444 days of captivity. Three aging Russian leaders, beginning with Leonid Brezhnev in 1982, died suddenly, thereby greatly reducing the influence of the Soviet Union. And when a disturbed gunman shot Reagan in the chest two months after his inauguration, the wounds were not life threatening. Even Reagan's critics admired his courage in the face of death.

The Reagan Agenda

In addition to luck, however, Reagan viewed the economic downturn as an opportunity to push for his revolution in government. He called for massive tax cuts, deregulation of the economy, and a reduction in spending for social programs. Only the military would be spared the budget cutters' ax, because Reagan planned a forceful foreign policy to contain Soviet power.

SUPPLY-SIDE ECONOMICS A commitment to **supply-side economics** became the cornerstone of the Reagan revolution. Supply-side advocates argued that high taxes and government regulation stifled business. The key to revival lay in a large tax cut—a politically popular proposal, though economically controversial. Lower tax revenues would not increase the massive and growing federal budget deficits, insisted supply-side economist Arthur Laffer. His calculations suggested that lower tax rates would stimulate the economy so greatly, tax revenues would actually grow, thanks to higher profits and a renewed prosperity. Broad cuts in social programs would further reduce deficits.

TAX CUTS After little more than half a year in office, Congress handed the president most of the cuts he requested. The Economic Recovery Tax Act (ERTA) lowered income tax rates over the following three years by 25 percent, capital gains by 40 percent, and investment income rates by 28 percent. Taxpayers in the highest brackets were far and away the biggest winners. At the same time, Reagan signed the Omnibus Budget Reconciliation Act, which slashed some $35 billion in spending from government programs. *The Wall Street Journal* hailed the two measures as a "spectacular tax victory," and news commentators suggested that Reagan had ended 50 years of liberal government.

Liberal government relied on the support of big labor. Here, too, Reagan struck a decisive blow. In 1981 members of PATCO, the air traffic controllers union, struck against what they claimed were dangerous and debilitating working conditions. PATCO workers were, however, both highly paid and public service employees. Reagan declared their strike illegal and, without addressing the issues they raised, summarily fired them. Large corporations seized on the antiunion climate to wrest significant concessions on wages and work rules.

Deregulating the Environment

Many conservatives viewed environmental policies as a strategy to regulate business. They were highly skeptical of the growing alarms over global warming. The National

| Striking air traffic controllers protest their firing.

Climate Program Office, created by Carter, was viewed by Reaganites as "an outpost in enemy territory." As for the Environmental Protection Agency, Reagan charged its new head, Anne Gorsuch, with the task of dismantling it. During her first year the EPA filed no new enforcement cases against hazardous waste sites, though the agency knew of some 18,000 that qualified for clean-up under the "Superfund" law, passed in Carter's final year in office. That law taxed the chemical and petroleum industries in order to provide money used to help clean up sites polluted by factories and refineries.

The Occupational Safety and Health Administration (OSHA) was also severely scaled back, ending efforts to set new health and safety standards or to regulate toxic work environments. Workers were at particular risk in plants that produced polyvinyl chloride (PVC) and similar chemicals, used in a wide array of consumer products. At a chemical plant in Louisiana run by German manufacturer BASF, members of the Oil, Chemical, and Atomic Workers union (OCAW) documented chemical wastes dumped into the Mississippi River. (They constantly smelled "this chlorine all day, twenty-four hours a day, depending on what job you're working at.") When OCAW called a strike to gain improved wages and working conditions, the company locked them out for five years. OSHA showed no interest in pursuing such cases.

Other conservative activists lobbied to allow private enterprise to develop more of the vast tracts of wilderness land and forests managed by the federal government. The spokespersons for cattle, mining, and timber interests—who referred to themselves as "**Sagebrush rebels**"—led the campaign to open up such lands to logging, cattle grazing, and real estate development. Reagan appointed James Watt, one such advocate, to head the Department of the Interior. Watt's abrasive style (he once denied the Beach Boys a concert permit, because he considered their music immoral) forced him to resign in 1983. But the administration continued to attack environmental regulations as an unnecessary restraint on free enterprise.

A Halfway Revolution

"REVENUE ENHANCEMENTS" Despite Reagan's tax-cut victories in the political arena, continued recession, rising interest rates, and crippling federal deficits sent the stock market into a tailspin. At first the president refused to compromise his commitment to lower taxes. Still, the evidence was clear that supply-side predictions of booming tax revenues had failed to materialize. So Reagan reversed course and accepted the Tax Equity and Fiscal Responsibility Act of 1982, a measure including $98 billion in tax increases disguised as "revenue enhancements." A year later Social Security reform led to further tax increases. In both cases Regan allowed pragmatism to trump ideology.

After the reversal on tax cuts, the economy began a strong upturn that extended through both of the president's

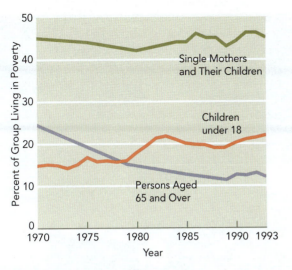
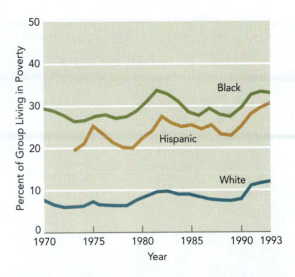

Poverty in America, 1970–1993

Social Security and other income supplements to older Americans reduced their rate of poverty. For all other traditionally impoverished groups the prosperity of the Reagan-Bush years left them slightly worse off than in 1980. The charts also indicate that poverty was most severe for single mothers and their children, and people of color.

terms in office. Labor productivity improved, inflation subsided to 4.3 percent, unemployment fell, and the stock markets rose sharply. Falling energy costs played a major role as OPEC members exceeded their production quotas. Having sold for as much as $30 per barrel, crude prices fell as low as $10.

ECONOMIC INEQUALITY

The benefits of an improved economy were distributed unevenly across economic classes and regions. For the wealthiest Americans the 1980s were the best of times. The top 1 percent commanded a greater share of wealth (37 percent) than at any time since 1929. Their earnings per year were 25 times greater than the 40 percent of Americans at the bottom of the economic ladder. Still, good times meant new jobs— over 14.5 million of them. Three million of these were concentrated in unskilled, minimum-wage areas such as hotels, fast-food restaurants, and retail stores. High-paying jobs in financial services, real estate, insurance, and law went largely (70 percent) to white males; only 2 percent went to African Americans.

OUTSOURCING

The 1980s also saw an acceleration of the trend toward **outsourcing** high-wage industrial jobs and polluting industries to areas such as Mexico and Asia. Given its commitment to free markets and free trade, the Reagan administration resisted proposals to keep jobs at home. Thus, even as the economy grew and inflation dropped below 2 percent, unemployment hovered above 6 percent, and poverty levels ranged from 11 to 15 percent. Cuts in programs such as food stamps, Medicaid, and school lunches increased the burden on the poor. The decision to classify ketchup as a vegetable and thereby meet government nutritional standards for a well-balanced diet symbolized for liberals the administration's indifference to those in need.

The Contours of Science and the Landscape of Technoburbs

THE PC REVOLUTION

New technologies and an increasingly global economy accounted for changes in Americans' work and wealth distribution. During the 1980s sales soared for such new electronic goods as VCRs, cell phones, fax machines, compact disc players, and, above all, computers. In the 1970s Steve Jobs and Steve Wozniak, two techies from California, founded Apple Computer and introduced an affordable and user-friendly home computer. A few years later IBM entered the market with the PC and adopted a rival operating system, MS-DOS, designed by two software programmers, Paul Allen and Bill Gates. Success in marketing computers transformed the ways in which Americans moved, managed, and stored information.

MEDICAL TECHNOLOGIES

Computer-assisted technologies were part of a larger revolution in medical technologies. The CAT scan (Computed Axial Tomography) generated three-dimensional images of the body from flat (that is, two-dimensional) X-ray pictures. Magnetic Resonance Imaging and Proton Emission Tomography (MRIs and PET scans) used different techniques to probe the human body. Neurochemistry made discoveries about brain functions that resulted in a new generation of psychotropic drugs, which modified moods and emotions. **Biogenetic engineering** was yet another dynamic technology. In 1977 Genentech Corporation used recombinant DNA research to produce a synthetic protein. Five years later, the company created a synthetic version of insulin, the first genetically engineered drug to win approval from the FDA. The health care industry in the 1980s was by far the biggest producer of new jobs.

Many high-technology companies build headquarter complexes much like college campuses. Oracle, a business software systems company, built this gleaming complex in Redwood City, California, near what has come to be known as Silicon Valley.

As these technologies began to change lives, they also changed the landscape—literally. Unlike manufacturing industries of old, high-tech companies did not depend on transportation networks to move raw materials or ship finished products to market. They could set up shop where the quality of life was high and office rents were low or near university centers that generated new ideas, researchers, and entrepreneurs. The 1980s saw an explosion of edge cities or "technoburbs" along interstate highways where office and industrial parks housed technology companies, pharmaceutical concerns, professionals, and providers of financial services. As developers turned open meadows and farmlands into office parks, the string of technoburbs stretching between Palo Alto and San Jose came to be known as Silicon Valley—so named because of the miniature silicon wafers at the heart of microprocessor technology.

Winners and Losers in the Labor Market

YUPPIES — Several characteristics distinguished workers in the new technology industries from those in older industrial sectors. In general they were much younger and better educated. Further, unlike the stuffy corporate culture of the 1950s, which stressed the idea of "go along to get along," the new businesses were far more informal. Casual clothing replaced the gray flannel suits; individualism and creativity marked the road to success, and those who flaunted authority were welcomed. The media began referring to young, upwardly mobile, urban professionals as Yuppies—part of the younger generation that repudiated the antimaterialistic values of their hippie forebears.

Access to computers marked a generational divide. To Gen-Xers, those born after 1963 (the end of the baby boom), computers and other electronic devices were second nature. Computerization and information technologies streamlined the workplace so that the time and cost of new product development and production fell sharply. Increased productivity also reduced the demand for low-skill workers. By contrast, demand for workers with education and technical skills rose (as did wages) and thereby increased the income gap between those at the top and bottom of the labor market.

WOMEN: HIGH-WAGE VS. LOW-WAGE JOBS — In an economy in which brains displaced brawn, educated women were among the big winners. Not only did they find more jobs in high-tech areas and computerized offices, but they also increased their presence in law, medicine, business, and other careers. Still, many women continued to flow into lower-paying jobs in health care, education, social services, and government. The net result was that well-educated women gained far more economic independence and a more substantial political voice, while women with fewer skills and less education saw their earnings eroded. Single mothers with children, many who worked in low-wage jobs, were the nation's most impoverished group.

Job displacement in the 1980s had a devastating impact on two other groups, African American men and organized labor. Beginning in the 1970s, black males lost much of the gains they had made over the previous three decades. The decline in manufacturing industries such as steel and autos struck hardest at the older industrial cities where blacks had gained a foothold in the economy. Often lacking the education required in the technology sector, black men had difficulty finding new jobs and many simply dropped out of the labor market. Sociologists began to describe an underclass, trapped in poverty, while middle-class blacks escaped devastated urban neighborhoods.

UNION DECLINE As manufacturing declined so, too, did membership in unions. Labor organized 27 percent of all workers in 1953, 20 percent in 1980, 16 percent in 1990. Only the increase in the number of unionized government workers helped offset the shrinkage in the industrial sector. A two-tier system emerged whereby younger workers received lower pay and hence had less incentive to join unions. Smaller numbers reduced labor's political clout, weakened the Democratic Party, and spurred the conservative revolution.

> ✔ **REVIEW**
>
> What were the goals of the Reagan revolution, and how did he hope to achieve them?

STANDING TALL IN A CHAOTIC WORLD

RONALD REAGAN'S VIEW OF WORLD affairs was primal. "The Soviet Union underlies all the unrest in the world," he stated in his 1980 campaign. Thus he made the defeat of the communist menace a central mission of his administration. To that end he believed Americans must put Vietnam behind them and once again stand tall in the world. Although he was pleased to see the Soviet threat dissolving by the end of his years in office, the president also discovered that firmness and military force alone were not sufficient to calm regional crises across the world.

The Military Buildup

DEFICITS Reagan described the Soviet Union as the "evil empire." His plan to defeat that enemy centered on a massive buildup of the American military. Whereas Richard Nixon had thought the United States needed enough force to fight one and one-half wars at any time, Reagan pushed for enough to fight three and one-half around the globe. That required expenditures of over $1.6 trillion in his first five years (Carter had planned for $1.2 trillion). The combination of massive defense spending and tax cuts created huge deficits. That drove up interest rates and thus the value of the dollar. The strong dollar slowed exports as the cost of American goods rose on world markets. Lower prices gave imports such as Japanese autos a large competitive advantage over American producers. The United States deficit of payments (the value of imports over exports) soared. From the end of World War I until the Reagan years, the United States had been the world's leading creditor nation. By 1986 it had become the world's largest debtor.

Debt was only one of the liabilities of the massive military buildup. Huge cost overruns and wasteful spending became widespread. Exposés of $600 toilet seats and $7,000 coffeepots symbolized spending run amok. Far more costly, however, were the multibillion-dollar weapons systems that either were unneeded or cost far more than planned. The air force, for example, persuaded Congress to fund the B-2 bomber, at a cost of $2 billion each and designed to penetrate Soviet air defenses. Only later did investigators determine that those Soviet air defenses did not exist. In general, advocates of the buildup exaggerated Soviet capabilities in order to pressure Congress to appropriate vast sums of money.

Talk of "standing tall" also spread fear. Reagan and his tough-talking defense planners spoke out about winning any nuclear exchange with the Soviet Union. Author Jonathan Schell debunked those claims in his book *Nuclear Winter*. In it, Schell described a war no one would win, in which debris in the atmosphere would create conditions fatal to all life on earth. Such warnings revived the antinuclear movement across East Asia, Europe, and America. Bishops of the American Catholic Church felt moved to announce their opposition to nuclear war.

Disaster in the Middle East

LEBANON The Middle East continued to be a flashpoint for U.S.-Soviet tensions. In 1982 Israel invaded neighboring Lebanon to destroy missiles supplied by Syria, a Soviet client state. Israeli general Ariel Sharon also used the invasion to strike a decisive blow against forces of the Palestine Liberation Organization (PLO) that were camped in Lebanon. As the Israeli offensive bogged down, however, international outrage over the massacre of Palestinians in Israeli-controlled camps forced Sharon to withdraw his troops.

Reagan then decided to send American troops to Beirut, Lebanon's capital, to protect the Palestinians and keep the peace between warring Christian and Muslim factions. Unfamiliar with the terrain or the politics, the Americans were drawn into supporting Christian militias. Muslim radicals responded first by bombing the American Embassy and then, in October 1983, a U.S. marine barracks. Some 239 troops died. Confronting a chorus of criticism from the media, Congress, and his own Defense Department, Reagan withdrew the American troops.

TERRORIST ATTACKS The president also searched with little success for a way to respond to terrorist attacks by Islamic fundamentalists. In 1982 agents of Libya's Muammar al-Qadhafi exploded a bomb on an American airliner flying over Lockerbie, Scotland. Three years later terrorists took hostages in Lebanon, hijacked American airline flights, killed an American hostage on a

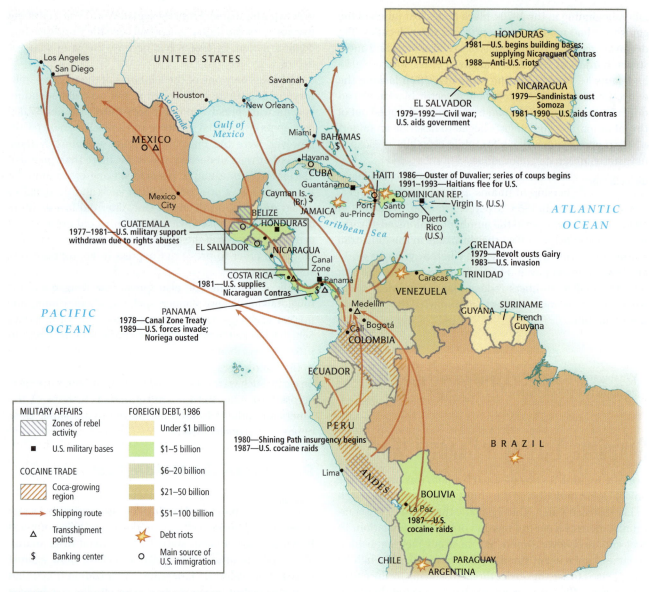

MILITARY AFFAIRS

Zones of rebel activity

■ U.S. military bases

COCAINE TRADE

Coca-growing region

→ Shipping route

△ Transshipment points

$ Banking center

FOREIGN DEBT, 1986

Under $1 billion

$1–5 billion

$6–20 billion

$21–50 billion

$51–100 billion

✳ Debt riots

○ Main source of U.S. immigration

Map labels:

UNITED STATES
Los Angeles
San Diego
Houston
Savannah
New Orleans
Rio Grande
Gulf of Mexico
MEXICO
Mexico City
Miami
BAHAMAS $
Havana
CUBA
Guantánamo
Cayman Is. (Br.) $
JAMAICA
Port-au-Prince
HAITI 1986—Ouster of Duvalier; series of coups begins
1991–1993—Haitians flee for U.S.
DOMINICAN REP.
Santo Domingo
Virgin Is. (U.S.)
Puerto Rico (U.S.)
ATLANTIC OCEAN
Caribbean Sea
BELIZE
GUATEMALA
1977–1981—U.S. military support withdrawn due to rights abuses
HONDURAS
EL SALVADOR
NICARAGUA
COSTA RICA
1981—U.S. supplies Nicaraguan Contras
Canal Zone
Panamá $
PANAMA
1978—Canal Zone Treaty
1989—U.S. forces invade; Noriega ousted
GRENADA
1979—Revolt ousts Gairy
1983—U.S. invasion
TRINIDAD
Caracas
VENEZUELA
GUYANA
SURINAME
French Guiana
PACIFIC OCEAN
Medellín
Bogotá
Cali
COLOMBIA
ECUADOR
PERU
1980—Shining Path insurgency begins
1987—U.S. cocaine raids
Lima
ANDES
BRAZIL
BOLIVIA
La Paz
1987—U.S. cocaine raids
CHILE
PARAGUAY
ARGENTINA

Inset map:
GUATEMALA
HONDURAS
1981—U.S. begins building bases; supplying Nicaraguan Contras
1988—Anti-U.S. riots
EL SALVADOR
1979–1992—Civil war; U.S. aids government
NICARAGUA
1979—Sandinistas oust Somoza
1981–1990—U.S. aids Contras

CENTRAL AMERICAN CONFLICTS, 1974–1990

*President Reagan's attempts to overthrow the Sandinista government in Nicaragua and to contain communism focused American attention on Latin America. So, too, did the staggering debts Latin countries owed to banks in the United States and elsewhere. Equally distorting to the hemisphere's social and economic fabric was the sharp rise in the drug trade organized by criminal syndicates. Most notorious was the Medellín **cartel**, which operated from a remote region in Colombia, shipping drugs through havens in Panama and the Bahamas into the United States while depositing its enormous profits in banks in Miami and offshore banking centers such as the Cayman Islands. The war on drugs led President Bush to invade Panama in December 1989 and bring its corrupt leader, Manuel Noriega, to the United States for trial.*

Mediterranean cruise ship, and bombed a West German nightclub popular with American troops. In response to such provocations, the president was always forceful and uncompromising: "Let terrorists beware: . . . our policy will be one of swift and effective retribution."

But against whom should the United States seek retribution? American intelligence agencies had only sketchy profiles of the many terrorist factions and their political allies. In 1986 the president launched an attack against Libya, which sponsored terrorism. But so too did Syria and Iran, against whom the administration did nothing.

Frustrations in Central America

At first, Reagan found he could stand tall closer to home. On the pretext of protecting American medical students studying on the Caribbean island of Grenada, American troops crushed a band of pro-Cuban rebels and evacuated the students, who were hardly at risk. But the action in Grenada was largely symbolic.

More challenging was Reagan's campaign to overthrow the left-wing Sandinista government in Nicaragua. The president justified arming the anti-Sandinista "Contras" as "freedom fighters" battling in the spirit of America's Founding Fathers. True, the Contras included a few democrats and disillusioned Sandinistas, but the majority had served in the brutal and corrupt dictatorship of Anastasio Somoza, which the Sandinistas overthrew in 1979.

CONTRAS Reagan had no desire to broker a settlement between the opposing forces. Instead, he allowed the CIA to help the Contras mine Nicaragua's harbor, in hopes of destabilizing the Sandinistas. When the mines damaged foreign ships—a violation of international law—conservatives and liberals alike condemned the president's actions. Congress adopted the Boland Amendment, which explicitly forbade the CIA or "any other agency or entity involved in intelligence activities" to spend money to support the Contras "directly or indirectly." Reagan reluctantly signed the measure, though he remained determined to overthrow the Sandinistas.

Neither mushrooming deficits nor frustrations in the Middle East and Central America dented Ronald Reagan's popularity. The booming economy kept his poll ratings high. In the 1984 election he easily won a second term, winning 59 percent of the popular vote against Walter Mondale of Minnesota. Mondale's choice of Geraldine Ferraro of New York as the first female running mate made the presidential campaign noteworthy. Reagan and his advisers entered his second term determined to force solutions to some of his most stubborn foreign policy problems. It was a decision that led to scandal and threatened the Constitutional system of checks and balances.

The Iran-Contra Connection

By mid-1985 Reagan policy makers felt two major frustrations. First, Congress had forbidden any support of the Contras in Central America, and second, Iranian-backed terrorists continued to hold hostages in Lebanon. In the summer of 1985 a course of events was set in motion that eventually linked these two issues.

ARMS FOR HOSTAGES DEAL The president made it increasingly clear that he wanted to find a way to free the remaining hostages. National Security Adviser Robert McFarlane suggested opening a channel to "moderate factions" in the Iranian government. If the United States sold Iran a few weapons, the grateful moderates might use their influence in Lebanon to free the hostages. But an agreement to exchange arms for hostages would violate the president's vow never to pay ransom to terrorists. Still, over the following year, four secret arms shipments went to Iran. One hostage was set free. McFarlane's successor as national security adviser, Admiral John Poindexter, had the president sign a secret intelligence "finding" that allowed him and his associates to pursue their mission without informing anyone in Congress or even the secretaries of defense and state. Because the president ignored the details of foreign policy, McFarlane, Poindexter, and their aides had assumed the power to act on their own.

Oliver North successfully took the offensive in his testimony before the congressional committee investigating the Iran-Contra scandals. Here North delivers a pro-Contra lecture to the committee.

OLIVER NORTH The man most often pulling the strings was Lieutenant Colonel Oliver "Ollie" North, a junior officer under McFarlane and later Poindexter. A Vietnam veteran with a flair for the dramatic, North was impatient with bureaucratic procedures. In January 1986 he hit on the idea that the profits made selling arms to Iran could be siphoned off to buy weapons for the Contras. The Iranian arms dealer who brokered the deal thought it a great idea. "I think this is now, Ollie, the best chance, because . . . we never get such good money out of this," he laughed, as he was recorded on a tape North himself made. "We do everything. We do hostages free of charge; we do all terrorists free of charge; Central America free of charge."

Cover Blown

The secret operation was exposed in the fall of 1986, when reports of the Iranian arms deal surfaced in a Lebanese newspaper. Astonished reporters besieged the administration, demanding to know how secret arms sales to a terrorist regime benefited the president's antiterrorist campaign. As the inquiry continued, the link between the arms sales and the Contras was discovered.

IRANGATE The press nicknamed the scandal "Irangate," comparing it to Richard Nixon's Watergate affair. But Irangate raised more troubling issues. During Watergate, President Nixon had led the cover-up to save his own political skin. But during the Iran-Contra congressional hearings, Admiral Poindexter testified that he had kept Reagan in ignorance "so that I could insulate him from the decision and provide some future deniability for the president if it ever leaked out." In that way Iran-Contra revealed a presidency out of control. An unelected segment within the government had taken upon itself the power to pursue its own policies outside legal channels.

From Cold War to *Glasnost*

Because few members of Congress wanted to impeach a popular president, the hearings came to a sputtering end. Reagan's prestige returned, in part because of substantial improvement in Soviet-American relations. By the 1980s the Soviet Union was far weaker than American experts, including the CIA, had ever recognized. The Soviet economy stagnated; the Communist Party was mired in corruption. The war in Afghanistan had become a Russian Vietnam. By accelerating the arms race, Reagan placed additional pressure on the Russians.

MIKHAIL GORBACHEV In 1985 a fresh spirit entered the Kremlin. Unlike the aged leaders who preceded him, Mikhail Gorbachev was young and saw the need for reform within the Soviet Union. Gorbachev's fundamental restructuring, or *perestroika,* set about improving relations with the United States. He reduced military commitments and adopted a policy of openness (*glasnost*) about problems in the Soviet Union. In October, the two leaders held their second summit in Reykjavík, Iceland. Gorbachev dangled the possibility of abolishing all nuclear weapons. Reagan seemed receptive to the idea, but in the end he and his advisers backed away from such a radical proposal. A summit in Moscow two years later eliminated an entire class of nuclear missiles with ranges of 600 to 3,400 miles. Both sides agreed to allow on-site inspections of missile bases and the facilities where missiles would be destroyed.

Thus, as the election of 1988 approached, the president could claim credit for improved relations with the Soviet Union. Loyalty to Ronald Reagan made Vice President George H. W. Bush the Republican heir apparent. The Democratic challenger, Governor Michael Dukakis of Massachusetts, pointed out that poor and even many middle-class Americans had lost ground during the 1980s. But Bush put the lackluster Dukakis on the defensive. With the economy reasonably robust, Bush won by a comfortable margin. The Reagan agenda remained on track.

 **REVIEW**

How did Reagan try to overcome the legacy of Vietnam?

AN END TO THE COLD WAR

PRESIDENT GEORGE HERBERT WALKER BUSH was born to both privilege and politics. The son of a Connecticut senator, he attended an exclusive boarding school and then Ivy League Yale University. That background made him part of the East Coast establishment often scorned by more-populist Republicans. Yet once the oil business lured Bush to Texas, he moved to the right, becoming a Goldwater Republican when he ran unsuccessfully for the Senate in 1964. Foreign policy interested him far more than domestic politics. But in the end, inattention to domestic issues proved his undoing as the economy slid into recession.

A Post–Cold War Foreign Policy

To the astonishment of most Western observers, Mikhail Gorbachev's reform policies led not only to the collapse of the Soviet empire but also to the breakup of the Soviet Union itself. In December 1988, Gorbachev spoke in the United Nations of a "new world order." To that end he began liquidating the Soviet cold war legacy, as the last Russian troops began leaving Afghanistan and then Eastern Europe.

 THE FALL OF COMMUNISM Throughout 1989 Eastern Europeans began to test their newfound freedom. In Poland, Hungary, Bulgaria, Czechoslovakia, and, most violently, Romania, Communist dictators fell from power. Nothing more inspired the world than the stream of celebrating East Germans pouring through the Berlin Wall in November 1989. Within a year the wall, a symbol of Communist oppression, had been torn down and Germany reunified. Although Gorbachev struggled to keep together the 15 republics that made up the U.S.S.R., the forces of nationalism and reform pulled the Soviet Union apart. The Baltic republics—Lithuania, Latvia, and Estonia—declared their independence in 1991. Then, in December, the Slavic republics of Ukraine, Belarus, and Russia formed a new Commonwealth of Independent States. By the end of December eight more of the former Soviet republics had joined the loose federation. Boris Yeltsin, the charismatic president of Russia, became the Commonwealth's dominant figure. With no Soviet Union left to preside over, Gorbachev resigned.

Although President Bush increasingly supported Gorbachev's reforms, he did so with caution. Even if he had wished to aid Eastern Europe and the new Commonwealth states, soaring deficits at home limited his options. The administration seemed to support the status quo in Communist China, too. When in June 1989 China's aging leadership crushed students rallying for democratic reform in Beijing's Tiananmen Square, Bush muted American protests.

The fall of the Soviet Union signaled the end of a cold war that, more than once, had threatened a nuclear end to human history. At a series of summits with Russian leaders, the United States and its former rivals agreed to sharp reductions in their stockpiles of nuclear weapons. The Strategic Arms Reduction Treaty (or START), concluded in July 1991, far surpassed the limits negotiated in earlier SALT talks. By June 1992 Bush and Yeltsin had agreed to even sharper cuts.

The Gulf War

SADDAM HUSSEIN With two superpowers no longer facing off against each other, what would the "new world order" look like? If anything, regional crises loomed larger. Instability in the Middle East produced the greatest foreign policy challenge. From 1980 to 1988 Iran and Iraq had battered each other in a debilitating

HISTORIAN'S TOOLBOX

THE BERLIN WALL

A "pioneer" cleaning squad is sweeping away garbage, as many residents from the right side of the Wall tossed empty bottles, boxes, and trash of all sorts into the other side.

This platform was erected in 1969 when President Richard Nixon visited the Berlin Wall.

In what way do these paintings suggest a difference between the public cultures of East and West Berlin?

Which side of the wall is East and which is West? Point out three details that suggest the answer.

No place in the world reflected cold war tensions more than the city of Berlin. And East Germany's erection of a wall there in August 1961—launched in great secrecy in the dead of night—struck many Americans as an escalation of the cold war. Suddenly, the outpouring of educated and skilled East Germans escaping to West Germany ceased. For some 28 years the Wall stood as a stark symbol of a divided Germany, and historians can use the Wall to help track the ups and downs of the long conflict between East and West.

Attempted escapes, the addition of barbed wire and guard posts, espionage novels such as *The Spy Who Came in from the Cold*, the periodic scaffolding erected so that American presidents could project their messages to captive citizens. . . . By 1987 tensions had begun to ease. President Ronald Reagan, while in the city commemorating Berlin's 750th anniversary, challenged Soviet Premier Mikhail Gorbachev to "tear down this wall." Two years later the wall came down.

Thinking Critically

What geographic difficulties prompted East Germany to build the Wall? (See the map on page 752.) What symbolic meanings does a wall suggest? Why did so many East Germans want to move to the West? Can you think of ways in which building a wall might have been a good thing?

WAR WITH IRAQ: OPERATION DESERT STORM

When Saddam Hussein invaded oil-rich Kuwait on August 2, 1990, the United States formed a coalition to force out the Iraqis. (Although Turkey was not a formal member, it allowed its airfields to be used. Israel remained uninvolved to avoid antagonizing Arab coalition members.) The coalition launched Operation Desert Storm in January 1991; land forces invaded on February 24 (Operation Desert Saber), routing Iraqi troops, who left Kuwait in ruin and its oil fields aflame. **Why did Saddam Hussein's invasion of Kuwait threaten American and European interests?**

war. During those years the Reagan administration assisted Iraq with weapons and intelligence, until at last it won a narrow victory over Iran's fundamentalists. But Iraq's ruthless dictator, Saddam Hussein, had run up enormous debts. To ease his financial crisis, Hussein cast a covetous eye on his neighbor, the small oil-rich sheikdom of Kuwait. In August 1990, 120,000 Iraqi troops invaded and occupied Kuwait, catching the Bush administration off guard. Would Hussein stop there?

Bush compared Hussein to Hitler and was determined to free Kuwait. He successfully coordinated a United Nations–backed economic boycott. Increasing the pressure further, he deployed half a million American troops in Saudi Arabia and the Persian Gulf. By November Bush had won a resolution from the Security Council permitting the use of military force if Hussein did not withdraw.

OPERATION DESERT STORM On January 17, 1991, air attacks by France, Italy, Britain, Saudi Arabia, and the United States launched Operation Desert Storm. After weeks of merciless pounding from the air, ground operations shattered Hussein's vaunted Republican

Guards in less than 100 hours. In an act of spite, Hussein resorted to ecoterrorism. His forces set Kuwait's oil fields ablaze and dumped huge quantities of crude oil into the rich Persian Gulf ecosystem. It did him no good: by the end of February Kuwait was liberated, and nothing stood between Allied forces and Iraq's capital, Baghdad. Bush was unwilling to advance that far—and most other nations in the coalition agreed. If Hussein were toppled, it was not clear who in Iraq would fill the vacuum of power or what power could contain the ambitions of neighboring Iran.

Domestic Doldrums

Victory in the Gulf War boosted the president's popularity so high that aides brushed aside the need for any bold domestic program. "Frankly, this president doesn't need another single piece of legislation, unless it's absolutely right," asserted John Sununu, his cocky chief of staff. "In fact, if Congress wants to come together, adjourn, and leave, it's all right with us." That attitude

DAILY LIVES

LIFE IN THE UNDERCLASS

During the 1880s Jacob Riis "discovered" a class of people he described as invisible. They were "individuals who have lost connection with home life, or never had any, or whose homes had ceased to be sufficiently separated, decent, and desirable to afford what are regarded as ordinary wholesome influences of home and family." A century later investigators for the *Chicago Tribune* discovered in American cities "a lost society dwelling in enclaves of despair and chaos that infect and threaten the communities at large." This ghetto world of dilapidated housing, poverty, and despair was home to as many as 5 million Americans. Yet while many of its spaces and avenues were public, it too was invisible, except when its private behavior became so violent or criminal that the news forced the broad middle class to pay attention.

Like Riis the *Tribune* reporters portrayed this urban blight through the story of individual lives. Dorothy Sands was one. In 1957 Dorothy, her mother, Ora Streeter, and the rest of her family lived in a one-room shack in rural Mississippi. To escape the South, her job, and her abusive husband, Ora took six small children to Chicago, where her mother lived. For her daughter Dorothy, "It was something like going to a new world."

Life in Chicago imposed disappointments and cruelties of its own. For several years Streeter struggled to make a decent life for her family. Arthritis finally prevented her from working and forced her to sign up for public assistance. Dorothy, the oldest child, assumed responsibility for the household. With what little time she had for herself, she reached the ninth grade. But at age 15 her dream of a nursing career ended when she discovered she was pregnant. In 1965, after her mother died, Dorothy began a relationship with Carra Little, a man who promised

he could not get her pregnant. Within a year Dorothy had her second child. She asked the doctors to sterilize her, but they refused. And the children kept arriving—four more. "When you are young, you don't really think about the future," Dorothy recalled.

After Little died suddenly of a heart attack in 1976, the household disintegrated. Dorothy's oldest daughter, Barbara, like her mother and grandmother before her, became pregnant at age 15. By 1985 Dorothy was a 37-year-old grandmother living in a three-room apartment with five of her six children, her daughter LaWanda's new boyfriend, two grandchildren aged 7 and 2, and two teenage runaways. In 20 years, the family had never been off welfare and no one in the household had held a regular job.

With public assistance money, Dorothy could afford only rooms in a dilapidated three-story building on Chicago's West Side. Each evening people pried open the building's front door to do "crack" or drink grain alcohol. Sometime in 1985 the family stopped bathing because every time they turned on the water, plaster fell into the tub. The building manager reneged on his promise to make repairs. So the children just stood over the sink and washed their clothes by hand. Meals were irregular affairs, because money was scarce and no one liked to cook. For two weeks each month the family splurged on eggs for breakfast and Spam for dinner. More often they got by on hot dogs, rice, and beans.

Of the neighborhood's 61,500 people, more than half received some form of welfare. People lucky enough to find work quickly moved away. One government official described "a caste of people almost totally dependent on the state, with little hope of breaking free."

The bleak spaces of public housing in the "Chicago projects" and in other decaying urban areas made life difficult for residents.

For the rest of the American people, more fortunate in their circumstances, a question persisted: How could the problems of the largely invisible underclass be solved before the violence and desperation of their private world overwhelmed the city streets?

Thinking Critically

How aware are Americans in the twenty-first century of the circumstances of the nation's poorest families?

---

suggested a lack of direction that proved fatal to Bush's reelection hopes.

ENVIRONMENTAL ISSUES At first Bush envisioned a "kinder, gentler" nation. Yet pressures from conservative Republicans kept the new president from straying too far from path of the Reagan revolution. When delegates from 178 nations met at an "Earth Summit" in Rio de Janeiro in 1992, the president opposed efforts to draft stricter rules to lessen the threat of global warming. Bush did sign into law the sweeping Clean Air Act passed by Congress in 1990. But soon after, Vice President Dan Quayle established a "Council on Competitiveness" to rewrite regulations that corporations found burdensome.

Similarly, the president called for reform of an educational system whose quality had declined through the 1980s. But, while he convened a well-publicized "Education Summit" in 1989, the delegates issued a modest set of goals only after the president was urged to do so by his co-chair at the summit, Governor Bill Clinton of Arkansas.

The Conservative Court

Although Presidents Reagan and Bush both spoke out against abortion, affirmative action, the banning of prayer in public schools, and other conservative social issues, neither made action a priority. Even so, both presidents shaped social policy through their appointments to the Supreme Court. Reagan placed three members on the bench, including in 1981 Sandra Day O'Connor, the first woman to sit on the high court. Bush nominated two justices. As more liberal members of the Court retired (including William Brennan and Thurgood Marshall), the decisions handed down became distinctly more conservative. The appointment of Antonin Scalia gave the Court its most outspoken conservative.

THE CLARENCE THOMAS HEARINGS
In 1991 the Senate hotly debated President Bush's nomination of Clarence Thomas, an outspoken black conservative and former member of the Reagan administration. The confirmation hearings became even more contentious when Anita Hill, an attorney who had worked for Thomas, testified that he had sexually harassed her. Women's groups blasted the all-male Judiciary Committee for keeping Hill's allegations private until reporters uncovered the story. Thomas and his defenders accused his opponents of using a disgruntled woman to help conduct a latter-day lynching. In the end the Senate narrowly voted to confirm, and Thomas joined Scalia as one of the Court's most conservative members.

The Court's conservative turn affected decisions on affirmative action—those laws that gave preferred treatment to minority groups in order to remedy past discrimination. State and federal courts and legislatures had used techniques such as busing and the setting of quotas to overturn past injustices. As early as 1978, however, the Court began to set limits on affirmative action. In *Bakke v. Regents of the University of California* (1978), the majority ruled that college admissions staffs could not set fixed quotas, although they could still use race as a guiding factor in trying to create a more diverse student body. Increasingly, the Court made it easier for white citizens to challenge affirmative action programs. At the same time, it set higher standards

In 1991 Justice Clarence Thomas survived a bitter Senate battle during his Supreme Court confirmation hearings. Here, he is sworn in by Chief Justice William Rehnquist as Thomas's wife and President George H. W. Bush and Barbara Bush look on. Thomas's conservative views on abortion and affirmative action were later confirmed by the votes he cast as a justice.

for those who wished to put forward a claim of discrimination. "An amorphous claim that there has been past discrimination in a particular industry cannot justify the use of an unyielding racial quota," wrote Justice O'Connor in 1989.

Disillusionment and Anger

Ronald Reagan had given a sunny face to conservatism. He had assured voters that if taxes were cut, the economy would revive and deficits would fall. He promised that if "big government" could be scaled back, there would be a new "morning in America." Yet a decade of hands-off conservative leadership left the deficit ballooning and state and local governments larger than ever. A growing number of Americans felt that the institutions of government were seriously off track. Indeed, the attacks on big government by Reagan and Bush fueled that cynicism.

S&L Crisis A series of longer-term crises contributed to this sense of disillusionment. One of the most threatening centered on the nation's savings and loan institutions. By the end of the decade these thrifts were failing at the highest rate since the Great Depression. To help increase bank profits, the Carter administration and Congress had agreed to cut back federal regulations. That move allowed savings and loan institutions to invest their funds more speculatively. Few depositors noticed or cared, because their money was insured by the Federal Savings and Loan Insurance Corporation. The government, however, had to pay depositors as these banks failed in large numbers. During the Bush administration it become clear that the cost of rebuilding the failed banks and paying off huge debts might run into hundreds of billions of dollars.

The late 1980s also brought a public health crisis. Americans were spending a higher percentage of their resources on medical care than were citizens in other nations, yet they were no healthier. As medical costs soared, more than 30 million Americans had no health insurance. The crisis was worsened by a fatal disorder that physicians began diagnosing in the early 1980s: acquired immunodeficiency syndrome, or AIDS. With no cure available the disease threatened to take on epidemic proportions not only in the United States but around the globe as well. Yet because the illness at first struck hardest at the male homosexual community and intravenous drug users, many groups in American society were reluctant to address the problem.

Bank failures, skyrocketing health costs, anger over poverty and discrimination—none of these problems by themselves derailed the conservative revolution. Still, the various crises demonstrated how pivotal government had become in providing social services and limiting the abuses of powerful private interests in a high-technology society.

As the AIDS epidemic spread in the 1980s, quilts such as these expressed sorrow for lost friends and loved ones. The quilts also served to raise public awareness of the need for a more effective policy to aid the afflicted and fight the disease.

The Election of 1992

Gramm-Rudman Act In the end, George Bush's inability to rein in soaring government deficits damaged his reelection prospects. "Read my lips! No new taxes," he pledged to campaign audiences in 1988. But the president and Congress were at loggerheads over how to reach the holy grail of so many conservatives: a balanced budget. In 1985 Congress had passed the Gramm-Rudman Act, establishing a set of steadily increasing limits on federal spending. These limits were meant to force Congress and the president to make hard choices needed to reach a balanced budget. If they did not, automatic across-the-board cuts would go into effect. By 1990 the law's automatic procedures were threatening programs such as Medicare, which Republicans and Democrats alike supported. Facing such unpopular cuts, Bush agreed to a package of new taxes along with budget cuts. Conservatives felt betrayed, and in the end, the deficit grew larger all the same.

WHITE-COLLAR UNEMPLOYMENT As the election of 1992 approached, unemployment stood at more than 8 percent, penetrating to areas of the economy not affected by most recessions. Wages for middle-class families had not increased since the early 1970s and had actually declined during Bush's presidency. Many Reagan Democrats seemed ready to return to the government activism of Franklin Roosevelt.

"IT'S THE ECONOMY..." Meanwhile, the Democrats nominated Governor Bill Clinton of Arkansas. During the campaign, Clinton was dogged by reports of marital infidelity, by his halfhearted admission that he had tried marijuana while a student but had not inhaled, and by his youthful opposition to the war in Vietnam. Still, he gained ground by hammering away at Bush for failing to revive the economy. "It's the economy, stupid!" read the sign tacked up at his election headquarters to remind Clinton workers of the campaign's central theme. Clinton painted himself as a new kind of Democrat: a centrist, willing to work with business, and not a creature of liberal interest groups.

At the voting booth, middle-of-the-road voters turned to Clinton and, in smaller numbers, to third-party challenger H. Ross Perot. Clinton captured 43 percent of the popular vote (to Bush's 38 and Perot's 19) in the largest turnout—55 percent—in 20 years. The election of four women to the Senate, including the first African American woman, Carol Moseley Braun, indicated that gender had become an electoral factor.

Candidate (Party)	Electoral Vote (%)	Popular Vote (%)
Bill Clinton (Democratic)	370 (69)	44,908,254 (43)
George H. W. Bush (Republican)	168 (31)	39,102,343 (38)
Ross Perot (Independent)	–	19,725,433 (19)

ELECTION OF 1992

 REVIEW

How did Reagan, Bush, and Gorbachev take steps to end the cold war?

CONCLUSION

THE WORLD AT LARGE

The 1992 election left the fate of the conservative revolution unresolved. Under Reagan and Bush the economy had grown and inflation had subsided. Yet prosperity benefited mostly those at the upper end of the income scale. The majority of Americans saw their finances stagnate or grow worse. Reagan and Bush both had supported a conservative social agenda that sought to restrict abortion rights, return prayer to the schools, and end affirmative action, but neither had done much to put that agenda into action. Both presidents significantly weakened the capacity of the federal government to implement social programs. No longer did Americans expect Washington to solve all the issues of the day. How, then, would the nation meet the future needs of the increasing numbers of poor, minority, elderly, and immigrant Americans?

Reagan and Bush had also presided over the end of the cold war. Despite a growing isolationist sentiment among Democrats and Republicans, both presidents had shown a willingness to assert American power—in Libya, in Lebanon, in Nicaragua, in Panama, in Somalia, in the Persian Gulf— though these were situations in which no major conflict threatened. What role would the United States play in the post–cold war era, when it stood as the lone superpower in the world arena? That was a question for William Jefferson Clinton as he sought to lead the United States into the twenty-first century. ◦◦◦◦◦

CHAPTER SUMMARY

DURING THE YEARS OF THE Ford, Carter, Reagan, and Bush administrations, the nation's political and social agenda was increasingly determined by a conservative movement, including newly politicized evangelical Christians, that sought to restore traditional religious and family values, patriotism, and a limited role for government.

■ An energy crisis brought on by Arab-Israeli conflict and an oil boycott by the OPEC nations worsened an already ailing American economy.

■ Secretary of State Henry Kissinger used shuttle diplomacy to bring an uneasy peace to the Middle East. He and President Ford sought to preserve American power and ease diplomatic tensions by pursuing détente with the Soviet Union.

■ Jimmy Carter, unable to end the recession at home, pursued a human rights policy abroad and the negotiation of the Camp David Accords between Israel and Egypt—only to have the Soviet invasion of Afghanistan and the Iranian hostage crisis undermine his foreign policy.

■ Ronald Reagan led the conservative tide with a program to limit the power of labor unions, reduce government regulation, lower taxes, and sharply increase spending on the military.

■ Despite a revived economy, Reagan's tax cuts had two undesirable outcomes: huge government budget deficits and a growing gap in income between the rich and poor.

■ Conservative appointments to the federal judiciary and the Supreme Court led to decisions increasing limits on government intervention in the areas of civil rights, affirmative action, abortion rights, and the separation of church and state.

■ Reagan's efforts to "stand tall" in foreign policy led to the Iran-Contra scandal, which revealed a broad pattern of illegal arms shipments to right-wing rebels in Nicaragua and the trading of arms to Iran in an unsuccessful attempt to win the release of hostages in Lebanon—actions for which the president was sharply criticized but not impeached.

■ Both Reagan and George Bush welcomed reforms set in motion by Mikhail Gorbachev that led by 1991 to the breakup of the Soviet Union, reductions in nuclear arms, and an end to the cold war.

■ In the post–cold war era, regional conflicts proved more troublesome as Iraq's invasion of Kuwait led Bush to form a UN coalition that routed the forces of Saddam Hussein in Operation Desert Storm.

■ For George Bush a continuing recession, high budget deficits, and high unemployment undermined his bid for reelection.

ADDITIONAL READING

BRUCE SHULMAN, *THE SEVENTIES* (2002), follows the transition from the 1960s to the Reagan era. An intriguing new look at the same subject is Philip Jenkins, *Decade of Nightmares: The End of the Sixties and the Making of Eighties America* (2006). An even-handed treatment of Jimmy Carter is Robert A. Strong, *Working in the World: Jimmy Carter and the Making of American Foreign Policy* (2000). Two books that do justice to Ronald Reagan and the politics of the right are John Ehrman, *The Eighties: America in the Age of Reagan* (2006), and Gil Troy, *Morning in America: How Ronald Reagan Invented the 1980s* (2005). Considering the transformation into the digital world is Fred Turner, *From Counterculture to Cyberculture: Stewart Brand, the Whole Earth Network, and the Rise of Digital Utopianism* (2006).

Randall Balmer, *Mine Eyes Have Seen the Glory: A Journey into the Evangelical Subculture in America* (2006), offers the perspectives of someone raised in the evangelical tradition. The issue of income inequality is well explained in Frank Levy, *The New Dollars and Dreams: American Incomes and Economic Change* (1999). Racial currents of the era are powerfully conveyed in Nicholas Lemann, *The Promised Land* (1995). The reasonably friendly treatment of George H. W. Bush by Ryan Barilleaux and Mark Rozell, *Power and Prudence: The Presidency of George H. W. Bush* (2004), can moderate the often insightful Kevin Phillips, *American Dynasty: Aristocracy, Fortune, and the Politics of Deceit* (2004). On the first Gulf War, see Alberto Bin, Richard Hill, and Archer Jones, *Desert Storm: A Forgotten War* (1998).

For a fuller list of readings, see the Bibliography at www.mhhe.com/eh8e.

SIGNIFICANT EVENTS

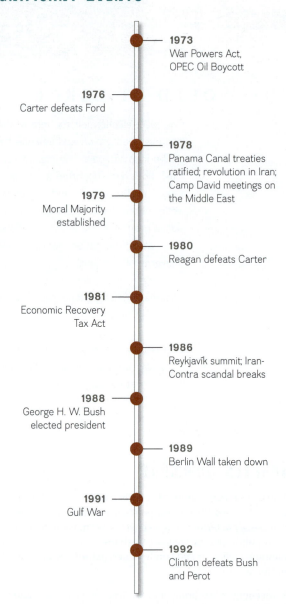

1973
War Powers Act, OPEC Oil Boycott

1976
Carter defeats Ford

1978
Panama Canal treaties ratified; revolution in Iran; Camp David meetings on the Middle East

1979
Moral Majority established

1980
Reagan defeats Carter

1981
Economic Recovery Tax Act

1986
Reykjavík summit; Iran-Contra scandal breaks

1988
George H. W. Bush elected president

1989
Berlin Wall taken down

1991
Gulf War

1992
Clinton defeats Bush and Perot

[Reagan and Bush: Conservative Revolutionaries or Pragmatic Leaders?]

CONSERVATIVE GOALS	CONSERVATIVE ACTIONS/*PRAGMATIC ACTIONS*

Foreign Policy

Restore U.S. power to the levels before the Vietnam War so that U.S. can "stand tall"

Invade Grenada and Panama

Increase defense spending sharply

Withdraw U.S. forces from Lebanon after the tragic barracks bombing

Isolate the Soviet Union as the "evil empire" and bring it down

Fail to agree to eliminate nuclear weapons

Negotiate with Soviets at Reykjavík and Moscow summits and accept sharp missile reductions under START treaty

Proclaim the superiority of American values and American freedom

Support "authoritarian" dictators who are pro-American

Deemphasize Carter's commitment to human rights

Fight global terrorism, insisting on no ransom for hostages

Bomb Libya

Attempt to free terrorist hostages by negotiating with Iranian "moderates"

Oppose Castro and leftist political movements in the Americas

Attempt to overthrow the Sandinistas in Nicaragua by aiding Contras

Sell arms to Iran and use profits to buy guns for the Contras

Domestic Policy

Shrink the power and size of government

Restrict the role of OSHA

Increase defense spending

Try to balance the federal budget by adopting "supply-side economics"

Cut income tax rates

Use "revenue enhancements" and Social Security taxes to reduce the deficit

Agree to tax increases to close budget gap, despite "Read my lips: no new taxes"

Reverse the liberal social agenda from the 1960s

Speak out for the Moral Majority agenda

Avoid major action on abortion rights, gay rights, and school prayer

Create a Supreme Court hostile to such decisions as *Engle v. Vitale* and *Roe v. Wade* and opposed to the civil and criminal rights agenda of the Warren Court

Appoint Sandra Day O'Connor as first woman justice on Supreme Court

Appoint conservative justices Rehnquist, Scalia, and Thomas

Support the "Sagebrush Rebellion" and reduce environmental regulations

Open public lands for development and reduce effectiveness of the EPA

It took three months to get across the U.S.-Mexican border, evading thieves and hostile border guards. Chanax carried little more than a letter introducing him to several Guatemalans. They suggested he apply at Randall's, an upscale Houston supermarket chain, which was eager to expand as high oil prices set the Texas economy to booming. The grocery chain did not want just any low-wage workers. It specialized in high-priced goods in fancy suburban stores. Its upscale customers received valet

| Juan Chanax

parking, hassle-free shopping, and service from uniformed employees. Chanax was happy to do any job without complaint. Even on his minimum-wage salary, he could wire money home to his family. And when the manager said Randall's would soon need more workers, Chanax arranged for his brother-in-law and an uncle to come north. Over time Randall's began to hire Guatemalans exclusively. Shortly before a new store opened, the managers would tell Chanax how many maintenance people they needed. He would then recruit more Mayas from San Cristobal and, along with other experienced Mayas, prepare the newcomers for their jobs. That meant more than learning to clean and stack. The recruits were also told to arrive on time, work hard, and disrespect no one. When a problem arose, they did not take it to a Randall's manager but to another Guatemalan. "That way," as Chanax observed, "if a man was sick or had to leave work early or anything, we would solve it ourselves."

Within five years after Juan Chanax reached Houston, over a thousand Mayas from San Cristobal worked at Randall's. A single person had created what scholars call a migration chain. Through Chanax, Randall's had found access to a minimum-wage workforce that would perform willingly—in the company's words—as "cheerful servants." The Mayas, in turn, found opportunities unavailable in Guatemala. In the process Chanax and other early immigrants had become department managers and supervising assistants; their wives often worked as maids and servants in the homes of Houston's rapidly growing upper-income communities.

In many ways Chanax and his fellow Guatemalans mirrored the classic tale of immigrants realizing the American dream. In suburban Houston they formed their own community in an area that came to be known as Las Americas. There, various Central American immigrant groups established churches and social clubs amid some 90 apartment complexes that a decade or two earlier had housed mostly young, single office workers. On weekends and evenings, rival soccer teams played in the nearby park. (Juan, also the soccer league's president, helped new teams fill out the forms required by the parks department to use its fields.) The growth of Las Americas in the late twentieth century echoed the pattern of immigrants who had come to the United States at the century's opening.

Yet those patterns had changed too. Cities remained the mecca of most immigrants, but many newcomers of the 1980s and 1990s settled in suburban areas, particularly in the West and Southwest. Industrial factories provided the lion's share of work in the 1890s, but a century later the service industries—grocery stores, fast-food chains, janitorial companies—absorbed many more immigrants. And the faces had changed, as European immigrants found themselves outnumbered by Latinos from Mexico and Central America as well as by Asians from the Philippines, China, Korea, Southeast Asia, and the Indian subcontinent, not to mention increasing numbers of Russians, Arabs from the Middle East, and Africans. Transportation and communications networks tied immigrants to their home countries more strongly than in the past, allowing newcomers like Juan to keep regularly in touch with former neighbors and relatives. Immigrants continued to participate in home-country politics more easily; they could wire money instantly to relatives and even build homes thousands of miles away where one day they planned to retire.

With the arrival of the twenty-first century, immigration was only one factor that linked American society to the world. The interwoven strands of global finance, the blossoming connections to the new Internet, and the politics of global terrorism all ensured that even if Americans wanted to, they could not ignore the rest of the world. ∞∞∞

THE NEW IMMIGRATION

THE IMMIGRATION ACT OF 1965 (see pages 815–816) altered the face of American life. The lawmakers who passed the act did not expect such far-reaching consequences, because they assumed that Europeans would continue to predominate among newcomers. Yet reform of the old quota system opened the way for a wave of immigrants unequaled since the beginning of the century.

ECONOMIC AND POLITICAL CAUSES OF IMMIGRATION

Turmoil abroad pushed many immigrants toward the United States, beginning in the 1960s with Fidel Castro's revolution in Cuba and unrest in the Dominican Republic. The war in Vietnam and its aftermath produced more than 500,000 refugees in the 15 years after 1975. Revolutionary conflicts in Central America during the 1980s launched new immigration streams. Yet economic factors played as great a role as the terrors of war. Although some Filipinos fled the repressive regime of Ferdinand Marcos, many more came to the United States in a more straightforward search for jobs. When Mexico suffered an economic downturn in the 1980s, emigration there rose sharply.

In all, over 20 million immigrants arrived in the United States between 1990 and 2010. The nation's foreign-born population rose to almost 12 percent, the highest proportion since World War I. By 2009 the Latino population approached 50 million and exceeded the population of African Americans. The Asian American population grew at an even faster rate to about 16 million. Throughout the 1990s a steadily expanding economy made immigrants a welcome source of new labor. The world economic crisis after 2007 provoked new debates over immigration and the problem of illegal aliens.

The New Look of America: Asian Americans

In 1970, 96 percent of Asian Americans were Japanese, Chinese, or Filipino. By 2000 those same three groups constituted only about half of all Asian Americans. As the diversity of Asian immigration increased, Asian Indians, Koreans, and Vietnamese came to outnumber Japanese Americans. The newcomers also varied dramatically in economic background, crowding both ends of the economic spectrum.

PROSPEROUS NEWCOMERS

The higher end included many Chinese students who, beginning in the 1960s, sought out the United States for a college education, then found a job and stayed, eventually bringing in their families. "My brother-in-law left his wife in Taiwan and came here as a student to get his PhD in engineering," explained Subi Lin Felipe. "After he received his degree, he got a job in San Jose. Then he brought in a sister and his wife, who brought over one of her brothers and me. And my brother's wife then came." Asian Indians were even more acculturated on arrival because about two-thirds entered

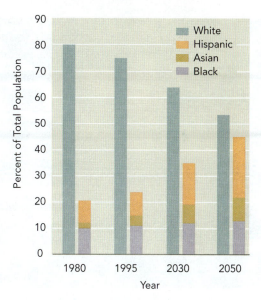

Projected Population Shifts, 1980–2050

Census figures project an increasing racial and ethnic diversity for the American people. White population is projected to drop from 80 percent in 1980 to about 53 percent in 2050, with the nation's Latino population rising most sharply.

the United States speaking English and with college degrees already in hand. Indian engineers played a vital role in the computer and software industries. Similarly, Korean and Filipino professionals took skilled jobs, particularly in medical fields.

BLUE-COLLAR ASIANS

Yet Asian immigrants also included those on the lower rungs of the economic ladder. Among the new wave of Chinese immigrants, or *San Yi Man,* many blue-collar workers settled in the nation's Chinatowns, where they worked in restaurants or sewed in sweatshops. Without education and language skills, often in debt to labor contractors, most remained trapped in Chinatown's ethnic economy. Refugees from war and revolution in Southeast Asia often made harrowing journeys. Vietnamese families crowded into barely seaworthy boats, sometimes only to be terrorized by pirates, other times nearly drowned in storms before reaching poorly equipped Thai refugee camps. By 1990 almost a million refugees had arrived in the United States, three-quarters of them from Vietnam, most of the others from Laos or Cambodia. Since 2000, immigrants from China, India, and the Philippines accounted for almost half the Asian total. Thus the profile of Asian immigration resembled an hourglass, with the most newcomers either relatively affluent or extremely poor.

ASIAN DOWNWARD MOBILITY

Finally, Asian Americans experienced two forms of downward mobility. First, highly educated Asian immigrants often found it difficult to land jobs in their professions. To American observers, Korean shopkeepers seemed examples of success, when in fact such owners often enough had been former professionals forced into the risky small-business

The Hmong people from Cambodia were among the many refugees fleeing Southeast Asia in the wake of the Vietnam War. While Chue and Nhia Thao Cha stayed in a refugee camp in Thailand, they stitched a traditional Hmong story cloth that, in this detail, shows refugees boarding a plane to come to the United States.

world. One Filipino doctor noted that strict state licensing standards prevented him from opening up his own medical practice. Instead, he found himself working as a restaurant meat cutter for employers who had no idea about his medical background. "They thought I was very good at separating meat from the bone," he commented ironically. Second, schools reported significant numbers of Asian American students who were failing. This "lost generation" were most often the children of families who entered the United States with little education and few job skills.

The New Look of America: Latinos

Like Asian Americans, Latinos in the United States constituted a diverse mosaic, reflecting dozens of immigrant streams. Although the groups shared a language, they usually settled in distinct urban and suburban barrios across the United States. Such enclave communities provided support to newcomers and an economic foothold for newly established businesses. Money circulated within a community; the workers and owners of an ethnic grocery, for example, spent their wages at neighboring stores, whose profits fueled other immigrant businesses in a chain reaction.

THE DOMINICANS OF WASHINGTON HEIGHTS
Washington Heights, at the northern tip of New York City, followed that path as nearly a quarter of a million Dominicans settled there during the 1970s and 1980s. A hundred blocks to the south, Manhattan's downtown skyscrapers seemed distant; shopkeepers' stereos along the major thoroughfares boomed music of trumpets and congas, while peddlers pushed heavily loaded shopping carts through busy streets, crying "¡A peso! ¡A peso!" ("For a dollar!"). In addition, Dominican social clubs planned dances or hosted political discussions. Similarly, in Miami

and elsewhere in South Florida, Cuban Americans created their own self-sustaining enclaves. A large professional class and strong community leadership brought them prosperity and political influence.

EAST LOS ANGELES
Along the West Coast, Los Angeles was the urban magnet for many Latino (and Asian) immigrants. Mexican immigrants had long flocked to East Los Angeles, which facilitated access to the jobs in factories, warehouses, and railroad yards across the river. Many Mexican Americans now owned their own businesses and homes. But beginning in the mid-1980s and 1990s, the neighborhood of MacArthur Park became the focal point for the newest immigrants from Mexico and Central America. MacArthur Park was less developed as a community, and many of its residents were transient, passing quickly to other neighborhoods or jobs.

As more factories and service industries became decentralized, locating themselves beyond urban downtowns, the barrios followed as well. Las Americas near Houston, where Juan Chanax lived, was one example; but suburban barrios could be found dotted all across the nation, from Rockville, Maryland, to Pacoima, California, near Burbank. Pacoima's well-kept bungalows housed working-class Mexican Americans who had lived in California for decades. But the front lawns of many residences were often paved over to hold the cars of additional workers or families, and the garages were converted to dormitories with a sink and toilet, where four or five newcomers from Central America could rent a spot to lay a bedroll on the cement floor.

Illegal Immigration

Because Mexico and the United States share such a long common border—and an equally long history of intermingling

At Our Lady of Guadalupe Catholic Mission, a family in the growing Mexican and Central American community of Muscatine, Iowa, held a quinceañera— a celebration of a girl's 15th birthday. In the 1990s, even rural towns from Iowa to Ohio and New York reflected the growing diversity of immigrant religious life.

of peoples and cultures—many Mexicans entered the United States illegally. But the number of illegal immigrants increased during the 1980s as Central Americans joined the northward flow, along with Mexicans escaping a sharp economic downturn in their own country. By 1985 the number of illegal immigrants in the United States was estimated at anywhere from 2 to 12 million.

IMMIGRATION AND CONTROL ACT OF 1986

Congress attempted to stem that flow by passing the Immigration and Control Act of 1986. Tightened border security was coupled with a new requirement that American employers bear the responsibility of certifying their workers as legal residents of the United States. At the same time, those illegal immigrants who had arrived before 1986 were granted amnesty and allowed to become legal residents. In the end, however, the terms of the law failed to create the clean slate Congress had hoped for. Legal immigrants continued to be intertwined with illegals in a host of different ways: as relatives helping loved ones make the transition to living in the United States, as landlords boarding newcomers until they could get on their feet, as links with communities in the home country—just as Juan Chanax continued to be after he received amnesty from the act in 1986.

 ## Links with the Home Country

Because systems of communication and transportation drew the world closer, the new immigrants found it easier to maintain links with their points of origin and wire money back to relatives. Pacoima, the suburban barrio outside Burbank, California, boasted only a small town center. But along that half-mile stretch, 13 different currency exchanges were open for business to handle immigrant funds.

By 1992 the amount of funds sent worldwide was so great that it was surpassed in volume only by the currency flows of the global oil trade.

BANDA MUSIC

And not just money traveled these routes. An immigrant entering La Curaçao, a furniture store in Los Angeles's MacArthur Park, could sign up to buy a bedroom suite on the installment plan. When the payments were completed, the furniture was released—not in Los Angeles but at a branch warehouse in El Salvador, where relatives could pick up the purchase. Cultural ties remained strong as well. Young Mexican immigrants flocked on Saturday night to popular dance halls such as the Lido in Los Angeles to hear a variety of music known as *banda.* Women wore tight tank tops and jeans or skirts, while the men's cowboy outfits were distinguished by their *cuarta,* a small riding whip at the belt, and by a kerchief hanging from the right hip pocket, with the name of the wearer's native Mexican state embroidered proudly for all to see.

Religious Diversity

The global nature of the new immigration also reshaped the religious faiths of America. During the 1950s most Americans' sense of religious diversity encompassed the mainline Protestant churches, Roman Catholicism, and Judaism. But immigrants brought with them not only their own brands of Christianity and Judaism but also Buddhist, Hindu, and Islamic beliefs. By 2001 there were perhaps a million Buddhists and a million Hindus living in the United States and anywhere from 2 to 6 million Muslims. (Precise figures are difficult to obtain.) The largest number of Muslims came from Pakistan and South Asia, but close to a million were from the Arab world, especially Lebanon, Egypt, and Syria. Mosques became common in New York City, Los Angeles, and Detroit.

Mainline Protestants and Catholics changed as well. The Presbyterian Church (U.S.A.) increased its Korean-speaking congregations from about 20 in 1970 to over 350 by 2000. In New York City, Episcopalian services were held in 14 different languages. And Catholic churches increasingly found themselves celebrating mass in both English and Spanish. Such arrangements took place not only in urban congregations such as the Church of the Nativity in South Central Los Angeles (where Latinos alternated services with African Americans) but increasingly even in rural areas like Columbus Junction, Iowa, whose Catholic church was energized by Mexican Americans working in a nearby meat-processing plant.

 REVIEW

How did the immigration populations from Asia and Latin America become more diversified during the 1980s and 1990s?

CLINTON AND THE NEW GLOBAL ORDER

IN 1993 WILLIAM JEFFERSON CLINTON became the first baby boomer to occupy the White House. His wife, Hillary Rodham Clinton, would be the most politically involved presidential wife since Eleanor Roosevelt. Like many couples of their generation, the Clintons were a two-career family. Both trained as lawyers at Yale University during the tumultuous 1960s. Bill chose politics as his career, while Hillary mixed private practice with public service. Their marriage had not been easy. Revelations of Clinton's sexual affairs as governor of Arkansas almost ruined his campaign for the presidency. The first couple seemed, however, more intent on making public policy than in defending their private lives.

President John Kennedy had inspired Clinton to enter politics. Like Kennedy, Clinton envisioned himself as an activist president, not a detached leader like Reagan. Unlike the senior George Bush he would concentrate on domestic policy. But Clinton's desire for major legislative initiatives ran up against the election results of 1992: he had received just 43 percent of the popular vote, while the Republicans had narrowed the Democratic majorities in Congress. Still, he pledged to revive the economy and rein in the federal deficit that had grown so enormously during the Reagan years. Beyond that, he called for systematic reform of the welfare and health care systems.

DON'T ASK; DON'T TELL — As one of his first acts, the new president attempted to eliminate a rule that banned homosexuals from serving in the military. In doing so, he fulfilled a campaign pledge to the gay community. Resistance from conservatives and the military forced Clinton to accept a compromise position satisfactory to no

one: "Don't ask; don't tell." As long as gay soldiers kept their sexual orientation private, they could serve their country.

Such early missteps could be set down partly to the stumbles of a newcomer learning his way around the office. But larger issues of character could not be dismissed. One observer shrewdly noted that there were two Bill Clintons—the idealistic young man from Hope, Arkansas (his hometown), and the boy from Hot Springs (his mother's home). The latter was a resort town associated with the seamier side of Arkansas high life. With increasing frequency, the leadership mustered by the idealistic politician from Hope seemed to be undermined by the character flaws of the boy from Hot Springs.

WHITEWATER — Although Clinton's conservative opponents disliked his politics, the president's moral lapses troubled them even more. Critics nicknamed him "Slick Willie" and sought continually to expose discreditable or illegal dealings from his past. Accusations arose that when Clinton was governor in the early 1980s, both he and his wife had received special treatment from a failed real estate venture known as Whitewater. Rumors also abounded about Clinton's womanizing, fanned in 1994 when a former Arkansas state employee, Paula Jones, filed a sexual harassment suit against the president. Under pressure from congressional conservatives, Attorney General Janet Reno appointed former judge Kenneth Starr as a special prosecutor to investigate Whitewater. But during Clinton's first term, Starr's investigations, as well as two Senate committees, produced no evidence that the Clintons had acted illegally.

 THE NEW WORLD DISORDER — Clinton entered office focusing on domestic, not foreign, affairs. He discovered that the "new world order," hailed by both Mikhail Gorbachev and George H. W. Bush, seemed more like a world of regional disorders. In sub-Saharan Africa corruption and one-party rule severely weakened most economies, tribal violence mounted, and AIDS became epidemic. Brutal civil wars broke out in both Somalia and Rwanda. As a presidential candidate, Clinton had supported President Bush's decision in December 1992 to send troops to aid famine-relief efforts in Somalia. But attempts to install a stable government proved difficult. Tragically, the United States as well as European nations failed to intervene in Rwanda before over a million people were massacred in 1994. By contrast, the United States joined a multinational effort in Haiti in 1994 that sustained an uneasy peace.

Yugoslavian Turmoil

CONFLICTS IN BOSNIA AND CROATIA — Europe's most intractable trouble spot proved to be Yugoslavia, a nation divided by ethnic rivalries within a number of provinces, including Serbia, Croatia, and Bosnia. After Bosnia became independent in 1992 both sides, but especially the Serbs, resorted to what was euphemistically referred to as "ethnic cleansing"—the massacre of rival

| American troops were part of the NATO peacekeeping force sent to Bosnia after the Dayton Accords of 1995. These marines were among the first arrivals, who encountered chilly, wet weather.

populations—to secure control. Serbs even set up "rape camps" where they brutalized Muslim women. The United States initially viewed the civil war in Yugoslavia as Europe's problem. Remembering Vietnam, many members of Congress did not want to see American troops bogged down in a distant civil war. But after the civilian death toll mounted to a quarter of a million, Clinton committed the United States to support NATO bombing of Serb forces. In 1995 the Serbs agreed to peace talks at a meeting in Dayton, Ohio. The Dayton Accords created separate Croatian, Bosnian, and Serbian nations. Some 60,000 NATO troops, including 20,000 Americans, moved into Bosnia to enforce the peace.

INTERVENTION IN KOSOVO
Having lost Croatia and Bosnia, Serbia was determined not to lose Kosovo, a province in which the Serb minority ruled over a mostly Albanian population. In fighting Albanian rebels, Serbian police and militia groups committed widespread atrocities against civilians. Hundreds of thousands of Albanian refugees poured into the surrounding countries. In the spring of 1999 Clinton committed U.S. forces to a NATO bombing campaign that forced Serbia to agree to a NATO occupation of Kosovo. Once again, American troops entered as peacekeepers.

Middle East Peace

Steps forward in Haiti and the Balkans could not quiet fears of a new Middle East crisis. Sporadic protests and rioting by Palestinians in the Israeli-occupied territories of Gaza and the West Bank gave way in the 1990s to negotiations. At a ceremony hosted by President Clinton in 1993, Palestinian leader Yasir Arafat and Israeli prime minister Itzak Rabin signed a peace agreement permitting self-rule for Palestinians in the Gaza Strip and in Jericho on the West Bank. In 1995 Arafat became head of the West Bank Palestinian National Authority.

MIDDLE EAST PEACE NEGOTIATIONS
Still, a full settlement remained elusive. As Clinton pursued negotiations, he found he had limited leverage. The assassination of Prime Minister Rabin in 1995, by an angry Orthodox Jew, began a period of increased suspicion on both sides as extremists sought to derail the peace process. Clinton engaged in two marathon negotiating sessions with the two sides, in 1998 and in 2000 at Camp David, in hopes of hammering out an agreement that would allow for a separate Palestinian state alongside Israel. But positions on both sides hardened. Whether in the Middle East, Eastern Europe, Africa, or the Caribbean, such regional crises demonstrated that a new global "world order" would be difficult to maintain.

✓ **REVIEW**

How did ethnic, religious, and cultural differences play a part in regional crises in Yugoslavia and the Middle East?

THE CLINTON PRESIDENCY ON TRIAL

THROUGHOUT CLINTON'S PRESIDENCY THE NATION experienced a powerful economic expansion. Despite low unemployment, there was little inflation. Prosperity allowed the president to eliminate the budget deficits that had soared during the 1980s. But increased government revenues did not persuade Congress to support Clinton's reform agenda.

Recovery without Reform

CLINTON PROGRAM
In his first speech to Congress, Clinton proposed a program that began reducing the deficit as well as providing investments to stimulate the economy and repair the nation's decaying public infrastructure. In contrast, Presidents Reagan and Bush had cut funds to rebuild schools, roads, dams, bridges, and other public structures. In August 1993 a compromise budget bill passed by only a single vote in the Senate, with Republicans blocking the stimulus portion of Clinton's program. Still, deficit reduction was a significant achievement.

NAFTA
The victory in the budget battle gave Clinton the momentum to hammer together a bipartisan coalition that passed NAFTA, the North American Free Trade Agreement. With the promise of greater trade and more jobs, the pact linked the United States economy more closely with those of Canada and Mexico. The president also helped supporters of gun control overcome the powerful opposition of the National Rifle Association to

Election officials in Broward County, Florida, examine a ballot for chads, punched paper from holes, in the hotly contested presidential election of 2000.

The impeachment controversy left the president weakened, but hardly powerless. Throughout the political tempest the nation's economy had continued to grow. By 1999 the rate of unemployment had dropped to 4.1 percent, the lowest in nearly 30 years, while the stock market reached new highs. Furthermore, as the economy expanded, federal tax receipts grew with it. By 1998 Bill Clinton faced a situation that would have seemed improbable a few years previous—a budget surplus. By balancing the budget the president had appropriated a key Republican issue.

Hanging by a Chad: The Election of 2000

Budget surpluses, Social Security reform, and tax cuts topped the list of issues in the 2000 election. Vice President Al Gore, running for the Democrats, had served in Vietnam and the Senate, written a book on the global environmental crisis, supported the development of the Internet, and was especially active as vice president. Despite these strengths, he was a stiff and uninspiring campaigner.

By contrast, the affable Texas governor George W. Bush (son of the 41st president) had little interest in world affairs. He once asked a Saudi diplomat why people expected him to know so much about a puny country such as North Korea. "I don't have the foggiest idea about what I think about international foreign policy," he confessed. Bush's previous record in business was mixed at best, and as governor he served in a state where the officeholder wielded little power. But Bush made character the central issue of his campaign—not his or Gore's, but Bill Clinton's. In that way, Bush deprived Gore of a vital campaign asset, because the president remained popular with voters.

HANGING CHADS

FLORIDA PUNCH-CARD BALLOT

The outcome of the election came down to one state—Florida, where Bush led by just 300 votes. Nationwide, Gore had a 500,000 edge in the popular vote, but without Florida's 25 electoral votes neither candidate had a majority in the Electoral College. Evidence immediately surfaced of widespread voting irregularities. Some Florida counties used ballots with complicated layouts that led voters to choose the wrong candidate.

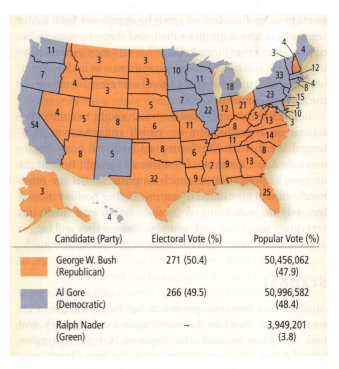

Candidate (Party)	Electoral Vote (%)	Popular Vote (%)
George W. Bush (Republican)	271 (50.4)	50,456,062 (47.9)
Al Gore (Democratic)	266 (49.5)	50,996,582 (48.4)
Ralph Nader (Green)	–	3,949,201 (3.8)

ELECTION OF 2000

Other counties used punch-card machines so old that they routinely failed to perforate the ballot or left partial holes that popularly became known as "hanging chads." More serious were allegations that the state had actively suppressed voting in heavily black counties. Those accusations were especially troubling since George Bush's brother, Jeb, was Florida's governor.

BUSH V. GORE   After weeks of wrangling, the U.S. Supreme Court entered the legal fray over Florida's contested votes. In *Bush v. Gore,* the Court's conservative majority, all Republican appointees, ruled 5–4 that the recount must end. The majority argued that because the recount applied to only three counties, it valued some votes more than others. Regardless of who had the better argument, in *Bush v. Gore,* the Supreme Court, not the American voters, made George W. Bush the 43rd president of the United States.

 **REVIEW**

How did partisan differences affect at least three political clashes between 1992 and 2000?

THE UNITED STATES IN A NETWORKED AND MULTICULTURAL WORLD

IN 1988 ECONOMIST LAWRENCE SUMMERS was working on the presidential campaign of Michael Dukakis. At a meeting in Chicago, the staff assigned him a car with a telephone. Summers was so impressed, he recalled, that "I used it to call my wife to tell her I was in a car with a phone." A decade later as deputy treasury secretary in the Clinton administration, he visited the Ivory Coast in Africa to help launch an American-supported health project. One village on his itinerary could be reached only by dugout canoe. As Summers stepped into the canoe for his return trip, an aide handed him a cell phone. "Washington has a question for you," the aide said. The same man who once marveled at a phone in his car in Chicago ten years later expected one in his dugout canoe in the interior of Africa.

The Internet Revolution

Like Lawrence Summers, most Americans by the beginning of the twenty-first century were linked to a global communications network. Computers, cell phones, iPads, MP3 players, and other electronic devices provided almost instant contact with a wider world.

THE WORLD WIDE WEB   Early Internet pioneers shared a democratic vision, a web open and free to all. Users could communicate without restriction and find access to any form of information. Such openness was the bane of authoritarian governments, which found it difficult to control public opinion in a world in which information flowed freely. The unregulated format of the web raised substantial legal, moral, and political questions in

the United States as well. By 1999 five million websites were in operation—among them sites promoting pornography, hate speech, and even instructions on how to build atomic bombs. A number of politicians and civic groups called for the censorship of the more extreme web content. Others argued that the greater danger lay in allowing the Internet to become dominated by large telecommunications companies. These advocates called for legislation protecting "Net neutrality."

E-COMMERCE   Business spending on technology jumped from 3 percent in the 1960s to 45 percent by the mid-1990s, fueled by the recognition that the web's interconnectivity gave it enormous commercial potential. Businesses could now interact with their customers without respect to physical location or time zone. E-commerce practitioners began using the Internet to disseminate company or product information, generate leads, take orders, and build customer databases. Business-to-business sales went from $40 billion in 1998 to some $1.1 trillion by 2007, while retail sales approached $400 billion. Online merchandiser Amazon.com began to challenge such giant brick-and-mortar retailers as Wal-Mart and Target.

American Workers in a Two-Tiered Economy

The benefits of the Internet revolution were not evenly distributed, however. Economists described the United States in the 1990s as a two-tiered labor market in which most increases in earning went to people at the top of the wage scale. Thus, despite the decade's prosperity, the median income of American families was barely higher in 1996 than in 1973. Indeed, the earnings of the average white male worker actually fell. Only because so many women entered the job market did the family standard of living remain the same. In the early 1970s some 37 percent of women worked outside the home; in 1999 about 57 percent did.

Education was a critical factor in determining winners in the high-tech economy. Families with college-educated parents were three times more likely to have home access to the web than were those families in which parents' education ended with high school. Because average education levels were relatively lower among African Americans and Latinos (and relatively higher among Asian Americans), the computer divide took on a racial cast as well. But the implications went beyond mere access to the web. More important, the high-wage sector of the computer economy required educated workers, and the demand for them drove up those workers' salaries.

WAGE STAGNATION   Unlike computer programmers or corporate executives who were in high demand, low-skill workers were not able to increase their earnings simply by switching jobs. Some economists concluded, "the most important economic division is not between races, or genders, or economic sectors, but between the college-educated and the non-college-educated."

DAILY LIVES

SOCIAL MEDIA

Humorist Will Rogers once described Americans as a nation of joiners. Three people, he joked, could barely pass each other on the street without pausing to hold a meeting. That might explain why in the 1990s sociologist Robert Putnam was startled to discover that Americans were increasingly disconnected from one another. Civic organizations that had once created communities of shared interests—in PTAs, church congregations, bowling leagues, or garden clubs—seemed to be disintegrating. In the process, Putnam argued, the United States had lost valuable "social capital." A society of isolated individuals was not so richly endowed as one "with a dense network of reciprocal social relations."

But Putnam made these observations at the dawn of an era in which the Internet was erecting a host of new communities built around social media. In 2003 the social network Myspace was founded; three years later it had become the most visited website on the Internet, popular especially with young adults. Myspace not only influenced pop culture and music, but it also launched gaming sites such as Zynga (Farmville) and Rock You (Zoo World and Galactic Allies). Facebook, launched at Harvard in 2004, quickly overtook Myspace, claiming over a billion users by 2012. Its members created personal profiles that included photographs, videos, and other media, as well as lists of "friends." Facebook members joined groups sharing common interests and organized friends into lists such as "People from School" or "Best Pals." Rival LinkedIn targeted business and professional members who reached out to connect with people who might be useful in their work lives.

In 2006 brainstormers at the podcasting company Odeo created a site through which individuals could send brief communications to small groups. From the code twttr came Twitter, an online social network and micro-blogging service whose users can send and read text messages of up to 140 characters, known as "tweets." In the early days some 60,000 tweets a day fluttered into the ether, but when pop idol Michael Jackson died in 2009 the tweets reached 100,000 per hour and company servers crashed. Social scientists began analyzing the flow for meaning, as they swirled, like flocks of starlings, around every conceivable subject from the doings of movie stars to the gaffes of politicians or the course of a flu epidemic.

The difficult question to answer, as Putnam observed, was whether these tweets, blogs, and gaming sites actually fostered "social capital and genuine community." Were social media profiles little more than pages on which one could "type oneself into being," as one observer commented? Unlike face-to-face conversations, virtual communications often provided limited or misleading information about the participants in these new communities. On the other hand, if the age, race, or physical appearance of individuals remained hidden, would the new social sites tend to be more egalitarian and their conversation more candid and outspoken? Or would anonymity spawn legions of trolls and flamers, who defaced social sites?

Given their huge memberships, social networks have begun to influence politics and society in larger ways. In his 2008 presidential race, Barack Obama led the way in using social media to raise money and motivate volunteers and voters. In 2011 a series of uprisings and rebellions known as the "Arab Spring" used social media to build crowds, communicate, and arouse

Social community or social isolation?

opposition in the Middle East, despite government efforts to censor the Internet. Businesses launched web advertising campaigns that they hoped would "go viral." Consumers used social media sites to find a plumber, rent an apartment, or meet a potential spouse. Police departments monitored gang activities by following Twitter; parents worried that children, using social networks, would attract predators.

So the full impact of these virtual communities remains to be determined. Their potential for civic engagement and social connectivity was "impressive," Putnam admitted. No longer did limits of time and space determine whom one could "friend," when one could Skype, or how often one could Tweet. In a mere matter of two decades, for better or worse, these new forms of community had thoroughly entrenched themselves.

Thinking Critically

In what ways does social media affect personal privacy?

The prosperity of the late 1990s produced an interesting dilemma. On the one hand, it eased many social tensions that had long divided the nation. Inner-city crime rates fell; the poor began to experience a marked improvement in their finances; consumer confidence reached an all-time high. But over the longer term, the boom's statistics were not encouraging. Despite the decline in the poverty rate, it remained above the rate for any year in the 1970s. If the strongest economy in 30 years left the poverty rate higher than during the inflation-plagued years of the 1970s, what would happen if the economy faltered?

African Americans and the Persistence of the Racial Divide

In the 1990s the highest-paid celebrity in the world was an African American—Michael Jordan. Oprah Winfrey, also an African American, was the highest-paid woman in America. Although the situation of African Americans had improved vastly compared with their position in the 1950s, race still mattered.

INNER-CITY RENEWAL By the late 1990s African Americans in increasing numbers were benefiting from a decade of economic expansion. Home-ownership reached 46 percent and employment increased from around 87 percent in 1980 to nearly 92 percent in 1998. African Americans in increasing numbers rose up the ladder in corporate America. Many started their own businesses. Economic success also brought new hope to the nation's inner cities. Crime and poverty decreased significantly, especially rates of murder and violence. Births to single mothers reached a postwar low. Fewer blacks lived below the poverty level and fewer were on welfare.

Yet many African Americans were reserved in their reaction to such statistics. "To the extent that you proclaim your success," one community leader remarked, "people forget about you." Furthermore, an economic downturn might reverse those gains, especially if employers resorted to the traditional practice of "last hired, first fired."

PROPOSITION 209 AGAINST AFFIRMATIVE ACTION Civil rights leaders were most concerned about the continued assault on affirmative action. In 1996 California voters passed a ballot initiative, Proposition 209, that eliminated racial and gender preferences in hiring and college admissions. Ironically, the leading advocate for Proposition 209 was a conservative black leader, Ward Connerly. Connerly argued that racial preferences demeaned black and other minority students by setting up a double standard that patronizingly assumed minorities could not compete on an equal basis. In any case, Proposition 209 had a striking effect. Enrollments of Latinos and blacks at the elite California university campuses and professional schools dropped sharply: at UC Berkeley, down 57 percent for black students and 34 percent for Latinos. What remained was a student body that was only 3 percent black and 9 percent Latino, in a state in which African Americans constituted 7 percent and Latinos 29 percent of the population. Major state universities in Washington, Texas, and Michigan also experienced declines after passing similar laws.

Also in 1996 a federal circuit court ruled in *Hopwood v. State of Texas et al.* that race could not be used as a factor in college admissions. The Supreme Court did not fully address that issue until 2003, in the case of *Gratz v. Bollinger,* when the Bush administration pressed the Court to strike down the use of any racial preference in the admissions programs of the University of Michigan. In deciding the case the justices did strike down a point system used by Michigan giving minorities preference in undergraduate admissions. However, the Court approved, 5 to 4, a separate program used by the university's law school, which gave race some influence in the admissions process. Affirmative action had been reduced in scope but not abolished.

Global Pressures in a Multicultural America

Clearly the enormous changes wrought by immigration and the new global economy gave the United States a more multicultural flavor. Salsa rhythms became part of the pop-cultural mainstream, and Latino foods competed with Indian curries, Japanese sushi, and Pad Thai. Baseball, the national pastime, became truly all-American as major league rosters filled with stars from Japan, the Dominican Republic, Mexico, Cuba, Panama, and Venezuela.

But the mix of cultures did not occur without friction. Throughout American history, the dominant culture has reacted defensively when immigrant flows increased from new sources or when jobs were hard to find. After reforming their immigration laws in the 1960s, Americans once again debated how diverse the United States could become without losing its traditional identity.

PROPOSITION 187 In 1990, Lawrence Auster echoed earlier nativists with *The Path to National Suicide,* in which he warned of the "browning of America." Four years later opponents of immigration in California put forward Proposition 187, a state ballot initiative that denied health, education, and welfare benefits to illegal aliens. Despite the opposition of most major religious, ethnic, and educational organizations, the measure passed with a lopsided 59 percent majority. In the end, however, Proposition 187 never went into effect because a federal judge ruled unconstitutional the provision denying education to the children of illegal aliens.

| Libertad *by Ester Hernandez*

HISTORIAN'S TOOLBOX

MAPPING THE INTERNET

Color of lines and height of arcs indicate the intensity of web traffic as of the mid-1990s; the hotter the colors (orange, yellow) the greater the traffic.

Note which areas of the world are shown in black.

Why is the southern tip the only colored area of Africa?

How does this map suggest a potential source of tension between the Islamic and Western nations?

The Internet is not so much a single vast network, but a network of networks. It grew out of the efforts of the United States government to link major research and defense centers with a communications system that could survive a nuclear attack. The networks it joins now range from small home and office users, to universities, large corporations, and national governments. Probably no phenomenon in the recent past has done more to create a truly global economy. Stephen G.

Eick of Bell Laboratories created this map, based on 1993 data, to visually portray the flows of Internet traffic. Experts estimate that about a quarter of the world's people (almost 2 billion) have access to the World Wide Web (www). Though many people think of the web and the Internet as the same thing, they are not. Hardware and software create the Internet (much like a railroad), while documents, sites, and other electronically accessible information make up the web.

Thinking Critically

What would be another way to graph the information on this map? In what ways do you anticipate that the map would change if it were brought up to date? In what ways is the Internet similar to earlier systems of communication (that is, telephone, telegraph) and transportation (that is, railroads, airlines, interstate highways)? In what ways different?

Traditionally, nativist conflicts pit the dominant majority culture against the minority cultures of more recent arrivals. But in a multicultural society, such polar opposites often broke down. In 1998 yet another ballot initiative passed in California (Proposition 227), mandating that schools phase out all their bilingual education programs. Students would be granted only one year of English-language immersion courses before receiving all instruction in English. In this instance both white and Latino voters approved the proposition by nearly the

same margin, within one or two points of 62 percent. And the measure itself had been proposed after a group of Spanish-speaking parents boycotted their elementary school until it agreed to teach their children to read and write in English.

The New Debate

In 2006 immigration and especially the status of the approximately 11 million illegal aliens became a hotly debated issue. On the one hand, immigrant groups organized a day of marches and demonstrations in major cities across the country, proclaiming their loyalty to the United States and asking Congress to make it possible for them to become citizens. On the other hand, advocates of a more restrictive policy insisted that illegal immigration imposed a heavy burden on wages and government services. Since aliens earned less than natives, these workers were also more likely to need means-tested government benefits such as Medicaid and food stamps. Thirty-one percent of Mexican households received some form of public assistance in 1999, compared with only 17 percent of non-Mexican immigrants and 14 percent of natives.

The debate revealed a split particularly among Republicans. President Bush and many in the business community hoped to keep open the flow of low-wage labor and supported a guest worker program along with a plan to legalize the status of millions of illegal aliens. Other Republicans, especially in states like Arizona with high immigrant populations, campaigned to close the borders and oust those who had entered the country illegally. All the two camps could agree on was a plan to build a 700-mile fence along the U.S.-Mexican border. Hispanics voiced their displeasure in the 2006 elections. Some 70 percent of them voted for Democrats, who tended to side with the president on the immigration debate. U.S. Customs and Border Protection claimed that 580 miles (930 km) of fence was in place as of January 2009. The barriers were part of three operations (Gatekeeper in California, Hold-the-Line in Texas, and Safeguard in Arizona) to control the flow of illegal drugs from Latin America and cut down illegal immigration.

Even in the 2012 election the question of how the United States would manage its borders remained unresolved. The idea of a "nation" takes on new meaning in a global economy in which jobs, people, and goods move wherever markets for them exist. As the communications superhighway speeds information to all corners of the globe and international migrations bring new people to America's shores, the American political system will continue to evolve ways of encompassing a diversity that now reflects the entire world.

Some science fiction films of the 1950s had imagined a Manhattan like this: debris everywhere, buildings in ruin, the city shrouded in smoke and ash (see the movie poster on page 768). On September 11, 2001, however, disaster on such a large scale came not from nuclear war with another superpower but through the actions of international terrorists. The attack made clear that in a post–cold war world, global threats could come from small groups as well as powerful nations.

 REVIEW

Did the rise of the Internet do more to unite or divide Americans? What about the rising multiculturalism of American society during the 1980s and 1990s?

Terrorism in a Global Age

Along the northeast coast of the United States, September 11, 2001, dawned bright and clear. In the World Trade Center, Francis Ledesma was sitting in his office on the sixty-fourth floor of the South Tower when a friend suggested they go for coffee. Francis seldom took early breaks, but he decided to make an exception. In the cafeteria he heard and felt a muffled explosion: a boiler, he thought. But then he saw bricks and glass falling by the window. When he started to head back to his office for a nine o'clock meeting, his friend insisted they leave immediately. Out on the street Francis saw the smoke and gaping hole where American Airlines Flight 11 had hit the North Tower. At that moment a huge fireball erupted as United Airlines Flight 175 hit the South Tower where they worked. "We kept looking back," Francis recalled as they escaped the area, "and then all of a sudden our building, Tower 2, collapsed. I really thought that it was a mirage."

That was only the beginning of the horror. Shortly after takeoff from Dulles Airport, American Airlines Flight 77 veered from its path and crashed into the Pentagon. Several passengers on United Airlines Flight 93 from Newark to San Francisco heard the news over their cell phones before hijackers seized that plane. Rather than allow another attack, passengers stormed the cockpit. Moments later the plane crashed into a woods in western Pennsylvania.

From a secure area at Barksdale Air Force Base in Louisiana, President George W. Bush addressed a shaken nation. He called the crashes a "national tragedy" and condemned those responsible. "Freedom itself was attacked this morning by a faceless coward, and freedom will be defended," he assured the American people.

GLOBAL DIMENSIONS OF THE ATTACK

In an age of instant global communications, the entire world watched as the tragedy unfolded. Three minutes after the first plane hit the World Trade Center, ABC News announced that an explosion had rocked the towers. British television was already covering the fire when the second plane reached its target at 9:03 a.m. Japanese networks were on the air with coverage of the Pentagon crash about an hour later, around midnight their time. TV Azteca in Mexico carried President Bush's statement from Barksdale Air Force Base, and China Central Television was not far behind. This was, indeed, an international tragedy. The aptly named World Trade Center was a hub for global trade and finance. Citizens of more than 50 nations had died in the attack.

ECONOMIC DOWNTURN

Not since Pearl Harbor had the United States experienced such a devastating attack on its homeland. Most directly the tragedy claimed approximately 3,000 lives. Before September 11 the booming economy of the 1990s was already showing serious signs of strain; the World Trade Center attack pushed the nation into a recession. Security fears compounded economic concerns. The attacks were not the work of an enemy nation but of an Arab terrorist group known as al Qaeda, led by a shadowy figure, Saudi national Osama bin Laden. How many of al Qaeda's terrorist cells were still undetected within the United States? After the World Trade Center attack, nations were no longer the only threat to national security. Smaller groups—subnational or international—possessed the capability of using weapons of mass destruction to make war against the most powerful nation in the world.

A Conservative Agenda at Home

Before the attacks George W. Bush's administration seemed to lack direction. Bush's claim to leadership was shaky partly because when he took office in January 2001, a majority of the electorate had voted for his opponent, Al Gore. The crisis of September 11, 2001, energized the president.

Bush in his inaugural address had promised a moderate course, but Karl Rove, the new president's trusted political adviser, urged him to govern from his base on the right. A tight group of advisers led by Rove, Vice President Dick Cheney, Defense Secretary Donald Rumsfeld, and lobbyist Grover Norquist steered the president's conservative program. Although he appointed women and minorities to his cabinet, Bush also placed evangelicals such as Attorney General John Ashcroft in key positions. Majorities in both Houses of Congress and opportunities to appoint two justices to the Supreme Court gave the Republicans control over all three branches of government.

ENERGY POLICY

The partisan tone of the administration became quickly apparent. When Vice President Cheney convened leaders of the energy industry to recommend new policies, he included no one from the environmental community. Rather than promote conservation, the gathering stressed ways to increase production: drilling in environmentally sensitive coastal areas and the Arctic National Wildlife Refuge.

EDUCATION

To improve education the administration pressed to make schools more accountable through the use of standardized tests. Liberals led by Senator Ted Kennedy joined the president in January 2002 when he signed into law the "No Child Left Behind" initiative. The bill allowed for $18 billion in funding, but the administration asked for only $12 billion, which left much of the burden of implementing the ambitious new program to financially strapped state and local governments. Evangelical Christians were pleased with the president's proposal for "faith-based initiatives" that would provide public funds to churches involved in education and social work. Critics complained that such aid blurred the line separating church and state.

TAX CUTS

Tax cuts formed the cornerstone of the Bush agenda. Many conservatives wanted lower taxes in order to limit the government's ability to initiate new policies—a strategy referred to as "starving the beast." With the threat of recession looming, Bush defended his proposals as a means to boost the economy and create

The Bush administration reversed a number of environment rulings put in place during the Clinton era, including a gradual ban of snowmobiles in Yellowstone and Grand Teton National Parks. In general the new administration was more receptive to deregulation and voluntary standards as ways of addressing environmental problems.

more jobs. Congress supported the proposed cuts, passing first the Economic Growth and Tax Reform Reconciliation Act of 2001 (EGTRRA) and then the Job Creation and Workers Assistance Act of 2002 (JCWA). Size alone did not make these tax bills controversial. Critics objected that the cuts did little for job creation and that those in high-income brackets received most of the benefits. Citizens for Tax Justice claimed that by the end of 2010, when the Bush tax reductions were set to expire, 52 percent of the total tax relief would have gone to the richest 1 percent of Americans. Further, tax cuts turned the federal budget surpluses of the late 1990s into massive deficits.

Unilateralism in Foreign Affairs

Even before the events of September 11 the president rejected the multilateralism in foreign affairs that since World War II had guided American presidents, including his father. President Bush was determined that the United States would play a global role, but largely on its own terms. The administration's unilateral approach was made clear when it rejected the 1997 Kyoto Protocol on global warming to which 178 other nations had subscribed. "We have no interest in implementing that treaty," announced Christie Whitman, head of the Environmental Protection Agency, arguing that it would unfairly burden American energy producers. Environmentalists around the globe protested. With only 4 percent of the world's population, the United States produced about 25 percent of the Earth's greenhouse gases.

KYOTO PROTOCOL REJECTED

After seven months in office, George Bush's conservative agenda at home and his unilateralism abroad had not stirred widespread enthusiasm. But September 11 changed perspectives around the world. "This is not only an attack on the United States but an attack on the civilized world," insisted German chancellor Gerhard Schroeder. Even normally hostile nations such as Cuba and Libya conveyed shock and regrets. At home the president was careful to distinguish between the majority of "peace-loving" Muslims and "evil-doers" such as Osama bin Laden. But he made it clear that "our enemy is a radical network of terrorists" and that governments around the world had a simple choice: "Either you are with us or you are with the terrorists."

In a war with so many shadowy opponents, it was not easy to agree on which radical groups most threatened American security. The "radical network of terrorists" worked underground, spread across dozens of nations. Even the states most hospitable to al Qaeda proved hard to single out. Afghanistan was an obvious target. It was the seat of the Taliban, the extreme Islamic fundamentalists who ruled the country, and the haven of bin Laden. Yet 15 of the 19 hijackers in the World Trade Center attacks hailed from Saudi Arabia, long an ally of the United States.

The Roots of Terror

Before September 11 few Americans had paid much attention to terrorist movements. Indeed, few American radicals had resorted to terrorist tactics. In 1995 Timothy McVeigh, a right-wing terrorist, exploded a bomb that killed 161 people in the federal building in Oklahoma City. Yet that event was shocking precisely because, in the United States, it was relatively rare.

Most terrorists resort to violence not because they are strong but because they are weak. By creating widespread

For most of the twentieth century, Americans were accustomed to thinking of terrorism as a problem encountered abroad, as in Northern Ireland, where this IRA mural was painted on a wall (left) or in Israel, where Palestinian terrorists used bombings to campaign for their own independent state (center). In 1995 terrorism at home shocked Americans, when Timothy McVeigh (right) was arrested for bombing a federal building in Oklahoma City.

fear they hope to undermine the legitimacy of governments or force their enemies to recognize their grievances. In both Northern Ireland and Israel, two centers of past terrorist activities, the ruling governments possessed far more power than the insurgents.

OSAMA BIN LADEN Between 1982 and 1992, when the Russians withdrew from Afghanistan, approximately 35,000 Muslim radicals traveled there to make holy war, or **jihad.** One of the militants who did was Osama bin Laden, a tall, lanky Saudi who during the 1980s founded al Qaeda to forge a broad-based alliance of Arab rebels. When Iraq invaded Kuwait in 1991, bin Laden called upon Saudi Arabia to help repel the invasion. To his dismay, the Saudis allowed the United States to use its lands to invade Iraq—not at all the kind of holy war bin Laden imagined. From his network of hidden camps in Afghanistan he began directing a worldwide terror network, including operatives in the United States.

A GLOBAL TERRORIST STRATEGY Bin Laden's organization differed from previous movements. As historian Walter LaFeber noted, earlier attacks came from nation-based groups, with nationalist objectives. The Irish Republican Army wanted a unified Ireland. Palestinians wanted an independent state of their own. Al Qaeda, in contrast, had no national home. It was born out of the global alliance of radical Muslims who gathered in Afghanistan in the 1980s; its primary motivation was religious rather than nationalist.

Al Qaeda's campaign against the United States began with the 1993 bombing of the World Trade Center. That attack killed six people but did only minimal damage to the building. Further attacks occurred in places far from the United States. Twice the Clinton administration retaliated against al Qaeda with missile attacks; once it narrowly missed killing bin Laden himself in one of his Afghan camps.

The War on Terror: First Phase

AFGHANISTAN The military offensive against terrorism began in early October 2001. Despite intense American pressure to deliver bin Laden "dead or alive," the Taliban rulers of Afghanistan refused to expel him or al Qaeda. The United States then launched air attacks followed by an invasion, which quickly routed the Taliban. The United States established a coalition government in Kabul to help in the slow and uncertain process of rebuilding the country. Although bin Laden had managed to escape the bombing campaign, this first stage of the war on terrorism went well. Many Afghans celebrated the end of Taliban rule, particularly women, whose rights had been severely restricted by the regime.

Domestically the war on terrorism faced a daunting task. The United States was an open society, where citizens expected to travel freely and valued their privacy. How aggressively should the government act to prevent terrorist incidents? A month after the World Trade Center attacks, the vulnerability of American society was further exposed by the deaths of five people from letters tainted with anthrax virus sent through the postal system. Evidence eventually pointed to a domestic rather than foreign source of the virus, but widespread fears led the administration to propose the USA Patriot Act. Congress passed it so quickly, some members did not even read the bill before voting for it. The act broadly expanded government powers to use electronic surveillance, monitor bank transactions (to fight money laundering), and investigate suspected terrorists.

Beyond locating and arresting terrorists, authorities moved to secure vital systems of transportation, communication, and energy production. To coordinate new measures, Bush created the cabinet-level Department of Homeland Security. The new department brought together such diverse bodies as the Drug Enforcement Agency (DEA),

Immigration and Naturalization Service (INS), and the Coast Guard.

The War on Iraq

With the war in Afghanistan seeming to wind down, the president's focus shifted from Osama bin Laden to Iraq's brutal dictator, Saddam Hussein. Indeed, in the first weekend after the September 11 attacks the administration had decided to overthrow Hussein. The only question, Deputy Defense Secretary Paul Wolfowitz acknowledged, "was whether [invading Iraq] should be in the immediate response or whether [the president] should concentrate simply on Afghanistan first."

In September 2002 the president appeared before the UN General Assembly, challenging it to step up its inspection program for weapons of mass destruction (WMD) in Iraq. "All the world now faces a test," concluded the president, "and the United Nations a difficult and defining moment. Are Security Council resolutions to be honored and enforced, or cast aside without consequence?" The speech proved effective. Under renewed pressure from the United Nations, Hussein allowed inspections to resume, but Bush grew impatient. "If we know Saddam Hussein has dangerous weapons today—and we do—," he proclaimed, "does it make any sense for the world to wait . . . for the final proof, the smoking gun that could come in the form of a mushroom cloud?" The president had already laid the groundwork for an attack by asserting that the United States would be "ready for preemptive action when necessary to defend our liberty and to defend our lives."

PREEMPTION VERSUS CONTAINMENT

This **doctrine of preemption**—announcing that the United States might attack before it was itself attacked—was a major departure from the cold war policy of containment. "A preventive war, to my mind, is an impossibility," President Eisenhower declared in 1954. But Bush argued that, in an era in which terrorist enemies struck without warning, containment would no longer work. In October 2002 Congress passed a joint resolution giving the president full authority to take military action against Iraq.

UN weapons inspectors, however, could find no evidence of WMDs or programs to build them. The Security Council refused to support an American resolution giving the United States the authority to lead a UN-sponsored invasion. Only the United Kingdom, Spain, and Italy, among the major powers, were willing to join the United States. So on March 19, 2003, without a UN mandate, a "coalition of the willing" (30 nations, though the actual troops were virtually all American and British) attacked Iraq. The invasion was accomplished with speed and precision. Within days U.S. forces were halfway to Baghdad. On May 1 Bush announced an end to major combat operations. Coalition casualties (135 dead and 1,511 wounded) were remarkably low. Vice President Dick Cheney predicted that coalition forces "would be greeted as liberators" by the Iraqis.

A Messy Aftermath

Although a large majority of Americans supported the invasion of Iraq, a vocal minority had opposed the war. Some believed that a doctrine of preemption was not only morally

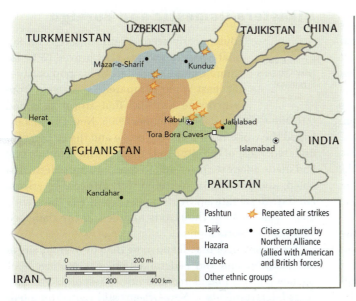

THE WAR ON TERROR: AFGHANISTAN AND IRAQ

*In Afghanistan, al Qaeda forces were concentrated in the mountainous region along the border with Pakistan. Ethnic and religious divisions influenced allegiances in both wars. In Iraq the most severe resistance to American occupation occurred from around Baghdad to Fallujah in the west and Tikrit to the north. In this "Sunni triangle," Sunni Muslims had prospered more under Saddam Hussein than had Shi'ite Muslims to the south. **Why might the war on terror threaten Iran?***

Among the leaders of the major powers, only Prime Minister Tony Blair (left) of the United Kingdom unreservedly supported President Bush's war in Iraq. The two leaders met in the Azores several days before the invasion of Iraq with the prime ministers of Spain and Portugal.

Governing from the Right

ENERGIZING THE BASE — Bush made the war on terror the centerpiece of his 2004 reelection campaign. His Democratic challenger, Senator John Kerry from Massachusetts, opposed the war and once again, the election's outcome came down to a single state—this time Ohio. Had 60,000 out of 5.6 million Ohio voters switched to Kerry, he would have won an electoral majority, though not the popular vote.

REFORMING SOCIAL SECURITY — With Republicans in control of all three branches of government, Bush began a politically risky campaign to reform Social Security, long a conservative goal. With the baby-boom generation closing in on retirement, the federal retirement system faced insolvency if steps were not taken to fix it, the president warned. But he met stiff opposition, even from some in his own party, to his proposal to **privatize** the system by creating individual retirement accounts. Critics worried that individuals risked losing their nest eggs if they chose unwisely, whereas the existing system guaranteed a return, even if it was less dramatic than private investment.

The president pressed what proved to be a second losing issue—tax cuts. In particular, he called for the cuts scheduled to end on December 31, 2010, to be made permanent and the estate tax (rebranded as a "death tax") to be eliminated. Yet the issue that had worked for Republicans so well and so long seemed to be losing its appeal. With deficits soaring and no end to the Iraq War in sight, even the Republican Congress would not deliver for Bush.

Disasters Domestic and Foreign

HURRICANE KATRINA AND NEW ORLEANS FLOODING — Bush's early second-term missteps on Social Security and tax cuts proved to be no more than a headwind to his popularity—at least when compared to the gale from Hurricane Katrina. That storm slammed into the Gulf Coast in September 2005. New Orleans escaped the worst until its levees broke and the city was inundated. Most of the city's well-to-do escaped, but no one had made adequate provision to evacuate the elderly, disabled, and poor, most of whom were African American. For days desperate survivors hung to rooftops. Thousands died, while tens of thousands huddled in the damaged Superdome sports arena.

The president at first did no more than fly over the site of the disaster, and the Federal Emergency Management Agency (FEMA) floundered in trying to respond. Over two years later, residents of New Orleans still waited for a federal plan to rebuild their city. Katrina reminded Americans that there were some problems that only effective government can solve.

With American casualties mounting in an unstable Iraq and drift in domestic affairs at home, voters voiced

wrong, but also dangerous. If the United States felt free to invade a country, what was to stop other nations from launching their own wars, justified by similar doctrines of preemption? Opponents also pointed out that no solid evidence linked the secular Saddam Hussein with the religious al Qaeda.

IRAQI CIVIL WAR — The administration found it impossible to ignore the practical problems arising out of swift victory. Ethnic and religious factions divided Iraq—**Shi'ite** Muslims in the southeast, **Sunni** Muslims around Baghdad, and Kurds in the north. Without Saddam's tyranny to hold the country together, the burden of peacekeeping fell to the American military. By the fall of 2004 the United States had spent over half a billion dollars in a futile search for the weapons of mass destruction. Hussein had never possessed the technology to build them. Even the creation of a provisional Iraqi government in June 2004 did not stop the violence from spreading. Meanwhile, the American cost of the war had risen to over $120 billion, at a time when the federal deficit at home was exceeding $550 billion.

The intangible costs of the war were also high. In the spring of 2004 Americans were stunned to learn that Iraqi prisoners of war being held in the Abu Ghraib prison near Baghdad had been abused and tortured by American soldiers guarding them. The Bush administration blamed a handful of "bad apples," but in fact the administration had encouraged such abuses. The Justice Department's Office of Legal Counsel prepared a memo that argued that cruel, inhumane, or degrading acts might not be classified as torture.

A plea from New Orleans residents threatened by Hurricane Katrina.

disciplined campaign that Barack Obama, a junior senator from Illinois, would run. Obama possessed the advantages of relative youth—he was 47 when he ran—as well as the hard-nosed skills of a former community organizer. His campaign made good use of the Internet by raising huge sums through small donations. Even more striking, Obama embodied contemporary multicultural trends. An African American, born in Hawaii to a white mother and a Kenyan father, he graduated from Columbia University and Harvard Law School.

John McCain, a Vietnam War hero and the senior senator from Arizona, faced the challenge of rallying a party demoralized by scandals and an unpopular president. He excited Republican conservatives and independents by choosing Sarah Palin as his vice presidential nominee. The little-known governor of Alaska and an evangelical conservative, Palin portrayed herself as a plainspoken truth-teller and "hockey mom." But many voters wondered whether only two years as governor provided the experience to stand a heartbeat away from a presidency occupied by the 72-year-old McCain.

The summer polls gave Obama a narrow lead. In the end, though, his strong margin of victory owed as much to an event neither he nor McCain anticipated: a sudden financial crisis that threatened to plunge the nation into another great depression.

their displeasure in the 2006 congressional elections. Democrats also tarred Republicans with a culture of corruption, after scandals exposed a number of lobbyists and members of Congress who had traded cash, campaign contributions, and gifts for legislative favors. For the first time since 1994, Democrats took control of both the House and the Senate.

THE SURGE   Despite the political setback, President Bush chose to double down on his approach to Iraq. In 2007 he sent more troops, rather than withdraw, and placed General David Petraeus in charge of implementing a new "surge" strategy. The new tactics succeeded in reducing violence, but it remained unclear whether the new stability in Iraq could be maintained once American forces began to withdraw. Furthermore, Taliban forces in Afghanistan had regrouped and regained territory.

The Election of 2008

The 2008 election was the first since 1952 in which no incumbent president or vice president campaigned for the office. And as President Bush's popularity plummeted, Democrats sensed victory. Former first lady and senator from New York, Hillary Clinton, seemed the odds-on favorite for their nomination. But Clinton underestimated the

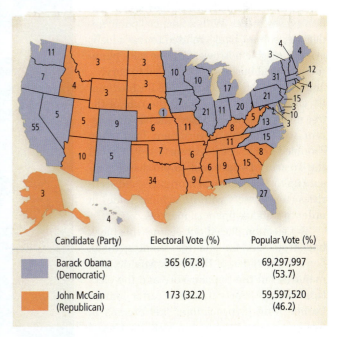

Candidate (Party)	Electoral Vote (%)	Popular Vote (%)
Barack Obama (Democratic)	365 (67.8)	69,297,997 (53.7)
John McCain (Republican)	173 (32.2)	59,597,520 (46.2)

ELECTION OF 2008

Financial Collapse

There had been rumblings over the previous two years, but few financial experts or regulators paid heed. Mortgage companies such as Countrywide Financial had been selling mortgages to prospective homeowners who possessed virtually no assets and little capacity to make monthly payments—mortgages whose "teaser" low rates would rise sharply. The financial markets took these subprime mortgages—trillions of dollars worth—and chopped them up, repackaging them into "derivatives," along with credit card debt, car loans, and even leases on jet aircraft. They sold them to banks, investment firms, and **hedge funds** as secure investments that earned much more than traditional financial products. The banks reasoned that if a few subprime mortgages failed, the losses would be spread out over a large number of investments, minimizing everyone's risk. But these "derivatives" were so complicated that few bankers understood them or the risks they entailed.

By 2007 the housing market had begun to contract. As banks foreclosed on more and more mortgages, a tipping point materialized. On September 15, 2008, Lehman Brothers investment bank suddenly filed for bankruptcy. The following day the Federal Reserve authorized $85 billion in loans to keep insurance giant American International Group (AIG) afloat. Nine days later the Office of Thrift Supervision closed Washington Mutual Bank, the nation's largest savings and loan association. It then became the nation's largest bank failure.

TOXIC ASSETS   "Toxic assets" was the phrase coined to describe these speculative investments. With a financial panic under way, solvent banks refused to make loans even to reliable borrowers. Home sales plummeted, small businesses struggled to survive, and unemployment soared. The Bush administration, which championed the rule of the free market, rushed in to save the banking system with massive government loans. The Troubled Asset Relief Program (TARP) allowed the Treasury Department to purchase or insure up to $700 billion of mortgages and securities (toxic assets with no evident value) in order to stabilize financial markets.

The election played out against this bleak backdrop. Obama and his running mate, Senator Joe Biden of Delaware, won decisive majorities in the popular vote and the electoral college. Forty-five years after Martin Luther King Jr. proclaimed his dreams of freedom on the Washington Mall, the United States had elected the first African American president.

Obama: Hope versus Pragmatism

A young president, an attractive wife with her own credentials as a lawyer, and two energetic young daughters made for an uplifting inaugural ceremony, attended by an estimated 1.8 million people. But Obama faced a host of problems. Not only had millions of Americans lost jobs and their homes, but major corporate icons such as General Motors and Chrysler stood on the brink of bankruptcy. Abroad, no timetable existed to bring American troops home from Iraq. Worse, pressure mounted to redeploy troops to Afghanistan, where Taliban insurgents threatened neighboring Pakistan.

On the one hand, the new president was widely hailed overseas as a leader who rejected the unilateral foreign policy of the Bush years. Obama traveled widely in his first year: to Africa, South America, Asia, and Europe. He paid the American overdue contribution to the United Nations and showed a willingness to listen to allies and open dialogue with enemies. Even so, after weeks of strategic discus-

| *The Obama family on election night, 2008*

sions the president announced in November 2009 a surge strategy in Afghanistan to combat deteriorating conditions. Another 30,000 troops were deployed "at the fastest pace possible," bringing troop strength there up to 100,000. Obama promised a withdrawal of forces would begin in 2011.

STIMULUS BILL In his effort to shore up the faltering economy, the president faced numerous obstacles. He needed to restore consumer confidence and spending, while also promoting an economy that reduced the greenhouse gases that contributed to global warming. The banks teetered toward insolvency, the stock market continued to retreat, and major American industries faced bankruptcy, including auto manufacturing and housing. In February 2009 the president announced an economic stimulus package that carried a $787 billion price tag. The bill included tax cuts and expanded unemployment benefits and social welfare provisions, as well as spending on education, police, health care, and infrastructure. The measure received no Republican votes in the House and only three in the Senate. In October 2010, Senate minority leader Mitch McConnell openly admitted the Republicans' partisan project. "The single most important thing we want to achieve is for President Obama to be a one-term president," he announced.

AMERICA'S HEALTH CARE SYSTEM Such partisanship complicated Obama's attempt to reform the nation's health care system. Americans paid more per capita for medical care than any other nation, but its citizens died younger on average than those in 17 other developed nations, including France, Great Britain, Germany, Japan, and Italy. Over 40 million Americans had no health insurance, and rising unemployment threatened the coverage of millions more. Mindful that the Clinton health care reforms of the 1990s were defeated when the president submitted a plan worked out by the administration in advance, Obama left the House and Senate to formulate their own bills. But Republicans threatened a filibuster in the Senate, where every single vote of the 60 Democrats and independents was required to pass a bill. Only after intense lobbying by the administration did Congress pass health care reform, the Patient Protection and Affordable Care Act, the signal accomplishment of Obama's first year in office. Most of its promised benefits did not go into effect until 2014, after the next presidential election, at which time all Americans would be required to purchase health insurance. The bill immediately allowed parents to extend insurance coverage to their children until the age of 26. Republicans condemned the reform as socialized medicine and dubbed it "Obamacare." They pledged to repeal it or defeat it in the courts.

IRAN SANCTIONS In foreign policy, Obama fulfilled his pledge to withdraw American troops from Iraq and turn power over to an elected government. That shifted the focus to Afghanistan, where resurgent Taliban forces and a corrupt government offset the surge of additional American troops. Iran and North Korea presented intractable problems of another kind: both were determined to acquire nuclear weapons, and both resisted the pressure of economic sanctions to change course. Iran posed a particular threat to Israel, long a key American ally. Neoconservative Republicans pressed the president to take military action or support an Israeli attack in order to prevent Iran from gaining a nuclear force. Obama, in cooperation with the international community, instead pushed economic sanctions and diplomacy. Growing unrest in Iran suggested that by 2012 the sanctions were working, though Iran continued to resist inspection of its nuclear facilities.

Restraint paid dividends in the Middle East when dissenters across the region began demonstrations that came to be known as "Arab Spring." They toppled the autocratic government in Tunisia and then the long-entrenched military dictatorship of Hosni Mubarak in Egypt. Since Mubarak had been a strong American ally, many of Obama's critics pressed him to defend the regime. Obama let the rising tide of democratic reform take its course even when that brought an Islamic party to power. In Libya he lent U.S. support to a NATO coalition that helped rebels overthrow Muammar al-Qadhafi, a longtime dictator and supporter of anti-American terrorist groups.

The president also pushed his intelligence team to redouble efforts to locate al Qaeda leader Osama bin Laden. In the spring of 2011 they believed they had finally tracked him to a house in Pakistan, though he had never been visually sighted. Obama now faced the most difficult decisions of his presidency: Should the United States launch a raid without warning its ally Pakistan, whose leaders might well either refuse permission or leak word of the operation to bin Laden? Should the raid use unmanned drones or send in a special operations team? Vice President Joe Biden warned that if the effort failed in any of the many ways it could, Obama would lose his chance for a second term. The president chose the special teams option. Without alerting Pakistan, Navy SEALS soon after broke into bin Laden's secret compound and in the assault killed the al Qaeda leader, escaping with his body as well as a cache of valuable intelligence.

Despite his foreign policy successes, had Obama promised too much and delivered too little? That issue framed the election of 2012. Republican candidates called the president a socialist bent on turning medical care over to the government and incapable of restarting the faltering economy. On the other hand, Americans on the left complained that the president had not been forceful on either health care or financial reform. That frustration inspired the Occupy movement, an international protest aimed to reduce economic and social inequality. Occupy members charged that large corporations and global financial institutions threatened to destroy the middle class and democratic government. In the United States, Occupiers at first targeted Wall Street, but soon set up protest camps in cities around the country. The lack of both effective leadership and a coherent platform soon undermined the movement.

As the 2012 election approached, a sluggish economy failed to generate substantial new jobs and unemployment

SIGNIFICANT EVENTS

1986
Immigration and Control Act

1992
Rodney King verdict; Los Angeles riots; Bill Clinton elected

1994
Health care reform fails; Republicans win control of Congress

1996
Welfare reform adopted

1998
Senate acquits Clinton of impeachment charges

2000
Supreme Court ends Florida recount; George W. Bush elected

2001
Terrorists destroy the World Trade Center; United States attacks Afghanistan's Taliban regime

2003
Department of Homeland Security created; United States and the "Coalition of the Willing" invade Iraq

2005
Hurricane Katrina devastates the Gulf Coast

2006
Democrats win control of Congress

2008
Financial crisis; Barack Obama elected

2009
Surge begins in Afghanistan

2010
Health care legislation passes

2011
Obama draws U.S. troops out of Iraq

2012
Obama defeats Romney

Hallmarks of Globalization

1990–2000

Changing flows of global immigration to United States, with broader inflows from Mexico and Central America, South Asia, Africa

New **immigrants influence American culture** in religion, music, food, and sports

Sharply **increased international currency transfers**

NAFTA and outsourcing of jobs to Mexico, South America, and Asia

World regional crises affecting U.S.:

- Middle East: Palestinians and Israelis, growing terrorism

  - Africa: Rwanada and Somalia

- Europe: Yugoslavia splinters into Bosnia, Croatia, and Kosovo

World Wide Web and the growth of the Internet and e-business

Kyoto Protocol on global warming

2000–2012

Renewed **debate over immigration** and illegal aliens

9/11 terrorist attacks and the global war on terror:

- Al Qaeda becomes global in orientation

- Invasion of Afghanistan, Taliban ousted

  - Invasion of Iraq, no weapons of mass destruction found; new mission: installing stable democracy

  - Taliban resurgent in Afghanistan and Pakistan, Obama increases U.S. commitment

Bush rejects **Kyoto Protocol;** Obama seeks new accord at **Copenhagen** (2009), but only modest progress made

Broader bandwidth penetration interlinking computers, cell phones, tablets, e-books

Arab Spring topples dictators in Egypt, Libya, and Yemen, while civil strife mounts in Syria

Iran and North Korea continue their efforts to develop nuclear weapons

Appendix

The Declaration of Independence

In Congress, July 4, 1776,

THE UNANIMOUS DECLARATION OF THE THIRTEEN UNITED STATES OF AMERICA

When, in the course of human events, it becomes necessary for one people to dissolve the political bands which have connected them with another, and to assume, among the powers of the earth, the separate and equal station to which the laws of nature and of nature's God entitle them, a decent respect to the opinions of mankind requires that they should declare the causes which impel them to the separation.

We hold these truths to be self-evident, that all men are created equal; that they are endowed by their Creator with certain unalienable rights; that among these, are life, liberty, and the pursuit of happiness. That, to secure these rights, governments are instituted among men, deriving their just powers from the consent of the governed; that, whenever any form of government becomes destructive of these ends, it is the right of the people to alter or to abolish it, and to institute a new government, laying its foundation on such principles, and organizing its powers in such form, as to them shall seem most likely to effect their safety and happiness. Prudence, indeed, will dictate that governments long established, should not be changed for light and transient causes; and, accordingly, all experience hath shown, that mankind are more disposed to suffer, while evils are sufferable, than to right themselves by abolishing the forms to which they are accustomed. But, when a long train of abuses and usurpations, pursuing invariably the same object, evinces a design to reduce them under absolute despotism, it is their right, it is their duty, to throw off such government and to provide new guards for their future security. Such has been the patient sufferance of these colonies, and such is now the necessity which constrains them to alter their former systems of government. The history of the present King of Great Britain is a history of repeated injuries and usurpations, all having, in direct object, the establishment of an absolute tyranny over these States. To prove this, let facts be submitted to a candid world:

He has refused his assent to laws the most wholesome and necessary for the public good.

He has forbidden his governors to pass laws of immediate and pressing importance, unless suspended in their operation till his assent should be obtained; and, when so suspended, he has utterly neglected to attend to them.

He has refused to pass other laws for the accommodation of large districts of people, unless those people would relinquish the right of representation in the legislature; a right inestimable to them, and formidable to tyrants only.

He has called together legislative bodies at places unusual, uncomfortable, and distant from the depository of their public records, for the sole purpose of fatiguing them into compliance with his measures.

He has dissolved representative houses repeatedly for opposing, with manly firmness, his invasions on the rights of the people.

He has refused, for a long time after such dissolutions, to cause others to be elected; whereby the legislative powers, incapable of annihilation, have returned to the people at large for their exercise; the state remaining, in the meantime, exposed to all the danger of invasion from without, and convulsions within.

He has endeavored to prevent the population of these States; for that purpose, obstructing the laws for naturalization of foreigners, refusing to pass others to encourage their migration hither, and raising the conditions of new appropriations of lands.

He has obstructed the administration of justice, by refusing his assent to laws for establishing judiciary powers.

He has made judges dependent on his will alone, for the tenure of their offices, and the amount and payment of their salaries.

He has erected a multitude of new offices, and sent hither swarms of officers to harass our people, and eat out their substance.

He has kept among us, in time of peace, standing armies, without the consent of our legislatures.

He has affected to render the military independent of, and superior to, the civil power.

He has combined, with others, to subject us to a jurisdiction foreign to our Constitution, and unacknowledged by our laws; giving his assent to their acts of pretended legislation:

For quartering large bodies of armed troops among us:

For protecting them by a mock trial, from punishment, for any murders which they should commit on the inhabitants of these States:

For cutting off our trade with all parts of the world:

For imposing taxes on us without our consent:

For depriving us, in many cases, of the benefit of trial by jury:

For transporting us beyond seas to be tried for pretended offences:

For abolishing the free system of English laws in a neighboring province, establishing therein an arbitrary government, and enlarging its boundaries, so as to render it at once an example and fit instrument for introducing the same absolute rule into these colonies:

For taking away our charters, abolishing our most valuable laws, and altering, fundamentally, the powers of our governments:

For suspending our own legislatures, and declaring themselves invested with power to legislate for us in all cases whatsoever.

He has abdicated government here, by declaring us out of his protection, and waging war against us.

He has plundered our seas, ravaged our coasts, burnt our towns, and destroyed the lives of our people.

He is, at this time, transporting large armies of foreign mercenaries to complete the works of death, desolation, and tyranny, already begun, with circumstances of cruelty and perfidy scarcely paralleled in the most barbarous ages, and totally unworthy the head of a civilized nation.

He has constrained our fellow citizens, taken captive on the high seas, to bear arms against their country, to become the executioners of their friends, and brethren, or to fall themselves by their hands.

He has excited domestic insurrections amongst us, and has endeavored to bring on the inhabitants of our frontiers, the merciless Indian savages, whose known rule of warfare is an undistinguished destruction of all ages, sexes, and conditions.

In every stage of these oppressions, we have petitioned for redress, in the most humble terms; our repeated petitions have been answered only by repeated injury. A prince, whose character is thus marked by every act which may define a tyrant, is unfit to be the ruler of a free people.

Nor have we been wanting in attention to our British brethren. We have warned them, from time to time, of attempts made by their legislature to extend an unwarrantable jurisdiction over us. We have reminded them of the circumstances of our emigration and settlement here. We have appealed to their native justice and magnanimity, and we have conjured them, by the ties of our common kindred, to disavow these usurpations, which would inevitably interrupt our connections and correspondence. They, too, have been deaf to the voice of justice and consanguinity. We must, therefore, acquiesce in the necessity which denounces our separation, and hold them as we hold the rest of mankind, enemies in war, in peace, friends.

We, therefore, the representatives of the United States of America, in general Congress assembled, appealing to the Supreme Judge of the world for the rectitude of our intentions, do, in the name, and by the authority of the good people of these colonies, solemnly publish and declare, that these united colonies are, and of right ought to be, free and independent states: that they are absolved from all allegiance to the British Crown, and that all political connection between them and the state of Great Britain is, and ought to be, totally dissolved; and that, as free and independent states, they have full power to levy war, conclude peace, contract alliances, establish commerce, and to do all other acts and things which independent states may of right do. And, for the support of this declaration, with a firm reliance on the protection of Divine Providence, we mutually pledge to each other our lives, our fortunes, and our sacred honor.

The foregoing Declaration was, by order of Congress, engrossed, and signed by the following members:

JOHN HANCOCK

NEW HAMPSHIRE
Josiah Bartlett
William Whipple
Matthew Thornton

MASSACHUSETTS BAY
Samuel Adams
John Adams
Robert Treat Paine
Elbridge Gerry

RHODE ISLAND
Stephen Hopkins
William Ellery

CONNECTICUT
Roger Sherman
Samuel Huntington
William Williams
Oliver Wolcott

NEW YORK
William Floyd
Philip Livingston
Francis Lewis
Lewis Morris

NEW JERSEY
Richard Stockton
John Witherspoon
Francis Hopkinson
John Hart
Abraham Clark

PENNSYLVANIA
Robert Morris
Benjamin Rush
Benjamin Franklin
John Morton
George Clymer
James Smith
George Taylor
James Wilson
George Ross

DELAWARE
Caesar Rodney
George Read
Thomas M'Kean

MARYLAND
Samuel Chase
William Paca
Thomas Stone
Charles Carroll, of Carrollton

VIRGINIA
George Wythe
Richard Henry Lee
Thomas Jefferson
Benjamin Harrison
Thomas Nelson, Jr.
Francis Lightfoot Lee
Carter Braxton

NORTH CAROLINA
William Hooper
Joseph Hewes
John Penn

SOUTH CAROLINA
Edward Rutledge
Thomas Heyward, Jr.
Thomas Lynch, Jr.
Arthur Middleton

GEORGIA
Button Gwinnett
Lyman Hall
George Walton

Resolved, That copies of the Declaration be sent to the several assemblies, conventions, and committees, or councils of safety, and to the several commanding officers of the continental troops; that it be proclaimed in each of the United States, at the head of the army.

The Constitution of the United States of America[1]

We the People of the United States, in Order to form a more perfect Union, establish Justice, insure domestic Tranquility, provide for the common defence, promote the general Welfare, and secure the Blessings of Liberty to ourselves and our Posterity, do ordain and establish this CONSTITUTION for the United States of America.

ARTICLE I

Section 1. All legislative Powers herein granted shall be vested in a Congress of the United States, which shall consist of a Senate and House of Representatives.

Section 2. The House of Representatives shall be composed of Members chosen every second Year by the People of the several States, and the Electors in each State shall have the Qualifications requisite for Electors of the most numerous Branch of the State Legislature.

No Person shall be a Representative who shall not have attained to the Age of twenty-five Years, and been seven Years a Citizen of the United States, and who shall not, when elected, be an Inhabitant of that State in which he shall be chosen.

[Representatives and direct Taxes[2] shall be apportioned among the several States which may be included within this Union, according to their respective Numbers, which shall be determined by adding to the whole Number of free Persons, including those bound to Service for a Term of Years, and excluding Indians not taxed, three fifths of all other Persons.][3] The actual Enumeration shall be made within three Years after the first Meeting of the Congress of the United States, and within every subsequent Term of ten Years, in such Manner as they shall by Law direct. The Number of Representatives shall not exceed one for every thirty Thousand, but each State shall have at Least one Representative; and until such enumeration shall be made, the State of New Hampshire shall be entitled to chuse three, Massachusetts eight, Rhode-Island and Providence Plantations one, Connecticut five, New York six, New Jersey four, Pennsylvania eight, Delaware one, Maryland six, Virginia ten, North Carolina five, South Carolina five, and Georgia three.

When vacancies happen in the Representation from any State, the Executive Authority thereof shall issue Writs of Election to fill such Vacancies.

The House of Representatives shall chuse their Speaker and other Officers; and shall have the sole Power of Impeachment.

Section 3. The Senate of the United States shall be composed of two Senators from each State, chosen by the Legislature thereof, for six Years; and each Senator shall have one Vote.

Immediately after they shall be assembled in Consequence of the first Election, they shall be divided as equally as may be into three Classes. The Seats of the Senators of the first Class shall be vacated at the Expiration of the second Year, of the second Class at the Expiration of the fourth Year, and of the third Class at the Expiration of the sixth Year, so that one-third may be chosen every second Year; and if Vacancies happen by Resignation, or otherwise, during the Recess of the Legislature of any State, the Executive thereof may make temporary Appointments until the next Meeting of the Legislature, which shall then fill such Vacancies.

No Person shall be a Senator who shall not have attained to the Age of thirty Years, and been nine Years a Citizen of the United States, and who shall not, when elected, be an Inhabitant of that State for which he shall be chosen.

The Vice President of the United States shall be President of the Senate, but shall have no vote, unless they be equally divided.

The Senate shall chuse their other Officers, and also a President pro tempore, in the absence of the Vice President, or when he shall exercise the Office of President of the United States.

The Senate shall have the sole Power to try all Impeachments. When sitting for that purpose they shall be on Oath or Affirmation. When the President of the United States is tried, the Chief Justice shall preside: And no person shall be convicted without the Concurrence of two thirds of the Members present.

Judgment in Cases of Impeachment shall not extend further than to removal from Office, and disqualification to hold and enjoy any Office of honor, Trust, or Profit under the United States: but the Party convicted shall nevertheless be liable and subject to Indictment, Trial, Judgment, and Punishment, according to Law.

Section 4. The Times, Places and Manner of holding Elections for Senators and Representatives, shall be prescribed in each State by the Legislature thereof; but the Congress may at any time by Law make or alter such Regulations, except as to the Places of Chusing Senators.

The Congress shall assemble at least once in every Year, and such Meeting shall be on the first Monday in December, unless they shall by Law appoint a different Day.

Section 5. Each House shall be the Judge of the Elections, Returns and Qualifications of its own Members, and a Majority of each shall constitute a Quorum to do Business; but a smaller number may adjourn from day to day, and may be authorized to compel the Attendance of absent Members, in such Manner, and under such Penalties, as each House may provide.

Each House may determine the Rules of its Proceedings, punish its Members for disorderly Behaviour, and, with the Concurrence of two thirds, expel a Member.

[1]This version follows the original Constitution in capitalization and spelling. It is adapted from the text published by the United States Department of the Interior, Office of Education.

[2]Altered by the Sixteenth Amendment.

[3]Negated by the Fourteenth Amendment.

Each House shall keep a Journal of its Proceedings, and from time to time publish the same, excepting such Parts as may in their Judgment require Secrecy; and the Yeas and Nays of the Members of either House on any question shall, at the Desire of one fifth of those Present, be entered on the Journal.

Neither House, during the Session of Congress, shall, without the Consent of the other, adjourn for more than three days, nor to any other Place than that in which the two Houses shall be sitting.

Section 6. The Senators and Representatives shall receive a Compensation for their Services, to be ascertained by Law, and paid out of the Treasury of the United States. They shall in all Cases, except Treason, Felony, and Breach of the Peace, be privileged from Arrest during their Attendance at the Session of their respective Houses, and in going to and returning from the same; and for any Speech or Debate in either House, they shall not be questioned in any other Place.

No Senator or Representative shall, during the Time for which he was elected, be appointed to any civil Office under the Authority of the United States, which shall have been created, or the Emoluments whereof shall have been increased, during such time; and no Person holding any Office under the United States shall be a Member of either House during his continuance in Office.

Section 7. All Bills for raising Revenue shall originate in the House of Representatives; but the Senate may propose or concur with Amendments as on other bills.

Every Bill which shall have passed the House of Representatives and the Senate, shall, before it become a Law, be presented to the President of the United States; If he approve he shall sign it, but if not he shall return it, with his Objections, to that House in which it shall have originated, who shall enter the Objections at large on their Journal, and proceed to reconsider it. If after such Reconsideration two thirds of that House shall agree to pass the bill, it shall be sent, together with the objections, to the other House, by which it shall likewise be reconsidered, and if approved by two thirds of that House, it shall become a Law. But in all such Cases the Votes of both Houses shall be determined by Yeas and Nays, and the Names of the Persons voting for and against the Bill shall be entered on the Journal of each House respectively. If any Bill shall not be returned by the President within ten Days (Sundays excepted) after it shall have been presented to him, the Same shall be a Law, in like Manner as if he had signed it, unless the Congress by their Adjournment prevent its Return, in which Case it shall not be a Law.

Every Order, Resolution, or Vote to which the Concurrence of the Senate and House of Representatives may be necessary (except on a question of Adjournment) shall be presented to the President of the United States; and before the Same shall take Effect, shall be approved by him, or being disapproved by him, shall be repassed by two thirds of the Senate and House of Representatives, according to the Rules and Limitations prescribed in the Case of a Bill.

Section 8. The Congress shall have Power To lay and collect Taxes, Duties, Imposts and Excises, to pay the Debts and provide for the common Defence and general Welfare of the United States; but all Duties, Imposts and Excises shall be uniform throughout the United States;

To borrow money on the credit of the United States;

To regulate Commerce with foreign Nations, and among the several States, and with the Indian Tribes;

To establish an uniform rule of Naturalization, and uniform Laws on the subject of Bankruptcies throughout the United States;

To coin Money, regulate the Value thereof, and of foreign Coin, and fix the Standard of Weights and Measures;

To provide for the Punishment of counterfeiting the Securities and current Coin of the United States;

To establish Post Offices and post Roads;

To promote the Progress of Science and useful Arts, by securing for limited Times to Authors and Inventors the exclusive Right to their respective Writings and Discoveries;

To constitute Tribunals inferior to the Supreme Court;

To define and punish Piracies and Felonies committed on the high Seas, and Offenses against the Law of Nations;

To declare War, grant Letters of Marque and Reprisal, and make Rules concerning Captures on Land and Water;

To raise and support Armies, but no Appropriation of Money to that Use shall be for a longer Term than two Years;

To provide and maintain a Navy;

To make Rules for the Government and Regulation of the land and naval forces;

To provide for calling forth the Militia to execute the Laws of the Union, suppress Insurrections and repel Invasions;

To provide for organizing, arming, and disciplining the Militia, and for government such Part of them as may be employed in the Service of the United States, reserving to the States respectively, the Appointment of the Officers, and the Authority of training the Militia according to the discipline prescribed by Congress;

To exercise exclusive Legislation in all Cases whatsoever, over such District (not exceeding ten Miles square) as may, by Cession of particular States, and the acceptance of Congress, become the Seat of the Government of the United States, and to exercise like Authority over all Places purchased by the Consent of the Legislature of the State in which the Same shall be, for the Erection of Forts, Magazines, Arsenals, Dock-yards, and other needful Buildings;—And

To make all Laws which shall be necessary and proper for carrying into Execution the foregoing Powers, and all other Powers vested by this Constitution in the Government of the United States, or in any Department or Officer thereof.

Section 9. The Migration or Importation of such Persons as any of the States now existing shall think proper to admit, shall not be prohibited by the Congress prior to the Year one thousand eight hundred and eight, but a tax or duty may be imposed on such Importation, not exceeding ten dollars for each Person.

The privilege of the Writ of Habeas Corpus shall not be suspended, unless when in Cases of Rebellion or Invasion the public Safety may require it.

No bill of Attainder or ex post facto Law shall be passed.

No capitation, or other direct, Tax shall be laid unless in Proportion to the Census or Enumeration herein before directed to be taken.

No Tax or Duty shall be laid on Articles exported from any State.

No Preference shall be given by any Regulation of Commerce or Revenue to the Ports of one State over those of another: nor shall Vessels bound to, or from, one State, be obliged to enter, clear, or pay Duties in another.

No Money shall be drawn from the Treasury, but in Consequence of Appropriations made by Law; and a regular Statement and Account of the Receipts and Expenditures of all public Money shall be published from time to time.

No Title of Nobility shall be granted by the United States: And no Person holding any Office of Profit or Trust under them, shall, without the Consent of the Congress, accept of any present, Emolument, Office, or Title, of any kind whatever, from any King, Prince, or foreign State.

Section 10. No State shall enter into any Treaty, Alliance, or Confederation; grant Letters of Marque and Reprisal; coin Money; emit Bills of Credit; make any Thing but gold and silver Coin a Tender in Payment of Debts; pass any Bill of Attainder, ex post facto Law, or Law impairing the Obligation of Contracts, or grant any Title of Nobility.

No State shall, without the Consent of the Congress, lay any Imposts or Duties on Imports or Exports, except what may be absolutely necessary for executing its inspection Laws; and the net Produce of all Duties and Imposts, laid by any State on Imports or Exports, shall be for the use of the Treasury of the United States; and all such Laws shall be subject to the Revision and Control of the Congress.

No state shall, without the Consent of Congress, lay any duty of Tonnage, keep Troops, or Ships of War in time of Peace, enter into any Agreement or Compact with another State, or with a foreign Power, or engage in War, unless actually invaded, or in such imminent Danger as will not admit of delay.

ARTICLE II

Section 1. The executive Power shall be vested in a President of the United States of America. He shall hold his Office during the Term of four years, and, together with the Vice President, chosen for the same Term, be elected, as follows:

Each State shall appoint, in such Manner as the Legislature thereof may direct, a Number of Electors, equal to the whole Number of Senators and Representatives to which the State may be entitled in the Congress: but no Senator or Representative, or Person holding an Office of Trust or Profit under the United States, shall be appointed an Elector.

[The Electors shall meet in their respective States, and vote by Ballot for two persons, of whom one at least shall not be an Inhabitant of the same State with themselves. And they shall make a List of all the Persons voted for, and of the Number of Votes for each; which List they shall sign and certify, and transmit sealed to the Seat of the Government of the United States, directed to the President of the Senate. The President of the Senate shall, in the Presence of the Senate and House of Representatives, open all the Certificates, and the Votes shall then be counted. The Person having the greatest Number of Votes shall be the President, if such Number be a Majority of the whole Number of Electors appointed; and if there be more than one who have such Majority, and have an equal Number of Votes, then the House of Representatives shall immediately chuse by Ballot one of them for President; and if no Person have a Majority, then from the five highest on the List the said House shall in like Manner chuse the President. But in chusing the President, the Votes shall be taken by States, the Representation from each State having one Vote; a quorum for this Purpose shall consist of a Member or Members from two-thirds of the States, and a Majority of all the States shall be necessary to a Choice. In every Case, after the Choice of the President, the Person having the greatest Number of Votes of the Electors shall be the Vice President. But if there should remain

two or more who have equal votes, the Senate shall chuse from them by Ballot the Vice President.][4]

The Congress may determine the Time of chusing the Electors, and the Day on which they shall give their Votes; which Day shall be the same throughout the United States.

No person except a natural-born Citizen, or a Citizen of the United States, at the time of the Adoption of this Constitution, shall be eligible to the Office of President; neither shall any Person be eligible to that Office who shall not have attained to the Age of thirty-five years, and been fourteen Years a Resident within the United States.

In Case of the Removal of the President from Office, or of his Death, Resignation, or Inability to discharge the Powers and Duties of the said Office, the same shall devolve on the Vice President, and the Congress may by Law provide for the Case of Removal, Death, Resignation, or Inability, both of the President and Vice President, declaring what Officer shall then act as President, and such Officer shall act accordingly, until the disability be removed, or a President shall be elected.

The President shall, at stated Times, receive for his Services a Compensation, which shall neither be increased nor diminished during the Period for which he shall have been elected, and he shall not receive within that Period any other Emolument from the United States, or any of them.

Before he enter on the execution of his Office, he shall take the following Oath or Affirmation:—"I do solemnly swear (or affirm) that I will faithfully execute the Office of President of the United States, and will, to the best of my Ability, preserve, protect, and defend the Constitution of the United States."

Section 2. The President shall be Commander in Chief of the Army and Navy of the United States, and of the Militia of the several States, when called into the actual Service of the United States; he may require the Opinion, in writing, of the principal Officer in each of the executive Departments, upon any subject relating to the Duties of their respective Offices, and he shall have Power to Grant Reprieves and Pardons for Offenses against the United States, except in Cases of Impeachment.

He shall have Power, by and with the Advice and Consent of the Senate, to make Treaties, provided two-thirds of the Senators present concur; and he shall nominate, and by and with the Advice and Consent of the Senate, shall appoint Ambassadors, other public Ministers and Consuls, Judges of the supreme Court, and all other Officers of the United States, whose Appointments are not herein otherwise provided for, and which shall be established by Law: but the Congress may by Law vest the Appointment of such inferior Officers, as they think proper, in the President alone, in the Courts of Law, or in the Heads of Departments.

The President shall have Power to fill up all Vacancies that may happen during the Recess of the Senate, by granting Commissions which shall expire at the End of their next Session.

Section 3. He shall from time to time give to the Congress Information of the State of the Union, and recommend to their Consideration such Measures as he shall judge necessary and expedient; he may, on extraordinary occasions, convene both Houses, or either of them, and in Case of Disagreement between them, with respect to the Time of Adjournment, he may adjourn them to such Time as he shall think proper; he shall receive Ambassadors and other public Ministers; he shall take care that

[4]Revised by the Twelfth Amendment.

the Laws be faithfully executed, and shall Commission all the Officers of the United States.

Section 4. The President, Vice President and all civil Officers of the United States, shall be removed from Office on Impeachment for, and Conviction of, Treason, Bribery, or other high Crimes and Misdemeanors.

ARTICLE III

Section 1. The judicial Power of the United States, shall be vested in one supreme Court, and in such inferior Courts as the Congress may from time to time ordain and establish. The Judges, both of the supreme and inferior Courts, shall hold their Offices during good Behaviour, and shall, at stated Times, receive for their Services, a Compensation, which shall not be diminished during their Continuance in Office.

Section 2. The judicial Power shall extend to all Cases, in Law and Equity, arising under this Constitution, the Laws of the United States, and Treaties made, or which shall be made, under their Authority;—to all Cases affecting ambassadors, other public ministers and consuls;—to all cases of admiralty and maritime Jurisdiction;—to Controversies to which the United States shall be a Party;—to Controversies between two or more States;—between a State and Citizens of another State;[5]—between Citizens of different States—between Citizens of the same State claiming Lands under Grants of different States, and between a State, or the Citizens thereof, and foreign States, Citizens, or Subjects.

In all Cases affecting Ambassadors, other public Ministers and Consuls, and those in which a State shall be Party, the supreme Court shall have original Jurisdiction. In all the other Cases before mentioned, the supreme Court shall have appellate Jurisdiction, both as to Law and Fact, with such Exceptions, and under such Regulations as the Congress shall make.

The trial of all Crimes, except in Cases of Impeachment, shall be by Jury; and such Trial shall be held in the State where the said Crimes shall have been committed; but when not committed within any State, the Trial shall be at such Place or Places as the Congress may by Law have directed.

Section 3. Treason against the United States, shall consist only in levying War against them, or in adhering to their Enemies, giving them Aid and Comfort. No Person shall be convicted of Treason unless on the Testimony of two Witnesses to the same overt Act, or on Confession in open Court.

The Congress shall have power to declare the Punishment of Treason, but no Attainder of Treason shall work Corruption of Blood, or Forfeiture except during the Life of the Person attainted.

ARTICLE IV

Section 1. Full Faith and Credit shall be given in each State to the public Acts, Records, and judicial Proceedings of every other State. And the Congress may by general Laws prescribe the Manner in which such Acts, Records and Proceedings shall be proved, and the Effect thereof.

Section 2. The Citizens of each State shall be entitled to all Privileges and Immunities of Citizens in the several States.

[5]Qualified by the Eleventh Amendment.

A Person charged in any State with Treason, Felony, or other Crime, who shall flee from Justice, and be found in another State, shall on demand of the executive Authority of the State from which he fled, be delivered up, to be removed to the State having Jurisdiction of the crime.

No Person held to Service or Labour in one State, under the Laws thereof, escaping into another, shall, in Consequence of any Law or Regulation therein, be discharged from such Service or Labour, but shall be delivered up on Claim of the Party to whom such Service or Labour may be due.

Section 3. New States may be admitted by the Congress into this Union; but no new State shall be formed or erected within the Jurisdiction of any other State; nor any State be formed by the Junction of two or more States, or parts of States, without the Consent of the Legislatures of the States concerned as well as of the Congress.

The Congress shall have Power to dispose of and make all needful Rules and Regulations respecting the Territory or other Property belonging to the United States; and nothing in this Constitution shall be so construed as to Prejudice any Claims of the United States, or of any particular State.

Section 4. The United States shall guarantee to every State in this Union a Republican Form of Government, and shall protect each of them against Invasion; and on Application of the Legislature, or of the Executive (when the Legislature cannot be convened) against domestic Violence.

ARTICLE V

The Congress, whenever two-thirds of both Houses shall deem it necessary, shall propose Amendments to this Constitution, or, on the Application of the Legislatures of two-thirds of the several States, shall call a Convention for proposing Amendments, which, in either Case, shall be valid to all Intents and Purposes, as part of this Constitution, when ratified by the Legislatures of three-fourths of the several States, or by Conventions in three-fourths thereof, as the one or the other Mode of Ratification may be proposed by the Congress; Provided that no Amendment which may be made prior to the Year One thousand eight hundred and eight shall in any Manner affect the first and fourth Clauses in the Ninth Section of the first Article; and that no State, without its Consent, shall be deprived of its equal Suffrage in the Senate.

ARTICLE VI

All Debts contracted and Engagements entered into, before the Adoption of this Constitution, shall be as valid against the United States under this Constitution, as under the Confederation.

This Constitution, and the Laws of the United States which shall be made in Pursuance thereof; and all Treaties made, or which shall be made, under the Authority of the United States, shall be the supreme Law of the Land; and the Judges in every State shall be bound thereby, any Thing in the Constitution or Laws of any State to the Contrary notwithstanding.

The Senators and Representatives before mentioned, and the Members of the several State Legislatures, and all executive and judicial Officers, both of the United States and of the several States, shall be bound by Oath or Affirmation to support this Constitution; but no religious Tests shall ever be required as a qualification to any Office or public Trust under the United States.

ARTICLE VII

The Ratification of the Conventions of nine States shall be sufficient for the Establishment of this Constitution between the States so ratifying the same.

Done in Convention by the Unanimous Consent of the States present the Seventeenth Day of September in the Year of our Lord one thousand seven hundred and Eighty seven, and of the Independence of the United States of America the Twelfth. In Witness whereof We have hereunto subscribed our Names.[6]

GEORGE WASHINGTON
PRESIDENT AND DEPUTY FROM VIRGINIA

NEW HAMPSHIRE
John Langdon
Nicholas Gilman

MASSACHUSETTS
Nathaniel Gorham
Rufus King

CONNECTICUT
William Samuel Johnson
Roger Sherman

NEW YORK
Alexander Hamilton

NEW JERSEY
William Livingston
David Brearley
William Paterson
Jonathan Dayton

PENNSYLVANIA
Benjamin Franklin
Thomas Mifflin
Robert Morris
George Clymer
Thomas FitzSimons
Jared Ingersoll
James Wilson
Gouverneur Morris

DELAWARE
George Read
Gunning Bedford, Jr.
John Dickinson
Richard Bassett
Jacob Broom

MARYLAND
James McHenry
Daniel of St. Thomas Jenifer
Daniel Carroll

VIRGINIA
John Blair
James Madison, Jr.

NORTH CAROLINA
William Blount
Richard Dobbs Spaight
Hugh Williamson

SOUTH CAROLINA
John Rutledge
Charles Cotesworth Pinckney
Charles Pinckney
Pierce Butler

GEORGIA
William Few
Abraham Baldwin

Articles in Addition to, and Amendment of, the Constitution of the United States of America, Proposed by Congress, and Ratified by the Legislatures of the Several States, Pursuant to the Fifth Article of the Original Constitution[7]

[AMENDMENT I]

Congress shall make no law respecting an establishment of religion, or prohibiting the free exercise thereof; or abridging the freedom of speech, or of the press; or the right of the people peaceably to assemble, and to petition the Government for a redress of grievances.

[AMENDMENT II]

A well regulated Militia, being necessary to the security of a free State, the right of the people to keep and bear Arms shall not be infringed.

[AMENDMENT III]

No Soldier shall, in time of peace, be quartered in any house, without the consent of the Owner, nor in time of war, but in a manner to be prescribed by law.

[AMENDMENT IV]

The right of the people to be secure in their persons, houses, papers, and effects, against unreasonable searches and seizures, shall not be violated, and no Warrants shall issue, but upon probable cause, supported by Oath or affirmation, and particularly describing the place to be searched, and the persons or things to be seized.

[AMENDMENT V]

No person shall be held to answer for a capital or otherwise infamous crime, unless on a presentment or indictment of a Grand Jury, except in cases arising in the land or naval forces, or in the Militia, when in actual service in time of War or public danger; nor shall any person be subject for the same offence to be twice put in jeopardy of life or limb; nor shall be compelled in any criminal case to be a witness against himself, nor be deprived of life, liberty, or property, without due process of law; nor shall private property be taken for public use, without just compensation.

[AMENDMENT VI]

In all criminal prosecutions, the accused shall enjoy the right to a speedy and public trial, by an impartial jury of the State and district wherein the crime shall have been committed, which district shall have been previously ascertained by law, and to be informed of the nature and cause of the accusation; to be confronted with the witnesses against him; to have compulsory process for obtaining witnesses in his favour, and to have the Assistance of Counsel for his defence.

[AMENDMENT VII]

In suits at common law, where the value in controversy shall exceed twenty dollars, the right of trial by jury shall be preserved, and no fact tried by a jury, shall be otherwise reexamined in any Court of the United States, than according to the rules of the common law.

---

[6]These are the full names of the signers, which in some cases are not the signatures on the document.

[7]This heading appears only in the joint resolution submitting the first ten amendments, known as the Bill of Rights.

[AMENDMENT VIII]

Excessive bail shall not be required, nor excessive fines imposed, nor cruel and unusual punishments inflicted.

[AMENDMENT IX]

The enumeration of the Constitution, of certain rights, shall not be construed to deny or disparage others retained by the people.

[AMENDMENT X]

The powers not delegated to the United States by the Constitution, nor prohibited by it to the States, are reserved to the States respectively, or to the people.
[Amendments I–X, in force 1791.]

[AMENDMENT XI][8]

The Judicial power of the United States shall not be construed to extend to any suit in law or equity, commenced or prosecuted against one of the United States by Citizens of another State, or by Citizens or Subjects of any Foreign State.

[AMENDMENT XII][9]

The Electors shall meet in their respective States and vote by ballot for President and Vice-President, one of whom, at least, shall not be an inhabitant of the same State with themselves; they shall name in their ballots the person voted for as President, and in distinct ballots the person voted for as Vice-President, and they shall make distinct lists of all persons voted for as President, and of all persons voted for as Vice-President, and of the number of votes for each, which lists they shall sign and certify, and transmit sealed to the seat of the government of the United States, directed to the President of the Senate;—The President of the Senate shall, in the presence of the Senate and House of Representatives, open all the certificates and the votes shall then be counted;—The person having the greatest number of votes for President, shall be the President, if such number be a majority of the whole number of Electors appointed; and if no person have such majority, then from the persons having the highest numbers not exceeding three on the list of those voted for as President, the House of Representatives shall choose immediately, by ballot, the President. But in choosing the President, the votes shall be taken by states, the representation from each state having one vote; a quorum for this purpose shall consist of a member or members from two-thirds of the states, and a majority of all the states shall be necessary to a choice. And if the House of Representatives shall not choose a President whenever the right of choice shall devolve upon them, before the fourth day of March next following, then the Vice-President shall act as President, as in the case of the death or other constitutional disability of the President.—The person having the greatest number of votes as Vice-President, shall be the Vice-President, if such number be a majority of the whole number of Electors appointed, and if no person have a majority, then from the two highest numbers on the list, the Senate shall choose the Vice-President; a quorum for the purpose shall consist of two-thirds of the whole number of Senators, and a majority of the whole number shall be necessary to a choice. But no person constitutionally ineligible to the office of President shall be eligible to that of Vice-President of the United States.

[AMENDMENT XIII][10]

Section 1. Neither slavery nor involuntary servitude, except as a punishment for crime whereof the party shall have been duly convicted, shall exist within the United States, or any place subject to their jurisdiction.

Section 2. Congress shall have power to enforce this article by appropriate legislation.

[AMENDMENT XIV][11]

Section 1. All persons born or naturalized in the United States, and subject to the jurisdiction thereof, are citizens of the United States and of the State wherein they reside. No State shall abridge the privileges or immunities of citizens of the United States; nor shall any State deprive any person of life, liberty, or property, without due process of law; nor deny to any person within its jurisdiction the equal protection of the laws.

Section 2. Representatives shall be apportioned among the several States according to their respective numbers, counting the whole number of persons in each State, excluding Indians not taxed. But when the right to vote at any election for the choice of electors for President and Vice-President of the United States, Representatives in Congress, the Executive and Judicial officers of a State, or the members of the Legislature thereof, is denied to any of the male inhabitants of such State, being twenty-one years of age, and citizens of the United States, or in any way abridged, except for participation in rebellion, or other crime, the basis of representation therein shall be reduced in the proportion which the number of such male citizens shall bear to the whole number of male citizens twenty-one years of age in such State.

Section 3. No person shall be a Senator or Representative in Congress, or elector of President and Vice-President, or hold any office, civil or military, under the United States, or under any State, who, having previously taken an oath, as a member of Congress, or as an officer of the United States, or as a member of any State legislature, or as an executive or judicial officer of any State, to support the Constitution of the United States, shall have engaged in insurrection or rebellion against the same, or given aid or comfort to the enemies thereof. But Congress may by a vote of two-thirds of each House, remove such disability.

Section 4. The validity of the public debt of the United States, authorized by law, including debts incurred for payment of pensions and bounties for services in suppressing insurrection or rebellion, shall not be questioned. But neither the United States nor any State shall assume or pay any debts or obligation incurred in aid of insurrection or rebellion against the United States, or any claim for the loss or emancipation of any slave; but all such debts, obligations, and claims shall be held illegal and void.

Section 5. The Congress shall have the power to enforce, by appropriate legislation, the provisions of this article.

---

[8]Adopted in 1798.
[9]Adopted in 1804.

[10]Adopted in 1865.
[11]Adopted in 1868.

[AMENDMENT XV][12]

Section 1. The right of citizens of the United States to vote shall not be denied or abridged by the United States or by any State on account of race, color, or previous condition of servitude—

Section 2. The Congress shall have power to enforce this article by appropriate legislation.

[AMENDMENT XVI][13]

The Congress shall have power to lay and collect taxes on incomes, from whatever source derived, without apportionment among the several States, and without regard to any census or enumeration.

[AMENDMENT XVII][14]

The Senate of the United States shall be composed of two Senators from each State, elected by the people thereof, for six years; and each Senator shall have one vote. The electors in each State shall have the qualifications requisite for electors of the most numerous branch of the State legislatures.

When vacancies happen in the representation of any State in the Senate, the executive authority of such State shall issue writs of election to fill such vacancies: Provided, That the legislature of any State may empower the executive thereof to make temporary appointments until the people fill the vacancies by election as the legislature may direct.

This amendment shall not be so construed as to affect the election or term of any Senator chosen before it becomes valid as part of the Constitution.

[AMENDMENT XVIII][15]

Section 1. After one year from the ratification of this article the manufacture, sale, or transportation of intoxicating liquors within, the importation thereof into, or the exportation thereof from the United States and all territory subject to the jurisdiction thereof for beverage purposes is hereby prohibited.

Section 2. The Congress and the several States shall have concurrent power to enforce this article by appropriate legislation.

Section 3. This article shall be inoperative unless it shall have been ratified as an amendment to the Constitution by the legislatures of the several States, as provided in the Constitution, within seven years from the date of the submission hereof to the States by the Congress.

[AMENDMENT XIX][16]

The right of citizens of the United States to vote shall not be denied or abridged by the United States or by any State on account of sex.

Congress shall have power to enforce this article by appropriate legislation.

[AMENDMENT XX][17]

Section 1. The terms of the President and Vice-President shall end at noon on the 20th day of January, and the terms of Senators and Representatives at noon on the 3d day of January, of the years in which such terms would have ended if this article had not been ratified; and the terms of their successors shall then begin.

Section 2. The Congress shall assemble at least once in every year, and such meeting shall begin at noon on the 3d day of January, unless they shall by law appoint a different day.

Section 3. If, at the time fixed for the beginning of the term of the President, the President elect shall have died, the Vice-President elect shall become President. If a President shall not have been chosen before the time fixed for the beginning of his term or if the President elect shall have failed to qualify, then the Vice-President elect shall act as President until a President shall have qualified; and the Congress may by law provide for the case wherein neither a President elect nor a Vice-President elect shall have qualified, declaring who shall then act as President, or the manner in which one who is to act shall be selected, and such person shall act accordingly until a President or Vice-President shall have qualified.

Section 4. The Congress may by law provide for the case of the death of any of the persons from whom the House of Representatives may choose a President whenever the right of choice shall have devolved upon them, and for the case of the death of any of the persons from whom the Senate may choose a Vice-President whenever the right of choice shall have devolved upon them.

Section 5. Sections 1 and 2 shall take effect on the 15th day of October following the ratification of this article.

Section 6. This article shall be inoperative unless it shall have been ratified as an amendment to the Constitution by the legislatures of three-fourths of the several States within seven years from the date of its submission.

[AMENDMENT XXI][18]

Section 1. The eighteenth article of amendment to the Constitution of the United States is hereby repealed.

Section 2. The transportation or importation into any State, Territory, or possession of the United States for delivery or use therein of intoxicating liquors, in violation of the laws thereof, is hereby prohibited.

Section 3. This article shall be inoperative unless it shall have been ratified as an amendment to the Constitution by conventions in the several States, as provided in the Constitution, within seven years from the date of the submission hereof to the States by the Congress.

[AMENDMENT XXII][19]

No person shall be elected to the office of the President more than twice, and no person who has held the office of President, or acted as President, for more than two years of a term to which some other person was elected President shall be elected to the office of the President more than once.

[12]Adopted in 1870.

[13]Adopted in 1913.

[14]Adopted in 1913.

[15]Adopted in 1918.

[16]Adopted in 1920.

[17]Adopted in 1933.

[18]Adopted in 1933.

[19]Adopted in 1951.

But this Article shall not apply to any person holding the office of President when this Article was proposed by the Congress, and shall not prevent any person who may be holding the office of President, or acting as President, during the term within which this Article becomes operative from holding the office of President or acting as President during the remainder of such term.

This article shall be inoperative unless it shall have been ratified as an amendment to the Constitution by the legislatures of three-fourths of the several states within seven years from the date of its submission to the states by the Congress.

[AMENDMENT XXIII][20]

Section 1. The District constituting the seat of Government of the United States shall appoint in such manner as the Congress may direct:

A number of electors of President and Vice-President equal to the whole number of Senators and Representatives in Congress to which the District would be entitled if it were a State, but in no event more than the least populous State; they shall be in addition to those appointed by the States, but they shall be considered, for the purpose of the election of President and Vice-President, to be electors appointed by a State; and they shall meet in the District and perform such duties as provided by the twelfth article of amendment.

Section 2. The Congress shall have power to enforce this article by appropriate legislation.

[AMENDMENT XXIV][21]

Section 1. The right of citizens of the United States to vote in any primary or other election for President or Vice-President, for electors for President or Vice-President, or for Senator or Representative in Congress, shall not be denied or abridged by the United States or any state by reason of failure to pay any poll tax or other tax.

Section 2. The Congress shall have the power to enforce this article by appropriate legislation.

[AMENDMENT XXV][22]

Section 1. In case of the removal of the President from office or of his death or resignation, the Vice-President shall become President.

Section 2. Whenever there is a vacancy in the office of the Vice President, the President shall nominate a Vice President who shall take office upon confirmation by a majority vote of both Houses of Congress.

Section 3. Whenever the President transmits to the President Pro Tempore of the Senate and the Speaker of the House of Representatives his written declaration that he is unable to discharge the powers and duties of his office, and until he transmits to them a written declaration to the contrary, such powers and duties shall be discharged by the Vice-President as Acting President.

Section 4. Whenever the Vice-President and a majority of either the principal officers of the executive departments or of such other body as Congress may by law provide, transmit to the President Pro Tempore of the Senate and the Speaker of the House of Representatives their written declaration that the President is unable to discharge the powers and duties of his office, the Vice President shall immediately assume the powers and duties of the office as Acting President.

Thereafter, when the President transmits to the President Pro Tempore of the Senate and the Speaker of the House of Representatives his written declaration that no inability exists, he shall resume the powers and duties of his office unless the Vice President and a majority of either the principal officers of the executive departments or of such other body as Congress may by law provide, transmit within four days to the President Pro Tempore of the Senate and the Speaker of the House of Representatives their written declaration that the President is unable to discharge the powers and duties of his office. Thereupon Congress shall decide the issue, assembling within forty-eight hours for that purpose if not in session. If the Congress, within twenty-one days after receipt of the latter written declaration, or, if Congress is not in session, within twenty-one days after Congress is required to assemble, determines by two-thirds vote of both Houses that the President is unable to discharge the powers and duties of his office, the Vice President shall continue to discharge the same as Acting President; otherwise, the President shall resume the powers and duties of his office.

[AMENDMENT XXVI][23]

Section 1. The right of citizens of the United States, who are eighteen years of age or older, to vote shall not be denied or abridged by the United States or by any State on account of age.

Section 2. The Congress shall have power to enforce this article by appropriate legislation.

[AMENDMENT XXVII][24]

No law, varying the compensation for the services of the Senators and Representatives, shall take effect, until an election of Representatives shall have intervened.

---

[20]Adopted in 1961.

[21]Adopted in 1964.

[22]Adopted in 1967.

[23]Adopted in 1971.

[24]Adopted in 1992.

Presidential Elections

YEAR	CANDIDATES	PARTIES	POPULAR VOTE	% OF POPULAR VOTE	ELECTORAL VOTE	% VOTER PARTICIPATION
1789	**George Washington**				69	
	John Adams				34	
	Other candidates				35	
1792	**George Washington**				132	
	John Adams				77	
	George Clinton				50	
	Other candidates				5	
1796	**John Adams**	Federalist			71	
	Thomas Jefferson	Dem.-Rep.			68	
	Thomas Pinckney	Federalist			59	
	Aaron Burr	Dem.-Rep.			30	
	Other candidates				48	
1800	**Thomas Jefferson**	Dem.-Rep.			73	
	Aaron Burr	Dem.-Rep.			73	
	John Adams	Federalist			65	
	Charles C. Pinckney	Federalist			64	
	John Jay	Federalist			1	
1804	**Thomas Jefferson**	Dem.-Rep.			162	
	Charles C. Pinckney	Federalist			14	
1808	**James Madison**	Dem.-Rep.			122	
	Charles C. Pinckney	Federalist			47	
	George Clinton	Dem.-Rep.			6	
1812	**James Madison**	Dem.-Rep.			128	
	DeWitt Clinton	Federalist			89	
1816	**James Monroe**	Dem.-Rep.			183	
	Rufus King	Federalist			34	
1820	**James Monroe**	Dem.-Rep.			231	
	John Quincy Adams	Indep.-Rep.			1	
1824	**John Quincy Adams**	Dem.-Rep.	113,122	31.0	84	26.9
	Andrew Jackson	Dem.-Rep.	151,271	43.0	99	
	Henry Clay	Dem.-Rep.	47,136	13.0	37	
	William H. Crawford	Dem.-Rep.	46,618	13.0	41	
1828	**Andrew Jackson**	Democratic	642,553	56.0	178	57.6
	John Quincy Adams	National Republican	500,897	44.0	83	
1832	**Andrew Jackson**	Democratic	701,780	54.5	219	55.4
	Henry Clay	National Republican	484,205	37.5	49	
	William Wirt	Anti-Masonic	101,051	8.0	7	
	John Floyd	Democratic			11	
1836	**Martin Van Buren**	Democratic	764,176	50.9	170	57.8
	William H. Harrison	Whig	550,816	49.1	73	
	Hugh L. White	Whig			26	
	Daniel Webster	Whig			14	
	W. P. Mangum	Whig			11	
1840	**William H. Harrison**	Whig	1,275,390	53.0	234	80.2
	Martin Van Buren	Democratic	1,128,854	47.0	60	

YEAR	CANDIDATES	PARTIES	POPULAR VOTE	% OF POPULAR VOTE	ELECTORAL VOTE	% VOTER PARTICIPATION
1972	**Richard M. Nixon**	Republican	47,169,911	60.7	520	55.2
	George S. McGovern	Democratic	29,170,383	37.5	17	
	John G. Schmitz	American	1,099,482	1.4		
1976	**Jimmy Carter**	Democratic	40,830,763	50.1	297	53.5
	Gerald R. Ford	Republican	39,147,793	48.0	240	
1980	**Ronald Reagan**	Republican	43,904,153	51.0	489	52.6
	Jimmy Carter	Democratic	35,483,883	41.0	49	
	John B. Anderson	Independent	5,719,437	7.0	0	
	Ed Clark	Libertarian	920,859	1.0	0	
1984	**Ronald Reagan**	Republican	54,455,075	58.8	525	53.3
	Walter Mondale	Democratic	37,577,185	40.5	13	
1988	**George H. W. Bush**	Republican	48,886,097	53.9	426	48.6
	Michael Dukakis	Democratic	41,809,074	46.1	111	
1992	**William J. Clinton**	Democratic	44,908,254	43.0	370	55.9
	George H. W. Bush	Republican	39,102,343	37.4	168	
	H. Ross Perot	Independent	19,741,065	18.9	0	
1996	**William J. Clinton**	Democratic	45,590,703	49.3	379	49
	Robert Dole	Republican	37,816,307	40.7	159	
	H. Ross Perot	Reform	8,085,294	8.4	0	
2000	**George W. Bush**	Republican	50,456,062	47.9	271	51.2
	Al Gore	Democratic	50,996,582	48.4	266	
	Ralph Nader	Green	2,858,843	2.7	0	
2004	**George W. Bush**	Republican	62,048,610	50.7	286	60.7
	John F. Kerry	Democrat	59,028,444	48.3	251	
	Ralph Nader	Independent	465,650	0.4	0	
2008	**Barack Obama**	Democratic	65,070,487	53	365	63.0
	John McCain	Republican	57,154,810	46	173	
2012	**Barack Obama**	Democrat	65,899,660	51.0	332	58.9
	Mitt Romney	Republican	60,929,152	47.2	206	

Justices of the Supreme Court

	TERM OF SERVICE	YEARS OF SERVICE	LIFE SPAN
John Jay	1789–1795	5	1745–1829
John Rutledge	1789–1791	1	1739–1800
William Cushing	1789–1810	20	1732–1810
James Wilson	1789–1798	8	1742–1798
John Blair	1789–1796	6	1732–1800
Robert H. Harrison	1789–1790	—	1745–1790
James Iredell	1790–1799	9	1751–1799
Thomas Johnson	1791–1793	1	1732–1819
William Paterson	1793–1806	13	1745–1806
*John Rutledge**	1795	—	1739–1800
Samuel Chase	1796–1811	15	1741–1811
Oliver Ellsworth	1796–1800	4	1745–1807
Bushrod Washington	1798–1829	31	1762–1829
Alfred Moore	1799–1804	4	1755–1810
John Marshall	1801–1835	34	1755–1835
William Johnson	1804–1834	30	1771–1834
H. Brockholst Livingston	1806–1823	16	1757–1823
Thomas Todd	1807–1826	18	1765–1826
Joseph Story	1811–1845	33	1779–1845
Gabriel Duval	1811–1835	24	1752–1844
Smith Thompson	1823–1843	20	1768–1843
Robert Trimble	1826–1828	2	1777–1828
John McLean	1829–1861	32	1785–1861
Henry Baldwin	1830–1844	14	1780–1844
James M. Wayne	1835–1867	32	1790–1867
Roger B. Taney	1836–1864	28	1777–1864
Philip P. Barbour	1836–1841	4	1783–1841
John Catron	1837–1865	28	1786–1865
John McKinley	1837–1852	15	1780–1852
Peter V. Daniel	1841–1860	19	1784–1860
Samuel Nelson	1845–1872	27	1792–1873
Levi Woodbury	1845–1851	5	1789–1851
Robert C. Grier	1846–1870	23	1794–1870
Benjamin R. Curtis	1851–1857	6	1809–1874
John A. Campbell	1853–1861	8	1811–1889
Nathan Clifford	1858–1881	23	1803–1881
Noah H. Swayne	1862–1881	18	1804–1884
Samuel F. Miller	1862–1890	28	1816–1890
David Davis	1862–1877	14	1815–1886
Stephen J. Field	1863–1897	34	1816–1899
Salmon P. Chase	1864–1873	8	1808–1873
William Strong	1870–1880	10	1808–1895
Joseph P. Bradley	1870–1892	22	1813–1892
Ward Hunt	1873–1882	9	1810–1886
Morrison R. Waite	1874–1888	14	1816–1888
John M. Harlan	1877–1911	34	1833–1911
William B. Woods	1880–1887	7	1824–1887
Stanley Matthews	1881–1889	7	1824–1889
Horace Gray	1882–1902	20	1828–1902
Samuel Blatchford	1882–1893	11	1820–1893
Lucius Q. C. Lamar	1888–1893	5	1825–1893
Melville W. Fuller	1888–1910	21	1833–1910
David J. Brewer	1890–1910	20	1837–1910
Henry B. Brown	1890–1906	16	1836–1913

*Appointed and served one term, but not confirmed by the Senate.

Note: Chief justices are in italics.

	TERM OF SERVICE	YEARS OF SERVICE	LIFE SPAN		TERM OF SERVICE	YEARS OF SERVICE	LIFE SPAN
George Shiras Jr.	1892–1903	10	1832–1924	Robert H. Jackson	1941–1954	13	1892–1954
Howell E. Jackson	1893–1895	2	1832–1895	Wiley B. Rutledge	1943–1949	6	1894–1949
Edward D. White	1894–1910	16	1845–1921	Harold H. Burton	1945–1958	13	1888–1964
Rufus W. Peckham	1895–1909	14	1838–1909	*Fred M. Vinson*	1946–1953	7	1890–1953
Joseph McKenna	1898–1925	26	1843–1926	Tom C. Clark	1949–1967	18	1899–1977
Oliver W. Holmes	1902–1932	30	1841–1935	Sherman Minton	1949–1956	7	1890–1965
William R. Day	1903–1922	19	1849–1923	*Earl Warren*	1953–1969	16	1891–1974
William H. Moody	1906–1910	3	1853–1917	John Marshall Harlan	1955–1971	16	1899–1971
Horace H. Lurton	1909–1914	4	1844–1914	William J. Brennan Jr.	1956–1990	33	1906–1997
Charles E. Hughes	1910–1916	5	1862–1948	Charles E. Whittaker	1957–1962	5	1901–1973
Edward D. White	1910–1921	11	1845–1921	Potter Stewart	1958–1981	23	1915–1985
Willis Van Devanter	1911–1937	26	1859–1941	Bryon R. White	1962–1993	31	1917–2002
Joseph R. Lamar	1911–1916	5	1857–1916	Arthur J. Goldberg	1962–1965	3	1908–1990
Mahlon Pitney	1912–1922	10	1858–1924	Abe Fortas	1965–1969	4	1910–1982
James C. McReynolds	1914–1941	26	1862–1946	Thurgood Marshall	1967–1991	24	1908–1993
Louis D. Brandeis	1916–1939	22	1856–1941	*Warren C. Burger*	1969–1986	17	1907–1995
John H. Clarke	1916–1922	6	1857–1945	Harry A. Blackmun	1970–1994	24	1908–1999
William H. Taft	1921–1930	8	1857–1930	Lewis F. Powell Jr.	1972–1987	15	1907–1998
George Sutherland	1922–1938	15	1862–1942	William H. Rehnquist	1972–1986	14	1924–2005
Pierce Butler	1922–1939	16	1866–1939	John P. Stevens III	1975–2010	35	1920–
Edward T. Sanford	1923–1930	7	1865–1930	Sandra Day O'Connor	1981–2006	24	1930–
Harlan F. Stone	1925–1941	16	1872–1946	*William H. Rehnquist*	1986–2005	18	1924–2005
Charles E. Hughes	1930–1941	11	1862–1948	Antonin Scalia	1986–	—	1936–
Owen J. Roberts	1930–1945	15	1875–1955	Anthony M. Kennedy	1988–	—	1936–
Benjamin N. Cardozo	1932–1938	6	1870–1938	David H. Souter	1990–2009	20	1939–
Hugo L. Black	1937–1971	34	1886–1971	Clarence Thomas	1991–	—	1948–
Stanley F. Reed	1938–1957	19	1884–1980	Ruth Bader Ginsburg	1993–	—	1933–
Felix Frankfurter	1939–1962	23	1882–1965	Stephen Breyer	1994–	—	1938–
William O. Douglas	1939–1975	36	1898–1980	*John G. Roberts Jr.*	2005–	—	1955–
Frank Murphy	1940–1949	9	1890–1949	Samuel A. Alito Jr.	2006–	—	1950–
Harlan F. Stone	1941–1946	5	1872–1946	Sonia Sotomayor	2009–	—	1954–
James F. Byrnes	1941–1942	1	1882–1972	Elena Kagan	2010–	—	1960–

YEAR	POPULATION	PERCENT INCREASE	POPULATION PER SQUARE MILE	POPULATION PERCENT URBAN/ RURAL	PERCENT MALE/ FEMALE	PERCENT WHITE/ NONWHITE	PERSONS PER HOUSEHOLD	MEDIAN AGE
1790	3,929,214		4.5	5.1/94.9	NA/NA	80.7/19.3	5.79	NA
1800	5,308,483	35.1	6.1	6.1/93.9	NA/NA	81.1/18.9	NA	NA
1810	7,239,881	36.4	4.3	7.3/92.7	NA/NA	81.0/19.0	NA	NA
1820	9,638,453	33.1	5.5	7.2/92.8	50.8/49.2	81.6/18.4	NA	16.7
1830	12,866,020	33.5	7.4	8.8/91.2	50.8/49.2	81.9/18.1	NA	17.2
1840	17,069,453	32.7	9.8	10.8/89.2	50.9/49.1	83.2/16.8	NA	17.8
1850	23,191,876	35.9	7.9	15.3/84.7	51.0/49.0	84.3/15.7	5.55	18.9
1860	31,443,321	35.6	10.6	19.8/80.2	51.2/48.8	85.6/14.4	5.28	19.4
1870	39,818,449	26.6	13.4	25.7/74.3	50.6/49.4	86.2/13.8	5.09	20.2
1880	50,155,783	26.0	16.9	28.2/71.8	50.9/49.1	86.5/13.5	5.04	20.9
1890	62,947,714	25.5	21.2	35.1/64.9	51.2/48.8	87.5/12.5	4.93	22.0
1900	75,994,575	20.7	25.6	39.6/60.4	51.1/48.9	87.9/12.1	4.76	22.9
1910	91,972,266	21.0	31.0	45.6/54.4	51.5/48.5	88.9/11.1	4.54	24.1
1920	105,710,620	14.9	35.6	51.2/48.8	51.0/49.0	89.7/10.3	4.34	25.3
1930	122,775,046	16.1	41.2	56.1/43.9	50.6/49.4	89.8/10.2	4.11	26.4
1940	131,669,275	7.2	44.2	56.5/43.5	50.2/49.8	89.8/10.2	3.67	29.0
1950	150,697,361	14.5	50.7	64.0/36.0	49.7/50.3	89.5/10.5	3.37	30.2
1960	179,323,175	18.5	50.6	69.9/30.1	49.3/50.7	88.6/11.4	3.33	29.5
1970	203,302,031	13.4	57.4	73.5/26.5	48.7/51.3	87.6/12.4	3.14	28.0
1980	226,545,805	11.4	64.0	73.7/26.3	48.6/51.4	86.0/14.0	2.76	30.0
1990	248,709,873	9.8	70.3	75.2/24.8	48.7/51.3	80.3/19.7	2.63	32.9
2000	281,422,426	13.1	79.6	79.0/21.0	49.0/51.0	81.0/19.0	2.59	35.4
2010	308,745,538	9.7	87.4	80.7/19.3	49.2/50.8	77.1/22.9	2.58	37.2

NA = Not available.

YEAR	BIRTHS	YEAR	VITAL STATISTICS (RATES PER THOUSAND) BIRTHS	DEATHS*	MARRIAGES*	DIVORCES*
1800	55.0	1900	32.3	17.2	NA	NA
1810	54.3	1910	30.1	14.7	NA	NA
1820	55.2	1920	27.7	13.0	12.0	1.6
1830	51.4	1930	21.3	11.3	9.2	1.6
1840	51.8	1940	19.4	10.8	12.1	2.0
1850	43.3	1950	24.1	9.6	11.1	2.6
1860	44.3	1960	23.7	9.5	8.5	2.2
1870	38.3	1970	18.4	9.5	10.6	3.5
1880	39.8	1980	15.9	8.8	10.6	5.2
1890	31.5	1990	16.7	8.6	9.8	4.6
		2000	14.7	8.7	8.5	4.2
		2010	13.8	8.0	6.8	3.6

NA = Not available.
*Data not available before 1900.

YEAR	TOTAL POPULATION	LIFE EXPECTANCY (IN YEARS)		WHITE MALES	NONWHITE MALES
		WHITE FEMALES	NONWHITE FEMALES		
1900	47.3	48.7	33.5	46.6	32.5
1910	50.1	52.0	37.5	48.6	33.8
1920	54.1	55.6	45.2	54.4	45.5
1930	59.7	63.5	49.2	59.7	47.3
1940	62.9	66.6	54.9	62.1	51.5
1950	68.2	72.2	62.9	66.5	59.1
1960	69.7	74.1	66.3	67.4	61.1
1970	70.9	75.6	69.4	68.0	61.3
1980	73.7	78.1	73.6	70.7	65.3
1990	75.4	79.3	75.2	72.6	67.0
2000	76.9	80.0	75.0	74.8	68.3
2010	78.3	80.8	80.3	75.7	74.5

THE CHANGING AGE STRUCTURE

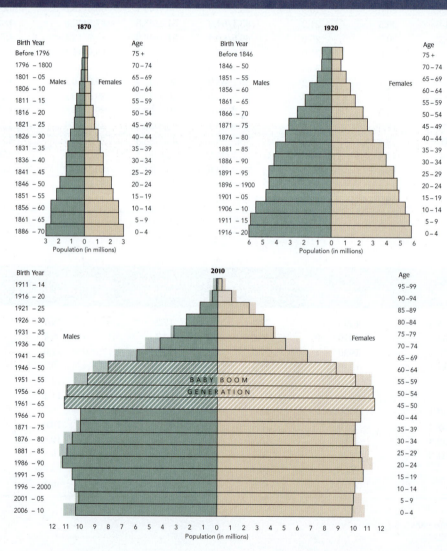

Before the twentieth century, the age distribution of Americans could be charted roughly as a pyramid, as seen in the figures for 1870 and 1920. High birthrates create a broad base at the bottom, while mortality rates winnow the population to a small tip of elderly. But by 2010, the pyramid had been transformed more nearly into a cylinder. Over the past two centuries fertility rates have undergone a steady decline, pulling in the base of the pyramid, while higher living standards have allowed Americans to live longer, broadening the top. Only the temporary bulge of the baby boom distorts the shape.

		REGIONAL ORIGIN OF IMMIGRANTS (PERCENT) EUROPE					
YEARS	TOTAL NUMBER OF IMMIGRANTS	TOTAL EUROPE	NORTH AND WEST	EAST AND CENTRAL	SOUTH AND OTHER	WESTERN HEMISPHERE	ASIA
1821–1830	143,389	69.2	67.1	—	2.1	8.4	—
1831–1840	599,125	82.8	81.8	—	1.0	5.5	—
1841–1850	1,713,251	93.8	92.9	0.1	0.3	3.6	—
1851–1860	2,598,214	94.4	93.6	0.1	0.8	2.9	1.6
1861–1870	2,314,824	89.2	87.8	0.5	0.9	7.2	2.8
1871–1880	2,812,191	80.8	73.6	4.5	2.7	14.4	4.4
1881–1890	5,246,13	90.3	72.0	11.9	6.3	8.1	1.3
1891–1900	3,687,546	96.5	44.5	32.8	19.1	1.1	1.9
1901–1910	8,795,386	92.5	21.7	44.5	6.3	4.1	2.8
1911–1920	5,735,811	76.3	17.4	33.4	25.5	19.9	3.4
1921–1930	4,107,209	60.3	31.7	14.4	14.3	36.9	2.4
1931–1940	528,431	65.9	38.8	11.0	16.1	30.3	2.8
1941–1950	1,035,039	60.1	47.5	4.6	7.9	34.3	3.1
1951–1960	2,515,479	52.8	17.7	24.3	10.8	39.6	6.0
1961–1970	3,321,677	33.8	11.7	9.4	12.9	51.7	12.9
1971–1980	4,493,300	17.8	4.3	5.6	8.4	44.3	35.2
1981–1990	7,338,000	10.4	5.9	4.8	1.1	49.3	37.3
1991–2000	9,095,417	14.9	4.8	8.6	1.6	49.3	30.7

Dash indicates less than 0.1 percent.

	RECENT TRENDS IN IMMIGRATION (IN THOUSANDS)				PERCENT		
	1961–1970	1971–1980	1981–1990	1991–2000	1971–1980	1981–1990	1991–2000
All countries	3,321.7	4,493.3	7,338.1	9095.4	100.0	100.0	100.0
Europe	1,123.5	800.4	761.5	1359.7	17.8	10.4	14.9
Austria	20.6	9.5	18.3	15.5	0.2	0.3	0.2
Belgium	9.2	5.3	7.0	7.0	0.1	0.1	0.1
Czechoslovakia	3.3	6.0	7.2	9.8	0.1	0.1	0.1
Denmark	9.2	4.4	5.3	6.0	0.1	0.1	0.1
France	45.2	25.1	22.4	35.8	0.6	1.3	0.4
Germany	190.8	74.4	91.6	92.6	1.7	2.2	1.0
Greece	86.0	92.4	38.3	26.7	2.1	0.4	0.3
Hungary	5.4	6.6	6.5	9.3	0.1	0.1	0.1
Ireland	33.0	11.5	31.9	56.9	0.3	0.9	0.6
Italy	214.1	129.4	67.2	62.7	2.9	0.2	0.7
Netherlands	30.6	10.5	12.2	13.3	0.2	0.1	0.1
Norway	15.5	3.9	4.2	5.1	0.1	1.1	0.5
Poland	53.5	37.2	83.3	163.7	0.8	0.5	1.8
Portugal	76.1	101.7	40.4	22.9	2.3	0.3	0.3
Spain	44.7	39.1	20.4	17.1	0.9	0.2	0.2
Sweden	17.1	6.5	11.0	12.7	0.1	0.1	0.1
Switzerland	18.5	8.2	8.8	11.8	0.2	0.1	0.1
United Kingdom	213.8	137.4	159.2	151.8	3.1	2.2	1.7
USSR	2.5	39.0	57.7	462.8	0.9	0.3	5.1
Yugoslavia	20.4	30.5	18.8	66.5	0.7	0.5	0.7
Other Europe	9.1	18.9	8.2	57.7	0.2	0.0	0.6

| RECENT TRENDS IN IMMIGRATION (IN THOUSANDS) | | | | | | | |
| | | | | | PERCENT | | |
	1961–1970	1971–1980	1981–1990	1991–2000	1971–1980	1981–1990	1991–2000
Asia	427.6	1588.2	2738.1	2795.6	35.2	37.3	30.7
China	34.8	124.3	298.9	419.1	2.8	4.1	4.6
Hong Kong	75.0	113.5	98.2	109.8	2.5	1.3	1.2
India	27.2	164.1	250.7	363.1	3.7	3.4	4.0
Iran	10.3	45.1	116.0	69.0	1.0	1.6	0.8
Israel	29.6	37.7	44.2	39.4	0.8	0.6	0.4
Japan	40.0	49.8	47.0	67.9	1.1	0.6	0.7
Korea	34.5	267.6	333.8	164.2	6.0	4.5	1.8
Philippines	98.4	355.0	548.7	503.9	7.9	7.5	5.5
Turkey	10.1	13.4	23.4	38.2	0.3	0.3	0.4
Vietnam	4.3	172.8	281.0	286.1	3.8	3.8	3.1
Other Asia	36.5	176.1	631.4	735.4	3.8	8.6	8.0
America	1716.4	1982.5	3615.6	4486.8	44.3	49.3	49.3
Argentina	49.7	29.9	27.3	26.6	0.7	0.4	0.3
Canada	413.3	169.9	158.0	192.0	3.8	2.2	2.1
Colombia	72.0	77.3	122.9	128.5	1.7	1.7	1.4
Cuba	208.5	264.9	144.6	169.3	5.9	2.0	1.9
Dominican Rep.	93.3	148.1	252.0	335.3	3.3	3.4	3.7
Ecuador	36.8	50.1	56.2	76.5	1.1	0.8	0.8
El Salvador	15.0	34.4	213.5	215.7	0.8	2.9	2.4
Haiti	34.5	56.3	138.4	179.6	1.3	1.9	2.0
Jamaica	74.9	137.6	208.1	169.2	3.1	2.8	1.9
Mexico	453.9	640.3	1655.7	2249.4	14.3	22.6	24.7
Other America	264.4	373.8	639.3	744.3	8.3	8.7	8.2
Africa	29.0	80.8	176.8	355.0	1.8	2.4	3.9
Oceania	25.1	41.2	45.2	55.8	0.9	0.6	0.6

Figures may not add to total due to rounding.

AMERICAN WORKERS AND FARMERS							
YEAR	TOTAL NUMBER OF WORKERS (THOUSANDS)	PERCENT OF WORKERS MALE/ FEMALE	PERCENT OF FEMALE WORKERS MARRIED	PERCENT OF WORKERS IN FEMALE POPULATION	PERCENT OF WORKERS IN LABOR UNIONS	FARM POPULATION (THOUSANDS)	FARM POPULATION AS PERCENT OF TOTAL POPULATION
1870	12,506	85/15	NA	NA	NA	NA	NA
1880	17,392	85/15	NA	NA	NA	21,973	43.8
1890	23,318	83/17	13.9	18.9	NA	24,771	42.3
1900	29,073	82/18	15.4	20.6	3	29,875	41.9
1910	38,167	79/21	24.7	25.4	6	32,077	34.9
1920	41,614	79/21	23.0	23.7	12	31,974	30.1
1930	48,830	78/22	28.9	24.8	7	30,529	24.9
1940	53,011	76/24	36.4	27.4	27	30,547	23.2
1950	59,643	72/28	52.1	31.4	25	23,048	15.3
1960	69,877	68/32	59.9	37.7	26	15,635	8.7
1970	82,049	63/37	63.4	43.4	25	9712	4.8
1980	108,544	58/42	59.7	51.5	23	6051	2.7
1990	117,914	55/45	58.4	44.3	16	3871	1.6
2000	135,208	54/46	61.3	45.7	15	3305	1.1

| | GROSS NATIONAL PRODUCT (GNP) (IN BILLIONS)* | FOREIGN TRADE (IN MILLIONS) | | | FEDERAL BUDGET (IN BILLIONS) | FEDERAL SURPLUS/DEFICIT (IN BILLIONS) | FEDERAL DEBT (IN BILLIONS) |
YEAR		EXPORTS	IMPORTS	BALANCE OF TRADE			
1790	NA	$20	$23	$−3	$0.004	$+0.00015	$0.076
1800	NA	71	91	−20	0.011	+0.0006	0.083
1810	NA	67	85	−18	0.008	+0.0012	0.053
1820	NA	70	74	−4	0.018	−0.0004	0.091
1830	NA	74	71	+3	0.015	+0.100	0.049
1840	NA	132	107	+25	0.024	−0.005	0.004
1850	NA	152	178	−26	0.040	+0.004	0.064
1860	NA	400	362	−38	0.063	−0.01	0.065
1870	$7.4	451	462	−11	0.310	+0.10	2.4
1880	11.2	853	761	+92	0.268	+0.07	2.1
1890	13.1	910	823	+87	0.318	+0.09	1.2
1900	18.7	1499	930	+569	0.521	+0.05	1.2
1910	35.3	1919	1646	+273	0.694	−0.02	1.1
1920	91.5	8664	5784	+2880	6.357	+0.3	24.3
1930	90.7	4013	3500	+513	3.320	+0.7	16.3
1940	100.0	4030	7433	−3403	9.6	−2.7	43.0
1950	286.5	10,816	9125	+1691	43.1	−2.2	257.4
1960	506.5	19,600	15,046	+4556	92.2	+0.3	286.3
1970	992.7	42,700	40,189	+2511	195.6	−2.8	371.0
1980	2631.7	220,783	244,871	+24,088	590.9	−73.8	907.7
1990	5803.2	394,030	495,042	−101,012	1253.1	−220.5	3206.6
2000	9872.9	1,102,900	1,466,900	−364,000	1788.8	+236.4	5629.0

THE ECONOMY AND FEDERAL SPENDING

*For 1990 and after, gross domestic product (GDP) is given.

Glossary

A

actual representation view that the people can be represented only by a person whom they have actually elected to office; this understanding of representation was the consensus among colonials during the imperial crisis and the basis of their objection to the British claim that Americans were virtually represented in Parliament.

affirmative action practice of actively seeking to increase the number of racial and ethnic minorities, women, persons in a protected age category, persons with disabilities, and disabled veterans in a workplace or school. Such measures sometimes include the setting of quotas or percentages in hiring.

amnesty general pardon granted by a government, usually for political crimes. Proposals of amnesty were made, with varying degrees of exception for high Confederate officials, by Presidents Lincoln and Johnson as well as by Congress in 1872. President Ford offered conditional amnesty in 1974 to draft evaders at the conclusion of the Vietnam War.

anti-Semitism hatred, prejudice, oppression, or discrimination against Jews or Judaism. *Semite* originally referred to the descendants of Shem, which included both Jews and Muslims in the Middle East. More recently the term has come to refer primarily to Jews.

appeasement policy of making concessions to an aggressor nation, as long as its demands appear reasonable, in order to avoid war. Hitler's full conquest of Czechoslovakia, violating his promises given at the Munich Conference in 1938, gave the term its negative connotation.

armistice mutually agreed-on truce or temporary halt in the fighting of a war so that the combatants may discuss peace.

artisan skilled craftworker, such as a blacksmith, a cooper, a miller, or a tailor. Master artisans constituted a large segment of the middle classes in American cities and towns from the beginnings of colonial settlement through the 1820s; they owned their own shops and employed a number of younger journeyman artisans, who owned only their tools, and trained even younger and less skilled apprentices in a craft.

assimilate to absorb a culturally distinct group into the dominant culture. The debate over the process of assimilation, of immigrants "becoming American," has been a persistent fault line in American politics. The debate revolves around what qualities are American and the degree to which a dominant culture should define them. The debate is extremely difficult in a society in which immigration plays a crucial role—in a "nation of nations," as Walt Whitman described the United States.

autonomy condition of being independent or, in the case of a political structure, the right to self-government.

B

balanced constitution view that England's constitution gave every part of English society some voice in the workings of its government. While the Crown represented the monarchy and the House of Lords the aristocracy, the House of Commons represented the ordinary people of England.

barter economy networks of trade based on the mutual exchange of goods and services with little or no use of coin or currency.

behaviorism school of psychology that measures human behavior, believes it can be shaped, and discounts emotion as subjective. Behaviorism was founded by psychologist John Watson and was first presented in his *Psychology as the Behaviorist Views It* (1913).

benign neglect policy also known as "salutary neglect," pursued by the British empire in governing its American colonies until the end of the Seven Years' War.

biocentric life-centered; also a theory of moral responsibility stating that all forms of life have an inherent right to exist and that humanity is not the center of existence.

biogenetic engineering process of changing the DNA of a plant or an animal to produce desirable characteristics. Examples of desirable characteristics include fast growth and unusually large size. The health and environmental safety of genetically modified food products is a subject of debate in the scientific and lay communities.

black codes series of laws passed by southern states in 1865 and 1866, modeled on the slave codes in effect before the Civil War. The codes did grant African Americans some rights not enjoyed by slaves, but their primary purpose was to keep African Americans as propertyless agricultural laborers.

bloody shirt political campaign tactic of "waving the bloody shirt," used by Republicans against Democrats; it invoked the tremendous loss of life and casualties from the Civil War as a reason to vote for Republicans as the party of the Union and not to trust Democrats, who had often opposed the war. The tactic continued to work, with diminishing success, throughout Reconstruction.

bonds certificates of debt issued by a government or corporation promising to repay the buyers of the bonds their original investment, plus interest, by a specified date of maturity. Bonds have been traditionally used by governments as a way to raise money during wartime or for large-scale projects.

boom-bust economy periods of expansion and recession or depression that an economy goes through. Also referred to as *business cycle*. Major downturns in the cycle have occurred in the United States beginning in 1819, 1837, 1857, 1873, 1893, 1907, and 1929, the start of the Great Depression.

bootlegging illegal transport or sale of goods, in this case alcoholic beverages during the 1920s. The term derived from the practice of hiding a container of alcohol in the upper part of a boot.

boycott tactic used by protesters, workers, and consumers to pressure business organizations through a mass refusal to purchase their products or otherwise do business with them.

brinkmanship policy of pushing a critical situation to the edge of catastrophe by using the implicit threat of nuclear war in order to persuade an opponent to back down. The strategy was developed by Secretary of State John Foster Dulles under President Dwight Eisenhower.

bureaucratic state government run by administrative bureaus or divisions and staffed by nonelected officials.

business cycle *see* **boom-bust economy.**

C

carpetbagger white Republicans, originally from the North, who came to live in the South after the Civil War. They received their nickname from hostile southerners who claimed that the newcomers arrived carrying all that they owned stuffed into a carpetbag and eager to get rich by plundering the South.

cartel organization of private businesses that join to control production, distribution, and prices.

caste system system of social stratification separating individuals by various distinctions, among them hereditary, rank, profession, wealth, and race. Slavery as a caste system not only separated whites from blacks but also assigned value to people according to shadings of color.

cede to give up possession of, usually by treaty.

celibate abstaining from sexual intercourse; also, unmarried. Celibacy is the abstention from intercourse, a state often motivated by religious teachings.

charter document issued by a sovereign ruler, legislature, or other authority creating a public or private corporation. England's rulers issued charters setting forth the authority of corporations or joint stock companies to colonize sections of the Americas; state legislatures have issued charters to corporations; and the British (including American colonials) traced basic rights of representation to the Magna Carta (Great Charter) granted by King John in 1215 CE.

checks and balances mechanism by which each branch of government—executive, legislative, and judicial—keeps the others within the bounds of their constitutional authority; James Madison emphasized this feature of the federal constitution to assure the Anti-Federalists.

Columbian exchange transition of people, plants, insects, and microbes between the two hemispheres, initiated when Columbus reached the Americas in 1492.

commercial economy economy in which individuals are involved in a network of markets and commercial transactions. Such economies are often urban, where goods and services are exchanged for money and credit; agricultural areas are also commercial when crops and livestock are sold in markets rather than consumed by those who grew or raised them. Commercial economies are less egalitarian, because wealth can be concentrated in the hands of fewer individuals. *See also* **semisubsistence economy.**

committees of correspondence strategy devised by Samuel Adams in 1772 to rally popular support among American colonials against British imperial policies. The committees of correspondence drew up statements of American rights and grievances, distributed those documents within and among the colonies, and solicited responses from towns and counties. This committee structure formed a new communications network, one that fostered intercolonial agreement on resistance to British measures and spread the resistance from seaports into rural areas.

community action programs programs designed to identify and organize local leaders to take steps to alleviate poverty and crime in their neighborhoods. Sociologist Saul Alinsky from Chicago organized the Industrial Areas Foundation to support community action programs in the 1960s.

conformity degree to which people adjust their behavior, values, and ideas to fit into a group or society.

conglomerate corporation whose various branches or subsidiaries are either directly or indirectly spread among a variety of industries, usually unrelated to one another. The purpose of a conglomerate is generally to increase shareholder value and ensure against market cycles by spreading its risk, rather than to improve market share or production efficiency by concentrating on excelling within a single industry.

Congregationalists members of a Protestant denomination that originated in sixteenth-century Britain as part of the Puritan movement. While some early Congregationalists, known as Separatists,

concluded that the Church of England was beyond reformation, most strove to reform English religion and society while remaining within the Church of England. Early modern Congregationalists embraced Calvinist theological beliefs and held that each individual congregation should conduct its own religious affairs, answering to no higher authority. The Separatists founded Plymouth, the first northern colony, and the Non-Separating Congregationalists predominated elsewhere in seventeenth-century New England.

conscription act of compulsory enrollment for military service, as opposed to a voluntary enlistment.

consensus point of view generally shared by a group, institution, or even a culture. Scholars have analyzed and debated the institutions that contribute to the construction of a consensus viewpoint, ranging from schools and churches to the media in their various forms.

constitution framework of government establishing the contract between rulers and ruled. American revolutionaries insisted on written constitutions to protect individual rights and liberties; by contrast, Britons understood the term *constitution* to mean the existing arrangement of government—not an actual document but a collection of parliamentary laws, customs, and precedents.

consumer goods products such as food and clothing that fill the needs and wants of individuals. *Producer* or *capital goods,* in contrast, are the factory equipment and other machines used to manufacture or transport other goods or services.

Continental Army main rebel military force, created by the Second Continental Congress in July 1775 and commanded by George Washington. After the 1776 campaign, most enlistments came from the poorest and most desperate in American society, and it was they who shouldered the burden of the fighting. During the harsh winter at Valley Forge in 1778/1779, the army acquired greater discipline and expertise and thereafter scored important military victories in the mid-Atlantic and the South.

contraband goods seized by a government during wartime, when the goods were being used by an enemy nation or being shipped to an enemy nation by a neutral nation. The term was also applied during the Civil War to escaped slaves who fled behind Union lines.

Copperhead derogatory term used by Republicans to label northern Democrats who opposed the war policies of the Lincoln administration and advocated a negotiated peace.

CORE   Congress of Racial Equality, an organization founded in Chicago in 1942. The group's inspiration was Krishnalal Shridharani's book *War without Violence,* which outlined Mohandas K. Gandhi's nonviolent philosophy for action. CORE believed that African Americans could use nonviolent civil disobedience to challenge racial segregation.

corporation   business entity that has been granted a charter granting it legal rights, privileges, and liabilities distinct from the individual members that are a part of it. A corporation therefore may survive the death of the individuals who created and run it.

Counter-Reformation   reform movement within the Roman Catholic Church in response to the Protestant Reformation, seeking to reform and reinvigorate the Church. Religious orders played a large role in the Counter-Reformation, particularly the Jesuit order, known formally as the Society of Jesus, and founded in 1534 by Ignatius of Loyola.

covert operations   military or political actions carried out in secret to allow the responsible government or party to deny its role. Governments have often relied on such operations when overt military force is impractical or dangerous or when public negotiations are likely to fail.

D

de facto segregation   spatial and social separation of populations brought about by social behavior rather than by laws or legal mechanisms. Segregation (especially in schools) has often existed without being sanctioned by law. When the practice is accomplished through explicit legal means, it is known as *de jure segregation.*

debt peonage   paying off a debt through labor when the debtor lacks sufficient cash or other assets.

Deep South   South Carolina, Georgia, Florida, Alabama, Mississippi, Louisiana, and Texas.

demographic   factors relating to the characteristics of populations. Demography is the study of populations, looking at such aspects as size, growth, density, and age distribution.

depreciated   decreased in value owing to market conditions. Depreciation in the value of banknotes can occur when too much paper money is put into circulation or when users doubt the ability of the government to back up the paper currency with reserves of gold or silver.

détente   relaxation of strained relations between nations, especially among the United States, the Soviet Union, and China in the 1970s and late 1980s. In seeking détente, once-hostile parties begin to emphasize their common interests and reduce their points of conflict.

deterrence   prevention of an action by fear of the consequences; during the cold war, the theory that war could be avoided because each side knew that the other possessed large numbers of nuclear weapons. Thus any nuclear exchange threatened the survival of both sides.

disenfranchise   to deny a citizen's right to vote.

disenfranchisement   denial of a citizen's right to vote.

doctrine of preemption   war undertaken in anticipation of imminent attack or invasion by another nation or in hopes of gaining a strategic advantage when war seems unavoidable. In that sense the Japanese government viewed its attack on Pearl Harbor as preemptive.

domesticity   devotion to home life, and a woman's place at the center of that life. The ideal of domesticity became popular during the nineteenth century as industrialization was increasingly separating work and home as individual spheres.

dove   *see* **hawks and doves.**

dry farming   farming system to conserve water in semiarid regions receiving less than 15 to 20 inches of rain a year. Methods include leaving some fields fallow or unplanted to reduce water use, keeping soil broken to absorb water, and growing drought-resistant crops.

due process   constitutional concept, embodied in the Fifth and Fourteenth Amendments, that no person shall be deprived of life, liberty, or property without legal safeguards such as being present at a hearing, having an opportunity to be heard in court, having the opportunity to confront hostile witnesses, and being able to present evidence.

E

ecosystem   a community and/or region studied as a system of functioning relationships between organisms and their environments.

ecumenism   movement encouraging unity among religions, especially among Christian denominations and between Christians and Jews. Ecumenical movements promote cooperation and better understanding among different religious denominations.

egalitarian   exhibiting or asserting a belief in the equality of humans in a social, political, or economic context.

elect   in theology, those of the faithful chosen, or "elected," by God for eternal salvation.

elites   class of people given special social, economic, or intellectual status within society. The singular noun *elite* can also be used as a plural, as in *the colonial elite.*

embargo   government act prohibiting trade with a foreign country or countries, usually to exert economic pressure.

enfranchise   *see* **suffrage** and **disenfranchisement.**

Enlightenment   intellectual movement that flourished in Europe from the mid-1600s through the eighteenth century and stressed the power of human reason to promote social progress by discovering the laws that governed both nature and society. In the American colonies, the Enlightenment's influence encouraged scientists such as Benjamin Franklin to experiment and discover useful scientific knowledge, and it also persuaded a growing minority to accept more liberal religious views, known as "rational Christianity."

escalation   process of steady intensification, rather than a sudden or marked increase, applied to the increasing American military presence in Vietnam. The term derives from an escalator, which gradually lifts its cargo to a higher level. Nuclear theorist Herman Kahn used the term geopolitically in his *On Escalation: Metaphors and Scenarios* (1968).

evangelical   term that derives from a Greek word meaning the bringing of good news—in this case, the Gospel. Protestant evangelicals stressed the need for individual conversion and rebirth stemming from an awareness of sinful guilt and Christ's act of atoning, through his death, for their sins.

excise tax   internal tax placed on the production or sale of a commodity, usually a luxury item or nonessential.

executive order   declaration issued by the president or by a governor possessing the force of law. Executive orders are usually based on existing statutory authority and require no action by Congress or the state legislature to take effect.

expatriate   one who leaves the country of one's birth or citizenship to live in another, usually out of a sense of alienation. The term is often applied to the group of writers and artists living in self-imposed exile in Paris during the 1920s and sometimes referred to as the "Lost Generation." That term was coined by the writer Gertrude Lawrence, describing the rootless generation of American expatriates who found life in the United States culturally sterile and promises of postwar freedom and democracy empty.

F

federalism   governing principle established by the Constitution in which the national government and the states divide power. A stronger commitment to federalism as the basis of a national republic replaced the system established by the Articles of Confederation, which granted virtually sovereign power to individual states.

fission   splitting of a nucleus of an atom into at least two other nuclei, accompanied by the release of a relatively large amount of energy. The splitting of the nucleus of the uranium isotope U-235 or its artificial cousin, plutonium, powered the atomic bomb.

Free Soil Party   antislavery party formed in 1848 by northern Democrats disillusioned with southern Democratic support for slavery. The party tried to widen its appeal by focusing less on outright abolition than on opposing the spread of slavery into the territories (the need to protect "free soil" and "free labor"). The party never gained strength, however; the Republican Party in the 1850s attracted the greater number of antislavery voters.

freedmen   former slaves; the term came into use during the Civil War, as greater numbers of slaves fled or were freed under the terms of the Emancipation Proclamation, and continued to be widely used during Reconstruction. More recently historians have also used the gender-neutral term, *freedpeople*.

G

graduated income tax   tax based on a percentage of an individual's income, the percentage increasing as total income increases. Under such a system, wealthy individuals are taxed at a higher rate than are poorer individuals.

Great Awakening   term used by some historians to describe periods of intense religious piety and commitment among Americans that fueled the expansion of Protestant churches. The First Great Awakening extended from the 1730s to the American Revolution; the Second Great Awakening includes the period from about 1790 to the 1840s; the Third Great Awakening took place during the late nineteenth and early twentieth centuries; the Fourth Great Awakening spans the latter half of the twentieth century.

H

habeas corpus   Latin phrase meaning, "you have the body." For centuries, the term referred in English law to the right of individuals to be brought before a court and informed of the crime alleged against them. The right of habeus corpus is meant to ensure that the government cannot arbitrarily arrest and imprison a citizen without giving grounds for doing so.

hawks and doves   nicknames for the two opposing positions in American policy during the war in Vietnam. Hawks supported the escalation of the war and a "peace with honor." Doves, the peace faction, argued that the United States had intervened in a civil war and should withdraw its troops.

hedge fund   an investment fund requiring high minimum contributions and thus used by a limited range of more affluent investors. Hedge funds are very lightly regulated by the government, often secretive, and undertake a range of high-risk investment and trading strategies.

Hessians   German soldiers who fought with the British Army during the American Revolution. Some Hessians taken as prisoners of war later served in the Continental Army and settled in the United States after the Revolution.

horizontal combination   strategy of business growth (sometimes referred to as "horizontal integration") that attempts to stifle competition by combining more than one firm involved in the same level of production, transportation, or distribution into a single firm.

http://   abbreviation for HyperText Transfer Protocol, the set of Internet rules governing the transfer of data between a server and a computer as well as for exchanging files (text, graphic images, sound, video, and other multimedia files) on the World Wide Web.

I

impeachment   under the U.S. Constitution, the process by which members of the House of Representatives bring charges against a high government official for "Treason, Bribery, or other high Crimes and Misdemeanors." Once an individual is impeached, he or she must stand trial before the Senate, where a two-thirds majority vote is required for conviction. Conviction results in removal from office.

imperialism   acquisition of control over the government and the economy of another nation, usually by conquest. The United States became an imperialistic world power in the late nineteenth century by gaining control over the Hawaiian Islands and, after the Spanish American War (1898), Guam, the Philippines, Cuba, and Puerto Rico.

indemnity   compensation for loss or damage.

indentures   contract signed between two parties, binding one to serve the other for a specified period of time. The term originated because two copies of the agreement were made, both indented in the same way at its edges, so that each party was provided an identical record of the agreement.

inflation   increase in the overall price of goods and services over an extended period of time; or a similar decrease over time of the purchasing power of money. The latter situation can be caused by an increase of the amount of currency and credit available in an economy. In such cases, when the perceived value of paper money declines (as often happens in wars, when the government tries to raise revenues by printing money), sellers raise the prices of their goods to compensate.

injunction   court order requiring individuals or groups to participate in or refrain from a certain action.

interstate commerce   trade in goods that crosses state lines. Regulation of interstate commerce is reserved in the Constitution for the federal government and has become the constitutional basis for much of federal regulation of business.

Iroquois League   Indian confederacy, also known as the Five Nations, that exerted enormous influence throughout the region. In 1712, a sixth tribe, the Tuscaroras, joined the confederation.

isolationism   belief that the United States should avoid foreign entanglements, alliances, and involvement in foreign wars. The tradition had its roots in President George Washington's farewell address, which warned in 1796, "It is our true policy to steer clear of permanent alliances with any portion of the foreign world. . . ."

Issei *see* **Nisei.**

itinerant traveling preacher attached to no settled congregation. Itinerants played an important role in the first Great Awakening, taking their inspiration from George Whitefield, who preached up and down the Atlantic seaboard. In the early nineteenth century, many Protestant denominations—especially the Methodists and the Baptists—made strategic use of itinerants to evangelize settlers on the frontier.

J

jihad Arabic term meaning "striving or struggling in the way of God." Although broadly the term can indicate a spiritual effort on the part of a Muslim believer to come closer to Allah, the expression is also used to denote a Muslim holy war against unbelievers.

joint stock company business in which capital is held in transferable shares of stock by joint owners. The joint stock company was an innovation that allowed investors to share and spread the risks of overseas investment. Instead of only a few individuals owning a ship and its cargo—which might sink and bring ruin to its investors—joint stock allowed for smaller sums to be invested in a variety of different ventures.

journeyman person who has served an apprenticeship in a trade or craft and who is a qualified worker employed by another person.

judicial review doctrine set out by Chief Justice John Marshall in *Marbury v. Madison.* The decision established that the judicial branch of the federal government possesses the power to determine whether the laws of Congress or the actions of the executive branch violate the Constitution.

L

laissez faire a French term ("allow [people] to do [as they choose]") referring to an economic doctrine that advocates holding government interference in the economy to an absolute minimum and ideally having none at all.

landed states and landless states some of the 13 colonies that became the United States had originally been granted land whose western boundaries were vague or overlapped the land granted to other colonies. During the Confederation period, the so-called landless states had boundaries that were firmly drawn on all sides, such as Maryland, New Jersey, and Massachusetts. The so-called landed states possessed grants whose western boundaries were not fixed. (See the map on page 186).

libertarian advocate of a minimalist approach to governing, in which the freedom of private individuals to do as they please ranks paramount. A libertarian philosophy contrasts with the outlook of modern liberals, in which government plays a more active role in meeting the needs of citizens or in managing social and economic life for the common good.

lien legal claim against property used to obtain a loan, which must be paid when the property is sold. Developing first in the South after the Civil War, the crop-lien system allowed merchants to claim a portion (or all) of current or future crops as payment for loans to farmers for seed, tools, and fertilizer. Merchants often insisted that indebted farmers raise a single cash crop, frequently cotton. That requirement helped to ensnare farmers in a cycle of debt as the price of such crops fell.

loyalists supporters of the king and Parliament and known to the rebels as "tories." At the outset of the American Revolution, loyalists made up about one-fifth of the white population, but their ranks diminished steadily after about 1777, as the British army alienated many civilians in every region that they occupied.

loyalty oath oath of fidelity to the state or to an organization. Plans for Reconstruction insisted that southerners returning to the Union take a loyalty oath of some sort, whether that they would be loyal henceforth to the United States or a more strict "ironclad oath" that they never had aided the Confederacy. At other times of stress—as during the Revolutionary era or during the cold war of the 1950s, loyalty oaths and loyalty investigations have been used by groups or governments to enforce obedience to the state or to a revolutionary movement.

M

managed economy economy directed by the government with power over prices, allocation of resources, and marketing of goods.

Manifest Destiny belief, as Democratic editor John L. O'Sullivan put it, that it had become the United States' "manifest destiny to overspread the continent allotted by Providence for the free development of our yearly multiplying millions." The roots of the doctrine were both religious and political. Protestant religious thinkers had long seen American settlement as setting a pious and virtuous example to the rest of the world. The political ideology of the Revolution encouraged the notion that the benefits of democracy would spread along with the political expansion of the nation. Yet Manifest Destiny was also racist in its assumption of the inferiority of other peoples and cultures; and it encompassed a purely economic desire to expand the nation's commerce and power.

"Maroon" communities collective attempts at escape typically undertaken by groups of newly arrived African slaves in the American South. Such slaves fled inland, often to the frontiers of colonial settlement, where they attempted to reconstruct the African villages from which they had been taken captive. Because of their size, such communities proved to be short-lived; they were quickly discovered by white slave patrols or by Indian tribes such as the Cherokees, who profited from returning runaways. "Maroon communities" in the Caribbean proved far more enduring and provided the bases for successful slave rebellions during the eighteenth and early nineteenth centuries.

mass media forms of communication designed to reach a vast audience, generally a nation state or larger, without personal contact between the senders and receivers. Examples would include newspapers, movies, magazines, radio, television, and—today—some sites on the Internet.

mercantilism European economic doctrine calling for strict regulation of the economy in order to ensure a balance of exports over imports and increase the amount of gold and silver in a nation's treasury.

merchants of death term popularized in the 1930s to describe American bankers and arms makers whose support for the Allied cause, some historians charged, drew the United States into World War I.

Mesoamerica the area stretching from present-day central Mexico southward through Honduras and Nicaragua, in which pre-Columbian civilizations developed.

Methodist denomination that originated as a reform movement within the Church of England during the mid-eighteenth century, much as the Puritans originated as a reform movement within the English church during the mid-sixteenth century. The distinctive features of early Methodism on both sides of the Atlantic included a strict devotional regimen, an ascetic moral discipline, and an emphasis on evangelical conversion. By the Civil War, Methodists had become the largest Protestant denomination in the United States among both whites and African Americans.

military-industrial complex combination of the U.S. armed forces, arms manufacturers, and associated political and commercial interests, which grew rapidly during the cold war era. It is another term for the mutually supportive relationship of military contractors, the Pentagon, and sympathetic members of Congress, an alliance also known as the "Iron Triangle."

militia local defense band of civilians comprising men between the ages of 16 and 65 whose military training consisted only of occasional gatherings known as musters. Militias were organized in towns and counties throughout the American colonies from the beginnings of settlement, but they played a crucial role in the war for independence by supporting the Continental Army whenever the fighting moved into their neighborhoods.

millennialism belief in the thousand-year reign of Christ predicted in the Bible's final book, the Revelation to John. The belief that dedicated Christians could help bring about this reign of holiness by converting the world to Christianity proved to be a powerful impulse to reform.

miscegenation marriage, cohabitation, or sexual relations between persons of different races. Since race is a socially constructed identifier rather than one with any scientific or genetic basis, *miscegenation* as a term is used only in its historical context.

monoculture growth of a single crop to the virtual exclusion of all others, either on a farm or more generally within a region.

mutiny refusal of rank-and-file soldiers to follow the commands of their superior officers. Mutinies plagued the Continental Army between 1779 and 1781 as resentments mounted among soldiers over spoiled food, inadequate clothing, and back pay.

mutually assured destruction (MAD) national defense strategy in which a nuclear attack by one side would inevitably trigger an equal response leading to the destruction of both the attacker and the defender. Deterrence theory suggested that when both sides possessed the capability to inflict nuclear annihilation, even after being hit by a first strike, neither side would dare use such weapons.

N

national debt cumulative total of all previous annual *federal deficits* or budget shortfalls incurred each year and owed by the federal government.

nativism outlook championing the supremacy of "native" cultural traits and political rights over those of immigrants from different backgrounds. Nativism flourished during the high immigration of the late 1840s and 1850s, evidenced by the rise of the American ("Know-Nothing") party. In the late nineteenth and early twentieth centuries, nativists pressed for the restriction of immigration and won their biggest victories when Congress enacted the National Origins Acts of 1921 and 1924. As immigrant numbers rose again in the late twentieth and early twenty-first centuries, the nativist debate again emerged.

naturalization act of granting full citizenship to someone born outside the country.

navalism theories of warfare and trade that rely on a nation's navy as a principal instrument of policy.

neo-isolationist term applied to those who after World War II believed the United States should avoid foreign entanglements. Neo-isolationists especially condemned the United Nations and its supporters, whom they contemptuously referred to as "one-worlders."

"new" immigrants called "new" because they differed substantially from earlier arrivals who had come mostly from northern and western Europe; these newcomers came to the United States between 1880 and 1920 from eastern and southern Europe. Unlike most earlier immigrants (with the exception of the Irish), these immigrants were non-Protestants: Catholics, Jews, and Russian Orthodox Christians.

Nisei American-born citizens of Japanese ancestry, contrasted with *Issei*, native-born Japanese who had moved to the United States. At the outbreak of World War II, Nisei referred specifically to Japanese Americans who lived on the West Coast (but not in Hawaii or the East Coast), who were interned during the war because of prejudice and the widespread fear that they sympathized with Japan.

nomad a member of a group of people who have no fixed home and who move about, usually seasonally, in pursuit of food, water, and other resources.

normal schools schools that trained teachers, usually for two years and mostly for teaching in the elementary grades.

Northwest Territory present-day states of Ohio, Indiana, Illinois, Michigan, and Wisconsin. The incorporation of this territory into the United States through the Northwest Ordinance of 1785 marked the major achievement of the national government under the Articles of Confederation.

O

Opposition diverse group of political thinkers and writers in Great Britain, also known as the Country Party and the Commonwealthmen, who elaborated the tradition of classical republicanism from the late seventeenth century through the eighteenth century. They warned that the executive branch of government (the king and his ministers) was conspiring to corrupt and coopt the legislative branch of government (the House of Commons), thereby endangering popular liberties, and they called for political reforms to make Britain's government more representative of and more accountable to the people. Dismissed in England as a disaffected radical minority, the Opposition exerted a decisive influence on the political thinking of an increasing number of American colonials in the decades leading up to the Revolution.

outsourcing the contracting of goods or services from outside a company or organization in order to maintain flexibility in the size of the organization's workforce. Increasingly, outsourcing has used suppliers outside the United States in low-wage countries such as Mexico, India, and China.

P

pandemic outbreak of disease that spreads across national boundaries or across the world.

partisan warfare armed clashes among political rivals, typically involving guerrilla fighting and the violent intimidation of civilians by militias. Partisan warfare between loyalists and rebels tore apart communities everywhere in the United States during the war for independence, but the fighting was especially fierce and protracted in the South. The success of rebel insurgencies there ultimately convinced many southern whites to support the cause of independence.

patent   legal document issued by the government giving the holder exclusive rights to use, make, and sell a process, product, or device for a specified period of time. The first patents in America were issued by colonial governments as early as 1641. Congress enacted the first patent law in 1790.

paternalism   attitude or policy of treating individuals or groups in a fatherly manner, by providing for their needs without granting them rights or responsibilities. The relation involves both a dominant and a subordinate party. Sometimes the dominance comes from gender, as in a male patriarchy, whereby females are given subordinate roles. But paternalism can also be expressed in relations between colonial and subject peoples, masters and slaves, or culturally different groups.

pays d'en haut   in the seventeenth century, the lands referred to by the French as the "upper country," the land upriver from Montreal as French fur traders passed into the Great Lakes beyond the southern shores of Lake Ontario. The trading lands stretched all the way to the Mississippi River.

peculiar institution   euphemism for slavery, perhaps revealing in its use. The institution was "peculiar" to the South in that it had been abolished in the North (and other parts of the world, increasingly). *Peculiar* also suggests the contradiction with the ideals of the Declaration of Independence, that "all men are created equal."

per capita income   average yearly income per person in a particular population; it provides one statistical measure of the relative wealth of a region.

pluralism   idea that identity cannot be reduced to a single shared essence. Under such a philosophy, distinct ethnic, cultural, and religious groups are tolerated and affirmed within a society. The philosophy contrasts with the belief, in American politics, that citizens should assimilate into a more uniform cultural identity of shared values. Contrasting metaphors portray an assimilationist United States as a melting pot versus a pluralist mixing bowl.

plurality   in elections, a candidate who receives a plurality wins more votes than any other candidate but less than half of all votes cast. Receiving more than half of the votes cast is called a *majority.*

pocket veto   means of vetoing a bill without formally doing so. Normally, if a president does not veto or sign a bill within 10 days of receiving it, the bill automatically becomes law. If it is received, however, within 10 days of Congress's adjournment, the president can simply "pocket" the bill unsigned, until Congress adjourns, and it does not go into effect.

political culture   patterns, habits, institutions, and traits associated with a political system. The political culture of the Jacksonian era, for example, was marked by a number of innovations: political nominating conventions, torchlight parades, campaign songs, badges, and other souvenirs.

political machine   hierarchical political organization developed in the nineteenth century that controlled the activities of a political party and was usually headed by a political boss.

popular sovereignty   doctrine that a territory could decide by vote whether or not to permit slavery within its boundaries. The doctrine was devised by Senator Stephen Douglas of Illinois as a way to placate southerners who wanted slavery permitted within Kansas Territory, forbidden under the Missouri Compromise. Meant as a compromise measure, the doctrine only inflamed the situation, as both sides worked to win a vote over slavery.

Populism   political outlook that supports the rights and powers of the common people in opposition to the interests of the privileged elite. The Populist Party evolved out of the economic distress of the 1890s among farmers and focused its anger against the era's large industrial corporations, railroad monopolies, and banks. But populism as an outlook and philosophy persisted long after the party had dissolved.

pragmatism   philosophical movement, led by philosophers Charles S. Peirce and William James, that stressed the visible, real-world results of ideas. Pragmatism was embraced by many progressives who wanted to promote the possibilities of change by abandoning the old notion that events were predetermined and inevitable.

predestination   basis of Calvinist theology and a belief that holds that God has ordained the outcome of all human

history before the beginning of time, including the eternal fate of every human being. Believers in this doctrine found comfort and meaning from its assurance that God was directing the fate of nations, individuals, and all of creation toward his divine purposes.

Presbyterians   members of a Protestant denomination that originated in sixteenth-century Britain as part of the Puritan movement. Like their fellow Puritan reformers, the Congregationalists, the Presbyterians embraced Calvinist theology beliefs; but unlike the Congregationalists, Presbyterians favored a more hierarchical form of church governance, a system in which individual congregations were guided by presbyteries and synods comprising both laymen and ministers.

presidio   military garrison; as Spanish colonizers moved north from central Mexico in the sixteenth and seventeenth centuries, they constructed presidios to consolidate claims over new territory. Presidios often encouraged the growth of nearby towns and ranches and were probably more important as sites of diplomacy with Indians than as centers of military power. Poor funding and political instability led to the decline of the presidios after Mexican independence in 1821.

privatize   transferral of an economic enterprise or public utility from the control of the government into private ownership. The Bush plan for Social Security reform sought to place retirement contributions into investment accounts managed privately, rather than into a fund managed by the Social Security Administration.

producer goods   goods, such as heavy machinery, used to manufacture other goods, often consumer goods.

psychedelic   characterized by or generating shifts in perception and altered states of awareness, often hallucinatory, and usually brought on by drugs such as LSD, mescaline, or psilocybin. Advocates of the psychedelic state spoke of euphoria, mystic visions, and philosophic insights produced. Critical observers pointed to the potential of inducing not only hallucinations but also sometimes psychoses.

public works   government-financed construction projects, such as highways and bridges, for use by the public.

Puritans   members of a reform movement within the Church of England that originated in the sixteenth century and that ultimately formed the Congregationalist and Presbyterian churches. Calvinist in their theology, the Puritans strove to reform English religion, society, and politics by restricting church membership to the pious and godly, by according the laity greater power in church governance, and by enlisting the state to enforce a strict moral code that prohibited drunkenness, gambling, swearing, and attending the theater.

Q

Quakers Protestant sect, also known as the Society of Friends, founded in mid-seventeenth century England. The Quakers believed that the Holy Spirit dwelt within each human being and that religious conviction was the source of their egalitarian social practices, which included allowing women to speak in churches and to preach in public gatherings. Quakers settled the mid-Atlantic colonies in large numbers and founded the colony of Pennsylvania.

R

racialism *see* **racism.**

racism form of discrimination based on the belief that one race is superior to another. Racism may be expressed individually and consciously, through explicit thoughts, feelings, or acts; it can be codified into a theory that claims scientific backing for its tenets. It can also be expressed socially and unconsciously, through institutions that promote inequality between races. In the early twentieth century, when racism became much more pronounced, the term *racialism* was also coined.

reconquista military reconquest of the Iberian Peninsula from Islamic Moors of Africa by European Christian rulers. The campaign lasted on and off from 718 to 1492 CE.

Redeemers southerners who came to power in southern state governments from 1875 to 1877, claiming to have "redeemed" the South from Reconstruction. The Redeemers looked to undo many of the changes wrought by the Civil War. Their goals included minimizing the role of African Americans in government and reducing their economic independence and strengthening the "New South" through industrial development.

red-light district area in cities reserved for prostitutes. The term, first employed in the United States, resulted from the use of red lights to show that prostitutes were open for business.

repatriation act of returning people to their nation of origin. The term often refers to the act of returning soldiers or refugees to their birth country.

republican motherhood redefinition of the role of women promoted by many American reformers in the 1780s and 1790s, who believed that the success of republican government depended on educated and independent-minded mothers who would raise children to become informed and self-reliant citizens. The ideal of republican motherhood fostered improvements in educational opportunities for women and accorded them an important role in civic life, but it also reinforced the notion that women should confine the sphere of their activities to home and family.

republicanism belief that representative government safeguards popular liberties more reliably than does either monarchy or oligarchy and that all citizens must practice vigilance and self-denying virtue to prevent their rulers from succumbing to the temptations of power and becoming tyrants. This "classical republicanism" profoundly influenced the political views of many Americans from the middle of the eighteenth century to the middle of the nineteenth century.

Romanticism intellectual and artistic movement that arose in the early nineteenth century out of a rejection of the Enlightenment values of reason and balance. Romanticism emphasized the individual's expression of emotion and intuition.

S

sagebrush rebels group of western cattlemen, loggers, miners, developers, and others who argued that federal ownership of huge tracts of land and natural resources violated the principle of states' rights. This group demanded that government transfer control to individual states, in respect of their right to make decisions about the management of both the land and the natural resources.

scalawag white southerners who supported the Republican Party. The derisive nickname was given by their opponents. Perhaps a quarter of all white southerners voted Republican at some time during Reconstruction.

scientific management system of factory production that stresses efficiency.

The system was pioneered by American engineer Frederick Winslow Taylor. In *The Principles of Scientific Management* (1911), his most famous work, he emphasized time-and-motion studies to enhance productivity. The book became the bible of efficiency experts and Taylor the "Father of Scientific Management."

sedition words or actions that incite revolt against the law or duly constituted government.

segregation system, imposed through law and custom, of separating people by race; first enacted into law in Tennessee (1875) with a statute separating blacks from whites on trains, one of the most prevalent public spaces for racial mingling.

self-determination principle in international law that people have a right to determine their own form of government free from outside control. The principle contrasts with colonialism and imperialism, under which people are subject to foreign rulers.

semisubsistence economy economy in which individuals and families produce most of what they need to live on. Such economies are overwhelmingly rural and also egalitarian, in that wealth is distributed fairly broadly. During the colonial period and early republic, much of the American economy was semisubsistence. *See also* **commercial economy.**

separate but equal rationale for a policy of segregation granting equal facilities and services to African American and whites in schools, hospitals, transportation and lodging facilities, and other public places. The Supreme Court upheld such laws in *Plessy v. Ferguson* (1896). In practice such facilities were separate but seldom equal.

separation of church and state principle that religious institutions and their representatives should exercise no civil or judicial powers and that civil governments should give no official sanction, privileges, or financial support to any religious denomination or organization.

separation of powers principle that each branch of government—the legislature (Congress), the executive (the President), and the judiciary (the Supreme Court)—should wield distinct powers independent from interference or infringement by other branches of government. During the debates of the Constitutional Convention in 1797, James Madison successfully argued that this separation of powers was essential to a balanced republican government.

settlement house   social reform effort that used neighborhood centers in which settlement house workers lived and worked among the poor, often in slum neighborhoods. The first settlement house, Toynbee Hall in London, was founded in 1884. The first settlement house in the United States (The Neighborhood Guild, later University Settlement House) came in 1886 in New York City and was founded by Stanton Coit.

Shi'ite and Sunni   two major branches of Islam, a division not unlike the Protestant-Catholic split in Christianity. After the death of the Prophet Muhammad, followers disagreed over who should be his successor. Most believers accepted the tradition of having their leader chosen by community consensus (the Sunni branch), but a minority supported the claim of Ali, the Prophet's cousin. Over the years theological differences have separated Shi'ite and Sunni Muslims as well. Today the Shi'ites are dominant largely in Iran and southeastern Iraq.

silent majority   phrase coined by President Richard Nixon in a 1969 speech, referring to the large number of Americans who supported his policies but did not express their views publicly.

sit-in   form of direct action in which protesters nonviolently occupy and refuse to leave an area. Mahatma Gandhi employed the tactic during the Indian independence movement, and autoworkers used it in Flint, Michigan, in the late 1930s. Student movements around the world widely adopted the tactic in the 1960s.

social mobility   movement of individuals from one social class to another. In general, the stronger the barriers of class, race, gender or caste, the less social mobility exhibited by a society.

socialism   philosophy of social and economic organization in which the means of producing and distributing goods is owned collectively or by government.

sociological jurisprudence   legal theory that emphasizes the importance not merely of precedent but of contemporary social context in interpreting the law.

specie   coined money of gold or silver. Also referred to as hard money or hard currency. In contrast, banknotes or notes are paper money or paper currency.

sphere of influence   geographic region beyond its border over which a nation exerts political or economic control.

spoils system   practice of rewarding loyal party members with jobs in government. Known more formally as "patronage," the practice drew its name from the old saying "To the victor belong the spoils," in this instance, meaning the rewards of election victories.

steerage   least expensive accommodation on a passenger ship, located below decks and often used by immigrants for passage to the United States in the late nineteenth and early twentieth centuries.

stock exchange   market at which shares of ownership in corporations are bought and sold. The creation of what were markets for investment capital made it easier to raise the large sums of money needed for large industrial projects.

stratified   layered; in this case, according to class or social station. A highly stratified society has a greater variety of social levels, from the richest or most socially esteemed to the poorest or least socially approved. A society can be stratified according to wealth, race, religion, or a number of other social markers.

subsistence farming   *see* **semisubsistence economy.**

subversive   one who seeks the destruction or overthrow of a legally constituted government; also used as an adjective (for example, *subversive conduct*) to refer more generally to behavior undermining the established social order.

suffrage   right to vote; also referred to as the franchise. To *disenfranchise* is to take away the right to vote.

Sun Belt   areas of the southern and western parts of the United States that experienced significant economic and population growth since World War II. That growth has been a contrast to the relative decline of the *Rust Belt*, the older industrial area from New England to the mid-Atlantic region across the upper Middle West.

Sunni   *see* **Shi'ite and Sunni.**

supply-side economics   theory that emphasizes tax cuts and business incentives to encourage economic growth rather than deficit spending to promote demand. Businesses and individuals, the theory assumes, will use their tax savings to create new businesses and expand old businesses, which in turn will increase productivity, employment, and general well-being.

T

tariff   duty on trade, the purpose of which is primarily to regulate the flow of commerce rather than to raise a revenue. The Molasses Act of 1733, for example, imposed a hefty customs duty on molasses imported from non-British Caribbean islands to encourage American distillers to purchase molasses exclusively from the British West Indies.

task system   way of organizing slave labor in the South Carolina low country during the eighteenth century. Masters and overseers of rice and indigo plantations assigned individual slaves a daily task, and after its completion, slaves could spend the rest of the day engaged in pursuits of their own choosing. Gang labor, the system practiced in the Chesapeake, afforded slaves less opportunity for freedom within slavery.

taxes   duty on trade (known as external taxation) or a duty on items circulating within a nation or a colony (known as internal taxation) intended primarily to raise a revenue rather than to regulate the flow of commerce. The Sugar Act of 1764 was an external tax, whereas the Stamp Act of 1765 was an internal tax.

Tejano   Texan of Hispanic descent. In the early stages of the rebellion against Santa Anna, more than a few Tejanos supported the Texan drive for independence. But as Americans continued to arrive in Texas in large numbers, many viewed Tejanos with suspicion, and they were marginalized in Texan society.

temperance movement   reform movement, begun in the 1820s, to temper or restrain the sale and use of alcohol. It achieved its greatest success when the Eighteenth Amendment took effect in 1920, outlawing the manufacture, sale, transportation, and importation of alcohol. The amendment was repealed in 1933.

tenement   building, often in disrepair and usually five or six stories in height, in which cheap apartments were rented to tenants. Such dilapidated housing sprang up in cities across the United States in the late nineteenth and early twentieth centuries to lodge the growing numbers of immigrants, African Americans, and other poor populations moving to urban centers.

theocracy   system of government dominated by the clergy.

totalitarian government   system in which the state controls all aspects of economic, political, and even social life, usually through some form of dictatorship. Nazi Germany under Adolf Hitler and the Soviet Union under Joseph Stalin are examples of totalitarian regimes.

trade association organization of individuals and firms in a given industry that provides statistical, lobbying, and other services to members.

trust business arrangement in which owners of shares in a business turn over their shares "in trust" to a board with power to control those businesses for the benefit of the trust. Following the example set by John D. Rockefeller and Standard Oil, trusts blossomed in the late nineteenth century as a means of consolidating power over production, marketing, and pricing, often crowding out other competitors.

U

union organization of workers designed to improve their economic status and working conditions. Such organizations come in two varieties: the horizontal union, in which all members share a common skill or craft, and the vertical union, composed of workers from all across the same industry.

Upper South the border states (Delaware, Maryland, Kentucky, and Missouri) and Virginia, North Carolina, Tennessee, and Arkansas.

V

vertical integration strategy of business growth that attempts to reduce costs by gaining control of the successive stages of a business operation, incorporating into a single firm several firms involved in all aspects of the manufacture of a product—from exploiting raw materials to manufacturing and distribution.

Victorianism constellation of middle-class values attributed to the proper virtues of Britain's Queen Victoria. Victorianism responded to the instabilities of an industrial age in which factory work dominated the lives of struggling workers and middle-class clerks as well as down-at-the-heels landed gentry. The culture's emphasis on "refinement" and "manners" established a social hierarchy offering some sense of stability.

virgin soil epidemic epidemic in which the populations at risk have had no previous contact with the diseases that strike them and are therefore immunologically almost defenseless.

virtual representation view that representation is not linked to election but rather to common interests; for example, during the imperial crisis the British argued that Americans were virtually represented in Parliament, even though colonials elected none of its members, because each member of Parliament stood for the interests of the whole empire. *See also* **actual representation.**

W

"watered" stock stock issued in excess of the assets of a company. The term derived from the practice of some ranchers who made their cattle drink large amounts of water before weighing them for sale.

welfare capitalism business practice of providing welfare—in the form of pension and profit-sharing programs, subsidized housing, personnel management, paid vacations, and other services and benefits—for workers. The practice was pioneered by Henry Ford under the philosophy that businesses in a capitalist economy should act for the common good of their workers. The philosophy, if not the businesswide practice, became popular in the 1920s as a way of reducing high rates of turnover among employees and integrating technological change into the workplace.

Wisconsin idea series of progressive reforms at the state level promoted by Robert La Follette during his governorship of Wisconsin (1901–1906). They included primary elections, corporate property taxes, regulation of railroads and public utilities, and supervision of public resources in the public interest. A nonpartisan civil service group, recruited mostly from faculty at the University of Wisconsin, provided a cadre of expert bureaucrats to run the new programs.

Y

yellow journalism brand of newspaper reporting that stresses excitement and shock over evenhandedness and dull fact. The term "yellow journalism" derived from the color of the ink used to print the first comic strip, which appeared in William Randolph Hearst's *New York Journal* in 1895. Hearst's newspaper specialized in yellow journalism and is often credited with igniting public passions for war with Spain in 1898.

Credits

Text Credits

CHAPTER 24

Page 662, Dueling Document 1
Quotation from Marcus Garvey, "Go Back to Africa," speech at Madison Square Garden, March 16, 1924. Reprinted in Amy Garvey, *Philosophy and Opinions of Marcus Garvey: African for the Africans* (NH: Ayer Company Publishers 2e, 1967), pp. 118–123. Reprinted with permission of Ayer Company Publishers.

Page 662, Dueling Document 2
"We must oppose all segregation" from W. E. B. Du BOIS, "On Being Ashamed of Oneself: An Essay on Race Pride," The McGraw-Hill Companies wish to thank the Crisis Publishing Co., Inc., the publisher of the magazine of the National Association for the Advancement of Colored People, for the use of this material first published in the May 1933 issue of Crisis Magazine.

CHAPTER 25
Page 690, Dueling Document 2
"Lorena Hickok to Harry Hopkins, January 1, 1935" in Richard Lowitt and Maurine Beasley, eds., *One Third of a Nation: Lorena Hickok reports on the Great Depression* (University of Illinois Press: Urbana, IL, 1981).

CHAPTER 28
Page 777
Figure: Average Annual Regional Migration, 1947–1960 from Frank Levy, "Major U.S. Migration Flows in the late 1940s and 1950s." In *Dollars and Dreams: The Changing American Income Distribution,* Figure 6.1. © 1998 Russell Sage Foundation, 112 East 64th Street, New York, NY 10065. Reprinted with permission.

Page 784
Reprinted courtesy of Pepsi-Cola Company.

CHAPTER 29
Page 820, Dueling Document 1
Quotation from Statement of Purpose of the SNCC (Student Non-Violent Coordinating Committee). Reprinted by permission of the SNCC Legacy Project, Inc.

Page 820, Dueling Document 2
Quotation from the Sharon Statement, 1960, Young Americans For Freedom. www.yaf.com, Young Americans For Freedom, 2300 M Street, NW, # 800, Washington, D.C. 20037.

Page 821, Dueling Document 3
Quotation from Port Huron Statement of the SDS, Michigan, 1962. Students for a Democratic Society, 1962, public document.

CHAPTER 30
Page 845, Dueling Document 1
Gloria Steinem, What Would It Be Like if Women Win? From Alexander Bloom and Wini Breines, eds., *"Takin' It to the Streets": A Sixties Reader* (New York: Oxford University Press, 1995), pp. 475–477. Reprinted by permission of the author.

Page 845, Dueling Document 2
Phyllis Schlafly, "What 'Women's Lib' Really Means." From the Phyllis Schlafly Report 5, no. 7 (February 1972). Reprinted by permission of the author.

CHAPTER 31
Page 866, Dueling Document 1
Quotation from *Listen America!* by Jerry Falwell, copyright © 1980 by Jerry Falwell. Used by permission of Doubleday, a division of Random House, Inc. Any third party use of this material, outside of this publication, is prohibited. Interested parties must apply directly to Random House, Inc. for permission.

Page 867, Dueling Document 2
Norman Lear, excerpt from "Liberty and Its Responsibilities," in *Broadcast Journalism 1979–1981: The Eighth Alfred I. DuPont Columbia University Survey,* Marvin Barnett, ed., (NY: Everest House, 1982). www.normanlear.com/backstory_writings.html. Used by permission.

Page 875
Figure: Poverty in America, 1970–1993 from Frank Levy, "Official Poverty Rates for Children, the Elderly, and the General Population." In *Dollars and Dreams: The Changing American Income Distribution* Figure 7.1. © 1998 Russell Sage Foundation, 112 East 64th Street, New York, NY 10065. Reprinted with permission.

CHAPTER 32
Page 926, Dueling Document 2
Reprinted by permission of the publisher from *The Discovery of Global Warming: Revised and Expanded Edition* by Spencer R. Weart, pp. 201–204, Cambridge, MA: Harvard University Press, Copyright © 2003, 2008 by Spencer R. Weart.

Photo Credits

Image Researcher: Deborah Bull; Assistant Researcher: Jullie Chung

CHAPTER 17
Opener: Library of Congress (LC-DIG-cwpb-00468); p. 440: Library of Congress; p. 441: Smithsonian American Art Museum, Washington, DC/Art Resource, NY; p. 442 (top): Harper's Weekly; (bottom): Library of Congress (LC-B8184-10690); p. 443: Library of Congress; p. 445: Puck, 1890; p. 447: "Portrait of Hiram Rhoades Revels," by Theodor Kaufmann, 1870. Oil on millboard, 12″ × 10″. Courtesy of the Herbert F. Johnson Museum of Art, Cornell University, Ithaca. NY. Transferred from the Olin 69.170; p. 448: The Granger Collection, New York; p. 450: © Corbis; p. 452: The New-York Historical Society (50475); p. 453: Schlesinger Library, Radcliffe Institute, Harvard University/The Bridgeman Art Library; p. 454: Library of Congress; p. 455: The Granger Collection, New York; p. 456: © David J. & Janice L. Frent Collection/Corbis; p. 457 (center): The New York Public Library/Art Resource, NY; (left and right): Library of Congress (cph 3c19565); p. 461: Library of Congress (cph 3a36683).

CHAPTER 18
Opener: The Granger Collection, New York; p. 464: Kansas State Historical Society (E185.1878.1); p. 465: Image copyright © The Metropolitan Museum of Art/Art Resource, NY; p. 467 (top): National Archives (NWDNS-102-LH-462); (bottom): Library of Congress (LC-USZ62-79320); p. 468: West Virginia and Regions History Collection, WVU Libraries (Image 035160); p. 470 (top): Archives of the Billy Graham Center; (bottom): LSU in Shreveport, Noel Memorial Library, Archives and Special Collections; p. 473: Image copyright © The Metropolitan Museum of Art/Art Resource, NY; p. 478: Private Collection/Peter Newark American Pictures/The Bridgeman Art Library International; p. 479: The Montana Historical Society Research Center (981-057); p. 482 (bottom): Library of Congress (LC-W7-938); p. 484: Idaho State Historical Society, (349); p. 486: M124.54, Clara McDonald Williamson *Old Chisholm Trail,* 1952, oil on canvas, 24 × 36 1/2. The Roland P. Murdock Collection, Wichita Art Museum; p. 487: Library of Congress; p. 488: Nebraska State Historical Society (RG2608 PH3535); p. 489: © 2014 Colorado State University/Communications and Creative Services, Photography. (B11041); p. 491: Image courtesy of Circus World Museum, Baraboo, Wisconsin; p. 492, 495, 496: Library of Congress; p. 497: Archive Photos/Getty Images; p. 498: Karl Bodmer, "Piegan Blackfeet Man," Joslyn Art Museum, Omaha, Nebraska, Gift of the Enron Art Foundation (1986.49.290); p. 499: Courtesy William Harlow, "Inside Wood: Masterpiece of Nature."

CHAPTER 19
Opener: Science and Society Picture Library, London; p. 502, 503: Library of Congress; p. 504: © Bettmann/Corbis; p. 505: Edison National Historic Site; p. 506 (top): The Granger Collection, New York; (bottom): Getty Images, RF; p. 507: The Granger Collection, New York; p. 508, 512: Library of Congress; p. 514: Hulton Archive/Getty Images; p. 515: Texas Energy Museum, Beaumont, TX; p. 516: Collier's, 1905; p. 518 (top): Brown Brothers; (bottom): Courtesy of the National Museum of Play® at the Strong™, Rochester, New York 2011; p. 519: Library of Congress; p. 520: Leslie's Illustrated Newspaper, 1888, Nov. 3, pg 191; p. 521: © Bettmann/Corbis; p. 522: Deutsches Historisches Museum; p. 523: Historical Society of Schuylkill County; p. 525: Culver Pictures, Inc.; p. 529: Library of Congress.

CHAPTER 20
Opener: Chicago History Museum/Archive Photos/Getty Images; p. 532: © Curt Teich Archives/HIP/The Image Works; p. 534: National Archives; p. 535: Library of Congress; p. 536: National Archives; p. 537: Collection of The New York Public Library, Astor, Lenox and Tilden Foundations; p. 539 (top and bottom): Library of Congress (3a47363); (right): Division of Political History, National Museum of American History, Smithsonian Institution (2004-26275); p. 540, 542: Library of Congress; p. 544: Courtesy of The Winterthur Library (RBR NK2740 R32 PF tc); p. 545 (top): National Archives (513360); (bottom): George Bellows, *New York 1911*. Collection of Mr. and Mrs. Paul Mellon, National Gallery of Art, Washington, DC (1986.72; p. 546: George Bellows, *The Sawdust Trail*, 1916. Oil on canvas, 63 × 45 1/8 inc. (160.02 × 114.62 cm), Milwaukee Art Museum, Layton Art Collection, Purchase L1964.7. Photo credit P. Richard Ellis; p. 547: Hulton Archive/Getty Images; p. 548: Winslow Homer, *Blackboard*, 1877. © 2000 Board of Trustees, National Gallery of Art, Washington, Gift (Partial and Promised) of Jo Ann and Julian Gans, Jr., in honor of the 50th Anniversary of the National Gallery of Art (1990.60.1./DR); p. 549: Harpers New Monthly Magazine, May 1893, pg 837; p. 550: Shinn, Everett, *Sixth Avenue Shoppers*, n.d. Pastel and watercolor on board, 21 × 26 1/2″. Santa Barbara Museum of Art, Gift of Mrs. Sterling Morton for the Preston Morton Collection; p. 552: Image courtesy of Circus World Museum, Baraboo, Wisconsin with permission from Ringling Bros. and Barnum & Bailey® THE GREATEST SHOW ON EARTH®; p. 557 (left): Welgos/Hulton Archive/Getty Images; (center and right): Library of Congress.

CHAPTER 21
Opener: © Bettmann/Corbis; p. 560: Library of Congress (3g03270); p. 562: © Courtesy Colorado Historical Society, All rights reserved; p. 563: Library of Congress; p. 564: Courtesy of the California History Room, California State Library, Sacramento, California (GL # 4216);

p. 565: Courtesy of Cornell University Library, Ithaca, NY; p. 566: Library of Congress; p. 569: Charles Dana Gibson; p. 571: Collection of David J. and Janice L. Frent; p. 572: Library of Congress; p. 576 (top): Library of Congress; (bottom): Philip P. Choy, Professor of Asian American Studies at San Francisco State University (Plate 50); p. 577: Hawaii State Archives; p. 579 (right): © David J. & Janice L. Frent Collection/Corbis; (left): Chicago History Museum (ICHi-08428); p. 580: © Museum of the City of New York, USA/The Bridgeman Art Library; p. 581: Huntsville Public Library, Huntsville, AL; p. 584 (right): National Archives; p. 587: Library of Congress; p. 588: Courtesy Frederic Remington Art Museum, Ogdensburg, New York; p. 590 (top); Theodore Roosevelt Collection, Harvard College Library; (bottom): New York Public Library/ Art Resource, NY; p. 591: New York Public Library/Art Resource, NY.

CHAPTER 22
Opener: Public Art for Public Schools/NYC School Construction Authority/Image © Stan Ries Photography; p. 594: Brown Brothers; p. 597: © Bettmann/Corbis; p. 598, 599: Library of Congress; p. 600 (top): Library of Congress (LC-DIG-ggbain-02461); (bottom): Illinois State Library; p. 602: *Gondolas in Venice Canal*, Venice, California, Photograph by Pacific Novelty Co. California Historical Society, San Francisco, [FN-29415]; p. 603 (top): Library of Congress; (bottom): Hulton Archive/Getty Images; p. 604: Without Sanctuary: Lynching Photography in America, plates 25 and 26 © 2000–2005 Collection of James Allen and John Littlefield/National Center for Civil and Human Rights; p. 605: (detail) National Portrait Gallery, Smithsonian Institutions, Washington, DC/Art Resource, NY; p. 606: Culver Pictures, Inc.; p. 608 (left): Brown Brothers; (right): Library of Congress; p. 609: Library of Congress; p. 610: From the Collections of the Henry Ford (00.4.5767); p. 611: Courtesy of The Bancroft Library, University of California, Berkeley (1971.031:1902.03.118); p. 613: Library of Congress (LC-H25-6497-MM); p. 614: Library of Congress; 616: Library of Congress (LC-DIG-ppmsca-06024); p. 619 (left): Illinois State Library; (right): Library of Congress.

CHAPTER 23
Opener: Imperial War Museum, London, UK/ The Bridgeman Art Library; p. 624: Library of Congress (LC-DIG-jpd-02531); p. 626: Brown Brothers; p. 627: Image copyright © The Metropolitan Museum of Art/Art Resource, NY; p. 629: National Archives; p. 631: © Hulton-Deutsch Collection/Corbis; p. 632: Courtesy New Mexico State Records Center & Archives, Santa Fe, NM. Read Collection, Private Papers, Folder 54a, Series II, Ellis & Jenkins, 1892–1920, Box #9, Serial Number 8425, WWI, Felix Sanchez Photo Number 7224; p. 633: Rubenstein Rare Book, Manuscript, and Special Collections Library, Duke University (n967);

p. 634: Library of Congress (3c00307); p. 635: © Bettmann/Corbis; p. 639: WPA Photo Collection, National Archives; p. 640: Cartoon by D.C. Boonzaier in "Die Burger," October 16, 1918; p. 643: Library of Congress; p. 644: (top): Culver Pictures, Inc.; (bottom): Library of Congress; p. 647: Library of Congress.

CHAPTER 24
Opener: The Granger Collection, New York; p. 650: © Bettmann/Corbis; p. 652: (detail) From the Collection of the Henry Ford (THF 25002); p. 653: Nebraska State Historical Society (RG2183-1933-0411-1); p. 654: Dover Publications; p. 655: Hartman Center for Sales, Advertising & Marketing History, Duke University (BH1567); p. 656: Image copyright © The Metropolitan Museum of Art, NY/Art Resource, NY; p. 657: © Bettmann/Corbis; p. 658: Library of Congress; p. 659: Leif Neandross, The Roxy Theater. Courtesy of the Rambusch Company Archives, NY; p. 660: Library of Congress; p. 661: Archibald John Motley, Jr., *Blues*, 1929. Photograph © 1993 The Art Institute of Chicago. All Rights Reserved. Collection of Mara Motley, M.D. and Valerie Gerrard Browne. Image courtesy of the Chicago History Museum; p. 663, 664: Library of Congress; p. 666: John Steuart Curry, 1897–1946, *Baptism in Kansas*, (1928). Oil on canvas, 40 1/4 × 50 1/4 in. (102.2 × 127.6 cm). Whitney Museum of American Art, New York; gift of Gertrude Vanderbilt Whitney 31.159. Digital Image, © Whitney Museum of American Art, NY. © Estate of John Steuart Curry; p. 667 (top): Courtesy of Christine Lesiak/NET Television; (bottom): Research Division of the Oklahoma Historical Society (OHS#16936); p. 668: Library of Congress (3c30973u); p. 669: © Corbis; p. 673, 677: Library of Congress.

CHAPTER 25
Opener: Library of Congress; p. 680: Library of Congress; p. 681: University of Washington Libraries, Special Collections (SEA0552); p. 682: Radio designed by Harold van Doren and J. G. Rideout. Made by Air-King Products CO., Brooklyn, 1930–33. The Brooklyn Museum of Art, purchased with funds donated by The Walter Foundation, [85.9] Photograph, Scott Hyde; p. 683: Hulton Archive/Getty Images; p. 684, 685: Library of Congress; p. 686: Louis Ribak, *Home Relief Station*, 1935–36. Collection of Whitney Museum of American Art, NY. Purchase. 36.148. Digital image, © Whitney Museum of American Art, NY; p. 687: *Riot at Union Square*, 1947 [date depicted: March 6, 1930]. Peter Hopkins, oil on canvas. Museum of the City of New York, Gift of the Artist, 66.82; p. 689: New York Daily News Archive/ Getty Images; p. 694, 695: The Granger Collection, New York; p. 696: Library of Congress; p. 697: USDA Photograph Archives; p. 698 (top): Library of Congress; (bottom): SuperStock; p. 699: Courtesy of The Bancroft Library, University of California, Berkeley; p. 700: Amy Jones; p. 701 (left): State Archives of Michigan, #05060; (right): Walter P. Reuther Library,

Wayne State University; p. 702: National Archives; p. 703: Library of Congress; p. 709: (top left): Wei/iStockphoto, RF; (center left): Oleg Kulakov/iStockphoto, RF; (top center): © Ingram Publishing/Fotosearch, RF; (bottom left): © IT Stock/PunchStock, RF; (bottom center): Anton Zhukov/iStockphoto, RF; (bottom right): Keith Webber, Jr./iStockphoto, RF.

CHAPTER 26

Opener: Private Collection/Peter Newark Military Pictures/The Bridgeman Art Library; p. 712: National Archives; p. 713: © 1942 Edward B. Marks Music Company. Copyright renewed. All rights reserved. Photograph courtesy Franklin Delano Roosevelt Library, Hyde Park, New York; p. 715: © Corbis; p. 716: Central Press/Getty Images; p. 717: © Corbis; p. 722 (top): Library of Congress; (bottom): National Archives; p. 723: Tillamook Air Museum/Image courtesy of James West Davidson; p. 724: National Archives; p. 726, 727: Library of Congress; p. 729: Photo by Bill Manbo. © Takao B. Manbo; p. 732: © Bettmann/Corbis; p. 734: D-Day Normandy. *The Rhino Ferry* by Orville Fisher. © Canadian War Museum, Beaverbrook Collection of War Art, 19710261-6230; p. 736: © Bettmann/Corbis; p. 738: National Archives; p. 739: Standish Backus Jr., Hiroshima, 1945. Courtesy of the Navy Art Collection, Naval Historical Center, Washington, DC; p. 741: Library of Congress (ppmsca 18531); p. 742 (top): National Archives; p. 743: National Archives (208-N-43440 [box 208 MO-105B]); p. 744 (top): © Brian Brake/Photo Researchers, Inc.; (bottom): National Archives.

CHAPTER 27

Opener: © Bettmann/Corbis; p. 748: © Corbis; p. 749: The Truman Presidential Museum & Library; p. 750: AP Images; p. 751: Hulton Archive/Getty Images; p. 754: stills from "Duck and Cover," Federal Civil Defense Administration; p. 755: Ben Shahn, *For Full Employment After the War Register to Vote*, 1944. The Museum of Modern Art, New York. Gift of the CIO Political Action Committee. Photo © 2014, The Museum of Modern Art, NY/Art Resource, NY. Art © Estate of Ben Shahn/License by VAGA, New York; p. 757: © Corbis; p. 758: Rare Books and Manuscripts, Benson Latin American Collection, University of Texas, Austin; p. 760: Center for Legislative Archives, US Senate Collection, National Archives (A-072_10-19-1948); p. 762: © Baldwin H. Ward & Kathryn C. Ward/Corbis; p. 763 (top); © Warner Bros./Photofest; (bottom): Eve Arnold/Magnum Photos, Inc.; p. 766: Interim Archive/Archive Photo/Getty Images; p. 767: Library of Congress (2a10935); p. 768 (top): The CONELRAD Collection, www.conelrad.com; (bottom): Private Collection; p. 771 (top): Library of Congress (3c17876); (bottom): Eve Arnold/Magnum Photos, Inc.

CHAPTER 28

Opener: Tom Kelly Archive/Archive Photo/Getty Images; p. 774: © Transtock/Corbis;

p. 776: © R. Krubner/ClassicStock//Corbis; p. 778: Printed by permission of the Norman Rockwell Family Agency. Copyright © 1959 the Norman Rockwell Family Entities. Courtesy Curtis Publishing; p. 779: © Corbis; p. 780 (top): Elliott Erwitt/Magnum Photos, Inc.; (bottom): © PoodlesRock/Corbis; p. 782: Los Angeles Public Library; p. 783: © Corbis; p. 785 (top): © Warner Bros./Photofest; (bottom): © Bettmann/Corbis; p. 788 (bottom): © Bettmann/Corbis; p. 791: Time & Life Pictures/Getty Images; p. 792 (left): Photofest; (center): © Corbis; (right): Photofest; p. 796: AFP/Getty Images; p. 799 (left): © Corbis; (right): Image Courtesy of the Advertising Archives.

CHAPTER 29

Opener: © Steve Schapiro/Corbis; p. 802: Drawing by Ruby. From *Children of Crisis: A Study of Courage and Fear, Volume I*, by Robert Coles. © 1964–67. By permission of Little, Brown and Company (Inc.); p. 804: Library of Congress (ppmsca 01271); p. 805 (top): Spencer Research Library, University of Kansas Libraries; (bottom): Dr. Hector P. Garcia Papers, Special Collections & Archives, Texas A&M University-Corpus Christi Bell Library; p. 807: John Bryson/Time & Life Pictures/Getty Images; p. 808: © Bettmann/Corbis; p. 809: Charles Moore/Black Star/Stock Photos; p. 810: AP Images; p. 811: Michael Alexander/Black Star/Stock Photos; p. 812: Ed Whitfield/AP Images; p. 813: Library of Congress (LC-DIG-ppsca-08102); p. 814: George Tames/New York Times, 1957/Redux; p. 816: © Bettmann/Corbis; p. 817: AP Images; p. 819: McCain Library and Archives, University of Southern Mississippi; p. 821: © Jeff Morgan 16/Alamy; p. 822: © Bettmann/Corbis; p. 824: AP Images; p. 827 (left): Comstock Images/Getty Images; (right): McGraw-Hill Companies.

CHAPTER 30

Opener: © Tim Page/Corbis; p. 830: © John Filo/Valley News Dispatch/Getty Images; p. 831 (left): AFP/Getty Images; (right): © Bettman/Corbis; p. 833: © Tim Page/Corbis; p. 834: AP Images; p. 836: © Bettmann/Corbis; p. 837: Julian Wasser/Time & Life Pictures/Getty Images; p. 839: © Bettmann/Corbis; p. 841: "Farm Workers' Altar" 1967, by Emanuel Martinez. Acrylic on wood. 37 1/2 × 53 × 35 1/2 in. Gift of the International Bank of Commerce in honor of Antonio R. Sanchez, Sr. Smithsonian American Art Museum (1992–95)/Art Resource, NY; p. 842: Arthur Schatz/Time & Life Pictures/Getty Images; p. 843: © Corbis; p. 844 (top): Courtesy of MS. Magazine; p. 844 (bottom): Courtesy of the James West Davidson; p. 847: © Bettmann/Corbis; p. 848: Hulton Archive/Getty Images; p. 850: NASA (AS11-40-5873); p. 852: AP Images; p. 855 (top): Library of Congress (ppmsca 11992); (bottom): National Archives; p. 856: Sandra Baker/Alamy; p. 857: Library of Congress (LC-USZ62-53278); p. 858: David Bookstaver/AP Images; p. 859 (top): James P

Blair/National Geographic Images; (bottom): Sandra Baker/Alamy, RF.

CHAPTER 31

Opener: © Wally McNamee/Corbis; p. 862: AP Images; p. 864: © Bettmann/Corbis; p. 865 (top): Dennis Cook/AP Images; (bottom): Michael Ochs Archives/Getty Images; p. 867: New York Daily News; p. 870: © Bettmann/Corbis; p. 872: Wally McNamee/Woodfin Camp & Associates; p. 874: Yvonne Hemsy/Getty Images; p. 876: © Gerald French/Corbis; p. 879: Lana Harris/AP Images; p. 881 (top): National Archives (NLNP-WHPO-MOF-0388[13A]); (bottom): © 2014 Artists Rights Society (ARS), New York/VG Bild-Kunst, Bonn; p. 883: Leonard Freed/Magnum Photos Inc.; p. 884: Dirck Halstead/Time & Life Pictures/Getty Images; p. 885: © Brad Markel/Corbis; p. 889 (top): National Archives; (bottom): Dirck Halstead/Time & Life Pictures/Getty Images.

CHAPTER 32

Opener: © Jenny E. Ross/Corbis; p. 892: Alicia Patterson Foundation/Image © Robert Suro; p. 894: (Detail) Hmong story cloth by Dia Cha and Chue & Nhia Cha. All Rights Reserved, Image Archives, Denver Museum of Nature & Science; p. 895: Buzz Orr; p. 897: Tom Haley/SIPA Press; p. 898: Ron Edmunds/AP Images; p. 899: Illustration by Anita Kunz for the New Yorker Magazine. Anita Kunz Limited. Reproduced by permission of the artist; p. 900: Robert Nickelsburg/Liaison/Getty Images; p. 902: Image Source/Getty Images, RF; p. 903: Library of Congress; p. 904: Stephen G. Eick/Advizor Solutions; p. 905: © Mark M. Lawrence/Corbis; p. 907: Raccardo Savi/The Image Bank/Getty Images; p. 908 (left): © Peter Turnley/Corbis; (center): Brian Hendler/AP Images; (right): © Ralf-Finn Hestoft/Corbis/SABA; p. 910: © Reuters NewMedia Inc./Corbis; p. 911: David J. Phillip/AP Images; p. 912: Doug Mills/The New York Times, November 5, 2008; p. 914: Pete Souza/The White House/Getty images; p. 916: © Andrew Lichtenstein/Corbis; p. 919 (left) Lourens Smak/Alamy; (right): AP Images.

ADDITIONAL CREDITS

Globe icon: Cartesia/Getty Images
Sun icon: Photodisc/Getty Images
Daily Lives (field): Design Pics/Michael Interisano/Getty Images
Dueling Documents (swords): Civil War Archive/Getty Images
Conclusion (map): Royalty-Free/Corbis
Historian's Toolbox (weathered wood): Darrin Kilmek/Getty Images

After the Fact images:
Magnifying glass: Richard Hutchings
Blank parchment paper: Christine Balderas/Getty Images
Roll of parchment, background: Oleksiy Maksymenko/Alamy
Antique books: Ingram Publishing/SuperStock
Row of books: Tetra Images/Getty Images

Index